Engaged Criminology

An Introduction

This book is dedicated to Mira.

Sara Miller McCune founded SAGE Publishing in 1965 to support the dissemination of usable knowledge and educate a global community. SAGE publishes more than 1000 journals and over 600 new books each year, spanning a wide range of subject areas. Our growing selection of library products includes archives, data, case studies and video. SAGE remains majority owned by our founder and after her lifetime will become owned by a charitable trust that secures the company's continued independence.

Los Angeles | London | New Delhi | Singapore | Washington DC | Melbourne

Engaged Criminology

An Introduction

Rena C. Zito

Elon University

Los Angeles | London | New Delhi
Singapore | Washington DC | Melbourne

FOR INFORMATION:

SAGE Publications, Inc.
2455 Teller Road
Thousand Oaks, California 91320
E-mail: order@sagepub.com

SAGE Publications Ltd.
1 Oliver's Yard
55 City Road
London, EC1Y 1SP
United Kingdom

SAGE Publications India Pvt. Ltd.
B 1/I 1 Mohan Cooperative Industrial Area
Mathura Road, New Delhi 110 044
India

SAGE Publications Asia-Pacific Pte. Ltd.
18 Cross Street #10-10/11/12
China Square Central
Singapore 048423

Printed in Canada

Library of Congress Control Number: 2022913661

ISBN (pbk) 978-1-0718-0193-2
ISBN (loose) 978-1-0718-8368-6

This book is printed on acid-free paper.

22 23 24 25 26 10 9 8 7 6 5 4 3 2 1

Acquisitions Editor: Josh Perigo

Content Development Editor: Adeline Grout

Production Editor: Rebecca Lee

Copy Editor: Colleen Brennan

Typesetter: diacriTech

Cover Designer: Scott Van Atta

Marketing Manager: Victoria Velasquez

BRIEF CONTENTS

DETAILED CONTENTS

LIST OF ACTIVITIES

PREFACE

Like most college instructors, I love to read—criminological research, historical fiction, memoirs, I love all of it! But in more than a decade of teaching criminology at the college level, I had yet to find a textbook that pulled me in. So, with support from SAGE, I wrote the book I wanted to use in my classes. That book—*this* book—would be written conversationally rather than in a dry, detached voice. Instead of bludgeoning students with encyclopedic coverage of every possible topic in criminology, it would focus on the most important topics, concepts, and theories with which an undergraduate student of criminology should be familiar. It would incorporate real-life examples and the kinds of hands-on activities that get students *doing* criminology rather than just retaining definitions. To this end, it would provide instructors the tools to incorporate low-stakes/high-effectiveness discussions and exercises that foster higher-order thinking (application, evaluation, synthesis, and creation) with an eye to time management in and out of the classroom and online. In other words, it would be engaging.

Engaged Criminology introduces students to the study of crime. Its overarching goal is to develop the learner's criminological imagination, encouraging them to "see the general in the particular" and understand individual experiences with crime and punishment as residing at the intersection of history (the macro-level) and biography (the micro-level). In its sociological approach, this book emphasizes social structural perspectives, highlighting the role of systemic inequalities as predictors and outcomes of criminal conduct and punishment. For example, students will read about systemic racism in mortgage lending, the yoke of legal debt in the U.S.'s offender-funded justice model, the school-to-prison pipeline, and the detrimental consequences of concentrated incarceration for children. This book asks students to interrogate inequalities, consider unintended consequences, appreciate the limitations of our knowledge, and envision solutions. Importantly, *Engaged Criminology* encourages students to adopt a critical lens without ever presenting one perspective as the "right" one. It is an invitation to learn and think like a criminologist.

What engages your students? If they fit the patterns described by scholars of teaching and learning, then they learn best when you as an instructor draw out and work with their prior knowledge. Students also respond to storytelling and examples. They benefit from the use of varied pedagogical techniques that are inclusive of students with diverse learning needs. When you assign tasks that build meta-cognitive skills, your students learn more deeply. And, most importantly, they find greater *joy* in learning when actively participating rather than passively absorbing. *Engaged Criminology* includes active-learning exercises and discussion prompts that foster joyful, deep learning through tasks like take-a-stand activities, concept photography, role-playing scenarios, cognitive mapping, hands-on data analysis, and reflection exercises. For example, students will measure and reflect on their own levels of legal cynicism. In another exercise, they will examine stock photo depictions of crime victims (overwhelmingly of white women) and compare their observations to empirical patterns in National Crime Victimization Survey data.

Engaged Criminology departs from the standard criminology textbook by adopting an active learning approach and by making that approach achievable across classroom settings. Each chapter features two student-facing *Engaged Criminology* exercises that can be completed in person or online, solo or in groups, in a 30-person seminar or a 200-person lecture course. An additional two or three exercises per chapter are available in the Instructors' Manual, as well. The four or five *Engaged Discussion* questions in each chapter can be used in in-person classes and synchronous online courses as think-pair-shares or as discussion board prompts in synchronous and asynchronous online settings. A book can only do so much to foster active engagement. After all, reading is passive. Nonetheless, I designed this book to equip instructors with ample resources for building a captivating learning experience, whether in person or online.

I served as the criminology area editor for the American Sociological Association's Teaching Resources and Innovations Library (TRAILS) for six years. I had the great fortune of reviewing and providing feedback on criminology assignments, exercises, and syllabi submitted by instructors passionate about teaching. Some of the *Engaged Criminology* exercises in this book are modified versions of the most effective TRAILS resources. Others take inspiration from activities found in *Teaching Sociology* and the *Journal of Criminal Justice Education*. Many instructors wish to incorporate active-learning strategies into their teaching but don't know where to begin, or they find the time required for these activities is too great. With this in mind, *Engaged Criminology* brings many resources together in one place, so criminology instructors don't need to spend time searching for ideas. In addition, the activities are designed for brevity, typically requiring no more than 15 minutes. Instructors can select the activities that best fit their daily learning goals, opting to use all of them or just a few.

Engaged Criminology differs from other criminology textbooks by avoiding the mile-wide-and-inch-deep approach. This book does not cover every criminological theory under the sun. I wrote my master's thesis on power-control theory and graduate school papers on control-balance theory. Neither appears in this book. Be assured, though, that *Engaged Criminology* addresses the major perspectives that are covered in any contemporary criminology course. And rather than offer a few dry paragraphs on each perspective in a mad dash to cram them all in, it offers deeper description, including real-world applications of each theory. For example, the section on social disorganization theory includes subsections on mass incarceration as a disorganizing condition, gentrification's effects on crime, and the opioid crisis in rural and suburban communities.

Many criminology textbooks are organized into three sections: an introduction/methods section, a crime theories section, and a crime types section—usually in that (utterly baffling) order. This book avoids that model. Sutherland wrote that criminology is concerned with (1) the making of laws, (2) the breaking of laws, and (3) reactions to law-breaking. Following Sutherland's lead, *Engaged Criminology* is ordered around the three main tasks of criminology—with some additional adventures built in. As with most texts, the book begins with an introduction to the discipline and its methods. Then, *before* criminological explanations are presented, students learn what crime is, including perspectives on the origins of law, processes of criminalization, and crime typologies. Rather than devote half of the book to crime types, however, this text contains only two chapters: one on common "street crime" typologies and another on white-collar crime, organized crime, cybercrime, hate/bias crime, and terrorism. This book also differs from other texts by devoting an entire chapter to empirical patterns in criminology (demographic correlates, institutional correlates, and temporal and ecological patterns) instead of treating them as an afterthought in the methods chapter. The theories described in the subsequent chapters then operate as tools students can use to make sense of established crime correlates. Another feature that distinguishes *Engaged Criminology* is its coverage of victimology as well as several chapters on Sutherland's third task of criminology: societal responses to law-breaking (including Chapter 13: Theories of Punishment and Chapter 14: Place-Based Approaches to Preventing Crime).

Engaged Criminology is meant to be flexible. Not all instructors wish to cover the history of criminology (Chapter 6: Origins of Criminology). Some may teach a separate course on victimology and will opt to omit Chapter 12. Others may want to address the major theoretical perspectives (like control, learning, and strain theories—Chapters 8, 9, and 10) *before* digging into contemporary schools of thought, like feminist criminology and biosocial perspectives (Chapter 7). Instructors should use *Engaged Criminology* and its active-learning resources in any order or quantity that meets their needs and their students' needs.

However you choose to use *Engaged Criminology*, you will find yourself with a ready supply of exciting strategies for generating student engagement and fostering critical interaction with the most central ideas in contemporary criminology. By pulling students in with an inviting tone, fascinating real-life examples, hands-on active-learning exercises, and discussion questions that foster higher-order thinking, *Engaged Criminology* will get your students thinking like criminologists.

TEACHING RESOURCES

This text includes an array of instructor teaching materials designed to save you time and to help you keep students engaged. To learn more, visit sagepub.com or contact your SAGE representative at **sagepub.com/findmyrep**.

ACKNOWLEDGMENTS

Thank you to the team at SAGE Publications for sharing my vision for this book and investing in me as an author. SAGE granted me the freedom to write this book as I thought it ought to be written. Thank you for putting your trust in me. The greatest thanks go to Sponsoring Editor Jessica Miller, who championed the *Engaged Criminology* approach from the outset, and Content Development Editor Adeline Grout, whose tireless attention to detail has often saved me from myself.

Thank you also to Elon University. This book was written during a sabbatical made possible by support from Elon University's Faculty Research and Development funds. I am fortunate to work at a liberal arts university that supports faculty scholarship in its many forms, including contributions that develop pedagogy and strengthen undergraduate education. I am also thankful for my Criminology students at Elon University. They were the first audience for the content in *Engaged Criminology*. Their responses to classroom activities, discussion prompts, real-life examples, and my particular style of explanation shaped what this book became.

I am eternally grateful to Dr. Maxine Atkinson (North Carolina State University) and Dr. Kathleen Korgen (William Patterson University), editors of *Sociology in Action* and *Social Problems in Action*. Maxine and Kathleen invited me into the world of textbook authorship and advocated for me as a SAGE author. This book would not have happened without their support and guidance.

There is no person more important in shaping the trajectory of my career than Dr. Stacy De Coster (North Carolina State University), my dissertation chair, mentor, coauthor, and friend. She encouraged me to pursue professional goals that would bring me joy, and I am forever grateful that I listened. I am thankful also for the mentorship of Dr. Barbara Costello (University of Rhode Island), who helped a know-nothing 19-year-old fall in love with criminology and envision themselves as a PhD student and college professor. Thank you for laughing at my jokes and convincing me to apply to graduate school.

My heartiest acknowledgment goes to Jim Zito, who has supported my career and been a wonderful partner over the past 15 years. Thank you for being on my team so that I could write this book despite the 24/7 presence of a remote-school fourth grader. You listened to all of my gripes with minimal complaint, for which you deserve a medal or, at the very least, an acknowledgment in print. I love you.

Finally, thank you to the following reviewers who provided invaluable feedback that made this book stronger:

Michael Barton, Louisiana State University
Joshua D. Behl, PhD, Flagler College
John J. Butler, Quincy College
Ellen G. Cohn, Florida International University
John M. Hazy, Youngstown State University
Daniel Hebert, JD, Dept. Chair, Springfield Technical Community College
Sarah Jakub, MA, JD, Bucks County Community College
Suman Kakar, Florida International University
Shelly A. McGrath, University of Alabama at Birmingham
David L. Monk, PhD, Southeastern Oklahoma State University
Cynthia Moore, Hillsborough Community College
Jacqueline M. Mullany, PhD, Triton College
Rocio Paez, University of Arkansas
Billi J. Patzius, PhD, Lindenwood University

Dawn Marie Peter, Palm Beach State College
Rebecca D. Petersen, PhD, Kennesaw State University
Leslie-Dawn Quick, Marshall University
Michelle Richter, St. Edward's University
Todd Scott, Ph.D., Schoolcraft College
Karin J. Storm, Brandman University
Frank Trost, William Rainey Harper College
Prabha Unnithan, Colorado State University
Ting Wang, University of North Carolina at Greensboro
M. Nicole Warehime, PhD, University of Central Oklahoma
Tiffany N. Williams, Sandhills Community College
Jan Yager, PhD, John Jay College of Criminal Justice
Egbert Zavala, University of Texas at El Paso

Special thanks are also due to the subject matter experts who scripted or reviewed the Concepts in Criminology animated videos that appear in the Vantage version of this text:

Viviana Andreescu, University of Louisville
Ellen Cohn, Florida International University
Terri Earnest, University of Texas at San Antonio
Paul Nunis, Arkansas State University
Gillian Pinchevsky, University of Nevada, Las Vegas
Michelle Richter, St. Edward's University
Nicole Sherman, California State University Chico
Andrew Walker, West Virginia University at Parkersburg
Jessica Warner, Miami University

ABOUT THE AUTHOR

Photo by Kim Walker

Rena C. Zito is Associate Professor of Sociology at Elon University, where she also serves as the coordinator of the Criminal Justice Studies program. Her research on families and delinquency, criminological theory, and intimate partner violence appears in the *Journal of Interpersonal Violence, Youth & Society, Australian and New Zealand Journal of Criminology, Journal of Youth and Adolescence, Journal of Contemporary Criminal Justice, Sociological Focus, Journal of Family Issues, Journal of Marriage and Family, Sociological Perspectives,* and in edited volumes, including *Preventing Crime and Violence, The Handbook on Race, Ethnicity, Crime, and Justice,* and *The Handbook of Teaching and Learning in Sociology*. In addition, she served as the criminology area editor for the American Sociological Association's Teaching Resources and Innovations Library in Sociology (TRAILS) for six years and is a contributing author on two active-learning undergraduate textbooks published by SAGE: *Sociology in Action* and *Social Problems in Action*.

⑤SAGE criminology&criminaljustice
arresting content. unlocking potential.

SAGE founder Sara Miller McCune pioneered publishing programs dedicated to social justice and equality. Over the decades, we have supported research and writing that challenge complacency, critique injustices, and seek to provide insights into how to create a more just and equitable world. We are proud of this legacy, but we can and need to do more.

OUR MISSION STATEMENT

Believing passionately in **the power of education** to transform the criminal justice system, **SAGE criminology & criminal justice** offers compelling content that explores questions of justice, equality, and ethics. With an extensive list written by renowned academics and practitioners, we are a committed partner in helping bring **innovative approaches** to the classroom. Our focus on critical thinking, application and **social justice** across the curriculum helps instructors prepare the next generation of criminal justice professionals to create meaningful, **real-world change**.

OUR COMMITMENT TO DIVERSITY, EQUITY, INCLUSION, AND SOCIAL JUSTICE

SAGE strongly condemns racism, police brutality, and injustice in any form and acknowledges the structural racism in American social institutions, including the criminal justice system, as well as housing, education, healthcare, and others.

As outlined in our mission statement, we firmly believe that education can help transform the criminal justice system and we are deeply committed to upholding principles of diversity, equity, inclusion, and social justice in our content. At SAGE, our goal is to ensure that we are doing our part to get instructors and students thinking critically and creatively about issues in the criminal justice system, so they have the skills that they need to address bias, make ethical decisions, and use evidence-based practices to affect change in a system distorted by centuries of structural racism.

Recognizing the need to address structural racism and systemic inequality at every opportunity, this charter codifies our commitment to publishing criminal justice content that has a strong focus on ethics, reform, social justice, inclusivity, and diversity.

What SAGE and Our Authors Are Doing to Achieve This:

- Continuing to publish content that advocates for criminal justice reform and elevates voices of marginalized groups

- Making SAGE a more attractive publishing house for authors of color and authors from other marginalized groups

- Revising and creating content to meet more diverse and inclusive standards, to connect with current events, critical research, and issues related to social justice to foster learning to dismantle structural racism within the criminal justice system

- Providing instructors the tools that they need to have what can be difficult and challenging conversations about race and criminal justice in the classroom

- Ensuring our content is accessible to all learners

- Recruiting talent and cultivating a work environment that advances greater inclusion

- Maintaining an equitable approach in our content, accurately and fairly presenting evidence-based practices and research in a way that facilitates critical thinking

- Actively working to use language that is inclusive, respectful, and person-centered and adheres to the SAGE guidelines for bias-free language

In order to hold ourselves accountable for all that we have mentioned here, we need you → the reader, the student, and the instructor. We truly value your feedback and if there are things you read in this book that are inaccurate, offensive, or need to be clarified, please do not hesitate to connect with us to share your concerns so we can hold true to our mission of educating future professionals and academics.

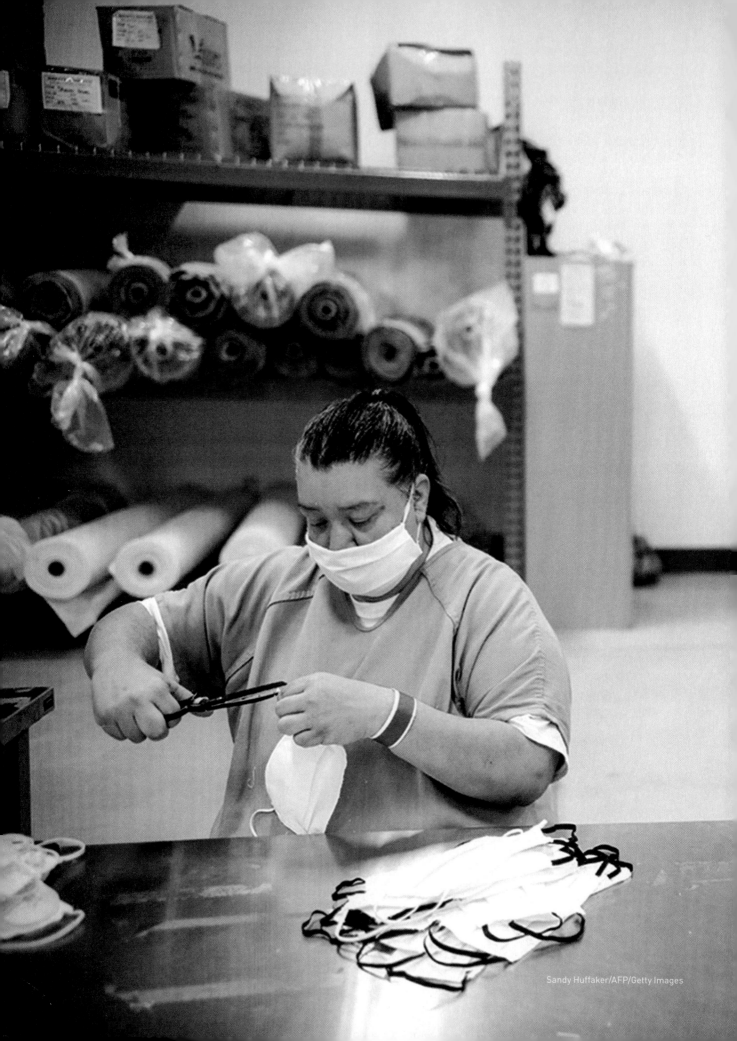

1 WHAT IS CRIMINOLOGY?

On January 4, 2020, the World Health Organization (WHO) reported a cluster of pneumonia cases, none of which had been fatal, in Wuhan, located in China's Hubei province. China reported its first death from the new virus one week later, on January 11. Exactly two months later, on March 11, 2020, the WHO declared the new virus, SARS-CoV-2, also called COVID-19, to be a global pandemic.[1] Around the globe, the spring of 2020 brought a wave of national and local policies restricting travel and nonessential services. Schools and businesses shuttered, and residents were encouraged or required to remain at home.

FIGURE 1.1 ■ Average weekly homicide rate in 22 U.S. cities, January 2018 to June 2021

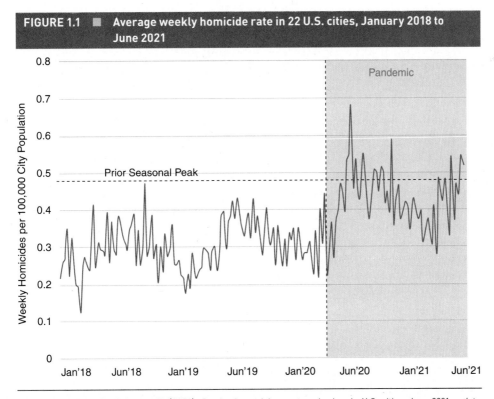

Source: Rosenfeld, R., & Lopez, E. (2021). *Pandemic, social unrest, and crime in U.S. cities: June 2021 update.* Washington, DC: Council on Criminal Justice.

1

As epidemiologists discussed infection rates and economists tracked unemployment numbers, criminologists were considering an entirely different set of outcomes.[2] What, they wondered, would this mean for crime? Will household burglaries plummet now that nearly everyone was at home? Will domestic violence and child abuse skyrocket as victims find themselves trapped with their abusers? What about robberies and murders now that bars are closed and fewer people are interacting in public? Will the inevitable financial stresses and a building sense of despair push people towards violence? Will crime run rampant when a large proportion of police officers cannot work due to illness or quarantine? Should jails and prisons release older and medically vulnerable incarcerated people? And what happens if lockdown orders stir antigovernment sentiment and public unrest, leading to violent confrontations? These were just a few of criminologists' concerns. Perhaps they were right to be concerned: Figure 1.1 displays the rise in homicides that corresponded with the start of the pandemic, though the pandemic's role in the uptick remains a source of criminological debate. Can you think of any other criminological questions about the virus's effects?

CRIMINOLOGY AS A SOCIAL SCIENCE

You were probably not expecting a book on criminology to begin with a description of a virus. After all, criminologists study crime. Best to leave the study of infectious diseases to medical researchers and public health experts, right? Maybe not. To understand why criminologists have something to teach us about a global pandemic, we first need to understand what criminology is.

One thing you need to know is that criminology is a *social* science. Modern criminology is a branch of sociology, the scientific study of society, including how individuals both shape and are shaped by society.[3] Sociology focuses on human groups and social behavior. We may think of crime as *anti*social behavior, but it is deeply social. What do prison gangs, hacker networks, corporate officials who collude to defraud consumers, and groups of teenagers who get drunk and destroy mailboxes have in common? They are human groups engaging in social behaviors. Even those who violate the law alone—criminologists call them solo offenders—are social creatures to the extent that they are influenced by the world around them, not to mention that crime often involves social interactions with victims. And what a society regards as serious crime, and who is regarded as dangerous, reflects that society's values and priorities. Criminal punishment, therefore, is a collective response to behavior that the community—or at least those with the power to make such decisions—deems unacceptable.

Now a disclaimer is in order: Not all criminologists are sociologists. Criminology, though sociological at its core, is multidisciplinary, meaning that people in a variety of fields conduct criminological research. Criminologists count psychologists, neuroscientists, economists, anthropologists, epidemiologists, and even some biologists among their ranks. For example, economists help us to understand how illicit markets for drugs and guns operate,[4] psychologists examine the role of mental illness in exposure to violent victimization,[5] and biologists and neuroscientists raise the alarm about the influence of toxins, such as lead, on the developing brain and the ability to control criminal impulses.[6] What unifies criminologists is their focus on the causes and consequences of crime, victimization, and punishment.

The second thing you need to know about criminology: it is a *scientific* study. That is the *-ology* part of criminology (the *crim-* part refers, unsurprisingly, to crime). The study of crime relies on systematic observation rather than just logic, intuition, or theory. That is not to say that criminology lacks theory. Quite the opposite, in fact! Criminologists develop and test many theories, or explanations, of crime, victimization, and punishment. It is the *testing* that makes criminology scientific, or empirical. The word *empirical* refers to the use of observational evidence to verify claims. Chapter 2 (Researching Crime) is an exploration of the many ways criminologists use empirical evidence to verify or disconfirm claims about crime.

The third thing to know about criminology is what *kinds* of claims criminologists examine using empirical evidence. So far, this chapter describes criminology as the study of crime. That is accurate but overly simplistic. Edwin Sutherland,[7] a titan of early 20th century criminology, offers a more nuanced definition:

> Criminology is the body of knowledge regarding delinquency and crime as social phenomena. It includes within its scope the process of making laws, breaking laws, and of reacting toward the breaking of laws. These processes are three aspects of a somewhat unified sequence of interactions. The objective of criminology is the development of a body of general and verified principles and of other types of knowledge regarding this process of law, crime, and reaction to crime. (p. 3)

Notice that Sutherland's definition includes three domains of criminological study: (1) law-making, (2) law-breaking, and (3) reactions to law-breaking. This remains true nearly a century after Sutherland first penned the statement, even though much of what criminologists study today would be unrecognizable to Sutherland (e.g., see the section on cybercrime in Chapter 4). In addition, contemporary criminology also includes the scientific study of victimization, called victimology, which is the focus of Chapter 12. We can thus define **criminology** as the scientific study of the characteristics of, extent of, causes of, and responses to crime and victimization. Now let's investigate the three domains of criminology identified by Sutherland, using the global pandemic to guide our exploration.

Making of Laws

North Carolina criminal statute 14-12.8 reads: "No person or persons shall in this State, while wearing any mask, hood or device whereby the person, face or voice is disguised so as to conceal the identity of the wearer, enter, or appear upon or within the public property of any municipality or county of the State, or of the State of North Carolina."[8] The statute, first introduced into law in 1953, sought to criminalize the masked activities of the Ku Klux Klan, a hate group that terrorized—and continues to terrorize—primarily Black, immigrant, Jewish (and, earlier in its history, Catholic), and LGBTQI individuals and communities.[9] As you might imagine, a law prohibiting the wearing of masks on public property poses serious problems during a pandemic. The 1953 law contained exceptions for "masquerade balls," "holiday costumes," and "gas masks for civil defense drills" but not for public health measures. On April 22, 2020, the North Carolina state legislature drafted a revision to the law exempting mask-wearing "for the purpose of ensuring the physical health or safety of the wearer or others."[10]

The law's revision meant that wearing a mask in public was no longer a crime in North Carolina. But what about failing to wear a mask while throwing a house party—definitely *not* a masquerade ball—in violation of the governor's month-long order prohibiting congregating for nonessential activities?[11] That became a Class 2 misdemeanor (a low-level offense typically resulting in fines or probation, if enforced), though not because of the face-showing. Mask-wearing was legal but not mandatory. The temporary law was not without discontents, with groups of armed protesters gathering in the state capital to decry the restrictions.[12]

These examples highlight how the creation of laws is an ongoing social process. Criminologists explore how some actions (or inactions) come to be defined as crime and some people as criminals. This part of criminology overlaps with the discipline of *legal studies* and another branch of sociology called the *sociology of law*. Importantly, criminologists do not always agree about the reasons that some, but not other, actions are prohibited by law. Their varied and conflicting views are explored in later sections of this chapter (see Origins of Law and Defining Crime).

Breaking of Laws

On May 22, 2020, William Sadleir, a former executive at Aviron Pictures, was arrested in his Beverly Hills home for fraudulently procuring $1.7 million from the Paycheck Protection Program, a federal loan program created to keep small businesses afloat during the COVID-19 pandemic.[13] Prosecutors claim he used the money on personal expenses, including making a $40,000 car payment and paying credit card bills. Four days later, New Jersey used car salesman Ronald Romano was arrested for wire fraud and conspiracy to commit wire fraud. Allegedly, Romano pretended to be an authorized dealer of personal protective equipment to get New York City to pay $45 million for nonexistent goods.[14] Romano did not invent the scam, however. One month earlier, Christopher Parris, of Georgia, attempted a $750 million scheme to sell the Department of Veterans Affairs 125 million masks that did not exist.[15]

What leads people like Sadleir, Romano, and Parris to risk prison time for the chance of an illicit windfall (allegedly)? Why do some people commit fraud, robbery, murder, sexual violence, or any other criminal act while the rest follow the rules? Criminologists are, above all, interested in answering the question: What causes crime? They investigate the factors that lead some individuals to break the law. For example, criminologists who study white-collar offenders like the COVID-19 pandemic fraudsters consider how they develop justifications for their actions—"insurance will pay for it," "no one got hurt," "everybody cheats"—that permit them to maintain a morally intact identity.[16] They look also to national, workplace, and peer cultures that support or tolerate unethical behavior that leads to crime, especially when combined with easy opportunities for lucrative dishonesty.[17]

The "Why do they do it?" question captures only one slice of the criminological pie, though. Some frame the question as "Why *don't* people commit crime?" Those who ask this question often assume that "money without work, sex without courtship, revenge without court delays"[18] is inherently appealing and, therefore, we must focus our attention on why so many are able to rein in their wayward impulses (see Chapter 8 Control Perspectives). They seek to explain sources of control rather than focus on explaining criminal motivation.

Most importantly, criminologists turn their attention to explaining large-scale patterns in crime. The William Sadleirs and Ronald Romanos of the world capture the public's attention, made evident by the popularity of true crime podcasts and Netflix documentaries that explore the psychology and misdeeds of individuals who violate the law. But criminologists mostly regard individuals as data points, or tiles in a broader mosaic of crime patterns. We ask different questions when we look at the mosaic instead of the tiles. For example, criminologists ask questions such as the following:

- Why do some nations have more fraud than other nations?[19]

- What causes household burglary rates to go up or down over time, as observed in Figure 1.2?[20]

- Why are rates of police brutality higher in some communities than others?[21]

- Why do men commit more homicide than women?[22]

In explaining any person's criminal behavior or any large-scale crime pattern, criminologists invoke three factors: (1) motivation to commit crime, (2) controls that prevent crime, and (3) situational opportunities for committing crime (Figure 1.3). A would-be pandemic fraudster might be incredibly motivated by a personal financial crisis or simply a strong desire for easy money. They may also lack any controls, either internally (low self-control) or externally (no significant others, commitments, or watchdogs keeping them in line). Yet the fraud is unlikely if they do not have the opportunity to pose as, let's say, a ventilator distributor because they lack access to city officials, or because they do not have the knowledge required to be a convincing imposter. Motivation minus control does not equal crime if opportunity is absent. Likewise, all the opportunity in the world will not produce crime if no one is motivated to do wrong.

Motivation, control, and opportunity also help us make sense of large-scale crime patterns, including crime trends over time, across geographic locations, and between groups. Table 1.1 shows how we

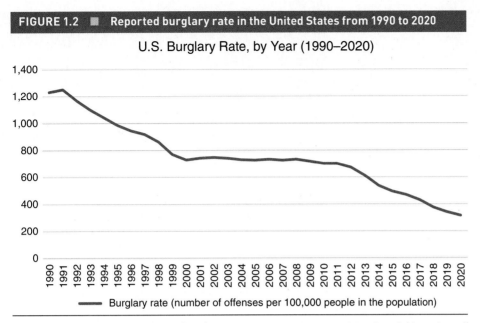

FIGURE 1.2 ■ Reported burglary rate in the United States from 1990 to 2020

U.S. Burglary Rate, by Year (1990–2020)

— Burglary rate (number of offenses per 100,000 people in the population)

Source: Federal Bureau of Investigation. (2021). Federal Bureau of Investigation Crime Data Explorer. https://crime-data-explorer.app.cloud.gov/pages/explorer/crime/crime-trend

FIGURE 1.3 ■ Three components of criminological explanations

can apply the three components to examples of crime patterns. Answering questions about the "breaking of laws" is the dominant task of criminology. That is why Chapter 5 (Patterns in Crime) takes a deep dive into a wide variety of trends criminologists observe. The chapters thereafter describe the theories—some focused on motivation, others on control or opportunity—criminologists develop to make sense of those empirical trends.

Engaged Criminology exercise 1.1 (Pandemic Criminology) asks you to think about and make claims regarding large-scale crime trends during the COVID-19 pandemic. You will use the three components—motivation, control, and opportunity—to hone your skills as a criminological thinker.

TABLE 1.1 ■ Applying the three components of criminological explanations to crime patterns

Example questions	Types of crime patterns	Possible questions	Example explanations
What causes household burglary rates to go up and down over time?	Crime patterns over time	Have opportunities increased or decreased over time?	Household burglaries increased in the 1960s and 1970s, as consumer goods became more portable and women's entrance into the labor force meant houses were more likely to be empty during the day. Rates declined in recent decades as security systems reduced easy access, and opportunities for other property offenses increased, such as phone thefts and identity fraud.
Why are rates of police brutality higher in some communities than others?	Crime patterns across geographic locations	Are there fewer controls in some locations than others?	Police brutality is less likely to occur in communities where police departments set clear administrative boundaries for use of force, citizen complaints are investigated, and sanctions are imposed when complaints are substantiated.
Why do men commit more homicide than women?	Crime patterns across groups	Are these groups differentially motivated?	Men are found to be more motivated than women to commit homicide because violence, especially the use of firearms, can be used as an avenue for asserting masculine status for men, but it does not help women to achieve feminine status.

ENGAGED CRIMINOLOGY 1.1

Pandemic Criminology

This activity requires you to make claims about the impact of the COVID-19 pandemic on various types of crime. Examine the criminal offenses listed in the table provided. Use the table to organize your answers to the following questions for each crime:

1. Are rates of offending likely to increase, decrease, or remain the same during a pandemic? If you come up with multiple predictions, write each of them down.

2. What are your reasons for the expected increases and decreases (or neither)? Record your reasons.

	Increase, decrease, or stay the same?	Reasons
Bank robbery *Definition:* Stealing money from a bank while subjecting employees or customers to force, violence, or a threat of violence		
Serial murder *Definition:* Murders of three or more people, with a significant time period between them and with the murders occurring over more than a month		

	Increase, decrease, or stay the same?	Reasons
Credit card fraud *Definition:* Form of identity theft in which an unauthorized person uses another's credit card information in order to charge purchases to the account or remove funds from it		
Vandalism *Definition:* Intentional destruction of, or damage to, public or private property		
Prescription drug trafficking *Definition:* Illegal sale, purchase, manufacture, delivery, or knowing possession at or above a specified quantity of prescription drugs		

Reactions to Law-Breaking

Laws prohibiting intentional spitting were in the news throughout the U.S. while the COVID-19 pandemic raged on. While such laws were not new, they took on a new level of seriousness, as many spitters—as well as coughers—claimed to have the virus. In one high-profile case, a 35-year-old Pennsylvania woman, Margaret Cirko, coughed and spat on approximately $35,000 worth of food at a grocery store, which had to be disposed of because she stated, "I have the virus. Now everyone is going to get sick." Cirko was not the only grocery store shopper expectorating maliciously. A 50-year-old New Jersey man, George Falcone, angered by a supermarket employee asking him to maintain physical distancing, leaned in to tell the worker he had the virus and intentionally coughed on her. Both Cirko and Falcone were charged with making terroristic threats, a felony. Cirko also faced one charge of threatening to use a "biological agent."[23]

Another kind of malady—one far more serious—was gripping the nation at the same time. On February 23, 2020, Ahmaud Arbery, a 25-year-old Black man, went for a jog in a suburban Georgia neighborhood near his home. Two white residents, a father and son armed with a shotgun and a .357 magnum revolver, followed Arbery, accosted him, and shot him twice, killing him, with a third man recording the murder on his cell phone.[24] Initially, police made no arrests and prosecutors did not seek criminal charges, citing Georgia's controversial "stand-your-ground" self-defense statute. "Stand your ground" laws allow people to use force, even lethal force, against threats or perceived threats to themselves or others. Unlike other self-defense laws, "stand your ground" laws can be invoked even if the person could have safely left the situation without using force. For this reason, "stand your ground" laws are also sometimes called "shoot first" laws. It took more than two months of public pressure and the release of graphic video footage for arrests to be made in Arbery's murder.

Less than three weeks after Arbery's murder, Breonna Taylor, a Black 26-year-old EMT, and her boyfriend, Kenneth Walker, were awakened after midnight by sounds of someone entering their Louisville, Kentucky, home. Taylor's boyfriend, a licensed gun owner, shot at the intruders in self-defense. They returned fire, striking Breonna Taylor eight times, killing her. Walker called 911, telling them "somebody kicked in the door and shot my girlfriend."[25] It turned out that "somebody" was police officers executing a "no-knock" warrant that permits law enforcement to enter without providing warning (i.e., knocking) or identifying themselves as police. Their apartment was raided because police suspected that two men being investigated for selling drugs, and who were already in police custody, had had packages delivered to Taylor's home, though no drugs were found. Walker was initially charged with first-degree assault and attempted murder of a police officer, but the charges were later dropped. No one has been charged in Taylor's homicide, though one police officer was indicted by grand jury for three counts of wanton endangerment for putting Taylor's neighbors at risk when shooting. The city of Louisville ultimately paid a $12 million settlement to Taylor's family and agreed to a series of reforms, including banning no-knock warrants and tracking police use-of-force incidents.[26]

Booking photos of Travis McMichael, his father Gregory McMichael, and William "Roddie" Bryan Jr., the three Georgia men found guilty in the murder of Ahmaud Arbery.

Glynn County Detention Center via AP, File

These cases—from malicious spitters like Margaret Cirko to the far more serious cases of the murder of Ahmaud Arbery and the police killing of Breonna Taylor—reveal something about modern-day responses to crime. They are, like all individual cases, tiles in a mosaic of broader patterns of criminal justice responses. The **criminal justice system** is comprised of the institutions and agencies, including policing, courts, and corrections (i.e., jail, prison, probation, parole), that are responsible for apprehending, prosecuting, defending, sentencing, imprisoning, and supervising individuals who are suspected, charged with, and convicted of criminal offenses. Criminologists study the functioning of criminal justice agencies and outcomes of criminal justice processing. Looking to our examples, criminologists might ask:

- Does the threat of jail time reduce the likelihood of low-level offending, like malicious spitting, relative to other forms of punishment, such as probation or fines?[27]

- What impact do "stand your ground" laws have on a finding of justifiable homicide (i.e., that the shooter will not face criminal charges)? And does it depend on the race of the offender and victim?[28]

- What are the predictors of police-involved shootings?[29]

- How does the public feel about militarized police tactics, like the use of "no-knock" raids?[30]

Some criminologists, observing patterns of injustice in the application of law and criminal justice processing based on race, ethnicity, and socioeconomic status, question whether *criminal justice* is the correct term for what we study. They offer alternatives, such as *criminal legal system* or *carceral system* (the word *carceral* refers to prison). People who favor the use of *carceral system* point to mass incarceration as the most prominent feature of U.S. crime control. **Mass incarceration** refers to the fact that United States has the highest imprisonment rate in the world, following a prison boom that began in the late 1970s and accelerated over the next 30 years, as in Figure 1.4. The U.S. is home to less than 5% of the world's population but more than 20% of the world's incarcerated population. Currently, 1.07% of all working-age adults in the U.S. are in local jails, state prison, or federal prison.[31] Furthermore, mass incarceration is experienced disproportionately by Black men, who are more than five times as likely as white men to be imprisoned.

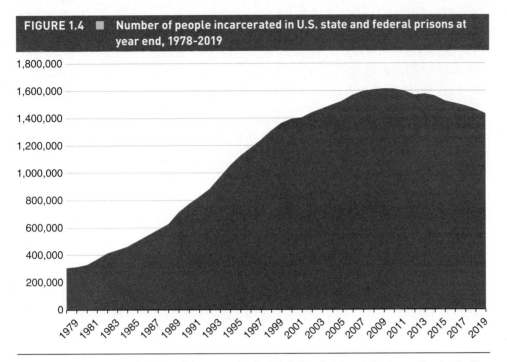

FIGURE 1.4 ■ Number of people incarcerated in U.S. state and federal prisons at year end, 1978-2019

Sources: Bureau of Justice Statistics. *Prisoners under the jurisdiction of state or federal correctional authorities, December 31, 1978-2019.* Correctional Statistics Analysis Tool - Prisoners. https://www.bjs.gov/index.cfm?ty=nps

ORIGINS OF LAW

Imagine that a cashier in Virginia is pocketing money that should be going into the cash register. Over the course of several months, the employee has stolen $500. In the state of Virginia, as in every U.S. state, it is a crime to steal money from one's employer. This type of workplace crime is called embezzlement, and in Virginia, it is a felony if the amount stolen is $200 or more; it is a misdemeanor if the amount is less than $200. A felony conviction is more serious than a misdemeanor conviction, as it carries a greater level of punishment, including the possibility of a prison sentence and a lifelong felony record. This is bad news for our cash register embezzler. But what if an employer steals money from workers by shorting their paychecks every week, amounting to a loss of $9,000? Fortunately for the victims in this case, Virginia recently passed a wage theft law,[32] which means that unscrupulous employers can face criminal penalties. However, in this case, the employer would only face misdemeanor charges, if charged at all. For wage theft, the threshold for a felony is $10,000 (versus $200 for employee theft). It bears noting here that Virginia's law is more extreme than in other U.S. states, most of which do not impose *any* criminal penalties for wage theft.[33]

Law is always a statement about what is acceptable and unacceptable in a society. But *whose* statement is it? Our answer depends on the assumptions we make about the origins of law. Is the more punitive legal response to the devious cashier than the devious employer a result of shared understanding of what is most harmful or immoral, or does it simply reflect power differences between businesses and the people who work for them? This is the distinction between a consensus perspective and a conflict perspective.

Consensus Perspective

The **consensus perspective** assumes that laws reflect general agreement (or consensus) in society about what is and is not acceptable behavior. Criminologists who adopt this position claim that there are shared values in society, and that law and its enforcement are expressions of an agreed-upon view about what is morally wrong. In sum, law and morality are inseparable. As a result, it is not criminalization or fear of legal repercussions that keeps most people from violating the law. Rather, people follow the rules because they have internalized social norms. Acts are criminalized *because* they are regarded as unacceptable by the society, and so criminalization is unnecessary for ensuring law-abiding behavior. In the words of Émile Durkheim, the famous 19th century sociologist and consensus thinker: "When mores are sufficient, laws are unnecessary; when mores are insufficient, laws are unenforceable." Mores (pronounced *mor-ays*) are social rules that have a moral dimension. The consensus perspective was common in late 19th century and early 20th century criminology but most contemporary criminologists have abandoned it, favoring a conflict perspective.

Émile Durkheim

Émile Durkheim (1858-1917), often called the father of sociology, is famous for two major contributions to criminology: (1) his concept of anomie, which is the focus of Chapter 10, and (2) his ideas about crime having important functions for society, which is addressed here. Understanding both requires diving into structural functionalism (also called functionalism), a perspective on human societies that dominated early 20th century sociology.

Let's start by imagining human societies like bodies. Human bodies contain many systems that work together to keep us alive and healthy—the central nervous system, the respiratory system, the circulatory system, and so on. The systems must work together in harmony to keep us chugging along. Functionalists use this as an analogy for societies. Like bodies, societies are also composed of many interrelated systems necessary to their survival. These systems are called social institutions, and they include family, education, economy, military, medicine, law, government, religion, and more. Change in one system requires adaptation in other systems so that harmony—or the status quo, if you're feeling critical—is maintained. For example, education must adapt to changes in the economy; as jobs become more technologically advanced, so too must education.

Functionalism presumes that features of social organization persist *because* they are functional for society. If they weren't functional, they would cease to exist (they would change through adaptation)! That brings up another important point about functionalism: It treats society as a thing that is separate from the individuals that comprise it. Conditions that are harmful to some—for example, inequality or crime—are presented as good for "society" because they serve a vital, positive purpose.

The spirit of functionalism infused Durkheim's position on crime. He began with two observations in his essay "The Normality of Crime":

1. Crime exists in all societies and in all time periods.

2. What is *called* crime differs across societies and time periods.

Durkheim reasoned that if a society without crime is impossible, then crime must serve an important function. It is an "integral part of all healthy societies."[34] Therefore, crime is normal, not abnormal or pathological (though too much or too little crime would indicate dysfunction). We generally regard crime as a bad thing—bad for victims, bad for businesses, bad for a fearful public. Can you think of any good outcomes of crime for society overall?

If you're struggling to come up with a positive consequence of crime, then follow Durkheim's suggestion to imagine a "society of saints." By our standards, the saints are exceptionally well behaved. They don't steal or fight or cheat on their taxes. But there will still be actions that are punished as crime. Crime might be spitting on the sidewalk or raising one's voice. The definition of crime will look different from our standards, but there must be *something* that is criminal. Why? Because it allows the saints to clarify their community's moral boundaries. In punishing the voice-raiser, they come together to passionately reaffirm their social solidarity, their sense of unity. Functionalism, therefore, is most assuredly a consensus perspective: It presumes that there is agreement in society about what is acceptable. Asserting their shared values strengthens their "collective consciousness." Durkheim dismisses deterrence and rehabilitation as punishment's goals. For him, punishment is about (and only about) strengthening the community's collective norms and values.[35] The audience for punishment is not the person who commits an offense but the honest onlookers.

The society of saints also depicts Durkheim's stance that the wrongfulness of crime is not in the act itself but in the social response to the act. That is why the definition of crime varies across places and time periods with different moral realities. He wrote,

> *The only common characteristic of all crimes is that they consist… in acts universally disapproved of by members of each society… crime shocks sentiments, which, for a given social system, are found in all healthy consciences.*[36]

A modern example is found in laws about child safety in vehicles. It was not unusual in the U.S. for unrestrained infants and toddlers to bounce around in backseats up through the 1980s, even though car seats were available and nearly all vehicles on the road had seatbelts. Today, however, it is considered a crime—albeit a traffic crime punishable primarily by fines—to fail to restrain a young child while driving.[37] Indeed, it "shocks the sentiments" of many people to see a toddler standing up on the passenger seat of a car going 70 miles per hour down the highway. Plus, actions that may shock the sentiments of U.S.-raised parents, such as motorcycle passengers holding babies, raise no eyebrows and invoke few penalties in other regions of the world.[38]

Many of Durkheim's ideas continue to shape criminology more than a century after his death, even though modern social scientists roundly reject functionalism. We will revisit the notion that social responses create "crime" in Chapter 11, on labeling theory. Plus, one of Durkheim's most important contributions to criminology—anomie theory (also called structural strain theory)—is so important that it gets its own chapter (Chapter 10).

Conflict Perspective

The **conflict perspective** assumes that law reflects the interests of those who are most powerful in society. Conflict thinkers assert that there are competing (or conflicting) values in society, and only some have their values written into law. In this view, law and its enforcement—or lack thereof—operates to maintain the advantages of the powerful. They draw attention to how the legal system deals disproportionately with the misdeeds of people with low incomes, criminalizing and punishing acts such as street-level drug sales, robbery, and behaviors associated with homelessness. Meanwhile, they argue, harmful actions of the wealthy are either not punished or not considered crime at all. For evidence, they

These demonstrators draw attention to Purdue Pharma's role in creating the opioid crisis, which aligns with the conflict perspective's emphasis on how power determines whose behaviors are worthy of punishment.

AP Photo/Seth Wenig

point to pharmaceutical company executives knowingly manufacturing and distributing highly addictive narcotics far in excess of legitimate demand, manufacturing and agricultural businesses polluting the environment through lax toxic waste disposal practices, and deaths or injuries caused by unsafe workplaces.

DEFINING CRIME

Tania Head was the president and director of the World Trade Center Survivors' Network and a ground zero tour guide. While leading tours, she would recount how she was working for Merrill Lynch on an upper floor of the south tower of the World Trade Center on September 11, 2001. Tania Head described how she was one of only 19 survivors who were at or above the area of impact when the plane hit the building. Her arm had been severely burned and she was close to death when someone picked her up and carried her to safety. Her fiancé Dave was not so lucky, having been killed while working in the north tower that day.

Only it never happened. Tania Head's real name was Alicia Esteve Head. She was not in the World Trade Center on September 11, 2001. In fact, she wasn't even in the United States. She was taking classes in Barcelona, Spain, where she grew up. Though her burn scars were real (the result of a car accident) and the man whom she falsely claimed was her fiancé did die tragically in the north tower, everything else in her story was fake. Tania Head's lies were exposed when the *New York Times* fact-checked details of her story for an article in September 2007. The public was appalled by Head's deception, and she was promptly removed from her position with the Survivors' Network. There is no doubting that Tania Head's—or Alicia Esteve Head's—acts were deviant and perhaps even immoral, but were they criminal? And should they be? Our answers depend on the approaches we adopt. We must, as criminologists, define our subject matter. The first step is to differentiate between crime and deviance.

Crime Versus Deviance

Proclaiming an act (or inaction) to be crime necessarily entails a judgment of social unacceptability, but not all frowned-upon behavior is against the law, like lying about being a 9/11 survivor for attention rather than financial gain. Furthermore, not all illegal acts violate social sensibilities, such as underage drinking. Social norms are rules of behavior that guide interaction, telling us what is desirable, allowable, and unacceptable in a given cultural setting. Deviance is the term given to violations of social norms, only some of which are codified in law. It helps to consider a Venn diagram whose overlapping circles are "crime" and "deviance," as in Figure 1.5. See if you can come up with examples of

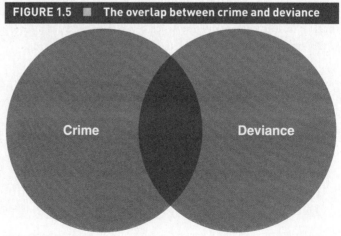

FIGURE 1.5 ■ The overlap between crime and deviance

Crime   Deviance

Use this Venn diagram to organize examples of acts that are (1) criminal but not deviant, (2) deviant but not criminal, and (3) criminal and deviant.

(1) criminal acts that are not generally regarded as deviant, (2) noncriminal acts that are typically considered to be deviant, and (3) acts that are both criminal and deviant.

Social norms include three types: folkways, mores, and laws. **Folkways** are the rules, often taken for granted, that govern everyday behavior. Think about the standards for how to act in a classroom (sit down, be quiet, don't wear a bear costume) or a public restroom (close the stall door, wash your hands, don't try to make friends). Those are folkways. Folkway transgressions usually evoke mild shows of disapproval. Mores, in contrast, are serious rules that dictate what is morally acceptable. For example, rules regarding religious rituals (e.g., prayer and handling of the deceased), human rights (e.g., freedom from slavery and torture), and acceptable sexual relationships (e.g., consenting, of age, and among nonrelatives) are mores. Transgressions of mores strike observers as morally wrong and therefore result in serious social sanctions. **Laws** are rules of behavior that have been formally codified by a governing authority, such as the state or federal government. Law violations result in formal punishments, including fines, probation, jail or prison time, and—where permitted—even death. Understandably, many mores, like those prohibiting killing and stealing, are written into law.

Think about each example you came up with for the Venn diagram in Figure 1.5. Are those violations of folkways, mores, laws, or some combination of the three?

The Harm Principle

Not all socially nonconforming acts are criminal, as your Venn diagram probably reveals. Why are some deviant acts (and nondeviant acts) criminalized while others are not? One answer is that criminal law, ostensibly, concerns only those acts that cause social harm (i.e., harm to others in society). The harm principle was famously asserted by 19th century British philosopher John Stuart Mill, who wrote:

> That the only purpose for which power can be rightfully exercised over any member of a civilized community, against his will, is to prevent harm to others. His own good, either physical or moral, is not a sufficient warrant. He cannot rightfully be compelled to do or forbear because it will be better for him to do so, because it will make him happier, because, in the opinions of others, to do so would be wise or even right. (p. 21)[39]

In other words, according to the **harm principle**, other people's distress, moral opposition, or belief that they know the "right way" to behave are not grounds for the criminalization of acts they do not like. Only that which causes harm to other people, such as physical injury, violations of privacy, or monetary loss, can justify criminalization.

We can see this principle in the U.S. legal system clearly in the landmark 2003 U.S. Supreme Court case, *Lawrence v. Texas,* in which the Court ruled in a 6-to-3 decision that laws prohibiting private sexual relations between same-sex consenting adults are unconstitutional. Justice Kennedy, writing for the majority, wrote, "The petitioners are entitled to respect for their private lives. The State cannot demean their existence or control their destiny by making their private sexual conduct a crime… the Texas statute furthers no legitimate state interest which can justify its intrusion into the personal and private life of the individual."[40] Others are not harmed by consensual sexual conduct that takes place behind closed doors; therefore, according to the majority opinion, the law is based only on moral beliefs about what people *ought* not to do, and that is insufficient justification for the law.

But which social harms are worthy of being outlawed? Though all may agree that murder and sexual assault represent harms to others, there is disagreement—or conflict—about what harms should be the domain of criminal law. Consider the following list of actions. All are criminalized in most or all U.S. states. Do you believe these acts cause harm to others, or just distress?

- Doctor-assisted suicide for the terminally ill
- Use of illicit substances by adults, such as cocaine or heroin
- Polygamy (marriage to more than one person)
- Providing sexual services for pay (or sex work)

Mala in Se Versus *Mala Prohibita* Crimes

Recall the crimes that you identified in your Venn diagram as violations of mores, or social norms that have moral weight. Those are *mala in se* offenses. *Mala in se* crimes are considered morally wrong irrespective of whether they are prohibited by law. The law, in this case, mirrors strong moral sentiments held by most people in society. *Mala in se* is Latin for "wrong in itself." In other words, the wrongfulness of the act is inherent in the act rather than in our labeling it "crime." Some examples include murder, assault, and child sexual exploitation.

Other offenses, called *mala prohibita* crimes, are regarded as wrong simply because they are against the law, not because they are inherently immoral, or a violation of mores. *Mala prohibita* is Latin for "wrong [because] prohibited." For example, think about the North Carolina law prohibiting public mask-wearing, from earlier, or laws banning the burning of garbage or public urination. Did your Venn diagram examples include criminal violations of folkways? If so, you identified *mala prohibta* offenses.

The photos in this Transgender Day of Remembrance memorial depict murder victims of anti-trans perpetrators whose *mala in se* offenses are violations of mores and laws.

Gillian Jones/The Berkshire Eagle via AP

Legalistic Definition

Criminologists study crime. But what do we mean by "crime"? There are several ways to answer this question. The most basic answer is: Crime is that which is illegal. Those who rely on a legalistic definition of crime believe that criminologists should focus on actions that violate criminal law. A *legalistic definition* of crime looks like this:

> Any culpable action or inaction prohibited by law and punishable by the state as a misdemeanor or a felony. (p. 30)[41]

Understanding the legal requirements of crime will help to explain each component of the legalistic definition. The two primary requirements of crime are *actus reus* and *mens rea.* The third requirement described—*nulla poena sine lege*—is a principle at the heart of the legalistic definition of crime.

1. ***Actus reus*** – A voluntary act must have occurred (or "guilty act" in Latin). *Actus reus* corresponds to the "action or inaction" portion of the legalistic definition. An act must be voluntary in that the person behaved with purpose rather than by reflex or accident. Your

professor has not committed a crime if they absentmindedly step on your foot, but they have committed a crime if they stomp on your foot in a fit of anger because your essay is late. In addition, conditions and beliefs are not subject to criminal penalty, as they are not actions. For example, it is not illegal to *be* a heroin addict (a condition), but it is criminal to manufacture, distribute, and possess heroin and other illicit substances.

There are exceptions to *actus reus*, called crimes of omission, which occur when there is a legal responsibility to act. For instance, adult citizens have a legal duty to pay taxes. Parents and legal guardians have a legal duty to provide basic education, medical care, shelter, and nutrition to dependent children. Tax evasion and child neglect are crimes of omission. It is the *failure* to act that presents the criminal conduct in crimes of omission.

2. ***Mens rea*** – An act or omission was committed with criminal intent (or "guilty mind" in Latin). *Mens rea* corresponds to the "culpable" portion of the legalistic definition. The word *culpable* means blameworthy. At the highest level of criminal intent, purposeful actions are intended to bring about a particular outcome, such as when Bryce Williams murdered his former coworkers during a live TV news broadcast. His was not a random act of violence. He fully intended to kill those individual victims. There is also criminal intent, albeit at a lower level, when people behave negligently or recklessly. For example, if a nursing home employee fails to provide food, water, and needed medication to a person in their care, and that person dies as a result, the employee might be charged with criminally negligent homicide. They may not have wanted the person to die, but they should have known it was a likely outcome. There are several legal defenses that counter claims of criminal intent, including claims of self-defense, entrapment, duress, and insanity. In those instances, the individual is denying *mens rea*.

Strict liability offenses constitute an exception to *mens rea*, as they do not require intent for a person to be legally responsible, or culpable. For example, traffic violations and driving while intoxicated are strict liability offenses. Even if a person claims ignorance of their driving speed or blood alcohol level, they are still subject to the law. In multiple states, statutory rape is also a strict liability crime, and claims that the offender did not know the child's age is not accepted as a defense.

3. ***Nulla poena sine lege*** – If there is no law, there is no crime (or "no penalty without a law" in Latin). *Nulla poena sine lege* corresponds to the "prohibited by law and punishable by the state" portion of the legalistic definition, as crime is an offense against the state, which creates laws and punishes the guilty. A person can intentionally engage in an act that harms another person, but if that act is not criminalized by the state, then the person cannot be punished for committing a crime. Consider the case of Hunter Moore, the self-proclaimed "professional life-ruiner" dubbed "the most hated man on the Internet" by *Rolling Stone*.[42] Moore created and ran a now-defunct "revenge porn" website called IsAnyoneUp, which hosted explicit images submitted by jilted exes, without the consent of the people in the photos. The images were often accompanied by personal details like phone numbers, social media profiles, and employer contact information so website users could harass the person, publicly shame them, and get them fired. At the time, in 2011, there was no federal or California state law criminalizing "revenge porn," or, more accurately, image-based sexual abuse of adults (Moore resided in California). Moore was ultimately convicted of hacking and identity theft because he had illegally gained access to email accounts to locate compromising photos, but he did not face criminal charges for hosting the website. Image-based sexual abuse of adults did not become a crime in the state of California until 2014.

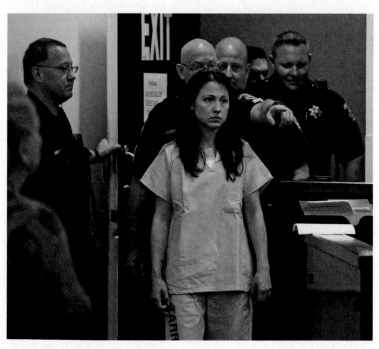

Sofya Tsygankova, who murdered her two daughters, was found not guilty by reason of insanity. The judge determined that Tsygankova, due to severe mental illness, lacked the *mens rea* necessary for a finding of guilt. She was committed to a state mental hospital.

Fort Worth Star-Telegram/Tribune News Service/Getty Images

ENGAGED CRIMINOLOGY 1.2

Considering Crime Seriousness

This activity requires you to rate the seriousness of criminal offenses and apply concepts from the chapter. Assign each offense a rating of 1 (very minor/should not be illegal) to 5 (very serious/deserving of life in prison).

| 1 very minor (should not be illegal) | 2 minor offense | 3 relatively serious offense | 4 serious offense | 5 very serious offense deserving life in prison |

1. A person is a vagrant (has no home and no visible means of support). This person sleeps on a public sidewalk.

2. A person attempts to kill a victim with a gun. The gun misfires, and the victim escapes injury.

3. A person, using force, robs a victim of $10.

4. A person plants a bomb in a public building. The bomb explodes and 20 people are killed.

5. A person is drunk in public.

6. A physician recommends and performs a surgery that they know to be unnecessary. The patient dies from complications.

7. A factory knowingly gets rid of its waste in a way that pollutes the water supply. As a result, 40 people die.

8. A person robs a victim at gunpoint. The victim struggles and is shot to death.

9. A person plants a bomb in a public building. The bomb explodes and one person receives minor injuries.

10. Several large companies illegally fix the retail prices of their products, costing consumers $100 million.

Answer the following questions:

1. Which was more important in determining your ratings—social harm or *mens rea*?

2. Identify one offense from the list that is a *mala in se* crime.

3. Identify one offense from the list that is a *mala prohibita* crime.

Source: Adapted from Wolfgang, M. E., Figlio, R. M., Tracy, P. E., & Singer, S. I. (1985). *The National Survey of Crime Severity* (pp. vi–x). Washington, DC: U.S. Department of Justice.

Criminal Law Versus Civil Law

Criminology concerns violations of criminal law, which differs from civil law (also called tort law). In criminal law, an individual has committed an offense against the state or federal government. Perhaps that sounds odd, given that we tend to view crimes as offenses against victims. But in legal terms, it is the government, which represents the people and establishes laws, that has been wronged. That is why criminal cases have names like *People of the State of California v. Brock Allen Turner*,[43] with the prosecutor representing the people at the state or federal level.

Criminal law can be sorted into two types: (1) substantive law and (2) procedural law. Substantive law pertains to the "substance" of law—it is about what is criminal and what punishments are associated with given offenses. The criminal statute that states that animal fighting is a third-degree felony in Florida, with animal fighting defined as "fighting between roosters or other birds or between dogs, bears, or other animals" is part of substantive law.[44] Procedural law is about the "procedures" or processes that occur in a criminal case. For example, the rules of court that state that a person facing animal fighting charges (or any other criminal charges) has a right to an attorney is part of procedural law. Elements of criminal procedural law also include the requirement of probable cause for an arrest, rules of evidence, presentation of witnesses, and the right to appeal, among others.

Civil law, in contrast, deals with disputes between parties. Lawsuits are the domain of civil law. In civil cases, plaintiffs, who are typically persons or businesses, claim to have been harmed by the actions of other persons, businesses, or other entities. That is why civil cases have names like *Franklin v. Peterson*.[45] Civil cases differ from criminal cases in other ways, as well, including the burden of proof required and the penalties incurred. Criminal cases require "proof beyond a reasonable doubt," whereas the burden of proof for civil cases is "a preponderance of the evidence," meaning that the winning side's evidence was more convincing than the other side's evidence. And while a criminal conviction usually results in probation or incarceration, losing a civil case never leads to imprisonment but instead results in a financial penalty (called damages) or an order to change behavior (called an injunction).

Interactionist Definition

The French Enlightenment author Voltaire wrote, "It is forbidden to kill; therefore all murderers are punished unless they kill in large numbers and to the sound of trumpets."[46] Voltaire died more than a century before the first criminologists put pen to paper, but we can see an interactionist spark in his observation.

The *interactionist definition* suggests that what we call crime depends upon our shared understandings of the behavior and the reactions it generates rather than simply that which is most harmful to society. It is rooted in the sociological perspective of social constructionism. Social constructionism holds that we create meaning through our interactions, and we act based on those meanings, thereby creating and re-creating our social reality. Money is a useful example of social construction. Imagine a $20 bill. The paper bill, itself, lacks any inherent value. However, it becomes valuable because we collectively define it as valuable and we act as if it is valuable. (You, your landlord, and the clerk at your local convenience store agree on this point.) According to the interactionist definition, the same is true of crime, deviance, and even harm itself. For example, interactionists point out that the commonly held stereotype of the "typical criminal" as young, male, low-income, and Black is created through a social process of criminalizing the harmful actions of people who lack social or economic power instead of the even-more-harmful actions of the wealthy and powerful.[47] Corporate crimes, like environmental violations and manufacturing of unsafe products, are not what comes readily to mind when we hear the word *crime* because we occupy a social world in which the legal system defines crimes of poverty—and those who commit them—as most dangerous.

The interactionist definition is based on **relativism**, or the notion that the deviance or moral wrongfulness of an act is dependent upon—or relative to—the cultural and historical context in which it occurs. Relativists argue that the wrongfulness of an act does not reside within the act itself but within the public's response to it. They point out that some acts that we regard as criminal today were considered socially acceptable in prior decades, such as driving while intoxicated or using a cane to discipline children. Other acts that were once considered immoral and criminalized are now regarded as ordinary, such as unmarried couples living together (or, according to an arcane Virginia statute, to "lewdly and lasciviously associate and cohabit together"[48]).

The relativist view of crime differs from **absolutism**, which posits that some behaviors are objectively, inherently wrong regardless of public sentiment or response. In essence, absolutists claim there are *mala in se* actions that are outside the reach of law. An absolutist might argue that doctor-assisted suicide for the terminally ill is morally wrong despite strong public support in favor of legalization (74% of Americans were in favor in a recent Gallup poll, as seen in Figure 1.6) and the fact that several states have legalized "medical aid in dying"—sometimes referred to as death with dignity laws—including California, Colorado, Hawaii, Maine, New Jersey, Oregon, Vermont, and Washington. From an absolutist perspective, this act would be viewed as criminal, regardless of law, and thus within the purview of criminology.

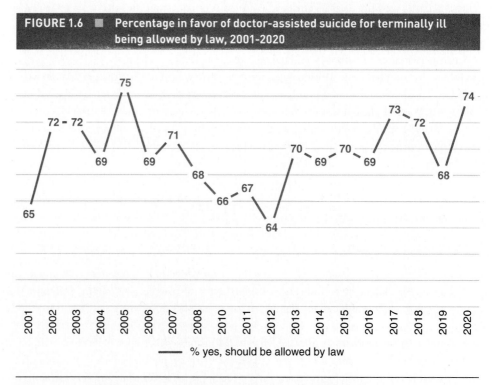

FIGURE 1.6 ■ **Percentage in favor of doctor-assisted suicide for terminally ill being allowed by law, 2001-2020**

——— % yes, should be allowed by law

Source: Jones, J., & Saad, L. (2020, May 1-13). *Gallup Poll social series: Values and beliefs.* https://compassionandchoices.org/wp-content/uploads/GALLUP-POLL-TOPLINE-2020.pdf

EXPLAINING CRIME

One project of criminology is to measure the extent of crime (the "how much" question). But, as you know, explaining law-breaking (the "why" question) is the dominant task of the discipline. Criminologists are interested in the etiology of crime. Etiology is the study of causes. Criminologists develop theories, which they test using data, to describe why crime occurs. A theory is an abstract explanation composed of proposed relationships between two or more concepts. For example, labeling theory, the focus of Chapter 11, proposes a relationship between the application of a deviant label (e.g., "felon," "delinquent," "addict," "sex offender") and heightened risk of subsequent law-breaking. According to the theory, deviant labels *cause* more deviance. In offering etiological theories, criminologists identify criminogenic conditions, or risk factors for crime (the suffix *-genic* means produced or formed by). For example, labeling theory suggests that deviant labels cause further criminal offending in part because they make it difficult for the labeled person to get quality employment, and financial stress is a criminogenic condition.

You will learn about many different etiological theories of crime in this book. That can be confusing. Students sometimes ask: Which one is right? The answer is that there is no one "right" theory of crime. In fact, theories are never "right"; instead, they are either supported or not supported by empirical evidence. And evidence can change depending on the time period, the location, the type of crime examined, and more. Plus, more than one theory, or portions of more than one theory, can be empirically supported simultaneously. Remember, theories are simply tools that we create to help us make sense of crime patterns. Some of our tools remain incredibly useful many decades after they were first developed (think of the timeless simplicity of a hammer!), but others deserve to be relegated to the dustbin of history.

Spotting Good Theories

The best way to understand what a "good" theory looks like is to start with a bad one. Imagine I develop a theory that sugar consumption causes criminal activity: People who eat more sugar are more criminal because the sugar rush causes them to lose all control over their actions. Ridiculous, right? Yes! But it's not that far off from an actual, though unsuccessful, criminal defense strategy—dubbed the Twinkie defense—that was used by defense attorneys for Dan White, who murdered San Francisco city supervisor Harvey Milk and Mayor George Moscone. The attorneys argued that White's excessive consumption of junk food exacerbated his mental health troubles, contributing to his violence.[49] There are many reasons why my sugar-crime theory is a terrible theory. Examine the list of characteristics in Table 1.2 and determine the reasons why my theory is, in fact, not sweet at all.

TABLE 1.2 ■ Characteristics of good criminological theories		
Characteristic	**What it means**	**Ask yourself...**
Parsimony	Theories that are concise and simple (or "elegant") are preferable to complex theories, all else being equal. When it comes to concepts and propositions of theories, smaller is better.	Is the theory simple rather than overly complex?
Scope	Theories with broader scope can explain more kinds of crime, such as property crime *and* violent crime or crime by juveniles *and* adults. When it comes to scope, bigger is better.	Does the theory explain many kinds of crime?
Logical consistency	Theories should pass the logic test given what we know to be true about crime patterns. Also, the claims of the theory must not be contradictory or built on incompatible assumptions about human nature or the origins of law.	Does the theory make sense?

(Continued)

TABLE 1.2 ■ Characteristics of good criminological theories (Continued)		
Characteristic	What it means	Ask yourself...
Falsifiability	Theories must be testable using data. Good theories can be falsified (or disconfirmed), whereas bad theories cannot be falsified no matter how much data one analyzes. Falsifiability requires that concepts in the theory are observable and measurable.	Can the theory be tested?
Empirical validity	Theories that are supported by evidence across multiple examinations are better than theories that receive partial, mixed, or no support.	Is the theory supported by evidence?

Source: Akers, R. L., Sellers, C. S., & Jennings, W. (2016). *Criminological theories: Introduction, evaluation, and application* (7th ed.). New York: Oxford University Press.

My sugar-crime theory has two things going for it: It is parsimonious and falsifiable. It is parsimonious in its simplicity (perhaps too much simplicity). Like nearly all contemporary crime theories, it is falsifiable in that I could measure and analyze individuals' sugar intake as well as their criminal conduct. However, as you probably figured out, it fails on the other three characteristics. Let's examine why the theory fails on scope, logical consistency, and empirical validity.

Scope: The theory is narrow in scope. It only explains impulsive crimes, such as assault. It cannot account for crimes that require planning or coordination, like accepting bribes, credit card fraud, or human trafficking (see Chapters 3 and 4 for descriptions of these and other crime types).

Logical consistency: The theory does not comport with what we know to be true about crime patterns. For example, we know that sugar consumption in the U.S. increased markedly over the past three decades. During those same decades, crime rates—particularly violent crime rates—decreased substantially. And countries with high per capita sugar consumption, such as Germany and the Netherlands, have very low crime rates relative to countries with less of a sweet tooth.[50] This, alone, is not enough to toss out the theory, though, as *individuals* who eat a lot of sugar may be more likely to engage in impulsive crimes, regardless of national patterns of sugar intake. Reaching conclusions about individuals based solely on nation-level evidence is inappropriate and called the *ecological fallacy*. This brings us to the third question: Is it empirical valid?

Empirical validity: We don't know. Criminologists have not tested the theory. After all, it is not a very good one. Other researchers have examined the impact of soft drink consumption on aggression in children or mice,[51] producing mixed findings. There is little logical or empirical reason to suspect, though, that adult crime can be predicted based on adults' taste for cookies and energy drinks. Other kinds of consumption, such as alcohol consumption, might be a better predictor of adult criminal conduct. Some criminologists even argue that the sharp decrease in violent crime during the 1990s in the U.S. was caused, in small part, by the fact that Americans were drinking much less than they had in previous decades.[52]

Determining Crime Causation

Criminological theories offer possible causes of law-breaking and other crime-related outcomes. For example, general strain theory, addressed in Chapter 10, suggests that stressful experiences, especially when they accumulate over time and undermine supportive connections to others, cause crime by producing frustration and anger. Chapter 8 includes a description of self-control theory, which argues that criminal offending is caused by low impulse control. Figuring out if those factors—strain, anger, low impulse control, or any others—are, in fact, causes of crime requires that three criteria are met:

1. *Statistical association* – To be a cause of crime, a factor must first be a correlate of crime. A correlate is a predictor, called a variable, that is statistically associated with an outcome, such as criminal conduct, incarceration, community crime rates, or risk of victimization. The predictor and the outcome are statistically associated (or correlated) if they vary together more

than would be expected by chance. For example, we know that having a parent who spent time in prison is a correlate of youth incarceration. Compared to children whose parents never went to prison, children of incarcerated parents are at much greater risk of ending up in juvenile or adult detention, a pattern referred to as the intergenerational transmission of incarceration.[53] Most children of imprisoned parents will not end up following in their parents' footsteps, and not all incarcerated young people have parents who also went to prison. However, by knowing whether a young person's parent spent time in prison, we can better predict whether the adolescent will spend time behind bars. Think about why that might be. Some possibilities include the loss of the parent's income and the emotional trauma of being separated, both of which might lead to youth law-breaking. But correlation does not equal causation. Two other criteria must be met.

2. *Temporal order* – For a correlate to be a cause, it must also precede the outcome in time. Temporal order is about the time ordering of the predictors and the outcome (notice the *tempo-* root, which refers to time or speed). Causes come before consequences. Let's stick with the parental incarceration example. A mother's incarceration cannot be a cause of her daughter's incarceration if the mother's stint in prison happened months or years after her daughter's imprisonment. In that case, the temporal ordering would be wrong. It is far more likely, though, that parental incarceration takes place prior to youth incarceration. We can be more confident in claims of causation if we find that to the be the case, as long as our last criterion is met.

3. *Nonspuriousness* – An association between a predictor and an outcome is spurious—and, therefore, *not* causal—if it is being driven by a third variable. We want the association to be nonspurious. In a spurious association, the predictor and the outcome have a shared cause (the third variable), which is making it appear that they are causally related even though they are not. A famous example of a noncausal, spurious association is the one between ice cream consumption and murder rates. When people eat more ice cream, more people get murdered. Of course, it's not that ice cream–induced brain freeze drives otherwise peaceful people into a lethal frenzy. The association is driven by a third variable: the weather. People eat more ice cream in warm weather months, and murder rates are higher in warm weather months. Our claim of a causal effect of parental incarceration on youth incarceration is far less outlandish. Nonetheless, it may also be spurious. Perhaps it is a matter of parents and their children experiencing similar conditions, such as substance abuse struggles or living in a high-crime, heavily policed community.

CAREER FIELDS THAT USE CRIMINOLOGY

Some college majors and minors have a clearly delineated career path. Nursing majors mostly become nurses. Education majors typically become teachers. For other disciplines, such as criminology, sociology, and psychology, the career path is not quite as proscribed. There are many options, with some but not all requiring education beyond a four-year degree. This section of the chapter will introduce you to career fields that interest students of criminology. The four fields described here do not encompass all possible criminology-related careers, but they do include a wide range of occupational paths.

Criminal Justice

The criminal justice system—or criminal legal system—includes policing, courts, and corrections (jail, prison, probation, and parole). Criminal justice is concerned primarily with official reactions of the state to violations of the law. In this way, the *study* of criminal justice is part of criminology: the part regarding reactions to law-breaking. But criminal justice, as a field, also includes the *practice* of criminal justice. For instance, a Department of Criminal Justice at a university might offer courses in Legal Procedure or Court Processes. Courses like these deal with the functioning of the legal system and the tasks of criminal justice professionals, including law enforcement, corrections officials, probation officers, prosecutors, defense attorneys, and judges.

Criminology offers insights that benefit criminal justice professionals. For example, criminologists study the impact of police practices on public trust, willingness to call for help, and cooperation with investigations.[54] They also examine what types of penalties and programs are most effective for reducing re-offending and improving life outcomes for people who have been convicted of crimes. For instance, learning from ample research on the detrimental effects of juvenile incarceration,[55] the state of Kentucky reformed its juvenile justice system to divert qualifying adolescents away from juvenile detention and into community-based services.[56] Criminologists also draw attention to stark inequalities in criminal justice processing, including disparities in police stops, searches, arrests, use of force, and sentencing on the basis of extralegal (legally irrelevant) characteristics, such as race, ethnicity, and social class.[57,58] Research-informed criminal justice agencies and institutions are able to implement practices shown to produce the highest levels of confidence, fairness, and public safety.

Forensic Fields

Forensic fields may appeal to you if you are drawn to the study of crime, but you have professional goals related to nursing, accounting, toxicology, pathology, clinical psychology, chemistry, molecular biology, or computer science. The word **forensics** refers to scientific techniques used in the detection of crime or in legal processes. The descriptor "forensic," therefore, is less about the type of work a person does and more about the context in which they do that work. For example, a forensic accountant is an accountant who identifies and gathers evidence of criminal activity in financial statements. Someone who works in computer forensics locates, maintains, recovers, and analyzes digital evidence for criminal or civil cases. Forensic nurses specialize in treating crime victims, and they are trained to collect and preserve medical evidence. All three work with law enforcement and may be called upon to present their findings in criminal proceedings.

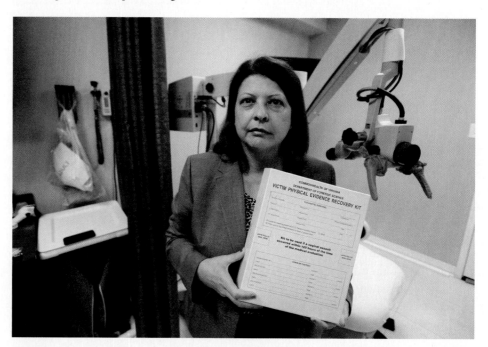

Forensic nurses use kits like this one to gather evidence used in rape cases. A national shortage of sexual assault nurse examiners means that rape survivors often must drive from hospital to hospital to find a nurse trained to examine them and collect physical evidence.

AP Photo/Steve Helber

Human Services

Human services is a broad career field that includes social workers, case managers, child advocates, crisis intervention counselors, substance abuse counselors, community outreach workers, and mediation specialists. The common theme among human services professionals is serving the needs of a specified group of people, with a focus on prevention and remediation of problems.[59] Many human services careers are in the public and nonprofit sectors, serving individuals who are involved in the justice system, at risk of becoming ensnared in the juvenile or adult criminal legal system, or are victims of crime. Some work within the criminal justice system as probation officers, parole officers, or juvenile court liaisons. Because human services is an interdisciplinary field, these professionals draw on insights from psychology, sociology, public health, criminology, and the study of criminal justice to inform their practices. Table 1.3 includes examples of human services careers that deal with issues in criminology.

TABLE 1.3 ■ Examples of human services careers that use criminology	
Career	**Description**
Child advocate	Serve as a liaison between neglected and abused children and state agencies. Speak on behalf of children in court and other settings. Responsibilities may include testifying in court, reporting to the child welfare system, interviewing children and family members, creating formal reports, and arranging services for children and caregivers.
Mediator	Work with parties in conflict to resolve disputes outside of the court system by providing neutral guidance. Responsibilities may include facilitating communication, interviewing witnesses and those involved in the dispute, and preparing court reports and other documents.
Juvenile court liaison	Ensure communication between school districts, parents, social services, police, attorneys, and juveniles. May work for the courts, a school district, or a private company that contracts with local governments. Responsibilities may include conducting screenings and assessments for the courts, working with families to rectify attendance issues, working on a supervisory team for juveniles on probation, filing legal documents, examining records, and making recommendations.
Victim services coordinator	Assist crime victims in accessing services and compensation, as well as assisting criminal justice agencies in working with victims. May work with prosecutors' offices or law enforcement agencies. Responsibilities may include assisting victims with court processes, interviewing victims and witnesses to direct them to appropriate services, educating the public about crime victimization, and instructing police on effects of practices on crime victims and witnesses.

Applied Research

Criminology, like all social sciences, is a research field. Some of that research is basic research and some is applied research. Basic research investigates the foundational principles in criminology, including theory testing. We learn about the causes and consequences of crime, in general, from basic research. This type of research is typically conducted by professors and other people with advanced degrees, usually PhDs, who work at universities and their affiliated research centers. Criminological applied research focuses on particular settings (e.g., Boston subway stations, high schools in Sacramento, a Toledo women's shelter) in order to identify immediate, real-world applications. It aims to solve practical problems. For example, the Crime Lab at the University of Chicago "partners with civic and community leaders to design, test, and scale promising programs and policies to reduce crime and violence."[60] One of their projects examined the impact of a Chicago City Schools youth mentoring and counseling program called Becoming a Man, which increased graduation rates and reduced the chances of arrest for boys and young men. Other examples can be found at RTI International, a nonprofit research firm that employs analysts to study crime, law enforcement, and corrections as part of their Social and Justice Policy area. In one study, researchers identified, and made recommendations for fixing, inefficiencies in the processing of sexual assault kits.[61] Sometimes called "rape kits," these kits contain physical evidence gathered during a forensic exam of sexual assault survivors, and they can be used to identify and convict offenders as well exonerate the innocent.

Research analysts have varied educational backgrounds, ranging from bachelor's degrees to doctoral degrees. Applied researchers are employed in many different settings, including

- Universities and affiliated research centers that partner with community agencies and organizations to solve local problems, like the Crime Lab;

- nonprofit and for-profit research institutes that apply for grants, conduct applied research, and publish research and policy briefs, like RTI International;

- Federal, state, and local government agencies that conduct research and publish reports on issues related to public safety; and

- Crime data analysis units of law enforcement agencies, who analyze police data to assist law enforcement in more effectively preventing and responding to crime.

CHAPTER SUMMARY

LO 1.1   Describe the three primary domains of criminological study.

Criminology is the scientific study of crime, including (1) the creation of criminal laws, (2) the causes of criminal offending, and (3) societal responses to crime when it occurs. The subdiscipline of victimology addresses the extent, causes, and consequences of victimization. A central task of criminology is developing and testing theories, or explanations, of crime, punishment, victimization, and other relevant outcomes using empirical evidence.

LO 1.2   Differentiate the legalistic and interactionist definitions of crime.

The legalistic definition describes crime as any action or inaction prohibited by criminal law. For a crime to have occurred, it must cause harm to others and have been committed voluntarily (*actus reus*) and with intent (*mens rea*). The interactionist definition, rooted in relativism, approaches crime as a social construction, acknowledging that what we define as crime, deviance, and harm depends on cultural and historical context.

LO 1.3   Compare the consensus and conflict perspectives on the origins of law.

The consensus perspective assumes that there is a shared morality in society regarding unacceptable behavior and that criminal law accurately reflects those sentiments. The conflict perspective assumes that there are competing interests and values in society among groups with differing levels of social power, and that the most powerful in society have their interests codified in law.

LO 1.4   Identify characteristics of good criminological theories.

High-quality criminological theories are simple (parsimony), explain a wide variety of crimes (scope), make sense (logical consistency), can be tested using evidence (falsifiability), and are supported by evidence (empirical validity). Theories address causality. The causes of crime identified in theories are causes only to the extent that they are correlated with the outcome (statistical association), occur prior to the outcome (temporal order), and the association with the outcome cannot be explained away by some other factor (nonspuriousness).

LO 1.5   Explore career fields that use criminology.

Career fields of interest to students of criminology include those within the criminal legal system (i.e., law enforcement, corrections officials, probation officers, prosecutors, defense attorneys, and judges), forensic fields, human services, and applied research. Educational requirements for careers in these varied fields vary tremendously, with some requiring doctoral degrees and others requiring associate's degrees or less.

ENGAGED DISCUSSION

1. What term do you think is best—criminal justice system, criminal legal system, carceral system, or some other term? Why?

2. Think of a recent high-profile criminal case that caused public moral outrage. Did punishing the person who committed the offense strengthen the community's sense of solidarity and shared values, as Durkheim describes? Why or why not?

3. Do you think Tania Head's deception (about being a 9/11 survivor) should have been considered criminal rather than just deviant? If so, what might that law look like? If not, why not?

4. Rank the five characteristics of good theories—parsimony, scope, logical consistency, falsifiability, empirical validity—from 1 (most important) to 5 (least important). Why does your ranking make sense?

5. If you had to pick one criminology career field to work in for the first five years after college (criminal justice, forensic fields, human services, or applied research), which would you select, and why?

KEY TERMS

Absolutism (p. 18)
Applied research (p. 23)
Basic research (p. 23)
Civil law (p. 17)
Conflict perspective (p. 11)
Consensus perspective (p. 9)
Criminal justice system (p. 8)
Criminal law (p. 17)
Criminogenic (p. 19)
Criminology (p. 3)
Deviance (p. 12)
Etiology (p. 19)
Folkways (p. 13)

Forensics (p. 22)
Harm principle (p. 13)
Laws (p. 13)
Mala in se (p. 14)
Mala prohibita (p. 14)
Mass incarceration (p. 8)
Mores (p. 10)
Procedural law (p. 17)
Relativism (p. 18)
Sociology (p. 2)
Substantive law (p. 17)
Theory (p. 19)

Jason Redmond/AFP/Getty Images

2 RESEARCHING CRIME

Gallup, a polling organization, has asked Americans "Is there more crime in the U.S. than there was a year ago, or less?" nearly every year over the past two decades. In all but two of those years, a majority stated that they believe there is more crime than in the previous year (see Figure 2.1). In 2020, 78% reported that there was more crime compared to only 14% who believed there was less (6% thought it was the same, and 3% reported no opinion).[1] If we are to believe the hunches of most Americans, then we must conclude that crime in the U.S. has increased year after year since 2002. But has it? We need accurate crime data to determine if our gut feelings are trustworthy. Our "common sense" beliefs about crime are subjective, shaped by political climate, media coverage, and personal experience.[2] Criminological research, in contrast, attempts to systemically measure crime to obtain as precise a count as possible.

FIGURE 2.1 ■ Responses to question "Is there more crime in the U.S. than there was a year ago, or less?"—percentages by year (2000-2020)

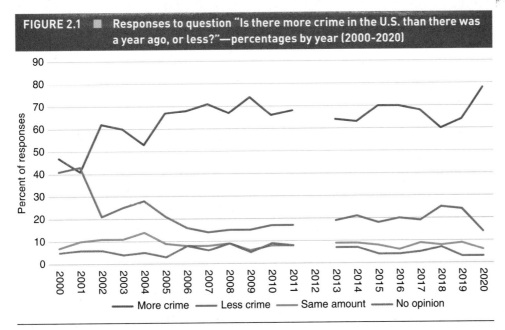

Note: Question not asked in 2012

Source: Gallup Historical Trends. (2021). *Gallup Poll: Crime.* In depth: topics A to Z. https://news.gallup.com/poll/1603/crime.aspx

Let's consider the consequences of relying on our intuition rather than systematic observation to determine the threat posed by crime. Fear of crime is a powerful predictor of psychological well-being and behavior.[3] Specifically, it keeps people anxious and indoors. Unjustified fears, then, reduce our quality of life unnecessarily. The belief that crime is always getting worse also shapes our political priorities and our trust in the agencies tasked with reining in law-breaking. Indeed, cultivating worries about crime is a tried-and-true campaign strategy dating back to the 1970s.[4] Having an accurate measure of crime is essential for making informed decisions, from deciding whether to avoid public transportation to determining who ought to represent us in government.

BASICS OF CRIMINOLOGICAL RESEARCH

Criminology is the scientific study of crime. This chapter is about *how* criminologists study crime, victimization, and criminal punishment scientifically. You will learn about the many methods researchers employ—in basic and applied research—to figure out (1) how much crime and punishment is occurring and (2) what predicts changes in crime and punishment Recall from Chapter 1 that criminology is etiological or concerned with causes. Criminologists also explore the consequences of crime and punishment (e.g., for victims and for formerly incarcerated people), attitudes towards crime and punishment, how criminal subcultures operate, and more. But before we get to the research methods used by criminologists, we must first address some basics regarding the purpose of our research (descriptive vs. explanatory), the kinds of data we collect (quantitative vs. qualitative), and the kinds of outcomes we are examining (levels of analysis).

Descriptive Versus Explanatory Research

Criminological research is either descriptive or explanatory. The roots of these words—*descript* and *explan*—clue us in about their meanings. Descriptive research seeks to describe the extent and characteristics of crime. It answers the "How much?" question: How many murders happened last year? What percentage of white-collar workers steal from their workplaces? How frequently do sex offenders re-offend after release from prison? Criminologists engage in descriptive research when they examine one variable at a time (a variable is a characteristic or property that can be measured and takes on multiple values). Notice that the example questions about murder, white-collar theft, and sex offender re-offending do not ask about the causes of these patterns, which would require mentioning two variables: a predictor and its outcome. Instead, those questions, as in all descriptive research, seek only to identify the patterns, not to account for them. They ask, simply, "How much?" We need descriptive research to determine whether the 78% of Gallup Poll respondents in 2020 who thought crime had increased since 2019 were correct. There are three primary data sources that criminologists rely on to answer the question of how much crime is happening in society:

1. Official crime statistics

2. Victimization survey data

3. Self-report survey data

Criminology, though, is etiological. We want to explain crime, victimization, and punishment. We are interested in causes. Explanatory research answers the "Why?" question: Why were there more murders in 2020 than 2019? Why do white-collar workers with high incomes commit money-generating crimes? Does age at release from prison predict whether a sex offender will re-offend? Note how the descriptive questions from earlier are transformed into explanatory questions by asking about predictors. Nearly all criminological research is explanatory, but describing the trends we wish to explain is a prerequisite to explanation. Both descriptive research and explanatory research are important.

Policy research is one type of explanatory research common in criminology. Policy research examines the impact of policy changes (like new laws, programs, and police practices) on crime and other outcomes. In this case, the predictor is the policy itself. Consider, for example, firearm restrictions for domestic violence perpetrators. People with histories of abusing their partners are prohibited by federal law, and some state laws, from purchasing or keeping guns if they are the subject of a domestic violence restraining order or they have certain misdemeanor domestic violence convictions (all felony convictions, regardless of domestic violence connection, result in the federal gun access restriction). Criminologists ask: Does restricting domestic abusers' access to guns reduce homicide? Policy research examining murders of abused partners and exes suggests that it does, in fact, have the intended effect.[5] And there is compelling evidence that the restrictions could also be effective for reducing mass murder, if implemented (many abusers fall through the cracks and there are loopholes for private gun purchases). A study of all mass shootings with four or more victims occurring between 2014 and 2017 revealed that nearly one-third of murderers had a history of domestic violence.[6]

Quantitative Versus Qualitative Research

Descriptive and explanatory research can be either quantitative or qualitative. Notice that these terms look like *quantity* and *quality*. That is a good starting place for understanding the distinction. *Quantitative research* relies on statistical evidence using numerical data. Criminologists Heap and Waters offer four main tasks of quantitative criminology: measurement ("How much crime?"), causality ("What causes crime?"), generalization ("Can findings apply elsewhere?"), and replication ("Can the research be repeated to yield similar findings?").[7] You are encountering quantitative criminology when you come across crime rates or descriptions of correlations between variables. Analysis of official crime statistics, surveys, and experiments are quantitative methods used by criminologists.

Qualitative research, in contrast, uses nonnumerical data, such as statements from people who are interviewed individually or in focus groups, descriptions of observations made by researchers (called field notes), or textual content from existing sources (e.g., Twitter posts, news articles, or offender manifestos). Qualitative data are typically comprised of words rather than numbers. They can also be images. Qualitative data are useful for gaining insight into "lived experiences," including how individuals create meaning.[8] Criminologists obtain qualitative data when conducting in-depth interviews and ethnographies, as well as when they use certain unobtrusive methods.

The type of data—quantitative or qualitative—criminologists opt to use is determined by their research questions. Some questions can only be answered using numerical data (e.g., Does widespread unemployment increase property crime rates?), and others require the discursive, or wordy, data of qualitative research (e.g., How do gang members create a moral code that permits some forms of violence while prohibiting other types?). Mixed-method studies combine qualitative and quantitative methods to gain a fuller understanding of their subject. For example, in a study of how abandoned housing—and its demolition—matters for nearby crime, criminologists analyzed two types of data from a high-crime Ohio community: (1) quantitative data from "calls for service" (911 calls and nonemergency calls to police) and video recordings of community properties and (2) qualitative data from interviews with law enforcement, ex-offenders, and community members.[9] The interviewees' observations about how vacant houses are perceived by residents and why people (don't) call 911 provided essential context for interpreting the statistical association between razing abandoned houses and a reduction in nearby crime.

In the ethnography *Down, Out, and Under Arrest*, researcher Forrest Stuart observed and interviewed police and those who are policed in LA's Skid Row. Stuart's research was qualitative.

AP Photo/Nick Ut

Levels of Analysis

When conducting research, criminologists observe the social world as though through the lens of a camera. Our level of analysis, or the scale or size of our research focus, determines what we see through the lens. We can zoom in to study individuals, asking questions like "Does moving to a low-poverty neighborhood reduce the risk of arrest for adolescents?" or "Does ADHD increase criminal activity in young adulthood?" Moving, having ADHD symptoms, being arrested, and criminal activity are individual variables: Some individuals move and others stay put, some individuals have ADHD symptoms and others don't, and so on. Therefore, we would need to examine data on individuals to answer these questions. This is individual-level research, which is also called micro-level research.

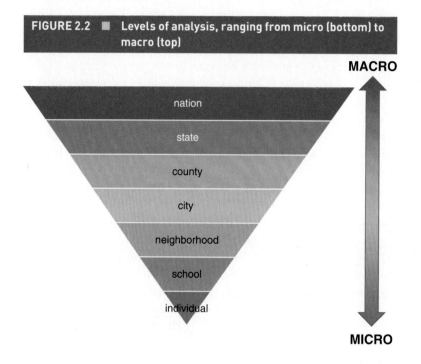

FIGURE 2.2 ■ Levels of analysis, ranging from micro (bottom) to macro (top)

MACRO

nation

state

county

city

neighborhood

school

individual

MICRO

Now let's zoom out a little to examine neighborhood variation instead of individual variation. With our lens focused on neighborhoods, we might ask questions like "Is there more robbery in neighborhoods with a higher density of pawn shops, payday lenders, and liquor stores?" or "Is there less vandalism in neighborhoods where residents know and trust one another?" We need neighborhood data, like neighborhood crime rates and counts of pawn shops per square mile. This is neighborhood-level research. If we zoom out even more, we might see cities through our lens. Even more zooming and we will analyze states. The most macro-level studies examine variation across nations or regions of the world. Figure 2.2 depicts levels of analysis commonly used in criminology, but it does not list all possibilities. For example, criminologists who study white-collar offending often focus their lens on workplaces.[10] And gang researchers, conducting gang-level research, compare gangs of different types to see which are the most violent.[11]

OFFICIAL CRIME STATISTICS

Criminologists have the formidable task of figuring out how much crime is happening in society, a descriptive and quantitative process. Official crime statistics are measures of crime—mostly in the form of crime counts and rates—provided by criminal justice agencies, including police, courts, and correctional agencies. Law enforcement are the first point of entry into criminal justice processing, making them the most important source of official crime data when attempting to measure the total amount of crime occurring.

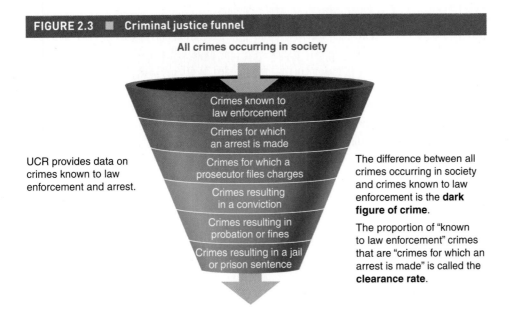

FIGURE 2.3 ■ Criminal justice funnel

All crimes occurring in society

Crimes known to
law enforcement

Crimes for which
an arrest is made

Crimes for which a
prosecutor files charges

Crimes resulting
in a conviction

Crimes resulting in
probation or fines

Crimes resulting in a jail
or prison sentence

UCR provides data on crimes known to law enforcement and arrest.

The difference between all crimes occurring in society and crimes known to law enforcement is the **dark figure of crime**.

The proportion of "known to law enforcement" crimes that are "crimes for which an arrest is made" is called the **clearance rate**.

The criminal justice system acts as a funnel. Most illegal activity goes on without detection. It never ends up in the funnel. The crime that happens without ever becoming known to officials is called the dark figure of crime. Think about the ways that crime comes to the public's attention. It typically begins with a complainant, a person who reports a crime to an appropriate agency, such as the police or Child Protective Services. Of all the crimes that go on, only a portion will ever become known to law enforcement. For offenses like drug trafficking and possession, there are no victims to report it. For offenses like identity theft and fraud, victims may not be aware that they have been targeted, or they may see it as something to report to their credit card company rather than the police. And victims are frequently reticent to report crimes like intimate partner violence and rape.

As the funnel narrows, the portion of all crimes measured becomes smaller. Once an offense becomes known to law enforcement, it *may* result in an arrest. Once an arrest is made, it *may* lead to a conviction. Once a person is convicted, they *may* serve time in a correctional facility. Therefore, crime statistics from police provide a more valid answer to the "How much?" question than do prison data.

This does not mean that data from further down the funnel are useless. After all, criminologists are interested in more than just counting crimes. Data on arrests, sentencing, and other criminal justice outcomes are especially helpful for answering explanatory questions about inequalities. For example, a criminologist used arrest data from the St. Louis Metropolitan Police Department to determine the role of racially discriminatory policing in drug arrests, finding evidence of "out-of-place" racial profiling, or targeting people whose race doesn't match that of most residents.[12] In another study, criminologists used data from the Pennsylvania Sentencing Commission to examine if women and men are punished equally when convicted of child neglect and child physical abuse. Male abusers, they found, were more likely than female abusers to be sentenced to prison, due—though only in part—to men's more extensive criminal histories.[13]

Uniform Crime Reporting (UCR) Program

The Uniform Crime Reporting (UCR) program is the longest running source of official crime data in the U.S. It was created in 1929 with data collection beginning the next year, following efforts by the International Association of Chiefs of Police to design a standardized (or uniform) system for reporting and tracking crime statistics. The Federal Bureau of Investigation (FBI) was tasked with compiling crime data submitted voluntarily by local, state, and federal police agencies. The percentage of law enforcement agencies submitting their data has increased substantially over time, with about 99% of the U.S. population now living in police jurisdictions that submit data to the FBI for the UCR program.[14] The UCR crime statistics are published annually in a report called *Crime in the United States.*

Initially, the UCR provided data on only seven criminal offenses, including four violent crimes (murder and nonnegligent manslaughter, aggravated assault, forcible rape, and robbery) and three property crimes (burglary, larceny-theft, and motor vehicle theft). An additional property offense, arson, was added in 1979. The UCR referred to the eight offenses as *index crimes* or *Part I offenses*, and it provided rates of index offenses known to law enforcement as well as arrest statistics (see Chapter 3 for index offense descriptions). Revisions in the 1980s added 21 offense categories for which arrest data were provided: simple assault, curfew offenses and loitering, embezzlement, forgery and counterfeiting, disorderly conduct, driving under the influence, drug offenses, fraud, gambling, liquor offenses, offenses against the family, prostitution, public drunkenness, runaways, sex offenses, stolen property, vandalism, vagrancy, and weapons offenses. These were *Part II offenses.*

For years, *Crime in the United States* presented aggregated counts and rates of Part I and Part II offenses as part of the Summary Reporting System (SRS), the principal data source for researchers attempting to measure and track crime in the U.S. But the SRS's critics pointed out three significant limitations that could be improved with a better data reporting system[15]:

- The SRS covered only a narrow range of offenses. It did not include data on specific forms of crime that are of interest to researchers, law enforcement, and policy makers (e.g., gang crime, firearm violence, domestic violence, crimes against children, white-collar offenses).

- The SRS only reported one crime per incident. Only the most serious crime was reported if multiple offenses took place during a single criminal event. This is called the *hierarchy rule.* For example, if a burglar happened upon a homeowner and killed them, only the homicide was counted (not the burglary).[16]

- The SRS used aggregate, or summed, monthly counts of crimes that obscured important factors like offense location, victim-offender relationship, and time of day.

Other limitations of the SRS were general critiques of official crime data and were not specific to the SRS. Among these were critiques that (1) the SRS only entailed crimes reported or known to police, (2) political pressures have occasionally led agencies to "fudge" the numbers to appear more effective at crime control, and (3) racial/ethnic and socioeconomic biases, in part, influence arrests and, therefore, arrest data.

Notice the use of past tense in describing the SRS. The reason is the recent phasing out of the summary reports in favor of a system that provides complex and detailed information on criminal incidents, including characteristics of the criminal events, the offenders, and the victims. The transition to the new system, called the National Incident-Based Reporting System (NIBRS), represents "one of the most significant changes in crime measurement in U.S. history" (p. 1030).[17] Today, the UCR program houses four data collections, with NIBRS now the primary source of official crime statistics in the U.S.:

1. The National Incident-Based Reporting System (NIBRS)

2. The Law Enforcement Officers Killed and Assaulted (LEOKA) Program

3. The Hate Crime Statistics Program

4. The National Use-of-Force Data Collection (newest addition)

National Incident-Based Reporting System

The **National Incident-Based Reporting System (NIBRS)**, which replaced the summary reporting system in 2021, is a clearinghouse for detailed crime data reported by local, state, tribal, and federal police agencies. It avoids the three major shortcomings of its predecessor: (1) a limited number of offenses included, (2) the hierarchy rule, and (3) reliance on aggregate counts that fail to supply offense details.

First, NIBRS expanded the crime categories for reported offenses and arrests, now providing information on 22 *Group A offense categories* containing 46 specific crimes. NIBRS also furnishes arrest data (only) for 10 additional *Group B offense categories* (see Table 2.1). In addition, it broadened the range of offenses included in the categories that had been previously reported in the summary reports. For example, the SRS reported aggravated assault, which was defined as an "unlawful attack by one person upon another for the purpose of inflicting severe or aggravated bodily injury," typically with the use of a weapon or "by other means likely to produce death or great bodily harm."[18] In other words, only the most serious form of assault. NIBRS reports multiple assault offenses, including aggravated assault, simple assault (assault without severe bodily harm), and intimidation.

TABLE 2.1 ■ Group A and Group B offenses reported in National Incident-Based Reporting System	
Group A offense categories (known offenses and arrests)	
Arson	Homicide offenses
Assault offenses	Kidnapping/abduction
Bribery	Larceny/theft offenses
Burglary/breaking and entering	Motor vehicle theft
Counterfeiting/forgery	Pornography/obscene materials
Destruction/damage/vandalism of property	Prostitution offenses
Drug/narcotic offenses	Robbery
Embezzlement	Sex offenses, forcible
Extortion/blackmail	Sex offenses, nonforcible
Fraud offenses	Stolen property offenses
Gambling offenses	Weapons law violations
Group B offense categories (arrests only)	
Bad checks	Family offenses, nonviolent
Curfew/loitering/vagrancy violations	Liquor law violations
Disorderly conduct	Peeping Tom
Driving under the influence	Trespass of real property
Drunkenness	All other offenses

Source: Federal Bureau of Investigation. (n.d.). *A guide to understanding NIBRS.* https://ucr.fbi.gov/nibrs/2012/resources/a-guide-to-understanding-nibrs

Second, NIBRS does not use the hierarchy rule. Multiple crimes can take place during a single incident (recall the homicidal burglar from earlier). NIBRS allows for up to 10 offenses to be reported in one criminal incident. Plus, unlike the earlier system, NIBRS data indicate if a criminal incident had multiple offenders and/or multiple victims. Simply put, it provides a fuller picture of crime. In fact, some law enforcement agencies early on worried that transitioning to NIBRS would give the appearance of a crime boom because the hierarchy rule would no longer suppress crime counts. To test if this was true, the FBI compared crime estimates supplied by the SRS and NIBRS over a 20-year period and found only minimal increases in Part I offenses when using NIBRS (less than a 1% increase for rape, robbery, aggravated assault, and burglary and a 3% increase for larceny-theft and motor vehicle theft).[19] The reasons? Most crimes were single-incident offenses. If they weren't, then the additional crimes were not Part I offenses.

Third, NIBRS is, as its name implies, an incident-based data source. It provides extensive details about criminal incidents not captured by traditional aggregate reports. Table 2.2 lists the data points, called elements, that NIBRS organizes into data segments: incident information, offense information, property information, victim information, offender information, and arrest information (see Table 2.2). In addition to offering demographic data on offenders and victims, NIBRS allows users to analyze what happened during criminal incidents, such as when they happened, where they happened, whether offenders were drunk or high, how many used weapons, and the nature of the relationships between offenders and victims. It also reveals the consequences of crime for victims, including the extent of injury and property loss.

Darryl McCauley, the half-brother of comedian Dane Cook, was sentenced to five to six years in prison for embezzling $10 million from the entertainer. His offense, embezzlement, would be counted as a "known offense" in NIBRS but not in the UCR's summary reporting system.

AP Photo/Lisa Poole, pool

TABLE 2.2 ■ Data reported in National-Incident Based Reporting System	
Data segment	**Data elements included**
Incident information	(1) incident date, (2) incident hour, (3) exceptional clearance, (4) exceptional clearance date
Offense information	(1) offense code, (2) attempted or completed, (3) offender suspected of using (alcohol, drugs, computers), (4) location, (5) type and number of premises entered, (6) type of criminal activity/gang information, (7) weapon/force used, (8) bias motivation
Property information	(1) loss type, (2) property description, (3) value of property, (4) date recovered, (5) number of motor vehicles stolen/recovered, (6) drug types and amounts
Victim information	(1) connection to offenses, (2) type of victim, (3) age, sex, race, ethnicity, and resident status, (4) assault and homicide circumstances, (5) injury types, (6) relationships to offenders
Offender information	(1) age, sex, and race of offender
Arrest information	(1) arrest date, (2) type of arrest, (3) arrest offense code, (4) age, sex, race, ethnicity, and resident status, (5) disposition of minor

Source: Federal Bureau of Investigation. (n.d.). *A guide to understanding NIBRS.* https://ucr.fbi.gov/nibrs/2012/resources/a-guide-to-understanding-nibrs

Understanding Rates

We measure crime to make comparisons—comparisons across time (e.g., Is there more fraud this year than last year?), comparisons across geographic locations (e.g., Is there more gang-related homicide in Phoenix than in Houston?), comparisons across groups (e.g., Do juveniles engage in dating violence more than adults?). Accurate comparisons are impossible without standardizing our measures of crime. Here is an example to illustrate using data from the UCR:

In 2020, California was home to 2,203 intentional homicides (murder and nonnegligent manslaughter). The same year, Delaware reported only 73 intentional homicides.[20] Wow, that's a big difference! It sounds like California is a much deadlier state than Delaware. Right? Not so fast. We cannot—or *should not*—compare the counts of homicides in California and Delaware without taking their population sizes into account. Fewer than a million people lived in Delaware in 2020 (989,948 at mid-year, to be exact). Compare that to the nearly 40 million people living in California that year. California may have had many more murders, but they also had many more people. Comparing them requires the calculation of crime rates, which are ratios of the number of crimes occurring in a location to the size of that location's population:

$$\frac{Number\ of\ crimes}{Number\ of\ people\ in\ the\ population} \times 100,000 = Crime\ rate\ per\ 100,000$$

Putting the population size in the denominator permits us to standardize and make comparisons across places (like California and Delaware), time periods, and groups that differ in population size. Technically, we *could* then compare what we calculated using only the division, but the result would not be intuitive. We multiply by 100,000 to make the values easier to interpret and compare. But there is nothing precious about the number 100,000. We could report rates per 1,000, per 10,000, or per 1 million. Traditionally, though, the UCR reports crimes rates per 100,000 inhabitants (or people in the population), which is why 100,000 is included here. Let's calculate rates with our California and Delaware homicide data.

California's rate of intentional homicide per 100,000 people in the population (2020):

$$\frac{2,203\ intentional\ homicides}{39,538,223} \times 100,000 = 5.57000 = 5.57\ intentional\ homicides\ per\ 100,000$$

Delaware's rate of intentional homicide per 100,000 people in the population (2020):

$$\frac{73\ intentional\ homicides}{989,948} \times 100,000 = 7.37000 = 7.37\ intentional\ homicides\ per\ 100,000$$

Delaware had a higher homicide rate than California in 2020 despite its far smaller count. In California, there were 5.57 intentional homicides in 2020 for every 100,000 people living in California that year, while Delaware saw 7.37 intentional homicides for every 100,000 people living in Delaware in 2020. It is important to always note the metric when reporting a crime rate: It is 5.57 *per 100,000*, not just 5.57 (5.57%? 5.57 per million? No one knows!). Note what would have happened if we had not multiplied by 100,000. California's rate would have been .0000557 and Delaware's would have been .0000737. Those values are not nearly as interpretable as 5.57 per 100,000 and 7.37 per 100,000.

The previously mentioned rates are incidence rates. In criminology, incidence refers to the occurrence or frequency of criminal events. The numerators—2,203 and 73—were frequencies of intentional homicide events. Their corresponding incidence rates—5.57 and 7.37 per 100,000—tell us how widespread crimes are. They do not tell us how widespread *criminals* are. It is possible that only a handful of people committed Delaware's 73 murders and nonnegligent manslaughters. It is also possible that each homicide was committed by a different person. The incidence rate does not shed light on either possibility. But prevalence rates do. Prevalence, in criminology, refers to the proportion of a population that engages in (or is a victim of) crime. The equation for prevalence rates looks similar to the equation for incidence rates, but the numerator is changed to the number of people involved in crime, as either offender or victim, rather than the number of criminal events:

$$\frac{Number\ of\ offenders\ (or\ victims)}{Number\ of\ people\ in\ the\ population} \times 100,000 = Prevalence\ rate\ per\ 100,000$$

ENGAGED CRIMINOLOGY 2.1
Are Our Crime Perceptions Correct?

This chapter began with polling data showing that most Americans have answered "more" to the question "Is there more crime in the U.S. than there was a year ago, or less?" every year since 2002. In this exercise, you will use data from the Uniform Crime Reporting program to determine if their perceptions were correct.

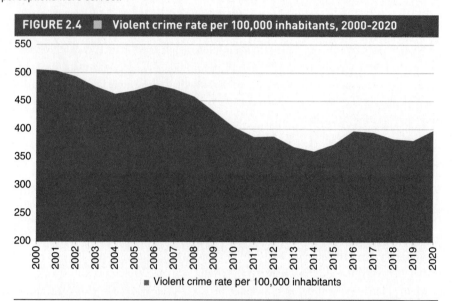

FIGURE 2.4 ■ Violent crime rate per 100,000 inhabitants, 2000-2020

■ Violent crime rate per 100,000 inhabitants

Source: Federal Bureau of Investigation. (2020). Crime Data Explorer. https://crime-data-explorer.app.cloud.gov/pages/explorer/crime/crime-trend

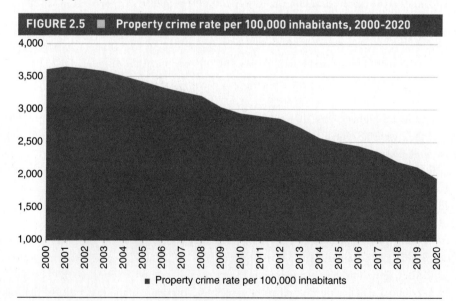

FIGURE 2.5 ■ Property crime rate per 100,000 inhabitants, 2000-2020

■ Property crime rate per 100,000 inhabitants

Source: Federal Bureau of Investigation. (2020). Crime Data Explorer. https://crime-data-explorer.app.cloud.gov/pages/explorer/crime/crime-trend

Use the figures to answer the questions:

1. Describe what happened to violent crime rates in the U.S. between 2000 and 2020 by reporting rates presented in Figure 2.4.

2. Describe what happened to property crime rates in the U.S. between 2000 and 2020 by reporting rates presented in Figure 2.5.

3. Are Americans' perceptions about increases in crime (every year since 2002) correct?

Incidence and prevalence rates are indirect measures of how well crime is being controlled, partially answering the question "Are police effective?" in addition to the "How much?" question. A better indicator of law enforcement performance, though, is the clearance rate, which is reported in NIBRS. A crime is cleared (or closed) if three things occur:

1. It leads to an arrest.

2. Criminal charges are filed.

3. The case is handed over to the prosecutor.

It can also be cleared by "exceptional means" if there is enough evidence for arrest and prosecution of an identified offender but circumstances prevented that from happening. For example, perhaps the offender died, the victim refused to cooperate, or the offender is in another country that refuses to turn the person over. The clearance rate indicates the proportion of known offenses that were cleared by either arrest or exceptional means. One person's arrest can clear multiple offenses, and several arrests are necessary for clearing crimes with more than one offender. The clearance rate, expressed as a percentage, is calculated using this equation:

$$\frac{Number\ of\ crimes\ cleared\ by\ arrest\ or\ exceptional\ means}{Number\ of\ crimes\ reported} \times 100 = Clearance\ rate$$

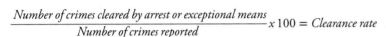

FIGURE 2.6 ■ Clearance rates (percent cleared), by offense, five-year averages (2016–2020)

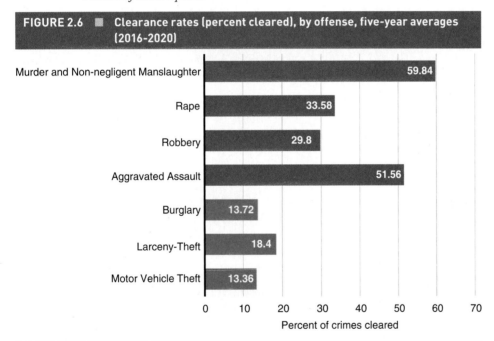

Source: Federal Bureau of Investigation. (2021). Crime Data Explorer. https://crime-data-explorer.fr.cloud.gov/pages/home

SURVEYS AND EXPERIMENTAL RESEARCH

Surveys and experiments are quantitative methods that criminologists use to examine relationships between variables with the goal of establishing causation. Statistical results from surveys and experiments help criminologists answer their explanatory research questions (survey data are useful for descriptive purposes, as well). Despite their shared quantitative focus, though, many features distinguish surveys from experiments.

Survey Research in Criminology

What percentage of robbery victims report the offense to police, and how do they make that decision? How frequently do adolescents abuse prescription drugs, and where do they get them? How widespread is the problem of prison sexual assault, and where in the prison is it most likely to happen? Why are some people more fearful of crime than others? Criminologists use surveys to answer descriptive ("How much?") and explanatory ("Why?") questions like these. To answer these questions, researchers must ask people—robbery victims, adolescents, inmates, the general public—about their experiences, behaviors, feelings, and thoughts.

Survey researchers administer questionnaires using a variety of modes: online, over the phone, face-to-face, through the mail. Some surveys are self-administered, which means that the respondents read the questions and mark their responses, as in mail-in and online surveys. Self-administered surveys are ideal for researchers asking about sensitive and socially undesirable topics, like histories of family violence, criminality, and substance use. In interviewer-administered surveys, including face-to-face and telephone surveys, researchers ask the respondents questions and note their responses. This way, researchers can clarify the meaning of questions. Online and telephone surveys are the least expensive and best for reaching large numbers of geographically dispersed respondents, but they tend to have low response rates, which means that only a small proportion of contacted people complete these surveys.

Like official crime statistics, survey data are quantitative. Survey responses are converted into numerical values through a process called coding, which are then analyzed using statistical methods (other, less common, survey questions are open-ended, allowing respondents to answer in their own words). Remember the issue of spuriousness addressed in Chapter 1, illustrated with the association between ice cream consumption and murder rates: Sometimes associations between variables are not causal. Instead, a third variable (like warm weather!) is making it appear that there is a causal relationship when there isn't. In statistical analysis, criminologists can control for, or rule out, alternative explanations for the results. In other words, survey data analysis is useful for determining the causes of crime and punishment and ruling out spuriousness.

Unlike official crime statistics, survey researchers typically rely on sample data. Let's use an example to illustrate. Imagine you have been given the task of determining the scale of sexual victimization among those incarcerated in U.S. correctional facilities. You believe, correctly, that you will get fuller information if you survey inmates, themselves, rather than rely purely on administrative records. But there are approximately 1.3 million people in U.S. prisons. You cannot possibly survey all of them! Fortunately, you don't need to. You can instead select a representative sample, or subset, of all prisoners. The sample is drawn from a population, which is comprised of all the people about which you wish to reach conclusions with your analysis.

Perhaps you will randomly select 10% of U.S. correctional facilities and survey the people incarcerated in them. You plan to generalize from your analysis of sample data to the population of all U.S. prisoners. In fact, the Bureau of Justice Statistics did exactly this with the National Inmate Survey. The survey, administered to inmates using computer-assisted questionnaires in 2007, 2008-2009, and 2011-2012, fulfills requirements of the Prison Rape Elimination Act of 2003. The act's purpose was to "provide for the analysis of the incidence and effects of prison rape in Federal, State, and local institutions and to provide information, resources, recommendations and funding to protect individuals from prison rape."[21]

The National Inmate Survey and the Survey of Prison Inmates are longitudinal surveys, conducted by the Bureau of Justice Statistics, that sample individuals from the population of prisoners in the U.S.

AP Photo/Ted S. Warren, File

Some surveys are **cross-sectional**, collecting data at one point in time. They provide a one-time snapshot of respondents' experiences, behaviors, feelings, or thoughts. Others, like the National Inmate Survey, have multiple periods of data collection. They are **longitudinal** (think "long" as in over a long time period). Longitudinal surveys are called panel studies if the same sample of people is surveyed at each period of data collection, permitting researchers to analyze how they change over time. They are trend studies if a new group of people is surveyed each time, which was the case for the National Inmate Survey.

National Crime Victimization Survey

The size of the dark figure of crime—the amount of crime that never becomes known to officials—varies immensely by offense. Rape and sexual assault, for example, have a large dark figure, whereas motor vehicle theft's dark figure is puny in comparison. That is probably not a surprise: Sexual victimization is notoriously underreported, and people typically alert law enforcement when their cars are stolen because cars are expensive, necessary, and, most importantly, insurance companies require that victims file police reports in order to claim benefits. But how on earth can we possibly know the size of each crime's dark figure? Isn't it, by definition, unknowable? The dark figure is beyond the reach of police-reported crime rates, but it *can* be estimated using victimization survey data.

The most important source of victimization data in the U.S. is the **National Crime Victimization Survey (NCVS)**, a nationally representative, household-based survey that collects data on household and personal victimization of people age 12 and older. Figure 2.7 displays the percentage of victimizations from the NCVS that were reported to law enforcement, giving a glimpse of the dark figure's size by type of crime. Over a span of five years, more than three-quarters of motor vehicle thefts become known to police compared to fewer than 30% of rapes and sexual assaults.

The NCVS, conducted since 1973 (and formerly called the National Crime Survey), is administered by the U.S. Census Bureau for the Bureau of Justice Statistics. Twice each year, researchers conduct face-to-face and telephone surveys with all members, age 12 and older, of a nationally representative sample of about 49,000 households, though sample size varies year to year based on budgetary

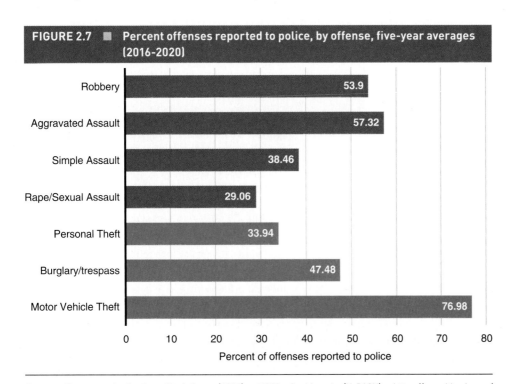

FIGURE 2.7 ■ Percent offenses reported to police, by offense, five-year averages (2016-2020)

Offense	Percent
Robbery	53.9
Aggravated Assault	57.32
Simple Assault	38.46
Rape/Sexual Assault	29.06
Personal Theft	33.94
Burglary/trespass	47.48
Motor Vehicle Theft	76.98

Percent of offenses reported to police

Source: Bureau of Justice Statistics. (2020). *NCVS Dashboard (N-DASH).* https://ncvs.bjs.ojp.gov/Home#hometopHome

constraints.[22] All told, approximately 160,000 people are surveyed each year in total.[23] When house-holds are selected and members agree to participate, they remain in the NCVS for three years and are surveyed every six months about personal and household victimization. Personal victimization occurs when the individual has been targeted, as in assault, rape, and thefts taking place outside of the home. Offenses that target households, like burglary and trespassing, result in household victimization (all members of the household were victims).

The NCVS has four primary objectives:

1. *Produce comprehensive information about victims and the consequences of victimization.* The NCVS provides the following information: demographic data on victims (e.g., sex, age, race, marital status, employment), household information (e.g., rented or owned, urban or rural, whether public housing), victim-offender relationships (e.g., spouse, roommate, neighbor, customer/client), victims' self-protective actions taken during crime events, outcomes of self-protective actions, context of victimization (e.g., location, whether others came to aid), consequences of victimization (e.g., how much money was lost, emotional distress, and school- and work-related outcomes).

2. *Determine the scale and scope of the dark figure of crime.* In addition to measuring crimes not reported to law enforcement, respondents are asked why they did not report them. Thus, the NCVS tells us which crime types and circumstances (e.g., types of victim-offender relationships, victim characteristics, locations of incidents) yield the largest dark figures. It also sheds light on the reasons some victims are unwilling or unable to inform police of what has transpired.

3. *Supply uniform estimates of certain crime types.* The NCVS provides estimates of crime incidence rates. NCVS personal victimization rates are presented per 1,000 persons age 12 and older (as compared to the UCR's metric of "per 100,000 inhabitants"). Household victimization rates are expressed per 1,000 households. The NCVS also provides victimization prevalence rates, indicating what percentage of people have been victims of various crimes.

4. The NCVS does not measure all forms of criminal victimization. For example, it does not provide homicide data (murder victims don't complete surveys). Nor does it include crimes committed against young children, commercial victimization (like shoplifting and burglaries of businesses), corporate crime, or victimless offenses. It also excludes some forms of personal and household victimization, like kidnapping and arson. Nonetheless, the NCVS provides valuable standardized estimates for major crime types: robbery, assault, rape and sex assault, burglary, theft, motor vehicle theft, vandalism, and more.

5. *Provide comparisons of crime victimization across areas, time periods, and groups.* As standardized measures, incidence and prevalence rates make comparisons possible. Moreover, criminologists can compare the nature and consequences of victimization across time, place, and group. For example, they can observe whether the proportion of victims of domestic violence who report the offense to police has increased over the years. Plus, because the survey includes victims and non-victims, researchers can determine the predictors of victimization risk, which is impossible when relying on police records.

The NCVS has undergone several redesigns to improve its accuracy and usefulness. The most recent revisions focus on (1) expanding the number of crimes to include offenses like stalking, identity theft, and fraud; (2) improving measurement of offenses that have been included in the NCVS for a long time, especially rape and sexual assault; (3) adding new demographic questions about disability status, veteran status, citizenship, gender identity, and sexual orientation; (4) measuring perceptions of police and their performance in interacting with victims; and (5) adding questions about the use of victim services. For decades after its inception, the NCVS provided only national estimates rather than state or city estimates (remember levels of analysis from earlier!). The recent redesign of the NCVS boosts the sample size in the largest U.S. states to allow for subnational—or state-level—estimates.[24]

The NCVS is, on its own, an exceptionally valuable source of data on the reach and impact of (some forms of) crime victimization in the U.S. It has even greater utility when combined with other sources of crime data. Criminologists get the most valid answer to the "How much?" question when they use triangulation. In triangulation, researchers rely on several data sources or research methods to gain a more complete and accurate understanding of their subject.[25] Criminologists combine what they observe in the Uniform Crime Reports (UCR), the NCVS, and offender self-report surveys to reach the most reliable conclusions possible about the extent and nature of crime in the U.S.

Offender Self-Report Surveys

The NCVS relies on victim reports. The UCR relies on police records. Who else can tell us about crime besides victims and law enforcement? People who violate the law, of course! In offender self-report surveys, researchers administer questionnaires to either

1. A sample of the general population, some of whom have engaged in criminal activity, or

2. A sample of known criminal offenders.

As with all criminological research methods, the type selected—general sample or offender sample—depends on the criminologist's research questions. Plus, the benefits and challenges differ between them, so it is best to address them one at a time.

Self-report surveys that rely on samples from the general population are useful for measuring the prevalence—the proportion of a population that engages in crime—of low-level criminal conduct, such as illicit substance use, shoplifting, drunk driving, and theft of services (what one criminologist calls the "crimes of everyday life"[26]). Plus, criminologists can examine the predictors of minor criminal activity by comparing the experiences, behaviors, feelings, and thoughts of the law-breakers and law-abiders in the sample. These surveys are good for answering questions about what differentiates people who skirt the rules from those who adhere to them.

The easiest way to address the limitations of using self-report surveys is to contemplate who—among the general population—is most likely to end up in a survey's sample. First, they are most likely to be young and in school. Unlike adults, who have greater autonomy and are not concentrated in a single location, high school students are ripe for inclusion. The focus on high schoolers is compounded by public concerns about the problem behaviors of adolescents, including drinking, drug use, unprotected sex, and other high-risk activities. Second, they are likely to be conventional. The individuals who are most embedded in a criminal lifestyle—whether adolescents or adults—are especially unlikely to participate in survey research (because, e.g., they have dropped out or been pushed out of school, are incarcerated, or are unstably housed). And even when they do, they represent a tiny proportion of the overall sample. Researchers would need an enormous sample size to get enough serious law-breakers included. The result is that general-population self-report surveys are ineffective for estimating the prevalence and predictors of serious crimes like murder, robbery, burglary, kidnapping, and human trafficking. On top of that, ensuring honesty is a major challenge. Though respondents are assured anonymity (data are stripped of names and other identifying information), concerns about judgments or legal consequences can cause respondents to underreport their serious illegal actions. In a reversed pattern, some adolescents exaggerate their involvement in low-level crime.

It is not all bad news, though. Self-report surveys capture offenses that other sources of crime data do not—namely, victimless crimes (like drug use) and other offenses that tend to escape police attention, such as shoplifting, drunk driving, and vandalism. For example, the National Survey on Drug Use and Health (NSDUH), a trend study begun in 1971, collects drug use data annually from a nationally representative sample of about 70,000 people age 12 and older.[27] The Monitoring the Future survey administers questionnaires to 8th-, 10th-, and 12th-grade students every two years, asking them about their behaviors, attitudes, and values regarding drugs, alcohol, and tobacco. A subset of the graduating seniors is selected for a follow-up survey that measures substance use among college students.

Some self-report surveys move beyond just drugs and alcohol. For instance, the National Longitudinal Survey of Adolescent to Adult Health (called Add Health) has followed a nationally representative sample of about 20,000 people from their middle and high school years (Grades 7 through 12) into middle age, surveying them five times: 1994-1995, 1996, 2001-2002, 2008, and 2016-2018. The surveys include questions about criminal activities like stealing, assault, selling illicit drugs, using weapons, damaging property, and committing intimate partner violence. They also contain measures of criminal justice involvement, like whether they have ever been arrested, charged, and convicted for a range of serious offenses. Table 2.3 presents a comparison of the three main sources of crime data.

TABLE 2.3 ■ Comparison of sources of crime data: NIBRS, NCVS, and self-report surveys			
	National Incident-Based Reporting System (NIBRS)	National Crime Victimization Survey (NCVS)	Self-report surveys
Includes crimes not reported to police?	No	Yes	Yes
Relies on sample data?	No	Yes	Yes
Includes "victimless" crimes?	Yes	No	Yes
Useful for estimating prevalence?	No	Yes, for victimization	Yes, for offending (and victimization)
Best for which type of offenses?	Serious and minor offenses	Serious and minor offenses	Minor offenses
Age of offenders and victims represented?	All ages included	Includes victims age 12 and older; offenders of any age	Better for understanding juvenile offending

Let's say you are not concerned with estimating prevalence, nor do you wish to compare lawbreakers and law-abiders. Instead, you want to study a select kind of criminal offender to understand their experiences, behaviors, feelings, and thoughts. Surveying an offender-only sample might be the best strategy for you. But you will need to clear some hurdles in your path. The biggest one is finding respondents. There isn't a Big Book of Identity Thieves or a Directory of Armed Robbers you can use to locate and contact participants. Moreover, surveys need sample sizes large enough for completing statistical analyses. That means you need to go where there are large concentrations of people who qualify to be in your study, and that is the criminal justice system.

An example of an offender-only survey comes from criminologists Griffin and Evans, who used a mail-in survey of 306 registered sex offenders living throughout Mississippi to examine racial differences in experiences with stigma (being treated as disgraced or with great disapproval).[28] They found that Black registered sex offenders reported fewer negative consequences—called collateral consequences—than white registered sex offenders (e.g., harassment, losing a job, trouble finding a place to live, property damage). The researchers offered two potential explanations: (1) Both groups do, in fact, get treated poorly, but white registered sex offenders are more apt to note their unequal treatment because they are less accustomed, generally, to discrimination than are Black respondents. (2) Black communities express greater forgiveness to people with criminal records as a "method of coping with discrimination and inequality in the dominant community" (p. 20).

Griffin and Evans wanted to know the consequences of registering as a sex offender, a form of criminal justice involvement. Surveying only sex offenders who have been caught and punished isn't a problem for them. Indeed, it is necessary. But that isn't the case for many survey researchers. Relying on the criminal justice system as a source for respondents creates complications if people who have been punished differ from those who have not. How might they be different? They might be less-skilled offenders, more likely to suffer from mental health or substance abuse problems, poorer and less educated, and their experiences in jail or prison might transform their perspectives. Always consider whether the sample is representative of the population of interest when interpreting survey results.

Experimental Research

People often (incorrectly) use the word *experiment* when describing any kind of study, but experiments are a very specific type of research. A study is an experiment *only* if the researcher manipulates a condition to observe if it causes a change in the outcome. In most cases, experiments include two or more groups that differ only in terms of receiving an experimental condition. The group that doesn't receive the experimental condition is called the control group. Typically, experimenters randomly assign participants (or locations or whatever else is receiving the experimental condition) to experimental and control groups to ensure that they are comparable, or as close to identical as possible. Because the experimental condition is the only thing that differentiates the groups, the researcher can be confident that any difference in the outcome is due to experimental condition and not some other factor. Experiments are considered the gold standard for determining causation for this reason. And remember, criminology is etiological, or concerned with causes.

Many criminological experiments investigate the impact of criminal justice interventions or policy changes on behavior. For example, a big problem for courts and defendants is the failure to appear for a scheduled court date. People miss court dates for lots of reasons: They forget, they are unaware that they are scheduled to appear in court, they must work or take care of children, they lack transportation, and more. One solution is to make reminder phone calls, just like a doctor's office. How can we know if this will work? After all, if the problem is work conflicts, child care, or transportation, then reminders are unlikely to be effective. Or maybe people don't show because they simply can't be bothered. Reminders won't work in that case, either. One criminologist sought to answer this question using an experiment in which people scheduled for court dates in New York City were randomly assigned to one of four groups: (1) no call, (2) reminder call three days in advance, (3) reminder call on same day as appearance, and (4) reminder call three days in advance and on the same day.[29] The experiment's results were encouraging. Reminder calls, regardless of when they occurred, reduced failures to appear by 37%. That's a significant causal impact of reminders!

You might wonder: If experiments are the gold standard for determining causation, then why isn't *all* criminological research experimental? The short answer is that most of the causes that interest criminologists are not things we can or *should* manipulate as researchers. Do you want to know if unemployment causes crime? As a researcher, you cannot randomly assign people to be fired from their jobs. Does the death of a parent contribute to juvenile delinquency? You aren't going to kill parents to find out. Many of the predictors that matter for crime, victimization, and how one is treated in the criminal justice system—poverty, education, sex, race and ethnicity, immigration status, mental health, trauma, family histories of incarceration or substance use, to name just a few—are outside the control of experimenters.

Natural experiments offer the benefits of experiments (isolating causation) without requiring criminologists to manipulate conditions that they cannot or should not manipulate. In a natural experiment, "natural" conditions mimic what would occur in an experiment. In other words, random assignment to experimental and control groups happened by chance or due to non-research-related circumstances. For example, assignment of cases to judges is a random or "natural" condition that creates comparable groups, just like experimental and control groups. Some judges are particularly lenient, and some are particularly punitive. As a result, equivalent defendants—same offense, same criminal history, same demographic characteristics—receive vastly different sentencing outcomes. What differentiates them? The answer is the criminal punishment they receive. For instance, one might receive probation while an equivalent defendant receives a prison sentence. Or one might receive a short prison sentence while their counterpart is locked up for years. The punishment mimics an experimental condition.

Now think about the many criminologists who study the impact of a criminal record on later (un)employment. Study after study reveals the difficulties ex-felons face in finding decent paid work.[30] The research is clear on this point. It is less clear on the reasons. It could be due to employers seeing a felony record—a "negative credential"[31]—and rejecting the applicant. Or it could be a result of time in prison rather than just the record; the longer the person is in prison, the larger the gap is in their employment history. Plus, potential employers might see incarcerated ex-felons as a riskier option than ex-felons who have never been to prison. Of course, researchers can't randomly assign people to receive a prison sentence, yet that is precisely what happens when cases are randomly assigned to lenient and punitive judges. Criminologists can then conduct natural experiments on the causal effects of prison on finding work.[32] They find that *any* felony conviction impedes employment, and that prison, relative to probation, adds an additional layer of impediment for defendants with strong preconviction employment histories.

QUALITATIVE RESEARCH AND UNOBTRUSIVE RESEARCH

Qualitative research is unconcerned with the "how much?" question. While quantitative research seeks to generalize, qualitative research aims for depth on a smaller number of cases in order to describe how people create meaning, maintain cultures, and understand their social world. Qualitative study may help to answer the "why?" question, but it does not test hypotheses about causal effects. Rather, it provides what early sociologist Max Weber called *Verstehen*: achieving understanding of action's meaning from the perspective of the actor. In-depth interviews and ethnographic study are qualitative methods through which criminologists can attain *Verstehen*.

Unobtrusive research (research that doesn't intrude into the lives of its subjects) can provide *Verstehen*, as well, especially when researchers employ qualitative techniques like covert observation. Other unobtrusive methods, however, like analysis of archival data or big data, are quantitative and better-suited to hypothesis testing.

In-Depth Interviews and Ethnography

In-depth interviews are exactly what they sound like. They are probing interviews of study participants conducted by researchers, ranging from unstructured free-flow interviews to highly structured interviews with predetermined questions. Many fall in between as semi-structured interviews guided by set questions but with researchers going "off script" to follow the flow of the conversation, ask follow-up questions, and press for deeper answers. Focus groups are similar, but they include multiple respondents being interviewed simultaneously, in groups. Interviews are typically audio-recorded and transcribed, or converted into text, for analysis. Qualitative researchers use a process called coding to locate and organize patterns in the transcript evidence.

Criminologists' research questions and goals govern the types of methods they use. Questions about emotions, decision-making, identity, and interpretation of experiences are best addressed with in-depth interviews or other qualitative techniques. Table 2.4 offers a few examples of criminological studies that use in-depth interviewing. Consider whether the research questions from the studies in Table 2.4 could have been answered effectively using quantitative methods like surveys or experiments.

Ethnography is "the study of groups of people in their natural setting, typically involving the researcher being present for extended periods of time in order to collect data systematically about their daily activities and the meanings they attach to them" (p. 115).[37] Unlike stand-alone in-depth interviews, ethnography is immersive, with researchers typically acting as participant observers. In criminological ethnographies, particularly studies of active offenders, ethnographers limit their participation to only noncriminal activities.[38] Nearly all ethnographies include in-depth interviews, as well. For example, ethnographer Lynne Haney spent three years conducting fieldwork in child support courts throughout Florida, New York, and California—in addition to interviewing 125 formerly incarcerated fathers—to examine how criminal justice and child support systems operate together in the post-incarceration lives of fathers who have been to prison.[39] Her ethnography set out to capture and analyze the impacts of mass incarceration on fathers who find themselves caught in a system of debts that hinder successful reintegration after prison.

TABLE 2.4 ■ Examples of in-depth interview studies in criminology		
Authors	**Research questions**	**How they studied it**
Jacobs and Cherbonneau (2017)	How do auto thieves manage "nerve" (controlling of fear and emotions) in making criminal decisions and accomplishing their crimes?	35 semi-structured interviews with active auto thieves in a large Midwestern city
Dickinson (2020)	How do sellers of illicit drugs understand their own identities and responses to drug debt (i.e., how they behave when people owe them money)?	33 in-depth interviews with active drug sellers in St. Louis, MO
Rios, Prieto, and Ibarra (2020)	How do police establish legitimacy through respectful interactions with gang-associated Latinos while simultaneously relying on stop-and-frisk tactics?	Observations during ride-alongs with police Gang Suppression Team (GST) and in-depth interviews with community members policed by the GST in a small California city
Trejbalová, Monaghan, Kennedy, Decker, and Cimino (2020)	How does being detained as a juvenile for prostitution and solicitation affect the lives and self-concepts of children who have been sexually exploited?	36 semi-structured interviews with formerly detained young women in Nevada

Sources: Jacobs & Cherbonneau[33]; Dickinson[34]; Rios, Prieto, & Ibarra[35]; Trejbalová, Monaghan, Kennedy, Decker, & Cimino.[36]

Ethnographies present challenges for any kind of researcher, but the hurdles are especially high for criminologists, who are usually interested in exploring criminal subcultures (like armed robbers or human traffickers) or criminal justice settings (like prison culture or police culture). Few other researchers, for instance, worry about being compelled by the courts to provide documents or testimony leading to a research participant's criminal conviction (researchers can obtain certificates of confidentiality from the National Institute of Health to protect against this).[40] For criminologists, ethnographic challenges include the following[41]:

- Negotiating access to highly controlled settings, including prisons, jails, and re-entry programs; plus, authorities controlling access may seek to dictate the content of the research, such as who is interviewed and what is asked in interviews.

- Negotiating access to "hidden populations" and criminal subcultures (e.g., criminal gangs, terrorist organizations, drug trafficking participants); requires the help of a "gatekeeper," a cultural insider who vouches for the researcher.

- Research participants might initially consider researchers untrustworthy and may test their trust throughout the study.

- The illegality of behavior—or stigma assigned to the behavior—may make people hesitant to fully participate or be completely honest.

Unobtrusive Research

Nearly every research method described in this chapter requires that people allow a researcher to intrude into their lives in some way—by asking questions, by exposing them to experimental conditions, by observing them. Intrusive techniques are required for answering some research questions. For instance, it is difficult to learn about people's motivations for shoplifting without asking them. Other questions, however, can be answered without making demands on others' time and attention with the use of unobtrusive methods. Unobtrusive research includes physical trace analysis, analysis of available (or archival) data, content analysis, and covert observation, none of which intrude into the lives of others.[42] A major benefit of unobtrusive techniques is that the behavior under investigation is immune to the presence of a researcher. It is nonreactive. Survey researchers worry about honesty, ethnographers fret that people alter their presentation of self, and interviewers fear that respondents seek to please them with socially desirable answers. These concerns evaporate with the use of unobtrusive methods.

Courtroom observational research is an example of an unobtrusive method used in criminology.

Chris Ryan/OJO Images/Getty Images

In *physical trace analysis*, researchers examine the material markers of human activity—that which is left behind—to learn about the behaviors of the people or places that created them. For example, publicly discarded drug use paraphernalia and empty liquor bottles could be counted and recorded, serving as markers of substance use and, potentially, community disorder. Litter, dog (and human) waste, and used condoms also serve as physical traces of criminologically relevant activity.

In *analysis of available data*, criminologists benefit from archived information collected for reasons that often have nothing to do with criminology. Emergency room data on treatment of drug overdoses provide insight into the scale of illicit drug use. Calls to nonemergency numbers like 311 alert researchers to the crime-related concerns of residents.[43] Foreclosure and eviction data indicate the magnitude of local housing crises.[44] These data already exist in the world and can be used without making demands on research participants.

Content analysis is the systematic examination of textual or image data to "appraise the meaning and messages" contained in the content.[45] The easiest way to understand this is to describe the kinds of content that criminologists analyze, including crime news articles,[46] advertisements for illicit services,[47] court decisions,[48] and even criminology textbooks.[49] Most, though not all, criminological content analysis explores trends in the depiction of crime and criminals in media, sometimes through journalistic content and other times through public responses to news coverage. For example, researchers have analyzed reader comments to news stories about parents of mass murderers Adam Lanza (Newtown) and Dylan Klebold and Eric Harris (Columbine) to study trends in sympathy and blame for mothers and fathers. They identified clear patterns of mother blame and a near absence of any mention of the fathers at all. When brought up, the fathers—unlike the mothers—were not held solely responsible by the commenting public for their sons' horrific crimes.[50]

Covert observation takes place without the awareness of observed parties. The word *covert* means secret or clandestine. There are ethical restrictions on observing people for research in private spaces— like at their homes, at school, in a doctor's office—without their consent, as is necessary in most research. However, clandestine public observation is sometimes permitted, such as observations on a public sidewalk. Criminologists interested in studying behavior often turn to video recordings as a form of unobtrusive observation, though gaining consent may still be necessary (see section Ethics in Criminological Research). Imagine, for example, that you wanted to understand how robberies unfold, including why some are successful—for the robbers, at least!—and others fail. You could, as others have done, analyze surveillance video footage of robberies.[51] Or perhaps you want to examine racial bias in police-citizen interactions. You ask: Are police quicker to use force and do they use *more* force against Black persons than otherwise similar white persons? Think about how you might use observation to answer that question. You could certainly do hours upon hours of police ride-alongs, but you're more likely to get high-quality observations (and save a great deal of time) by analyzing video footage from police officers' body-worn cameras. Criminologists do just this, observing that police are quicker to use force against people who are Black, even when the level of resistance is the same.[52]

Covert research, which takes place without the awareness of observed parties, is permitted when occurring in public settings.

Marco Piunti/E+/Getty Images

ENGAGED CRIMINOLOGY 2.2
Analyzing Surveillance Videos

In this activity, you will analyze patterns in convenience store robberies using an unobtrusive method of observation: analysis of surveillance video footage.

Step 1: Locate surveillance videos.

Search for "convenience store robbery" on YouTube. This will bring up many videos. Only select videos that feature surveillance footage of robberies posted by either (1) law enforcement agencies or (2) news organizations. Locate four videos that meet these criteria.

Step 2: Watch and analyze the videos.

As you watch each video, pay attention and take notes on the following characteristics:

- How many people are committing the robbery?
- Are there other people present in the store during the robbery (other than the clerk)?

- How do the robbers behave during the robbery? For example, do they show a weapon? Do they appear excitable or calm? What emotions do they display?
- How do the victims (clerks) behave during the robbery?

Note whether there are similarities across the videos in how convenience store robbers enact their crimes. What patterns do you see?

Step 3: Evaluate the method.

In about 10-12 minutes, write down your responses to the following questions:

1. What can we learn about convenience store robberies from video surveillance footage that we cannot learn from other methods, like surveys or ethnographies?

2. What *can't* we learn about convenience store robberies when we rely on observation of video surveillance footage?

3. Do you think these four videos are a representative sample of all convenience store robberies? Why or why not? And does it matter?

4. Does the perspective of the observer matter for what patterns are identified? That is, might you interpret what you see differently than what a classmate interprets?

Your instructor will let you know whether to complete this activity solo or in groups, as well as how to submit and share your findings and evaluation of the method.

Big Data

Even as you read this chapter, you are emitting a kind of digital dust—a residue of your online activity that can be scraped up and analyzed. Maybe you are wearing a fitness tracker? Posting on Instagram? Making online purchases? Using your phone's mapping app? Every tap of a credit card, every post or photo, every online search creates data. *Lots* of data. So much data that it's called big data, referring to enormous data sets too complex for traditional data analysis software. Think of big data as any large data set containing information from networked devices or any Internet activity. Just as advertisers, insurance companies, and governments benefit from the datafication of our lives, so too can criminologists, especially those interested in the new field of computational criminology.[53] For example, criminologists analyzed eight months' worth of geolocated tweets (i.e., Twitter posts with latitude/longitude coordinates) in southern California to track where people are, and when.[54] Then they linked that information to location-specific crime rate data from law enforcement to see if the flow of people influenced patterns of victimization.

The use of big data in criminology is still in its infancy, and many are doubtful that it will transform the discipline.[55] Their concerns center on the quality of data. Criminologists warn that big data are "messy, noisy, and unstructured" (p. 323).[56] They also lack the richness of information provided by data collected specifically for criminological purposes—we learn much more useful details from answers to researcher-created survey or interview questions than from tweets or Google searches. Plus, big data can suffer from problems of selection bias, meaning that only a select group's online activity is captured in the data. This is especially true of social media data, which are a common type of big data explored by criminologists. Nonetheless, the future of criminology, like the future of all disciplines, will be shaped by the technologies that define our world. Ultimately, though, criminologists' research questions will dictate the value of big data.

ETHICS IN CRIMINOLOGICAL RESEARCH

Imagine that your criminology instructor has assigned a research project. Every student in your class must collect and analyze their own data on college student criminal conduct, your instructor tells you. Your classmates conduct the following studies:

- Informal interviews with five drug dealers who supply illicit drugs to the campus community. The student doesn't tell the suppliers the reason for the interviews (they think is just a conversation), and the student includes the suppliers' first names in the research paper.

- An online survey of 300 enrolled students in which they are asked to report their recent criminal behaviors, including theft, assault, and substance use. They also provide their university email address in order to be entered into a drawing to win a $100 gift card.

- An experiment in which underage students are offered the purchase of a fake ID to see under what conditions they are willing to buy it. The interactions are video-recorded and analyzed. The students do not know they are part of an experiment and that there are no fake IDs being sold.

Can you think of any ethical problems with these studies? The word *ethics* refers to moral principles of right and wrong, so ethical problems in research are those that violate a code of proper—or "right"—conduct.

Criminologists and all other researchers who study humans must adhere to a well-defined code of ethics. Before conducting their studies, researchers must gain approval from their institution's **Institutional Review Board (IRB)**. IRBs examine researchers' proposed procedures to ensure that they follow certain guidelines that protect the people being studied, including:

1. *Participants are not harmed by the research.* This principle—also called beneficence—is similar to the physicians' creed "first, do no harm." The physical harms done by an unscrupulous doctor are obvious (see the section on health care crimes in Chapter 4 if you are unsure!), but what are the harms done by criminological research? Potential harms include (1) legal repercussions for exposed criminal activity; (2) personal consequences, such as job loss, relationship loss, eviction, school expulsion, violent retaliation, and harms to reputation or social standing; and (3) psychological harms, including those caused by revisiting past traumas, such as the traumas of child abuse, sexual violence, and other forms of victimization. Researchers should eliminate or minimize these harms by following the next principles listed.

2. *Participation in research is voluntary.* This principle—also called respect for persons—emphasizes that participants must consent to being involved in the research, and they must consent freely. Their participation is only truly voluntary if the nature of the research and its potential risks are known; they cannot consent to something they don't understand. The criminologist leading the study must obtain participants' informed consent before proceeding with the study, typically with an *informed consent* form. Informed consent forms must include each of these items:

   - Title of study
   - Researchers' names and contact information
   - A brief and clearly worded description of the research's purpose
   - A concise description of what will happen during the research
   - Description of potential risks and benefits of participation
   - Assurance of either anonymity or confidentiality, including how that will be achieved through data collection and storage procedures
   - Information about participants' right to withdraw from the research at any time

   Some populations have a diminished ability to freely consent to research. These populations include minors, individuals with severe mental illness, people with intellectual disabilities, individuals unfamiliar with or uncomfortable using the language used in the research, and—especially relevant for criminology—people under some form of criminal justice supervision, including jail inmates, prisoners, probationers, and people in court-mandated substance abuse treatment. IRBs require special protections be put in place when working with vulnerable populations whose involvement may be coerced or based on limited comprehension of what they are agreeing to.

3. *Participants are granted anonymity or confidentiality.* Protecting the identities of research participants is of utmost importance in criminological research. Think of the sensitive nature of what we study! Some researchers avoid collecting data on identifiers, including names,

birth dates, email addresses, phone numbers, and IP addresses, so even the researcher has no clue who is included. Or, alternatively, they strip the data of this information to achieve anonymity. *Anonymity* occurs when researchers cannot link participants' identities to information about them. Anonymity is not always possible, though. For example, identifiers must be maintained to follow participants over time in longitudinal panel surveys, and qualitative interviewers know their respondents' identities. In these cases, researchers must ensure *confidentiality*. Data are confidential when researchers can link participants' identities to information about them, but they conceal their identifies from others. Ethnographers and other qualitative researchers accomplish this in part by assigning pseudonyms, or fake names, to participants.

4. *Participants are not deceived unless under certain approved circumstances*. Deception involves presenting false information about the research, concealing information about the nature of the study, or concealing that research is taking place at all. It is, essentially, lying to participants (active deception) or, at the very least, withholding information (passive deception). Deception undermines informed consent, and it must be "justified by compelling scientific or administrative concerns."[57] And there are compelling reasons. Some degree of deception is necessary in many experiments, but experimenters alert participants of this in their informed consent procedures and debrief them, or fully explain the deception, later. Plus, covert observation necessarily entails deception, typically of the passive variety.

CHAPTER SUMMARY

LO 2.1   Differentiate descriptive and explanatory research in criminology.

Some descriptive research seeks to answer the "how much?" question—it is about the extent of crime. Explanatory research, in contrast, attempts to answer the "why?" question and thereby assess causes of crime, victimization, punishment, and other outcomes.

LO 2.2   Identify strengths and weaknesses of official crime statistics.

Official crime statistics, like those produced by NIBRS, provide information on criminal offenses known to police, arrests, and clearance rates. They include all known incidences rather than relying on sample data. They are limited by reliance on police for the data. They do not capture the dark figure of crime, they require honesty, and they are influenced by racial, ethnic, and socioeconomic biases.

LO 2.3   Describe the uses and limitations of survey and experimental research in criminology.

Survey research, including the National Crime Victimization Survey and offender self-reports, is useful for measuring crime that goes unreported to law enforcement as well as respondents' experiences, behaviors, feelings, and thoughts about crime, criminal justice, and related topics. Surveys are limited in that they rely on sample data and respondent accuracy. Experiments are best for determining causation, but ethical and practical concerns limit their use.

LO 2.4   Demonstrate understanding of how and why criminologists conduct qualitative research and unobtrusive research.

Qualitative research (like in-depth interviews and ethnographies) allows criminologists to study subcultures, identity formation, and decision- and meaning-making. It also allows for follow-up questioning and in-depth elaboration not possible in quantitative reports. Qualitative research seeks to understand action's meaning from the perspective of the actor. Unobtrusive research (like covert observation, content analysis, and analysis of archival data) is immune to the presence of a researcher because it does not require intrusion into the lives of its subjects.

LO 2.5   **Describe the ethical concerns in criminological research.**

In ethical criminological research, participants are not harmed, they participate voluntarily (with informed consent), their responses or other data remain anonymous or confidential, and they can only be deceived under certain approved circumstances. Criminologists must obtain approval for their research from an Institutional Review Board, which scrutinizes research methods to verify adherence to an established code of ethics.

ENGAGED DISCUSSION

1. Consider the crime of drunk driving. Develop one descriptive question about drunk driving. Then develop one explanatory question about it.

2. Imagine that you calculate your county's incidence rate and prevalence rate for murder this year and the values are the same. What can you conclude?

3. The NCVS excludes homeless persons. What is one way the criminal victimization of people experiencing homelessness might differ from the criminal victimization of those who are housed?

4. Come up with one type of text, image, or video content that you think might be useful in criminological research. What research questions could be answered by analyzing that content?

5. What are some ethical issues with conducting research on prisoners? What could researchers do to make their research on prisoners ethical?

KEY TERMS

Big data (p. 48)

Clearance rate (p. 37)

Crime rate (p. 35)

Cross-sectional (p. 39)

Dark figure of crime (p. 31)

Descriptive research (p. 28)

Ethnography (p. 44)

Experiment (p. 43)

Explanatory research (p. 28)

Incidence (p. 35)

In-depth interviews (p. 44)

Institutional Review Board (IRB) (p. 49)

Level of analysis (p. 30)

Longitudinal (p. 39)

National Crime Victimization Survey (NCVS) (p. 39)

National Incident-Based Reporting System (NIBRS) (p. 32)

Natural experiment (p. 43)

Policy research (p. 28)

Population (p. 38)

Prevalence (p. 35)

Sample (p. 38)

Triangulation (p. 41)

Uniform Crime Reporting (UCR) program (p. 31)

Unobtrusive research (p. 45)

3 COMMON CRIME TYPOLOGIES
Violent, Property, and Public-Order Crimes

LEARNING OBJECTIVES

3.1 Explain what crime typologies are and identify some common crime typologies.

3.2 Differentiate violent crime from other types of crime and identify examples.

3.3 Distinguish property crime from other types of crime and identify examples.

3.4 Identify the characteristics and subtypes of public-order crimes.

Throughout the 18th and 19th centuries in the U.S., "resurrectionists" committed the crime of body snatching, stealing corpses from fresh graves or using alternative methods to illegally access the recently deceased, such as by claiming bodies from poorhouses under false pretenses. Unlike grave robbery, in which criminals sought jewelry, gold teeth, or other valuables, resurrectionists set their sights on corpses. Cadavers were in high demand by medical schools and by physicians eager for anatomical knowledge. The popularity of body snatching declined over a century ago, though, as states began to supply medical schools with legal cadavers and individuals began leaving their bodies to science.

The graveyard resurrectionist may be a relic of a long-forgotten past, but the illicit trade in bodies—or, more precisely, body parts—for medical purposes endures. It is illegal to purchase or sell organs, such as hearts, kidneys, and livers, for transplant. But there is a thriving (and legal) business for nearly every other part of the human body. Bones are used to repair fractures. Veins are transplanted during bypass surgeries. Donor cartilage is integral to many facial remodeling surgeries. Tendons. Ligaments. Membranes. Skin. Corneas. Collagen. All are used routinely in the course of modern medicine, and they are supplied by tissue banks, many operating for profit, that harvest tissues from cadavers for medical use. There is one big problem, though: The demand for human tissues far outstrips the supply of donor bodies. Any half-awake student in Econ 101 can tell you that this will drive up the price of cadavers. Enter body snatching, 21st century edition.

Michael Mastromarino, president of Biomedical Tissue Services, was convicted in 2008 of illegally purchasing, harvesting, and selling human bodies and their tissues. He and his employees had forged consent forms, death certificates, and medical history forms, altering the documents so the cadavers appeared "younger and healthier on paper."[1] Tissues from diseased cadavers, including those with cancer, HIV/AIDS, and syphilis, and many far too old to be eligible for donation, were sold using the forged documents, and ultimately implanted in thousands of unsuspecting patients. The more than 1,000 bodies, purchased for $1,000 apiece from funeral homes, were stored for too long and in unsafe, unrefrigerated conditions. Mastormarino was charged with body stealing, opening graves, unlawful dissection, corruption, and forgery. He ultimately pled guilty and was sentenced to no less than 18 years in prison, where he died from bone cancer in 2013 at age 49.

How should we classify modern-day body snatchings? Descriptions of Mastromarino's crimes are grisly, but are they violent offenses? Who is the victim—the deceased person, their families, or the patients who received the compromised tissues? Are offenses against cadavers offenses against persons or against property? This chapter will explain the differences between various types of crimes, and perhaps even help you to categorize body snatching.

CRIME TYPOLOGIES

The illicit sale of body parts. Murder. Drunk driving. Communicating threats. Breaking and entering. Elder abuse. Insider trading. Motor vehicle theft. Do these acts have anything in common beyond their illegality? In some instances, yes. For example, breaking and entering and motor vehicle theft are crimes against property. Murder and elder abuse (in some forms) are violent crimes. **Crime typologies** are organizational tools for grouping together criminals or criminal offenses that have common characteristics. This chapter describes the common classification of crimes into types, including violent crime, property crime, and public-order crime. It provides ample examples to demonstrate the range of actions that share a label. Criminal offenses can be organized in other ways, as well, such as by level of severity, type of victim, and type of rewards generated by the offense.

By Severity

Criminal law in the U.S. sorts offenses into types based on level of severity of the punishment, which—at least in theory—reflects the seriousness of the criminal act. The two broad categories are felonies and misdemeanors. **Felonies** are serious offenses that carry the possibility of a prison sentence of a year or longer. Many states distinguish among felony offenses based on "class" or "degree." In Wisconsin, for instance, Class A felonies, like murder, are the most serious crimes and can result in life sentences. At the other end of the seriousness spectrum, Class I felonies, such as theft of property worth $5,000-$10,000, are capped at three and a half years of incarceration and a fine of no more than $10,000.[2] **Misdemeanors** are less-serious offenses with penalties that include fines, community service, probation, and jail terms of under one year. Like felonies, many states distinguish between levels of misdemeanors.

Notice that felonies can result in prison time whereas misdemeanors result in jail time, if the convicted person serves any time at all. Prisons and jails are not the same. State and federal **prisons** house individuals convicted of felonies. **Jails** are short-term holding facilities, usually operated by a city or county, that house individuals who have been arrested, are awaiting case disposition (trial or plea agreement) or sentencing, or are completing a short sentence for a misdemeanor or low-level felony.

Pelican Bay State Prison is a 275-acre facility in Del Norte County, California, that houses men convicted of violent crimes, two-fifths of whom are serving life sentences.

The least serious offenses are infractions, also called violations or petty offenses. Many infractions are violations of ordinances, municipal codes, or administrative regulations rather than criminal codes. However, some misdemeanors can result in a citation for an infraction under specified circumstances, such as first-time nonviolent offenses. Traffic violations, jaywalking, drinking in public, disturbing the peace, and littering are examples of infractions. In states that have decriminalized possession of small amounts of marijuana, citations are issued, much as would happen for traffic violations. In Ohio, for instance, possession of less than 100 grams of marijuana is an infraction that incurs a $150 fine, no risk of jail time, and does not create a criminal record, though it is still considered a misdemeanor offense.[3]

Criminologists and the public often talk about "the criminal justice system" in the U.S., but there is not one single, unified system. Rather, there are *many* criminal justice systems in the U.S., including the federal system and 50 distinct state systems, each with its own criminal statutes, felony and misdemeanor designations, court systems, and prison systems. What constitutes a felony in one state might be a misdemeanor in another. For example, a theft of $600 is a felony in New Mexico but a misdemeanor in Arizona. Plus, the class or level of a felony offense, and its accompanying penalty, can also vary from state to state, or between the federal and state systems. Take the case of fentanyl, an incredibly powerful prescription opioid that is trafficked for illicit use. A first-time offender convicted of trafficking (distributing and selling) 100 grams of fentanyl has committed a Class C felony in the state of Nevada and will face between one and five years in Nevada state prison with a possible fine capped at $50,000.[4] That same offender, if convicted in the federal system, faces no less than five years (and no more than 40 years) in federal prison and a fine not exceeding $5 million.[5]

By Type of Victim

Criminologists classify offenses based on the type of victim, distinguishing between (1) crimes against persons, (2) crimes against property, (3) crimes against the public order, and (4) crimes against the state.

- *Crimes against persons:* These are offenses that target or harm individuals, like murder, assault, sex offenses, kidnapping/abduction, and human trafficking.

- *Crimes against property:* The target of crimes against property is—to no one's surprise— property. Examples include arson, burglary, fraud, larceny/theft, and extortion/blackmail. Even though individuals are harmed by these acts (just ask the person who was blackmailed!), the object of the offense was the property rather than physical harm to the person.

- *Crimes against the public order* (also called *crimes against society*): These crimes violate a code of conduct inscribed in law, disrupting daily life and posing harm to the social good, but they are often victimless. Victimless crime is crime in which there is no aggrieved or injured party. Drug offenses, gambling offenses, prostitution/sex work offenses, public intoxication, and weapons law violations are crimes against public order. Some public-order offenses, like indecent exposure, have identifiable victims.

- *Crimes against the state*: These offenses target the existence of the state or government. They include crimes like treason (waging war or aiding others in waging war against the state), espionage (providing information to a foreign agent), and terrorism.

By Type of Rewards or Purpose

You may have heard the phrase "crime pays" before. Instrumental crimes certainly pay, as these acts provide financial rewards or status benefits to offenders. The criminal conduct is an *instrument* for achieving a desired end. For example, consider the case of David Player and Gerald Hardin III.[6] The two sawed off the right hand of Michael "Porky" Weaver, a man with severe intellectual disabilities who believed the offenders were his friends. Player and Hardin had convinced Weaver to go along with a scheme to fake an accidental dismemberment in order to collect $671,000 in homeowners and disability insurance payments. Player used the proceeds of the fraud to cover his living expenses, make luxury purchases, build an auto repair shop, and cover the costs of his divorce. His ex-wife discovered evidence of his crimes and turned him in. Instrumental crimes like Player and Hardin's often yield material rewards, such as money, drugs, or consumer goods, but not all instrumental rewards are tangible. Status rewards are those that elevate the offender's social position or allow them to save face.

Expressive crimes, in contrast, allow the offender to let out, or express, negative feelings like anger or frustration, often spontaneously. They are emotionally driven acts, such as an assault or property damage prompted by an insult or perceived slight. Expressive crimes yield phenomenological rewards. The word *phenomenological* refers to the person's experience of the act while committing it. The benefits of expressive crime are derived from the experience itself and include physiological and psychological satisfactions (e.g., thrill, excitement, sense of power, emotional release). Tangible and phenomenological rewards are not mutually exclusive. A single offense can provide both kinds of rewards. Armed robberies, for example, are instrumental crimes with clear material benefits in the form of money and goods. But armed robbers also recount the thrill of dominating victims, especially when the robbery is in retaliation for a previous wrongdoing.[7]

VIOLENT CRIME

In violent crime, the offender harms or threatens to harm a victim. Violent crime is a direct-contact crime, which means that the perpetrator and the victim come together in the same place and time at the moment of the offense (compare this to a crime like motor vehicle theft, during which the victim and offender are unlikely to interact). Harm to the victim is often the objective of violent crime, as in murder or assault, but this is not true of all interpersonal violence. Armed robbers, for instance, use violence and threats of violence instrumentally in committing their crimes against property. The Federal Bureau of Investigation (FBI), which compiles data on violent crime, identifies several major categories of violence, including murder and nonnegligent manslaughter, aggravated and simple assault, rape and sexual assault, and robbery.

Homicide

Homicide is any intentional and unlawful killing of a person by another person. Murder and manslaughter are types of homicide, differentiated by levels of intent. Murder involves *malice aforethought*, or the purposeful intent to kill or seriously injure the victim. Manslaughter, in contrast, occurs when the offender kills another person but without malice aforethought; rather, they act in "the heat of passion." For example, 20-year-old Gabriela Paulino committed voluntary manslaughter when she shot and killed 34-year-old Marc Devoe in a parking lot near the Lowell, Massachusetts, commuter rail station following a road rage confrontation in 2018. At Paulino's sentencing, the judge stated that "both people involved in that exchange on that day were provokers… No [one] was willing to put their anger to the side, which resulted in the death of a young man."[8] Paulino did not plan to kill Devoe or anyone else when she got behind the wheel. Nonetheless, she acted deliberately when she shot her victim, and was ultimately sentenced to 9.5 years in state prison. Read the descriptions of homicide types in Table 3.1 to see why Paulino's crime was neither second-degree murder nor involuntary manslaughter.

Homicide resulting from criminal negligence or recklessness is called involuntary manslaughter. The offender in involuntary manslaughter acts without intent. Nonetheless, their unlawful actions (or inactions) brought about the death of another person. Consider the tragic deaths Juan Rodriguez's one-year-old twins, Phoenix and Luna, whom he accidentally left in his overheated car while he was at work, believing that he had dropped them off at day care. Rodriguez was initially charged with manslaughter and criminally negligent homicide, but the charges were reduced to two counts of reckless endangerment. Over the past two decades, more than 440 sleep-deprived parents have accidentally left their infants in hot cars, causing their deaths, typically on days when their usual driving routines have been upended.[9] Such deaths meet the criteria for involuntary manslaughter, though prosecutors, juries, and judges tend to be lenient with grief-stricken parents who have suffered immeasurably and do not pose a danger to public safety. Other cases of involuntary homicide evoke less sympathy, including vehicular homicides in which the offending driver was intoxicated. Table 3.1

TABLE 3.1 ■ Types of homicide

Type of homicide	What it means
First-degree murder	Murder committed with premeditation or planning rather than on impulse. In some states, it includes non-premeditated murders of children, legal system actors (e.g., judges), law enforcement, and murders with multiple victims.
Second-degree murder	Murders committed without premeditation but with malice aforethought. The intent to kill or seriously injure in the moment is present but not planned.
Felony murder	Murder committed in the course of committing another felony, such as rape or robbery. Typically treated as first-degree murder by the courts.
Voluntary manslaughter	Killing committed with intent and provocation but without malice aforethought. The offense is deliberate but not planned. Considered "heat of passion" crimes.
Involuntary manslaughter	Killing committed without intent or planning. It is often the result of negligence, called negligent homicide, or occurs in the course of a low-level misdemeanor. Vehicular manslaughter is one type.
Justifiable homicide	Killing committed without criminal culpability. The offender's act is justified under the law, as when acting in self-defense.

Homicide Weapons

The story of intentional homicide in the U.S. is largely a story of gun violence. Of the 21,571 murders and nonnegligent manslaughters known to have taken place in 2020, law enforcement reported weapon information for 17,813 (82.58%) of them. Of these 17,813 homicides, 77% were gun-involved homicides (see Table 3.2). Indeed, it is the U.S.'s high level of gun violence that accounts—in large part but not completely—for the nation's high rate of homicide relative to other nations that are like the U.S. in terms of economic development and political structure. If we were to omit all gun homicides from the U.S. homicide rate, the U.S.'s homicide rate would be 1.52 homicides per 100,000 people in the population—versus 6.5 per 100,000 with gun homicides included.[10] This would put the U.S. close to the Australian homicide rate in 2020 (1.54 per 100,000) and Canadian homicide rate in 2020 (1.95 per 100,000). However, it would still be higher than many comparable nations, including Japan (0.74 per 100,000), Italy (0.46 per 100,000), Germany (0.34 per 100,000), and the U.K. (0.89 per 100,00). And those countries' rates included gun *and* non-gun homicides! The takeaway point is that the U.S.'s homicide rate is high because of guns but it's not *just* about guns. There is simply more intentional killing in the U.S., with much but not all of it facilitated by firearms.

Mass Murder

On the afternoon of April 23, 2018, Alek Minassian drove a rented van onto several Toronto sidewalks to intentionally strike pedestrians, murdering 10 and injuring an additional 15 people. A witness described Minassian making direct eye contact with victims and looking as though he was "playing a video game, trying to kill as many people as possible."[11] Just before his rampage, Minassian posted a message on Facebook stating the "incel rebellion has already begun" and praised "the Supreme Gentleman Elliot Rodger." The term *incel* is short for involuntary celibate. Self-identified incels are heterosexual men who do not have sex despite their desire to do so; they angrily blame women for denying them sex to which they feel entitled. Elliot Rodger, mentioned in Minassian's post, murdered 6 people and injured 14 others in Isla Vista, California, in 2014, before taking his own life. He described the motivation for his crimes as revenge against women who rejected him sexually and against attractive men of whom he was jealous in a YouTube video titled, "Elliot Rodger's Retribution" and a manifesto he called "My Twisted World: The Story of Elliot Rodger." Some online incel communities, including the one of which Minassian was a part, grant Rodger icon status.

TABLE 3.2 ■ Murder victims by type of weapon used, 2020	
Murder weapon	Number murder victims
Handguns	8,029
Firearms, type not stated	4,863
Knives or cutting instruments	1,739
Other weapons or weapons not stated	983
Personal weapons (hands, fists, feet, etc.)	662
Rifles	455
Blunt objects (clubs, hammers, etc.)	393
Shotgun	203
Narcotics	113
Other guns	113
Fire	106
Asphyxiation	71
Strangulation	58
Poison	16
Drowning	5
Explosives	4

Source: Federal Bureau of Investigation. (2021). Expanded homicide data. https://crime-data-explorer.fr.cloud.gov/pages/explorer/crime/shr

People gathered for the #Torontostrong vigil on April 29, 2018, to remember those murdered, injured, and terrorized in the Toronto van attack by mass murderer Alek Minassian.

Chris Young/The Canadian Press via AP

Minassian, like Rodger, committed mass murder. **Mass murder** occurs when an offender kills several victims—typically defined as four or more—in a single incident or during a brief crime spree.[12] A related term, *active shooter*, refers to a particular form of mass murder during which an offender, armed with one or more guns, kills or attempts to kill large numbers of people indiscriminately in a public space.[13] Active shooters seek to maximize the number of victims and appear to behave methodically to achieve this goal. Mass murderers who target specific victims in private spaces, such as family members (called family annihilators), would not be considered active shooters. As observed in Table 3.3, active shooter mass murders are often characterized as revenge killings, even when victims are selected at random (called proxy victims).[14] These violent acts are disproportionately committed by boys and men, to an even greater extent than in other homicides. Some scholars attribute their behavior to aggrieved entitlement, or the feeling that they have been denied the respect and status that they deserve as men, with violent retaliation adopted as an alternative avenue to masculine dominance: If you won't respect me, then I will make you fear me.[15] Mass murders borne of aggrieved entitlement are often masked suicides, or suicides concealed as a different act—in this case, as murder.[16]

TABLE 3.3 ■ Types of mass murder	
Type of mass murder	**What it means**
Family annihilators/familicide	Familicide is murder of one's family. Offenders, typically men, target spouses or partners, children, and other family members, killing all household members, including pets. Usually ends with the offender's suicide. It is the most common form of mass murder.
Workplace avengers	Offenders, typically middle-aged men, seek revenge on current or former coworkers as punishment for their perceived mistreatment or in response to being fired or anticipating being fired.
School rampage murders	Offenders, typically current or former students who are male, commit mass murder as either revenge against those perceived to have mistreated them or as a source of stardom and martyrdom. Includes both targeted and random victims.
Other public mass murder	Workplace and school mass murders are considered public incidents. Other public mass murders include those taking place in additional settings in which people congregate, including houses of worship, festivals, nightclubs, or public sidewalks. Victims are unknown to the offender and killed indiscriminately.
Felony mass murder	Murders of four or more people in a single incident where the "murders are attributable to some other underlying criminal activity or commonplace circumstance (e.g., armed robbery, criminal competition, insurance fraud, argument, or romantic triangle)."[17] Includes mass murders committed to cover up another felony.

Sources: Fridel, E. E. (2017). A multivariate comparison of family, felony, and public mass murders in the United States. *Journal of Interpersonal Violence*, 1-27; Fox, J. A., Levin, J., & Fridel, E. E. (2019). *Extreme killing: Understanding serial and mass murder.* Thousand Oaks, CA: SAGE.

Mass murders, including active shooter murders, are only a small portion of all homicide incidents in the U.S. and elsewhere. In 2020, for example, 611 people in the U.S. were killed in mass shootings (using a definition of four or more victims being shot or killed; count excludes offender deaths).[18] In the same year, 21,571 people were victims of murder or nonnegligent manslaughter.[19] Some quick math reveals that mass murder victims represented 2.8% of all homicide victims in 2020. Nonetheless, the number of mass shooting incidents does appear to be increasing over time (see Figure 3.1) and these violent crimes generate a great deal of public attention and fear, in part due to media coverage of the most extreme cases. Consistent with an "if it bleeds, it leads" principle, the greater the number of victims, the more coverage a mass murder receives.[20] Newsworthiness of mass murders is also determined by the socioeconomic status of the community in which it occurs: Violence in well-to-do places garners greater media attention.

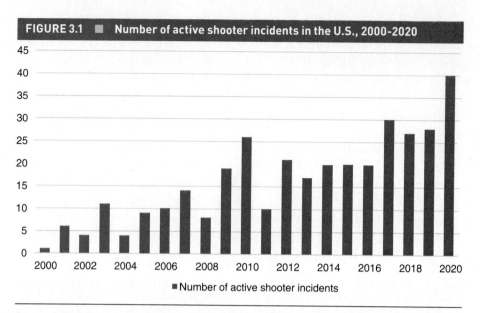

FIGURE 3.1   ■   Number of active shooter incidents in the U.S., 2000-2020

■ Number of active shooter incidents

Sources: Federal Bureau of Investigation (2018). *Quick look: 277 active shooter incidents in the United States from 2000 to 2018.* https://www.fbi.gov/about/partnerships/office-of-partner-engagement/active-shooter-incidents-graphics; Federal Bureau of Investigation (2019). *Active shooter incidents in the United States in 2019.* https://www.fbi.gov/file-repository/active-shooter-incidents-in-the-us-2019-042820.pdf/view; Federal Bureau of Investigation (2020). *Active shooter incidents in the United States in 2020.* https://www.fbi.gov/file-repository/active-shooter-incidents-in-the-us-2020-070121.pdf/view

ENGAGED CRIMINOLOGY 3.1

Applying Concepts to Mass Murder

This activity requires you to apply learned chapter concepts to a real-life case of mass murder. Read the case description and select the concepts that apply to it.

Amy Bishop sitting with her attorneys during a hearing in the Madison County Courthouse in Huntsville, Alabama, on September 22, 2011.

AP Photo/ The Huntsville Times, Glenn Baeske

Case: Amy Bishop

On February 12, 2010, University of Alabama biology professor Amy Bishop shot and killed three colleagues and injured three others during a routine biology department meeting. Bishop had been denied tenure, which meant that her job at the university would end when the spring semester ended. Bishop had appealed the decision but lost the appeal. Her department colleagues had not supported her in the tenure process, with some expressing concern about her erratic behavior. Bishop sat in the February 12, 2010, meeting for 40 minutes before committing the murders. One survivor reported, "This wasn't random shooting around the room; this was execution style."[21]

1. Make a case for whether Amy Bishop's crime was an expressive crime or an instrumental crime.

2. What type of mass murder was Amy Bishop's offense: familicide, workplace avenger, school rampage shooting, or felony murder? Explain your choice.

Serial Murder

On July 14, 2020, 46-year-old Reta Mays pled guilty to seven counts of second-degree murder. Mays had intentionally injected patients with lethal doses of unprescribed insulin while working as a nursing assistant at a Veterans Affairs (VA) hospital in West Virginia. She is an "angel of death" murderer, a type of serial murderer who commits their crimes within a health care setting.[22] Serial murder occurs when an offender kills multiple victims over three or more incidents with a cooling off period between each act. Mays clearly fits the bill. Researchers identify four primary types of serial murderers, including visionary, mission-oriented, hedonistic, and power and control–oriented murderers (see Table 3.4).[23]

TABLE 3.4 ■ Holmes and Holmes's serial murder classification	
Types of serial murder	**What it means**
Visionary	Offender has lost sense of reality; believes they are being directed by God, angels, demons, or others to kill persons or types of persons.
Mission-oriented	Offender is on a mission to purge the world of people they deem unacceptable. They are compelled by their own beliefs, not hallucinatory commands.
Hedonistic	Offender kills for pleasure. Includes three subtypes: (1) lust killing – offender obtains pleasure from the act of murder and sex is the focus of the murder, both during and after; (2) thrill killing – offender obtains pleasure from the thrill of the killing or torture prior to killing, which ends once the murder is complete; and (3) comfort killing – offender obtains pleasure from the material gains of murder rather than from the murder itself, as in the case of murder-for-hire.
Power and control–oriented	Offender achieves satisfaction from dominating and exerting power over their victims and regards themselves as a "master" of what they do.

Reta Mays does not conform to common stereotypes about serial murderers. First, she is a woman. Second, it appears that she did not commit her crimes for sexual pleasure. Third, her crimes were not performatively violent. Few types of criminals generate as much public fascination—in true-crime podcasts, in TV and movies, even in tourism and memorabilia markets—than serial murderers.[24] And the form of serial murder that is commodified for audiences constructs a typical depiction of serial murderers as highly intelligent white men, either evil geniuses or troubled loners, compelled by sexual urges to kill, which does not reflect the true heterogeneity (or variety) of those who commit this form of violence. Though some who commit three or more murders separated by periods of dormancy fit the stereotype (like Ted Bundy and Jeffrey Dahmer), many do not. Serial murderers display varying levels of intellect and come from all socioeconomic classes, racial identifications, and ethnic groups. As in other forms of murder, most—though obviously not all—offenders are men.

Like mass murder, serial murder is exceedingly rare, even among murders, which are, themselves, exceedingly rare. Only 0.28% of index crimes reported by the FBI in 2020 were murders or nonnegligent manslaughters (21571,214 nonnegligent homicides out of 7,729,734 total index crimes). And a very small proportion of that 0.28% is committed by serial offenders. According to a report from the FBI's Behavioral Analysis Unit, "Serial murder is a relatively rare event, estimated to comprise less than one percent of all murders committed in any given year."[25] Unlike homicide generally, there are few data sources that are specifically designed to count serial murderers and their victims. One exception is the Radford University/FGCU Serial Killer Database, which estimates that there were three serial murderers actively operating in the U.S. in 2020 (using a definition of three or more victims), down from 54 a decade earlier.[26] As you can see, serial murder occupies a highly disproportionate amount of the collective imagination considering its exceptional rarity.

Rape and Sexual Assault

On October 5, 2017, the *New York Times* published an investigative piece titled, "Harvey Weinstein Paid Off Sexual Harassment Accusers for Decades." The article was the first to publicly expose movie producer Harvey Weinstein's history of sex offenses and his efforts to conceal them. In the following days, many more women—including high-profile actors like Gwyneth Paltrow, Rosanna Arquette, and Rose McGowan—came forward with accounts of Weinstein's behavior, including sexual harassment, rapes, and other sexual assaults. Weinstein was ultimately sentenced to 23 years in prison for his crimes. The social media hashtag #MeToo went viral in the wake of the revelations about Weinstein's crimes (the phrase was first used on MySpace in 2006 by activist Tarana Burke but gained widespread recognition beginning in October 2017).[27]

Despite efforts such as #MeToo to encourage victims to speak up, rape and sexual assault remains one of the most underreported offenses. Researchers identify multiple reasons for this, including (1) stigma upon disclosing the victimization to peers or others;[28] (2) fear of not being believed;[29] (3) fear of retaliation;[30] (3) self-blame and humiliation;[31] (4) adherence to rape myths that "real rape" involves weapons, visible marks of physical injury (e.g., black eyes), and stranger attacks (quotation marks used to denote inaccurate perception);[32] and (5) the belief that nothing will be done by law enforcement or the courts. And it turns out that many victims are correct to assume that they will be treated differently than victims of other kinds of violent crime. Police and courtroom actors also frequently adhere to myths about what constitutes "real rape,"[33] such that victims' credibility is called into question.[34]

Myths about what constitutes a "real rape" reflect outdated and inadequate definitions of rape. Until 2012, the FBI defined rape as "the carnal knowledge of a female, forcibly and against her will," referred to as the legacy definition in the Uniform Crime Reports (UCR).[35] The definition excluded many forms of violence that are recognizable as rape, such as male victimization, and was ambiguous regarding what acts are criminalized as rape (what, exactly, *is* "carnal knowledge"?). The FBI's more recent definition of **rape**—"Penetration, no matter how slight, of the vagina or anus with any body part or object, or oral penetration by a sex organ of another person, without the consent of the victim"—provides a far more inclusive and specific description of the offense. Unlike the legacy definition, it includes victims and offenders of any biological sex. It also incorporates offenses during which the victim was incapacitated, such as by alcohol or drugs or when asleep or unconscious. The adoption of the revised definition revealed the extent to which sexual violence was undercounted in official statistics (on top of the notoriously large dark figure for sex offenses). In 2013, the first year for which data were reported using the new definition, there was a 41.7% increase in the number of rapes tallied in the UCR using the revised versus the legacy definition. The legacy definition excluded 611 rapes involving male victims, 7,602 rapes involving "sodomy" (i.e., oral or anal penetration), and 3,043 rapes involving objects.[36] Interpret these UCR numbers with the knowledge that only 34.8% of rape victims in the National Crime Victimization Survey (NCVS) reported the crime to police in that year.[37]

Acquaintance rape is especially unlikely to be reported to law enforcement. The acquaintance descriptor is used to distinguish offenses committed by rapists known to victims from those committed by strangers. Rapes committed by classmates, neighbors, coworkers, romantic partners, friends, people known only in passing, and even family members are, by definition, acquaintance rapes. Nonetheless, some researchers exclude assaults committed by relatives and current or former intimate partners (e.g., spouses) when offering statistics on acquaintance rape. Regardless of definitions, one thing is clear: Most rapes are committed by non-strangers. According to victimization data reported by the U.S. Department of Justice, about 7 out of 10 assailants are known to victims (see Figure 3.2).[38] The proportion is likely higher, though, as stranger rapes are more likely to be recognized *as* rape. Many victims of acquaintance rape understand their experiences as "bad sex" or a "miscommunication," and this is especially true of young victims, including college students.[39]

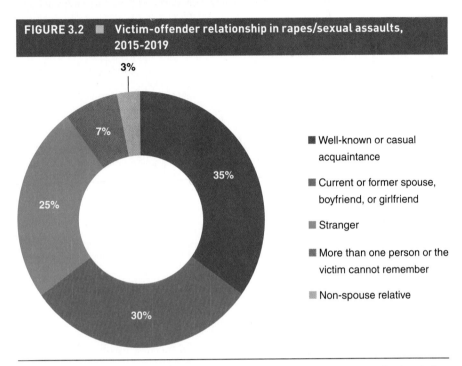

FIGURE 3.2 ■ Victim-offender relationship in rapes/sexual assaults, 2015-2019

- Well-known or casual acquaintance
- Current or former spouse, boyfriend, or girlfriend
- Stranger
- More than one person or the victim cannot remember
- Non-spouse relative

Source: Bureau of Justice Statistics. (2021). Number of rape/sexual assaults by victim-offender relationship, 2015-2019. Generated using the NCVS Victimization Analysis Tool (NVAT) at www.bjs.gov.

News coverage of the Weinstein case and the #MeToo movement shed light on the prevalence of sexual violence but left many to be confused about terminology, as the terms *rape* and *sexual assault* were used interchangeably. Table 3.5 clarifies the distinctions between sexual assault and rape, as well as sexual abuse and sexual harassment. One key point is that sexual assault is a broad category that includes multiple forms of nonconsensual sexual contact, including groping, rubbing, unwanted kissing, forcing a victim to touch an offender in a sexual manner, child sexual abuse, and rape.

Robbery

Have you ever heard someone say something along the lines of "My house was robbed"? What that person probably meant was that their house was burglarized (someone entered unlawfully for the purpose of committing a felony) or someone committed theft while in their home without entering unlawfully. Robbery, in contrast, is a violent crime. It is "the taking or attempting to take anything of value from the care, custody, or control of a person or persons by force or threat of force or violence and/or by putting the victim in fear."[43] The element of force or threatening force characterizes this form of theft as a violent, direct-contact offense rather than a property crime. Nonviolent forms of direct-contact theft, such as pickpocketing, are not considered robberies for this reason. It may help to think of robbery as a hybrid of two crimes: Robbery is theft (also called larceny) that is achieved using assault or threats of assault. The next time you hear "My house was robbed," you will—like a criminologist—imagine an armed robber pointing a gun at the side of a house and demanding that the house hand over all its valuables.

TABLE 3.5 ■ Types of sexual violence	
Type of sexual violence	**What it means**
Sexual assault	Broad category including a wide range of criminal acts of a sexual nature against victims of any age. Includes intentional sexual touching of another individual without their consent and physically forcing or coercing another individual to engage in a sexual act against their will.[40]
Rape	"Penetration, no matter how slight, of the vagina or anus with any body part or object, or oral penetration by a sex organ of another person, without the consent of the victim." (*FBI definition*)
Sexual abuse	Criminal acts against children that are of a sexual nature, including touching, forcing or coercing a child to touch an adult, forcing children to watch sexual activity, and other forms of sexual assault. Children under the legal age of consent (varies by state, usually 16-18) are, by law, incapable of giving consent for sexual contact. Also includes sexual assaults of adults unable to give consent, such as those with intellectual disabilities or age-related dementia.
Sexual harassment	Broad category that includes inappropriate and unwelcome sexual attention or advances, requests for sexual favors (*quid pro quo* harassment), and gender harassment—"conduct that disparages people based on gender but implies no sexual interest"[41]—in a work environment, learning environment, or social situation. Sexual harassment, itself, is not a violation of criminal law unless it involves sexual assault or criminal conduct. It may, however, violate Title VII of the Civil Rights Act of 1964.[42]

Robberies can be classified based on the type of force used or threatened. *Armed robberies* are committed with weapons, either used, brandished, or threatened, including firearms, knives or cutting instruments (e.g., box cutters), or other weapons (e.g., baseball bats or crowbars). *Strong-arm robberies*, in contrast, are committed using hands, fists, feet, or threats to use one's body to cause injury. As you can see in Figure 3.3, among the 434,141 robberies for which the FBI had access to weapons data through NIBRS between 2016 and 2020, most were armed robberies, with firearms the most frequently reported weapon.[44]

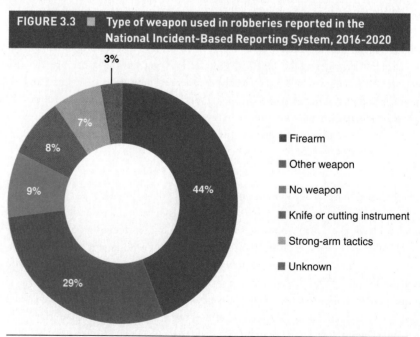

FIGURE 3.3 ■ Type of weapon used in robberies reported in the National Incident-Based Reporting System, 2016–2020

3%
7%
8%
9%
44%
29%

■ Firearm
■ Other weapon
■ No weapon
■ Knife or cutting instrument
■ Strong-arm tactics
■ Unknown

Source: Federal Bureau of Investigation. (2021). *Robbery offense characteristics: Type of weapon involved by offense* [Data set]. Crime Data Explorer. https://crime-data-explorer.fr.cloud.gov/pages/explorer/crime/crime-trend

Robberies are also categorized based on the target of the robbery and the context in which it occurs. Robberies that take place in public spaces such as streets or parking lots are called *muggings.* Figure 3.4 shows that this is the most common type of robbery based on location, comprising 24% of all robberies known to police, as reported in NIBRS between 2016 and 2020. *Carjacking* is a form of robbery that specifically targets vehicles for immediate use. Carjacking is distinct from motor vehicle theft in that it entails force or threats of force against the vehicle's occupants. *Bank robbery,* or robbery taking place in a bank or credit union, is the least common form of robbery reported in Figure 3.4. Nonetheless, bank robberies do occur, and the FBI maintains a database of wanted bank robbers, including serial offenders.

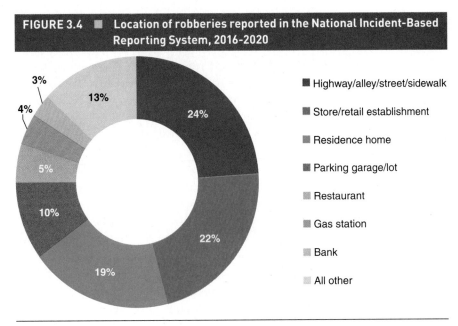

FIGURE 3.4 ■ Location of robberies reported in the National Incident-Based Reporting System, 2016-2020

Source: Federal Bureau of Investigation. (2021). *Robbery offense characteristics: Location type* [Data set]. Crime Data Explorer. https://crime-data-explorer.fr.cloud.gov/pages/explorer/crime/crime-trend

Criminologists do not just classify robberies; they also organize *robbers* into types. Specifically, they offer up a spectrum of robbery offenders ranging from amateurs to professionals. Amateurs are opportunists who act without planning when a low-risk chance for robbery presents itself. Amateurs' robberies "appear as little more than acts of desperation, usually because the person needs money quickly to pay off debts, to buy necessities or to support a drug habit" (p. 22) while professionals carefully plan their offenses and make efforts to disguise their appearance.[45] Amateurs, who make up the largest group of robbery perpetrators, are especially likely to target individual victims, whereas professionals tend to commit their crimes in commercial settings. And the proceeds of robbery differ by level of professionalism: Amateurs engage in low-risk, low-reward robberies, like muggings, whereas professionals plan and execute high-risk, high-reward robberies, such as robberies of armored trucks or known drug traffickers. Many robbers fall somewhere in the middle of the amateur-professional spectrum.

PROPERTY CRIME

In November of 2017, New Jersey couple Mark D'Amico and Kate McClure created a GoFundMe fundraiser they called "Paying it Forward" (GoFundMe is a crowdfunding web platform). According to their GoFundMe description, Kate's car had run out of gas while she was traveling on I-95 near Philadelphia. A homeless, heroin-addicted veteran named Johnny Bobbitt Jr. came to her aid, selflessly giving her his last $20 so she could buy gasoline and return home safely. Mark and Kate implored people to donate money to assist Johnny in getting back on his feet, stating:

> *"I am raising money for Johnny. With the money, I would like to get him first and last month's rent at an apartment, a reliable vehicle, and 4-6 months worth of expenses. He is very interested in find-ing a job, and I believe that with a place to be able to clean up every night and get a good night's rest, his life can get back to being normal.*

> *Truly believe that all Johnny needs is one little break. Hopefully with your help I can be the one to give it to him.*

> *Please help this man get into a home. It is already getting so cold out in Philadelphia, and I can't imagine what it will be like to be out there all winter. Any little bit will help."*[46]

The fundraiser far exceeded Mark and Kate's expectations after the story was picked up by local and national news outlets, netting a whopping $402,826. The couple claimed to have purchased a trailer for Johnny and to have established a trust that would manage his money. Johnny told a different story, claiming that the couple was withholding funds that were rightly his. He sued, and the lawsuit ultimately revealed the true nature of Mark and Kate's—and Johnny's—intentions. Johnny Bobbitt Jr. was, in fact, a homeless veteran struggling with substance abuse. But Mark and Kate had fabricated the story of the incident on I-95.[47] The couple were familiar with Johnny from their travels to nearby casinos. They had hatched a scam to defraud well-intentioned donors with a heartwarming tale of a Good Samaritan, and Johnny agreed to go along with the hoax. The plan had been to share the profits of their crime, but the couple became greedy, spending much of Johnny's share of the ill-gotten gains on a new car and trips to Disneyland, Disney World, and casinos in Las Vegas and Atlantic City. Their greed was their undoing. Mark D'Amico pled guilty to second-degree misapplication of entrusted property and was sentenced to five years in prison. Kate McClure pled guilty to second-degree theft by deception, agreeing to a four-year prison term. Johnny Bobbitt Jr. pled guilty to one count of con-spiracy, having incriminated himself when he exposed the scam. He was placed in a drug rehabilita-tion program.

The GoFundMe scam is an example of property crime. The primary objective of property crime is to take or do damage to property—including money, belongings, homes or businesses, vehicles, identification documents—without consent of its rightful owner. It includes a wide range of offenses, from impulsive acts of vandalism and shoplifting to highly sophisticated frauds and arson-for-profit schemes. This section of the book will address three types of property crime: Larceny-theft, burglary, and arson. The following chapter goes into depth on additional forms of property offenses, including white-collar and organized crimes.

Larceny-theft

Theft—in its myriad forms—is at the heart of many property crimes. The word *larceny* is used inter-changeably with the word *theft* and derives from the Anglo-Norman word for theft, *larcin*. Larceny is the unlawful appropriation of personal property belonging to an individual or business with the intention of permanently depriving them of it. What is included under the umbrella category of lar-ceny depends on who is using the term. When the FBI uses it for reporting crime rates, they limit it to tangible—or "constructive"—property and they exclude any theft that is committed using fraud, forg-ery, or confidence games.[48] The GoFundMe scam would not be considered larceny according to the FBI for this reason; it was *fraud*, which is the criminal use of deception for personal or monetary reward. Tangible personal property is something that can be seen and felt, such as money, bicycles, jewelry, or guns. If someone unlawfully takes something intangible, such as intellectual property or services, that may be a criminal act but not larceny, at least not according to the FBI. Nonetheless, in practice, thefts of service—for example, skipping out on a hotel or restaurant bill ("dine and dash") or stealing WiFi or cable services—are typically charged as larceny.

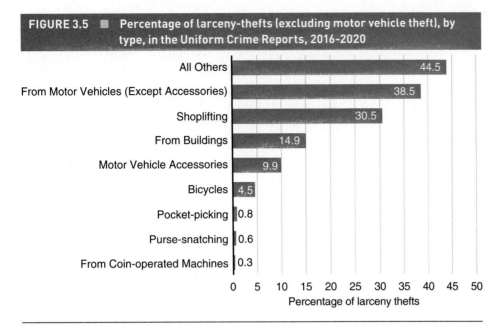

FIGURE 3.5 ■ Percentage of larceny-thefts (excluding motor vehicle theft), by type, in the Uniform Crime Reports, 2016-2020

Source: Federal Bureau of Investigation. (2021). *Offense analysis: Larceny-theft (except motor vehicle theft), larceny-theft by type, 2016-2020.* https://ucr.fbi.gov/crime-in-the-u.s

As with robbery, criminologists organize thieves along a continuum ranging from amateurs who occasionally and opportunistically steal to professional thieves who engage frequently in skilled offenses to support their day-to-day lives. Professionals plan whereas occasional thieves respond to *situational inducements,* which are aspects of an environment or circumstances that momentarily motivate them to break the law, such as a sudden and pressing need for money or being surrounded by friends who are stealing. The occasional thief finds way to justify or excuse their periodic misdeeds, freeing them from having to adopt a criminal identity. Perhaps the occasional thief sounds familiar to you, describing a friend or acquaintance who pockets items from convenience stores on impulse, albeit infrequently. Professional thieves, in contrast, cannot deny their criminal identity and are committed to developing a portfolio of illicit skills through both individual practice and learning from more experienced criminals. The distinction between occasional amateurs and seasoned professionals is especially apparent among shoplifters.

Shoplifting

Shoplifting is a form of larceny in which the offender takes goods from a retail establishment during business hours, and it comprises a significant portion of known larceny-thefts, as seen in Figure 3.5. In an interview for the "Why I Steal" episode of the podcast *Death, Sex, & Money,* shoplifter Alice (not her real name) described how she uses Tumblr, a web platform that is a hybrid of a social media and a blogging site, to connect with other thieves who use the site to share tips and boast about their frequent "lifting hauls."[49] Like other Tumblr shoplifters, Alice strategically selects easily secreted items with high resale value, like popular luxury cosmetics, from stores known to have lax security, stealing hundreds or even thousands of dollars' worth of store merchandise. She then sells the stolen goods using online marketplaces.

Alice and the other Tumblr shoplifters are a type of thief that criminologist Mary O. Cameron, in her classic work on shoplifters, called *boosters.*[50] Boosters are skilled shoplifters who earn a significant portion of their income from retail theft. Some boosters rely on *fences,* people who make a living by buying and reselling stolen goods. Technological advances—eBay and resale apps—have cut out the middleman for solo boosters like Alice. Boosters, along with professional burglars and fences, engage in *organized retail crime* when they collaborate with others in committing their offenses. Retailers lose over $30 billion (with a B!) each year due to organized retail crime, according to the National Retail Federation.[51] That value does not include loss from solo shoplifters like Alice.

Like other professional and semi-professional shoplifters, Alice employs learned techniques for efficiently stealing without drawing attention from store personnel. For example, she knows how to identify areas of stores that are free of cameras, and she describes using her daughter's diaper bag to hide stolen goods. Some professional boosters use items specifically designed to facilitate theft by concealing stolen property and shielding it from detection by security devices, including aluminum-lined bags called "booster bags."[52] Alice resides somewhere in the middle of the extreme ends of the continuum between occasional and professional thieves. Unlike true professionals, Alice does not think of herself as a criminal and she hid her crimes from her spouse for years. Her immersion in a criminal subculture exists only online. And like an occasional thief, Alice adopts a code of conduct that enables her to consider herself a noncriminal:

> *Alice: I mean I do have rules that I follow. I don't ever lift from small mom and pop kind of stores, and um, I don't lift from thrift stores, even though that's insanely easy because they never have cameras, mostly because somebody else is more likely to get hurt because of it. When you lift from somewhere like Walmart they already have it built into their insurance where they have like you know, loss insurance, and so they've already budgeted for a certain amount of stealing, I guess. And, I, it just, it lessens the impact.*

> *Interviewer: So you—it feels like it's like a victimless crime.*

> *Alice: Um, I would say it feels more like maybe a paper cut as opposed to like stabbing someone.*[53]

The shoplifters of Tumblr reveal multiple motivations for their crimes. In addition to boosters who make money selling what they steal (or bringing it back to stores for full-credit returns), some steal primarily for the thrill of the "five-finger discount," called *snitches*. Snitches are nonprofessional "pilferers" who act impulsively.[54] The booster-snitch distinction aligns with the professional-occasional distinction: Boosters lean professional while snitches are more apt to be amateurs who occasionally dabble in opportunistic theft.

John Patrick Weismiller was sentenced to one year in federal prison for stealing $73,000 worth of retail merchandise over the course of seven months, which he then resold in online auctions.

Federal Bureau of Investigation. (2012, April 17). *'Booster' behind bars: professional shoplifter gets prison terms.* https://www.fbi.gov/news/stories/booster-behind-bars

Burglary

Burglary occurs when someone enters a structure without permission in order to commit certain forms of crime, such as theft, assault, rape, or arson.[55] Burglary, a property crime, is characterized by unlawful entry. Structures subject to burglary include houses, apartments, barns and stables, house trailers, offices, stores, vessels (i.e., ships), and other dwellings that have a physical construction, though the types of structures specified vary from state to state.[56] The FBI excludes car break-ins, called auto burglaries, from their count of offenses, but vehicles can be the site of burglaries according to state laws. State laws also offer a range of definitions regarding whether force must be used to gain entry, such as breaking a window or prying open a garage door. You may have heard the term *breaking and entering* before. Burglaries that involve force are synonymous with breaking and entering, and they range from amateur "smash and grabs" to sophisticated entries using burglars' tools (lockpicks, master keys, acetylene torches, and more). A burglar who breaks a display window with a hammer, snatches valuables, and takes off running before security personnel can respond has committed a smash-and-grab burglary. It requires opportunity, speed, and force but little in the way of skill. *Ram raiding* is a particularly forceful strategy in which an offender drives—or rams—a vehicle through the windows or doors of a business to gain entry.[57]

Most modern definitions of burglary, including the FBI's, count unlawful entries without force as burglaries, as well; no "breaking" is required. For example, consider *distraction burglary*, wherein an offender lies their way into a home, often of an older adult, causing a diversion while their criminal partner commits theft.[58] Distraction burglars sometimes adopt credible guises, donning uniforms and acting as trusted visitors, like gas meter readers, water board officials, or contractors offering services (e.g., roofers or housepainters). Others knock on doors and present themselves as people in need of emergency assistance. "Bogus official" deceits tend to be more skilled than those committed by opportunistic fake assistance-seekers.

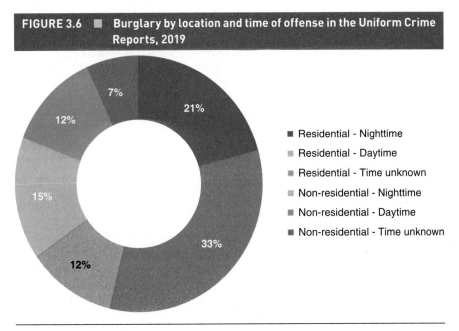

FIGURE 3.6 ■ Burglary by location and time of offense in the Uniform Crime Reports, 2019

- Residential - Nighttime
- Residential - Daytime
- Residential - Time unknown
- Non-residential - Nighttime
- Non-residential - Daytime
- Non-residential - Time unknown

Source: Federal Bureau of Investigation. (2019). Table 23. Offense analysis: Burglary, burglary by location. Crime in the United States, 2019. https://ucr.fbi.gov/crime-in-the-u.s/2019/crime-in-the-u.s.-2019/topic-pages/tables/table-23

Criminologists who study patterns of (non-auto) burglary distinguish between residential and nonresidential crimes, as well as by whether they occur during the daytime or nighttime, as seen in Figure 3.6. They also focus on the motivation for the burglary. Studies of offense characteristics reveal a variety of incentives beyond just the desire for money, including excitement, as an expression of anger towards the victim, and to secure a vacant place to live temporarily.[59] Sexual burglaries have—no surprise—a sexual motivation, sometimes paired with a financial incentive, as when a burglar sexually assaults a homeowner they were surprised to find asleep in bed. Other sexual burglaries have a singularly sexual motivation, either fulfilling fetishistic desires that do not require direct contact with victims (e.g., covert voyeurism or stealing undergarments) or committed for the purpose of sexual assault.[60]

Arson

In June of 1975, the *New York Times* ran a front-page story on the indictment of eight property owners and their associates who had set fire to their South Bronx apartment buildings so they could collect insurance payouts. The eight arsonists were, as the author of the article put it, "a drop in the bucket."[61] The South Bronx was the site of more than 5,500 arsons over a 17-month period spanning 1974 and 1975, many of them started by negligent landlords whose dilapidated properties were "worth more dead than alive."[62] The fires continued to burn. And in 1977, during the second game of the 1977 baseball World Series at Yankee Stadium, an ABC news helicopter captured footage of a burning building, famously discussed throughout the game by sportscasters Howard Cosell and Keith Jackson.[63] The South Bronx had lost almost 80% of its housing stock by the end of the decade.[64]

President Jimmy Carter surveying the damage done by widespread arson in the South Bronx, much of it committed by landlords. His visit took place one week prior to Game 2 of the 1977 World Series.

Jimmy Carter Library/National Archives and Records Administration

Arson is "the intentional and wrongful burning of someone else's property (as to destroy a building) or one's own property (as to fraudulently collect insurance)."[65] Sometimes called the "invisible" crime because it is rarely the focus of criminological study,[66] arson is a property crime because its defining feature is destruction of property, even though it may lead to injury or death. Criminologists distinguish arsons based on the type of property set ablaze—residential arson, nonresidential arson (e.g., office buildings), motor vehicle arson, and arson of natural resources, such as forests or wildlands. Vehicle arson is the most common type.

Deliberate fire-setting presents challenges for criminologists who wish to understand it. There are several reasons for this. Some arsons, called "hidden arsons," are not identified as the result of deliberate fire-setting.[67] Plus, arson has a low clearance rate, with only about one in five identified arsons leading to an arrest.[68] The result is that the available information on arson comes from a limited subset of fire-setters: those who are most likely to be apprehended (i.e., young male arsonists with intellectual impairment and mental health difficulties). Nonetheless, criminologists find some distinct motivations among arsonists, including the search for excitement through vandalism, attempts to conceal other crimes (e.g., burning stolen vehicles), achieving political goals as in terrorist attacks or rioting, self-injury or suicide attempts, as a form of revenge, and—as seen in the South Bronx of the 1970s—to swindle insurance companies.[69]

PUBLIC-ORDER CRIME

Public-order crime are unlawful actions that violate moral sentiments of a community (or a powerful segment of the community) or impede societal functioning.[70] Public drunkenness, sleeping on sidewalks (also called vagrancy), use and distribution of illicit substances, illegal gambling, and exchanging sexual services for money are public-order crimes, at least where they are outlawed. Because these offenses are typically without victim complainants to report them, they become known only when law enforcement seek them out proactively, often at the behest of community members troubled by their presence.

Critics of public-order laws argue that they criminalize the survival-centered actions of the most vulnerable groups in society, including runaway youth, throwaway youth who are forced to leave home by unsupportive caregivers, and other homeless populations.[71] As evidence, they point to "quality-of-life" initiatives, such as anti-panhandling ordinances, "camping" laws that make outdoor sleeping a crime, and laws that prohibit "public feeding" of the homeless.[72] Critics also point to the contested nature of public morality. Immorality, unlike direct harm to a victim, is in the eye of the beholder. So, whose eye matters most? The successful moral entrepreneur's.

Public-order crimes *become* crimes through a process of moral entrepreneurship. Consider the definition of the word *entrepreneur*: an organizer or operator of a business enterprise who, through risk and initiative, seeks to make a profit. A **moral entrepreneur** is "in the business of manufacturing public morality."[73] They attempt to alter social norms, including laws, to bring them into alignment with their own moral worldview. This idea should sound familiar. The idea of moral entrepreneurship relies on the interactionist definition of crime described in Chapter 1.

Consider Mothers Against Drunk Driving (MADD), a nonprofit organization, founded in 1980, whose mission is "to end drunk driving, help fight drugged driving, support the victims of these violent crimes and prevent underage drinking."[74] MADD has lobbied successfully to change both federal and state laws. It advocated for the 1984 National Minimum Drinking Age Act (the reason the drinking age is 21 in all 50 states) and lobbied to reduce blood alcohol content limits for criminal penalties arising from alcohol-impaired driving at the state level, typically from 0.15 to .08. Note the part of MADD's mission that describes drunk driving incidents as "violent crimes." In addition to changing laws, MADD has sought to alter the culture surrounding drunk driving by reframing driving under the influence as the catalyst for violent crime (i.e., alcohol-related collisions) rather than simply as a public-order offense.

Substance Use

Twenty-seven-year-old pitcher for the Los Angeles Angels, Tyler Skaggs, was found dead in his hotel room on July 1, 2019. He had asphyxiated (suffocated) on his vomit after ingesting a combination of alcohol, fentanyl, and oxycodone—the latter two are powerful opioid drugs. Skaggs's tragic death was one of many thousands of similar deaths, most not nearly as high-profile. In 2018, the year before Skaggs's death, more than 67,000 people in the U.S. died from a drug overdose, and 70% of those overdoses resulted from prescription (e.g., fentanyl and oxycodone) or illicit opioids (e.g., heroin).[75] Figure 3.7 displays how opioid abuse has increased over time in the U.S. Substance use may be victimless in the sense that no one is harmed directly and without their consent, but the costs of opioid abuse—to users, to their families, and to the broader society—are clear. Far less clear is the proper role of criminal punishment in addressing substance use, a public-order crime.

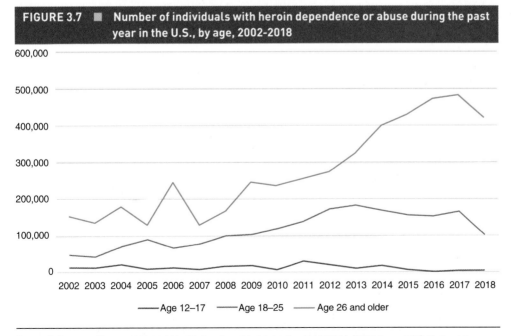

FIGURE 3.7 ■ Number of individuals with heroin dependence or abuse during the past year in the U.S., by age, 2002-2018

Source: Substance Abuse and Mental Health Services Administration (SAMHSA). (2019, August 20). *National Survey on Drug Use and Health.* https://www.samhsa.gov/data/report/2018-nsduh-detailed-tables

From the pre-Prohibition anti-alcohol crusades of the 19th and early 20th centuries to the War on Drugs a century later, many moral entrepreneurs have called upon political leaders to use criminal law to enforce sobriety and thereby control "dangerous" classes. For example, drug policy scholar David Musto described racialized anti-marijuana campaigns of the 1930s as a result of white laborers' economic insecurities about competing with Mexican immigrants—who cultivated and used marijuana—for scarce jobs during the Great Depression.[76] Efforts to frame marijuana as a Mexican menace threatening America's youth culminated in the Marihuana Tax Act of 1937. Its chief architect, Harry Anslinger, commissioner of the Federal Bureau of Narcotics, characterized the drug as inciting users to crime, writing:

How many murders, suicides, robberies, criminal assaults, holdups, burglaries and deeds of maniacal insanity it causes each year, especially among the young, can only be conjectured… No one knows, when he places a marijuana cigarette to his lips, whether he will become a joyous reveller in a musical heaven, a mad insensate, a calm philosopher, or a murderer." (p. 18)[77]

Similarly racialized claims—though with different ethnic groups as targets—had been made in campaigns to pass the San Francisco Opium Den Ordinance (1875), which vilified Chinese immigrants, and the Harrison Narcotics Tax Act (1914), which was passed following racist claims about the effects of cocaine on Black men's violence, especially sexual violence towards white women[78] (see Table 3.6). The War on Drugs began officially in 1971 when President Nixon declared drug abuse to be "public enemy number one." However, the major legislative successes of the War on Drugs came in the 1980s, and they relied on a characterization of crack cocaine as a drug of Black Americans that was responsible for urban disorder and poverty that threatened to bleed into middle-class, white communities if left unchecked.[79]

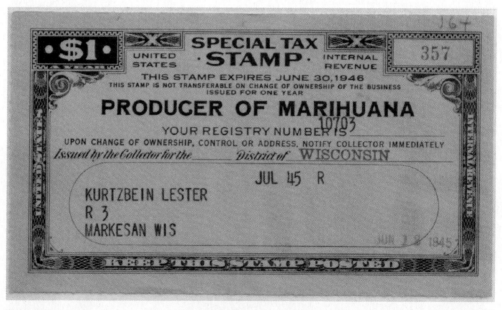

This marijuana producer tax stamp, issued in July 1945, was likely granted as part of the Hemp for Victory campaign during World War II.

Photo of "Producer of marihuana," by U.S. Government. https://commons.wikimedia.org/wiki/File:Producer_of_marihuana.jpg

Drug abuse violations are the most common public-order arrest. The U.S. Department of Justice reported over 1.65 million drug abuse arrests in 2018 (see Table 3.6), with the number of arrests bouncing between 1.48 and 1.70 million annually throughout the previous decade.[80] A recurring theme in drug-related moral entrepreneurship—and among those favoring a strong criminal justice response to substance use—is that drug use causes other forms of crime, including serious violent crime. There are, in fact, three ways that drugs and crime may be linked[81]:

1. *Psychopharmacological effects* – When substance use has a physiological impact that induces violent action, as when users become agitated, irrational, or incapable of controlling their anger.

2. *Economic-compulsive effects* – When the need for money to purchase illicit substances motivates users to employ illegal means of obtaining money or drugs, such as through burglary or robbery.

3. *Systemic effects* – When the criminalization of substances generates a lifestyle and business model among drug traffickers and distributors that relies on violent strategies to maintain market control.

Those who favor reforms, particularly legalization (or production, distribution, and sale regulated by the state, as with alcohol), point to systemic effects as justification.[82] Just as prohibition of alcohol emboldened violent organized criminals in the 1920s, they contend, prohibition of other substances gives rise to violent turf wars among local dealers, fuels drug cartel violence in other nations, and floods the market with substances of unknown quality and safety. Whether proponents of legalization or decriminalization (i.e., downgrading possession from a felony or misdemeanor to an infraction while trafficking remains criminalized), reformers call for a renewed focus on rehabilitation and argue that a harm reduction approach is more effective and humane than locking up users. The *harm reduction* model seeks to minimize the negative consequences of substance abuse—for the user and for

TABLE 3.6 ■ A brief history of drug laws in the U.S.	
San Francisco Opium Den Ordinance of 1875	The first U.S. drug law passed, this city ordinance made it a crime for Chinese immigrants to use and distribute opium in "dens." The ordinance did not affect the use of opium and its derivatives by non-Chinese populations. At the time, it was legal to purchase opium, morphine, and heroin without a prescription.
Harrison Narcotics Tax Act of 1914	This federal law taxed and regulated the production, distribution, and importing of opiates and coca products (including cocaine). Its goal was to restrict availability of opiates. Only registered companies and individuals could distribute cocaine. Doctors could still prescribe the substances but not for the treatment of addiction.
Eighteenth Amendment to the U.S. Constitution (1920); repealed 1933	The Eighteenth Amendment banned the manufacture, transportation, or sale of intoxicating liquors (i.e., Prohibition). The Twenty-First Amendment, ratified in 1933, overturned the Eighteenth Amendment.
Marihuana Tax Act of 1937	This federal law taxed the sale of marijuana and hemp, legal only among registered producers and importers. The law did not criminalize the possession or use of marijuana.
Controlled Substances Act of 1970	Created a federal drug policy regulating the manufacture, sale, importing, distribution, possession, and use of certain substances, which were categorized into "schedules" based on medical uses and potential for abuse. Schedule I substances—psychedelics (e.g., LSD), heroin, marijuana, MDMA (e.g., ecstasy), etc.—are considered to have no medical use and a high abuse potential. The act specifies fines and prison terms for violations.
Anti-Drug Abuse Act of 1986	The cornerstone of the War on Drugs, this federal law transformed the legal response to drug abuse from rehabilitation to punishment. It established and expanded mandatory minimum sentences for federal drug offenses, including possession. It famously imposed a five-year minimum sentence for possession of 5 grams of crack cocaine. A person would have to possess 100 times as much powder cocaine to receive an equivalent sentence. The 100:1 ratio was reduced to 18:1 in 2010 with the passage of the Fair Sentencing Act, which also eliminated the mandatory minimum of five years for simple possession of crack cocaine.

Source: Hari, J. (2015). *Chasing the scream: The first and last days of the War on Drugs.* New York: Bloomsbury.

the community—rather than to eliminate it entirely.[83] Harm reduction strategies include providing clean needles and safe injection sites, education on safer practices, methadone replacement therapies, overdose prevention drugs (like Narcan) and strategies, and easy access to drug treatment. The best way to address substance use—criminalization, legalization, harm reduction—is, as with nearly all public-order offenses, hotly debated.

Sex for Sale

Commercial sex—the exchange of sexual services for money or something else of value—dates back thousands of years. Licensed brothels operated in ancient Greece, around 500 BCE. Even earlier, Sumerian records dating to about 2400 BCE describe the "sacred prostitution" occurring within temple walls as well as the more commonplace prostitution of inns.[84] Sometimes called "the oldest profession," prostitution endures around the globe and is the source of moral handwringing, on one side, and movements to acknowledge prostitution as a legitimate form of labor, on the other. The term *sex work*, coined by activist Carol Leigh in 1978, describes multiple forms of commercial sex, some criminalized and some not—prostitution, stripping, pornography and camming, phone sex, and more.[85] Anti-obscenity and anti-prostitution laws are evidence of successful moral entrepreneurship by those wishing to use criminal law to uphold their vision of decency.

Obscenity

Obscenity laws criminalize the distribution, receipt, and broadcasting of materials deemed unacceptable using the Miller test, named for the 1973 Supreme Court ruling in *Miller v. California*. The test requires three criteria be met for materials to be considered obscene and, therefore, not protected by the First Amendment right to free speech:

1. "Whether the average person, applying contemporary adult community standards, finds that the matter, taken as a whole, appeals to prurient interests"

2. "Whether the average person, applying contemporary adult community standards, finds that the matter depicts or describes sexual conduct in a patently offensive way"

3. "Whether a reasonable person finds that the matter, taken as a whole, lacks serious literary, artistic, political, or scientific value."[86]

Obscenity laws have historically been used to restrict pornographic films, images, and texts produced for public, adult commercial consumption. In their modern-day application, obscenity laws are used to punish those who expose minors to pornographic materials, create and share child sexual abuse imagery (the more accurate term for child pornography) online, distribute unsolicited and nonconsensual explicit images of adults, and expose themselves sexually in public.

Prostitution

The FBI defines prostitution and commercialized vice as "the unlawful promotion of or participation in sexual activities for profit."[87] This is an umbrella category that contains those who sell sex (sex workers and sex-trafficked persons), purchase sex ("Johns"), and manage the selling of sex (traffickers, pimps, and madams). Prostitution is outlawed in all U.S. states though some forms are legal in a handful of Nevada counties, home to 20 legal brothels. Researchers classify prostitution based on the context in which sellers and customers interact for transactions. Brothel prostitution, as in Nevada, differs from other transaction contexts, such as (1) street-level prostitution (or "strolling"), some occurring in "red light districts," or informally designated vice zones, (2) massage parlors and other indoor erotic businesses, (3) agency-operated escort services, and (4) technology-mediated transactions that rely on web platforms or apps, some that exclusively advertise sexual services.[88]

The U.S Department of Justice reports that 26,710 prostitution and commercialized vice arrests occurred in 2019, as seen in Table 3.7. Of these, 9,880 (36.99%) arrestees were male and 16,830

(63.01%) were female, making prostitution a rare case in which women outnumber men in official statistics (it bears noting that some transgender persons—transgender women especially—are misgendered in these counts). Sex is not a stand-in for one's role in a commercial sex transaction; for example, a sizable minority of sex workers and sex-trafficked persons are male.[89] However, data from individual cities reveal how arrests differ for sellers versus buyers. For example, in Chicago in 2013, three-quarters of prostitution arrests were of sellers; their customers presented only one-quarter of prostitution arrests. This pattern was in line with data from other cities. Chicago was in the news later, though, as the arrest gap between sellers and buyers grew over the following years: By 2017, 91% of Chicago prostitution arrests were of sellers and only 8% were of customers (less than 1% of arrests were for pimping or "other offenses" in both years).[90]

TABLE 3.7 ■ Arrest counts for public-order offenses in the U.S., 2019	
Arrest offense	**Number of arrests**
Drug abuse violations	1,558,860
Driving under the influence	1,024,510
Disorderly conduct	310,330
Drunkenness	316,030
Liquor laws	175,550
Weapons – carrying, possessing, etc.	153,160
Offenses against the family and children	85,690
Prostitution and commercialized vice	26,710
Vagrancy	21,900
Curfew and loitering law violations	14,650
Gambling	2,460

Source: U.S. Department of Justice. (2019). Estimated number of arrests by offense and age group, 2019, all ages. *Office of Juvenile Justice and Delinquency Prevention: Statistical briefing book.* Retrieved from https://www.ojjdp.gov/ojstatbb/crime/ucr. asp?table_in = 1

Do not confuse commercial sex work by consenting, autonomous adults with sex trafficking. Sex trafficking is one type of human trafficking, which the U.S. Department of Homeland Security defines as the "use of force, fraud, or coercion to obtain some type of labor or commercial sex act."[91] It is a myth that traffickers rely primarily on violent tactics to control those they seek to exploit. According to hotline data from the Polaris Project, a nonprofit anti-trafficking organization, isolation/confinement, economic abuse (i.e., withholding money), threats, and emotional abuse were more common than physical violence in compelling victims to engage in unwanted commercial sex acts or sexual labor, such as working in illicit massage parlors or strip clubs.

Some criminology texts lump commercial sex trafficking in with consensual sex work in describing public-order crimes. The blurriness between sex trafficking and sex work—many sex workers report being trafficked as their entry into prostitution—may contribute to this.[92] While it may be true that both offenses are violations of moral sentiments, sex trafficking harms individual victims (remember the harm principle!) rather than some abstract notion of harm to "society." The same is true of certain other forms of commercialized vice, like sexual abuse imagery (photos or videos of trafficked persons or other crime victims that are distributed for pornographic consumption). Moreover, there is no such thing as a "child prostitute" or an "underage prostitute" despite use of these terms in some texts. These phrases position the child as a law violator rather than as a victim of crime. Minors who are induced to perform commercial sex acts are victims of trafficking, even in the absence of force or coercion, according to federal and state laws.[93]

ENGAGED CRIMINOLOGY 3.2

Crimes on the Docket

This activity requires you to identify crime types in an excerpt from a real-life criminal court docket in Wake County, North Carolina, on November 8, 2021. (Names have been altered for privacy.) A docket is a schedule of court cases.

TABLE 3.8 ■ Criminal Court Docket, Wake County, NC	
Defendant name	**Offense**
Alameda, Louis	Possession with intent to sell or distribute marijuana
	Maintaining a vehicle, dwelling, or place for controlled substances
Allen-Morgan, Devonte	Assault with a deadly weapon with intent to kill or seriously injure
	Possession of a firearm by a felon
Allen, Tre	Robbery with a dangerous weapon
	Possession of stolen goods or property
	Obtaining property under false pretenses
Andriaccio, Ina	Robbery with a dangerous weapon
	Common law robbery (without firearm or dangerous weapon)
	Second-degree kidnapping
	Identity theft
	Obtaining property under false pretenses
	Resisting public officer
Ashford, Thomas	Simple possession of a Schedule II controlled substance
	Simple possession of a Schedule III controlled substance
	Simple possession of a Schedule IV controlled substance
	Assault by strangulation
Baskins, James	Larceny of a motor vehicle
	Breaking or entering of a motor vehicle
Bradley, Anthony	Indecent exposure
	Indecent exposure with defendant >18 years and victim <16 years

The docket contains a list of criminal charges for each person who is to appear in court. As is common, the defendants have multiple charges. Your focus (or unit of analysis) is the individual criminal charges, not the people. **Use the docket excerpt to answer the following questions:**

1. Identify one example of a violent crime on the docket.
2. Identify one example of a property crime on the docket.
3. Identify one example of a public-order crime on the docket

CHAPTER SUMMARY

LO 3.1 Explain what crime typologies are and identify some common crime typologies.

Crime typologies are organizational tools for grouping together criminal offenses that share characteristics. Common crime typologies include organizing by (1) type of victim, including offenses against persons, property, the public order, or the state; (2) level of severity, as in misdemeanors versus felonies; and (3) type of rewards generated by the offense, including instrumental and expressive offenses.

LO 3.2 Differentiate violent crime from other types of crime and identify examples.

Violent crimes are direct-contact offenses (where the perpetrator and victim come to together in place and time) that produce physical harm or the threat of physical harm. While the target of a violent crime is often a person, violent offenses can also be crimes against property if physical force or the threat of physical force is used. Examples include homicide, assault, rape and sexual assault, and robbery.

LO 3.3 Distinguish property crime from other types of crime and identify examples.

Property crimes are offenses in which a person takes, does damage to, or attempts to take or do damage to property (e.g., money, belongings, homes or businesses, vehicles, identification documents) without consent of the rightful owner. Examples include larceny-theft, fraud, burglary, vandalism, and arson.

LO 3.4 Identify the characteristics and subtypes of public-order crimes.

Public-order crimes, unlike violent and property crimes, do not cause harm to specific individuals. Rather, they are regarded as causing harm to "society" and become criminal through a process of moral entrepreneurship. Examples include public drunkenness, sleeping on sidewalks (or vagrancy), use and distribution of illicit substances, illegal gambling, and exchanging sexual services for money.

ENGAGED DISCUSSION

1. Which do you think poses a greater risk to public safety—instrumental crime or expressive crime? In what ways?

2. Robbery is a violent crime as well as a crime against property. Which is more important to you in categorizing this offense: the ultimate goal (property) or the way it is carried out (violence)?

3. How would you rank the property crimes larceny, burglary, and arson in terms of their seriousness (with 1 = least serious and 3 = most serious), and why? Does your answer depend on the value of the stolen or damaged property?

4. Imagine if all U.S. states were to decriminalize consensual commercial sex work by adults. Do you think this would increase, decrease, or have no impact on sex trafficking (which would still be criminal)? Why?

KEY TERMS

Arson (p. 70)

Burglary (p. 69)

Crime typologies (p. 54)

Direct-contact crime (p. 56)

Expressive crimes (p. 56)

Felonies (p. 54)

Homicide (p. 56)

Infractions (p. 55)

Instrumental crimes (p. 55)

Jails (p. 54)

Larceny (p. 66)

Manslaughter (p. 56)

Mass murder (p. 59)

Misdemeanors (p. 54)

Moral entrepreneur (p. 71)

Murder (p. 56)

Prisons (p. 54)

Property crime (p. 66)

Public-order crime (p. 70)

Rape (p. 62)

Robbery (p. 63)

Serial murder (p. 61)

Sexual assault (p. 63)

Victimless crime (p. 55)

Violent crime (p. 56)

PLEASE SEE ASSOCIATE FOR ASSISTANCE

Tim Boyle/Getty

4 WHITE-COLLAR CRIME, ORGANIZED CRIME, CYBERCRIME, HATE CRIME, AND TERRORISM

LEARNING OBJECTIVES

4.1 Describe characteristics of entrepreneurial and ideologically motivated crime.

4.2 Classify types of white-collar crime, including occupational and corporate crime.

4.3 Explain what organized crime is and the forms it takes.

4.4 Identify multiple forms of cybercrime.

4.5 Discern between hate/bias crime and terrorism.

If you have ever strolled among the packs of diapers in the baby aisle at a grocery store, you may have noticed infant formula stored behind locked plexiglass or a notice stating that the formula is stored behind the customer service desk. Maybe you have seen a sign warning that you are being watched on a surveillance camera. Few items in the grocery store are so heavily monitored. Loss prevention experts—people who study and provide guidance on reducing retail "shrinkage" due to theft—inform retailers that infant formula is among the most frequently pilfered items on their shelves.[1] You probably have a good idea why if you have ever raised a formula-fed infant. Formula is expensive. Really expensive. It costs about $25 to $35 per 30-ounce can, more if the baby needs specialty formula due to gastrointestinal problems, and most babies will go through a can or more per week. But it's not just shoplifting by cash-strapped parents that created the grocery store formula fortress. Many formula thieves aren't parents at all. They are low-level players in organized crime.[2]

The phrase "organized crime" evoke images of gambling, prostitution, drug trafficking, and loan sharks. Rarely do they elicit the image of a can of infant formula. Yet there is a fertile black market for formula, an expensive product with small profit margins for retailers. The black market's customers aren't parents, though. The customers are the operators of independent stores, some in the U.S., some in other countries, who cannot afford to make the less-expensive bulk purchases that chain retailers can. Imagine a family-owned convenience store. Their customers need baby formula, but the store only sells 15 cans per month. The only way to afford to stock the small number of cans and make any money on those sales is to buy them below the wholesale price. Someone—many someones—saw the demand and stepped in to provide the product.

Some operations appear legitimate. They buy up unused, unopened cans of formula from parents and resell them. They are part of an innovative "gray market": The purchases and sales exist outside of formal distribution channels, but that is the only illegitimate part of the process. The product and the strategies for obtaining the product are legal.[3] The organized crime begins when formula procurers collude with cargo thieves, professional shoplifters (hence the plexiglass formula cases), and crooked employees to supply and operate a black market.

The organized underground market for stolen formula has operated for years, first hitting the U.S. news in 2005 when two traffic stops on I-75 in Tennessee turned up 1,224 and 3,300 cans of stolen infant formula, respectively. The director of the FBI at the time, Robert Mueller, stated that he suspected that proceeds from black market sales of infant formula were being used to fund terrorist organizations abroad.[4] Asked about the Tennessee cases (neither of which turned out to be linked to terrorism), FBI agent Tim Burke reported, "Some of these types of operations are used as fronts for terrorism financing... Some of them are just black market profit-making efforts. Others have more nefarious connections."[5]

Formula crime rings straddle multiple types of crime covered in this chapter. The black market operations are organized crime. They are often supplied by cargo workers and retail employees who use their workplace positions to commit theft, a type of occupational crime. If Director Mueller's and Agent Burke's claims had been founded and the black market profits were, in fact, used to fund terrorism, then formula crime rings would have had links to ideologically motivated crimes, as well.

ENTREPRENEURSHIP AND IDEOLOGY IN CRIME

The previous chapter described many types of crime that captivate the public's imagination and populate its fears, including violent crimes (like homicide, rape, and armed robbery) and property crimes (like burglary, arson, and motor vehicle theft). Those offenses are usually referred to as *street crimes,* and they are disproportionately committed by individuals who are poor. This chapter covers crime types that extend beyond typical street crime. Perpetrators of the crime types in this chapter—white-collar crime, organized crime, cybercrime, hate crime, and terrorism—often have (or are seeking) social or economic power. Their offenses are either entrepreneurial or driven by ideology.

In the business world, entrepreneurs are people who create new businesses and take on risks in order to make a profit. Entrepreneurial crime shares the elements of risk-taking and profit-making, but it relies on illegal methods for generating financial proceeds. It is, by definition, instrumental rather than expressive in nature. Another term for entrepreneurial crime is *enterprise crime,* as in business enterprise. The lion's share of white-collar crime, organized crime, and cybercrime is entrepreneurial crime. The criminal infant formula suppliers described at the chapter's outset were most assuredly entrepreneurial.

Ideologically motivated crime, in contrast, is driven by the offender's desire to use criminal action—often violence—to express or further a worldview. The word *ideology* refers to systems of ideas that

(a) offer an account of the existing order, usually in the form of a "world view"

(b) advance a model of a desired future, a vision of the "good society"

(c) explain how political change can and should be brought about – how to get from (a) to (b). (p. 10)[6]

Of course, most crime has an underlying ideological system; for example, entrepreneurial crime is rooted in capitalist ideology with its emphasis on competing for profit. What makes ideologically motivated crime distinct is that the crime is a tool for making a statement *about* ideology (rather than just lining one's pockets). Its purpose is to advance political and social agendas. Terrorism and hate/bias crime are ideologically motivated crimes, as are some forms of cybercrime.

WHITE-COLLAR CRIME

The term *white-collar crime* is part of the modern American vocabulary—the existence of a six-season TV show called *White Collar* attests to this—but that was not always so. The label and its place within criminology originates with Edwin Sutherland. As president of the American Sociological Society (now called the American Sociological Association, or ASA, a much better acronym) in 1939, Sutherland delivered an address in which he called upon criminologists to study crimes of "respectable, or at least respected businessmen and professionals" (p. 1).[7] The speech, which birthed the moniker "white-collar crime" laid out several propositions, including the following:

1. White-collar crime is real crime.

2. What differentiates white-collar crime from "lower-class criminality" (or street crime) is that it is treated differently in the administration of criminal law, with white-collar offenders avoiding criminal punishment.

3. Criminologists' explanations of street crime are insufficient for explaining white-collar crime. Indeed, they are insufficient for explaining street crime, too, because they cannot explain *all* forms of criminality.

4. Criminological theories should explain the crimes of both the higher and lower classes.

For Sutherland, white-collar crime was "crime committed by a person of respectability and high social status in the course of their occupation" (p. 9).[8] Compare his description to this more contemporary definition:

Illegal or unethical acts that violate fiduciary responsibility or public trust committed by an individual or organization, usually during the course of legitimate occupational activity, by a person of high or respectable social status for personal or organizational gain. (p. 330)[9]

You will notice that Sutherland's original definition distinguishes white-collar crime from other forms of crime (i.e., "blue-collar" or street crime) on two grounds: (1) characteristics of offenders ("person of respectability and high social status") and (2) the context of offending ("in the course of their occupation").[10] The more recent definition, crafted by a large group of criminologists seeking consensus on the meaning of the term, similarly emphasizes high social status and the workplace setting. White-collar crime is universally depicted as *elite crime*, or "crime in the suites" rather than "crime in the streets." The term *gray-collar crime* is adopted occasionally to describe white-collar offenses, like fraud or embezzlement, when committed by lower- or middle-status offenders (see Figure 4.1).

FIGURE 4.1 ■ A rainbow of collars: Variants on and distinctions from white-collar crime

Gray-collar crime	Red-collar crime	Blue-collar crime
• Offenses that have characteristics of white-collar crime but are committed by low- to middle-status persons in either an occupational or non-occupational context.	• Violent crimes committed by white-collar offenders trying to conceal their criminal acts, typically by targeting those who have detected and/or might disclose their offenses.	• Crimes committed by persons of lower social class; the term differentiates common forms of violence, property offending, and public-order violations ("street crime") in a non-occupational setting from white-collar crime ("elite crime").
• **Example case:** In California in 2018, Sarah Sandoval pled guilty to three counts of bank fraud and one count of aggravated identity theft. Sandoval was a DMV employee who, along with a co-offender, used stolen mail and DMV databases to select victims foe debit and credit card frauds.	• **Example case:** In California in 2008, Reginald Robinson, who attempted a $375,000 bank fraud, solicited the murder of his business partner, real estate developer Kashmir Billon, because Billon had discovered the scam and confronted Robinson about it.	• **Example case:** In Rochester, NY, in 2019, James Houston, Raekwon Fuqua, and others committed a robbery at an AT&T store, making off with 32 cell phones after holding an employee at gunpoint.

Sources: Brody, R. G., & Kiehl, K. A. (2010). From white-collar crime to red-collar crime. *Journal of Financial Crime, 17,* 351-364; California Statewide Law Enforcement Association. (2018, July 23). *Former DMV employee sentenced for bank fraud and identity theft scheme.* https://cslea.com/2018/07/former-dmv-employee-sentenced-for-bank-fraud-and-identity-theft-scheme/; Associated Press. (2011, March 9). Man gets 11 years for murder solicitation, fraud. *San Diego Union-Tribune.* https://www.sandiegouniontribune.com/sdut-man-gets-11-years-for-murder-solicitation-fraud-2011mar09-story.html; Department of Justice, U.S. Attorney's Office. (2020, December 23). *Rochester man pleads guilty to armed robbery of cell phone store.* Bureau of Alcohol, Tobacco, Firearms, and Explosiveshttps://www.atf.gov/news/pr/rochester-man-pleads-guilty-armed-robbery-cell-phone-store

The modern understanding of white-collar crime is narrower than Sutherland's in some ways and broader in others. It is more restrictive in identifying the motivation underlying white-collar offending ("personal or organizational gain"). It also describes white-collar offenses specifically as violations of trust, such as between a professional and their client or customer, or between a politician and the public they serve. The definition expands in acknowledging that not *all* white-collar crimes take place in an occupational setting and by including acts committed by organizations. In fact, in studying crimes of—and rewards to—both individuals and organizations, contemporary scholars of elite crime recognize two forms of white-collar offending: (1) occupational crime (individuals) and (2) corporate crime (organizations).

Occupational Crime

Occupational crime is crime committed for personal gain in the context of a legitimate occupation that is "fundamentally related to the opportunities that the occupation provides" (p. 95).[11] A legitimate occupation is any job that is not illegal. For example, consider the opportunities for income-generating crime that the following workers have at their occupations:

- Car dealership employees who check credit scores and offer lines of credit to buyers

- Department of Motor Vehicle (DMV) employees who issue new and replacement IDs

- Human Resources employees who administer workers' payroll and benefits

- Medical billing employees who manage patient records for payment purposes

- Real estate brokers who work with clients and lenders to facilitate transactions

These workers have ample opportunities to violate trust in order to secure illicit financial rewards, such as by diverting funds for personal use or accessing personally identifying information for committing fraud. In addition, some occupational crimes bring individual benefits that are not necessarily financial, at least not directly. For example, the occupational offenses in political and criminal justice contexts often involve the use of unethical strategies for gaining or maintaining power and influence (e.g., bribery and other forms of corruption).

Trust violations can occur in nearly any occupational setting. Some contexts give rise to unique opportunities for white-collar wrongdoing, including sales, housing, health care, politics, criminal justice, and the economic system. Table 4.1 provides examples of setting-specific occupational offenses. The victims of these occupational crimes can include customers, patients, clients, the general public, financial institutions, insurance companies, governmental agencies, and the organization that employs the offender.

Many occupational crimes involve some form of fraud. Fraud victims are deceived into giving money or property to perpetrators who have misrepresented facts. Fraud is, essentially, theft. But unlike other thefts, the victim of fraud—tricked by the offender's lies—willingly hands over their assets.[12] Three primary forms of occupational fraud are (1) asset misappropriation, (2) corruption for monetary gain, and (3) financial statement fraud.[13]

A perpetrator misappropriates assets when they use their occupational position to steal from the employing organization. They might falsify expense reports (expense reimbursement scheme) or claim they made payments to a nonexistent vendor (purchase order scheme) or "ghost" employee (payroll schemes). According to the Association of Certified Fraud Examiners (ACFE), asset misappropriation constitutes 86% of occupational frauds.[14] In the second form of occupational fraud—corruption for monetary gain—perpetrators collude, or cooperate in secret, with others to commit their crimes. For example, they might collude with vendors to make false payments, splitting the illicit proceeds between the vendor and themselves. Other forms include bribery (also called illegal gratuities), as when an employee provides organizational funds to another person or organization in exchange for personal benefits or a business advantage. Employees who alter balance sheets, cash flow statements, or income statements have engaged in financial statement fraud, the third type of occupational fraud. Financial statement fraud is the least common of the three types, comprising only 1 in 10 occupational frauds. However, it is the most damaging, with a median loss of $954,000 per case (versus a median loss of $100,000 for asset misappropriation and $200,000 for corruption).[15]

TABLE 4.1 ■ Settings, types, and descriptions of selected occupational crimes

Occupational crime setting	Example offenses	Offense descriptions
Sales	Embezzlement	Theft or misappropriation of money or property from an employer, business partner, or other person who entrusted the offender with money or property (e.g., the treasurer of an organization diverting funds into a personal account).
	Chiseling	Using deception to cheat clients, customers, or organizations such as by claiming to provide goods and services never rendered or by altering weights and measures (e.g., a mechanic charging for fake repairs).
Housing	Appraisal fraud	Deliberately inflating the appraised value of a property by a fraudulent appraiser or others altering accurate documents. Inflated appraisals are used to assist sellers in over-charging, to assist buyers in obtaining better loan terms, or as part of a mortgage fraud in which offenders secure large loans for low-cost properties.
	Foreclosure rescue scams	Scam targeting homeowners facing foreclosure. Offender takes over ownership of the home temporarily while former owners remain in the home and pay rent, which they are told will go towards a buyback of the home. The offender evicts the victims and sells the home.
Health care	Medical fraud	Filing dishonest medical claims, such as billing Medicare, Medicaid, private insurance companies, or patients for medical services, medications, or devices never provided. Alternatively, physicians may provide medically unnecessary services, medications, or devices in exchange for kickbacks or bribes from pharmaceutical companies, laboratory testing companies, or other organizations.
	Unnecessary surgeries	Physicians performing unneeded surgeries on deceived or uninformed patients in order to bill Medicare, Medicaid, private insurance companies, or patients, for financial gain.
Politics	Political corruption	Public officials misusing their position, to the detriment of the public's interests, to secure private benefits, including benefits to third parties. Can include bribery (offering, giving, soliciting, or receiving something of value to secure desired conduct or to influence judgment) or extortion (securing benefits through coercion).
	Campaign finance law violations	Violation of rules regarding how much money can be contributed to a political campaign, who can contribute, and how contributions can be used. Limitations were imposed to limit the influence of money on the political process.
Criminal justice	Police corruption	Violations of trust often involving bribery of law enforcement. Includes police demands for bribes from stopped citizens, bribery of police by individuals or organizations seeking desired outcomes related to policing, or collusion with criminal organizations. Also includes police violating rules not for personal benefit but for what they believe is the public good.
	Prosecutorial misconduct	Violations by a prosecutor, typically to influence a jury to wrongly convict a defendant or to impose a punishment that is harsher than appropriate, or to extract a guilty plea from a wrongly convicted defendant. Can include presentation of false evidence or concealing exculpatory evidence (i.e., evidence proving innocence).
Economic system	Insider trading	When a corporate insider discloses or uses information that is not available to the public and makes stock market trades based on nonpublic information. Also includes noncorporate persons who receive nonpublic information from those privy to it and then make trades based on that information.
	Ponzi schemes	Scams that involve paying profits to investors using funds from more recent investors. The defrauded investors are unaware that the so-called profits are being drawn from other investors rather than actual sales or other legitimate sources due to deceptive financial statements. The success of the scam relies on luring more and more investors indefinitely.

Source: Payne, B. (2016). *White-collar crime: The essentials.* Thousand Oaks, CA: SAGE.

The investment fraud offense known as a Ponzi scheme is named after Charles Ponzi, who gained notoriety in the 1920s for perpetrating the scheme.

Photo of Charles Ponzi, dated August 1920. Boston Library. https://commons.wikimedia.org/w/index.php?curid = 3153479

Corporate Crime

Between September 2008 and April 2009, an outbreak of salmonella poisoning linked to contaminated peanut butter sickened at least 714 people (unreported cases are estimated to be closer to 22,000) and killed 9 people.[16] Investigators traced the tainted peanut butter to a factory in Georgia run by the Peanut Corporation of America (PCA). Outbreaks of foodborne illness are not uncommon, but the peanut butter case was especially egregious. Email exchanges revealed that the CEO of PCA, Stewart Parnell, and other executives were aware of the contamination, sought to conceal it, and approved the distribution of the tainted product. During the outbreak, the company assured its customers that their peanut butter had been tested and was safe, which was a lie. Parnell was ultimately sentenced to 28 years in federal prison, the longest sentence ever imposed in a foodborne illness case. Four others were also sentenced to prison, with sentences ranging from 3 years to 20 years.[17]

The Peanut Corporation of America case is an example of corporate crime. Corporate crime is crime committed by business entities, or individuals acting on behalf of business entities, for organizational gain. That is the primary distinction of corporate crime from occupational crime: It is crime committed by and for the organization. Corporate crime nets corporate rewards. Nonetheless, the individuals who orchestrate the offenses benefit individually, as well. The profit, after all, is the point. Common forms of corporate wrongdoing include the following:

Antitrust crimes – The price of goods and services is supposed to be determined by supply and demand based on the principles of open market competition. Antitrust crimes restrict competition, in violation of the Sherman Antitrust Act of 1890.[18] The most frequently prosecuted antitrust crimes are price fixing, bid rigging, and market allocation.[19] *Price fixing* occurs when competitors collude "to raise, fix, or otherwise maintain the price at which their goods or services are sold,"[20] thereby undermining open competition and raising prices for consumers. *Bid rigging* occurs when competitors for a contract—typically a federal, state, or local government contract—decide in advance who will submit the winning bid. This undermines the competitive bidding process and drives up the cost of goods or services to taxpayers. *Market allocation* occurs when competitors split up markets, thus gaining a monopoly over the portion of the market they control. They may allocate, or divide, geographic territories, types of customers, or products.

False advertising – Businesses are prohibited from making deceptive or untrue claims. This may include the promise of nonexistent sale items, selling used items as new, or making inaccurate statements about what a product can do or where it was manufactured.[21] Though law violators may be subject to criminal penalties, most false advertising cases are settled in civil courts, such as Volkswagen's false "clean diesel" claims and the app Luminosity's claims that its product could prevent dementia.[22] In a high-profile case of false advertising, Mustafa Hassan Arif was sentenced to six years in federal prison for owning and operating over 1,500 commercial websites on which he sold nonprescription drugs presented as treating or curing multiple conditions or diseases, including Alzheimer's disease, cerebral palsy, and Parkinson's disease. The websites made false claims about clinical research, drug effectiveness, side effects, and the location of the drugs' origins (e.g., German customers were led to believe the drugs were being sold by a German company when all the drugs came from Pakistan).[23]

Harmful consumer products – This occurs when businesses knowingly or recklessly sell contaminated, defective, or dangerous products.[24] The Peanut Corporation of America case is an example of this type of corporate crime. In another high-profile case, the company Candy Color Lenses knowingly sold counterfeit and misbranded colored contact lenses, some of which were contaminated with bacteria that caused serious eye injury to customers.[25] The sale of harmful consumer products may occur alongside other criminal offenses, including false advertising regarding product safety and the sale of counterfeit products.

Unfair and unsafe labor practices – These happen when organizations harm employees through exploitation or maintaining workplace conditions that can result in death, injury, or illness.[26] Exploitation involves taking advantage of workers, such as requiring them to work extra hours without pay. Such cases rarely lead to criminal penalties, even when employers' blatantly reckless behavior results in fatalities (e.g., lack of basic safety precautions for construction workers).[27] Some cases are so egregious, however, that executives are criminally sanctioned. One example is the one-year sentence handed to Don Blankenship, former chairman and CEO of the Massey Energy Company, whose company's safety shortcuts contributed to the Upper Big Branch mine collapse, which killed 29 workers in 2010. Blankenship was found guilty of conspiring to willfully violate mine safety and health standards.[28]

Environmental offenses – These happen when businesses or organizations knowingly or negligently violate the Clean Air Act, the Clean Water Act, federal hazardous waste laws, or other environmental protection laws. They include offenses such as emission of toxic pollutants, illegal disposal of hazardous waste and pesticides, and illegal asbestos removal. For example, in February 2014, a broken stormwater pipe at a retired Duke Energy coal plant spilled 39,000 tons of coal ash into the Dan River in North Carolina, along with 27 million gallons of wastewater. Coal ash is a toxic by-product of power plants containing mercury, lead, cadmium, arsenic, and radioactive materials. Duke Energy pled guilty to nine charges of criminal negligence under the Clean Water Act and was required to pay $102 million in criminal fines and restitution.[29]

Most corporate crime convictions result in fines rather than prison time despite the large financial and health costs to consumers, taxpayers, workers, and residents. For example, the Environmental Protection Agency (EPA) released a list of the biggest criminal cases involving environmental offenses in 2017.[30] Of the 11 cases reported, which the EPA puts forth as the most serious environmental crimes of the year, only 5 resulted in *any* prison time at all. Indeed, the 28-year sentence for the CEO who approved the distribution of peanut butter contaminated with salmonella is noteworthy for its unusual length. In 2012, another foodborne illness outbreak, this time involving cantaloupe, killed at least 33 people. The two owner-operators of Jensen Farms, where the cantaloupe was prepared, packed, and stored in unsafe conditions, received no prison time. Instead, each was sentenced to five months' probation, 100 hours of community service, and was ordered to pay $150,000 in restitution to victims.[31] One reason for the lesser punishment in the cantaloupe case is the lower level of intent. Unlike in the peanut butter case, the owner-operators of Jensen Farms did not know that the cantaloupe posed a public health risk—even if they *should* have known the rule-violating conditions were ripe for the *Listeria* contamination—nor did they attempt to cover up the problem.

ENGAGED CRIMINOLOGY 4.1
White-Collar Crime in the News

This activity requires you to apply concepts in the study of white-collar crime to three real-world examples of white-collar perpetrators. Read the descriptions of three individuals who have been convicted of white-collar offenses and answer the questions.

Case #1: Christopher Lischewski, former CEO of Bumble Bee

Christopher Lischewski, the former CEO of the seafood company Bumble Bee, was sentenced to 40 months in prison and ordered to pay a $100,000 fine for "orchestrating, implementing, and enforcing" a tuna price-fixing scheme involving other seafood companies. The offense generated an estimated $600 million in illicit profits, which benefited Bumble Bee and the other participating seafood companies. In sentencing Lischewski, the judge stated, "The product in question is a basic food staple. It is not expensive LCD screens, it is not some part of high price consumer goods ... This is food ... for people who I think it's fair to assume includes those who are at the lower end of the socioeconomic scale based on the pricing of this product."[32]

Case #2: Dr. Farid Fata, hematologist/oncologist

Dr. Farid Fata, a Michigan hematologist/oncologist, was sentenced to 45 years in prison after pleading guilty to charges of health care fraud, conspiracy to pay and receive kickbacks, and money laundering. Acting on his own and for his own financial benefit, Dr. Fata had been knowingly administering chemotherapy to healthy patients who did not, in fact, have cancer, as well as to cancer patients for whom chemotherapy was unnecessary. In some instances, patients died as a result of these unnecessary treatments. Dr. Fata prescribed unwarranted treatments to defraud Medicare and private insurance companies of $34 million. Chief Richard Weber of the Criminal Investigations office of the Internal Revenue Service described Dr. Fata's actions as "the most egregious case of fraud and deception that I have seen in my career."[33]

Case #3: Steve Warshak, founder of Enzyte

Steve Warshak, former CEO of Berkeley Premium Nutraceuticals, was sentenced to 25 years in prison (later reduced to 10 years) and ordered to pay $93,000 in fines, after being found guilty of 93 counts of conspiracy, money laundering, and mail, wire, and bank fraud. The criminal charges pertained to the selling of Enzyte, an herbal supplement marketed as "the once daily tablet for natural male enhancement" (i.e., erectile size and function). Warshak was found to have fabricated studies supporting the product, made false claims about the product, and auto-enrolled customers in credit card payment schemes without their knowledge (after they had canceled their purchases), netting Berkeley Premium Nutraceuticals $100 million illicitly.[34]

1. Which of the three cases are occupational crimes and which are corporate crimes?
2. Are the harms of these offenders more serious, less serious, or equally as serious as instrumental street crimes like burglary or larceny/theft? Explain your thinking.
3. Do you regard any of these offenses as violent crimes? Why or why not?

White-Collar Crime as Violent Crime

There is a tendency to view occupational and corporate crimes as types of property crime, as they are typically committed for material gain or to avoid material loss. Nonetheless, many thousands of people are killed, injured, or made sick by illicit cost-cutting strategies and income-generating scams.[35] This is apparent in the criminal cases involving foodborne illnesses, like those at the Peanut Corporation of America and Jensen Farms. Unsafe workplaces also result in physical harms. The U.S. Bureau of Labor Statistics reported 5,333 fatal injuries[36] and 2.8 million nonfatal workplace injuries and illnesses in 2019.[37] It is difficult to determine how many workplace injuries and deaths resulted from violations of labor laws and safety regulations because such cases rarely end up in criminal courts.[38] It is far more likely to be a civil case if a courtroom is involved. One indicator of wrongdoing is a citation from the federal or state Occupational Safety and Health Administration (OSHA). Table 4.2 presents workplace fatalities occurring in one week in June 2020 that resulted in an OSHA citation. Unnecessary surgeries imperil the lives of patients, as well. There is rarely a bright line between "necessary" and "unnecessary" procedures, though, so many offenders escape criminal prosecution, even if they face civil suits.[39]

TABLE 4.2 ■ Fatality inspection data – examples of workplace deaths resulting in OSHA citations						
Date of Incident	City	State	Hazard Description	Inspection Number	Federal or State Plan	Citation Issued Related to Fatality
6/15/2020	Letart	WV	Worker fatally injured in building collapse.	1478912	Federal	Yes
6/15/2020	Houston	TX	Worker died in fall from ladder.	1479252	Federal	Yes
6/16/2020	Huntingdon Valley	PA	Worker trimming tree electrocuted when lanyard contacted power line.	1479380	Federal	Yes
6/17/2020	Hopkinsville	KY	Worker fatally crushed by transit table.	1479836	State	Yes
6/18/2020	Saint Cloud	MN	Worker died from heat exhaustion.	1481366	State	Yes
6/18/2020	Palm Beach	FL	Worker trimming palm tree electrocuted when frond contacted power line.	1479927	Federal	Yes
6/19/2020	Flint Hill	VA	Worker fatally struck by falling tree.	1479881	State	Yes
6/19/2020	Fresno	CA	Worker electrocuted while installing conduit in attic.	1482128	State	Yes
6/19/2020	Lynchburg	VA	Worker fatally burned when vapors from drums containing alcohol ignited.	1482114	Federal	Yes
6/19/2020	Austin	TX	Worker died in fall from deck.	1480104	Federal	Yes
6/19/2020	Dickinson	TX	Worker electrocuted when engineering rod contacted power line.	1480179	Federal	Yes

Source: U.S. Department of Labor, Occupational Safety and Health Administration (OSHA). Fatality inspection data. https://www.osha.gov/fatalities

Wrongful convictions due to prosecutorial or police misconduct cost victims their lives when the death penalty is imposed, and years are lost behind bars in noncapital cases.[40] According to the National Registry of Exonerations report, 143 incarcerated men and women were exonerated (proved innocent) in 2019. Seventy-five percent of exonerations in wrongful homicide cases in 2019 involved prosecutorial misconduct, police misconduct, or both.[41] The 2019 exonerees lost a total of 1,908 years behind bars for crimes they had not committed. Figure 4.2 displays the number of exonerations for wrongful convictions, by state, since 1989. Collectively, exonerees lost over 20,000 years to wrongful imprisonment. Importantly, exonerations are only possible when cases are taken on by professional exonerators, including nonprofit innocence organizations (e.g., the Innocence Project) and conviction integrity units (CIUs), which operate within prosecutors' offices to "prevent, identify, and remedy false convictions."[42] Innocence organizations understandably prioritize cases involving long sentences or the death penalty, particularly those with exculpatory DNA (i.e., violent crimes). And CIUs are a recent phenomenon, with most created after 2015. This means that there are likely many more people serving time for crimes they did not commit due to professional misconduct but whose cases have not been examined.

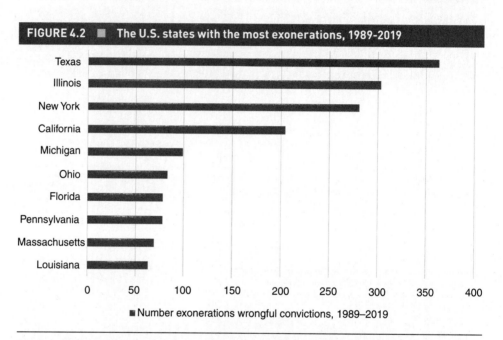

FIGURE 4.2 ■ The U.S. states with the most exonerations, 1989–2019

■ Number exonerations wrongful convictions, 1989–2019

Source: Neal Davis Law Firm. (2019, July 23). *The U.S. states with the most exonerations.* Statista. https://www.statista.com/chart/18772/number-of-exonerations-for-wrongful-convictions/. Licensed under CC BY-ND 3.0. https://creativecommons.org/licenses/by-nd/3.0/

Theophalis Wilson was exonerated of a 1989 triple murder after it was revealed that now-fired prosecutors engaged in misconduct, including withholding evidence that proved Wilson's innocence.

Jessica Griffin/The Philadelphia Inquirer via AP

State Crime as White-Collar Crime

States (including nations) have, in the words of sociologist Max Weber, a "monopoly on the legitimate use of physical force." He argues further that states are "considered the sole source of the 'right' to use violence."[43] Weber's argument is that governments, in creating and enforcing laws, necessarily dominate those they govern. The violent actions of states—including waging war or executing law-breakers—are defined by the state as legitimate uses of their authority. Nonetheless, states and state actors (like politicians, government officials, and intelligence officers) may commit crimes that violate international laws—or they may violate their own national laws—in pursuit of maintaining power or the interests of the state. **State crime**, therefore, is

An act or omission of an action by actors within the state that results in violations of domestic and international law, human rights, or systematic or institutionalized harm of its or another state's population, done in the name of the state regardless whether there is or is not self-motivation or interests at play. (p. 102)

State crimes include assassinations, genocide, crimes against humanity, police brutality, state-sponsored terrorism, the "disappearing" of political dissidents, and willful neglect leading to human suffering and death. These acts are regarded as crime by critical criminologists even when they are defined as lawful by the states committing them, as they are violations of basic human rights.[44]

A modern-day example of state crime is found in Myanmar (formerly called Burma), in the state-led genocide of the Rohingya, a Muslim minority. Genocide is committed "with intent to destroy, in whole or in part, a national, ethnical, racial or religious group" through mass violence and killing, creating conditions of life intended to bring about the group's destruction, implementing measures to prevent births, or forcibly transferring children from the targeted group to another group.[45] The genocide in Myanmar killed an estimated 22,000 Rohingya between 2017 and 2018. In addition, 75% of Rohingya villages were burned and destroyed. Of the 1.2 to 1.4 million Rohingya living in Myanmar, about 800,000 Rohingya fled to refugee camps in nearby Bangladesh, and the majority remaining in Myanmar were held in a "no man's land" on the border, in detention camps, or in prison villages. Interviews with survivors revealed that Myanmar's army and Border Guard Police (BGP) enacted the mass killing, mass rapes, and torching of villages with help from local extremists.[46]

State crime has elements of white-collar crime. State crime is committed on behalf of the state (an organization), much like corporate crime is committed on behalf of the corporation (also an organization). Plus, state crime is perpetrated by individuals of high social status in the course of their legal occupational activity. The white-collar connection is even more apparent in instances of **state-corporate crime**, in which governments and corporations, acting together to achieve shared goals, produce significant harm.[47] In state-initiated state-corporate offenses, the government employs corporations that it directs or allows to violate the law. In other instances, called state-facilitated state-corporate crime, the government fails to regulate and limit the dangerous and illegal actions of corporations.

ORGANIZED CRIME

What is the first thing you think of when you hear the phrase "organized crime"? Movies like *The Godfather* or *Goodfellas*? The TV show *The Sopranos*? The Japanese Yakuza? Transnational drug cartels? All of these would be considered organized crime. They are (or they depict) enduring, highly structured groups that engage in criminal conduct—violence, extortion, bribery, the operation of criminal industries—to make money and to obtain power and influence.

Like white-collar crime, organized crime is entrepreneurial. The profit is the point. Some profits are generated through operation of illicit businesses, such as gambling, drug trafficking, prostitution, and the sale of stolen goods. Other sources of income include payment for protection as well as abductions and demands for ransom. These forms of criminal conduct clearly distinguish organized crime from white-collar crime, which takes place within a legitimate occupational setting. However, some organized crime operates within the sphere of legal business. Organized crime groups sometimes operate businesses that, on their face, are legal (e.g., construction, shipping, or waste management), but they use violence, intimidation, extortion, and corruption to gain a monopoly and generate profit. Table 4.3 lists examples of criminal offenses typical of criminal organizations, divided by type.

TABLE 4.3 ■ Typology of organized crime	
Type of activity	**Criminal offenses**
Provision of illicit goods and services	• Illicit gambling • Loansharking • Human trafficking/prostitution • Drug trafficking • Arms trafficking • Stolen property offenses (including theft of interstate goods) • Smuggling of persons • Murder for hire • Trafficking in counterfeit goods
Infiltration of legitimate business or government	• Extortion • Bribery • Embezzlement • Money laundering • Tax evasion • Racketeering

Source: Adapted from Albanese, J. (2015). *Organized crime: From the mob to transnational organized crime* (7th ed.). New York: Routledge. Additions from Title 18 of the United States Code, Section 1961 (1).

The distinction between white-collar crime and organized crime is that white-collar crime is an aberration within the occupation setting. It is a deviation from what typically occurs, or from what *should* occur. In contrast, the occupational setting exists primarily to facilitate criminal profit-making in organized crime.[48] Nonetheless, there are overlaps, with organized crime drawing in participants who engage in white-collar offenses that further the goals of the criminal organization, such as corrupt public officials and business executives.

The term *organized crime* has a far shorter history than the behavior. Organized crime in the U.S. dates to at least the early 1800s. Nineteenth-century criminal gangs like the Forty Thieves were comprised of desperately poor Irish immigrants who came together for protection, preyed upon other immigrants, and relied on public corruption to facilitate their vice crimes until the group dissolved around 1850.[49] It would be more than a century before criminologists would identify organized crime as a distinct form of criminal conduct. Criminologist Donald Cressey was the first, in 1969, to offer a definition of organized crime:

> An organized crime is any crime committed by a person occupying, in an established division of labor, a position designed for the commission of crimes providing that such division of labor include at least one position for a corrupter, one position for a corruptee, and one position for an enforcer. (p. 319)[50]

Cressey's definition emphasizes two elements of organized crime: (1) a division of labor, which is the structure that makes it "organized," and (2) corruption, which is a strategy the group uses to engage in criminal conduct successfully. Corruption refers to criminal actions and abuses of power by persons in positions of authority for personal gain, such as a politician accepting a bribe in exchange for a favorable decision. Another example would be police or security personnel accepting payments for looking the other way during illegal activity or otherwise violating the law to assist criminals.

Organized-crime scholar Jay Albanese reviewed books and governmental reports on organized crime in search of common features of authors' definitions.[51] His analysis turned up 11 characteristics, some of which were mentioned in all or most definitions—a continuing organized hierarchy, rational profit through crime, use of force or threats, and corruption of public officials. Other characteristics were less common but appeared in several definitions, such as being nonideological, specialized, and having a code of secrecy. The word cloud in Figure 4.3 displays the relative frequency of the features. Albanese offers a useful definition of organized crime based on his review:

Organized crime is a continuing criminal enterprise that rationally works to profit from illicit activities that are often in great public demand. Its continuing existence is maintained through the use of force, threats, monopoly control, and/or the corruption of public officials. (p. 4)[52]

FIGURE 4.3 ■ Word cloud of common features in definitions of organized crime

Restricted membership
Corruption of public officials
Use of force or threat
Extensive planning   Specialization
Organized hierarchy
Public demand for services
Rational profit through crime
Code of secrecy
Monopoly over particular market
Nonideological

Source: Created with data from Albanese, J. (2015). *Organized crime: From the mob to transnational organized crime* (7th ed.). New York: Routledge.

Some of the crimes typical of criminal organizations will be familiar to readers, such as prostitution (a public-order offense addressed in Chapter 3) or embezzlement (an occupational offense addressed in this chapter's section on white-collar crime). Others are self-explanatory, like murder for hire. But a few crime types may be less familiar. Table 4.4 defines criminal offenses that are common to organized crime, including loansharking, money laundering, extortion, bribery, and racketeering.

Transnational Organized Crime

Globalization (the movement of people and goods between nations) and telecommunications innovations have given rise to transnational organized crime.[53] Some criminologists argue, in fact, that "transnational organized crime characterizes the 21st century in the same way that traditional street crimes characterized the 20th century" (p. 1).[54] Unlike criminal organizations specific to one region or nation, transnational organized crime (TOC) operates across geographic boundaries using many of the strategies common to region-specific organized crime, such as public corruption, violence, and extortion. Transnational criminal organizations exploit systems of international commerce and communication in carrying out their offenses, and they exist throughout the world.[55] The structure of TOC spans a range of forms, including hierarchies, familial and ethnicity-based clans, and sprawling cross-national networks. TOC is a major focus of the United Nations, INTERPOL (International Criminal Police

TABLE 4.4 ■ Select types and descriptions of organized-crime offenses	
Offense	**What it means**
Loansharking	Informal loans with exorbitant interest rates are extended to desperate customers, typically followed by intimidation, threats, and violence if the debtor has not paid off the loan.
Money laundering	Money laundering "cleans dirty money." It intentionally obscures the identification of the origin, tracing, or forfeiture of assets originating from a felony. Includes hiding illicitly gained assets, manipulating accounting records, and/or the fabricating evidence. Investment in noncash assets (e.g., real estate, gold, diamonds) is a common strategy for concealing assets. Cryptocurrencies (e.g., Bitcoin) are emerging as a preferred strategy, as well.
Extortion	Use of coercion—intimidation, threats, and/or violence—to obtain benefits (e.g., money, property, services, or official acts). Instills fear in the victim that something bad will happen if they do not comply with the extortionist's demands, such as physical injury, kidnapping, exposure to criminal charges, or release of personally damaging information. Includes blackmail and demands for payment in exchange for protection ("protection rackets").
Bribery	Someone, such as a public official, private employee, witness, or juror, voluntarily solicits or accepts some benefit (e.g., money, property, or services) in exchange for an act desired by the person providing the bribe. Bribery differs from extortion in that both parties consent to the agreement; there is no coercion.
Racketeering	Engaging in an ongoing criminal conspiracy. Covers a broad range of felony actions conducted as part of a criminal enterprise, including but not limited to extortion, bribery, murder, kidnapping, arson, robbery, gambling, and dealing in obscene materials or controlled substances. The Organized Crime Control Act of 1970 established the crime of racketeering. The Racketeering Influenced and Corrupt Organizations (RICO) portion of the act makes it illegal to run or generate income from a criminal enterprise. Criminal enterprises include both legal and illegal businesses and organizations that engage in a pattern of illicit activity, defined as two or more felonies within a 10-year period.

Sources: Albanese, J. (2015). *Organized crime: From the mob to transnational organized crime* (7th ed.). New York: Routledge; Teichmann, F. M. J. (2017). Twelve methods of money laundering. *Journal of Money Laundering Control, 20*, 130-137; 18 U.S. Code § 1961 – Definitions ("Racketeering activity").

Organization), the World Bank, the FBI, and other agencies. These organizations note that transnational organized crime flourishes where the rule of law is weak.[56]

The types of offenses committed by transnational criminal organizations include traditional forms of organized crime, such as drug trafficking, prostitution, cargo theft, and money laundering. However, TOC presents a host of other types of crimes that threaten public health and well-being, including the following:

Environmental crimes – These include illegal timber operations, trafficking of protected marine species and wildlife, illegal fishing and fisheries, marine pollution, and hazardous waste trafficking.[57] The formal global market for the collection and recycling of waste—including plastics, e-waste, medical waste, and chemical waste from manufacturing—is valued at $410 billion (USD) annually.[58] Criminal organizations skirt environmental laws by illegally shipping waste, engaging in unsafe waste management and treatment practices, and dumping hazardous waste (e.g., at sea or in ports). Tax fraud and money laundering usually accompany environmental offenses.[59]

Human trafficking – Trafficking in persons refers to the use of threats, force, fraud, or coercion to recruit, transport, transfer, harbor, or receive persons. Exploitative labor is at the center of human trafficking; it includes sex exploitation (prostitution or other sexual services), manual labor exploitation, and domestic servitude.[60] Unlike Hollywood depictions of abducted,

A multi-agency team involving INTERPOL and Kenya Revenue Authority officers stops a shipment of trafficked ivory elephant tusks being sent to Cambodia.

Stringer/AFP/Getty Images

chained-up victims, which are rare, most human trafficking is accomplished through deception and fraud. Investigations reveal that victims are often deceived with recruiters' false promises of work (as in restaurants, hotels, or child care) and are then compelled to work off exorbitant debts through labor that does not reflect what was promised. Traffickers wield control by claiming they can get the victim arrested or deported, shaming them or threatening their reputation (e.g., by revealing the nature of their work to relatives), seizing passports or other identity documents, and threatening or using physical violence.[61] Organized-crime groups capitalize on people's desperation for economic opportunities. One report shows that about 6 out of 10 (58%) prosecuted traffickers in the U.S. were working as part of an organized-crime group.[62] Some schemes, though, are orchestrated by traffickers working in small groups or alone, including "loverboys" who lure women into coerced prostitution by posing as doting boyfriends.[63] The International Labour Organization estimates that human trafficking produces a global annual profit of $150.2 billion (USD), though accurate counts of victims and profits are difficult to establish given the hidden nature of the crime.[64]

Migrant smuggling – Smuggling of persons is a "form of illegal trade in which the commodity is an assisted illegal entry into a country" (p. 471).[65] The absence of force, fraud, or coercion differentiates migrant smuggling from human trafficking—the smuggled person has solicited the help of the smuggler. Nonetheless, smugglers often exploit those seeking their assistance by charging outrageous fees and demanding more than the agreed-upon cost of their services once the smuggled person is particularly vulnerable. Indeed, a case that starts as migrant smuggling can quickly become human trafficking upon reaching the destination, with the conditions of the agreement changing (e.g., refusal to release the person until they pay additional fees or work off a debt). Migrant smuggling harms the state, whereas human trafficking harms the person who is trafficked.[66]

Trafficking in counterfeit and pirated products – Transnational organized crime groups engage in the manufacture, import, export, and distribution of counterfeit or pirated goods (fraudulent imitations and reproductions that violate copyright, trademark, or patent laws) deceptively presented to purchasers as legal products. Common counterfeits include pharmaceuticals, weapons, food products, medical devices, clothing, cigarettes, and forged identification documents. Counterfeit pharmaceuticals comprise an estimated 10% to 30% of all pharmaceuticals sold in the developing world, and their illegal proceeds make up about one-quarter of the total counterfeit market.[67] Counterfeit medications are especially dangerous to public health, as they can contain inferior ingredients, contaminants, or insufficient quantities of (or no) active ingredients.[68] International shipping of counterfeit goods is made possible by corruption, especially bribery. Counterfeit trade also creates a mechanism for laundering money gained from other criminal conduct.[69] Conservative estimates put the annual value of illicit trafficking of counterfeit and pirated products between $923 billion and $1.13 trillion (USD), making it the largest and most lucrative criminal enterprise globally.

Criminal Enterprise Versus Organized Crime

The FBI offers a term closely related to organized crime, criminal enterprise, which it defines as "a group of individuals with an identified hierarchy, or comparable structure, engaged in significant criminal activity."[70] Businesses that exist for the purpose of violating the law, such as those trafficking drugs, arms, people, or wildlife, would be considered criminal enterprises. The FBI's description does not emphasize corruption as a necessary component, but it does not preclude it either. Based on the FBI's definition, a criminal enterprise can operate without infiltration of legitimate business or government (see Table 4.3). The FBI's "most wanted" list includes individuals allegedly involved in criminal enterprises. Which of the following would you consider to be participating in "organized crime," based on the information provided?

- "Tomas Alberto Roque Espinoza was serving as a Harris County constable when he accepted payment to escort and protect a vehicle he believed was transporting over 5 kilograms of cocaine. Roque was also allegedly pulling over vehicles and keeping any drugs or money he found."[71]

- "Fausto Isidro Meza-Flores is the alleged leader of the Meza-Flores [transnational drug trafficking organization] based in Sinaloa, Mexico. The Meza-Flores [organization] is allegedly responsible for the possession, distribution, and importation of large quantities of heroin, methamphetamine, cocaine and marijuana into the United States, and has predominately controlled drug distribution in parts of Sinaloa, southern Sonora, and Nayarit, Mexico."[72]

- "Gerard L. Trice Jr. is wanted for his alleged involvement with a drug-trafficking organization in Arkansas from 2011 to 2013. Trice was allegedly a mid-level cocaine distributor who purchased cocaine from the organization's leaders and distributed the cocaine throughout the central Arkansas area."[73]

Perhaps you noticed a theme: Drugs. In fact, at the time of this writing, all 34 people on the FBI's "criminal enterprise" most-wanted list are wanted for drug trafficking, though some also face charges related to money laundering, firearms possession, and hostage-taking.[74] The criminal investigations office of the Food and Drug Administration (FDA) reports additional forms of criminal enterprise, including the following example. Again, think about whether you would regard this case as "organized crime."

- A federal grand jury returned indictments in a multimillion-dollar, multistate "fence" operation in which professional thieves stole over-the-counter medications, diabetic test strips, and health and beauty supplies from large retailers. The operators of the criminal enterprise purchased the stolen items, removed security labels and stickers, and shipped pallets of repackaged merchandise to wholesale companies for a profit.[75]

Are these examples of organized crime? Maybe, maybe not. Organized crime is a somewhat blurry term.[76] Organized-crime scholars point to two ways of assigning the organized crime descriptor, one focused on *who* does it and the other on *what* is done. The "who" approach emphasizes long-lasting, hierarchical criminal organizations, such as the Cosa Nostra (Sicilian Mafia), the Yakuza (Japanese Mafia), or Los Zetas (exceptionally violent organized-crime group based in Mexico but operating throughout Central and South America). The "what" approach emphasizes criminal activities that require a degree of organization, also called criminal enterprises. Think of it as the difference between Organized Crime (upper-case) and organized crime (lower-case).[77] Not all organized crimes—or criminal enterprises—are operated by Organized Crime groups. The Meza-Flores transnational criminal organization, whose leader the FBI is seeking, meets the criteria for Organized Crime. The three other examples appear to be of the lower-case variety: The participants engaged in crimes that required some level of organization, but they were not carried out by established crime syndicates.

Are Street Gangs Organized Crime?

Do street gangs qualify as organized crime? The answer is: It depends. It is a myth that most gangs have a well-coordinated, formal organizational structure with strong leadership and expertise that they use to efficiently conduct illicit business, as seen in Table 4.5.[78] Gangs exist on a spectrum, with some lacking any structure whatsoever (like short-lived youth gangs) and others displaying much higher degrees of organization (like drug-trafficking gangs).

Part of the difficulty in providing a decisive yes-or-no answer to "Are street gangs organized crime?" resides in the exceptionally broad definition of gangs. The federal government and 43 U.S. states have enacted legislation that defines **gangs**.[79] Though their definitions vary somewhat, a composite of their common criteria includes: (1) Gangs are organizations, associations, or groups of at least three people; (2) gangs engage in illegal activity; and (3) gangs have an identifying name, sign,

TABLE 4.5 ■ Myths and realities about gangs	
Myth	**Reality**
Most gangs have a formal and well-organized structure	Though some adult criminal gangs are highly structured, most street gangs, especially youth street gangs, are "generally loosely organized that are constantly changing—consolidating, reorganizing, and splintering" (p. 31). Small and less cohesive gangs tend to dissolve quickly.
Gangs that share a name are connected	Small local gangs often adopt the names and symbols of larger gangs. It is imitation, not affiliation. Creating an image of a gang with many "sets" contributes to a tougher image, though only some gangs are, in fact, comprised of connected, geographically dispersed sets.
Most crime by gang members is done on behalf of the gang (i.e., gang-motivated)	Though gang members engage in more crime than their otherwise similar non-gang counterparts, including turf-based violence, most of their crime is not committed to further the gang's interests. Gang member violence is often *gang-related* rather than *gang-motivated* (or committed at the behest of gang leadership). Gang members are especially likely to carry weapons and get into disputes that they settle violently.
Gangs are only comprised of racial minority group members	Gangs include members with varied racial and ethnic identities, though individual gangs tend to be comprised of members of a single race or ethnicity. The states' definitions of gangs include predominantly white groups that typically avoid the "gang" designation in the public imagination, including neo-Nazi/white supremacist groups and outlaw motorcycle gangs. U.S. prison gangs, which have influence outside of prisons, include Hispanic/Latino gangs (e.g., La eMe, Nuestra Family), Black gangs (e.g., Black Guerilla Family, Folk Nation), and white gangs (e.g., Aryan Brotherhood, Dead Man Inc.).
Once a young person joins a gang, they are a member for life	Most gang involvement is short-lived, with studies showing that about half of young people leave gangs within one year and only about 1% to 3% belong four or more years. However, prison gangs and some highly structured adult gangs adopt a "blood in, blood out" credo, meaning that those who leave may be killed.

Sources: Howell, J. C., & Griffiths, E. (2019). *Gangs in America's communities* (3rd ed.). Thousand Oaks, CA: SAGE; S. Decker & D. Pyrooz (Eds.). (2019). *The handbook of gangs*. Hoboken, NJ: John Wiley & Sons.

or symbol.[80] Law enforcement observe additional characteristics, including claiming territory or turf, wearing or displaying colors that identify membership, and the presence of members hanging out together.[81] A vast array of crime-involved groups fit this broad definition, ranging from a loosely knit group of five delinquent teenagers mimicking the symbols and postures of established gangs to highly structured adult drug-trafficking and prison gangs with hierarchical roles and articulated codes of conduct.

One example of a gang meeting the criteria for operating a criminal enterprise comes from South Carolina, where 40 prison inmates, allegedly acting on behalf of the Insane Gangster Disciples, were charged in December 2020 in the largest federal racketeering conspiracy in the state's history. The indictment alleged a "sprawling criminal enterprise whereby inmates with the South Carolina Department of Corrections (SCDC), often through the use of contraband cell phones, orchestrated murder, kidnapping, firearms distribution, and an international drug operation."[82] The defendants face RICO (Racketeer Influenced Corrupt Organizations) conspiracy charges, and are alleged to have committed, attempted to commit, or conspired to commit typical organized-crime offenses, including extortion, drug trafficking, and money laundering. In this case, the answer to "Are street gangs organized crime?" is clearly a yes.

CYBERCRIME

Decades ago, getting your wallet stolen could ruin your week. Wallets contained—and still do contain—identifying documents, like drivers' licenses and credit cards. Today, you're probably much more worried about having your phone stolen. Phones, themselves expensive, hold far greater value than most wallets: banking credentials, social media logins, questionable photos, and more. And it turns out that your phone can be stolen without ever leaving your sight. Here is how it can happen: (1) Someone (not you!) calls your phone service provider and persuades them to switch your service over to a SIM card in their possession. They claim to be you, they have just enough personal information to be convincing, and they state their old phone was stolen, destroyed, or that they just bought a replacement. (2) Once your service is transferred to their phone, they can change your logins. Do you use two-factor authentication? It doesn't matter. All those two-factor authentication texts are coming to their phone now. Everything on your phone is now theirs and you are left with a service-less phone, wondering what happened. It is a cybercrime called SIM swapping (a more accurate descriptor is SIM hijacking).[83] And there is a bustling underground market for the fruits of the offender's labor. For instance, maybe you had an unusual and highly sought-after Instagram handle (an "OG handle"). Think "Moneyman" or "Froggy." SIM hijackers sometimes target phones specifically to steal and sell these handles to anyone with enough Bitcoin.[84]

Cybercrime, also called cyber-dependent crime, is any criminal action that is facilitated using a computer and network, or a crime that targets a computer or network. Much cybercrime involves hacking (or cracking), which is "unauthorized access of a computer system with criminal intention" (p. 193).[85] While the goals of cybercrime are almost universally instrumental rather than expressive, the motivations—or type of criminal intentions—for cybercrime are diverse. Some have purely economic motivations while others are ideological, sexual, revenge-oriented, recreational, rooted in the desire for prestige within hacker subcultures, or some combination thereof.[86]

Cybercrime includes crimes against persons (e.g., cyberstalking and cyberharassment), crimes against property (e.g., hacking, credit card frauds, and online extortion scams), and crimes against the state (e.g., cyberterrorism). It is a broad category defined by the technology used by offenders. As a category, cybercrime has more in common with "gun-related crime" than, say, "corporate crime," as its defining feature is the *tools* that offenders use rather than their goals, gains, or social status. As such, it overlaps with other classifications described in this chapter: Dome white-collar crime is cybercrime, some cyber offenses can be characterized as organized, and some terrorists engage in hacking and other cybercrime offenses. The level of expertise necessary for committing cybercrime offenses varies tremendously, with some crimes requiring minimal technical skill, like cyberharassment, and others requiring advanced knowledge, such as cyberextortion scams using DDoS attacks (distributed denial-of-service attacks) made possible with botnets (remotely controlled zombie networks).

Table 4.6 presents multiple strategies used by cybercriminals, but it does not list the offenses that are facilitated using these techniques. For example, information obtained illegally using social engineering and phishing can be put to a myriad of criminal uses: identity theft, credit card fraud, cyberstalking, SIM swapping (as in the example at the start of this section), extortion, state or corporate espionage, and more. Criminologists differentiate between (1) "cyber-dependent criminal offenders," like individuals who phish, hijack SIM cards, and steal identities online to commit fraud, and (2) "cyber-dependent crime enablers," whose actions aid cybercriminals.[87] Enablers include people who operate illegal online marketplaces for malware, stolen data, specialized services, and automated hacking tools (e.g., botnet infrastructures for lease).[88] Cybercriminals use these platforms to offer hack-for-sale services. The programmers and coders who create malware (without using it themselves) are also enablers, as are those who instruct others on how to access networks illegally.

TABLE 4.6 ■ Types and descriptions of selected cybercrime techniques		
Type of cybercrime	Cybercrime technique	Offense description
Crimes that target networks or devices	Botnets	A botnet is a network of computers that have been infected with malware (malicious software) without the users' knowledge. The network is controlled by the offender, who uses the infected computers to commit other cybercrimes, including sending spam messages, committing DDoS attacks (see below), and accessing data illegally.
	Ransomware	Ransomware is a type of file-encrypting malware used to extort victims. Using malware, the offender takes over the victim's computer and prevents them from accessing their data. They then demand payment, often in the form of cryptocurrency, in order to restore the victim's access.
	DDoS attacks	A distributed denial-of-service (DDos) attack maliciously floods a server or network with Internet traffic to overwhelm its capacity, thereby shutting it down.
Crimes that use devices to commit offenses	Social engineering	Victim is tricked into sharing information, such as passwords, by an offender who impersonates someone who can be trusted with information, such as IT support staff. Social engineering relies on psychological tactics for obtaining protected or sensitive information rather than technical strategies (as in phishing scams).
	Phishing, vishing, smishing, or pharming	Victim is tricked into sharing information, such as login credentials, by clicking on a malicious email attachment or URL that appears to be from a legitimate website or email/text sender.
	Spoofing	Contact information is intentionally falsified to appear legitimate and mislead, as when phone numbers are spoofed to make mass robo-calls, email addresses are spoofed to send mass spam, or websites are spoofed to gather personal information from misled visitors.

The strategies presented in Table 4.6 require specialized skills, but some computer-facilitated crimes require nothing more than an Internet connection and the technological proficiency of a typical middle schooler. For example, participation in illicit online markets for illegal drugs, firearms, child pornography (a more precise term is *sexual abuse imagery*), and sexual services—as operators, distributors, sellers, or customers—is considered cybercrime. Cyberstalking and cyberharassment, including doxing (locating and publishing private information about a person online as a form of harassment and to encourage subsequent harassment), also require little in the way of sophisticated know-how. In fact, research on hackers consistently shows a relatively low level of technical proficiency, though a small percentage of offenses require a great deal of expertise.[89]

Some cybercrime is ideologically motivated. The term *hacktivism*, coined by a member of the Cult of the Dead Cow hacker collective in 1996, refers to the use of illegal digital strategies to make a political point and push for social change.[90] For example, individuals claiming affiliation with the international hacker movement Anonymous have engaged in hacktivism through online attacks targeting copyright protection agencies, child pornography websites, government agencies, hate groups (e.g., the KKK and the Westboro Baptist Church), corporations (e.g., PayPal and Sony), and others they regard as threats to free speech or human rights. Most cybercrime, however, is not hacktivism.

Supporters of Ross Ulbricht hold signs outside the courtroom where Ulbricht was standing trial for running the Silk Road, an online marketplace for illegal goods (including narcotics) and services (including computer hacking services).

AP Photo/Seth Wenig

Extent of Cybercrime

Cybercrime has gained greater attention from criminologists over the past decade, but our understanding of this type of crime is still limited due to insufficient data. We do not have reliable measures of the incidence of cybercrime, though the transition to the National Incident-Based Reporting System (NIBRS) means somewhat better data will be available moving forward. NIBRS has one offense category, "fraud offenses," containing an offense type that is specifically cybercrime, called "hacking/computer invasion." Even so, most cybercrime victimization—of individual victims and of corporations—is never reported to law enforcement.[91] In 2019, the FBI's Internet Complaint Center (IC3) reported 467,361 known cybercrime incidents; Table 4.7 lists the top 10 most frequent cybercrimes reported to the IC3.[92] Yet polling data suggest that incidence of cybercrime is far higher, with about one-quarter of surveyed households reporting being targeted.[93] The director of the FBI's IC3 estimates that only 1 in 10 cybercrime incidents are reported to law enforcement, with the true number closer to 3.5 million. Polling data on victimization, though, suggest that the true number is even greater. In fact, victimization reports establish that approximately half of the financial loss from property crime is due to cybercrime, signaling the presence of a cybercrime wave even as other forms of property crime have declined.[94]

Crime type	Victims	Loss
Phishing/vishing/smishing/pharming	241,342	$54,241,075
Nonpayment/nondelivery	108,867	$265,011,249
Extortion	76,741	$70,935,939
Personal data breach	45,330	$194,473,055
Spoofing	28,218	$216,513,728
Misrepresentation	24,276	$19,707,242
Confidence fraud/romance	23,751	$600,249,821
Harassment/threats of violence	20,604	$6,547,449
Business or individual email account compromise	19,369	$1,866,642,107
Credit card fraud	17,614	$129,820,792

TABLE 4.7 ■ FBI's Internet Complaint Center's 10 most frequent cybercrime incidents in 2020

Source: Federal Bureau of Investigation. (2021, February 11). *2020 Internet crime report.* https://www.ic3.gov/Media/PDF/AnnualReport/2020_IC3Report.pdf

HATE/BIAS CRIME AND TERRORISM

On June 17, 2015, white supremacist Dylann Storm Roof entered the Emanuel African Methodist Episcopal Church in Charleston, South Carolina, where he murdered nine African American congregants and injured three more. Roof espoused his racial hatred and desire to provoke a race war, the motivation for his crimes, in an online manifesto prior to the mass murder and in his confession. He continued to outline his white supremacist beliefs in a journal he kept while in jail. Several years later, on October 27, 2018, white supremacist Robert Bowers murdered 11 congregants of the Tree of Life synagogue in Pittsburgh, Pennsylvania, wounding six others. Bowers left an extensive online trail detailing his support for anti-Semitic conspiracy theories and white nationalism. Similar to Roof, Bowers left no doubt about the hate-based motivation for his crimes.[95] Less than a year later, on August 3, 2019, Patrick Crusius murdered 23 people in an El Paso Walmart in an anti-Latino attack. The manifesto he posted online just prior to committing his crimes adopted the rhetoric of white power ideology. In it, he describes his anti-immigrant beliefs, praises the anti-Muslim mass shooting in Christchurch, New Zealand, and provides a tactical roadmap for others who wish to follow in his footsteps.[96] All three men faced state and federal charges of murder and hate crimes.

Hate/bias Crime

Roof, Bowers, and Crusius are (alleged) perpetrators of hate crimes. Note that they would have faced serious criminal penalties even if their offenses hadn't been motivated by hatred. Murder is illegal. The classification of crime as hate crime (also called bias crime) is used to enhance criminal penalties rather than criminalize actions that would not otherwise be considered crime. Hate crimes can include a range of offenses, including vandalism, assault, arson, and murder, as well as threats to commit these offenses and conspiracies to commit them.

The specifics of hate crime laws differ across the federal and state levels, but they have common features, captured in the FBI's definition of hate/bias crime:

> A criminal offense against a person or property motivated in whole or in part by an offender's bias …[97]

The most important words in the definition are "motivated by." Hateful people can commit crimes against victims about whom they hold extreme biases (unfavorable, prejudiced attitudes), but their

Crusius's mass shooting in an El Paso Walmart in 2018 was an anti-Latino and anti-immigrant hate crime.
UPI/Newscom

offenses would not be hate crimes unless the biases were the *reason* for the attacks. Sometimes called "message crime," hate crime is ideologically motivated—it is intended to send a message to victims and the surrounding community that its targets are unwanted and unvalued.[98] The FBI's definition continues:

> …*against a race, religion, disability, sexual orientation, ethnicity, gender, or gender identity.*

These are the identity categories currently protected by federal hate crime law, as required by the Matthew Shepard and James Byrd Jr. Hate Crimes Prevention Act of 2009. Between 1968 (when the Civil Rights Act of 1968 established the first federal hate crime statute) and 2009, protected categories only included "race, color, religion, or national origin."[99] Plus, federal prosecutors could only pursue hate crime convictions if the victim was engaged in "federally protected activity" at the time of the offense, such as voting or attending school. The Shepard-Byrd Act transformed how the federal government defines, pursues, and counts hate crimes. Its noteworthy impacts include the following:

- Broadening the scope of the law by eliminating the federally protected activity requirement.

- Expanding protections by including crimes motivated by actual or perceived gender, sexual orientation, gender identity, or disability.

- Requiring the FBI to collect and report statistics on gender and gender identity hate crimes (they already tracked other types).

- Providing the federal government freedom to investigate and prosecute hate crimes that local authorities opt not to pursue.[100]

The Shepard-Byrd Act applies only to federal hate crimes. All U.S. states but two (South Carolina and Wyoming) also have hate crime statutes, but they vary wildly in what classes are protected under the law.[101] Some states' laws pertain to all protected classes listed in the Shepard-Byrd Act (e.g., Minnesota and New Mexico), while other states' hate crime laws exclude gender, gender identity, and sexual orientation, as depicted in Figure 4.4. In addition, some states cover additional bias motivations, such as age (e.g., Nebraska) and political affiliation (e.g., Iowa).

President Obama met with Byrd's sisters, Louvon Harris (left) and Betty Byrd Boatner (right), and Shepard's mother, Judy Shepard (center), at a reception commemorating the enactment of 2009 federal hate crime legislation.

Official White House Photo by Pete Souza

FIGURE 4.4 ■ Sexual orientation and gender identity in state hate crime laws

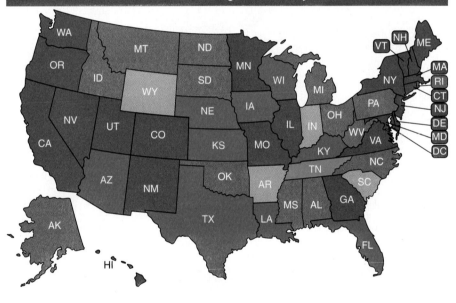

■ Law enumerates sexual orientation and gender identity *(22 states, 2 territories, + D.C.)*

■ Law enumerates only sexual orientation *(11 states)*

■ State explicitly interprets existing hate crimes law to include sexual orientation and/or gender identity *(1 state)*

■ Existing hate crime law does not cover sexual orientation or gender identity *(13 states)*

■ No hate crime law *(4 states)*

*Note: Tennessee state law explicitly enumerates sexual orientation, but not gender identity. However, the law does enumerate "gender," and the state attorney general affirms that this means transgender people are also protected.

Source: Map Advancement Project. "Equality Maps: Hate Crime Laws." https://www.lgbtmap.org/equality-maps/hate_crime_laws

Nature and Extent of Hate/Bias Crime

The FBI tracks hate crime statistics voluntarily reported by local, state, tribal, college and university, and federal law enforcement. Figure 4.5 displays the types of bias motivations in the 8,052 single-bias hate crimes reported by the FBI in 2020, which had 11,126 victims. The figure does not include the 211 multiple-bias hate crimes (with 346 victims) recorded by the FBI in the same year. More than three-fifths (62%) of FBI-reported hate crimes had a race/ethnicity/ancestry bias motivation in 2020. One in five hate crimes targeted victims due to their actual or perceived sexual orientation (21%), and 13% were motivated by bias based on the victims' actual or perceived religion. The remainder of FBI-reported hate crime victims were targeted because of their gender identity (2%), disability (1%), and gender (1%), as seen in Figure 4.5.

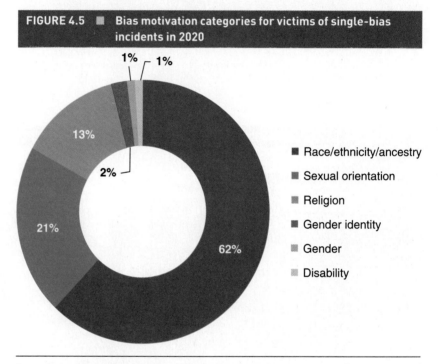

FIGURE 4.5 ■ Bias motivation categories for victims of single-bias incidents in 2020

- Race/ethnicity/ancestry
- Sexual orientation
- Religion
- Gender identity
- Gender
- Disability

Source: Federal Bureau of Investigation. (2021). *Hate crime statistics, 2020.* https://www.justice.gov/hatecrimes/hate-crime-statistics.

Comparisons of official hate crime data and victimization reports reveal an immense dark figure for hate crime. According to National Crime Victimization Survey (NCVS) data, an average of 232,586 bias-motivated criminal incidents occurred annually between 2015 and 2019; the annual average was 210,660 for violent hate crimes and 20,796 for property hate crimes.[102] During the same span of years, the FBI's Uniform Crime Reports (UCR) tallied an annual average of 6,716 hate crime incidents with 8,249 victims, a far lower count.[103]

Obtaining accurate official hate crime statistics requires two things to happen: (1) Victims report the incident to police, and (2) police appropriately classify the offense as motivated by bias. Victim underreporting is one reason for hate crime's dark figure. In fact, victims of bias-related crimes are less likely than victims of "ordinary" crimes to report the offense to law enforcement.[104] However, many report the crime to alternative organizations, such as outreach centers and community support groups. Expectations about police treatment and effectiveness also impact decisions not to report hate crime victimization. For example, victims targeted due to sexual orientation or gender identity (e.g., transgender persons) describe how they are discouraged from reporting bias-motivated victimization due to past interactions with unsympathetic and unkind law enforcement.[105] Even victims who report bias-motivated crimes to police (such as assaults by offenders who yell racial or ethnic slurs) are frequently left out of official hate crime counts.[106] Misclassification as non-bias-related crimes by law enforcement comprises another reason for the large dark figure.[107]

ENGAGED CRIMINOLOGY 4.2

Analyzing Hate Crime Offenders

Table 4.8 displays the characteristics of offenders in violent hate crime and non–hate crime incidents, as reported by victims in the National Crime Victimization Survey. The values in the table are percentages (e.g., 68.5% of violent hate crimes had one offender).

TABLE 4.8 ■ Offender characteristics in violent hate and non–hate crime incidents, 2015-2019		
Offender characteristics	Violent hate crime incidents	Violent non–hate crime incidents
Number of offenders		
1 offender	68.5%	82.8%
2-3 offenders	13.6%	7.8%
4 or more offenders	9.5%	4.9%
Unknown number	8.4%	4.5%
Sex of offender		
Male	65.1%	70.4%
Female	18.0%	17.9%
Both male and female	6.8%	4.0%
Unknown sex	10.1%	7.6%
Age of offender		
11 or younger	0.0%	2.1%
12-17 years old	10.1%	12.6%
18-29 years old	18.8%	24.0%
30 years or older	46.5%	42.7%
Two or more age groups	8.6%	4.3%
Unknown age	16.0%	14.4%
Relationship to victim		
At least casually known	30.7%	53.3%
Stranger	56.2%	36.9%
Unknown	13.1%	9.8%

Source: Kena, G., & Thompson, A. (2021, September). *Hate crime victimization, 2005-2019.* Washington, DC: U.S. Department of Justice. https://bjs.ojp.gov/library/publications/hate-crime-victimization-2005-2019

Answer the following questions using the data presented in Table 4.8.

1. Are violent hate crimes more likely than other violent crimes to be committed by more than one person? Use percentages from Table 4.8 in your answer.

2. Are violent hate crimes more likely than other violent crimes to be committed by a stranger? Use percentages from Table 4.8 in your answer.

3. What is one finding from the table that surprised you, and why?

Terrorism

You may be thinking: Aren't mass murderers Dylann Roof, Robert Bowers, and Patrick Crusius terrorists? Why were they discussed in the section on hate crime instead of the section on terrorism? The answer to the second question is more straightforward, so let's start there. Roof, Bowers, and Crusius were charged with committing hate crimes, so their offenses were presented in the section on hate crime. And they certainly *did* commit hate crimes. It is also a fair characterization to call them domestic terrorists, though there is some disagreement on this point. For instance, commenting on Dylann Roof's crimes, then-director of the FBI, James Comey, described how the FBI regards Roof's offenses as hate crimes but does not consider them terrorism:

> *Terrorism is [an] act of violence done or threatened in order to try to influence a public body or citizenry, so it's more of a political act, and again, based on what I know, I don't see this as a political act. Doesn't make it any less horrific, but terrorism has a definition under federal law.*[108]

Terrorism *does* have a definition under federal law, differing somewhat for international terrorism and domestic terrorism. According to the FBI, domestic and international terrorism are defined as follow:

- **Domestic terrorism**: "Violent, criminal acts committed by individuals and/or groups to further ideological goals stemming from domestic influences, such as those of a political, religious, social, racial, or environmental nature."

- **International terrorism**: "Violent, criminal acts committed by individuals and/or groups who are inspired by, or associated with, designated foreign terrorist organizations or nations (state-sponsored)."[109]

The FBI-provided definition of domestic terrorism is less nuanced than the federal *laws* regarding terrorism. The laws determine the criminal charges available to federal prosecutors. According to federal criminal statutes, domestic terrorism

A involve[s] acts dangerous to human life that are a violation of the criminal laws of the United States or of any State;

B appear to be intended—
  i to intimidate or coerce a civilian population;
  ii to influence the policy of a government by intimidation or coercion; or
  iii to affect the conduct of a government by mass destruction, assassination, or kidnapping; and

C occur primarily within the territorial jurisdiction of the United States.[110]

While both terrorism and hate/bias crime are ideologically motivated, hate/bias crime is not typically committed with the intention of influencing governmental conduct or policies. Plus, terrorism is usually—though not always—an "upward crime" in which an offender of lower social status targets a higher-status group. In contrast, hate/bias crime is typically a "downward crime" involving a powerful or majority group member attacking a less-powerful victim.[111]

Social scientists who study terrorism devise their own definitions, with most offering a variant of "an act of violence carried out by a non-state actor against a civilian target with some political aim."[112] Violence committed to further religious, social, racial, or environmental goals is necessarily political. Thus, the FBI's definition does not differ much from criminologists' conceptualization of terrorism. Both acknowledge that terrorism is more than just a *statement* of ideology—it is about *advancing* ideological goals. It seeks to instigate change. Terrorism expert Brian Michael Jenkins adds an additional element, arguing that "terrorists want a lot of people watching" and "terrorism is theater" (p. 83).[113] In Jenkins's understanding, terrorism is different from other violent crimes because it is audience-oriented; it is ideologically motivated violence intended to *get attention* in an effort to further political aims.

Criminologists often discuss hate crime and terrorism in the same breath. Comparisons of multiple forms of hate crime and domestic terrorism in U.S. counties show that several of these types of crimes increase together, leading researchers to conclude that hate crime and domestic terrorism are "close cousins" rather than "distant relatives."[114] Where one type of extremist behavior increases, so too does the other type. Hate crime and domestic terrorism are best thought of as variations on a common theme, or at least as two overlapping circles in a Venn diagram.

Nature and Extent of Extremist Violence

Terrorism scholars distinguish between participants in terrorist organizations and "lone wolf" (or lone actor) terrorists. Lone wolf terrorists are individuals who become radicalized and commit terrorist attacks on their own. For example, Anders Breivik was a far right domestic terrorist in Norway who acted alone in killing 77 people in 2011, 69 of whom were attending a Workers' Youth League summer camp on Utøya Island in Norway. Breivik killed the other 8 in a bombing outside the office of the Norwegian Prime Minister in Oslo.[115] He detailed his nationalist, anti-Muslim, anti-multiculturalism, and anti-feminist ideology in a manifesto he disseminated through email shortly before his attacks. He targeted the summer camp as retribution against the Labour Party (a political party in Norway), which operated the camp.[116] Breivik's violence is considered lone wolf terrorism because he developed his extremist ideology and carried out his crimes alone.

Skeptical terrorism researchers argue that the lone wolf descriptor is inaccurate.[117] First, they observe that even those who engage in violence alone are typically radicalized through online and offline interactions with other extremists who provide justifications for violence and act as role models. Second, they reject the reference to lone actors as wolves, as it "implies a high level of cunning and lethality" that is simply not characteristic of most terrorism perpetrators who act alone (p. 772).[118] For example, researchers find that most lone actor terrorists display amateurism, typically revealing (or "leaking") their intentions in advance of their crimes and taking few, if any, precautions against detection (e.g., no data security and leaving evidence of bomb-making in plain sight).[119]

In post-9/11 America, the word *terrorism* often conjured images of jihadist (or Islamist) international terrorism of the sort experienced in the U.S. on September 11, 2001. But domestic terrorism, especially right-wing extremist terrorism, is far more pervasive in the U.S. than international terrorism of any kind. And far-right domestic terrorism is much more common than domestic terrorism committed by "homegrown" jihadists in the U.S.

The National Consortium for the Study of Terrorism and Responses to Terrorism (START) collects data on radicalization and extremist violence. Radicalization is "increasing extremity of beliefs, feelings, and behaviors in directions that increasingly justify intergroup violence and demand sacrifice in defense of the in-group" (p. 416).[120] START's data set Profiles of Individual Radicalization in the U.S. (PIRUS) contains anonymized information, spanning 1948-2018, on violent and nonviolent extremists who were members of officially designated terrorist organizations or were arrested, indicted, or killed based on ideologically motivated activities.[121] Table 4.9 presents data from a random selection of 1,503 cases reported in the PIRUS. What patterns do you see in the Table 4.9?

Terrorism scholars observe patterns common to individuals who commit extremist violence irrespective of their ideology and geographic location. They observe phases in the radicalization process of domestic and international terrorists. For example, the "staircase" model of radicalization offers a narrowing series of steps leading towards involvement in terrorism, as seen in Figure 4.6.[123] The model uses the metaphor of staircases in a building comprised of six floors, with only those who reach the top floor engaging in terrorist violence. Notice that several conditions must occur for extremist violence to take place: (1) perceptions of unfairness that produce frustration; (2) rigid, categorical thinking that divides the world into "us" versus "them," with frustrations projected onto "them"; (3) replacing ordinary morality with a new morality in which the ends—creating the "ideal" society—justify the means; and (4) reframing victims as representing the enemy ("them") to break down personal inhibitions against harming the innocent. Terrorist violence, though seen as the embodiment of evil to observers, is believed by its perpetrators to be morally acceptable or even obligatory; to them, it is "virtuous violence."[124]

TABLE 4.9 ■ Extremist outcomes by ideology using data from Profiles in Individual Radicalization in the United States (PIRUS)

Ideology	Behavioral outcome			
	Noncriminal	Nonviolent criminal	Violent	Total
Far left	22 (26.8%)	83 (17.0%)	209 (22.4%)	314 (20.9%)
Far right	40 (48.8%)	197 (40.3%)	400 (42.9%)	637 (42.4%)
Islamist	1 (1.22%)	100 (20.4%)	125 (13.4%)	226 (15.0%)
Single issue	18 (22.0%)	101 (20.7%)	183 (19.6%)	302 (20.1%)
Hybrid	1 (1.2%)	8 (1.6%)	15 (1.6%)	24 (1.6%)
Total	82 (100%)	489 (100%)	932 (100%)	1,503 (100%)

Notes: "Single issue" extremists are motivated by one issue rather than a broader ideology, such as anti-abortion extremists, anarchist extremists, and extremists with idiosyncratic ideologies (e.g., Ted Kaczynski anti-technology ideology). The "hybrid" category includes anyone who fits into two or more categories.[122]

Source: Sawyer & Hienz (2016). Reprinted with permission.

FIGURE 4.6 ■ Staircase model of terrorism

Terrorist act and sidestepping inhibitions: Psychological distancing from civilians as out-groups (enemy), enabling violence

Solidification of categorical thinking and perceived legitimacy of terrorism: Deep involvement and beliefs in its rightfulness

Moral engagement: Commit to an alternate morality that justifies creating an "ideal" society by any means possible

Displacement of aggression: Frustrations are targeted at out-groups

Perceived options to fight unfair treatment: Perceptions of possibility for personal mobility and procedural justice

Psychological interpretation of material conditions: Perceived injustice, frustration, and shame

Source: Adapted from Moghaddam, F. M. (2005). The staircase to terrorism: A psychological exploration. *American Psychologist, 60*(2), 161-169.

Criminologists note further that some worldviews are more prone to extremism and justification of violence than others. Worldviews are ways of making sense and meaning of the world and our experiences in it. Extremist worldviews tend to include the following overlapping characteristics:

- *Authoritarianism* – Rigid intolerance for ambiguity and preference for dualistic thinking. Authoritarianism emphasizes staunch conventionalism, submission to authority, and aggression towards out-groups.[125]

- *Apocalypticism* – Perceive the past and the future as predetermined and believe they know how it will play out. Adherents "believe they have a divine mission to help bring about the end of the present evil age by sparking a global catastrophe that will lead to a cosmic showdown between the forces of good and evil" (p. 780).[126]

- *Fundamentalism* – Characterized by "dualistic thinking, paranoid ideas, an apocalyptic orientation, focus on a charismatic leader, and a totalized conversion process" (p. 22).[127]

Of course, these descriptions are not a perfect fit for all who engage in terroristic violence. Some non-extremists participate in terrorism groups because they are committed to an extremist individual rather than to the ideology. Plus, many who engage in extremist violence are, in fact, poorly versed in the ideology to which they supposedly subscribe.[128]

CHAPTER SUMMARY

LO 4.1   Describe characteristics of entrepreneurial and ideologically motivated crime.

Entrepreneurial (or enterprise) crime generates financial proceeds using planned, organized, illegal methods. Most white-collar crime, organized crime, and cybercrime is entrepreneurial. Ideologically motivated crime attempts to advance political and social agendas through illegal action. Hate/bias crime, terrorism, and some forms of cybercrime are ideologically motivated.

LO 4.2   Classify types of white-collar crime, including occupational and corporate crime.

Occupational crime is white-collar crime committed for individual gain in the context of a legitimate job. Many occupational crimes involve fraud (asset misappropriation, corruption, or financial statement fraud). Corporate crime is white-collar crime committed by business entities, or individuals acting on behalf of businesses, for organizational gain (e.g., antitrust violations, environmental crimes, unsafe labor practices)

LO 4.3   Explain what organized crime is and the forms it takes.

Organized crime is an ongoing criminal enterprise that is sustained through violence, threats, monopoly control, and/or corruption. It involves (1) provision of illicit goods and services (e.g., trafficking of drugs or arms) and (2) infiltration of legitimate business or government (e.g., extortion and bribery). Transnational organized crime operates across geographical boundaries, exploiting systems of international commerce and communication to generate illicit profits.

LO 4.4   Identify multiple forms of cybercrime.

Cybercrime is any criminal action that (1) is facilitated using a computer and network, and/or (2) targets a computer or network. Cyber-facilitated crimes range from low-skilled offenses like cyberharassment and online solicitation of illicit sexual services to higher-skilled crimes like phishing and spoofing. Cybercrimes that attack computers or networks include provision and use of botnets, ransomware, and DDoS attacks.

LO 4.5   Discern between hate/bias crime and terrorism.

Hate/bias crime and terrorism are both ideologically motivated. Hate/bias crime is an offense against a person or property that is motivated by the offender's bias (against a religion, race, ethnicity, sexual orientation, disability, gender, or gender identity), and offenders tend to target victims of lower status. Terrorism is violence committed to further religious, political, social, racial, or other ideological goals by intimidating civilian populations and influencing governmental conduct or policies.

ENGAGED DISCUSSION

1. Come up with one example of an entrepreneurial crime. What makes it entrepreneurial?

2. Which do you think is more important in classifying a crime as white-collar: the social status of the offender or the kind of offense they have committed?

3. Do you believe corruption of public officials is a necessary component of organized crime? Why or why not?

4. The line between IRL (in real life) experiences and online experiences is grows blurry as we spend more and more time online. Considering this, develop an argument regarding whether the category "cybercrime" is still necessary.

5. What would go in the overlap of a Venn diagram of hate/bias crime and terrorism? What would go in the non-overlapping portions?

KEY TERMS

Corporate crime (p. 84)

Corruption (p. 90)

Criminal enterprise (p. 94)

Cybercrime (p. 96)

Domestic terrorism (p. 104)

Entrepreneurial crime (p. 80)

Fraud (p. 82)

Gangs (p. 95)

Hacking (p. 96)

Hate/bias crime (p. 99)

Ideologically motivated crime (p. 80)

International terrorism (p. 104)

Lone wolf terrorists (p. 105)

Occupational crime (p. 82)

Organized crime (p. 90)

Radicalization (p. 105)

State crime (p. 89)

State-corporate crime (p. 89)

Transnational organized crime (p. 91)

White-collar crime (p. 81)

AP Photo/Candice Choi

5 PATTERNS IN CRIME

LEARNING OBJECTIVES

5.1 Explain what correlates of crime are, and what they are not.

5.2 Describe demographic patterns in criminal offending.

5.3 Identify structural-level institutional predictors of crime rates.

5.4 Differentiate between temporal and ecological patterns in criminology.

5.5 Describe patterns in co-offending, weapon use, and offender substance use.

On March 26, 2021, 21-year-old Robert Aaron Long murdered eight people, six of them Asian women, at massage spas in the Atlanta area.[1] The crime, committed with a 9-mm handgun purchased hours before the offense, took place at three spa locations between 4:40 p.m. and 6:00 p.m. on a Tuesday. Long claimed to have a "sexual addiction" that conflicted with his religious beliefs and that he targeted women who worked at the spas to "eliminate the temptation," language which denied the victims their full humanity.[2]

About one week earlier, prosecutors in Chicago charged two 20-year-old men, Dakari Davis and Ladon Braxton, with attempted murder, aggravated unlawful use of a weapon, attempted vehicular hijacking, and aggravated possession of a stolen vehicle.[3] The two allegedly shot at the 45-year-old victim with a handgun while unsuccessfully attempting to steal his car, and they then stole the vehicle of a woman who witnessed the attack. Davis, who left high school before his senior year, had a history of weapons offenses dating back to his adolescence, while Braxton had a clean record.[4]

Just days before that, police in Bradenton, Florida, arrested a 15-year-old boy for his involvement in the fatal drive-by shooting of 20-year-old Antonio Aguirre.[5] A second 15-year-old boy was arrested several days later.[6]

One day earlier, police in Mesa, Arizona, arrested 24-year-old Rodrigo Garcia for stealing a BMW parked outside a convenience store. The story made the news because there was a sleeping toddler in the backseat. The perpetrator abandoned the vehicle upon discovering the child.[7] Police used surveillance video to identify the suspect. Garcia was charged with kidnapping, theft of means of transportation, and vehicle burglary.[8]

These crimes all occurred within a two-week span in March 2021. They occurred in different regions of the country. Some targeted property while others targeted people. Ages differed across the (alleged) offenders and their victims, as did their race and ethnicity. Several committed their offenses alone, but others had co-offenders. All are part of broader patterns in criminal offending and criminal events.

UNDERSTANDING CRIME PATTERNS

Each person who commits a crime and each criminal event—including the five people and four events described in the preceding paragraphs—is like a tile in a mosaic. It is the mosaic, not the individual tiles, that interests criminologists. The mosaics are not usually random pops of color and texture. Rather, they form into predictable designs, or patterns. The goal of the criminologist, in part, is to identify and explain patterns. Why do they exist? Under what circumstances do they look different? What changes to social and legal policies might alter them for the better?

One form of crime patterns is correlates of crime. A crime correlate is a variable that is statistically associated with criminal behavior or crime rates. The predictor and the outcome (crime) are statistically associated, or correlated, if they vary together more than would be expected by chance. For example, sex is a correlate of serious violent crime. We know this because the proportion of violent crimes like robbery, aggravated assault, homicide, and sex offenses committed by men is far greater than their proportion in the general population.[9] If sex were *not* a correlate, then about half of violent crimes would be committed by men and half by women.

Accurately interpreting crime correlates requires that we acknowledge a few facts about correlations. First, correlation does not equal causation. It only means that there is an observed statistical association. That association may be driven by other, more important, factors. For example, criminologists observe that Indigenous populations have higher rates of criminal offending, victimization, and incarceration than other groups in the U.S., Canada, Australia, and elsewhere.[10] For example, Indigenous peoples represent 15.6% of the population in Alaska but 31% of incarcerated Alaskans.[11] The homicide victimization rate for Native American boys and men in Montana is about four times greater than for the rest of the state.[12] The correlation between Indigenous status and crime is due largely to concentrated disadvantage, collective trauma, and residential isolation brought about by generations of mistreatment (by colonization, by governments, by individuals who wield power). It is not being Indigenous, per se, that causes these outcomes; rather it is the result of all that has been done to Indigenous populations. A correlation, alone, cannot capture this deeper complexity. Bear this in mind while reading about correlational patterns in this chapter.

A second fact about correlation is that they don't tell us exact, or one-to-one, relationships. If we say that dropping out of high school is a correlate of criminal offending, we are not saying that *all* people who didn't complete high school commit crime (that would be ridiculous!). Nor are we saying that *only* people who left high school early commit crime (equally ridiculous!). Instead, we are saying that the likelihood of criminal conduct is increased by not having a high school diploma, at least relative to those who did complete high school.

This chapter addresses demographic correlates (age, sex, social class and poverty, race and ethnicity, and immigration status) as well as institutional correlates (family, employment, religion, and political factors). These correlates sometimes operate on the individual level, as characteristics of individual offenders, and sometimes on the structural level, as characteristics of societies. Often, it is both. For example, a person's history of joblessness may predict their likelihood of committing theft (individual level), and the unemployment rate may predict community theft rates (structural level). This chapter attends to both kinds of patterns.

Patterns in criminal events represent another crime pattern. How often do crimes involve more than one offender? When do they occur during the day and during the year? Do they happen more in some regions than others, or in some time periods than others? This chapter explores large-scale patterns in rates of criminal events, including temporal (time-based) and ecological (location-based) patterns. It also describes empirical patterns in criminal incidents, such as the presence of co-offenders, weapons, and use of drugs or alcohol.

A Note of Caution

Our knowledge of patterns in crime is only as good as our data. Remember from Chapter 2 that criminologists studying the extent of crime (the "How much?" question) rely primarily on official statistics and victimization surveys. Victimization data tell us more about the predictors of victimization than of offending, yet we are able to glean insight into patterns in criminal events from sources like the National Crime Victimization Survey (NCVS). Official statistics from the National Incident-Based Reporting System (NIBRS) provide a window into demographic correlates of criminal behavior, co-offending patterns, and more. Plus, criminologists studying structural correlates of crime rates, like unemployment rates and wealth inequality, depend on official statistics to complete their analyses. Studies of arrestees, probationers, and incarcerated populations also provide information about the characteristics of offenders, their crimes, and the communities and families that produced them.

We ought to exercise caution given the sources of our information. Official police statistics and studies of people caught up in the criminal legal system only tell us about (1) the crimes that are treated as worthy of scrutiny by law enforcement, (2) individuals whose behaviors come to the attention of law enforcement, and, in the case of probationers and imprisoned persons, (3) individuals whose criminal cases prosecutors deemed worthy of pursuing.[13] In the case of lower-level and public-order offenses, like drug possession, trespassing, drunkenness, and weapons law violations, available data reflect patterns of policing.[14] Residents of neighborhoods where people are routinely stopped and searched are more likely to face citation or arrest, and they are more likely to end up in crime data than those who live in communities with low or congenial police presence.[15] In sum, the data available to us tell us more about some crimes—and some groups' crimes—than others:

- We have more information on crimes of the poor (like burglary) than crimes of the wealthy (like corporate crime).

- We have more information on direct-contact crimes (like robbery and homicide) than crimes with diffuse effects (like environmental crimes and securities fraud).

- We have more information on crimes with adult victims (like motor vehicle theft) than crimes without victims (like gambling offenses) or with child victims (like child sexual abuse).

- We have more information on crimes that people are more apt to report to police (like motor vehicle theft) than crimes with low rates of reporting (like sexual assault and intimate partner violence) or crimes for which people may not know they have been victimized (like identity theft).

- We have more information on behaviors, places, and groups that are more scrutinized by law enforcement, reflecting police priorities and patterns of criminalization, especially for offenses with a lower level of seriousness (like drug possession).

Residents of communities where people are frequently stopped and searched face higher rates of citation or arrest, and they are more likely to appear in crime data.

AP Photo/Seth Wenig, File

This does not mean that examining patterns in crime is a futile task. It means that when studying the correlates of crime and criminal event patterns, we must realize that we are studying specific kinds of patterns: street crimes, "gray-collar" crimes (i.e., white-collar offenses, like fraud or embezzlement, committed by lower- or middle-status offenders), and public-order crimes disproportionately committed by heavily policed populations. Plus, many researchers rely on index crime rates, sometimes broken down into violent crime rates (murder and nonnegligent manslaughter, aggravated assault, robbery, and rape/sexual assault) and property crime rates (burglary, larceny, motor vehicle theft, and arson) to examine large-scale patterns. Though index offenses do not capture the full range of criminal conduct, they do represent many offenses that harm us.

DEMOGRAPHIC CORRELATES

Demography is the scientific study of populations, and individuals' demographic characteristics indicate the population groups to which they belong or are assigned. Demographic characteristics include age, sex, social class, race, ethnicity, and immigration status. Demographic patterns in criminology— or demographic correlates of crime—tell us which demographic groups exhibit higher or lower rates of criminal offending and criminal punishment.

Age

Age is one of the most consistent predictors of criminal conduct. In the U.S. and elsewhere, today and in other time periods, people in their late teens through their mid-20s exhibit greater criminality than older groups. Some criminologists even declare it a universal truth, or "brute fact," that the young commit more crime than older people.[16] They describe an age-crime curve that rises sharply in the teenage years, peaks in late adolescence and the early 20s, and then gradually declines thereafter. The age-crime curve is not symmetrical; instead, it has an inverted-J shape. Moreover, the age-crime curve in the U.S. holds across types of offenses, including violent and property offenses, both serious and minor.

There are some exceptions to the established shape of age-crime curve, however. For example, in Taiwan, which has a more collectivist culture (an emphasis on group harmony rather than conflict or aggression) than the U.S., the age-crime curve peaks in the late-20s or later and has a much flatter curve, with more than half of arrests involving people in their mid-30s or older.[17] Also, even within the U.S., where the inverted-J is well-established, the peak age of offending differs somewhat across offenses, as seen in Figure 5.1. The current wisdom is that the age-crime curve is universal but not invariant. In other words, it is seen all over the world and for nearly all crimes, but its shape differs by location and crime type.

There are additional ways that age-crime curves vary. For example, the peak age of offending is somewhat earlier for women than for men.[18] In addition, the curve is taller and wider for young men who grow up in extremely poor neighborhoods, showing a strikingly steep increase in the teenage years and a relatively slow exit from offending.[19] This effect is driven almost entirely by neighborhoods rather than individual characteristics: Young men who are similar in nearly every way (e.g., in education, in family relationships, in mental health) but live in economically prosperous neighborhoods have much flatter and narrower age-crime curves. Plus, because violent offenders usually target victims who are the same age as them, the age-victimization curve for violence looks awfully like the age-crime curve.[20]

There are two ways to approach the age-crime curve: (1) Study individuals' changes in criminal conduct over age periods of their life courses by conducting longitudinal research, or (2) study crime rates among different age groups in society. Both approaches tend to show the curve, though some individuals are persistent, or chronic, offenders throughout their lives, beginning their criminal careers in childhood and continuing well past the age when most have stopped (see Chapter 8 for more on life-course criminology).[21] Figure 5.1, which uses NIBRS data, adopts the second approach, showing how crime rates go up and down as we move from the youngest (age 11–15) to the oldest group (age 66 and older).

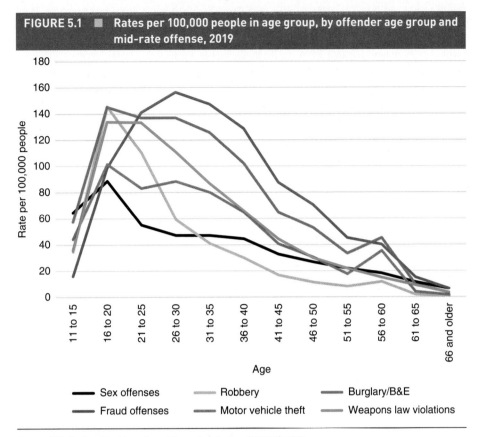

FIGURE 5.1 ■ **Rates per 100,000 people in age group, by offender age group and mid-rate offense, 2019**

Legend:
- Sex offenses
- Fraud offenses
- Robbery
- Motor vehicle theft
- Burglary/B&E
- Weapons law violations

Source: FBI, National Incident-Based Reporting System (NIBRS), 2019.

ENGAGED CRIMINOLOGY 5.1

Exploring the Age-Crime Curve

In this activity, you will examine Figure 5.1 to explore and analyze variation in age-crime curves.

1. Which offense has the steepest decline after its peak at age 16–20? Develop an explanation for the extreme age-crime pattern for this offense.

2. Which offense has the oldest peak age (where the highest part of the curve is farther to the right)? Devise an explanation for the later age peak for this offense.

As a person who has been young (or is still young), you probably have your own ideas about why crime rates are so much higher among 19-year-olds than 49-year-olds. Criminologists offer several reasons. The first is brain maturation. This explanation points to the still-developing brain as the cause of poor judgment in youth.[22] As we age, development in the frontal region of the brain brings greater impulse control.[23] Second, and related to maturity, adolescents are more susceptible than adults to peer influence.[24] In interview studies, incarcerated men express how adulthood changed their capacity to learn from past mistakes, to weigh consequences before acting, to make and follow through on long-term plans, and to make better choices when choosing friends.[25] Other explanations focus on the social rather than the neurodevelopmental circumstances of adolescent life: the desire for independence, boys' concerns with proving their manhood, the failures of schools and families to control behavior, and the absence of adult responsibilities.[26]

Sex

The **gender gap** in crime—or the high rates of criminal offending among men and boys relative to women and girls—is observed for most offenses. The more violent the crime, the wider the gulf between male and female rates. The sex difference is particularly stark for sex offenses, robbery, and homicide. For instance, of the 10,297 people known to have committed homicide in the U.S. in 2020 and whose sex was reported by FBI in the National Incident-Based Reporting System, 87% were male and 13% were female.[27] Figure 5.2 shows the sizeable width of the gender gap for multiple offenses. The gender gap is much slimmer for property and public-order offenses, and it is even flipped for select offenses like prostitution.

Some criminologists have questioned whether the gender gap is actually as large as it appears in police data.[28] The chivalry hypothesis claims that police treat women more leniently than men, or more chivalrously.[29] While there is evidence of preferential treatment for *some* women (i.e., white women who commit minor, stereotypically feminine offenses like shoplifting), most crime-involved women receive no such kindness.[30]

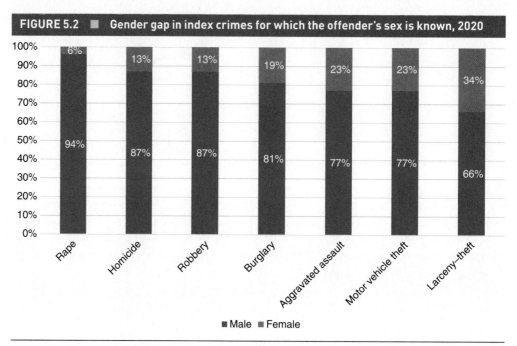

FIGURE 5.2 ■ Gender gap in index crimes for which the offender's sex is known, 2020

Source: FBI, National Incident-Based Reporting System (NIBRS), 2020.

Criminologists point to the gendered meaning of aggression to explain why men and boys commit so much more violence and weapons-related crime than women and girls.[31] A man can assert his masculinity by brutalizing (or threatening to brutalize) other men, but aggression serves no femininity-enhancing function for women.[32] In other words, crime is a setting for gender performance: Men and boys can perform (or act out) masculinity by taking risks, drinking to excess, and physically dominating rivals.[33] This does not mean that women don't engage in violence, or that their violence isn't connected to gender. For example, girls' and women's aggressive responses to reputation challenges (like being called a sexist slur like "bitch" or "slut") are common in high-violence neighborhoods and institutions where a cultivating a tough persona provides protection.[34]

Opportunities for crime are also tied to gender.[35] Women and girls are often denied access to—or relegated to minor roles in—drug trafficking organizations, burglary crews, car theft networks, and corporate crime schemes.[36] Together, gender performance and opportunities can account for the relatively equal numbers of male and female embezzlers as well as the small gaps for fraud and larceny. These instrumental offenses can be committed solo, require no direct contact with victims, and pose no threat of violence.

The gender gap in crime has narrowed over time, piquing the interest of criminologists.[37] The shrinking ratio of male-to-female crime prompted two possible conclusions: (1) Women's behavior is becoming more like men's behavior (or vice versa), a "behavior change" explanation, or (2) women's behavior hasn't changed, but female offenders are more likely to be identified by law enforcement now than in the past, a "criminal justice change" explanation.

Incarcerated women at Las Colinas Women's Detention Facility in Santee, California, sewing protective masks in April 2020. The gender gap in incarceration narrowed as women's rates of incarceration increased more steeply than men's rates between the 1980s and 2010s.

Sandy Huffaker/AFP/Getty Images

There are two "behavior change" explanations. The first is the liberation hypothesis. First devised in the 1970s and also called the "emancipation hypothesis," this explanation suggested that growing gender equality (in education, in work, in family roles) was creating greater gender equality in criminal behavior. No longer stuck at home, women could go to work (and steal), go to the bar (and get in drunken altercations), and adopt men's orientations towards risky behavior. The hypothesis has long been refuted on two grounds. First, the shrinking gap was mostly due to men's declines in crime rather than increases in women's law-breaking.[38] Second, the women who do commit serious crimes are on the economic margins of society, not the liberated women depicted by the hypothesis.[39]

The second "behavior change" explanation is the economic marginalization hypothesis, which focuses on women's growing hardships relative to men's—their levels of poverty, low wages, and single parenthood—as the source of the narrowing gap. For example, 56% of Americans living in poverty are female, and the percentage is closer to 59% if we only include adults.[40] One in four unmarried mothers with children under age 18 is poor.[41] As women's economic lives become more precarious as compared to men's lives, sex differences in criminal behavior, especially property offending, begin to dwindle. According to researchers, women's economic vulnerability is, in fact, a strong predictor of their property offending.[42]

The primary "criminal justice change" explanation is the policy change hypothesis. Imagine that police and prosecutors wield a net that they use to scoop up criminal offenders (i.e., arrest them and charge them). This hypothesis claims that the net got wider over time due to changes in arrest policies and charging decisions. In the past, the net scooped up only the more serious offenders (robbers, burglars, assaulters who caused significant injury) and minor crimes—or those considered minor at the time—were handled differently. Rising concern about domestic violence and school shooters, as well as growing intolerance for any criminal behavior, led to policy shifts that lowered the threshold for behaviors deemed worthy of arrest and criminal charges. For example, mandatory arrest policies intended to hold domestic abusers accountable had the unintended consequence of increasing arrests of women and girls. Why? Because women's and girls' interpersonal conflicts are more likely than men's and boys' conflicts to take place at home, such as teenage daughters becoming physically aggressive in confrontations with parents.[43] As the net widened to scoop up more simple assaults and other minor crimes, the proportion of arrestees who were female increased.[44]

Social Class

Social class refers to one's income, occupational status, and education. The higher each is, the higher one's social class position is. For example, most surgeons make lots of money, have lots of prestige, and have medical degrees, making them upper class. Social class is linked to criminal offending, but not in a linear, or step-by-step, way. In other words, criminal conduct does not decline steadily as we move from "lower class" to "lower middle class" to "middle class" to "upper middle class" to "upper class." Instead, there is a gulf between the poor (or "lower class") and the nonpoor (everyone else), at least for index crimes like robbery and burglary. Poverty is the real correlate.[45] Ancient Greek philosopher Aristotle was correct when he wrote, "Poverty is the parent of crime." Unsurprisingly, the relationship is reversed for most corporate and elite occupational offenses, with only the most economically advantaged in society having the opportunity to commit crimes like price-fixing and violating labor laws.[46] Wealth, it seems, is the parent of corporate crime.

Imagine the classic story of a person stealing a loaf of bread to feed their family, like Jean Valjean's crime in the book and musical *Les Misérables*. This is poverty's direct effect: committing crime to secure what is needed due to impoverishment. Direct effects of poverty are observed by criminologists who study "survival crimes" among people experiencing chronic homelessness, including stealing food or personal hygiene products, and trespassing to secure a warm place to sleep.[47] Direct effects are explained by the economic model of crime. In this view, crime is the result of a rational decision-making process in which potential offenders weigh the probable costs (or risks) of crime against its potential benefits.[48] Poverty heightens the incentives to violate the law by increasing crime's benefits relative to its costs. In one innovative study, a researcher examined trends in crimes that produce economic gain across cities with different public assistance payment schedules.[49] They found that money-generating crimes rose as more time passed since payments were distributed (and money had run out for recipients); there was no effect on other types of crime. Property crime, it seemed, was the direct result of an increasing number of desperately poor, cash-strapped people. Plus, joblessness and underemployment (not having enough work) make participation in illicit markets, like drug markets, more attractive.[50]

Homeless "survival crimes," like trespassing and stealing personal hygiene items, fit the economic model of crime.
AP Photo/Michael Dwyer

Poverty's effects can also be indirect. Poverty molds people's lives in ways that increase crime and victimization. For example, being poor limits options for where a family can afford to live. As a result, low-income parents face greater difficulties in shielding their children from criminal influences in their neighborhoods and schools.[51] In addition, poverty can be destabilizing, leading to frequent residential moves, job changes, and instability in romantic partnerships.[52] Social bonds and social support—important protective factors against crime—suffer as a result.[53] In addition to creating economic pressures to skirt the law, poverty leads to conditions—poor housing conditions, neighborhood conditions, and school conditions—that make law-breaking more likely.

Note that this section has focused entirely on poverty as an individual experience. Poverty is also a characteristic of places. Criminologists ask: Is crime more likely in communities with concentrated poverty (where a large proportion of residents are poor)?[54] The straightforward answer is yes. As community poverty rates increase, so too do crime rates, at least up until 30% or more of the population is poor, at which point the rates level off.[55] The reasons are plenty. Concentrated poverty transforms social life. Its impacts include the absence of conventional role models, weakened social institutions (such as struggling families and underfunded schools), low levels of trust among neighbors, having too little political power to address problems, and cultural outlooks that view violence as a necessary self-protective strategy.[56]

"He who opens a school door closes a prison," a remark usually attributed to 19th century author Victor Hugo, remains relevant today. Educational attainment, or how much schooling a person completes, is a correlate of criminal offending.[57] As with social class generally, education is not associated with crime in a linear step-by-step fashion with offending rates dropping a small amount for each additional year of schooling. Instead, dropping out or being pushed out of school is the real correlate. Pushouts include students—disproportionately students of color, LGBTQI students, and students with disabilities—who are expelled or discouraged from continuing to attend school as a result of zero-tolerance and biased disciplinary practices.[58]

Researchers document the overrepresentation of high school dropouts and pushouts in jails and prison.[59] By 2010, 52.7% of white jail and prison inmates ages 20 to 34 had neither a high school diploma nor a GED (general equivalency degree); 61.8% of Black jail and prison inmates had no high school or equivalent credentials.[60] As mass incarceration was rising in the 2000s, 3 in 10 white male high school dropouts and 6 in 10 Black male high school dropouts had served time in state or federal prison at some point during their lives.[61] Formerly incarcerated people are twice as likely to have no high school credential (diploma or GED) than the general public, as seen in Figure 5.3. Additionally,

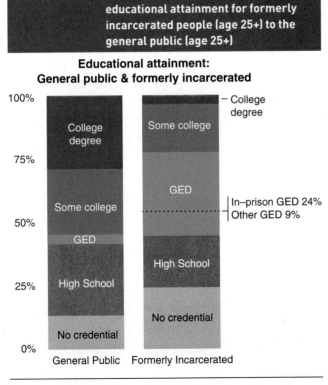

FIGURE 5.3 ■ Comparing the highest level of educational attainment for formerly incarcerated people (age 25+) to the general public (age 25+)

**Educational attainment:
General public & formerly incarcerated**

Source: Prison Policy Initiative. https://www.prisonpolicy.org/reports/education.html

GEDs are more common than high school diplomas among people who have been to prison, with about 73% of those GEDs completed during incarceration (24% in prison vs. 9% not in prison).

The correlation between high school non-completion and criminal offending is largely spurious, or noncausal. Leaving high school is the "the final event in a long, gradual process of disenchantment and disengagement from school" (p. 44).[62] Many young people who exit high school before graduation day are already on a path towards adult legal problems long before they decide not to return to the classroom, due to substance use, impulse control difficulties, and involvement in the juvenile justice system.[63] In contrast, students who leave school for other reasons, like working full-time to contribute financially to their family, are not at increased risk of criminal behavior as a result of dropping out.[64]

Dropping out has a causal effect on crime-related outcomes in some contexts. For example, longitudinal research following serious delinquent offenders over time shows that exiting high school has no effect on their criminal behavior, but it does increase their risk of being arrested. This suggests that police are less tolerant of known "dropouts" who are negatively stereotyped.[65] In addition, one study—the first to focus on college non-completion and crime—finds that dropping out of college increases criminal offending. Perhaps unexpectedly, the rise in offending is strongest for students who were, in fact, most likely to finish their degrees had they not gotten off track.[66]

Race and Ethnicity

Race is a social construction.[67] Race scholars Zuberi and Bonilla-Silva express this idea when they write, "Human biological variation is real, yet race is a distorted way of organizing this variation... Racial stratification is real, but biology is not its root cause" (p. 10).[68] What they mean is that racial categories (e.g., Black, White, Asian, Native American) and racial inequality (another word for stratification) are human creations, not expressions of inherent, fixed differences. The same applies to ethnic categories, like Latinx or Arab. That's why racial and ethnic categories differ across countries and over time periods. For example, people from African nations who move to the U.S. describe a kind of culture shock upon discovering their national and ethnic identities are swallowed up into a category called "Black."[69] Any variation observed between racial and ethnic groups—in education, in employment, in health, in crime, in incarceration, to name a few—must therefore be understood as arising from the racialized experiences of those groups. Being Black or white or Asian or Native Hawaiian or Latinx or any other categorization doesn't *cause* GPAs or homeownership or criminal conduct or any other social outcome. Rather, the *experience* of being Black or white or Asian or Native Hawaiian or Latinx (and so on) shapes opportunities, how one is treated, where one is likely to live, and other important factors.

Information about race, ethnicity, and rates of criminal offending come from official sources like NIBRS as well as victimization data (NCVS), which rely on simplistic categories. For example, NIBRS arrest data include five racial categories: "White," "Black or African American," "American Indian or Alaska Native," "Asian," and "Native Hawaiian or Pacific Islander," as well as "two or more races." The only ethnicity category reported in NIBRS is "Hispanic/Latino." The NCVS, which relies on the victim's perception and memory of the offender's characteristics, contains similar racial and ethnic groupings.

Comparisons of racial/ethnic patterns in official data and victimization data are valuable, despite the simplistic categories. Remember that NCVS data come directly from victims, whereas NIBRS data come from police. Any differences between the racial/ethnic patterns in the two sources indicate possible racial or ethnic disparities. A **disparity** is an inequality or a difference that is unfair. In this case, we might observe disparities in either reporting to police or the likelihood of arrest based on the offender's race or ethnicity. An example is illustrative. In the U.S. Department of Justice's 2021 report on violent offenders' and arrestees' race and ethnicity,[70] the author noted,

> *White offenders were underrepresented among persons arrested for nonfatal violent crimes (46%) relative to their representation among offenders identified by victims in the NCVS (52%).*

In other words, when there is no police involvement in counting violent offenders, more than half of offenders are identified (by victims) as white, yet white people make up less than half (46%) of those arrested by police for all violent offenses (homicide excluded). The author goes on to note the source of this disparity:

> *When limited to offenders in incidents reported to police, white people were found to be arrested proportionate to their criminal involvement.*

This means that the disparity arose from the lower likelihood of white offenders being reported to police by victims, not due to police arresting white violent offenders at a lower rate, once reported. Put another way, white violent offenders disproportionately fly under law enforcement's radar.

Though white persons comprise the majority of offenders and arrestees in the U.S., they are under-represented for multiple offenses relative to their proportion in the population (61.6% identified as white in the 2020 U.S. Census), whereas Black/African American persons are overrepresented relative to their proportion in the population (12.4% identified as Black or African American, and another 1.8% reported being Black or African American in combination with another race). This is called racial disproportionality, which occurs when a racial group's representation in crime statistics is not equal to their representation in the general population. For instance, Figure 5.4 shows that, according to NIBRS, 70.0% of all arrestees for whom race was known in 2020 were white, 26.0% were Black or African American, 2.5% were American Indian or Alaska Native, 1.2% were Asian, 0.3% were Native Hawaiian or Pacific Islander. Notice that 26.0% (percentage of arrestees who were Black or African American) is greater than 14.2% (percentage of U.S. population that was Black or African American alone or in combination). Asian persons are also disproportionately underrepresented in arrest statistics, comprising 6.0% of the U.S. population but only 1.2% of arrestees. These are patterns of racial disproportionality.[71]

NIBRS reports Hispanic or Latinx ethnicity separately from race, revealing a pattern of ethnic disproportionality in arrests. In 2020, 18.7% of the U.S. population identified as Hispanic or Latino.[72] In the same year, 22.5% of all arrestees were Hispanic or Latino. While Hispanic or Latino persons were overrepresented in some offense categories (like gambling offenses [42.1%], driving under the influence [28.4%], and sex offenses [30.4%]), other offenses display a pattern of Hispanic/Latino underrepresentation, including larceny-theft (15.2%) and fraud (14.8%).

The *size* of racial disproportionality may be a bit overstated, though. That's because researchers rely on the racial composition of the U.S., in general, to make comparisons. The U.S. population includes people of all ages. But the racial composition of Americans over, say, age 65 is far from the racial composition of people under age 30. And it is young people who make up the bulk of people represented in crime data. Consider this: 72% of Baby Boomers (born 1946 to 1964) are white/non-Hispanic compared to 55% of Millennials (born 1981 to 1996).[73] And the share of the population that is Hispanic/Latinx nearly doubled (from 11% to 21%) between those generations. Among Generation Z (born 1997 to 2012), 25% are Hispanic/Latinx and 51% are white.[74] We also know that, at the same time, about 29% of people in the U.S. population were Baby Boomers or older![75] All this translates into comparisons between the racial/ethnic compositions of a relatively young group (people in crime data) and a relatively old group (the U.S. population).

Many criminologists, subscribing to the racial invariance hypothesis, argue that the causes of crime are the same for all people, regardless of race or ethnicity. It's just that race and ethnicity are linked to those shared causes—like poverty, unemployment, educational outcomes, and residence in economically distressed neighborhoods—due to structural legacies of racist policies. Other criminologists question whether the causes of crime are completely racially invariant. They argue that a "long history of public dishonor and ritualized humiliation" of Black Americans by white Americans—extending from chattel slavery through the Jim Crow era and into modern-day police violence—creates a worldview that has no equivalent counterpart among other Americans (p. 8; critics argue that Native Americans' experiences are comparable).[76] This perspective sees perceptions of discrimination as essential for understanding criminal offending, much more so for African Americans than others. Anti-Black stereotypes and unjust treatment produce "shame, anger, hostility, and defiance," and the law loses its legitimacy when it is seen as a "means to disrespect, harass, bully, and unfairly imprison" (p. 173).[77]

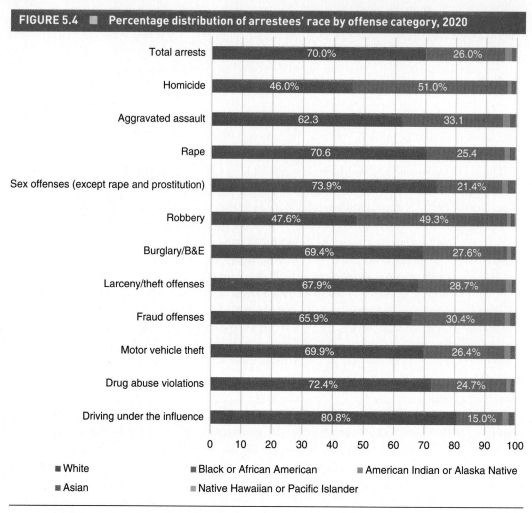

FIGURE 5.4 ■ Percentage distribution of arrestees' race by offense category, 2020

Offense	White	Black or African American
Total arrests	70.0%	26.0%
Homicide	46.0%	51.0%
Aggravated assault	62.3	33.1
Rape	70.6	25.4
Sex offenses (except rape and prostitution)	73.9%	21.4%
Robbery	47.6%	49.3%
Burglary/B&E	69.4%	27.6%
Larceny/theft offenses	67.9%	28.7%
Fraud offenses	65.9%	30.4%
Motor vehicle theft	69.9%	26.4%
Drug abuse violations	72.4%	24.7%
Driving under the influence	80.8%	15.0%

■ White   ■ Black or African American   ■ American Indian or Alaska Native
■ Asian   ■ Native Hawaiian or Pacific Islander

Source: Federal Bureau of Investigation, NIBRS, 2020.

Note: NIBRS data excluded Hispanic/Latino ethnicity or "two or more races." Percentages sum to 100% regardless of the incidence rate. Final three categorizations too small to display percentages.

Immigration

Politicians who hold nativist attitudes often raise alarm bells about the criminal threat that immigrants pose.[78] Sometimes their claims focus exclusively on undocumented immigrants who are in the country without legal documentation. Their message has resonated with a large segment of the U.S. population. Almost half (45%) of Gallup poll respondents in 2017 stated that they believe that immigrants make the crime situation worse in the U.S. (compared to 9% who said "better"; 43% thought immigrants had no effect on crime).[79] But do immigrants, in fact, make the crime situation worse? In short, no.

Researchers consistently find that immigration either reduces crime somewhat or has no effect on crime whatsoever.[80] There are two explanations. The first is about *who* immigrates. Immigrating, regardless of legal authorization, is an arduous, or difficult, process. Only those with high levels of initiative and ambition are willing to take on this challenging task. Plus, some immigrant groups are comprised of many highly educated professionals. Both factors lead to a scenario in which the people who immigrate are unlikely to be criminally inclined.[81] On top of this, being caught committing a crime could jeopardize one's immigration status or lead to deportation. The costs of crime are especially great for immigrants.

The second explanation is about how immigrants transform neighborhoods. When a large number of immigrants settle in an economically distressed community, that community's fortunes often improve, including a drop in crime. For example, a study of 194 "new destination communities" found that recent increases of Latinx immigrants reduced property crime rates: The larger the inflow of immigrants, the sharper the decline in crimes like burglary, larceny, and motor vehicle theft.[82] The **immigrant revitalization hypothesis** explains this effect: Immigrants bring their robust family and community ties, their entrepreneurship creates jobs and economic activity, and they reduce housing vacancy rates.[83]

Communities that have large foreign-born populations, like Minneapolis's Cedar-Riverside neighborhood, benefit from the revitalizing effects of immigration.

Doug Glass/AP Photos

   Of course, it would be ridiculous to lump all immigrants into a single category. In the words of one scholar, "There is no one 'immigration-crime' link any more than there is one type of immigrant or one type of job or one type of crime" (p. 1397).[84] Immigrants leave their nations of origin for a host of reasons, including the pursuit of economic and educational opportunity, seeking political asylum, escaping the horrors of war, and fleeing stigma and persecution. Some have been in the U.S. for decades and others for only months. Some immigrated as toddlers and others as middle-aged adults. And immigrants come from all over the world, bringing a vast spectrum of languages, customs, and religious beliefs. Some were doctors and lawyers before immigrating; others have only a few years of formal schooling. Some immigration is legally authorized; some isn't. While criminologists have not investigated all of these variations, they have addressed the unique effects of undocumented immigration on crime.

   What we know about the approximately 11 million undocumented immigrants in the U.S. is that they are disproportionately concentrated in low-skilled jobs, and they are poorer, younger, and more likely to be male relative to the general population. These facts, alone, might lead observers to conclude that they are more likely to engage in crime.[85] But, as with legally authorized immigration, criminologists find either no effects of undocumented immigration on crime or a small crime-suppressing effect for offenses ranging from burglary to homicide to intimate partner violence.[86] Plus, contrary to public perceptions, upswings in undocumented immigration bring down states' rates of drug- and alcohol-related problems, like drug arrests, drug overdoses, and drunk driving deaths.[87] This finding—that immigrants engage in less crime than native-born people despite their higher levels of social disadvantage—is called the immigrant paradox (or "Latino paradox" when applied specifically to immigrants from Latin America).[88] It's a paradox because it contradicts what is reasonably expected.

Most studies of immigration and crime focus on rates: immigration rates and their effects on crime rates. It is impossible to know from these studies, alone, if immigration reduces crime because (1) immigrants commit less crime than nonimmigrants, or (2) immigration changes social life in ways that reduce *everyone's* criminal behavior. Fortunately, some criminologists use longitudinal survey data to figure out if option 1 is true. Their evidence suggests it is. For example, criminologists find that foreign-born adolescents engage in less delinquent behavior and violence than their native-born peers, and this difference lasts into adulthood. U.S.-born respondents are also more likely than immigrants to be arrested, plead guilty to criminal charges, get sentenced to probation, and be incarcerated.[89] Moreover, the longer families have been in the U.S., and the more assimilated young people are into American culture, the more likely they are to offend, at least for some groups (e.g., Asian and Latinx immigrant groups).[90]

INSTITUTIONAL CORRELATES

Institutional patterns are about trends in social institutions. Social institutions are complex systems that serve the basic functions of society and support its survival. They include family, the economy, religion, and more. The people who enact roles in these social institutions change over time, but the institution persists. Lots of people enact the roles of "mother" or "father," for instance, and those roles will continue to exist long after our own mothers and fathers are gone. Social institutions undergo change despite their long-lasting nature. For example, how families are organized (e.g., the extent of two-parent vs. single-parent families) and family norms (e.g., using corporal punishment) vary over time, across locations, and between families. This section addresses how patterns in families, employment, religion, and politics impact—or fail to impact—crime.

Family

Families are the most basic building block of human societies. Most people's first relationships are with family members. When we are young, our families—if they are able—provide for our material needs (food, clothing, a roof over our head) and socialize us through interactions (how to speak, how to share, how to wait our turn).[91] Families can be a source of deep emotional support or of lasting trauma, occasionally both. Our experiences of family life shape our behaviors, criminal or otherwise.[92] These experiences include childhood family structure (e.g., married parents, single parents, presence of stepparents or live-in partners), family conflict, and parental disciplinary tactics. Adult family lives also matter, including living with a partner, getting married, splitting up, and having children of one's own.

Families differ in their structure. About one in four children in the U.S. lives with a single parent (21% with single mothers and 4% with single fathers).[93] The proportion rises to one in three if we include all families with non-married parents. This represents a major shift in how families look over the past half-century. Adolescents who spend all or much of their childhood in single-parent families are at a somewhat increased risk of criminal behavior, though most lead conventional lives. Family structure is a correlate of crime because family structure is intertwined with other known predictors of law-breaking, like poverty, stress, and conflict.

Children are expensive. The costs of day care, new shoes, dentist appointments, after-school programs, and apartments with extra bedrooms add up. Single parents struggle with finances more so than families in which two adults work for pay.[94] Plus, poor parents are less likely to get and stay married in the first place; economic difficulties predict family structure rather than the other way around.[95] We are often talking about poverty when we talk about family structure. Raising children alone and being the sole earner is stressful for parents, and stressed-out parents sometimes lash out at their children.[96] Children who bear the brunt of their caregiver's despair, anger, and frustration are prone to externalizing problems (aggression, lying, cheating) in childhood and criminal conduct in older years.[97] We are often talking about parental stress when we talk about family structure. In general, happy marriages (and committed cohabitations) do not end, but unhappy ones do.[98] Parental fighting in the months and years leading up to a breakup, as well as conflict in months and years after a split (e.g., over child support), predict child and adolescent behavior problems.[99] Plus, the movement of a stepparent, boyfriend, or girlfriend into the home creates tensions that undermine family functioning when children and the new adult do not get along.[100] We are often talking about family conflict when we talk about family structure.

Families differ in how they discipline children, as well. Dimensions of parenting include (1) responsiveness, or parental warmth towards the child and (2) behavioral control, or parental communication of consistent expectations for appropriate behavior and monitoring of children's behavior. In general, behavioral control is a positive thing for children, especially when paired with parental warmth, but some forms are criminogenic. Specifically, adolescents act out in response to harsh forms of behavioral control that involve physical or verbal punishments. Harsh control is common among authoritarian parents who assert their power by demanding obedience, issuing orders, and punishing any deviation from their strict rules. Parenting styles that are insensitive, unresponsive (i.e., lack warmth), and rejecting also lead to child aggression and criminality. The absence of parental control, or permissiveness, increases delinquent behavior, as well, but for different reasons. Harsh and rejecting parenting weakens parent-child relationships and generates hostility among young people, whereas permissive parenting results in opportunities for wrongdoing in the absence of watchful adults.[101]

Children are less likely to be aggressive or delinquent when parents display high levels of responsiveness, or warmth, whereas harsh and rejecting parenting has the opposite effect.

Nick David/DigitalVision/Getty Images

Adults' criminal behavior is shaped by family life, as well. For example, married people commit less crime than single people. Plus, criminal offenders slow down or end their criminal careers upon getting married.[102] Criminologists examine whether this is due to a "taming" effect of marriage or the fact that certain kinds of people get married (i.e., rule followers and people wanting to make a change). They find evidence of both.[103] Becoming a parent reduces criminal involvement under some conditions, too, as "parenthood is fundamentally incompatible with the partying, drug dealing or other actions that are linked to continued legal problems" (p. 413).[104] For example, studies of gang members show that parenthood reorders priorities and discourages risky behavior more profoundly for mothers than fathers.[105] Nonetheless, becoming a father restrains law-breaking, too, though typically only when fathers live with their children.[106]

Families serve a function for the individuals that comprise them. They also serve a function for society at large. Grandparents often step in when their own children are unable to provide adequate care to their grandchildren due to incarceration or substance abuse, serving as a buffer against foster care.[107] In the best circumstances, parents look out for neighbors' children as well as their own,[108] and they intervene when children misbehave or are being mistreated.[109] The phrase "it takes a village" captures the public functions of families. But when many families under stress are clustered together, they are less able to perform their "village" functions. For example, neighborhood crime rates are higher in communities with high percentages of households headed by single mothers, in part because such neighborhoods struggle to maintain informal networks that enable neighbors to look out for one another.[110]

Employment

Something counterintuitive happened in the late 2000s. The housing bubble burst, catapulting the U.S. into the Great Recession, which was, at the time, the most substantial economic downturn since the Great Depression 80 years earlier. Unemployment rates shot up, more than doubling between December 2007 (5%) and their peak in January 2010 (10.6%).[111] These effects were even more extreme among Black workers, with Black men, in particular, enduring the greatest job losses and unemployment rates; 17.8% of Black men were unemployed in July 2010.[112] Less-educated workers also suffered far more than highly educated workers: 17.9% of people without a high school diploma were unemployed at the peak versus only 5.3% of people with a bachelor's degree.[113] Importantly, these values only counted people who were actively looking for work. The full scope of joblessness was even greater, as many people stopped seeking jobs entirely (they were called "discouraged workers"). It's no wonder that people were dismayed: The median length of unemployment was six months in 2010, up from the typical eight weeks.[114] Logic dictated that crime rates should have skyrocketed. Instead, they dropped. And they dropped for *everyone,* even the groups hit hardest by the economic crisis.[115]

The public may have been shocked by what happened to crime rates in the late 2000s, but criminologists knew that the relationship between economic conditions, employment, and crime is complicated.[116] They might point to the 1960s as a case in point: The economy was in full swing and unemployment rare throughout the 1960s, yet crime rates climbed year after year. Unemployment matters for crime, but not in the oversimplified sense of "bad economy = more crime." After all, more unemployment translates into more people staying at home during the day, informally keeping watch over their homes and their neighborhoods.[117]

To start, let's imagine a worker who has been stably employed for 10 years, earning $45,000 per year. They own their home, they have children, they have no criminal record. An economic crisis descends, and their job disappears. They look for work for months, unsuccessfully. They qualify for unemployment insurance benefits, but those eventually run out. They cannot make their mortgage payments, so they sell their home and move in with their 70-year-old mother, where they use the meager proceeds from the house sale to pay her utility bills. They keep looking for work and plan to move into an apartment once securely employed again. Is this person likely to turn to crime to make ends meet? Probably not.

Now let's imagine another person whose employment history is inconsistent at best. Even in good economic times, they have difficulty maintaining a job due to substance use, unreliability, and frequent conflicts with coworkers and supervisors. When they are working, the pay is hourly and barely enough to cover living expenses. They take out their stresses on their spouse, often violently, especially during periods of joblessness when their drinking escalates. They have a record of offenses like DUIs, simple assaults, and drug violations. An economic crisis descends, and their temporary bouts of unemployment transform into a permanent state of joblessness. Is this person likely to engage in crime as a result of worsening economic conditions? Yes, or at least much more so than the first person.

Unemployment matters for crime, but it matters more for some people than others. Think of unemployment as a hand pushing a person standing on a diving board. If the person falls off the diving board, they engage in crime. Only those standing close to the edge—people already marginally employed and predisposed to crime—are likely to be nudged off the diving board by job loss. Criminologists distinguish between people who are (1) unemployed but looking for work; (2) out of the labor force for socially accepted reasons, like schooling, disability, or becoming a stay-at-home parent; and (3) out of the labor force for socially unaccepted reasons, like choosing not to work, earning income through alternative underground sources, or being unable to work due to substance dependence. Joblessness only leads to criminality when the reasons for it are socially unaccepted.[118] Unemployment also matters more for some crimes than others, especially money-generating property crimes.[119] Intimate partner violence also rises during times of unemployment.[120]

Unemployment also operates as a property of communities. When joblessness rates are very high, it is a problem for everyone who lives in the area rather than just a problem for the person out of work. Concentrated joblessness, more so than poverty itself, is the primary driver of violent crime rates in economically troubled neighborhoods: Places with joblessness *and* poverty fare much worse than poor communities where joblessness rates are low.[121]

We must acknowledge the role of criminal punishment when discussing unemployment. There are several ways the criminal legal system complicates the unemployment-crime correlation. First, the association could be spurious (or noncausal), owing to tightening police budgets during times of economic crisis.[122] Second, criminal conduct can be a cause of unemployment, rather than just the reverse. More precisely, a criminal record makes it difficult to get a job.[123] About 1 in 12 Americans has a felony conviction record.[124] It can be difficult to tease out how much of the link between unemployment and crime is, in fact, due to crime causing criminal records, which, in turn, cause joblessness. Nonetheless, researchers conclude that job loss promotes recidivism (or re-offending) among people with felony records, above and beyond the effects of a criminal history.[125]

A society's financial health can be measured using macro-level economic factors besides unemployment. For example, consumer sentiment—how optimistic or pessimistic individuals feel about their own economic situation and the general state of the economy—is a strong correlate of acquisitive (or money-generating) crimes.[126] Inflation also predicts acquisitive crime rates, with crimes like burglary, robbery, larceny, and motor vehicle theft increasing during periods of rising consumer prices.[127] In fact, the absence of inflation during the Great Recession is one explanation for its failure to propel crime rates upward.

Religion and Religiosity

All major world religions condemn killing. They offer blueprints for correct living through conformity to religious norms. We could reasonably surmise, then, that religion suppresses crime, but under what circumstances does it fail to do so?

We must start with an important distinction: Religion versus religiosity. Religion refers to particular systems of supernatural belief, such as Hinduism, Christianity, Islam, Judaism, Buddhism, and others. It also includes the many denominations or subgroups within these broad religions (e.g., Catholics, Seventh-day Adventists, and Methodists are all Christians). Religiosity, in contrast, is the strength of religious belief or feeling. It is usually measured as the frequency of prayer, regularity of attendance at religious services, and acceptance of religious beliefs (e.g., in God or an afterlife). Most research on religion and crime is actually about religiosity and crime.

What we find about the religiosity-crime relationship depends on our level of analysis. The world's 10 most secular (i.e., nonreligious) nations—Sweden, Denmark, Norway, Czech Republic, Estonia, Japan, Britain, France, the Netherlands, Germany, South Korea, New Zealand, Australia, Vietnam, Hungary, China, and Belgium—have some of the world's lowest crime rates.[128] The U.S. states with the highest levels of religiosity—Alabama, Mississippi, Tennessee, Louisiana, Arkansas, South Carolina, West Virginia, Georgia, Oklahoma, and North Carolina—are among the most violent.[129] However, this does not mean that religiosity promotes crime. Secular nations tend to be wealthy nations with robust social welfare policies. Religious U.S. states are mostly lower-income states located in the South. Religiosity is a correlate but not necessarily a cause of state- and nation-level crime rates.

Religiosity is a protective factor against crime on the individual level. On average, people who are very religious engage in less law-breaking than those who are less religious.[130] Religious adolescents report lower rates of nonviolent crimes and substance use than their less-religious peers.[131] The same is true of adults.[132] Even prisoners who are or become religious engage in less prison misconduct than their fellow inmates.[133] Religiosity—whether in prison or not—can alleviate depression and provide a positive way of coping with negative feelings.[134] Criminologists credit religion as a source of proso-cial values and social bonds that keep people from pursuing acts that violate religious principles.[135] Religious practice also demands self-control that, in turn, prevents criminal behavior.[136]

Religiosity is especially important for desistance (i.e., leaving crime behind).[137] It allows prisoners to build "desistance narratives" both during and after incarceration. Desistance narratives are stories people tell themselves and others about why they used to commit crime and why crime no longer fits in their lives. Religion supplies "redemption scripts" that emphasize one's former life as a sinner, as con-trasted with an optimistic "new self" that can persevere through tough times with social and spiritual support.[138]

There are exceptions, of course. Few studies examine atheists (i.e., nonbelievers) and agnostics and crime, but those that do exist find no difference in the criminality of nonbelievers and believers.[139] Plus, people who espouse Christian fundamentalist religious beliefs are more likely than others to also espouse support for intimate partner violence and to engage in these violent acts.[140] They are also more likely to condone beliefs that support child physical abuse ("spare the rod, spoil the child").[141] Fundamentalism is characterized by belief that religious texts are the literal word of God, strict adher-ence to religious principles, intolerance of other views, and opposition to secularism. Support for rigid hierarchies and a male-dominated home life help explain the link between fundamentalism and fam-ily violence. Fundamentalist beliefs also predict support for honor-based violence in Muslim-majority nations, including killing of relatives who have dishonored one's family through premarital or extra-marital sex.[142] Fundamentalism matters for violence because

> *To people with religious fundamentalist attitudes, acting against religious norms might, thus, not just represent behavioral transgression, but might constitute an existential threat to their social iden-tity and worldview, which consequently might elicit extreme responses to punish the offender. (pp. 12-13).*[143]

TEMPORAL AND ECOLOGICAL PATTERNS

What time of day do you think household burglaries are most likely to occur? What day of the week do you think there are the most sex offenses? Which season has the most assault? And which year was the worst for homicide in the U.S.? These are all questions about temporal patterns in crime, which are time-based. They range from small units like hours in the day to yearly trends and even variation across historical eras, as observed in Figure 5.5. The answers, by the way, are: (1) Residential burglaries are more likely to occur during daytime hours when the home is left unoccupied.[144] (2) There isn't a day with more sex offenses than other days, though outdoor rapes, which are more likely than other sex offenses to be committed by strangers, are more common on weekends during nighttime hours.[145] (3) Summer has the most assaults, and seasonal variation in crime is especially noticeable in places where the climate changes a great deal from season to season.[146] (4) The year with the highest homicide rate in the past century in the U.S. is 1980 (10.2 homicides per 100,000 people in the population).

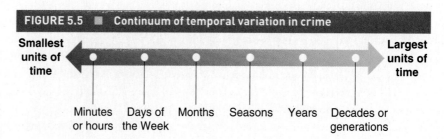

FIGURE 5.5 ■ Continuum of temporal variation in crime

Smallest units of time → Largest units of time

Minutes or hours | Days of the Week | Months | Seasons | Years | Decades or generations

Studying hour-to-hour and day-to-day patterns in crime requires thinking in terms of the "crimino-logical day" rather than the calendar day.[147] Imagine two assaults, one that takes place at 11:30 p.m. on Friday night and another that takes place an hour later. If we use midnight as the break between Friday and Saturday, then these assaults occurred on different days. But did they *really*? Criminologists who study temporal patterns think not. Instead, they consider the "criminological day" to start at 5:00 a.m. or thereabouts.[148] Using this approach, they find that crimes do, in fact, follow distinct daily patterns.[149] For example, criminologists find that burglaries and thefts are much more likely to occur on weekdays than weekend days when examining data from the Vancouver police.[150]

Another factor we need to consider is that timing of crime changes depending on location. For instance, violent crime in public transportation areas, like bus and subway stations, is greater in winter months as passengers crowd indoors to avoid the cold.[151] This runs counter to the typical finding that homicides, assaults, and sex offenses peak in warm-weather months when people are outside, coming into contact (and conflict) with one another.[152]

No temporal topic captures criminologists' attention more than yearly patterns in crime rates, especially homicide rates.[153] Understanding what drives crime up and then back down has spawned the creation of numerous theories about the likely contributors. There are two eras of homicide trends that fascinate criminologists: (1) the rapid rise of homicide rates from the late 1960s through early 1980s, and (2) the steep decline of homicide rates from the early 1990s through the 2000s, which are depicted in Figure 5.6. The sharp increase in homicides in 2020 also captures the attention of crime scholars, but most conclude that short-term fluctuations are insufficient to declare a trend, especially considering the unusual pandemic circumstances of the year.[154]

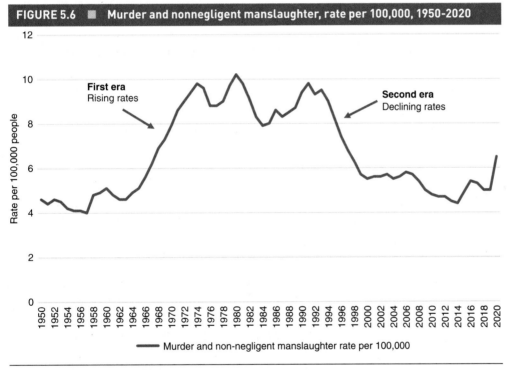

FIGURE 5.6 ■ Murder and nonnegligent manslaughter, rate per 100,000, 1950–2020

Legend: —— Murder and non-negligent manslaughter rate per 100,000

Source: Federal Bureau of Investigation, Crime in the United States.

Let's begin with the first era, when homicides skyrocketed. The size of the youth population is a favored explanation.[155] The share of the U.S. population in their crime-prone years—late teens to early 20s—ballooned as Baby Boomers (born in the post-WWII years) reached maturity in the late 1960s and early 1970s. More young people equals more crime. Others noted that the economic plight of city dwellers, particularly African Americans, worsened substantially in the 1970s as jobs disappeared and the middle class—first whites and then middle-class African Americans and others—fled to the suburbs, taking businesses and tax dollars with them. The result was the kind of extremely concentrated poverty in which violence flourishes.[156] A third likely contributor is the expansion of gun manufacturing and imports during this era. There were far more firearms in circulation in the 1970s in the U.S. than in the early 1960s, and gun availability is a strong predictor of lethal violence.[157]

It's not always true that what goes up must come down, but that was certainly the case for U.S. homicide rates. The "great crime decline" of the 1990s and 2000s, as it is now known, is a source of speculation.[158] Theories of its causes can be sorted into two types: (1) changes in specific opportunities for offending, and (2) changes that broadly affected ways of life.[159] Table 5.1 displays crime decline explanations that receive at least some empirical support or make logical sense and have yet to be disconfirmed. It is likely that all or most had some small hand in bringing down the U.S. crime rate.

TABLE 5.1 ■ Crime decline explanations	
Category	**Explanation**
Changes in specific opportunities for offending	Effective security devices that increase the risk of detection proliferated during this period.
	This era saw substantial changes in policing, including policing strategies and increased numbers of police officers.
	The scale of punishment and incarceration exploded during this era in the U.S., locking up more people who might otherwise commit crime.
	The spread of offender re-entry programs helped people exiting prison get back on their feet and avoid re-offending.
	Crack cocaine markets, which had been the setting for violent turf disputes and had encouraged young men to carry handguns, faded.
	Drug prices for heroin, crack, and cocaine fell, which decreased competition-fueled crimes among sellers and reliance on crime to finance drug habits among users.
	Increasing reliance on credit cards, e-commerce, and electronic welfare payments (EBT) reduced cash transactions. Crimes for economic gain declined with the reduction in cash circulating.
Changes that broadly affected the way of life	The proliferation of cell phones, the Internet, and the rise of home entertainment altered how and where people interact (i.e., keeping them at home). May have reduced direct-contact crime while increasing cybercrime.
	Improving labor market factors, including reduced unemployment, suppressed crime rates.
	Aging of the population has meant that a shrinking proportion of the population is in the crime-prone years of their late teens and early 20s.
	An overall decline in alcohol and drug consumption reduced aggression and violence.
	Reductions in exposure to lead in infancy and childhood in the 1970s produced a lagged effect on crime 20-25 years later by cutting the number of people with lead-related cognitive impairments, including poor impulse control.
	Increases in prescriptions for effective psychotropic medications, including antipsychotics, reduced aggression, violence, and impulsive behaviors.
	The growth of nonprofit organizations in high-crime communities, including programs for youth recreation, job training, and substance abuse prevention, suppressed the crime rate.

Sources: Tcherni-Buzzeo, M. (2019). The "great American crime decline": Possible explanations. In M. Krohn, N. Hendrix, G. P. Hall, & A. Lizotte (Eds.), *Handbook on crime and deviance* (pp. 309-335). Cham: Springer; Sharkey, P., Torrats-Espinosa, G., & Takyar, D. (2017). Community and the crime decline: The causal effect of local nonprofits on violent crime. *American Sociological Review, 82*(6), 1214-1240; Wright, R., Tekin, E., Topalli, V., McClellan, C., Dickinson, T., & Rosenfeld, R. (2017). Less cash, less crime: Evidence from the electronic benefit transfer program. *Journal of Law and Economics, 60*(2), 361-383.

Ecological patterns are about differences across space, or geographic location, in rates of crime. Like time, units of geographic space range from very small (intersections of streets) to enormous (regions and nations), as seen in Figure 5.7. For example, homicide rates vary tremendously across countries, as shown in Figure 5.8. Within each nation, there are regions—including states, provinces, counties, cities and towns, and communities—with vastly different rates of crime. Consider, for instance, the rate of violent crime was greater than 750 offenses per 100,000 people in New Mexico and Alaska in 2020 while it was under 150 offenses per 100,000 in Maine and New Hampshire.[160] Even cities with similar population sizes within the same state can look very different. For example, California cities Oakland and Long Beach have about the same number of residents (440,646 in Oakland and 466,742 in Long Beach), but Oakland's rate of violent crime was more than double Long Beach's rate in 2020.[161]

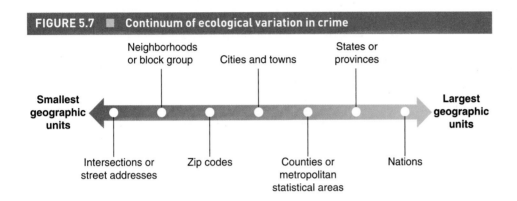

FIGURE 5.7 ■ Continuum of ecological variation in crime

Rates of crime differ across large geographic regions. High rates of interpersonal violence, including homicide, in the U.S. South (relative to other regions of the U.S.) have prompted the development of the "Southern culture of violence" explanation. This perspective views Southern tolerance of violence as the result of honor-based norms that endured over the past several centuries, first emerging prior to the Civil War in response to the absence of formal law.[162] Within this culture, argument-based threats to masculine honor, family, and property can be resolved through violent confrontation, though other forms of violence (e.g., indiscriminate violence or violence in the course of a felony) are not tolerated or condoned.[163] Criminologists apply this cultural explanation specifically to white violence in the South.[164] Some point to the brutalizing effects of slavery as responsible for an enduring Southern proclivity towards violence.[165] The heavy concentration of early Scots-Irish settlers, said to have imported a culture of honor, fierce independence, and tolerance for violent dispute resolution, is another explanation.[166] Skeptics counter that Southern violence is a product of structure, not culture: The South is poorer and has greater inequality than other regions of the country.[167] Nonetheless, even taking structural disadvantages into account, criminologists document excessive rates of white dispute-based lethal violence in Southern states and cities.[168] Additionally, in surveys, rural Southern white men endorse the use of violence in response to hypothetical confrontations more so than do other racial, regional, and gender groups.[169]

Ecological analyses in criminology often focus on intersections of roads, street segments (both sides of a street between two intersections), or neighborhood blocks, as crime tends to concentrate in these areas.[170] The small percentage of places responsible for the majority of crime in a geographic location are called **crime hotspots**.[171] Hotspots can include types of facilities in addition to the intersections and street segments. Bus stops, bars, payday lending businesses, motels, and abandoned buildings can be hotspots for drug offenses, assaults, robberies, or other forms of crime.[172] The primary criminological explanations for hotspot concentration of crime emphasize either opportunities for offending (e.g., high-traffic locations like subway stations and bars provide ample opportunities for offenders and victims to come together) or social disorganization, in which some locations lack behavioral controls that prevent crime.[173]

Ecological and temporal patterns happen in tandem. Because crime is clustered at hotspots (ecological pattern), crime rates can change dramatically over time (temporal pattern) as a result of changes in a small number of places. For example, just 24% of street segments were responsible for 87% of Albany's crime decline between 2001 and 2013.[174]

FIGURE 5.8   ■   Homicide rate per 100,000 people in population, by nation, 2017

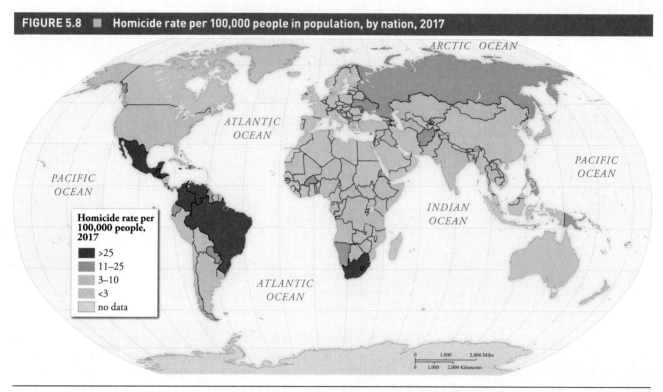

Source: Max Roser and Hannah Ritchie. (2013). Homicides. Published online at OurWorldInData.org. Licensed under CC BY 4.0. https://ourworldindata.org/grapher/share-of-deaths-homicides?tab=chart

Crime tends to concentrate in micro-places like specific intersections or street segments.

iStockphoto / Photo Italia LLC

ENGAGED CRIMINOLOGY 5.2

Analyzing Temporal Patterns

This activity asks you to analyze temporal patterns in criminal offenses in a U.S. city. Figure 5.9 depicts day-to-day patterns in all reported assaults, burglaries, and robberies in Chicago, Illinois, occurring during the four-week period of November 15, 2021, to December 12, 2021. Use the figure and your knowledge of the "criminological day" to answer the questions.

FIGURE 5.9 ■ Number of assaults, burglaries, and robberies by day of the week in Chicago, Illinois, November 15, 2021, to December 12, 2021

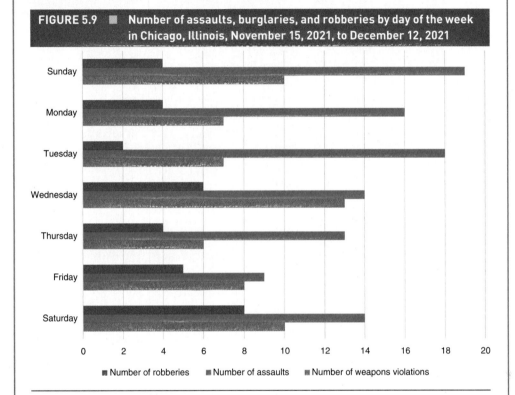

Source: Chicago Police Department.

Answer the following questions using evidence from the figure:

1. Do there appear to be day-to-day temporal patterns in assaults, burglaries, and robberies in Chicago? Provide numbers from Figure 5.9 in your answer. Offer an explanation for what you observe.

2. Figure 5.9 uses 5:00 a.m. as the cutoff for the "criminological day," instead of midnight. In one or two sentences, make a case for whether midnight or 5:00 a.m. is a more appropriate cutoff.

3. Do you think you would observe different patterns if the data came from summer months instead of November 15 to December 12? Explain.

CRIMINAL INCIDENT PATTERNS

A criminal incident is a single criminal event, like the mass murder in Atlanta, the attempted carjacking in Chicago, the drive-by shooting in Florida, and the foiled Arizona car theft described at the chapter's start. What takes place during a criminal incident—the number of offenders, the use of weapons, whether the offenders are drunk or high on drugs—is part of the foreground of crime. The foreground refers to the dynamics of the crime situation in the moment when the offense takes place.[175] It stands in contrast to the background of crime, or what happened in the offender's life prior to, and predicting, criminal offending. Demographic and institutional correlates of crime tell us about the background of crime, whereas criminal incident patterns tell us about the foreground of crime.[176]

Number of Offenders

Co-offending is the commission of crime by two or more people. Offenses with multiple participants are often referred to as group crimes, but this is misleading, as most co-offending involves only two offenders.[177] "Lone offenders" or "solo offenders" are individuals who commit offenses by themselves. Most violent crimes are committed by lone offenders; according to the Bureau of Justice Statistics, 87.6% of violent offenses in 2018 had just one perpetrator.[178] The remaining 12.4% had multiple offenders, and the average number of offenders across all violent incidents was 1.29 people.

Criminal events with multiple perpetrators are more violent and produce greater injury than crimes committed by lone offenders.[179] This is frequently attributed to the diffusion of responsibility, wherein no one person feels fully responsible for the harm done in groups, leading to reduced inhibitions.[180] Consistent with this, there is an inverse relationship between the size of the offending group and the anticipated likelihood of punishment.[181] In other words, group offenders are less fearful about the legal consequences of their actions. Their perceptions are incorrect, however, as NIBRS data show that robbery co-offenders are, in fact, more likely to be arrested than lone offenders.[182]

Individuals in co-offending pairs and groups usually share characteristics—they are typically around the same age, the same ethnicity, the same gender, from the same area of residence, and with the same level of criminal experience.[183] This pattern is called *homophily*, which is the tendency of people to select into groups comprised of people like themselves. In addition, offending groups form based on the people most readily available. The pool of potential accomplices tends to be composed of people with similar life circumstances and demographic characteristics. Co-offenders come together in "convergence settings," like schools, street corners, and jails or prisons, which furnish a steady stream of potential accomplices and provide opportunities for collaborative law-breaking.[184]

Patterns of co-offending map onto age-crime curves.[185] Young people are more likely to commit their crimes with other people than are older offenders.[186] This is especially true for offenses like homicide, burglary, and robbery. Among adolescents, the majority of arrests for these crimes are of co-offenders (68% for homicide, 64% for burglary, and 58% for robbery, in one study using NIBRS data). The co-offender percentages drop off for adults over age 24 (to 25%, 21%, and 23%, respectively).[187]

There are several explanations for the tendency of the young to co-offend. First, relative to adults, young people spend more of their social time doing things in groups, with crime just one of many group activities.[188] Second, young people are more susceptible than adults to group influence. Worry about peer ridicule and the desire to attain status and demonstrate group loyalty compels young people to engage in acts that they would not pursue on their own.[189] Many youth accomplices (or "followers") desist from crime once adolescence ends, while co-offending instigators ("leaders" or "recruiters" who convince others to commit group crimes) are more apt to persist into adulthood.[190] Third, some co-offenders transform into lone offenders as they age, due to developing criminal expertise and a dwindling pool of potential accomplices. There are fewer co-offenders available as their peers begin to age out of crime, consistent with the age-crime curve.[191]

Weapons

By definition, crimes committed with weapons are violent crimes. That is why robbery, which necessarily involves force or threat of force, is a violent offense whereas larceny is not. Some violent crimes do not involve weapons like firearms or knives. Instead, they involve physical force or "personal weapons," such as the use of hitting, kicking, biting, or strangulation. Table 5.2 displays the frequency of weapon/force types across multiple violent offenses reported by NIBRS in 2020.

It is important to distinguish between presence of weapons and use of weapons. Consider that more than half (55.1%) of victims of serious violent crime (aggravated assault, robbery, and rape or sexual assault) report being injured when no weapon was used, compared to 13.7% of victims whose offenders possessed a firearm and 22.9% whose offenders possessed a knife.[192] This seemingly counterintuitive finding—that the presence of weapons is associated with lower risk of injury—arises from the low likelihood of a gun being fired or a knife being used to stab a victim during the criminal incident.[193] A person can possess a knife or gun and use it to threaten a victim to gain their compliance without injuring them.[194] In contrast, there is no "possession" equivalent when it comes to physical force. After

TABLE 5.2 ■ Offense category by type of weapon or force involved, 2020 (NIBRS)				
Type of weapon/force	Aggravated assault	Homicide	Rape	Robbery
Total firearm	**123,669**	7,482	1,234	47,482
Knife/cutting instrument	**61,924**	877	800	8641
Personal weapon	**74,403**	415	36,529	30,607
All other	**97,954**	960	27,891	18,580
Blunt object	39,643	203	285	3,348
Motor vehicle	0	0	0	0
Poison	485	3	10	83
Explosives	250	2	0	43
Fire/incendiary device	865	48	7	37
Drugs/sleeping pills	456	88	747	36
Asphyxiation	10,640	51	211	119
Other weapon	29,497	150	2,092	3,793
Unknown weapon	7,772	415	5,958	3,300
None reported	8346	n/a	18,581	7,821

Notes: "None reported" includes offenses for which no weapon/force was reported by law enforcement (does not indicate absence of weapon/force). Reporting agencies must report weapon/force for homicide. "Personal weapons" are parts of the body, such as fists, feet, or teeth.

Source: FBI, NIBRS, "Type of weapon involved by offense, 2020."

all, we all have bodies. By default, all non-weapon violence involves use or threatened use of a "personal weapon" (one's body). Indeed, 100% of aggravated assaults involving personal weapons result in injury, by definition.[195]

The *use* of weapons in a criminal incident, especially the use of a firearm, substantially increases the risk of serious injury or death.[196] Gunshot victims are seven times as likely to die as victims of knife attacks.[197] Gun assaults are 11 times more lethal than unarmed (or personal weapon) assaults.[198] Other studies find even larger fatality gaps across weapon types.[199] Importantly, these differences in injury persist even when controlling for the offender's intent to kill.[200] In other words, the difference in lethality is not due to gun assailants possessing a stronger desire to kill their victims than knife-wielding assailants.

Criminal offenders use weapons to "facilitate compliance, inflict pain, or mete out punishment" (p. 42).[201] Their motivations, in part, determine the type of weapon or force selected. For example, an analysis of 705 homicide incidents in Newark, New Jersey, identified three general forms of motivation with distinct patterns of weapon use.[202] The three types were

1. *Doing crime* – Offenders and victims immersed in a criminal lifestyle, including drug market participation and gang activity.

2. *Establishing moral order* – Offenders target intimates whom they perceive as violating moral ideals such as sexual fidelity or parental authority.

3. *Demanding esteem* – Offenders use violence in response to direct challenges to their status in an effort to save face and avoid humiliation or disrespect.

Most firearm homicides (73%) involved "doing crime," and they frequently involved planned aggression that took place in a public setting. For this group, carrying a firearm was part of a crime-involved lifestyle. In fact, in firearm homicides involving "doing crime" and "demanding esteem," it was common for both the offender and victim to be armed. Homicides committed with blunt objects, knives, or fists were largely unplanned acts committed against intimates or acquaintances in private residences. These expressive offenses were likely to involve "establishing the moral order."[203]

Substance Use

If you have ever heard alcohol referred to as liquid courage, then you are familiar with the notion that substances can reduce behavioral inhibitions. Alcohol and drug use shape criminal involvement in several ways, and not always in a "liquid courage" way. Ethnographic studies of instrumental offenders—residential burglars, armed robbers, identity thieves—show that crime is typically a way to "keep the party going," facilitating continued drug and alcohol use once money has run dry.[204] In such situations, acute intoxication, or being drunk or high in the moment, does not necessarily lead to offending. Instead, the desire to obtain more substances drives offenders' behavior. The same motivation is observed among individuals who commit acquisitive crimes to stave off opiate withdrawal.[205] These are substances' "economic-compulsive" effects (like needing money to get drugs or alcohol) rather than "psychopharmacological effects," which are physiological effects of substance use that induce violence and lower inhibitions against crime.[206]

But what about the role of substance-altered states during the course of a criminal incident? Indeed, the decline of alcohol use is offered as a contributor to the substantial decline in U.S. crime rates during the 1990s and 2000s (recall Table 5.1). NIBRS data demonstrate that alcohol and drug use is observed among a small but not insubstantial percentage of offenses. NIBRS offenses are only marked as drug- or alcohol-involved if offenders display obvious signs of impairment, resulting in undercounts.[207] Surveys of prisoners suggest much higher rates of alcohol use during criminal events, with more than a third of incarcerated men reporting being drunk at the time of the offense that landed them in prison.[208] Violent crimes, in particular, are likely to involve alcohol, with simple assault and aggravated assault most likely to be committed by an intoxicated offender.[209] These results aren't specific to the United States. In a study of homicide across nine nations, 48% of homicide offenders were drinking at the time of the killing.[210]

TABLE 5.3 ■ Percentage of violent offenses with suspected drug or alcohol use, 2019 (NIBRS)		
Offense	Percentage of offenses with suspected offender alcohol use	Percentage of offenses with suspected offender drug use
Assault	10.3%	2.5%
Homicide	6.5%	5.1%
Kidnapping	9.6%	5.3%
Sex offenses	7.2%	3.3%
Robbery	1.9%	2.0%

Source: FBI, NIBRS, "Offenses Involving Offender's Suspected Use, Drugs/Narcotics and Alcohol by Offense Category, 2019."

Alcohol is a central nervous system depressant. It affects the reward center of the brain, producing a sense of pleasure while also slowing down cognitive processing (i.e., thinking) and interrupting anticipatory processing of cues about rewards, or understanding of consequences. Intoxication causes people to become present-oriented rather than future-oriented.[211] The result is impulsive decision-making and risk-seeking, precursors to aggression.[212] "Liquid courage" is better characterized as "liquid disinhibition," including disinhibitions against violence and other conduct with serious long-term consequences, like incarceration.

CHAPTER SUMMARY

LO 5.1   Explain what correlates of crime are, and what they are not.

Correlates of crime are individual- or structural-level variables that are associated with individual offending or crime rates in a statistical sense. They do not indicate perfect, or one-to-one, relationships, nor do they indicate causation.

LO 5.2   Describe demographic patterns in criminal offending.

Established demographic correlates of street crime offending include age, sex, social class, race and ethnicity, and immigration status. Criminologists document an age-crime curve, a gender gap in offending, impacts of poverty and high school non-completion, and racial disproportionality in crime. They find an inverse relationship between immigration status and crime. Demographic correlation does not equal causation.

LO 5.3   Identify the structural-level institutional predictors of crime rates.

Structural correlates are macro-level societal conditions that influence individual offending and crime rates. They include levels of family disruption, unemployment rates and consumer sentiment, concentrated poverty, and immigration rates.

LO 5.4   Differentiate between temporal and ecological patterns in criminology.

Temporal patterns are time-based patterns in crime frequency. They range from small units like hours of the day to large units like decades or generations. Ecological patterns are crime rate variations across geographic space. They range from small units like street segments and intersections to large units like regions and nations.

LO 5.5   Describe patterns in co-offending, weapon use, and offender substance use.

Most violence crime is committed by lone offenders, but adolescent offenders co-offend at high rates, especially in homicides, robberies, and burglaries. Weapon use, especially firearm use, increases the risk of serious injury or death irrespective of the intent to kill, despite the lower overall risk of injury when a weapon is present. Substance intoxication, especially alcohol use, is common during violent criminal incidents.

ENGAGED DISCUSSION

1. Think of an example of a real-life criminal case (from this book or elsewhere). Consider the broader patterns of which that case is a part. What correlates of crime do you observe in those patterns?

2. Come up with one criminal offense that you believe is not linked to any demographic characteristic (like age, sex, and social class). Explain your thinking.

3. Why do you think intimate partner violence increases more than other forms of violence during periods of unemployment?

4. Which of the explanations in Table 5.1 can also explain the crime decline observed in countries other than the U.S., such as Germany and Australia, during the same time period?

5. Which type of violent offending do you think is especially likely to involve co-offending: "doing crime," "establishing moral order," or "demanding esteem"? Explain.

KEY TERMS

Age-crime curve (p. 114)

Chivalry hypothesis (p. 116)

Co-offending (p. 134)

Correlates of crime (p. 112)

Crime hotspots (p. 131)

Disparity (p. 120)

Ecological patterns (p. 130)

Economic marginalization hypothesis (p. 117)

ORIGINS OF CRIMINOLOGY

On January 24, 2019, at 7:45 in the morning, a 911 dispatcher received a call for help. They heard a woman screaming and referring to a knife. Police were dispatched to an off-campus apartment near Radford University in Virginia where they expected to find a domestic disturbance. Instead, they found 21-year-old university student Luisa Cutting covered in blood and confessing to murdering her best friend and roommate, 20-year-old Alexa Cannon. She turned around, put her hands behind her back, and said, "Arrest me" and "I killed her."[1] The police found Cutting's victim inside the apartment. She had been stabbed between 30 and 40 times.

Police described Cutting's interrogation as a "rambling and bizarre series of episodes" that included reciting the Hail Mary in Spanish over and over, talking about the apocalypse, praying, and claiming that she did "cocaine with the devil."[2] At one point while being held in jail, Cutting attempted to stuff her whole hand into her mouth and was transferred to a mental health facility.

Details of events leading up to the crime emerged as Cutting's criminal case proceeded. Cutting and Cannon had been friends since 2016, and both appeared to be ordinary college students. They traveled together, left funny comments on each other's Instagram posts, and held campus leadership positions. But Cutting's party lifestyle had escalated since the young women moved in together. She admitted to using a variety of illicit and legal substances on the night before and on the morning of the murder, and police found evidence of her claims in the apartment. Experts concluded that a combination of cocaine, Adderall, Xanax, psilocybin (hallucinogenic) mushrooms, alcohol, and sleep deprivation brought on Cutting's psychotic episode that ended in murder. Cutting eventually pleaded guilty to second-degree murder and was sentenced to 20 years in prison to be followed by 10 years of probation.[3]

Today, we understand this tragic murder as a result of an acute mental health crisis prompted by excessive substance use. Cutting's punishment reflected the seriousness of the crime and her level of culpability (she became intoxicated voluntarily but did not premeditate the murder). But how would Cutting's crime have been understood in previous centuries? Her sudden criminality would likely have signaled demonic possession in pre-criminology societies. Certainly, her claims of "doing cocaine with the devil" and her religious incantations after the crime would have evoked a supernatural explanation. Crime scholars of the 18th century, like Cesare Beccaria, may have disregarded her impaired judgment, instead seeing crime as flowing from calculating decisions of rational people. In any event, they would argue that she should be punished as all murderers are punished—with a sentence proportional to the seriousness of her offense. Nineteenth and early 20th century criminologists, like Cesare Lombroso, would have wondered about her natural tendencies towards crime and whether her body bore the markers of biological and moral inferiority.

Perspectives on crime and people who commit crimes have come a long way over the past few centuries, and it is easy to look back on criminology's forebearers with amusement or horror. Yet we owe a debt of gratitude to these early scholars of crime. The rights granted to criminal defendants like Luisa Cutting would probably not exist without classical school criminologists. Positivist school criminologists' emphasis on objective, systematic research on crime ultimately led to our present-day understanding of the psychological predictors of violent behavior (and the knowledge that most people experiencing mental health crises do not engage in criminal violence). In fact, the high-profile nature of Cutting's homicidal behavior is due, in part, to its unusualness, or the fact that it does not comport with well-established empirical patterns in crime.

THE EARLIEST EXPLANATIONS OF CRIME

Criminology, as a discipline in the social sciences, has existed for only about two centuries. It had its first rumblings in the 18th century, though crime-focused thinkers of the 1700s were primarily philosophers and legal scholars rather than researchers. Of course, humans had plenty of folk theories about crime and deviance stretching back far before the development of the scientific method. The term *folk theories* refers to everyday "commonsense" explanations rather than abstract explanations composed of proposed, testable relationships between two or more concepts. There is, however, little in common between the common sense of one time period and the common sense of another. For instance, the practice of bloodletting, either through cuts or use of leeches, was a commonsense response to illness for three millennia in Europe and beyond.[4] Contemporary U.S. common sense tells us to run from any doctor recommending leech therapy for your asthma. Novelist L. P. Hartley may have put it best: "The past is a foreign country; they do things differently there."[5]

Two commonalities across eras and geographic locations are that (1) explanations of crime and deviance reflect the overall concerns, ideas, and philosophies of the societies in which they were developed, and (2) those explanations determine how the society responds to rule breakers. Since the 18th century, criminological thought has reflected a secularized view of the world. Sociologist Peter Berger describes *secularization* as "the process by which sectors of society and culture are removed from the domination of religious institutions and symbols" (p. 107).[6] This does not mean that individuals' or groups' religious involvement and beliefs don't factor into some criminological theories (they do!), but rather that the *sources* of criminal behavior are no longer believed to be otherworldly or supernatural. In other words, no criminologists suggest "the devil made them do it." In contrast, pre-classical theories of crime—those dating before the 18th century rise of the classical school in criminology—are largely demonological.[7]

Pre-Classical Demonic Perspective

The demonic perspective on crime, the earliest recorded explanation, conflates crime and deviance with sin. Deviance is understood as an offense against God, the gods, or some other supernatural entity (the word *deviance* encapsulates both criminal actions and nonnormative behaviors that are punished regardless of formal prohibitions). In this view, people, torn between the supernatural forces of good and evil, engage in deviant behavior when either (1) tempted by demonic forces or (2) possessed by evil spirits.[8] Supernatural explanations, though varied in their details, proliferated throughout the pre-classical world.[9]

The temptation-possession distinction plays out in the witchcraft trials of the Massachusetts Bay Colony in 1692.[10] It began when two girls, ages 9 and 11, started having violent fits, contorting their bodies and screaming out. A local physician diagnosed them with bewitchment, a "taking over" of the innocent by a demonic spirit, or possession. Soon after, more girls and young women in the community began showing similar markers of possession. They incriminated three particularly vulnerable women—an enslaved woman from Barbados (Tituba), a disliked older woman (Sara Good), and a woman who had scandalized her Puritan neighbors by being romantically involved with a man to whom she was not married (Sara Osbourne). The women, accused of consorting with the devil (or temptation), were convicted and executed. The possessed girls were pressed for more names. They offered them. In the end, 20 people were executed after being convicted of witchcraft; contrary to popular imagination, none were burned at the stake (19 were hanged, and 1 was crushed to death with heavy stones).

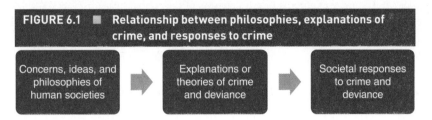

FIGURE 6.1 ■ **Relationship between philosophies, explanations of crime, and responses to crime**

Concerns, ideas, and philosophies of human societies ⇒ Explanations or theories of crime and deviance ⇒ Societal responses to crime and deviance

The concerns, ideas, and philosophies of the Puritans of the Massachusetts Bay Colony informed their explanation of deviance and their response to it, as depicted in Figure 6.1. They believed that the human world was a battlefield for the forces of good and evil and that those lacking extreme self-discipline were vulnerable to the temptations of the devil. In fact, their definition of witchcraft *as crime* mirrored their supernatural concerns. In turn, their response to deviance made sense in the logic of their demonological theory. Those tempted by evil spirits cannot be corrected through 30 days in jail, after all. Only execution would ensure the spiritual safety of the community. Another option used in societies that embraced demonic thinking—exorcism, or "dispossession"—was off the table for the Puritans, who were prevented by church doctrine from engaging in the practice or in "magic rites."[11]

Matteson's 1853 painting "Examination of a Witch" took inspiration from the Salem witch trials. It depicts the examination of a woman's body for signs of the devil, including moles and birthmarks.

"Examination of a Witch" painting by Tompkins Harrison Matteson, 1853, accessed via Wikimedia Creative Commons.

"Criminal Justice" in the Demonic Perspective

Demonological explanations are evident in the widespread use of trial by ordeal to determine guilt, especially during its peak in the Middle Ages (5th to 15th centuries). Trial by ordeal was a "pain-producing diagnostic technique" used to identify signs of divine presence to sort good (faithful and innocent) from evil (deviant and guilty).[12] In short, it was torture. In the demonic view, only innocents protected by a higher power could persevere through the ordeal or heal afterwards. For example, in a form of trial by fire used in England, the accused would be required to walk nine feet across red-hot ploughshares (metal component of a plow) while carrying a red-hot iron bar. If their wounds were festering three days later, they were determined to be guilty. Cleanly healing wounds announced innocence.[13] In trial by poison, the accused was required to ingest a poisonous substance. For example, the Efik people of West Africa used the poisonous calabar bean,[14] and the toxic tangena nut was used in Madagascar.[15] If the defendant vomited up the tangena nut or survived ingestion of the calabar bean? Innocent! Otherwise, they were proclaimed guilty (and proclaimed dead, as well, in many cases; 1 out of 10 poison-takers died in Madagascar). Additional forms used throughout the world included trial by water and trial by combat.

In Medieval Europe, during the height of the demonic perspective and trial by ordeal, the type of deviance—adultery, murder, heresy (violating religious doctrine)—was unimportant: All were the devil's handiwork. Therefore, the punishments for the guilty were imbued with religious fervor. Brutal, excruciating punishments and mutilating executions "underscored the subordination of natural bodies to supernatural struggles between good and evil" (p. 29).[16] Burning as torture and execution spiked during the Spanish Inquisition, with the belief that fire would provide the sinner a sample of hell prior to death.[17] Apotropaic rituals, or rituals intended to purge evil spirits, accompanied the executions of deviants. Instruments and practices were developed to inflict the maximum amount of damage to the physical form, to compel confessions, punish the sinner, drive out the evil, and provide a gruesome spectacle for onlookers.[18]

Have you ever heard these expressions before?

- "To cut off your nose to spite your face"
- "To hold one's feet to the fire"
- "A slow burn"
- "To be drawn and quartered"
- "To be racked with pain"

All refer to methods of punishment meted out in earlier centuries. In Medieval Europe, cutting off someone's nose was the ultimate spiteful act, and laws called for cutting off noses for crimes such as prostitution, heresy, and treason.[19] Amputation of hands, ears, and tongues were also codified in law, as were branding and blinding.[20] Punitive limb amputations, in fact, have a long history in human societies, with evidence of the practice in the Babylonian Code of Hammurabi (around 1750 BCE), for the physician's crime of accidentally blinding or killing nobles or for enslaved people who assaulted free citizens, as well as in ancient Peru (starting 300 BCE) and in the Roman and Byzantine empires.[21]

The phrases that invoke fire imagery have their roots in the use of burning as torture and execution. And the reference to being "drawn and quartered" harks back to an execution method for the crime of treason, first sentenced in England in 1283. The convicted person was tied to a horse and dragged to the gallows (or drawn) where they were then faced some combination of further torments, including being hanged (but not typically to death), being disemboweled while still alive, having their entrails burned, and being beheaded. Quartering, the final stage, was the splitting of the body in four, sometimes accomplished by tying each limb to a different horse and sending them running in four directions. The practice was outlawed in England in 1870.[22]

The roots of "being racked with pain" are found in a torture device dating back to ancient Greece and popular during the Middle Ages. An accused person would be fastened to the rack by their wrists and ankles. Rollers at either end of the rack would be turned to pull painfully on the elbow, knee, shoulder, and hip joints, ultimately dislocating them, while the accused was interrogated.[23] Other instruments designed to maximize pain included the breaking wheel, an execution device that looked like a large, spoked wheel, used—depending on the time period—to punish street thieves, highway robbers, arsonists, and murderers. The purpose of the wheel was to mutilate the body prior to execution, and this was accomplished by crushing the bones in the limbs before braiding them into the wheel's spokes. What happened next varied. Some were decapitated, some were thrown into a fire, and others were left to die on the wheel over the course of several days while animals scavenged their bodies for food.[24]

Most criminal punishments were not quite so elaborate or torturous as the wheel. Ordinary people who committed crimes—or those convicted of crimes, at least—were more likely to be hanged than drawn and quartered or broken on the wheel. In fact, the introduction of "drop hanging" (hanging by dropping a person a far enough distance to break the neck) in 1783 England was regarded as a moral innovation because it produced instant death.[25] Death sentences were not reserved solely for the most serious offenders. By 1800, there were over 200 capital offenses listed in English law, later called the "Bloody Code."[26] Many of them were nonviolent: poaching, counterfeiting, forgery, theft from a rabbit warren, larceny of 12 pence or more (one-twentieth of a week's wages at the time). And the sentence of death was imposed arbitrarily. Most convicted persons did not pay for their crimes at the gallows. The winners (pardoned) and losers (executed) of the "lottery of justice" were determined by the whims of individual judges.[27]

During the heyday of the demonic view, and particularly in 17th and 18th century Europe and the American colonies, many public punishments inflicted shame rather than mutilating the body. Some accomplished both ends. For example, the punishment for a fishmonger who sold bad fish might be wearing a string of decaying smelts around the neck.[28] The stocks, which restrained the legs, were originally built to hold the accused much like a jail, but they became a source of public humiliation used primarily for nuisance offenses like drunkenness, gambling, and slandering.[29] The pillory similarly transformed the offender into an object of ridicule, restraining them by the neck and wrists; the offender's ears were often nailed to the pillory, as well. In the American colonies, pillory offenses included forgery, cheating, slandering, coin clipping (shaving down coins for counterfeiting), blasphemy, beating one's wife, fortune-telling, arson, sedition, and treason. Public whipping was also common.[30] It was also not unusual for offenders to be branded, typically a letter on the hand, though sometimes on the forehead. For example, well into the 18th century in Maryland, people were branded with a T for thief, M for manslaughter, R for rogue, and S. L. for seditious libel.[31]

The earliest rumblings of criminology emerged from philosophical reactions to the brutality and arbitrariness of pre-classical criminal justice (if it can be called that) in Europe and, to a lesser extent, the American colonies. Explanations of crime and justifications for punishment left the realm of the supernatural as the prevailing perspective shifted from the demonic view to the secularized, rational view put forth by Enlightenment thinkers.

THE CLASSICAL SCHOOL

The history of criminology unfolds in a series of schools of thought. The first school of criminology, the classical school, emerged in mid-18th century Europe, adopting Enlightenment ideas about human nature and society. Said to have taken place during the "long 18th century" (1685-1815), the Enlightenment (also called the Age of Reason) transformed politics, science, and philosophy by questioning forms of authority that dominated in earlier centuries, such as the authority of the church and divine authority of monarchs. Enlightenment thinking centered on humans' free will and their capacity for rationality.[32] Human nature was mutable, or alterable, and therefore human societies could be improved through rational changes. Classical school ideas focused primarily on reforming criminal justice by building a system in which the most rational choice is to not commit crime.

The Social Contract

Classical school thinkers were influenced by early Enlightenment philosophers' ideas about the social contract, first described in Thomas Hobbes's 1651 text *Leviathan*. To understand the social contract, we must first imagine a life in the absence of any government. Hobbes (1588-1679) wrote of the State of Nature, or a lawless state of human existence without a common authority. The consequence is "war of all against all," according to Hobbes.[33] He argued that people are self-centered and greedy in their most primitive state. Their self-interest, when combined with competition over scarce resources and fear of attack from others, leads to endless violence—violence to take from others and violence to defend oneself from others. Even in the absence of quarrel, people strike one another preemptively, fearing that they may otherwise become a target. Hobbes described the consequences of the State of Nature in stark terms:

> In such condition, there is no place for industry; because the fruit thereof is uncertain: and conse-
> quently no culture of the earth; no navigation, nor use of the commodities that may be imported by

sea; no commodious building; no instruments of moving, and removing, such things as require much force; no knowledge of the face of the earth; no account of time; no arts; no letters; no society; and which is worst of all, continual fear, and danger of violent death; and the life of man, solitary, poor, nasty, brutish, and short.[34]

The terrifying conditions of "war of all against all" motivate people, who are presumed rational, to submit to a common authority, or government, who will act as an intervening bystander to violence. Law and criminal punishment for aggressors remove the burden of retaliation from the victim, as well as the need to establish reputation through preemptive attacks. Individuals agree to abide by the government's laws in exchange for the government protecting them from others who wish to do them harm. For example, you have given up the right to enter your neighbor's apartment and take their Xbox by force in exchange for the law protecting you from people who wish to enter your apartment and take *your* Xbox by force. That is the essence of the social contract: "The idea that people invest in the laws of their society with the guarantee that they will be protected from others who violate such rules" (p. 33).[35] Law interrupts the cycle of predation (or predatory attack) and retaliation found in the State of Nature.

The social contract entails two elements that make cooperative living possible. First, people must "collectively and reciprocally renounc[e] the rights they had against one another in the State of Nature."[36] Second, people must give one person or a group of people (like a sovereign or government) the power and authority to enforce the contract. But why would people agree to give up their rights to the state? Self-interest! The State of Nature is a miserable ordeal. When we no longer must focus all attention on protecting ourselves, we can focus our energies elsewhere. Daily life becomes more predictable, and human progress can flourish. Even later Enlightenment philosophers like John Locke, who didn't see the State of Nature as quite so terrible as Hobbes (he saw it as a state of liberty), acknowledged that personal property was not safe without the social contract.[37]

Enlightenment thinkers agreed that people will only buy into the law—that is, the social contract will only be effective—if they have a say in government. Plus, they argued that the social contract will break down under conditions of inequality in the application of law and criminal punishment. It was not uncommon in the 18th century (and centuries prior) for an impoverished, starving bread thief to be sentenced to the gallows while a high-status habitual criminal was dealt with "by the purse," meaning that they purchased a pardon.[38] The social contract is only as strong as people's belief in it, and injustice undermines that belief.

Cesare Beccaria

The most famous thinker of classical school criminology is Cesare Beccaria (1738-1794), more formally known as Cesare Bonesana, Marchese di Beccaria. Beccaria was an Italian legal scholar and author of the 1764 essay *On Crimes and Punishments* (*Dei Delitti e Delle Pene*). His treatise, initially published anonymously at age 26, laid the Enlightenment-inspired foundation for a rational system of justice. It established principles that would come to form the philosophical basis of contemporary legal systems in democratic nations worldwide. It was also the first statement of deterrence theory in criminology.

Beccaria, like any good Enlightenment scholar, believed firmly in the importance of the social contract. He subscribed also to the principle of utilitarianism, another Enlightenment mainstay. Utilitarianism is the notion that law should produce the greatest overall good, or happiness, for society. In this view, both crime and punishment are incompatible with happiness, so both must be minimized. This is best accomplished by applying only the amount of punishment necessary for preventing further

Cesare Bonesana, Marchese di Beccaria (1738-1794), is regarded as the father of classical school criminology.

Painting of Cesare Beccaria by Eliseo Sala, after 1864, accessed via Wikimedia Creative Commons.

law-breaking. Any penalty in excess of what is necessary for inhibiting crime—and any crime not met with an appropriate sanction—creates surplus unhappiness, violating the utilitarian principle. This is a "consequentialist" perspective: It centers on the consequences of punishment for future behavior and future happiness.[39]

Beccaria championed a legal code that was transparent (including public trials), rooted in reason, and applied consistently and equally to all people. Decisions about punishment should not be shaped by vengeance, retaliation, or judges' whims, he wrote. *On Crimes and Punishments* was a repudiation of the arbitrary, brutal, and secretive Medieval version of justice.[40] It is safe to say that Beccaria would not have approved of punitive nose amputation!

Public, uniform, and proportional application of the law are necessary to both maintaining the social contract and preventing crime.[41] Beccaria believed people to be rational actors with free will, as did other Enlightenment thinkers. Thus, they will choose (or use their free will) to commit crime if the benefits of crime outweigh the costs. Punishment is the cost. Likewise, they will opt to abide by the law if the costs of crime exceed its rewards. These are the underpinnings of **deterrence**, the notion that crime can be reduced by altering the costs and benefits associated with offending.

Why, then, did Beccaria disapprove of the cruel punishments of yesteryear if he thought the costs of crime must outweigh the benefits? Flogging, branding, blinding, drawing and quartering, and breaking on the wheel are steep and excessive costs. But in their excess, Beccaria argued, there is a **brutalization effect**. The public becomes accustomed to the savagery and, in turn, behaves even more inhumanely against one another. Criminality, itself, grows more brutal, and this effect outweighs any potential deterrent of extreme sentences.[42] This is one of the reasons Beccaria opposed capital punishment.[43] He reasoned further that the "perpetual wretchedness" of a life in prison was a more effective deterrent than a death sentence, which could end misery or enable martyrdom.[44] Plus, Beccaria, ever concerned with the legitimacy of the social contract, observed that law is nothing more than individual liberty in collective form. It is the will of the people. "Who," he asked rhetorically, "has ever willingly given other men the authority to kill him?"[45]

Beccaria argued that torture-executions like that of Robert-François Damiens, who attempted to assassinate King Louis XV, produced a brutalizing effect on the public. This is an illustration of Damiens's 1757 torture-execution in Paris.

Drawing of the torture of Robert-François Damiens, 1757, Gallica/National Library of France, accessed via Wikimedia Creative Commons.

Beccaria argued that crime stems from a flawed system of justice rather than from flawed people. He was not naïve, however. He understood that crime would always exist even under ideal circumstances. Nonetheless, he wrote that a rational legal system had the greatest potential to maximize societal happiness. Such a system would have the following characteristics:

- *It is public* – Accusations, witness testimony, and criminal trials must not happen in secret. Defendants should be permitted to confront their accusers and cross-examine witnesses. The law and its application should be visible to the public.

- *It is applied equally* – Fairness requires that all people, regardless of wealth or social standing, are subject uniformly to the law and receive equivalent punishments for equivalent crimes. Following democratic principles, guilt should be determined by a jury of fellow citizens or peers, rather than by one person in a position of authority.

- *It punishes the act* – Criminal acts harm society and so the legal system should respond to the severity of the act's harm rather than the individual offender's circumstances or intent. (Beccaria's sole emphasis on *actus reus* to the neglect of *mens rea* is a point of controversy.)

- *The punishment fits the crime* – The severity of punishment is proportional to the severity of the crime—the more serious the crime, the more serious the penalty. This is called **proportionality**. Further, the severity of the punishment must only be as great as required to deter crime. If murder invokes the same sanction as robbery, then robbers have no reason to spare the lives of victims who might act as witnesses against them.

- *It prioritizes certainty over severity* – There are three elements of deterrence: (1) severity of punishment, (2) certainty of punishment, and (3) celerity, or swiftness, of punishment. Certainty is the most important feature. Imagine a scenario in which one thief has a 99% chance of punishment (a 90-day jail term) while another thief has a .01%—or 1 in 10,000—chance of punishment (being hanged). The certain-but-less-severe punishment is a greater deterrent than the severe-but-unlikely punishment.

- *It emphasizes celerity (or swiftness) of punishment* – Determination of guilt and sentencing should follow quickly after crime occurs. Lengthy pretrial detention, or being held in jail without being convicted, is both unjust and a detriment to deterrence. The link between the criminal conduct and its penalties breaks down in the minds of offenders when action and outcome are separated by many months or years.

ENGAGED CRIMINOLOGY 6.1
Translating Beccaria

This activity requires you to read and answer questions about several quotes from Beccaria's *On Crimes and Punishments*. These sentences were written over 250 years ago, and it shows. Your task is to identify the "translation" using modern-day language that best captures the idea in each quote.

1. Which translation best captures the classical school idea in this Beccaria quote?

   It is clear that the purpose of punishments is not to torment and afflict a sentient being or to undo a crime which has already been committed ... The purpose of punishment, then, is nothing other than to dissuade the criminal from doing fresh harm to his compatriots and to keep other people from doing the same. (p. 24)

   a. We should punish people who commit crime because they deserve it.
   b. Punishing law-breakers prevents people from committing crimes in the future.
   c. Punishment is pointless because the crime already happened and you can't turn back time.

2. Which translation best captures the classical school idea in this Beccaria quote?

> *Crimes of every kind should be less frequent, in proportion to the evil they produce to society ... If an equal punishment be ordained for two crimes that injure society in different degrees, there is nothing to deter men from committing the greater as often as it is attended with greater advantage."(pp. 21-25)*

    a. Deterrence requires serious punishments for serious crimes and minor punishments for minor crimes.

    b. Preventing crime requires punishing all crimes harshly, regardless of how serious the crime is.

    c. Crime shouldn't happen because it is evil, and most people aren't evil.

3. Which translation best captures the classical school idea in this Beccaria quote?

> *In proportion as punishments become more cruel, the minds of men, as a fluid rises to the same height with that which surrounds it, grow hardened and insensible; and the force of the passions still continuing, in the space of an hundred years the wheel terrifies no more than formerly the prison.* (p. 99)

    a. Extremely cruel punishments are effective deterrents because they scare people out of committing crime.

    b. We shouldn't use extremely cruel punishments because they make us insensitive to cruelty and they don't prevent crime.

    c. We need extremely cruel punishments because people aren't rational thinkers.

4. In one or two sentences, describe one classical school idea that aligns with your own thinking about crime and punishment. Explain why you agree with this idea.

Sources: Quote 1: Beccaria, C. (1986/1764). *On crimes and punishments* (D. Young, Trans.). Indianapolis: Hackett. Quotes 2-4: Beccaria, C. (1775/1764). *An essay on crimes and punishments* (translated from the Italian; with a commentary attributed to Mons. De Voltaire, translated from the French). London: K. Newberry.

Beccaria's logic plays out in today's legal realm. For example, Beccaria's claims about severity's limitations are evident in the failure of extreme punishments, such as mandatory minimum sentences, to deter would-be offenders. Mandatory minimums are base-level sentences that are applied automatically for certain offenses; a judge can sentence a longer term but not a term shorter than the minimum. Each U.S. state has its own version of mandatory minimums, but it is the federal system that is best known for its severe minimum penalties, especially for drug offenses. For example, the minimum sentence for a person convicted of possessing 10 grams or more or LSD is 10 years in federal prison.[46] In 2019, 26.1% of all federal cases that came up for sentencing were subject to mandatory minimums; 72.7% of those were drug trafficking convictions. Most received "no relief," meaning that the defendant received at least the minimum sentence.[47]

One goal of mandatory minimums aligns with Beccaria's perspective: They create uniformity across offenders regardless of individual circumstances. In reality, though, they are used to compel guilty pleas from people terrified of receiving the minimum. They plead guilty to a lesser charge to avoid the longer sentence if found guilty at trial.[48] This might sound like a classical school idea: People plead guilty because they are afraid of the severity. Yet realize that they still committed the crime in the first place. They were not deterred. Studies show that mandatory minimum policies do not reduce law-breaking,[49] possibly because people are unaware of sentencing laws or their minds are elsewhere while committing crime.[50] The biggest critique of these controversial policies is their disproportionality. The sentence does not fit the crime. Beccaria would be displeased.

Proportionality, integral to Beccaria's philosophy, plays a central role in U.S. Supreme Court decisions about criminal punishment. For example, the Court ruled that the death penalty was cruel and unusual (i.e., disproportionate) in cases that don't involve homicide, including the 1977 case *Coker v. Georgia* regarding the constitutionality of capital punishment in non-homicide rape cases with adult victims.[51] Or consider the case of *Solem v. Helm* (1983). Jerry Helm was convicted of writing a "no account" check for $100, a minor offense. He was sentenced to life in prison without the possibility of parole under South Dakota's habitual felon statute. Mr. Helm had six previous nonviolent convictions dating back to the 1960s. The Supreme Court ruled that the life sentence violated the principle of proportionality, but they stopped short of striking down habitual offender statutes.[52]

Beccaria's prioritizing of punishment's certainty continues to be relevant today. When the risk of apprehension is high, people are less likely to skirt the rules.[53] You understand this if you've ever avoided parking illegally when tow trucks are at the ready. Similarly, a field experiment on probationers in New Jersey pointed to "the miracle of the cells": People on probation are much more likely to pay their delinquent fines when they are convinced that nonpayment will result in a brief and immediate days-long stint in jail.[54] Establishing certainty's effects among the general public (not just probationers) is far more challenging. Recall clearance rates from Chapter 2: The proportion of known offenses that led to charges being filed or that were cleared by exceptional means (i.e., "solved"). Researchers have sometimes relied on clearance rates to measure the certainty of punishment, but others warn against it because most people are unaware of the risk of apprehension.[55] This is where Beccaria's ideas begin to break down. He neglected the role of perception, or what people *believe* about certainty, severity, and celerity. You can learn about how perception matters in the modern-day, or neoclassical, version of Beccaria's ideas in Chapter 7 (Contemporary Schools of Thought).

Jeremy Bentham

Beccaria's ideas inspired British legal scholar and philosopher Jeremy Bentham (1748-1832), who also became a classical school theorist, though his ideas are largely regarded as less transformational than his predecessor's. Bentham's writing echoed Beccaria's ideas about the utilitarian goal of deterrence, but Bentham was more explicit about several key ideas. For example, he theorized more extensively about the rational cost-benefit analysis assumed in Beccaria's deterrence argument in his writing on the **hedonistic calculus**, a "theoretical algorithm" for establishing the moral worth and value of an action.[56] It is sometimes referred to as the felicific calculus, but that doesn't quite roll off the tongue. Bentham famously wrote that "nature has placed mankind under the governance of two sovereign masters, pain and pleasure."[57] All humans seek pleasure and try to avoid pain. They will weigh possible pleasures against potential pains—by considering their intensity, duration, certainty, remoteness, and tendency to create more pleasures and pains—and rationally select the course of action that produces the greatest satisfaction with the least discomfort.

Borrowing from Beccaria and others, Bentham offered the *greatest happiness principle*, which is mostly a restatement of the utilitarian aim of using law to maximize pleasure (or happiness) for the greatest number of people while minimizing overall pain (or unhappiness). Bentham is credited with adding a fourth pillar to Beccaria's three components of deterrence (certainty, severity, and celerity of punishment) based on the greatest happiness principle; this fourth pillar is parsimony. Bentham argued explicitly that punishments must not cause greater pains to the offender than the pains they would prevent among possible victims. For instance, executing a horse thief is not parsimonious because the pain of death is greater than the pains endured by the owners of stolen horses. Bentham took this position because he regarded punishment as evil, just as crime is evil:

> But all punishment is mischief: all punishment in itself is evil. Upon the principle of utility, if it ought at all to be admitted, it ought only to be admitted in as far as it promises to exclude some greater evil.[58]

Bentham is also well-known for his development of the **panopticon**, a prison design that ensures control by enabling a single guard to observe all inmates simultaneously (*pan-* means "of everything"; *opti-* refers to sight). Of course, the overseer cannot, in fact, observe everyone at the same time, but the prisoners are unable to tell whether they are being watched. For Bentham, "power should be visible and unverifiable."[59] As such, inmates must constantly regulate their behavior. This was achieved architecturally by housing inmates in cells placed in a rotunda surrounding a central inspection house. Bentham subscribed to an *inspection principle*, arguing that the behavior of both inmates and guards must be transparent. Just as the guards must be able to monitor the behavior of the prisoners, so too must the public be able to monitor the behavior of the guards. Despite early interest in Bentham's design among British officials, and some efforts among prison architects to create his vision in Europe, the U.S., and Cuba, the panopticon has largely been abandoned, though some modern prisons, like Lelystad Prison in the Netherlands, adopt a "digital panopticon" approach by using electronic wristbands.[60]

This now-abandoned prison building at Presidio Modelo, Isla de Pinos, in Cuba, was one of four Cuban prisons modeled on Jeremy Bentham's panopticon design.

Photo of "Inside of prison building" by Friman, https://commons.wikimedia.org/wiki/File:Presidio-modelo2.JPG, licensed under CC BY-SA 3.0, https://creativecommons.org/licenses/by-sa/3.0/deed.en

THE POSITIVIST SCHOOL: BIOLOGICAL ORIGINS

Enlightenment notions of free will and rationality paved the way for the classical school of criminology in the 18th century. The rise of science in the 19th century began a new chapter in criminological history: the positivist school. Scholars of the classical period had primarily been "armchair theorists." They had plenty of ideas about crime and justice, but they did not attempt to test their explanations with data. The positivist school, in contrast, was empirical. Indeed, positivism is a doctrine claiming that society is ordered, measurable, and can be understood objectively through research. Positivists hold that the true nature of the social world can be uncovered—or *positive* knowledge obtained—using the scientific method.[61] Just as physicists and biologists could identify the laws of the natural world through rigorous observation and experimentation, early positivists sought to reveal laws (or "social facts") governing the social world.

Classical school philosophers found the causes of crime in the rational choices of people enacting free will. In contrast, positivist school criminologists argued that the root causes of crime were forces outside of the individual's control. These could take the form of either individual pathologies (biological, psychological, or personality deficiencies) or social pathologies (dysfunctions in the social, economic, or political environment). In other words, positivists were determinists. Determinism is the premise that human behavior is caused (or determined) by forces external to the individual will. For example, *biological determinism* locates the causes of criminality in biological traits. *Psychological determinism* argues that psychological predispositions determine criminal behavior. *Environmental determinism* points to the influence of one's social surroundings as the determining factor.

Agency (the ability to make choices) and powerful external forces can coexist, of course. Criminologists differentiate between hard determinism and soft determinism. Hard determinism disregards agency entirely: "If X, then Y *will* follow."[62] Soft determinism, in contrast, is not nearly so black-and-white. Soft determinists argue that people enact free will within constraints set by biological, psychological, or environmental forces.[63] A brain injury or exposure to family violence might be important determinants of criminal conduct, but those determinants are filtered through individual decision-making. Soft determinists might say: "If X, then Y is *more likely* to follow." In this way, many modern criminologists are positivists of the soft determinism variety.[64]

Early positivists edged closer to hard determinism. This is one reason (among numerous others) that 19th century positivist ideas have been relegated to the dustbin of history. But it is imperative that we not mistake the two-century-old theories of positivist school criminologists for positivism as a way of understanding the world. *Positivism is not a theory*. It is general approach to studying the social world that centers on predicting crime using scientific principles. Early positivists are important not because they got it right (they often didn't!) but because they transformed *how* we study crime. Criminology as a social science would not exist without them. In fact, it was positivist school criminologist Raffaele Garofalo who coined the term *criminology* (*criminologia* in Italian) in 1885.[65]

Early Biological Positivists

The earliest positivists were biological determinists. They were on the hunt for a list of traits that differentiated people who commit crimes from people who do not, or the "inferior" from the "superior." The belief that humans could be sorted into a hierarchy of types fit within the dominant views held by many academics in Europe and the U.S. in the 19th century. The global slave trade, efforts to quash uprisings against European colonial rule, and mass immigration in the U.S. motivated the powerful in society to draw a line between "desirable" and "undesirable" groups and individuals. This belief system infused 19th and early 20th century criminological thought. Biological defects or differences were thought to be the key to sorting the undesirable criminal classes from the upstanding citizens. This line of thinking supported eugenics.[66] Eugenics is the unscientific and racially biased study and practice of controlling reproduction to improve the human race.

One of the first biological differences believed to separate the inferior from the superior was brain size: the bigger, the better. This pseudoscience was called craniometry. Craniometrists used devices to measure the skull and determine brain mass under the faulty assumption that larger brains were more intelligent.[67] These studies were intended to give a sheen of scientific respectability to racist ideologies (called *scientific racism*) that supported eugenics.[68] In a wonderfully ironic twist, the brains of dead craniometrists proved to be of average or smaller than average volume. Surviving craniometrists then changed their tune: Now they argued that convoluted brain structures—like those of dead craniometrists—indicated superiority.[69] Their claims did not hold up under rigorous scrutiny.

Phrenology, a cousin of craniometry, also assumed that researchers could identify the physiological markers of superiority and inferiority. Phrenologists claimed that individuals' dispositions, including criminal dispositions, could be read in the bumps and contours of their skulls.[70] They thought that the brain's form matched the skull's form. Therefore, they incorrectly interpreted an abnormal lump on the skull as evidence of an abnormality in the corresponding portion of the brain. It is true that certain regions of the brain are responsible for specific functions (e.g., the frontal lobe controls emotional expression and memory). However, reliance on skull bumps as indicators of criminal propensity has been thoroughly discredited.

Craniometry and phrenology are criminology's "disreputable ancestors."[71] Their practitioners were not criminologists, per se. Rather, they were interested in all manner of human characteristics. Nonetheless, they had a lasting impact on the field. They brought scientific methods, however poorly applied, to the study of criminal behavior. They drew attention to individual-level differences in criminality, which was absent from classical school thinking. They offered a medical view of people who commit crimes as sick rather than bad or sinful, and they favored rehabilitation for offenders. Plus, they set the historical context for Cesare Lombroso, widely described as the father of positivist criminology.

Cesare Lombroso and the Birth of Positivist Criminology

Cesare Lombroso (1835-1909) was an Italian physician and criminologist who offered the first comprehensive theory of criminality that was subjected to empirical testing. His 1876 text, *Criminal Man*, incorporated several prominent ideas of his era.[72] First, Lombroso was a social Darwinist. Charles Darwin had published his groundbreaking work on biological evolution and natural selection just 17 years earlier.[73] Social Darwinists took Darwin's ideas about the natural world and applied them (incorrectly) to the social world. They regarded human social life as a competition operating on a "survival of the fittest" principle. Only the most evolved or "fittest" come out on top. The impoverished masses were viewed as less evolved and biologically inferior. Their oppression was therefore justified, in this now-discredited view.[74] Second, Lombroso embraced physiognomy. Physiognomy was the practice of determining an individual's personality or character based on their physical features, especially their face. Physiognomy was to the face what phrenology was to the skull. He also used craniometry as part of his measurement of the human form.

Lombroso wove these two approaches—social Darwinism and physiognomy—into a theory of criminal atavism. *Atavism* is reversion to an earlier evolutionary stage. Lombroso believed that people who committed serious crimes were a less-evolved, more "savage" form of human. Because they were in a more primitive state of evolutionary development, his theory went, their criminality was innate, or something that they were born with.[75] They were biologically and morally inferior "born criminals."[76] Lombroso did not think that *all* law-breakers were atavists, however. His writings included multiple criminal types[77]:

- *Born criminals*: Evolutionary failures (atavists) whose criminal disposition is innate, causing serious and chronic criminal behavior. Lombroso believed about one-third of people who commit crimes were "born criminals."

- *Criminaloids, pseudo-criminals, and habitual criminals*: Occasional offenders who are neither biologically nor psychologically abnormal. They commit crime due to environmental circumstances ("criminaloids") or necessity and self-defense ("pseudo-criminals"). Opportunistic crime has become a habit for "habitual offenders." Lombroso argued that more than half of people who commit crimes fit this category.

- *Criminals by passion*: Those who commit sudden emotional acts of violence absent of planning, or "crimes of passion."

- *Insane criminals*: People whose mental illness "completely upsets their moral nature."[78] They are not atavists.

Lombroso focused most of his attention on "born criminals" even though he claimed that non-atavists make up the largest slice of the criminal pie. Atavistic offenders were the gravest threat to society, he argued. They were chronic, violent criminals in need of containment. Lombroso theorized that "born criminals" could be identified using physiological markers of atavism.

Atavistic Stigmata

Lombroso argued that atavistic stigmata, or physiological traits indicating atavism, could alert observers to a person's innate criminality. The "revelation" came to him while he autopsied the body of Giuseppe Villella, an imprisoned Italian bandit.[79] Villella had a skull abnormality—a median occipital dimple—observed in lemurs (a lower primate) as well as human fetuses prior to the fifth month of gestation.[80] Inspiration struck Lombroso: Perhaps physiological abnormalities corresponded to criminal tendencies. They would mark the person who committed a crime as a lower form of humanity. Lombroso presumed that physical features that departed from the average form (i.e., unusually big, unusually small, differently shaped) signified the degree of the person's moral degeneracy.

The practice of offender profiling based on physical features was called criminal anthropology. Its practitioners, like Lombroso, developed criminal anthropometry to measure physiological peculiarities for criminal identification (the suffix *-metry* refers to measurement; *anthro* means human). The bodily and facial features said by Lombroso to mark "born criminals" included the following:

- Long arms relative to lower limbs
- High cheekbones
- Unusual skull sizes
- Abnormally large or small ears, eyes, or jaws

- Asymmetry of the facial bones

- Large and protruding chins

- Low, sloping foreheads

- Handle-shaped ears

- Drooping eyes

- Flattened or hawk-like noses

- Pain insensitivity (as indicated by tattoos)

Why use atavistic stigmata to sort the born criminals from the rest? Because, in Lombroso's thinking, the criminal punishment ought to depend on the type of person who committed an offense. Departing from the classical school, Lombroso favored punishing the individual rather than the act. He wrote that "crime is like an illness that requires a specific remedy for each patient."[81] And who is the person to determine the illness and appropriate treatment? The criminal anthropologist! Lombroso recommended that the courts follow the advice of experts in the measurement of atavistic stigmata, saving the most isolating punishments for "born criminals" and "habitual criminals." Lombroso reasoned that born and habitual criminals lacked the capacity for rehabilitation. Therefore, he advocated for life sentences to be served in "prisons for incorrigibles," ideally located on islands, where they would do manual labor for the nation's benefit, such as building roads. He also favored the death penalty for violent repeat offenders.

For non-atavists, such as "criminaloids" and "criminals by passion," Lombroso believed in reform. He preferred alternatives to prison for individuals who lacked innate criminality. He endorsed legal warnings, fines matched to the offender's ability to pay, forced labor without imprisonment, and house arrest with enforced discomforts like cold showers or restricted diets. When incarceration of non-atavists was required, Lombroso argued for moral education, hard work, and increasing freedoms based on a merit point system.[82]

The Death of an Idea

Lombroso may be well-known for introducing data analysis into the study of individual criminality, but his own research suffered from crucial flaws. Specifically, Lombroso failed to use a control group as a basis of comparison in most of his research. Maybe people who did not commit crimes also had flattened or hawk-like noses! Plus, he favored anecdotal evidence (or evidence based on single cases) that confirmed his hypotheses over systematic studies that might prove them wrong.[83] French journalist Émile Zola, who admired Lombroso, said of him: "Like all men with a thesis, he marshals all the facts that support his own … while ignoring all those that conflict with it."[84] Lombroso finally provided statistical analyses using a comparison to 55 "normal" subjects in the last edition of his book *Criminal Man* in 1896.[85] The results were underwhelming. Only a handful of proposed stigmata were observed more frequently in the criminal group: facial asymmetry, plagiocephaly (flat spot on the head), frontal microcephaly (underdevelopment of the frontal lobe), and bulging eyebrow arches. And even these characteristics were uncommon among the individuals he studied.[86]

Lombroso's ideas survived scathing criticism during his lifetime (called "scientific fiction," "a mixture of facts and nonsense,"[87] and "false science"[88] by various skeptics), but they were discarded soon after his death in 1909. Charles Goring, a prison medical officer and researcher, conducted comprehensive and methodologically superior tests of Lombroso's hypotheses, publishing his results in 1913.[89] He took measurements of about 3,000 incarcerated people as well as of hospital residents, university students, and officers with the British Royal Engineers. He found no physiological differences between the people convicted of crime and the others.[90] He also compared his measurements with prisoners' skulls discovered in 1893 at London's Whitechapel prison. Goring saw none of the abnormalities that Lombroso had claimed to observe.[91] Just four years after his death, Lombroso's theory of criminal atavism was thoroughly debunked, and it would be a source of ridicule over the ensuing century.[92]

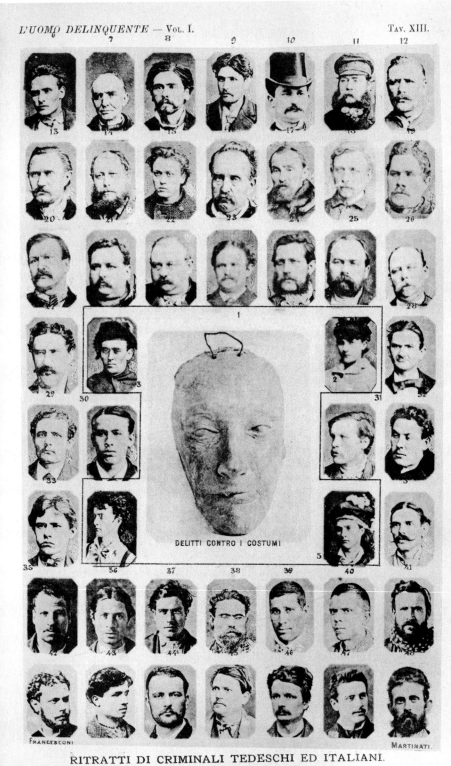

This image appeared in Lombroso's *l'Uomo Delinquente* with the title "Portraits of German and Italian Criminals"; the title below the mask reads "Crimes against Morals" [translated from Italian].

Lombroso's Legacy in Criminology

Lombroso has two divergent legacies. One is a dark legacy of lending scientific legitimacy to eugenics and a pseudoscience called "criminal biology" that the Nazi regime used to justify genocide during the Holocaust (several decades after Lombroso's death).[93] He continues to be a source of ridicule also because his theory was based on a profound misunderstanding of evolutionary principles. Indeed, many of the anatomical features described by Lombroso were, in fact, a consequence not of atavism and criminality but of malnutrition due to extreme poverty.[94]

Yet criminologists still talk about Lombroso, and not just because he is a cautionary tale. Lombroso's other legacy is found in the development of criminology as a scientific discipline, even if the greatest advances were made by those seeking to prove him wrong. And wrong though he was about atavism, his attention to the body endures in biosocial criminology (see Chapter 7 for details about the biosocial perspective).[95] He put the spotlight on the criminal (the person) rather than on the crime (an event), an approach to which many criminologists still adhere. Plus, it turns out that Lombroso was right about *some* things. Several anatomical traits he noted among incarcerated people are now understood as markers of abnormal brain development in early pregnancy.[96] For example, Lombroso observed low-set ears and facial asymmetry among some "born criminals." We now know that these are indicators of fetal alcohol spectrum disorders (FASDs), which can occur when a mother drinks alcohol during pregnancy. Consequences of FASDs include intellectual disability, behavior problems, and weak impulse control. People with FASDs continue to be overrepresented among incarcerated people.[97] Lombroso wasn't observing atavism. But he wasn't wrong that the body tells a story that aids in understanding behavior.

Lombroso transformed criminology in other ways, as well. For example, he was the first to take women who commit crimes seriously as a research topic.[98] Additionally, some of his non-atavism ideas maintain their relevance even today. His writings on political violence draw attention to social conditions, religious grievances, and psychological states that continue to appear in modern studies of terrorism.[99] He was also one of the first scholars to study prison subcultures; he analyzed prison tattoos, and he published prisoners' art and writings in his 1888 book *Prisoner Palimpsests*.[100] Few things in life are all good or all bad. Lombroso's legacy is no different.

THE POSITIVIST SCHOOL: STRUCTURAL ORIGINS

Lombroso brought attention to the individual as a focus of study. Earlier in the 19th century, other European scholars were offering criminological insights about social structure. Their attention was on the organization of people and groups in society, or large-scale societal patterns, rather than why one person committed crime and another did not. In France and Belgium, and before Lombroso had even said his first words, André-Michel Guerry and Adolphe Quetelet were developing fields called *moral statistics* and *social physics*, precursors to modern-day quantitative criminology and sociology.

Adolphe Quetelet wrote, "Society itself contains the germs of all the crimes committed. It is the social state, in some measure, that prepares these crimes, and the criminal is merely the instrument that executes them."[101] He published this in 1835, the year Lombroso was born. The sentiment of the quote is that the causes of crime are social, or that places and environmental conditions matter. Along with André-Michel Guerry, Quetelet was a pioneer in the ecological (or spatial) study of crime.[102] They were major voices in the creation of positivist criminology.

André-Michel Guerry and the Cartographic Approach

We take national crime statistics for granted in the U.S. and elsewhere today, but the collection and publication of crime rates has only been around for about two centuries. When these statistics became available from the French Ministry of Justice, André-Michel Guerry (1802-1866), a lawyer and statistician, plotted them on maps, broken down by region. His was a **cartographic approach**: He used maps to show the spatial distribution of crime and other social problems. He referred to quantitative analysis of social behaviors as **moral statistics**. Moral statistics would measure "the mind of man... his capabilities, his morals and customs, his feelings and sentiments, and his passion."[103] This was a novel idea in the 1830s.

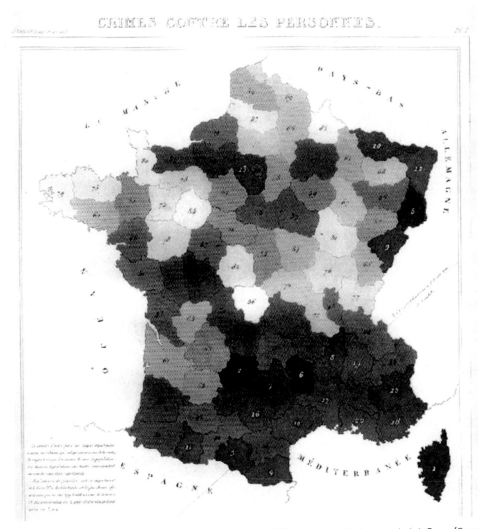

André-Michel Guerry's "Crimes against Persons" map from his 1833 *Essai sur la statistique morale de la France* [*Essay on the moral statistics of France*]

Photo of "Crimes against persons," from *Essai sur la statistique morale de la France,* by André-Michel Guerry, 1833, accessed via Wikimedia Creative Commons.

Guerry's 1833 *Essay on the Moral Statistics of France* contained a multitude of maps detailing the geography of crime (including by age, sex, and motive) as well as suicide, literacy, wealth and poverty, children born outside of marriage, prostitution, infanticide (killing of babies), charitable donations, and military desertion.[104] Guerry observed that violent crimes were more common in impoverished areas, whereas property crime rates were higher in wealthy regions.[105] His explanation? Opportunities for theft: Wealthy areas have desirable belongings available for the taking. This conclusion fits contemporary ideas about "attractive targets" for theft in affluent communities (see the section on Routine Activities Theory in Chapter 14).

ENGAGED CRIMINOLOGY 6.2

Be a Cartographic Criminologist

In this data activity, you will adopt Guerry's cartographic approach to the study of region, poverty, and crime rates. You will use analyze modern-day data from New Mexico counties to see if Guerry's observations hold up 200 years later.

The U.S. Census Bureau reports the percentage of population living below the federal poverty line by county. Note the location of the most and least impoverished counties in New Mexico.

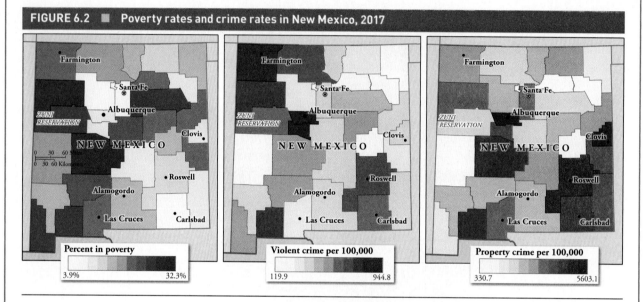

FIGURE 6.2 ■ Poverty rates and crime rates in New Mexico, 2017

Source: Adapted from datawrapper.du using Uniform Crime Reports and U.S. Census Bureau data.

Now examine the map of New Mexico displaying violent crime rates and property crime rates per 100,000. Focus on those counties you identified as the most and the least impoverished.

In 1833, Guerry observed that the most impoverished areas in France had the highest violent crime rates while property crime rates were highest in more affluent areas. Provide a one- or two-sentence response to each of the following questions using the New Mexico maps.

1. In what ways does Guerry's observation hold up or fail to hold up, based on what you see in the three New Mexico maps?

2. What are some problems with relying on county-level data to determine the influence of social environment on crime?

Adolphe Quetelet and Social Physics

Just two years after publication of Guerry's influential essay on moral statistics, Belgian astronomer and statistician Adolphe Quetelet (1796-1874) made a similar argument in his own influential book, whose title translates to *On Man and the Development of His Faculties*.[106] Quetelet, who had recently discovered the normal distribution in statistics (a symmetrical bell curve with known properties), argued for the development of social physics, or the application of statistical principles to the study of social behavior, including crime. This should sound familiar. It was nearly the same as Guerry's moral statistics! Unlike Guerry, though, Quetelet argued that the "average man," or the statistical mean, should be the yardstick against which all social behavior was measured.[107]

Quetelet showed the usefulness of social physics by analyzing how French crime rates varied by season (June had the most crime).[108] Like Guerry, he also examined crime rates across regions, including *arrondissements* (administrative districts), provinces, and countries. He demonstrated patterns by age, sex, and education across many forms of crime. The same—or at least similar—idea struck Quetelet and Guerry at precisely the same historical moment.

Quetelet joined Guerry in describing how crime was concentrated in some regions and among some demographic groups (poor, less-educated young men who were unemployed or in "lowly occupations"). But Quetelet went beyond Guerry's argument about criminal opportunities in explaining the patterns. He saw the yawning gap between rich and poor as criminogenic. He was quick to point out that some of the poorest and most illiterate regions of France and the Low Countries (e.g., Luxembourg) were among those with the least crime.[109] Poverty, alone, did not produce crime, according to Quetelet. It was poverty amidst wealth—or wealth inequality—that mattered. In highly unequal regions, the poor are "surrounded by subjects of temptation" and are frustrated and disheartened by exposure to inaccessible luxuries. Criminologists today call this *relative deprivation*, and it features prominently in strain perspectives on crime (the topic of Chapter 10).

Quetelet described other patterns modern criminologists continue to analyze, as well. These included the sex gap in criminal offending, the age-crime curve, and the problem of unknown crimes, later called the dark figure. He also noted the constancy of crime, which was the steady level of crime observed over time: Concentrations of crime among types of people and places were persistent and predictable.[110] Therefore, he reasoned, there must be something about the organization of society that gives rise to crime. It is not simply a matter of individual personalities and free will. Quetelet's social determinism—his belief that human behavior is caused by forces external to the individual—was a rejection of classical school ideas. This attracted many angry critics. If the causes of crime are social and not simply a matter of rational choices, the critics speculated, then how can criminals be held accountable for their wrongdoing?[111] Nonetheless, Quetelet's (and Guerry's) new way of thinking stood the test of time, ultimately leading to the 20th century Chicago school of criminology, which is described in detail in Chapter 8.[112]

ORIGINS OF SOCIAL STRUCTURE IN U.S. CRIMINOLOGY

Across the pond, U.S. social scientists developed their own structural approaches to crime, influenced in part by their European counterparts. The Chicago school of criminology, which began in the early 20th century at the University of Chicago, adopted Guerry's cartographic approach and aspects of Quetelet's structural view on crime. Chapter 8 describes the Chicago school and its primary, enduring perspective: social disorganization theory. But in the late 19th century, several decades before the start of the Chicago school, one U.S. social scientist highlighted how the unique structure of U.S. social life, which was marked by extreme racial inequalities, shaped crime and punishment. His name was W. E. B. Du Bois.

W. E. B. Du Bois

W. E. B. Du Bois (1868-1963), an African American scholar born just a few years following the official end of slavery, is an important but historically underappreciated figure in the development of criminology. Du Bois spent his academic life moving between his home state of Massachusetts (he was the first African American to earn a doctoral degree at Harvard University, in 1895), Fisk University in Nashville, and the University of Berlin, where he studied with the world's most prominent social scientists of the period.[113] The contrast of life in North and South was jarring, ultimately shaping Du Bois's commitment to studying the social world.

Du Bois's early works were explorations of white slave traders' "notorious infractions" of, and efforts to circumvent, international laws prohibiting the transatlantic slave trade.[114] Thus began Du Bois's career examining crime, particularly crimes committed against and by Black Americans. In his classic book *The Souls of Black Folk,* Du Bois famously stated, "The problem of the twentieth century is the problem of the color-line."[115] Racism (another word for the color-line), he wrote, created a **double consciousness** among Black people in the U.S., or a sense of having a dual self, or a "two-ness" wrought by oppression and devaluation. Of double consciousness, Du Bois wrote in 1897,

> *After the Egyptian and Indian, the Greek and Roman, the Teuton and Mongolian, the Negro is a sort of seventh son, born with a veil, and gifted with second-sight in this American world, — a world which yields him no self-consciousness, but only lets him see himself through the revelation of the other world. It is a peculiar sensation, this double-consciousness, this sense of always looking at one's*

self through the eyes of others, of measuring one's soul by the tape of a world that looks on in amused contempt and pity. One feels his two-ness, — an American, a Negro; two souls, two thoughts, two unreconciled strivings; two warring ideals in one dark body, whose dogged strength alone keeps it from being torn asunder.[116]

W. E. B. Du Bois, pictured here circa 1907, was a famous historian and sociologist who wrote extensively on race, crime, and justice.

Photo of W. E. B. Du Bois, 1907, accessed via Wikimedia Creative Commons.

Rather than seeking to compare the crimes and punishments of Black and white Americans, Du Bois instead focused his analysis almost exclusively on Black people's experience. The color-line, after all, ensured that the circumstances of white and Black life in America at the turn of the 20th century were not the same, nor could they be. Slavery—in its legal form, at least—was only several decades in the past. And the indignities of everyday racial oppression ensured that the criminalization, law-violating actions, policing, and punishment of Black and white people in the U.S. required distinct explanations.[117]

Unable to find faculty employment at any major universities despite his elite preparation and multiple Harvard degrees, and after a short spell teaching at a small historically Black university in Ohio, Du Bois was offered a nonfaculty research position in Pennsylvania. He was to study poverty and crime in a Philadelphia community to assist social welfare agencies. The result of his study, *The Philadelphia Negro: A Social Study,* would establish Du Bois as a pioneer in criminology, though he was denied this acknowledgment during his lifetime (and for several decades thereafter).[118] Keep in mind that the language used in Du Bois's works reflected the time period in which he was writing.

The Philadelphia Negro demonstrated the immense value of ethnography in criminology, and it was the first comprehensive use of the method in the study of crime. Du Bois rejected a purely positivist approach rooted solely in statistical analysis. Instead, he opted to live among those he studied in Philadelphia's Seventh Ward. He and his wife Nina embedded themselves in the culture of the community. They stayed 15 months, during which time Du Bois conducted extensive surveys, made systematic observations, and reviewed official sources of statistics. In other words, Du Bois used triangulation to paint a holistic picture of life in the Seventh Ward.[119]

Du Bois located the source of Black crime in the Seventh Ward in the displacement unique to Black Americans, first in the transatlantic slave trade and later in the movement from South to North. The racial apartheid (i.e., system of segregation) of slavery gave way to another form of racial apartheid in which the law was used to deny Black persons employment opportunities as workforce competition increased. These structural conditions also appear in his later analysis of Black crime in the rural South, for which he identified four causes[120]:

1. The convict-lease system

2. The attitude of the courts

3. Lawlessness and brutality of lynch mobs

4. Racial segregation

The convict-lease system refers to the use of free or cheap labor of people who were convicted of crimes, protected by the Thirteenth Amendment, by landowning white people and business owners in the post-Emancipation decades. Du Bois described how racially discriminatory laws called Black Codes, backed by Southern courts, were used to unofficially reinstitute slavery by limiting basic freedoms of Black Americans and enforcing low-wage labor. Black Codes criminalized everyday actions of Black people in the U.S. South (e.g., "vagrancy" or being unemployed, selling farm products without written permission from a white employer, practicing any occupation other than farmer or servant). These laws ensured a large reserve of cheap and free labor, which was in high demand after the official end of slavery, by Black Americans whose everyday behaviors had been

Du Bois wrote about the unjust practice of convict-leasing in the U.S. South, a criminogenic system supported by racially discriminatory laws. The young men in this 1915 photo were leased as convict labor for timber harvesting.

Photo of "Convicts Leased to Harvest Timber," 1915, via the Library of Congress.

criminalized. Black Codes were transformed into Jim Crow laws in the 20th century, having much the same effect.

Lynch mobs are a form of premeditated vigilante violence wherein groups commit informal executions, often accompanied by torture, to punish persons suspected or convicted of crimes, or as a form of terroristic intimidation. Many early U.S. lynchings were in the western territories and arose from lack of an established judicial system for dealing with people suspected of having committed crimes; most victims of "Wild West regime" lynch mobs were white or Hispanic (though *rates* of victimization were still higher for Black Americans during these years).[121] But by 1888, lynchings had moved primarily to the South, and victims were almost exclusively Black, as observed in Figure 6.3. According to the Equal Justice Initiative, there were more than 4,400 racial terror lynchings of Black people by white mobs between 1877 and 1950 in the U.S.[122] Du Bois observed how systemic patterns—using the law and courts to criminalize even the most mundane actions of Black Americans, the unofficial enslavement of Black people after Emancipation, the racial terror of mob violence, and segregation—undermined efforts at law-abiding behavior and trust in the law by rendering it untrustworthy. On this point, Du Bois wrote in 1899,

> *Let a Negro be simply accused of any crime from barn-burning to rape and he is liable to be seized by a mob, given no chance to defend himself, given neither trial, judge nor jury, and killed. Passing over the acknowledged fact that many innocent Negroes have thus been murdered, the point that is of greater gravity is that lawlessness is a direct encouragement to crime. It shatters the faith of the mass of Negroes in justice; it makes race hatred fiercer; it discourages honest effort; it transforms horror at crime into sympathy for the tortured victim; and it binds the hands and lessens the influence of those race leaders who are striving to preach forbearance and patience and honest endeavor to their people. It teaches eight million wronged people to despise a civilization which is not civilized.* (p. 50)[123]

Du Bois's legacy in criminology cannot be understated, and few early criminologists offered insights that remain so thoroughly relevant today. His work does not fit neatly into an identified historical school of thought (like the positivist school or Chicago school), but Du Bois's social analysis laid the groundwork for modern criminology, including his indictment of structural inequality as the source of criminalization, crime, and unequal punishment: "[In] convictions by human courts the rich always are favored somewhat at the expense of the poor, the upper classes at the expense of the unfortunate classes, and whites at the expense of the Negroes" (p. 249).[124] Du Bois, though occasionally moralistic in his tone towards those who violate the law, saw racial discrimination as criminogenic, an idea that would later infuse strain theories in criminology.[125] He rejected notions about diminished intelligence and crime that had been favored by positivists like Lombroso, instead offering that "crime comes either in spite of intelligence or as a result of misdirected intelligence under severe economic or moral strain" (p. 254).[126] In other words, Du Bois advanced a structural view of crime that points the finger at unequal social systems. For Du Bois and a parade of criminologists after him, crime is a "symptom of countless wrong social conditions" (p. 241).

Du Bois's contributions do not stop there. He was a methodological trailblazer who modeled how ethnography could provide the *Verstehen*—interpreting action's meaning from the perspective of the actor—necessary for a complete understanding of crime. In addition, Du Bois was one of the first scholars to document a pattern wherein a small number of people who commit crime were responsible for the bulk of crimes committed, a finding even more extreme for serious crimes. Criminologist Marvin Wolfgang would become a prominent scholar of this pattern in the 1960s and 1970s, labeling high-rate criminals "habitual offenders," a term that Du Bois had, in fact, used in 1899.[127]

Why, then, is Du Bois rarely mentioned in criminology textbooks? Why has he been what one writer calls a "scholar denied" until quite recently?[128] Criminology was dominated by white scholars, nearly all of them men, who acted as gatekeepers to the discipline during Du Bois's lifetime and in decades after.[129] Contemporary criminologists are working to remedy the longstanding neglect of crime scholars like Du Bois who have been denied the historical prominence they deserve due to race, gender, or other factors.

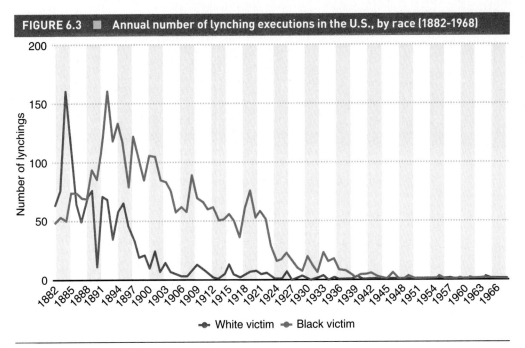

FIGURE 6.3   ■   Annual number of lynching executions in the U.S., by race (1882-1968)

◆ White victim   ◆ Black victim

Source: Lynchings Stats Year Dates Causes. (2021, January 14). Tuskegee University Archives. http://archive.tuskegee. edu/repository/digital-collection/lynching-information/lynchings-stats-year-dates-causes/

CHAPTER SUMMARY

LO 6.1   Describe pre-classical perspectives on crime and punishment.

Pre-classical explanations of crime were largely supernatural, focusing on demonic influence. Torture to elicit confessions, determination of guilt through trial by ordeal, and mutilating criminal punishments reflected supernatural beliefs about the battle between the forces of good and evil.

LO 6.2   Identify classical school views on crime and deterrence.

Classical school scholars like Beccaria and Bentham argued that the law should be applied publicly and uniformly, and that punishments should be certain, swift, and proportional to the seriousness of the crime. They believed this was necessary to achieve specific and general deterrence. Disproportionately harsh punishments were to be avoided because they have a brutalizing effect on people and violate the principles of utilitarianism.

LO 6.3   Contrast the positivist approach of Lombroso with the classical approach to theorizing crime.

Positivism suggests that the true nature of society can be measured and understood using the scientific method. Positivist criminologists like Lombroso collected data to test their claims (even if their methods and conclusions were flawed), whereas classical school thinkers were primarily philosophers or legal scholars. Positivist criminologists argued that forces outside of individuals' control, such as biological factors in Lombroso's "born criminal" concept, cause crime, whereas classical school philosophers asserted that crime results from people's rational choices.

LO 6.4   Summarize the structural explanations of positivist criminologists like Guerry and Quetelet.

Guerry and Quetelet pioneered the ecological, or spatial, study of crime. Their *moral statistics* and *social physics* were precursors to modern-day statistical analysis of crime rates. Guerry and Quetelet argued that environmental conditions affected crime rates. Their explanations of the varying rates of crime among different regions and demographic groups emphasized opportunities for crime (Guerry) and economic inequality (Quetelet).

LO 6.5   Describe the contributions of Du Bois to contemporary criminology.
   Du Bois saw structural inequality, including racial inequality, as the cause of criminalization, crime, and unequal punishment. These insights align with modern-day strain and labeling perspectives in criminology. Additionally, he wrote about habitual criminals, the small percentage of all offenders responsible for most crimes. He also pioneered ethnographic methods in the study of crime.

ENGAGED DISCUSSION

1. Imagine a world without law. What would that world look like? What assumptions are you making about human nature while envisioning that world?

2. Describe a time in the past week when you used the hedonistic calculus to decide on a course of action. What pleasures and pains did you weigh?

3. What are some alternative explanations for the presence of the physiological features listed as "atavistic stigmata" by Lombroso? What can cause those characteristics?

4. How might social media transform the relationship between location, relative deprivation, and crime described by Quetelet? Does place still matter?

5. What parallels exist between Du Bois's observations over 100 years ago and contemporary claims about race, policing, and mass incarceration?

KEY TERMS

Atavistic stigmata (p. 153)
Brutalization effect (p. 147)
Cartographic approach (p. 157)
Classical school (p. 145)
Criminal anthropology (p. 153)
Demonic perspective (p. 142)
Determinism (p. 151)
Deterrence (p. 147)
Double consciousness (p. 159)
Enlightenment (p. 145)
Eugenics (p. 152)

Hard determinism (p. 151)
Hedonistic calculus (p. 150)
Moral statistics (p. 157)
Panopticon (p. 150)
Positivism (p. 151)
Proportionality (p. 148)
Social contract (p. 146)
Social physics (p. 158)
Soft determinism (p. 151)
Utilitarianism (p. 146)

7 CONTEMPORARY SCHOOLS OF THOUGHT

LEARNING OBJECTIVES

7.1 Explain the central ideas in neoclassical criminology.

7.2 Contrast the four types of modern biosocial criminology.

7.3 Identify the primary arguments in radical criminology.

7.4 Describe the core principles of feminist criminology.

7.5 Summarize the central claims in critical race, queer, and green criminology.

On April 20, 2021, a jury found Minneapolis police officer Derek Chauvin guilty of murdering 46-year-old George Floyd.[1] In the course of an arrest for suspected use of a counterfeit $20 bill at a convenience store on May 25, 2020, Chauvin, who is white, used a prohibited tactic to suffocate Floyd, who was Black and unarmed, after he had already been subdued. A video shot by a teenage bystander showed how Chauvin held his knee on Floyd's neck for nine minutes and 29 seconds as Floyd begged for his life, while dismissing concerns from fellow officers about his treatment of Floyd. According to expert testimony presented during the trial, Floyd was dead for three minutes before Chauvin removed his knee. All the while, Chauvin's three fellow officers watched on and held off bystanders as they attempted to intervene.[2]

Floyd's murder at the hands of police sparked a summer of widespread racial justice protests throughout the U.S. and other parts of the world. Between 15 million and 26 million people in the U.S. participated in Black Lives Matter protests in the early weeks of the summer of 2020, making it one of the largest social movements in U.S. history.[3] Black Lives Matter is an anti-racist social movement that calls for justice, equity, and an end to police brutality. Black Lives Matter advocates are critical of existing structures—laws, policies, and practices—that perpetuate racial (and other) inequalities, including the disproportionate policing of and use of force against persons of color.[4] Activists call for reimagining the role of police in society. Instead of tasking police with managing every social problem (mental illness, homelessness, addiction, and school troubles, to name just a few), activists demand greater investment in community services—like education, child care, medical clinics, and mental health treatment—that improve the quality of life for all people.[5] As the chapter will demonstrate, the Black Lives Matter movement's perspectives and goals match those of critical criminologists.

Contemporary criminologists often align with a particular school of thought, or intellectual tradition. A criminological school of thought is composed of assumptions about how the social world operates, beliefs about what ought to be the focus of criminological analysis, and ideas about the best ways to conduct research. In short, it offers ways of thinking about crime, law, and punishment. The classical school and the positivist school, from Chapter 6, are examples of early schools of thought in criminology, and both have modern-day corollaries in neoclassical criminology and biosocial criminology.

The other contemporary schools of thought covered in this chapter—radical criminology, feminist criminology, critical race criminology, queer criminology, and green criminology—are critical schools of thought that provide visions for a more humane and just society. Critical criminology is *critical* because it questions social structures, including economic systems and criminal legal systems, that create and maintain social inequalities. It emphasizes social justice and reducing social harms through abolition of racist, classist, sexist, homophobic, and ableist systems, laws, policies, and practices. Critical criminologists approach their subject matter from the point of view of marginalized groups in society.

You may be wondering what the difference is between a criminological theory and a school of thought. Theories are explanations of a specified outcome (e.g., neighborhood crime rates), whereas schools of thought are broad perspectives on the nature of law and human behavior. Some theories fit within particular schools of thought. For example, routine activities theory, which explains victimization rates, is one of many theories within the neoclassical school of thought. (Routine activities theory is addressed in depth in Chapter 14.) As you read about each contemporary school of thought, ask yourself: Which of these ideas most closely aligns with my own views on the nature of law and human behavior?

NEOCLASSICAL CRIMINOLOGY

Ohio Judge Michael Cicconetti received national attention for his unorthodox sentences. He sentenced men convicted of soliciting sex for pay to walk around in chicken suits. He required a man who called a police officer a "pig" to stand with an actual pig and hold a sign reading, "This is not a police officer." Other judges have adopted the same sign-carrying tactic. A man on probation for drunk driving in Texas was ordered to hold a sign reading, "I killed Aaron Coy Pennywell while driving drunk" at the site of the crash for four Saturdays, from 9:00 a.m. to 5:00 p.m.. Cleveland Magistrate Judge Pinkey Carr ordered a woman to carry a sign stating, "Only an idiot drives on the sidewalk to avoid a school bus." Another person who came through her courtroom was required to hold a sign reading, "I apologize to officer Simone & all police officers for being an idiot calling 911 threatening to kill you. I'm sorry and it will never happen again."[6]

Public humiliation is unpleasant, and the unpleasantness is the point. Sometimes the unpleasantness is downright dangerous, as when vigilantes issue death threats (as in the Texas drunk driver's case) and threaten, assault, or kill people convicted of sex offenses whose crimes are made public through registries, local crime websites, and social media. Punishments of all kinds—prison stays, fines, having one's mugshot displayed online, in the local paper, or on a billboard—are imposed, in part, with the goal of deterring people who would commit an offense otherwise. Of her unconventional sentences, Judge Carr said, "Whenever I utilize any type of creative punishment, it's to hopefully teach people a lesson… I think it's a deterrent. No one likes to be publicly humiliated, so it sends a clear message."[7]

Deterrence is at the heart of neoclassical criminology. Recall the classical school ideas of thinkers like Beccaria and Bentham during the Enlightenment era (from Chapter 6): People have free will, they rationally weigh the costs and benefits of action, and the law ought to impose costs and reduce benefits of criminal conduct to achieve deterrence. **Neoclassical criminology** adopts these classical school principles of utility maximization

Sign-wearing humiliation-based punishments are intended to achieve deterrence, a central concept in neoclassical criminology.

AP Photo/Tony Dejak

(the idea that people will make decisions that maximize, or increase as much as possible, pleasures relative to pains).[8] Classical school thinkers were primarily philosophers, whereas neoclassical criminologists today engage in empirical analysis to determine the promise and pitfalls of policies that alter the cost-benefit calculus. Another difference is that neoclassical criminologists appreciate that achieving deterrence—making the costs of crime outweigh the benefits—requires a nuanced understanding of decision-making contexts and the limits of rationality.

Deterrence theory is not the only neoclassical perspective in criminology. Multiple perspectives rely on classical school assumptions that all people will rationally choose to engage in crime if its benefits outweigh its costs. These include control perspectives (Chapter 8), routine activities theory, and situational crime prevention (Chapter 14), in addition to deterrence theory (Chapter 13). This chapter will not delve deeply into each perspective, as all are discussed at length elsewhere in the book. Instead, the focus now is on what links them together as well as the current state of neoclassical thinking, in general. Table 7.1 presents the common thread among several neoclassical perspectives, that is, the emphasis on rational calculation of costs and benefits in criminal decision-making.

TABLE 7.1 ■ Claims about costs and benefits of crime in criminological theories adopting the neoclassical perspective	
Neoclassical perspective	**Primary claim about costs and benefits of crime**
Deterrence theory	Formal sanctions prevent crime by increasing the perceived costs of law-breaking. The more certain the anticipated punishment is, the less likely the individual is to offend, all else being equal.
Social control theory	People engage in crime when attachments to others and prosocial commitments fail to make law-breaking costly enough. In the absence of social bonds (like those to family, school, or work), the individual has little to lose.
Situational crime prevention	Changes to the physical environment can prevent crime by making it less rewarding (e.g., by concealing or removing targets, disrupting markets, or denying benefits) and more costly (as by increasing natural and formal surveillance, reducing anonymity, or using place managers).
Routine activities theory	Victimization occurs when daily routines bring potential targets into contact with people motivated to commit an offense who perceive the target (person, location, or object) as rewarding (or "attractive") and the risks of detection as low due to the absence of capable guardianship.

Another term for neoclassical perspectives is rational choice theory. Rational choice theory, like the name implies, assumes that humans use their free will to make the rational choice to break the law (or not). Neoclassical/rational choice perspectives are about crime (the occurrence of criminal events) rather than criminality (individual traits). They take criminal propensity for granted.[9] Rational choice criminologists instead seek to explain what prevents, rather than motivates, crime and victimization. Seven principles form the basis of rational choice views on crime:

1. *Rationality* – Human beings are rational actors.

2. *Utility* – Rational actors engage in means-ends calculations. In other words, they try to figure out whether the action (or means) is worth the outcome (or ends).

3. *Hedonism* – Rational actors are pleasure-seeking. They try to get the greatest possible pleasure (or benefits) with the least amount of pain (or costs) when making the means-ends calculation.

4. *Punishment* – Legal and informal punishments are potential pains/costs whose effectiveness depends on their certainty, celerity (or swiftness), and severity.

5. *Expectations* – Anticipation of pleasures/benefits and pains/costs is the driving force in decision-making. Expectations need not be accurate reflections of actual risks of costs and benefits.

6. *Social exchange* – The rational actor's ultimate decision is the end point of a series of cost-benefit calculations of multiple courses of action that could be taken at a given moment.

7. *Bounded rationality* – Consideration of alternative courses of action are limited (or bounded) by the actor's abilities and knowledge. Human beings are rational, but their rationality has limits.

The final principle, bounded rationality, is a neoclassical response to criticism of classical school ideas. If people are truly rational, the critiques goes, then they must "know all of the probabilities associated with a given course of conduct" (p. 1741).[10] They must know the risk of getting caught, the likelihood of being charged, the length of the sentence they would receive, and so on. In reality, though, people are poor estimators of these probabilities. Their expectations of legal sanctions (principle #5), also called subjective risks, rarely match their actual, or objective, risks.[11]

Imagine a person who is texting and driving while speeding down a narrow road. With their attention elsewhere, they drift across the lines and hit another moving vehicle. In the moment, several courses of action run through their mind, including (1) stopping and calling for help or (2) driving away. Imagine all the probabilities they must estimate if a hit-and-run is an option under consideration— the probability that a witness could identify their vehicle, the probability that the accident was caught on camera, the probability that the other driver was injured, the probability that they will be charged with a misdemeanor or felony if caught, the probability of having to serve time in prison, plus the length of the sentence or the amount of the fines. And then there are the probabilities of the alternative, lawful course of action—the probability that insurance costs will increase and how much they will increase, the risk of being charged with a crime related to reckless driving, the probability of losing their license, the cost of moving violation fines.

The driver is unlikely is to have complete and accurate knowledge about all (or any) of the possible outcomes. Their rationality is bounded. That makes it difficult to maximize utility (select the optimal course of action for increasing pleasures relative to pains). As a result, they will probably engage in satisficing, which is making the best decision they can with the information available. The word *satisficing* is a combination of "satisfy" and "suffice." In satisficing, decision-makers select a satisfactory (or "good enough") course of action rather than the optimal one. Satisficing is common in criminal decision-making.[12]

Incomplete or inaccurate knowledge is just one source of bounded rationality. Let's now imagine that the irresponsible texter-driver has been drinking. Their inebriation will alter the cost-benefit calculation, of course, as calling the police now means greater certainty of criminal punishment, now for driving under the influence, or DUI. More importantly, though, alcohol alters decision-making, causing people to disregard long-term consequences in favor of present concerns. This is called discounting. In discounting, criminal behavior becomes a rational choice because the person "consider[s] immediate rewards and underweight[s] future sanction costs."[13] Sources of discounting include intoxication (as in our example), cognitive impairment, and situational factors that make immediate needs especially pressing, such as time pressures, a personal economic crisis, or substance withdrawal.

Another source of bounded rationality is emotions. Anger, jealousy, fear, and excitement interrupt rational calculations, causing people to engage in what appear to be irrational acts, like excessive use of violence and spontaneous offenses without thought to risk of detection. Expressive crimes are typically impulsive and chaotic. In a qualitative study on violence in cities, perpetrators described how moralistic or righteous anger influenced their decisions to retaliate violently against those who had wronged them. Their intense emotional state resulted in "errors of scale" (using too much violence) and "errors of target" (lashing out at available but innocent victims; p. 1747).[14] In a study of 898 people convicted of sex offenses, criminologists found that rapists engage in "myopic decision-making," focusing narrowly on immediate rewards rather than more distant risks. In other words, they engage in discounting. For example, the decision to use a weapon, which substantially increased the perpetrators' prison sentences when convicted, was guided by desire to ensure the victim's compliance and the offender's arousal in the moment.[15] Their sensation-seeking state reduced their capacity to be deterred by fears of punishment.

Situational factors like substance withdrawal can lead to discounting, in which immediate rewards are weighed more heavily than more distant costs.

John Moore/Getty Images News/Getty Images

Policy Implications of Neoclassical Criminology

Neoclassical criminology aligns with right realism. Right realism is an ideological view that disregards structural contexts of people's lives (like poverty and inequality) as root causes of crime and instead places attention on the individual and their choices. Right realists favor conservative "law-and-order" or "tough-on-crime" policies that seek to change individual decision-making through punishment rather than policies that fix underlying social conditions that motivate offending. For example, right realists favor zero-tolerance policies, aggressive policing strategies, and lengthy prison sentences, such as mandatory minimum sentences and three-strikes laws. The "right" part of right realism refers to the political leaning of its strict adherents.[16] This view fits with neoclassical thinking, which suggests that any rational person will break the law if the rewards of crime far exceed the anticipated punishment. The solution, in the neoclassical view and in right realism, is to punish sufficiently to make crime an irrational decision.

There are other paths to crime reduction than punishment in the neoclassical view. The costs and rewards of crime can be manipulated by altering the physical environment, as in situational crime prevention (see Chapter 14 for specific strategies). Routine activities theory supports increased surveillance and monitoring (like cameras, security personnel, and well-lit streets) to improve capable guardianship and reduce victimization (see Chapter 14). Plus, programs and policies that support the formation of pro-social bonds early in life—youth mentoring programs, parenting classes, school dropout prevention—increase the informal costs of crime, consistent with social control theory (see Chapter 8).

BIOSOCIAL CRIMINOLOGY

Biosocial criminology analyzes the ways that biological factors and social factors interact to produce criminal behavior. Criminology has a "tortured history" with biology that has only recently improved (p. 289).[17] Most social scientists rejected biological thinking about crime following the Second World War. This was, in part, a response to empirically unsound positivist school ideas about the biological roots of criminality (recall Lombroso's criminal atavism). Plus, biological perspectives grew unpopular with the ascendency of critical criminology beginning in the 1960s (see the section on radical criminology later in this chapter).[18] The decline of biological views in criminology was also a rejection of a form of thinking that provided a veneer of (pseudo)scientific legitimacy for the atrocities of the Nazi regime as well as the eugenics movement in the United Sates (see Chapter 6 for more on eugenics). The Third Reich's reliance on "criminal biology" to justify genocide was "criminology's darkest hour" (p. 287).[19] In the decades that ensued, the *social* roots of crime—poverty, inequality, segregation—took criminology's center stage and biological perspectives were purged from the discipline.

The past few decades have witnessed a resurgence of biological thinking in criminology. This time around, however, the research is more sophisticated, carefully designed, and ethically sound than its early precursors.[20] Contemporary biosocial criminologists see sociological and biological studies of crime as complementary. They argue that biological risk factors help us to understand why harmful social environments lead to criminal conduct for some individuals but not for others.

Biosocial criminology is not a form of biological determinism (the premise that human behavior is caused solely by biological traits). Instead, the social is central. In biosocial perspective, the body provides the potential, or predisposition, with the environment either amplifying the risk of crime or serving as a protective buffer, preventing its expression.[21] An individual with a genetic, physiological, or neurological predisposition towards aggression and antisocial behavior is likely to offend if raised or residing in an adverse environment. We can think of biological traits as creating different susceptibilities to environmental influences. Some individuals, due to genetic or neurological traits beyond their control, are highly vulnerable to the crime-producing effects of social conditions like child maltreatment and living in a violent neighborhood.[22]

There are several types of modern biosocial research on crime, including biological criminology (the study of hormones and heart rates), behavioral genetics, molecular genetics, and neurocriminology.[23] Each type acknowledges the complex interplay between individual bodies and the social environment in producing antisocial behavior.

Hormones and Heart Rates

Current research in biological criminology can be sorted into two primary domains of study: hormones and resting heart rates.[24] Testosterone garners the most attention from biosocial criminologists. Testosterone is an androgen, or a male sex hormone. All bodies, regardless of assigned biological sex, produce testosterone, though levels of testosterone vary *across* sex categories and *within* sex categories. In other words, biologically male bodies, in general, produce more testosterone than biologically female bodies (variation across sex categories), and some biologically male bodies make more testosterone than other biologically male bodies (variation within a sex category). Across many studies, high levels of testosterone are linked to increased delinquency, aggression, and risk-taking.[25] As such, biosocial criminologists assert that at least part of the gender gap in criminal behavior is due to men's higher levels of the hormone relative to women's levels.

The testosterone-aggression association in humans is not straightforward. For one thing, an individual's testosterone levels can fluctuate throughout the day as well as over their life course.[26] Additionally, the causal order may be reversed, with testosterone levels increasing in response to social provocation.[27] In fact, baseline levels of testosterone, or one's typical day-to-day levels of testosterone, are not consistently found to predict aggression. Instead, dominance behaviors, like using violence, are associated with acute increases in testosterone in the context of interpersonal conflict and competition, at least for men.[28] The biological is also social.

Find your pulse on your wrist after you have been sitting for a while. Now set a timer and count your heartbeats for one minute to obtain your resting heart rate. You have this information at your fingertips already if you wear a fitness tracker with a heart rate monitor. A normal resting heart rate is between 60 and 100 beats per minute. Very low, naturally occurring resting heart rates are correlated with aggression and risk-taking behavior, including criminal behavior.[29] This pattern holds for adolescents as well as adults, for women and men, and across national contexts. Moreover, in longitudinal studies, low resting heart rates early in life are associated with criminal behavior years—even decades—later.[30]

Biosocial criminologists study the resting heart rates of incarcerated populations to determine whether and how this biological function is tied to criminal conduct. A study of adolescents incarcerated by the California Youth Authority showed that young people who had committed serious offenses had lower resting heart rates than adolescents who were not incarcerated.[31] Low resting heart rates were linked to more criminal convictions and earlier ages of criminal onset among adult male prisoners in Ontario, Canada, as well.[32] Another study suggested that low resting heart rates are associated with violent arrests more so than property crime arrests among people in U.S. jails.[33] In a rare study of resting heart rate and white-collar crime, researchers found no connection between this biological marker and occupational crime.[34]

Two explanations dominate heart rate crime research: the fearlessness hypothesis and the sensation-seeking hypothesis.[35] Understanding both requires some baseline knowledge about heart rates: Heart rates are controlled by the sympathetic (SNS) and parasympathetic (PNS) branches of the autonomic nervous system. When not under stress, the PNS keeps the heart rate low to conserve energy. When faced with stress, the PNS pulls back and the SNS operates, increasing the heart rate and metabolic output. This is why our hearts race in moments of extreme anxiety. The fearlessness hypothesis states that a low resting heart rate indicates a lack of fear, including fear of punishment and other consequences, in people with antisocial traits. The sensation-seeking hypothesis, which receives more support, claims that people with low resting heart rates engage in risky behaviors, including illegal behaviors, because they require greater stimulation to experience arousal of the autonomic nervous system.[36] In other words, they need more intense experiences to get that exciting, heart-pumping feeling.

There are many ways to experience exhilaration that are perfectly legal. Motorcycles, rock climbing, rollercoasters, sexual adventures, and a trip to the casino provide arousing sensations. A low resting

The sensation-seeking hypothesis states that people with low resting heart rates engage in crime, like joyriding in stolen vehicles, because they seek out arousing, high-risk activities.

heart rate need not lead to criminal behavior. The biological (resting heart rate) and the social (environment) interact. This is apparent in a study on the interplay of neighborhood conditions and resting heart rates on boys' delinquency.[37] The results showed that living in a distressed neighborhood had a stronger effect on the criminal conduct of boys with low heart rate reactivity.

Genetics and Crime

When 17-year-old Stephen Spahalski was booked into Chemung County Jail following his confession to the brutal murder of 48-year-old storeowner Ronald Ripley in 1971, police found that Spahalski's identical twin brother, Robert Spahalski, was also there, serving time for a parole violation. Over the ensuing decades, Stephen and Robert Spahalski cycled in and out of prison. Following his sentence for Ripley's killing, Stephen Spahalski served time for burglary, armed robbery, and various other offenses. His twin brother Robert committed four murders between 1990 and 2005, along with other less-serious offenses, eventually turning himself in to police. In the third murder, Robert Spahalski bludgeoned his victim, Charles Grande, with a hammer, just as Stephen Spahalski had done to Robert Ripley back in 1971. Stephen Spahalski expressed surprise when learning of his twin brother's murders, stating, "I thought I was the only murderer in the family."[38] The true story of the Spahalski twins draws attention to the possibility that their identical genetics played a role in their shared criminality.

Biosocial research on genetics and criminal behavior falls into two categories: Behavioral genetics and molecular genetics. **Behavioral genetics** is a field of study devoted to determining the extent of genetic heritability in predicting social behaviors, including aggression and law-breaking.[39] Genetic heritability refers to how well differences in people's genes account for the differences in their traits. Behavioral geneticists seek to answer questions about "nature versus nurture," or the relative influence of genes versus the social environment. Behavioral genetics helps answer the question: How much of the Spahalski twins' shared criminality was written in their identical genetic code (versus their similar experiences while growing up)?

Twin studies are the gold standard in behavioral genetics. Researchers compare monozygotic (identical) and dizygotic (fraternal) same-sex twins to tease out the role of genetic heritability.[40] Monozygotic twins have identical DNA, whereas fraternal twins only share 50% of their DNA, as is true of all full siblings. Yet both twin types in these studies share social environments—twin pairs are raised by the same parents, attend the same schools, and experience the same economic deprivations and privileges. If twins' aggression and criminal activity are much more similar among identical twins than fraternal twins, researchers conclude that genetics explains the difference in levels of similarity. A landmark study examining 50 years' worth of twin studies on over 17,000 different traits among 14 million twins demonstrated that roughly half of the variation in human traits, including antisocial traits, is inherited.[41] Adoption studies—where genetically related (biological) and genetically unrelated (adoptive) parent-child groups are compared—also assist biosocial criminologists in determining the relative impact of genes and environment.[42]

Biosocial criminologists caution that, while useful for understanding within-group differences in criminal behavior, we should *not* look to behavioral genetics when explaining differences in criminality across population or demographic groups.[43] For example, genetic heritability might help us to understand why some adolescents who grow up in extreme poverty engage in delinquent behavior while others do not. However, genetic heritability does not help us understand differences in rates of delinquency between adolescents raised in low-income, low-opportunity neighborhoods relative to adolescents raised in high-income, high-opportunity neighborhoods. To illustrate, imagine you have a barrel of many different corn seeds mixed together. The corn seeds represent individuals with many different genetic traits. You grab two handfuls from the barrel. You plant the first handful in nutrient-rich soil, which represents a high-quality social environment. You plant the second handful in nutrient-poor soil, which represents a low-quality social environment. The seeds grow and you observe that there is variation in the height of the corn plants in the nutrient-poor soil. Because they share an environment, any variation in height (a metaphor for behavior) is the result of heritability. The same is true among the corn plants in the nutrient-rich soil—their height depends on the individual seed. But the difference in average corn plant height between the two fields is entirely due to the quality of the two soils (social environments), *even though heritability explains within-field variation.*[44]

Twin studies allow researchers to determine how much of the variation in antisocial traits is due to genetics versus the environment.

Edwin Tan/E+/Getty Images

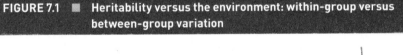

FIGURE 7.1 ■ Heritability versus the environment: within-group versus between-group variation

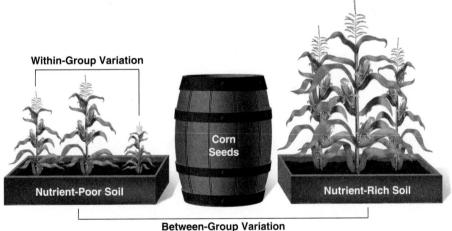

The second type of research on genetics and crime comes from molecular genetics. **Molecular genetics** in biosocial criminology involves the identification of specific genes that may be correlated with antisocial behavior.[45] Genetics, as a field, took a giant leap forward around the turn of the 21st century, when scientists first successfully mapped the human genome, allowing researchers to identify specific genetic traits. Returning to the Spahalski twins example, molecular genetics helps answer the question: Which, if any, genetic traits account for the Spahaski twins' criminality?

A beginner-level explanation of genes is useful here: There are 23 pairs of chromosomes inside every nucleus of every cell in the human body, with the exception of red blood cells. DNA (deoxyribonucleic acid) is wrapped around each chromosome. DNA has a helical, or twisted ladder, structure. The ladder's rungs are comprised of four nucleic acid base pairs, which are called A, T, C, and G (the genetic alphabet), and a portion of DNA is represented by strings of these four letters. Genes are made up of segments of this code that are responsible for functions in the body. Geneticists estimate that there are between 20,000 and 30,000 genes in the human body, and most of our genetic sequence is exactly the same across humans. The small fraction of our genes that differ from person to person are called genetic polymorphisms. Genetic polymorphisms code for the same genes, but the small differences in DNA sequences produce differences across individuals in their bodily functions (like the production of serotonin or dopamine) and physical characteristics (like eye color or height). Genetic polymorphisms are the focus of molecular genetics.

There is no "crime gene." Instead, there are genes that are associated with traits that are statistically correlated with criminality. For example, the MAOA (monoamine oxidase A) enzyme is responsible for breaking down neurotransmitters—like serotonin, dopamine, and norepinephrine—that influence aggression, emotion, and cognition. Abnormal variants of the MAOA gene can lead to increased aggressive behavior due to excessive levels of neurotransmitters in the brain (dopamine is involved in mood, motivation, and reward; serotonin is involved in impulse control and emotional regulation; norepinephrine is involved in the fight-or-flight response). The MAOA gene has been nicknamed the "warrior gene" for this reason.[46]

Many studies show that certain variants of the MAOA gene are linked to aggression and antisocial behavior among boys and men,[47] as well as psychopathic traits among girls and women.[48] Similar results are found for other genetic traits that affect neurotransmitter levels (like DAT1 and DRS2).[49] But DNA is not destiny when it comes to complex social behaviors like crime. Instead, genetic predisposition interacts with the social context. Gene-environment interactions are two-way relationships.[50] First, the influence of the environment (e.g., a violent home life or an unsafe school) on crime depends on the presence of genetic traits. Second, the expression of genetic traits depends on the environment.

Consider the case of child abuse and neglect, an environmental factor. Maltreated children are at a 50% increased risk of adult criminality relative to non-maltreated children, yet most children who are abused or neglected grow up to be law-abiding adults. The reason may be, in part, genetic. In a study that tracked 1,037 children from age 3 to age 26, researchers found that childhood maltreatment predicted adolescent conduct problems and violent convictions in adulthood much more strongly for those with genetic deficiencies in MAOA activity, at least for males.[51] The combination of abuse and neglect with genetic predisposition—far more than either alone—predicted violent behavior. For example, abused and neglected boys with low MAOA activity (a genetic deficiency) were nearly 10 times as likely as non-maltreated boys with the same genotype to be convicted of a violent crime in adulthood. This told the researchers that genes can create vulnerabilities to risky environments.

Neurocriminology

In 1991, Barbara Weinstein fell 12 stories onto Manhattan's East 72nd Street. Shortly afterward, her husband Herbert Weinstein confessed to hitting and strangling his wife and then throwing her from their 12th-story apartment window. He had tried to make it look like a suicide. Weinstein seemed an unlikely murderer. The 65-year-old retired advertising executive had no criminal record and no history of violence. He didn't even have a short temper according to people who knew him well. What he did have was an orange-sized cyst buried in his brain's arachnoid membrane. The cyst was putting pressure on his brain's frontal lobe, the region of the brain responsible for impulse control and judgment. In a first for U.S. criminal courts, the judge in Weinstein's trial permitted the defense to present MRI (magnetic resonance imaging) evidence, or brain scans, at trial. Worrying that the MRI results would sway the jury, the prosecution offered a reduced sentence for manslaughter in exchange for Weinstein's plea of guilty before the jury could even be selected. He accepted.[52]

Neurocriminology is a subdiscipline of biosocial criminology concerned with the anatomy, physiology, and chemistry of the brain. It is the neuroscience of crime.[53] Neurocriminologists come from a variety of disciplines, most outside of criminology, including neuroscience, neurology, law, and psychiatry.[54] Neurocriminologists' studies reveal many sources of impaired brain structures and functions that contribute to antisocial behavior. They include birth complications, brain dysfunction with organic causes (like Herbert Weinstein's cyst), traumatic brain injuries (TBIs) resulting from accidents or violent victimization, harmful environmental effects (like fetal alcohol exposure and lead poisoning), and toxic stress early in life.[55] Adverse childhood experiences like witnessing parental violence, sexual or emotional abuse, and enduring neglect can alter functioning in parts of the brain that govern emotional processing and decision-making.[56]

There are higher rates of neurological impairments among crime-involved populations than in the general public. An estimated 51% to 60% of incarcerated adults have sustained a traumatic brain injury, which is five to six times greater than the rate of TBIs in the general population (8%-12%).[57] And longitudinal studies following children as they grow into young adulthood find that prenatal and postnatal exposure to lead, a neurotoxin, increases the risk of delinquency[58] and of later arrest.[59] Whether TBIs and lead exposure *cause* crime is up for debate (e.g., the high-risk lifestyles of people who commit offenses might make them vulnerable to being injured), yet the correlations are clear, as observed in Figure 7.2.

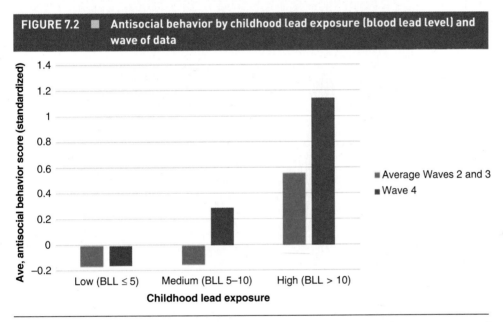

FIGURE 7.2 ■ Antisocial behavior by childhood lead exposure (blood lead level) and wave of data

Source: Sampson, R., & Winter, A. (2018). Poisoned development: Assessing childhood lead exposure as a cause of crime in a birth cohort followed through adolescence. *Criminology*, 56(2), 269-301. © 2018 The Authors. *Criminology* published by Wiley Periodicals, Inc. on behalf of American Society of Criminology.

Notes: Participants were age 16-18 at Wave 4. Wave 2 and 3 data were collected in early childhood.

Genes and hormones are "neuro," too, in that they operate indirectly through their effects on the brain. After all, the brain is "the epicenter for all human behavior and emotions" (p. 80).[60] The link between genes and the brain goes even deeper. Genetics accounts for an estimated 60% to 80% of variation in the brain's structure, though it explains only 40% of the variation in brain functioning.[61] This tells us that the environment matters a great deal in forming the brain's wiring, or neural connections. The brain has the "ability to calibrate itself to the environment," called plasticity (p. 97).[62] Social experiences shape the brain, just as the brain influences social behavior.

Neurocriminologists rely on neuroimaging techniques to study the brain's structures and functions, including functional magnetic resonance imaging (fMRI), which measures brain activity by identifying changes in the brain's blood flow. Figure 7.2 displays an example of MRI results. Typically, they compare the imaging results of antisocial individuals (including people incarcerated for committing violence offenses) and a control group, or they compare imaging results for different categories of antisocial populations, like people who commit domestic violence offenses versus people who commit property offenses. In some studies, antisocial participants will be given moral decision-making tasks during imaging, allowing researchers to examine how their brains respond, in the moment, to problems of right and wrong.[63]

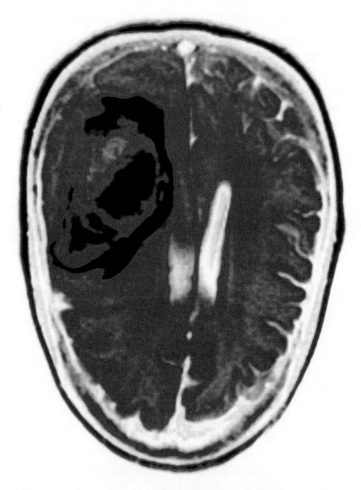

Traumatic brain injuries, like the one observed in this MRI scan, can impact criminal conduct by altering functioning in parts of the brain that govern emotional processing and decision-making.

Ted Kinsman/Science Source

Using brain imaging, neurocriminologists find that the most consistent neurological predictor of antisocial behavior, including crime, is reduced functioning in the brain's frontal lobe, as was the case for Herbert Weinstein.[64] This makes sense once we consider the activities of the frontal lobe's various regions. For example, the dorsolateral prefrontal cortex is involved in self-regulation processes; poor functioning in this part of the brain is associated with impulsive behavior.[65] The anterior cingulate cortex is responsible for avoidance learning and conflict monitoring; damage to this region of the brain leads to aggression, disinhibition, and difficulties processing emotions. And decision-making is impaired, including the ability to learn from rewards and punishment, among people with injury to the ventral prefrontal cortex.[66]

Brain imaging studies of people incarcerated for chronic violent offending also point to altered functioning of the amygdala.[67] The amygdala is involved in decision-making and emotional responses, including fear. Reduced volume in this region of the brain, observed more among people convicted of serious violent offenses than among people who have not been convicted of such offenses, is associated with psychopathic traits, like calculated aggression and reduced empathy.[68]

ENGAGED CRIMINOLOGY 7.1
Take a Stand

In this take-a-stand activity, you must take a position on whether a person who commits a serious violent crime should be punished less severely if they have a genetic and neurological predisposition towards criminality.

The scenario: *You are the judge responsible for sentencing a person who has been found guilty of an aggravated assault that resulted in serious injury to the victim. The offender, in a moment of anger and frustration, attacked the victim (a neighbor) with a baseball bat until passersby pulled them off. The defense attorney presented evidence that the offender had several conditions that predisposed them to impulsivity and emotional dysregulation, including a history of traumatic brain injuries damaging the frontal lobe (based on fMRI evidence) and low MAOA activity (a genetic variant linked to antisocial behavior).*

1
Not culpable:
No criminal
punishment at all

10
Equally culpable:
Same exact punishment
as an offender without
biological, genetic, or
neurological
predisposition

1. Where do you fall on the continuum, which ranges from 1 (not culpable/no punishment) to 10 (equally culpable/same punishment)? Indicate your position by selecting a value between 1 and 10.

2. In one or two sentences, explain the reason(s) for your score.

Policy Implications of Biosocial Criminology

In making policy recommendations, biosocial criminologists look to prevention science.[69] Prevention science is a field of research whose goal is to prevent or mitigate human dysfunctions through the study of risk and protective factors. There are two main biosocial approaches to crime prevention. The first is to create targeted interventions for young people, especially for "dual risk" individuals, or those who are at a high risk of offending due to biological risk and environmental risk, such as family dysfunction.[70] The second approach seeks to lessen the harmful physical and social states that create criminogenic neurological conditions in the first place.

Biosocial interventions often focus on temperament, the mostly innate and stable way in which people experience and respond to their environment. Two interrelated aspects of temperament are associated with lifelong behavior problems: effortful control (ability to regulate one's behavior, focus attention, and suppress unnecessary thoughts and emotions) and negative emotionality (predisposition to frustration, anger, fear, and irritability). Intervention programs aim to build self-regulation and anger management skills. Some programs target parents of young children, providing training in modeling resilience and positive interpersonal skills. An experimental study of one such program—Strong African American Families (SAAF)—found that the intervention was especially effective for children with high-risk genetic traits.[71] Other interventions are implemented in schools, like Promoting Alternative Thinking Strategies (PATHS), whose goals include developing emotional competence and regulation in children.[72]

Biosocial criminologists also call for policies that fix harmful physical conditions that cause neurological disruption. Examples include lead abatement (removing lead from products, homes, and the physical environment) and nutrition programs for pregnant people, infants, and children.[73] Improving social conditions is an additional policy goal. Complex trauma—exposure to chronic and prolonged traumatic experiences like abuse, neglect, and witnessing intimate partner violence or community violence—alters brain functioning, changing cognitive and emotional competencies.[74] Policies that provide a safety net for economically struggling families, as well as funding for early childhood home visitation programs and parenting training programs, align with the biosocial approach.[75]

RADICAL CRIMINOLOGY

From Santa Fe, New Mexico, to Boise, Idaho, to Winston-Salem, North Carolina, hundreds of home-less tent encampments dot the American landscape.[76] These communities range in size, with about one in six serving as home to over 100 homeless residents. They have become semi-permanent features of U.S. cities, with about two-thirds lasting more than a year and one-quarter lasting more than five years. City officials feel pressure to "do something" about visible homelessness. Most have employed punitive measures, criminalizing encampments and survival behaviors of the homeless. Encampments are routinely destroyed, and residents' belongings along with them, as "camping bans" are enforced. Homeless persons are issued citations for violating "sit-lie ordinances" when they sit or sleep in public spaces, as well as when they panhandle, urinate outdoors, or sleep in a vehicle overnight.[77] Unable to afford the fines, they often cycle in and out of jail. It is even illegal to give food to homeless people in some cities.[78] When citations aren't issued, homeless persons are often told by police "you can't be here" and are compelled to move to another unwelcoming location.[79] Criminologists call these policies "rabble management." Rabble refers to socially undesirable people.[80] Anti-homeless ordinances are the state's way of containing the poorest of the poor. Contemporary radical criminologists can point to the criminalization of the homeless as evidence of their claims.

Police interacting with a resident of a homeless encampment in Sacramento, California. Police are responsible for "rabble management," which radical criminologists describe as criminalization of the poor.

Justin Sullivan/Getty Images News/Getty Images

Radical criminology, which grew in prominence during the 1960s and 1970s, shines a critical light on the very definition of crime and conventional thinking about its causes. It is one of multiple critical schools of thought, all of which question social structures that create and reproduce inequalities. (The remainder of this chapter covers various critical schools of thought.) In **radical criminology**, capitalism—and the unequal class system it requires—is the core cause of crime.[81] Radical criminologists challenge the state's overcriminalization of the poor and powerless, as well as its failure to address harmful actions of the powerful in society, including the actions of corporations and the state itself.[82] In this view, over-criminalization and undercriminalization—called criminal selectivity—reflects the dominant inter-ests of the powerful and serves to maintain their position at the top of economic and social hierarchies.

Radical criminologists regard harms committed by the state (e.g., war, genocide, and imperial-ism) and harms committed by corporations (e.g., dangerous workplaces, exploitative wages, and toxic dumping) to be *real* crimes. Meanwhile, they argue, jails and prisons are filled with marginalized peo-ple who engage in offenses—drug possession, burglary, robbery—that are a response to their position at the bottom of hierarchies that sort people into haves and have-nots. Their crimes are an expression of either economic need or social demoralization. They are beaten down by a system that strips them of their humanity. Thus, criminal law is seen as a coercive instrument used by the state "to preserve the existing economic and social order" (p. 241).[83] The idea that the legal system ensures that "the rich get richer and the poor get prison" is a radical criminological stance.[84]

Marx and Engels's Economic Analysis

Radical criminology is largely rooted in Marxist analysis of capitalist society, though Marx, himself, wrote very little on the subject of crime. Karl Marx (1818-1883) was a 19th century social philosopher and historian who argued that a society's economic development determined all of its human relations. Marx and his colleague Friedrich Engels based their analysis on a concept called historical material-ism. **Historical materialism** treats the historical development of human societies, including the devel-opment of their cultural institutions (like religion, law, and morality), as arising from their material conditions. In other words, the way people develop and produce material goods—the society's mode of production—determines everything else in the society, including its political and legal structure.

Marx's expansive analysis of capitalism is far too complex to fit into a few paragraphs, but a brief primer will suffice for our purposes. The first thing to understand is the word *capitalism*. Capitalism is an economic system in which industry and trade are controlled by private owners for profit. Marx and Engels argued that there are two primary classes in capitalist society: the bourgeoisie (the ruling class) and the proletariat (the working class). The *bourgeoisie* controls the facilities and resources necessary for producing goods, called the means of production. In the 19th century, when Marx and Engels were writ-ing, this mostly meant factories. The *proletariat*, in comparison, own little and their survival requires selling their labor to the bourgeoisie.[85] A contemporary example would be the distinction between Jeff Bezos (bourgeoisie), the founder and CEO of Amazon (and the richest person in the world as of this writing), and the warehouse workers and drivers that make Amazon's operations possible (proletariat).

There is a third class, as well: the *lumpenproletariat*. This group occupies the lowest position in the class hierarchy. They are the "surplus population" of unemployed or underemployed people that serves as a reserve pool of low-wage labor that can be drawn on when needed. They accept the worst (and worst-paid) jobs when the proletariat will not. Because of their impoverished circumstances, some of the lumpenproletariat resort to illegal or disreputable means to survive, like prostitution, theft, or panhandling. They are regarded by the rest of society as the criminal classes who threaten the capitalist system even though capitalism requires a reserve pool of desperate workers willing to accept undesir-able jobs for low pay. Therefore, crime is inevitable in capitalism, according to this perspective.[86]

Exploitation is central in Marx's analysis of capitalism. He and Engels claimed that the bourgeoisie exploit the proletariat by paying them less than their labor is worth. By paying their workers little, the bourgeoisie can maximize their profits. For this reason, the interests of the ruling class and the work-ing class are fundamentally at odds.[87] Yet many exploited workers (and unemployed people) do not realize that their interests are opposite that of the bourgeoisie; they lack a "class consciousness." Marx and Engels argued that if workers understood their shared predicament of exploitation under capital-ism, they would band together to solve their problem through the formation of unions or, in extreme conditions, revolution. Workers may, in fact, possess a "false consciousness," Marx and Engels assert, in which they fail to see how they are being exploited and instead blame their circumstances on something other than the economic system, such as immigration.[88]

Contemporary Radical Thinking in Criminology

Contemporary radical criminologists draw on Marx's analysis of capitalism to critically evaluate crimi-nal law and its enforcement. Though their perspectives vary somewhat, they can be synthesized into four main propositions:

1. *Capitalism produces crime.*
   Capitalism necessarily leads to the creation of an underclass comprised of those at the bottom of the class hierarchy (the lumpenproletariat). This group—alienated and

despairing—engages in crimes of survival.[89] Marxism suggests that capitalism is a criminogenic system for others, as well, because of the competitive, self-interested ideology it promotes. People must compete for scarce jobs and resources, especially in light of technological transformations that replace human workers. Classmates, coworkers, and neighbors are transformed into competitors. Those who are more readily exploited, such as immigrants, are vilified. The moral imperative to care for and show concern for others diminishes. This is compounded by the alienation people feel when they toil at work without purpose. Engels wrote that when people look out only for themselves, whether one

injures declared enemies is simply a matter of selfish calculation as to whether such action would be to [their] advantage or not. In short, everyone sees in [their] neighbor a rival to be elbowed aside, or at best a victim to be exploited for [their] own ends. (pp. 145-146)[90]

Self-serving elbowing and exploiting are not reserved only for the powerless. The dominant class is also in fierce competition among themselves, leading to cheating and white-collar offenses in efforts to beat out rival capitalists, typically at the expense of less-wealthy customers, clients, and community members.[91]

2. *Criminal law under capitalism enables and hides crimes of domination.*

Richard Quinney, a radical criminologist, differentiates between "crimes of accommodation" and "crimes of domination."[92] Crimes of accommodation, he wrote, are the predatory or personal offenses committed by the poor or working class as a direct result of their marginalized position. Examples include theft, assault, and burglary. Crimes of domination, in contrast, are committed by the state or members of the ruling class to keep the poor in their place and hold on to their position of power. These include offenses like political corruption, price fixing, and police brutality. Crimes of domination are undercriminalized because they generate and maintain wealth or power for the ruling class. When treated as harms, they are dealt with in civil courts (as lawsuits) instead of criminal courts. If they are treated as criminal harms, they result in "slap on the wrist" consequences, such as fines instead of prison time.

In radical criminological view, crimes of domination extend beyond acts codified in law as crime. They also include harms created by unjust systems, including racist, classist, and sexist governmental policies, as well as state acts of violence and violations of human rights that are legal but unethical.[93] Demeaning treatment of migrants and asylum seekers, forced sterilization of poor women, oppressive treatment of Indigenous populations (like land seizures and forced removal of Indigenous children), and enforcement of punitive anti-homeless ordinances (described at the start of the section) are a few examples of crimes of domination in this perspective.

3. *Crime serves important functions for capitalism.*

Radical criminologists suggest that crime serves a useful function for the ruling class because it diverts attention away from capitalism's exploitative nature and towards the criminal behaviors of the poor.[94] As a result, the thinking goes, the public's anger is misplaced. It is a sleight of hand, drawing attention down to the bottom of the social hierarchy rather than up to the top—or to the hierarchy itself.

In addition, crime control is a lucrative industry. Cracking down on marginalized groups who commit crimes of accommodation and survival (substance users, the chronically homeless, people who cannot find legal work due to criminal records) ensures jobs for law enforcement, probation officers, correctional staff, and others. Moreover, for-profit companies capitalize on mass incarceration. About 1 out of 12 state and federal prisoners in the U.S. is housed in a private—or for-profit— prison.[95] The profits flow to the corporation that runs the prison, not to the state that contracts with the corporation. Private probation services operate in a similar fashion, with private companies contracted by local governments to supervise probation for minor crimes like misdemeanors and criminal traffic offenses. Probationers must pay for their own probation services, including drug screening fees, treatment fees, and probation supervision fees. They pay the fees directly to the private company.[96] A common critique, shared by radical criminologists, is that privatization of criminal justice turns prisoners and probationers into commodities.[97] They argue that capitalism creates perverse incentives to continue enacting harmful policies, like the War on Drugs, that fail to improve public safety and serve only to deepen human suffering of groups least able to resist criminalization.

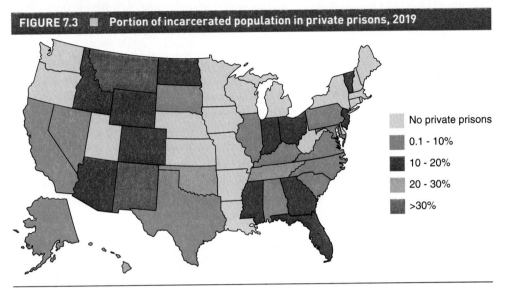

FIGURE 7.3 ■ Portion of incarcerated population in private prisons, 2019

Legend:
- No private prisons
- 0.1 - 10%
- 10 - 20%
- 20 - 30%
- >30%

Source: The Sentencing Project. (2021, March 3). *Private prisons in the United States.* https://www.sentencingproject.org/publications/private-prisons-united-states/

4. *Capitalism determines how society responds to crime.*

      Radical criminologists argue that the content of law reflects the ruling class's concerns about subordinated groups making trouble for capitalism. What makes trouble for capitalism? Actions that threaten ownership under capitalism (like theft) make trouble and are targeted for punishment. The same goes for actions that undermine productivity (like substance use) and do not contribute to production (like homelessness). Actions that threaten institutions that uphold the dominant ideology are also criminalized.

      Radical criminologist Steven Spitzer organized threats to capitalism targeted by law into two groups: social junk and social dynamite. Social junk is, from the perspective of the dominant class, a "costly yet relatively harmless burden to society" (p. 645).[98] Individuals regarded as social junk are unable or unwilling to participate in productive roles. That is what renders them "junk" in the dominant view—they are worthless to those seeking profit because they do not work or support others who work for pay. This group includes people with substance dependencies and severe mental illness. Populations who live in tent encampments would fall into this category (though a sizeable minority work in legal jobs).[99] Social dynamite, in contrast, holds the potential to "blow up" relations of production and domination. They challenge the existing social order. Compared to social junk, they tend to be younger, angrier, more alienated, and more politically volatile. Social dynamite is viewed by the dominant class as an organized political threat. The Black Lives Matter movement, discussed at the start of the chapter, is regarded as social dynamite by many who benefit from the status quo.

Policy Implications of Radical Criminology

Nothing short of transforming the economic structure of society will solve the crime problem, according to true radical/Marxist perspective. Tweaking or even overhauling criminal justice policies will be ineffective because the fundamental cause of exploitation, class conflict, and crime—that is, the capitalist mode of production—remains in place. Marx and Engels entreated their readers to revolt, writing "Workers of the world, unite! You have nothing to lose but your chains!"[100] Nonetheless, many radical criminologists today advocate for reforms, such as ending prison privatization and mass incarceration, rather than revolution.[101]

Radical criminologists question definitions of crime that characterize the poor as dangerous people who commit crime and ignore the harms of the powerful. They see repressive crime control as a tool of the ruling class, used for controlling and managing the poor.[102] As such, radical criminologists propose a shift towards punishing people who commit "crimes of the powerful" and corporations that do criminal harm. In addition, they favor providing an adequate social safety net to decrease crimes of economic desperation, as through higher minimum wages, universal health care, paid family leave, universal high-quality child care, and accessible community mental health treatment. These ideas are in line with a perspective called left realism.

Left realists regard "street crimes" as a real social problem (hence *realism*) in need of a solution, while holding the view that capitalism is at the heart of the crime problem. Left realism, in contrast to the right realism associated with neoclassical criminology, is an ideological view that locates the root causes of crime in social structures, or the unequal organization of groups in society. Crime control measures favored by right realists—zero-tolerance policies, aggressive policing, and long prison sentences—will only increase crime by further marginalizing the powerless, in the left realist perspective. Left realists prefer policies that address harmful social conditions at the root of the crime problem without advocating revolution. In this view, punishing law-breakers is insufficient for reducing crime, as the social system that gave birth to crime in the first place remains unchanged.[103] Left realist solutions to crime include alternatives to prison (like restorative justice and community service) along with socialist policies—for example, government-funded housing and child care subsidies—that protect vulnerable groups who might otherwise turn to crime to meet their needs.[104]

FEMINIST CRIMINOLOGY

Feminist criminology is a critical school of thought that calls for greater attention to the role of gender in crime and criminal justice experiences. Feminism is the idea that all people, regardless of gender, should have equal legal and political rights, autonomy, and self-determination. Feminist movements advocate for structural and cultural changes that will achieve economic, social, and political equality. Feminist criminologists approach the study of crime from this perspective.

Feminist criminologists acknowledge that gender inequalities (or sexism), in combination with other social inequalities (on the basis of race and ethnicity, social class, ability, age, and sexualities), shape social life in ways that matter for crime, victimization, and punishment.[105] In other words, intersectionality—the notion that people's overlapping identities shape the disadvantages and privileges they experience—is central in contemporary feminist criminology, thanks to the contributions of Black feminist thinkers like Kimberlé Crenshaw.[106] And feminist scholars of crime link research to activism, pushing for evidence-informed policies and practices that improve women's (and others') lives. Their research and activism often address gender-based violence, women's incarceration, and gendered injustices in the application and administration of law.[107]

Up until the 1980s, criminology was, in the words of feminist criminologists Kathleen Daly and Meda Chesney-Lind, stuck in an "androcentric slumber" (p. 507).[108] Androcentrism is the centering of masculinity, male points of view, and male experience (*andro-* means male). Androcentrism treats men and masculine traits as normal and all non-male gender experiences as "other." Criminologists were overwhelmingly white and male until about 40 years ago. Their focus of study was primarily men's crime and men's incarceration. For example, a content analysis of 20th century American and British criminological research revealed that fewer than 11% of research articles in criminology journals focused on female crime, and a similarly small proportion relied on samples that contained equivalent numbers of women/girls and men/boys.[109] During these years, explanations of female criminality and the gender gap in crime invoked ideas from theories designed to explain male criminality rather than consider women's and girls' experiences *as women and girls*. Feminist scholars called this the "add gender and stir" approach.[110]

Feminist criminologists don't just bring women and girls into the study of crime. They bring gender into it, as well, acknowledging how gender shapes the lives of *all* people, including men, boys, and, more recently, transgender and nonbinary persons.[111] Feminist criminology, like feminism is general, is not "only" about women. The core principles of feminist criminology include the following:

1. *Gender organizes social life.* Norms and expectations about male and female behavior are transmitted and enforced through social interaction. These include interactions with parents, peers, strangers in public, police, correctional officers, and others. Though there is a biological component to gender development, which feminist criminologists recognize, their focus is on the ways that gender is socially constructed.[112] In this perspective, gender is understood as a "situated accomplishment," or something that one *does* in response to context-specific norms rather than something that one *is*. ("Gender identity," a distinct concept, refers to one's sense of self as a woman, a man, neither, or both.) People "do gender" continuously in social interactions, and how they enact gender can change over time and from situation to situation.[113] Consider, for example, how the expected performance of masculinity might be different in prison versus at home with one's children.

2. *Most societies differentially value men and women.* In other words, they are characterized by sexism. This is expressed interpersonally in daily interactions, and it is a feature of macro-level social structures, including the organization of family roles, work, the law, and politics. Sexism is baked into **patriarchy**, a social system in which men dominate women and masculinity is believed to be superior to femininity.[114] Sexism can be hostile or benevolent. Hostile sexism is openly anti-woman (or misogynistic), regarding women as manipulative and deserving of objectification or of being degraded. In hostile sexism, women's demands for equal treatment are perceived as threats to masculinity or "traditional values," evoking anger, resentment, and aggression.[115] An example of hostile sexism is found in violence of self-proclaimed "incels" who seek to punish women (and men) who represent their sexual rejection.[116] Benevolent sexism, in contrast, regards women as moral, pure, fragile, and in need of men's protection. Women who adhere to a docile feminine stereotype and occupy traditionally feminine roles (e.g., stay-at-home mothers) are granted esteem; other women are not. Although benevolent sexism appears more positive than hostile sexism, it, too, "presumes and reinforces women's subordinate status" (p. 295).[117] Benevolent sexism shapes attitudes towards female victims of sexual assault, intimate partner violence, and stalking—those who hold these attitudes are more likely to see women who do not fit feminine stereotypes as deserving victims.[118]

Liberal Versus Radical Feminist Criminology

There are several branches of feminist thought, all of which subscribe to the core principles regarding gender as an organizing principle and sexism as a problem. However, they adopt different ways of thinking about and solving the problems of gender inequalities, gender-based violence, and gender bias in the criminal legal system. Two types of feminism that have influenced the study of crime and criminal justice reform are liberal feminism and radical feminism.

Liberal feminism (or mainstream feminism) is concerned with ensuring women have rights and opportunities equal to men's. Abolishing gender discrimination in all realms of life is a central aim of liberal feminism.[119] Liberal feminists support legal reforms that eliminate gender bias in policing, sentencing, and other forms of criminal justice decision-making. Another path to gender equality runs through childhood socialization, with liberal feminists championing a change to traditional gender socialization, with girls and boys instead learning similar attitudes and behaviors. The liberation hypothesis (the claim that increased gender equality means women's crime will become more like men's crime) and the economical marginalization hypothesis (the claim that women's increasing economic vulnerability causes an increase in women's crime relative to men's crime), both addressed in Chapter 5, are examples of liberal feminist criminological explanations of the shrinking gender gap in crime.

Feminist criminologists study gender-based violence, including trafficking and criminal punishment of sexually exploited girls and women like this 17-year-old in South Central Los Angeles who was criminally charged with prostitution.

Robert Nickelsberg/Getty Images News/Getty Images

Radical feminism foregrounds patriarchy (versus socialization) in its analysis of gender inequality, arguing that women's structural oppression, or sexism, is the most fundamental form of oppression in human societies. Radical feminist criminologists assert that patriarchal gender relations result in men's violent attempts to control women's sexuality, including rape, stalking, intimate partner violence, sex trafficking, and gender-based war crimes.[120] In this perspective, the criminal legal system, like all patriarchal social structures, maintains male dominance and female subjugation.

Radical feminists spearheaded the study of violence against women, and they drew attention to the failures of the legal system to protect women and girls from men's and boys' violence.[121] Their efforts have resulted in major legislative reforms and changes to enforcement practices, including revised rape laws that encompass a broader range of sexual violations (and focus attention on the actions of perpetrators instead of the actions of victims) and the treatment of intimate partner violence as a criminal action worthy of prosecution.[122] Detractors, however, accuse radical feminists of neglecting female criminality as well as overlooking how other systems of oppression, like racism, class inequality, and heterosexism, interact with sexism to produce very different criminal justice outcomes for women of color, poor women, immigrant women, trans women, and lesbians.[123]

Policy Implications of Feminist Criminology

Feminist activists and scholars transformed violence against women from a private problem into a public issue, as captured in the feminist slogan, "The personal is political." A signature achievement of the feminist movement, informed by the work of feminist criminologists, was the passage of the 1994 Violence Against Women Act (VAWA), which created and provided funding support for programs addressing domestic violence, sexual assault, dating violence, and stalking. VAWA reauthorization, approved by the House of Representatives on March 8, 2021, entailed updates that responded to the complexities of survivors' lives.[124] It included support for

- Legal services for survivors;

- Restorative justice practices;

- Housing protections and victim relocation vouchers;

- Prevention programming, including the Rape Prevention and Education Program;

- Closing of loopholes in federal domestic violence–related firearms laws; and

- Nondiscrimination guarantees that extend VAWA protections regardless of a survivor's gender.

Feminist criminologists also call for changes to how the criminal legal system responds to girls and women, favoring gender-responsive incarceration and re-entry programming. Gender-responsive programs acknowledge and address traumatic pathways that characterize many girls' and women's pathways to substance use and law-breaking, as well as their unique experiences with pregnancy and motherhood.[125] Scholars of women's incarceration note further that such programming ought to be community-based, not just within the confines of jails and prisons, which are, themselves, traumatizing institutions.[126]

Feminists today are split regarding ideal policy solutions when it comes to perpetrators of gender-based violence. There are two broad camps: carceral feminism and abolitionist feminism. Critical of the state's inadequate response to rape and other crimes that disproportionately harm women, *carceral feminism* "promotes state-based responses to sexual violence (and gender violence more generally), primarily through the traditional criminal justice system" (p. 50).[127] For example, demands that Brock Turner, the perpetrator in the high-profile Stanford rape case, face substantial prison time reflect the priorities of carceral feminism. *Abolitionist feminism*, in contrast, opposes incarceration as the primary or sole response to sexual violence (and other offenses), arguing that imprisonment fails to actually reduce the risks of sexual assault, if the perpetrator is ever, in fact, punished at all.[128] Instead, abolitionists propose restorative justice initiatives, which focus on healing, giving victims a voice, building empathy in people who commit offenses, and requiring them to take responsibility for the harms they have caused.[129]

QUEER CRIMINOLOGY, CRITICAL RACE CRIMINOLOGY, AND GREEN CRIMINOLOGY

There are multiple additional critical schools of thought in criminology, most of them overlapping with or emerging from radical and feminist criminology. As critical perspectives, they all challenge social structures—the criminal legal system among them—that maintain inequalities and produce social harms, and each offers a vision for a more just society. This section addresses three such perspectives: queer criminology, critical race criminology, and green criminology.

Queer Criminology

Queer criminology critiques the status quo in in the study of crime, victimization, and punishment by bringing LGBTQ issues and perspectives into the foreground, just as feminist criminology does with gender and critical race criminology does with race.[130] The word *queer* in queer criminology is an umbrella term for individuals and communities who identify as lesbian, gay, bisexual, queer, transgender, gender-expansive, intersex (when one's reproductive or sexual anatomy does not fit typical definitions of male or female), and other identities outside of cisgender heterosexuality. The word *cisgender* refers to when one's gender identity and presentation correspond to their assigned sex at birth. As with other critical perspectives, queer criminology seeks to expose injustices, with a focus on inequalities based on sexual orientation and gender identity, intersecting with other identities. Queer criminology also addresses the lack of attention to LGBTQ issues in criminal justice. It challenges the heteronormativity of mainstream criminology and of the criminal legal system. Heteronormativity is the belief that heterosexuality is the default (or "normal") sexual orientation and the assumption that all people are heterosexual.

Queer criminology highlights how the criminal legal system is used as a tool to stigmatize and criminalize the LGBTQ community.[131] The most basic example of this is found in laws that criminalized particular sexual acts, including those between people of the same biological sex, called "anti-sodomy" laws. Starting in the late 1960s, with the rise of the gay liberation movement, anti-sodomy laws specifically targeted gay people (versus heterosexual people engaging in prohibited sex acts). Kansas was the first state, in 1969, to rewrite its anti-sodomy law to apply only to same-sex intimacy. Seven other states followed suit, and two additional states' laws only applied to same-sex contact despite sexuality-neutral writing. Anti-sodomy laws—whether specifically targeting same-sex relations or not—were then used as justification for employment discrimination and preventing lesbians and gay men from maintaining custody of their own children as well as adopting or fostering children.[132]

The U.S. Supreme Court struck down laws that criminalize sexual behaviors between consenting adults in *Lawrence v. Texas* (2003), though laws prohibiting same-sex intimacies persist around the globe, with at least 69 nations criminalizing consensual same-sex relations. Additionally, at least nine nations have laws that target transgender and gender-expansive persons, prohibiting specific forms of gender expression.[133] Throughout the mid-20th century in the U.S., "masquerade laws," which prohibited "cross-dressing," were used to regulate gender expression and punish those who did not conform.[134] Though transgender identities and presentation are no longer criminalized in the U.S., laws that target transgender persons persist, such as "bathroom bills" that criminalize transgender persons who use public restrooms that align with their gender identity and expression. Critics point out that these laws rest on inaccurate stereotypes that malign transgender people as a sexual threat.[135] They also note that it is trans people who are at greatest risk of victimization while accessing public accommodations. In fact, a study of 27,715 transgender persons found that 59% of respondents avoided using public bathrooms in the previous year due to fear of harassment and violence.[136]

Queer criminologists highlight the risks of criminal victimization specific to the LGBTQ community as a result of homophobia and transphobia. For example, they draw attention to the disproportionate risk of murder victimization among trans women of color, especially trans women engaged in sex work.[137] They give voice to victims of anti-gay and anti-trans hate crimes, including attention to how victims think about and respond to these attacks.[138] LGBTQ victims of bias-motivated crimes, and transgender victims especially, are often hesitant to report to law enforcement for fear of further discriminatory treatment.[139] Furthermore, queer criminologists describe how homophobia and transphobia at home, in school, in religious congregations, and in other institutions push young LGBTQ people into homelessness, where they are vulnerable to further victimization on the streets and within the criminal legal system.[140]

Much of queer criminology focuses on LGBTQ experiences—of victims, people who commit offenses, and employees—within the criminal legal system, including jails and prisons.[141] Incarcerated people and correctional staff who are LGBTQ report high levels of discrimination and harassment, as well as feelings of isolation and alienation. And the risk of physical attacks by fellow incarcerated people or corrections personnel among gay and transgender persons are far higher than for the general population of people who are incarcerated, especially in men's facilities.[142] Prison officials often opt to place vulnerable people—including trans women held in men's prisons—in segregation units (isolation cells).[143] Though protection is important, these practices violate the Prison Rape Elimination Act (PREA), and they have profound negative consequences for mental and physical health.[144]

Jarvis "Lady Jae" Clark, pictured here with drama therapist Rezal Martínez-Gillies, is a transgender woman housed at the San Quentin State Prison for men.

Michael Macor/The San Francisco Chronicle/Getty Images

ENGAGED CRIMINOLOGY 7.2
Criminology Product Reviews

This activity requires you to create a positive product review of a school of thought in criminology. The product review will be in the style of a positive, five-star review you would see on a site like Amazon or Yelp. Select one school of thought to review.

1. Which school of thought did you select? Pick one.
   a. Neoclassical criminology
   b. Biosocial criminology
   c. Feminist criminology
   d. Radical criminology
   e. Critical race criminology
   f. Queer criminology
   g. Green criminology

2. Create a five-star review for your selected school of thought. Write the review like you would review a product on an online marketplace. The language can be informal. Consider: What is good about this school of thought? How is it useful to criminologists? Why should others consider adopting the perspective?

Critical Race Criminology

Critical race criminology, born of the critical legal studies movement of the 1970s, addresses the relationship between race/ethnicity, racism, and power in the creation of crime and society's response to it. It is the application of critical race theory, which "expose[s] the easily obscured and often racialized power structures of American society," to the study of crime and criminal justice (p. 1).[145] Critical race criminologists question the foundations of the criminal legal system, arguing for alternatives systems (like restorative justice) and seeking to correct historical and ongoing injustices. This sets the critical race perspective apart from the civil rights approach, which advocated incremental changes to the status quo.[146] Five ideas are at the core of critical race criminology[147]:

Guided by these five ideas, critical race criminologists have two principal aims. The first aim is to expose the role of law in perpetuating racial oppression and white supremacy, both historically and in modern times.[150] White supremacy is the ideology that white people are superior to people of color, as maintained by beliefs, values, and social structures. For example, critical race scholars argue that the War on Drugs deepens racial hierarchies.[151] It has been called a "purveyor of mass injustice" (p. xi)[152] that has "created a new racial caste system" (p. 11).[153] As evidence, they note that Black persons have been 6 to 10 times more likely to be incarcerated for drug offenses than white persons despite similar levels of substance use across racial groups.[154] They further describe how mass incarceration, which has disproportionately affected Black and (to a lesser extent) Latinx and Native American communities, was driven in part by War on Drugs policies.[155] Between 1992 and 2009, years of unprecedented prison growth and the War on Drugs, the federal sentences of Black persons convicted of drug offenses were, on average, almost four years (47 months) longer than those of white persons sentenced to federal prison for drug crimes. This was due primarily to sentencing policies that appeared race-neutral but punished Black persons convicted of drug crimes excessively relative to white persons. For example, lengthy mandatory minimum sentences for possessing small amounts of crack cocaine disproportionately affected Black federal defendants (powdered cocaine, which was more likely to be used by white persons, resulted in much shorter federal sentences). The racial gap for federal drug sentences disappeared entirely following reforms to these policies.[156]

The second aim of critical race criminology is to prevent the law from being used to perpetuate white supremacy and racial oppression.[157] This is the activist part of the critical race school of thought. Attention is given to specific laws and practices that disproportionately impact communities of color, including racial profiling, police brutality, wrongful convictions, and mandatory minimum sentences.[158] Here we can see how the Black Lives Matter movement, discussed at the start of the chapter, aligns closely with critical race criminology; there is a shared commitment to centering the voices of people of color (through "legal storytelling") and transforming the legal order to achieve racial justice.

Green Criminology

Green criminologists are critical of mainstream criminology's preoccupation with street crimes, arguing that "green crimes" are a more pressing and existential threat to human safety, to say nothing of the safety of nonhuman animals and the Earth's ecosystem. **Green criminology** is best defined as

the study of those harms against humanity, against the environment (including space) and against non-human animals committed both by powerful institutions (e.g., governments, transnational corporations, military apparatuses) and also by ordinary people. (p. xiii)[159]

The harms described in this definition are **green crimes**, or "human behaviors that cause ecological destruction" and dangerous disruptions to ecosystems, negatively impacting human and nonhuman animals (p. 10).[160] They include acts that are criminalized, like illegal dumping of toxic waste, as well as those that are "lawful but awful," like monopolization of natural resources, which includes the privatization of water (p. 3).[161] And these green crimes—whether illegal or not—are committed in the pursuit of accumulating capital, or wealth.[162]

Green criminology is concerned with human rights, animal rights, and environmental justice.[163] It entails the study of (1) the causes, consequences, and extent of environmental harms (illegal or otherwise); (2) societal responses to environmental harms, including social movements and legal system responses (criminal, civil, or regulatory); and (3) media representations of environmental harms.[164] Be sure not to confuse green criminology with environmental criminology, which focuses on the spatial distribution of crime (see Chapter 14).

Green criminology began in the early 1990s, in response to a series of human-made environmental catastrophes. In 1984, a gas leak at a Union Carbide plant in Bhopal, India, killed an estimated 16,000 people; many more were injured. In 1986, a nuclear meltdown at the Chernobyl power plant in Pripyat, Ukrainian Soviet Socialist Republic, caused widespread contamination, killing between 4,000 and 93,000 people (the exact number is impossible to know because radiation contamination is widespread and can takes years or even decades to cause fatal disease). In 1989, the *Exxon Valdez* oil tanker crashed, spilling at least 11 million gallons of oil along the coast of Alaska. These catastrophes were described in new stories as "accidents" and "disasters" rather than as crimes, even though they involved criminal negligence and cover-ups. When criminal sanctions were imposed, the wheels of justice turned slowly. For example, it took until 2010 (26 years later) for anyone to be convicted and sentenced for the Union Carbide gas leak. And the criminal penalties were mild, at best. For instance, only the captain of the *Exxon Valdez* faced criminal charges; he pled guilty to a misdemeanor (and the company paid a $125 million fine).[165]

Green crimes, including the examples from Union Carbide, Chernobyl, and *Exxon Valdez*, are typically corporate crimes, which are crimes committed on behalf of a corporation or for corporate gain, or state crimes, which are crimes committed by nation-states. In addition, green crimes may be the result of business-as-usual production (e.g., pollution or deforestation) rather than an aberration during production, such as a gas leak or oil spill.

Today, we live under the specter of "global ecosystem collapse" due to climate change, which is the primary focus of contemporary green criminology (p. 57).[166] Green criminologists point out that nation-states enable "lawful but awful" green crimes that contribute to the climate crisis, often in concert with corporations, because "these institutions have the capacity to shape official definitions of environmental crime in ways that allow or condone [or perpetuate] environmentally harmful practices" (p. xiv).[167] They recognize that economic interests influence the creation of law—and what is considered environmental crime.

CHAPTER SUMMARY

LO 7.1   Explain the central ideas in neoclassical criminology.

Neoclassical criminology adopts the classical school's assumption that people rationally weigh the costs and benefits when deciding whether to commit a crime. Contemporary theories of deterrence, social control, situational crime prevention, and routine activities are examples of neoclassical thinking, also called the rational choice perspective. Unlike earlier thinkers, neoclassical criminologists recognize the reality of bounded rationality.

LO 7.2   Contrast the four types of modern biosocial criminology.

Behavioral genetics, using twin studies, focuses on the relative contribution of genetics and the environment to social behavior. Molecular genetics uses genotyping to identify genetic traits associated with criminality. Neurocriminology uses neuroimaging to identify brain structures and functions related to criminality. Biological criminology concerns other biological correlates, including hormones and heart rates.

LO 7.3   Identify the primary arguments in radical criminology.

Radical criminologists argue that (1) capitalism causes crime by creating an alienated underclass and fostering a competitive culture of exploitation; (2) the law in capitalist society conceals and fosters crimes of the powerful; (3) crimes of powerless people serve important functions for capitalism by diverting attention toward people who are poor and creating a lucrative punishment industry; and (4) capitalism determines how society responds to crime.

LO 7.4   Describe the core principles of feminist criminology.

Feminist criminologists, including both liberal and radical feminist criminologists, assert that (1) gender is a "situated accomplishment" that organizes social life, and (2) societies differentially value women and men, resulting in structural gender inequality, or sexism. Both matter for understanding the gendered character of crime, victimization, and punishment.

LO 7.5   Summarize the central claims in critical race, queer, and green criminology.

Critical race criminology seeks to expose the role of law in perpetuating white supremacy and racial oppression and to prevent the law from being used in this way. Queer criminology brings LGBTQ issues and perspectives into the study of crime, victimization, and punishment. Green criminology draws attention to "green crimes," which are actions, illegal or legal, that destroy or disrupt ecosystems, harming human and nonhuman animals.

ENGAGED DISCUSSION

1. Do you think people are still "rational" decision-makers if they engage in satisficing and discounting? Why or why not?

2. Devise an explanation for the finding that low resting heart rates are correlated with serious violent crime but not with white-collar crime.

3. Come up with an example (not one mentioned in the chapter) of either "social junk" or "social dynamite." Which one is it, and why?

4. Which criminal offenses provide opportunities for boys and men to "do gender"? Which provide the opportunities for girls and women to "do gender"?

5. Is it possible to subscribe to multiple schools of thought simultaneously? For example, can you be a biosocial criminologist and a green criminologist? Are any two schools fundamentally incompatible?

KEY TERMS

Behavioral genetics (p. 174)

Biosocial criminology (p. 171)

Bounded rationality (p. 170)

Critical race criminology (p. 189)

Discounting (p. 170)

Feminist criminology (p. 184)

Gene-environment interaction (p. 176)

Green crimes (p. 190)

Green criminology (p. 190)

Heteronormativity (p. 187)

Historical materialism (p. 181)

Intersectionality (p. 184)

Left realism (p. 184)

Molecular genetics (p. 175)

Neoclassical criminology (p. 168)

Neurocriminology (p. 176)

Patriarchy (p. 185)

Queer criminology (p. 187)

Radical criminology (p. 180)

Rational choice theory (p. 169)

Right realism (p. 171)

Satisficing (p. 170)

Sensation-seeking hypothesis (p. 173)

Harris-Moore was escorted home by a sheriff's deputy who accused him of having stolen it. Soon after, his beloved dog was struck by a car and died. One year later, Harris-Moore's stepfather died, and his mother's drinking intensified.[6] She described her subsequent live-in boyfriend in court records as "not playing with a full deck."[7] Child Protective Services visited the home on 12 separate occasions due to suspicions of neglect and physical abuse. Harris-Moore ran away after being violently attacked by his father at age 12. He then embarked on a years-long series of residential and store burglaries and other crimes that ultimately landed him in detention.

Despite the made-for-Hollywood Barefoot Bandit narrative of the "swashbuckling adventures of a rakish teenager,"[8] the truth of Colton Harris-Moore's crimes is a tragic story of family dysfunction and a child failed by the institutions that exist to protect them. The forensic psychiatric evaluation presented to the court reported,

> *On September 10, 2001, clinicians wrote: "Assertive, talkative 10-year-old who can become quite angry—but the situation with mother and her boyfriend drinking, living in a tiny trailer, mother drinking all the time, and the physical abuse Colton has gotten from boyfriend makes his anger easy to understand..." He was treated with antidepressant medications, but subsequently in December of 2001, he was also placed on the anti-psychotic medication, Geodon. Records are not clear as to why such a potent medicine was tried, but most likely it was to assist in behavioral control. He was diagnosed with Intermittent Explosive Disorder, Depressive Disorder, NOS [not otherwise specified] and Parent-Child Relational Problem in 2003.[9]*

The evaluation depicts Colton Harris-Moore as a child with emotional struggles whose social environment deprived him of the supports he needed to thrive. Lacking strong prosocial bonds, Harris-Moore simply followed his impulses. And his impulses were strong. His mother stated in a report to the court that her son "does things without thinking of the end results."

WHAT ARE CONTROL PERSPECTIVES?

Colton Harris-Moore was a young man with nothing to lose, undaunted by the risk of punishment, and free to follow his most destructive drives. It is a tale of weak controls. Control perspectives focus attention on the forces that constrain, or control, crime. Remember from Chapter 1 the difference between "Why do they?" and "Why don't they?" questions in criminology. Control theorists ask, "Why *don't* people commit crime?" Rather than ask why Harris-Moore pursued an adolescent life of crime, control theorists wonder why more of us don't follow in his footsteps.

Some control perspectives draw our attention to individual control and criminality. In other words, they identify the reasons some people become Barefoot Bandits while the rest follow the rules, presumably with shoes on. This chapter describes three individual-level control perspectives in criminology: (1) Hirschi's social bond theory, (2) Sampson and Laub's age-graded theory of informal social control, and (3) Gottfredson and Hirschi's self-control theory. The chapter also addresses Shaw and McKay's social disorganization theory, a structural-level control perspective focused on places and their crime rates, or the reasons some communities keep residents in check to a greater extent than others.

Control Perspective Assumptions

All criminological perspectives make assumptions about morality and human nature. Control perspectives assume (1) value consensus (morality assumption) and that (2) humans are naturally hedonistic but rational (human nature assumption). These should sound familiar as they are Classical School assumptions. As a refresher, let's begin with the first assumption. Think back to the distinction between consensus and conflict perspectives described in the first chapter. Control theories assume value consensus, or a belief that there is general agreement in society about what behaviors are wrong and therefore ought to be criminal.[10] They presume that when people commit criminal acts, they do so *despite* knowing that their behavior is unacceptable (or despite *consensus* that the action is wrong), not because they believe that it is right.

According to one of criminology's most cited control theorists, Travis Hirschi, we must ask not why people break the rules, but why they follow them: "Deviance is taken for granted; conformity must be explained" (p. 10).[11] But why is deviance taken for granted by control theorists? Control perspectives regard the roots of criminal conduct as uncomplicated: People engage in crime because of their natural desires.[12] Plainly put, crime feels good. Control theorists assume, like Classical School thinkers, that people are pleasure-seeking, or naturally hedonistic. And many things that produce quick pleasure are violations of the law. When you are angered by another, the natural desire is to retaliate. When you want something, the natural desire is to take it, just like Colton Harris-Moore stole an airplane because, quite simply, he wanted it. We do not need to learn that crime is good, according to control theories. Watch an angry or envious three-year-old and you will see that the hedonistic impulse towards crime is in us all. Rather, we must be properly constrained so that we do not act out of our inborn desires. Most control perspectives assume also that people are rational: We seek pleasure, but we also wish to avoid pain. We are hedonistic and utilitarian (practical or focused on usefulness).[13] Effective controls ensure pain in the form of punishment and thus restrain behavior.

Types of Control

Restraints, or controls, come in several forms. Social control refers to the processes by which conformity to social norms is regulated, encouraged, and enforced. Criminologists distinguish between formal and informal social controls. Formal control occurs when one is compelled to conform by the state or others with the official capacity to enforce codified rules. Formal control is operating if fear of arrest prevents you from hurting others. It is also operating if fear of expulsion keeps you from cheating on your Criminology exam. In contrast, informal control originates from unwritten social rules rather than laws. Disapproval, gossip, rejection, and ridicule are examples of sources of informal control. Informal control is operating if the fear of embarrassment or letting down your loved ones is what keeps you from taking off your shoes to burglarize a hardware store like the Barefoot Bandit.

Security guards are an example of direct control: They control behavior through their physical presence.

Bill Varie/The Image Bank/Getty Images

Social control can be either direct or indirect. Direct control involves the source of control being physically present to restrain behavior. You are familiar with this process if you have ever slammed your car's breaks upon noticing a police cruiser parked along the side of the road. Surveillance efforts, like identified security personnel in stores and doorbell cameras on homes, also operate on the principle of direct control.

Studies show that direct control makes a difference. Consider the unanticipated effects of the terror alert system in Washington, D.C., following the attacks of September 11, 2001. The Department of Homeland Security implemented a color-coded system to indicate terrorism threat levels, including red (severe), orange (high), and yellow (elevated). On orange days, extra police were dispatched to high-risk areas of high-risk cities, particularly Washington, D.C. As a result, and seemingly at random, there would be extra direct control in some areas of the capital. This created experiment-like conditions, which are hard to come by; the extent of police presence is usually tied to the amount of crime in an area, making it difficult to tease out cause from effect. The goal was to prevent terrorism, but amplified direct control had an added effect: a 7% reduction in (non-terrorism) crime in Washington, D.C., on high-alert days.[14]

Indirect control occurs when the source of control is psychologically present, rather than physically present. The indirectly controlled person considers committing criminal acts but ultimately decides to conform because they also think about what they have to lose, including relationships and investments in work or school. Importantly, direct control is unnecessary when indirect control is strong.[15] Only the unrestrained would-be criminal requires direct monitoring. These forms of social control—formal, informal, direct, and indirect—are not mutually exclusive. For example, many informal controls operate indirectly, like worries about disappointing one's mother or child. Plus, social control differs from self-control, or internal control, which is regulated by one's conscience and exercised from within rather than through a social process.

Signs like this seek to create an image of a community that exercises direct and formal controls.

Smith Collection/Archive Photos/Getty Images

HIRSCHI'S SOCIAL CONTROL THEORY

Few ideas in criminology have endured quite so long as Hirschi's social control theory (also called social bonding theory). First described in Travis Hirschi's 1969 book *Causes of Delinquency,* social control theory offered a view of juvenile crime—later applied to adult crime by other criminologists—that saw weakened connections to conventional society as the source of law-breaking.[16] The theory claims that informal, indirect controls matter more for ensuring conformity than do formal, direct controls. If all people are assumed pleasure-seeking, then the most important barrier against criminality is their bond to society. A strong social bond guarantees that people develop a moral compass and have something to lose if they offend.

Four Elements of the Social Bond

Social control theory identifies four elements of the social bond, each of which promotes conformity to law:

1. Attachment – Emotional closeness to and affection for prosocial others (such as family, friends, colleagues) and institutions. People with strong, healthy relationships more readily internalize conventional, noncriminal norms. They care about the opinions of the people they love or respect. It is the most important element of the bond that acts as a prerequisite for the establishment of the remaining three, which are commitment, involvement, and belief. Attachment is the affective element of the social bond.

2. Commitment – Calculation of the costs of law violation for future goals. Hirschi offers up a Hobbes quote to illustrate: "Of all passions, that which inclineth men least to break the laws, is fear."[17] His point is that we are rational and we consider (and fear) consequences. Commitment is a deterrent to crime. A person who has invested time and energy in pursuing their goals—like completing school, getting and keeping a decent job, or raising children well—has something to lose if they break the law. Commitment is the cognitive element of the social bond.

3. Involvement – Time spent in conventional activities. The proverb "idle hands are the devil's workshop" fits here. Hirschi writes, "The person involved in conventional activities is tied to appointments, deadlines, working hours, plans, and the like so the opportunity to commit deviant acts rarely arises." The involved person is, essentially, too busy for crime. Involvement is the behavioral element of the social bond.

4. Belief – Ideas about the moral validity of the law, which support a conventional orientation. A person who believes wholeheartedly that it is wrong to steal is more constrained when tempted than the person who adheres only weakly to anti-theft values. Remember that the theory assumes value consensus. Therefore, it is not that the person believes stealing is *right*; rather, they understand that it is wrong. They are just less morally bound by that belief. Belief is the evaluative element of the social bond.

The theory states that weakened or broken bonds to conventional society—inadequate attachments, too few commitments, insufficient involvement in prosocial activities, and a failure to believe the law is morally valid—lead to delinquency and crime. A person is free to follow their wayward impulses when the social bond breaks down or was never formed in the first place. Hirschi refers to attachment and commitment as **stakes in conformity**. The person has something valued or invested (at stake) that can be jeopardized if they don't follow the rules (conform).

Few ideas in criminology have been tested empirically to the extent of Hirschi's. The theory stands the test of time, in part, because of the evidence in its favor, especially as it pertains to adolescent delinquency. Parental attachment consistently emerges as a predictor of youth crime,[18] with commitment to conventional lines of action (like schooling and work) a close runner-up.[19] The element of belief receives the least amount of attention from social control researchers, but studies on morality and crime fit the expected pattern. For instance, one study found that parental hostility increases the odds of juvenile property crime through its effects on moral disengagement, a result consistent with Hirschi's arguments.[20] Other parts of the theory receive less support. Idle hands are *not* the devil's workshop—there is little evidence that people who spend a lot of time involved in prosocial activities are more law-abiding. For example, teenagers who work many hours in paid employment are, in fact, more delinquent than other youths, even when controlling for financial hardship.[21]

Evaluating Hirschi's Social Control Theory

Despite vast empirical support in investigations of juvenile delinquency, Hirschi's theory is not without its shortcomings. For example, critics argue that theory is useful when explaining minor crime and delinquency (think petty theft, vandalism, and fighting) but it is less helpful for understanding serious crimes like rape, domestic terrorism, or intimate partner homicide.[22] In other words, they claim the theory has limited scope. Nonetheless, criminologists who study terrorist violence and hate crime do, indeed, observe a loosening of social controls directly prior to criminal action.[23] It also falls short in explaining many occupational and corporate crimes. For example, some people who commit white-collar offenses choose crime because it is a convenient avenue to status and the "inner circle" at work.[24] Can weak stakes in conformity explain the use of fraud to succeed in one's career? Perhaps not. However, some studies show that occupational crimes are often preceded by a breakdown in social control, including failed marriages and employment instability.[25]

The most common refrain among critics of social control theory is that it does not adequately address the criminogenic influence of crime-involved relatives, friends, and others. Decades of research shows, again and again, that deviant associates promote law-breaking. Every parent who has forbidden their teenage child from hanging around "the bad crowd" feels this in their bones. Social control theory offers that this is a "bird of a feather flock together" phenomenon rather than a causal effect. In other words, they claim the temporal ordering is backwards. Further, Hirschi contended that weakly bonded people are too selfish to form close and trusting friendships with others; he described friendships among crime-involved youth as "cold and brittle."[26] Yet studies suggest otherwise.[27] For example, having crime-involved older siblings increases younger brothers' and sisters' criminality, and this causal connection is even stronger when the siblings are emotionally close, contrary to the theory's claims.[28] Close bonds can promote rather than hinder crime when the bonds are to law-breakers.[29] Plus, criminal youth develop emotional ties to friends that are equally or even stronger than among youth who are not delinquent.[30] Hirschi, himself, acknowledged delinquent peer effects, but he regarded this influence as "beyond the reach of control theory" (p. 161).[31]

ENGAGED CRIMINOLOGY 8.1
Social Control Theory Through Photos

In this activity you will examine two photos and decide which concept from Hirschi's social control theory best fits each one.

Sam Edwards/OJO Images/Getty Images

Oliver Rossi/Digital Vision/Getty Images

1. Which one of the four elements of the social bond best fits what is depicted in Photo #1?

2. Which one of the four elements of the social bond best fits what is depicted in Photo #2?

3. What term does Hirschi use to refer to the two elements of the bond depicted in the photos?
  a. Direct control
  b. Formal control
  c. Value consensus
  d. Stakes in conformity

SAMPSON AND LAUB'S AGE-GRADED THEORY OF INFORMAL SOCIAL CONTROL

Sampson and Laub's age-graded theory of informal social control applies social control theory ideas to patterns in crime over the life course, including continuity and change in offending.[32] The theory acknowledges that our social relationships and life circumstances develop as we age in ways that can either prevent or promote crime. It is one of several criminological perspectives rooted in the life-course criminology paradigm. We must appreciate what life-course criminology entails before diving into the details of the age-graded theory of informal social control.

Life-Course Criminology

Age is one of the strongest correlates of criminal offending: Crime typically increases in late adolescence and declines throughout adulthood.[33] Even career criminals, or those who habitually commit offenses, usually desist (reduce or cease crime) over time.[34] Explaining why most people reduce their criminal behavior as they age—and why some persist in chronic offending until older ages—is a primary task of life-course criminology. Life-course criminologists aim to explain within-individual variation in crime, or why people engage in crime during only some periods of life. They examine criminal careers, which are the developmental trajectories of law-breaking that characterize an individual's life.[35] Life-course criminologists train their lenses on several patterns in crime[36]:

- Age of onset –- The life-course period at which a person begins engaging in criminal behavior. Criminologists differentiate between early or childhood onset, later adolescent onset, and adult onset of offending. Earlier age of onset—usually defined as prior to age 14—is a risk factor for a lengthier criminal career and serious violent offending in adulthood.[37]

- Escalation – A period of increasing frequency and severity of criminal conduct. Some escalation is due to age and maturation. For example, 23-year-olds get into more serious trouble than 13-year-olds. Other escalation is due to criminal experience, including exposure to the criminal justice system.[38]

- Persistence –- Continuation of criminal behavior over several life-course periods. The length of time that a person persists in committing crime is equal to the length of their criminal career. Most people with extensive criminal careers follow an intermittent, or "zigzag," pattern rather than maintaining a constant level of criminal involvement over time.[39]

- Desistance – Reduction in the frequency or severity of criminal conduct over the life course, including termination of a criminal career. Desistance involves both a structural element and a subjective element. Structural factors include life changes that reorganize daily routines, such as employment. The subjective aspect is about reconstructing one's identity and making a genuine commitment to "do good."[40]

Social Control as Age-Graded

In their age-graded theory, Sampson and Laub borrowed Hirschi's ideas about attachment, commitment, involvement, and belief (especially the first two) and considered how they apply to life-course patterns in age of onset, escalation, persistence, and desistance. They point out that the social forces that keep us in line (or fail to) are dependent on age, or age-graded.[41] A 15-year-old is controlled by parents and teachers. They might be constrained by attachments to coaches or pastors, as well as by their commitment to adolescent goals, like graduating high school. A 45-year-old's life is quite different. Parents and teachers are replaced by romantic partners, spouses, and employers. Their commitments—to raising their children, being a good provider, serving as a strong role model—are distinctly adult. Understanding why and when people begin to offend (onset), accelerate the involvement (escalation), continue to engage in crime (persistence), and stop offending (desistance) requires us to examine how social controls change throughout their lives.

The idea for the age-graded theory of informal social control was birthed in the basement of the Harvard Law School Library in the 1980s.[42] Criminologist John Laub chanced upon boxes of long-forgotten data. Decades earlier, a criminological duo—Eleanor and Sheldon Glueck—had gathered longitudinal data on adult parolees and boys in Boston juvenile court. The boys' data followed them from age 7 to 32 years old. Laub, along with criminologist Robert Sampson, reanalyzed the data using contemporary statistical methods unavailable during the Gluecks' time. But they didn't stop there. They tracked down the boys—now old men—to see what had happened in the intervening years. Examinations of criminal records, death records, and interviews with 52 of the surviving delinquent boys told a story of lives derailed and lives turned around. Ultimately, even the most delinquent boys desisted from crime in adulthood, but the timing of desistance varied tremendously from person to person. Laub and Sampson published their results and theoretical claims in a book titled *Shared Beginning, Divergent Lives: Delinquent Boys to Age 70*.[43]

One conclusion of Laub and Sampson's research, and life-course criminologists generally, is that the bonds people form in each stage of life are determined, in part, by what occurred in the previous stages. The past is prologue in life-course criminology. Crime early in the life course begets more crime in later years, as precocious law-breaking can produce ballooning consequences for social bonds in a pattern of cumulative disadvantage. The term *cumulative disadvantage* refers to a piling up, or snowballing, of harmful effects. Weak social bonds lead to crime, which leads to even weaker social bonds. And so on.

Imagine a 15-year-old named Kim. She, like the Barefoot Bandit, is growing up amidst chaos and conflict, and with few attachments to caring adults. She gets in frequent fights and is chronically truant from school. After one particularly bad fight in which the other girl suffered a brain injury, Kim is placed in juvenile detention. She attends high school classes while in detention, but she is learning alongside adolescents with varied educational needs and grade levels. Upon release and readmission to her public high school, she discovers that she is far behind everyone else, even more so than before. She will need to stay an extra year to graduate. Fed up, Kim stops attending classes. She had once dreamed of operating her own daycare center after getting an associate's degree in early childhood development, but now that goal is receding. Instead of being enrolled in college at age 19, she is now sleeping on friends' couches and working part-time as a convenience store clerk. With few commitments to work towards, Kim jumps at the chance to make some money with a few friends who have been stealing credit cards. The thieves are male but the names on the cards are women's names, so they ask Kim to use the cards in stores to purchase luxury items for resale. After several successful purchases, Kim is caught. She is convicted of credit card fraud. She serves 30 days in county jail, followed by probation, and now she has a criminal record. The terms of her probation require that she looks for or holds a job, but no one is willing to hire her. Each time she is caught and punished, her tenuous bond to society is frayed even further and crime becomes likelier. The more she loses, the less she *has* to lose.

Another conclusion of *Shared Beginnings, Divergent Lives* is that turning points can thoroughly alter the direction of an off-course life, or "knife off" a criminal past from a law-abiding present.[44] Despite the cumulative nature of weakened informal controls, people do desist. Trajectories change. Turning points are life changes that link a person to institutional sources of informal control such as well-paying employment, a stable marriage or partnership to a conventional mate, involved parenthood, or a residential move.[45] The trajectory of Kim's life might be changed substantially if an employer took a chance on her or she became a mother. She would suddenly have stakes in conformity. Studies of fathers reveal that residential fatherhood (living with one's child) promotes desistance from crime, and this is equally true of teenage and adult fathers.[46] The men in the *Shared Beginnings, Divergent*

Lives research experienced stable employment, marriage, and military service as most consequential. Of course, work and parenthood are transformative only for some. The age-graded theory of informal social control acknowledges the role of agency, which is the capacity to make context-specific choices, however constrained those choices might be.[47] Faced with similar potential turning points, some desist while others persist or "waver," not quite fully prepared to make a change.[48]

Gainful, stable employment is an important turning point that supports desistance.

Tom Williams/CQ Roll Call via AP Images

Evaluating the Age-Graded Theory of Informal Social Control

Like the theory on which it is based (Hirschi's social control theory), the age-graded theory of informal social control receives a great deal of empirical support. Nonetheless, critics point to several problems with the theory's claims. First, they argue that it suffers from a "chicken or the egg" problem.[49] It might be that marriage, military service, employment, and parenthood don't cause desistance by creating informal controls; rather, people predisposed to desist might seek out these changes. Turning points might be the egg (outcome) rather than the chicken (cause) when ceasing crime. This creates measurement challenges for researchers seeking to establish temporal ordering of bond formation and transitions out of crime.

Another criticism pertains to agency, or behavioral choice. The theory recognizes that people are not simply at the mercy of their social environments. They make decisions based on preferences that change over time. They can be motivated for self-change. In other words, there are objective transformations (like getting a job or moving in with a girlfriend) and subjective transformations (like desiring a change in identity).[50] Agency matters, but it can also become a catch-all for anything the theory cannot explain. Why did one 30-year-old who got a decent job stop offending while an otherwise similar 30-year-old lost that job after two weeks and persisted in a criminal lifestyle? Agency. Also, critics ask how criminologists are supposed to measure this thing called agency, taking aim at the theory's falsifiability.[51]

SHAW AND MCKAY'S SOCIAL DISORGANIZATION THEORY

The app and website nextdoor.com bills itself as "cultivat[ing] a kinder world where everyone has a neighborhood they can rely on."[52] The service provides a platform for residents who live within a certain distance of one another to "greet newcomers, exchange recommendations, and read the latest local news… support local businesses and get updates from public agencies… borrow tools and sell couches."[53] Local law enforcement participate, alerting community members of reported car break-ins and burglaries. While in practice the platform has its fair share of problems (gossiping, ranting, busy-body complaints, harassment), in *theory,* it is a technological solution to the problem of disorganized communities.

This chapter thus far has described social control as a property of individuals: Some people are more controlled than other people. Social disorganization theory, in contrast, posits that social control is a property of places, as well: Some neighborhoods are more controlled, or less disorganized, than others. It explains the spatial distribution of crime, or community crime rates. Importantly, social disorganization theory offers a "kinds of places" explanation of crime rather than a "kinds of people" explanation. The theory points to the type of social life that proliferates in disorganized communities. It is less about the specific individuals living in the neighborhood and more about the structure of the neighborhood. Regardless of who lives there, crime will continue if the neighborhood is disorganized.

Social disorganization theory holds that neighborhoods are less effective at reining in crime when residents do not know or trust one another as well as when communities are unable to access essential services like safe housing, medical care, and education. When neighborhoods deteriorate, people move away as soon as they are able, if they are able. Residents, therefore, do not invest in their communities. Everyone has one foot out the door. They do not get to know their neighbors, nor do they look out for one another. They may even fear them. As a result, residents hesitate to intervene or report deviant behavior to authorities. Public norms promoting law-abiding behavior crumble. The typical sources of social control (like schools, families, social service organizations, religious institutions, local businesses, youth organizations, and law enforcement) become weakened and unable to fulfill their functions. Children are exposed to adult criminals, and young people—free from adequate constraints—develop street corner subcultures in the form of gangs. The result is widespread crime.[54]

Origins of Social Disorganization Theory: Social Ecology

Social disorganization theory emerged from the Chicago School of criminology, which dominated the field in the first half of the 20th century. To understand the theory, we must first understand the social context of Chicago in the early 20th century. Chicago's population grew faster than any other U.S. city's during the 19th century, doubling every 10 years.[55] In 1800, only 5,000 people lived in Chicago; by 1900, two million people lived in the city. Cities today have formal agencies to address community problems: Social workers, firefighters, garbage collectors, building inspectors, and more. In the first half of the 1800s, few such agencies existed.[56] Chicago didn't have its own police force until 1851, and even then, they were focused primarily on locating lost children and arresting vagrants and intoxicated persons.[57] Communities were left to solve their own problems, a task complicated by the fact that most Chicago residents did not speak the same language: After decades of immigration, roughly 70% of residents were foreign-born, according to U.S. Census Bureau data from this era,[58] many drawn to the city by the promise of work in the stockyards and meat-packing plants (as depicted in the Upton Sinclair novel *The Jungle*).

The theory's architects, Clifford Shaw and Henry McKay, examined the distribution of people and social problems across city neighborhoods in early 20th century Chicago. They noted vast differences in concentrations of juvenile crime across locations, which prompted them to argue that some neighborhoods were criminogenic. But they were hardly the first social scientists to argue for the importance of place. For example, Du Bois made that case in his 1899 book, *The Philadelphia Negro,* writing "Crime is a phenomenon of organized social life, and is the open rebellion of an individual against its social environment."[59] Social disorganization theory was heavily influenced by the work of social ecologists. Social ecology (also called human ecology) took principles from biological ecology and applied them to human societies. Ecology is a branch of biology that examines the relationship of organisms to one another and their physical surroundings, including how ecosystem changes impact the health and population size of endangered species. Social ecology is the study of relationships of *people* to one another and their physical surroundings.

About a century ago, social ecologists at the University of Chicago were considering the impact of the city's rapid changes, including industrialization, urbanization, immigration, and population growth. They believed that people compete for scarce resources and space, just as wildlife do in the natural ecology.[60] Their *concentric zone model* described the city as a series of socially distinct regions, or "natural areas," that are arranged in successive rings around the city's central business district, or downtown. Social ecologists Park and Burgess described patterns of invasion and domination of city areas. Just as invasive plant species can expand and take over adjacent regions, so too can portions of the city. The contemporary idea of urban and suburban sprawl is similar, as it involves the gradual encroaching of urban or suburban spaces on rural areas. In the concentric zone model, the central business district was expanding into surrounding residential communities. As a result, residential properties surrounding downtown fell into disrepair as people moved away to avoid the commotion of the central business district and the stench of factories. Plus, landlords did not invest in their residential properties; rather, they waited until they could sell them off as commercial areas expanded. Only the most economically pressed groups, including newly arrived immigrants, settled in the derelict neighborhoods outside the central business district, at least until they could afford higher-quality housing. This was called Zone II, or the transitional zone, in Park and Burgess's model (see Figure 8.1), which included five zones:

- *Zone I* – The innermost zone containing the central business district. It included large buildings, retail establishments, courthouses and government offices, and other nonresidential properties.

- *Zone II* – The deteriorated area on the outskirts of the central business district marked largely by factories and other industry. It was a zone in transition, switching from a residential zone to an industrial zone. It was the least desirable and most criminogenic residential zone, occupied mostly by renters limited by economic circumstance.

- *Zone III* – Lower-class residential area containing humble apartment buildings. Though the housing was relatively inexpensive and the standard of living low, it was pricier and more desirable than the options found in Zone II.

- *Zone IV* – Middle-class area containing more expensive single-family homes and apartments.

- *Zone V* – Middle- and upper-class suburban commuter zone.

FIGURE 8.1 ■ Park and Burgess's concentric zone model

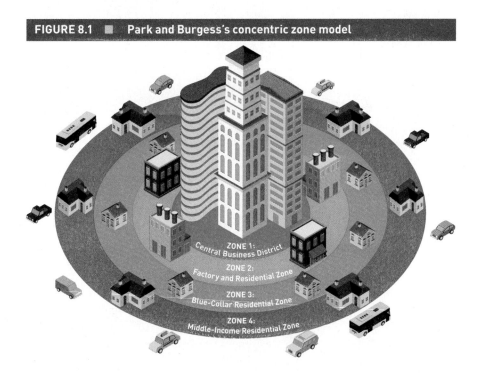

It was Zone II, the zone in transition, that would interest criminologists like Shaw and McKay. They applied the model's insights to the study of juvenile delinquency. Their publication *Juvenile*

Delinquency and Urban Areas described their analysis of 20 years of juvenile court data in 21 U.S. cities.[61] Using a cartographic approach, they mapped out the residential location of adjudicated delinquents, noting a clear pattern of concentration of juvenile delinquents in transitional zones. Children and adolescents with juvenile records became increasingly dispersed as one moved away from the cities' dilapidated industrial centers. Their research yielded several conclusions that formed the foundation of social disorganization theory[62]:

1. Crime and community-level social and economic disadvantage (like the percentage of families receiving public assistance, median rents, rates of home ownership) vary in tandem. Crime and other social problems follow the same pattern of ecological distribution: plenty in the transitional zone and fewer and fewer towards the outer zones.

2. High-crime areas remain high-crime areas regardless of the race, ethnicity, and nativity of the individuals who live there. Complete population turnover—that is, new groups of people moving in and supplanting old residents—does not alter the crime rate. This is the basis for the "kinds of places" (rather than "kinds of people") argument.

Physical dilapidation, or housing in disrepair, as seen in this photo of a Baltimore neighborhood, is one of the hallmarks of socially disorganized neighborhoods that struggle with high crime rates.

AP Photo/Patrick Semansky, File

Characteristics of High-Crime Areas in Social Disorganization Theory

Social disorganization theory is a "kinds of places" explanation. What kinds of places, then, produce concentrations of law-breaking? Shaw and McKay offer several characteristics of high-crime communities. It is necessary to note that these characteristics, though consequential, do not cause crime directly, according to the criminologists. Rather, they operate indirectly through their impact on social disorganization, which limits the capacity of neighborhoods to control crime, as seen in Figure 8.2.

The first characteristic is concentrated poverty and joblessness. People reside in high-crime communities not by choice but because they cannot afford to live elsewhere. Only the poorest families are left behind as upwardly mobile residents move to more prosperous neighborhoods. The second, related characteristic is physical dilapidation, or a community in disrepair. Broken windows and staircases remain unrepaired by landlords, roofs leak, trash sits uncollected and attracts pests, black mold and other environmental toxins pervade. Conditions are unsafe and unsanitary. The third characteristic is unsurprising given the physical state of housing: **residential mobility**. In other words, people move frequently.

This is due partially to the low rate of owner-occupied homes, as renters move more than homeowners. But mostly it results from economic pressures that require frequent changes in living circumstances, on one end, and a desire to move to neighborhoods with better conditions, on the other end.

The fourth characteristic is ethnic or cultural heterogeneity. The word *heterogeneity* refers to diversity of content (*hetero-* means different; *-geneity* means state or composition). Shaw and McKay noted that high-crime neighborhoods were composed of many different ethnic groups living side by side. Each had a distinct language and set of cultural norms, which were often in competition with the cultural norms of other residents. Lastly, high-crime areas were plagued with additional social ills, including high levels of disease, alcoholism, family violence and neglect, and infant mortality. Contemporary criminologists also note that high-crime neighborhoods experience a great deal of family disruption, including single-parent families, grandparent-headed households, and children in foster care.[63]

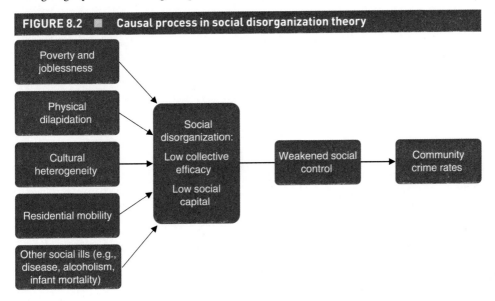

FIGURE 8.2 ■ Causal process in social disorganization theory

Defining Social Disorganization

What, exactly, is social disorganization? Contemporary criminologists describe social disorganization as the "inability of local communities to realize the common values of residents or solve commonly experienced problems" (p. 199).[64] Think of a few commonly experienced problems that neighborhoods might face; these might include uncollected garbage or litter, insufficient access to safe play areas for children, unleashed dogs behaving aggressively, loud music at all hours, and, of course, crime. Disorganized neighborhoods lack collective efficacy, or an orientation towards collective problem-solving action.[65] Imagine if a neighborhood had a problem with speeding or otherwise dangerous motorists. A community with a high level of collective efficacy might engage in the following:

1. *Informal surveillance* – Residents might set up a neighborhood watch that monitors problematic roadways, marking down license plate numbers of reckless drivers. Adults in the neighborhood supervise community children to ensure that they do not play in the road.

2. *Direct intervention* – Residents might chasten their neighbors who are observed driving dangerously, or they might contact parents of teenage drivers seen speeding, requesting that they admonish their children.

3. *Access public resources* – Residents might solicit and receive support from police in the form of increased traffic patrolling or speed-monitoring signs. They might also successfully petition for speed bump installation.

In sum, people are willing to intervene on behalf of the common good in socially organized areas. Note that social disorganization and collective efficacy are characteristics of communities, not of individuals.

Neighborhoods that lack dense networks of social ties are unable to mobilize collectively to address problems like dangerous drivers or crime.[66] They have insufficient social capital. Social capital refers to social relationships that operate as resources.[67] A person with mutually trusting social ties to many friends and neighbors that they can call on in a time of crisis has plenty of social capital. An especially valuable form of social capital is ties to institutional gatekeepers, including city council members, school board members, and chiefs of police. In one innovative quasi-experimental study, criminologists examined the formation of crime prevention and community-focused nonprofit organizations on urban crime.[68] They found that for every 10 of these nonprofits created, the murder rate was reduced by 9%, overall violence declined 6%, and property crime went down by 4%. The authors conclude that "local organizations are a core component of the informal networks that are essential to generating social cohesion and informal social control" (p. 1218). Nonprofits—neighborhood development groups, substance abuse prevention programs, job training organizations, and youth recreation programs—generate social capital.

Modern social disorganization thinkers typically subscribe to a systemic model of the theory, arguing that disorganization occurs at multiple levels. The systemic model of social disorganization includes three levels: private, parochial, and public.[69] This three-tiered approach presents a kind of continuum of (dis)organization, ranging from personal, individual-level sources of control (private level) to impersonal, community-level controls (public level), as seen in Table 8.1. Crime increases when organization breaks down at the private, parochial, and/or public level.

TABLE 8.1 ■ Bursik and Grasmick's systemic model of social disorganization

Level of organization	How it works	Example
Private	Informal controls fostered by intimate primary groups in the form of attachments; mirrors Hirschi's social bond theory. Control is achieved through threats to withdraw support, esteem, or warm sentiment.	Adolescent residents with strong emotional connections to trusted adults refrain from criminal conduct.
Parochial	Interpersonal social networks within the broader community of individuals and institutions, such as schools, houses of worship, community organizations, and stores. Social ties facilitate trust, communication, and intervention, but not close emotional bonds.	Neighbors observe and intervene (e.g., voicing disapproval, calming people down, calling authorities) when crime occurs.
Public	Community can access public goods and services controlled by agencies located outside the neighborhood, including social services and law enforcement. These goods and services are instrumental in preventing and responding effectively to crime.	Police show up when residents call for service, and the needs of residents in crisis (e.g., food insecurity or mental health emergencies) are addressed by local organizations.

Source: Bursik, R. J., Jr., & Grasmick, H. G. (1993). *Neighborhoods and crime*. New York: Lexington Books.

Much of our contemporary knowledge of neighborhoods and crime in the U.S. comes from the Project on Human Development in Chicago Neighborhoods (PHDCN), which includes surveys of community members living in 343 neighborhoods, video-recorded observations of 80 neighborhood blocks, and longitudinal studies of 6,000 randomly selected Chicago children, adolescents, and young adults.[70] Criminologists who analyze PHDCN data find that collective efficacy does, indeed, link neighborhood deprivation to serious violent crime.[71] Importantly, disadvantaged neighborhoods that manage to foster a high degree of collective efficacy see substantially lower homicide rates relative to economically similar neighborhoods with a frayed social fabric.[72] In other words, it's not *just* poverty, residential mobility, and cultural heterogeneity that lead to crime; it's the kind of social life they engender. Spatial patterns of crime outside the U.S.—for example, in Brazil,[73] South Korea,[74] Finland,[75] and China[76]—fit the tenets of social disorganization theory, as well.

ENGAGED CRIMINOLOGY 8.2

Eviction Rates and Social Disorganization

In this activity, you will examine spatial patterns of evictions in Cleveland, Ohio, and apply concepts from social disorganization theory to what you observe. An eviction occurs when a landlord expels tenants from their rental property, typically because they are behind on rent. Figure 8.3 displays the rate of evictions, with the size of the red circle indicating the percentage of renters who were evicted in a single year, by city block group. For example, on the city block directly above Emery Rd., 17.1% of renters were evicted (large red circle), while fewer than 3% of tenants living just north of Harvard Rd. experienced eviction (small red circle).

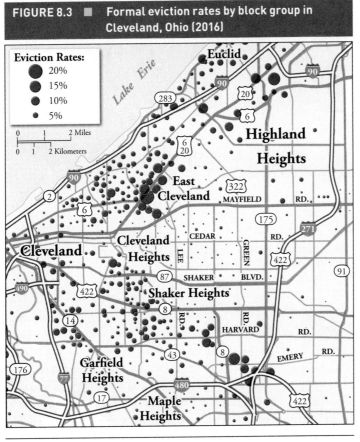

FIGURE 8.3 ■ Formal eviction rates by block group in Cleveland, Ohio (2016)

Source: Courtesy of the Eviction Lab at Princeton University.

1. Based on Figure 8.3, which statement is true?
   a. Evictions are evenly distributed across Cleveland neighborhoods.
   b. Evictions are concentrated in some Cleveland neighborhoods.

2. In one sentence, describe how the social disorganization concept of residential mobility relates to the pattern of evictions seen in Figure 8.3.

3. Criminologists find that crime rates are higher in neighborhoods with high eviction rates than otherwise similar neighborhoods with low eviction rates. In one or two sentences, devise an explanation for the eviction-crime link using the concept of collective efficacy.

Mass Incarceration, Social Disorganization, and Crime

Any discussion of community crime rates must include an acknowledgment of mass incarceration's impacts. Imprisonment of dangerous individuals who pose risks to public safety (like serial rapists and others who habitually commit violent offenses) is a benefit to communities. However, mass incarceration—including people held in jail, most of whom are awaiting case disposition for nonviolent offenses because they are too poor to afford bail[77]—casts a wide net, capturing many more "dolphins" than "sharks." And incarceration is unevenly distributed across communities.[78] In a recent study of incarceration in Massachusetts, criminologists found that more than half of all prison admissions came from census tracts containing just 15% of the state's population (Figure 8.4 shows the distribution by town and city).[79]

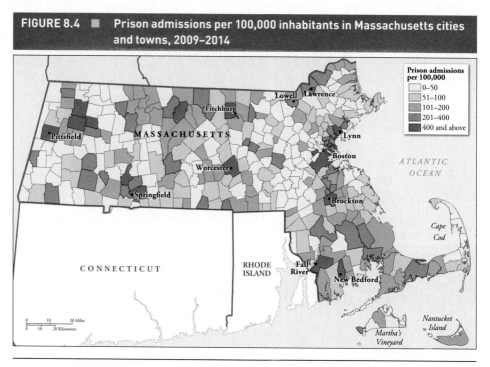

FIGURE 8.4   ■   Prison admissions per 100,000 inhabitants in Massachusetts cities and towns, 2009–2014

Source: Simes, J. T. (2018). Place and punishment: The spatial context of mass incarceration. *Journal of Quantitative Criminology, 34,* 513-533.

There is also wide variation within census tracts. In Houston, for example, just seven neighborhoods containing only 5% of the city's residents are home to more than a quarter of people returning from prison.[80] Some neighborhoods are virtually incarceration-free while nearby communities are the sites of concentrated imprisonment and prisoner re-entry. If you drive east on Amherst Street in Buffalo, you will pass through two adjacent neighborhoods: Starin Central to your left and Leroy to your right (see Figure 8.5). Despite their proximity, the neighborhoods are miles apart in social conditions. In 2010, Leroy had an incarceration rate of 14.49 per 1,000, which was 10 times higher than the rate in adjacent Starin Central (1.46 per 1,000). Leroy residents were more than four times as likely to live below the federal poverty line (43.2% in Leroy vs. 10.4% in Starin Central), and their rate of unemployment was 55.2% higher than among their neighbors to the north. Note that the data presented in this section so far refer only to people held in state prisons, not to the many people who cycle through city and county jails.

Crime is a cause of incarceration, of course, but incarceration—when high in magnitude—can be a cause of crime at the neighborhood level.[81] Think about how a social disorganization theorist would approach the subject of concentrated incarceration and re-entry. How might a high rate of imprisonment and return matter for poverty and joblessness? Residential mobility? Cultural heterogeneity? Family disruption? Criminologists Dina Rose and Todd Clear refer to incarceration as *coercive mobility*.[82] It is movement—removal and re-entry—that is involuntary (coerced or forced). The churning of residents through juvenile detention, jails, and prisons destabilizes the neighborhood for those left behind by disrupting social networks that operate as forms of informal social control, including families. Plus, they write, people exiting prison often return to their communities with a deviant orientation that exacerbates cultural heterogeneity. Criminal and prison norms clash with prosocial norms, undermining social cohesion and trust among neighbors. When social ties do form, they often promote crime rather than prevent it. Furthermore, legal cynicism pervades among residents personally affected by mass incarceration, including formerly incarcerated people and their family members and friends. Legal cynicism is a "cultural orientation in which the law and the agents of its enforcement are viewed as illegitimate, unresponsive, and ill-equipped to ensure public safety" (p. 443).[83] Residents are unwilling to report crime to authorities or to cooperate with law enforcement when legal cynicism prevails.[84] The community's capacity to enact social control suffers even further.

FIGURE 8.5 ■ A tale of two Buffalo neighborhoods

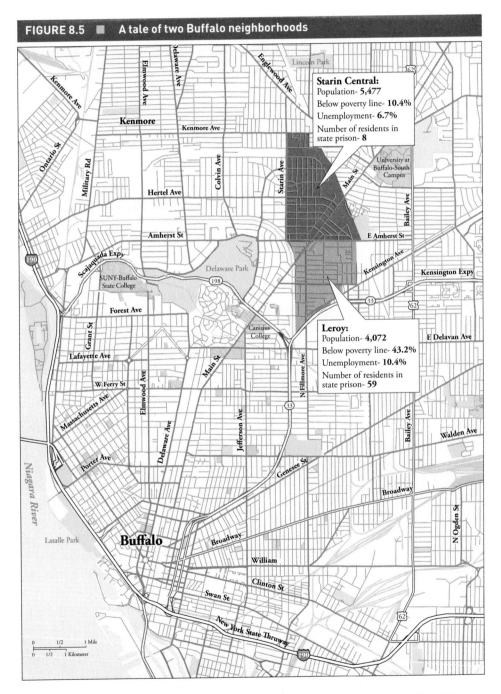

These two northeastern Buffalo neighborhoods—Starin Central and Leroy—sit on opposite sides of Amherst Street yet they are worlds apart when it comes to poverty and incarceration.

Source: Prison Policy Initiative and VOCAL-NY. (2020, February 19). *Mapping disadvantage: The geography of incarceration in New York State.* Prison Policy Initiative. https://www.prisonpolicy.org/origin/ny/report.html

Gentrification, Social Disorganization, and Crime

Most U.S. cities today bear little resemblance to the industrial northern cities of the early 20th century that fascinated social disorganization theorists. This is certainly true of the large cities of California, Texas, and Arizona, which are characterized today by traffic and sprawl, with few concentric zones in sight. Even the once-industrial metropolises of Chicago and Philadelphia have experienced massive economic and social transitions over the past 70 years that have gutted and revitalized neighborhoods. Deindustrialization, white flight, and disinvestment transformed urban neighborhoods between the 1960s and 1980s. Employment dried up as urban manufacturing and heavy industry jobs moved overseas or were replaced by automation.[85] At the same time, white families were fleeing the city center for the suburbs, and government investment followed them, with taxpayer dollars flowing to suburban infrastructure development and maintenance. Once-vibrant communities were ravaged by urban depopulation and political abandonment. Only the most economically vulnerable residents remained.[86]

City centers today—from Austin to Baltimore to Pittsburgh—are home to a new urban transformation: gentrification. Gentrification occurs when lower-income households are displaced by higher-income residents moving into the neighborhood, ultimately altering the "essential character and flavor" of the community (p. 5).[87] Cities have experienced a resurgence in population after decades of abandonment. Between 2000 and 2015, population growth in cities outstripped growth in suburban areas, though the urban boom has slowed down since 2015.[88] The back-to-the-city movement of affluent residents has once again transformed the urban core. Coffee shops, restaurants, upscale grocery stores, and other amenities appear. Vacant housing is demolished or rehabilitated. Housing values and rental costs creep—or lurch—upwards.[89] Many of the original residents, especially renters, can no longer afford to stay. Those who do stay may experience cultural displacement, as the social norms and built environment of the neighborhood begin to favor the newly arrived, who are disproportionately wealthy, white, and U.S.-born.[90]

Criminologists who study gentrification and crime reach for social disorganization theory as their guide.[91] Gentrification has the capacity to both increase and decrease collective efficacy and, therefore, law-breaking.[92] On the one hand, gentrification increases residential mobility and cultural heterogeneity.[93] Rifts and racial tensions emerge between old and new residents who hold conflicting attitudes about what constitutes problematic behavior in the neighborhood.[94] On the other hand, the influx of affluent neighbors reduces concentrated poverty and joblessness (in the gentrifying neighborhood, at least) and improves the physical environment. Perhaps most importantly, middle- and upper-class residents bring much-needed public resources, including investment in public schools, safe recreation, and public transit.[95]

Criminological research on gentrification and crime has exploded over the past two decades. The results differ depending on the city under investigation, the form of crime studied (e.g., homicide vs. burglary), how gentrification is measured (some criminologists have even used counts of upscale coffee shops!), and the timing of crime's measurement (immediate vs. long-term effects). For example, one study of gentrification in New York City over a 29-year period examined whether violent crime changed over time in neighborhoods that saw rapid increases in home prices and the educational profile of residents.[96] The researchers found that gentrification reduced assault, robbery, and homicide over the long term. Others find that gentrification increases crime in the short term as neighborhoods undergo change.[97] A study of majority-Latinx neighborhoods in East Los Angeles found that gentrification had no effect on gang homicide over a 30-year period and it even increased non-gang homicide. This was potentially due to newcomers being targeted for robberies that go "sideways" because they do not know the best ways to protect themselves during a violent confrontation.[98] And the diffusion of coffee shops—a prominent cultural symbol of gentrification—is, in fact, linked to reduced homicide and robbery in Chicago neighborhoods.[99] In sum, gentrification is neither all good nor all bad when it comes to crime prevention.

The Opioid Crisis, Social Disorganization, and Nonurban Crime

Historically, criminologists—social disorganization theorists among them—have neglected crime in rural communities, regarding cities as pathological and rural areas as idyllic.[100] Suburbia has been

Some criminologists use counts of coffee shops to measure the extent of gentrification and its impact on crime.

Westends61/Getty Images

similarly ignored.[101] Although, empirically speaking, rates of violence are greater in urban regions in the U.S., non-city communities also struggle with crime and, increasingly, mass incarceration. In fact, jail incarceration rates are higher in rural communities than in urban areas.[102] In the foreword to a report on rural jails by the Vera Institute of Justice, research director Christian Henrichson wrote,

> *Rural counties have been out of sight and out of mind in much of America…. Their burgeoning jails are a window into the pain in those places, and a symptom of the challenges many of them confront — such as shrinking economies, deteriorating public health, negligible services and pervasive addiction.*[103]

Though substance dependence bridges the rural-suburban-urban spectrum, pervasive addiction to opioids, including heroin and prescription painkillers, is a burden borne disproportionately by rural communities.[104] Recall from Chapter 3 the three ways that drugs and crime may be linked: (1) psychopharmacological effects, (2) economic-compulsive effects, and (3) systemic effects. The jails in economically depressed rural areas—along with struggling suburbs and small postindustrial cities— are housing people who have committed crimes to support their addiction (economic-compulsive effects) and those who have been caught possessing or distributing illicit substances (systemic effects). In some rural jails, like in Hamblen County, Tennessee, nearly every person is there because of addiction.[105]

Can social disorganization theory account for crime—including crimes associated with the opioid epidemic—in nonurban regions? There are two questions at play: (1) Does social disorganization predict substance use the same way it predicts violent and property crimes? (2) Do high-crime rural areas have the same criminogenic social conditions as urban areas? Let's take them one at a time. Most studies of social disorganization and substance dependence focus on alcohol, not opioids.[106] Nonetheless, these studies provide compelling arguments for why neighborhood characteristics might matter for opioid misuse:

- There is great availability of illicit substances in disorganized communities.

- Residents of disorganized communities suffer from high levels of stress and poor mental health.

- Community norms fail to prevent illicit drug use, or it may be more socially acceptable in disorganized communities.

Mahoning County, home to Youngstown, where this photo was taken, has an opioid overdose death rate that is 2.75 times greater than the national rate.

Spencer Platt/Getty Images News/Getty Images

These factors may account for why adolescents who live in disorganized neighborhoods are more likely to abuse prescription drugs, including opioids.[107]

But are rural communities disorganized? Some of the social conditions described by Shaw and McKay certainly apply across the rural-urban divide; these include poverty and joblessness, physical dilapidation, and family disruption.[108] But rural residents are far less likely to move frequently, and their communities tend to be culturally homogeneous.[109] The anonymity of the bustling urban center stands in stark contrast to the dense, generations-long kinship networks of the heartland. Put simply, people know one another. But that doesn't necessarily mean they trust one another. Criminologists have found that crime diminishes social trust and collective efficacy in rural communities and small towns.[110] Some also find that the key predictors of urban community crime rates—economic risk, residential mobility, and cultural heterogeneity—similarly explain rural crime,[111] while others find little support for the theory's claims in the rural context.[112] Nearly all of these studies, though, focus on violent crime rather than crimes of the opioid crisis.

Evaluating Social Disorganization Theory

Social disorganization has seen a major revival over the past several decades, following years of neglect as criminology swung in favor of individual-level explanations of delinquency (e.g., social control theory) and interactionist examinations of deviance (e.g., labeling theory) between the 1960s and 1980s.[113] And the theory continues to prove relevant, even if the structure of U.S. cities has been transformed by deindustrialization, gentrification, and other forces that render the concentric zone model outdated.

Some of the theory's earliest critiques—especially the argument that Shaw and McKay never clarified what social disorganization *is* and how it is distinct from crime itself—have been addressed by contemporary criminologists.[114] Modern ideas about collective efficacy and social capital put this critique mostly to bed. Contemporary critics take issue with the idea that there are well-defined and mutually agreed upon neighborhoods. Ask any two residents of the same apartment building where the borders of their neighborhood lie, and you will get two different answers. Plus, criminologists' lines of neighborhood demarcation—typically measured by U.S. Census Bureau block groups, tracts, or zip codes—often bear no resemblance to residents' perspectives on where their neighborhood ends and another begins.[115] Criminologists attend to this critique by asking residents about their perceptions of neighborhood boundaries rather than relying on administrative definitions. Some argue that we should use "egohoods," in which "persons are in the center of their geographic space" and occupy multiple overlapping neighborhoods.[116]

Critics argue further that social disorganization theory and its contemporary adherents fail to sufficiently address reciprocal effects. Crime is both a cause *and* a consequence of neighborhood characteristics, the critics point out.[117] Fear of crime drives residents' choices of where to live, when to move, whether to participate in community life, and willingness to enforce behavioral standards when faced with disorderly neighbors.[118] This creates a feedback loop wherein crime creates social conditions that lead to more crime.

As with many criminological perspectives, social disorganization theory offers an explanation only of street crime. Crimes of the powerful—corporate wrongdoing, political corruption, and the like—are outside the scope of the theory. Moreover, it is primarily a theory of urban crime. Suburban and rural crime are neglected, though contemporary criminologists find that social disorganization theory has some, albeit limited, relevance to crime outside the city.[119] This is especially important given that most people in the U.S. live in the suburbs, which are home to a good deal of law-breaking, much of it is less visible than crimes in urban centers.[120]

GOTTFREDSON AND HIRSCHI'S SELF-CONTROL THEORY

The year is 1970. Two psychologists at Stanford University have published the results of an experiment on delayed gratification that will come to shape popular thinking in a way that few academic studies ever do. The researchers Walter Mischel and Ebbe Ebbesen had 32 young children in their lab, all of them students at Stanford University's Bing Nursery School. The children, all between 3½ and 5½ years old, were shown a snack—animal crackers or pretzel sticks. They were told that the experimenter was going to leave the room and return after 15 minutes. The child could call the experimenter back in to get a snack before the 15 minutes was up, or, if they could resist temptation for the entire 15 minutes, they would be rewarded with an additional treat.[121] The experimenter then left the room and the child's behavior was observed. Some gave in; others distracted themselves until it was time to claim their prize.

It was not until a 1972 replication experiment that marshmallows were used as a possible reward, giving rise to the "marshmallow study" moniker that came to define this series of experiments that included, in total, 653 preschoolers.[122] The so-called marshmallow study didn't enter the public's imagination, though, until after a 1990 follow-up investigation.[123] Mischel, along with several colleagues, tracked down the parents of 185 of the 653 children. Parents reported on their (now adolescent) child's coping capacities, cognitive abilities, and SAT scores. The researchers found that children who were able to delay gratification in preschool grew into teenagers who were better at coping with stress and scored higher on their SATs than those who gave in to temptation quickly. Another follow-up study in 2011 used brain imaging techniques to examine the preschoolers, now in their 40s, revealing differences in brain activity between the gratification delayers and non-delayers.[124] Character, it seemed, was destiny.

While Mischel's self-control studies were dominating the psychology corner of pop culture, criminology was undergoing its own self-control transformation. And the cast of characters will sound familiar. Twenty-two years after publishing *Causes of Delinquency,* his landmark book that catapulted social control theory into the criminological spotlight, Hirschi did an about-face. He abandoned social bonds in favor of self-control as the primary source of criminal conduct (or, more accurately, its absence). His book *A General Theory of Crime,* written with criminologist Michael Gottfredson, laid out the foundation for an individual-level theory that would vie with a handful of other perspectives for domination of the field for several decades to come.

Like social control theory, Gottfredson and Hirschi's self-control theory is built on the Classical School assumption that all people are naturally motivated to engage in self-interested, pleasurable action; that is, people are hedonistic. Their definition of crime reflects their concern with self-interest and eschews the legalistic definition used by most other criminologists. In self-control theory, crime refers to "acts of force or fraud undertaken in the pursuit of self-interest" (p. 14).[125] Some acts of force or fraud are illegal but others—cheating on a girlfriend, lying to one's parents, screaming at one's child—are not. They also make the following assertions:

- Crimes provide *immediate* gratification of desires.

- Crimes provide *easy* or *simple* gratification of desires.

- Crimes are *exciting, risky*, or *thrilling*.

- Crimes provide *few or meager long-term benefits*.

- Crimes require *little skill or planning*.

- Crimes often result in *pain or discomfort for the victim*.

These characteristics of crime—immediate, easy, risky, unplanned actions that give little thought to others and provide few benefits over the long term—are the domain of the person with few internal restraints. Contrary to the view of the calculating self-interested criminal, self-control theory depicts criminal action as short-sighted and reactive, arguing that "the major benefit of many crimes is not pleasure but relief from momentary irritation" (p. 90).[126] The momentary irritation of having an empty wallet on a Friday night. The momentary irritation of being insulted at the bar. The momentary irritation of one's child talking back. In these instances, criminal action—theft to line one's wallet, assault to defend one's status, or child physical abuse—provides short-term relief. It also risks long-term negative consequences. Therein lies a departure from Classical School assumptions: Self-control theory does not assume that we all are rational and utilitarian. In fact, it is the failure to act rationally (i.e., weigh the costs and benefits) that defines the person with low self-control.

What Is Self-Control?

Do you have high self-control? If you are reading this chapter as part of your college coursework, then you must have at least a modicum of internal restraint. Otherwise, you would not have made it this far in your education. What individual characteristics do you possess—or lack—that helped you to answer the question of your own self-control? Perhaps they correspond to the six characteristics of people with low self-control described by Gottfredson and Hirschi:

1. *They are impulsive.* They have a "here and now" orientation and act without thinking about the long-term consequences.

2. *They prefer simple rather than complex tasks.* Simple tasks require less long-term planning and provide greater immediate satisfaction than complex tasks, which present frustration.

3. *They are risk-seeking.* They enjoy the excitement of in-the-moment adventure; they are not cautious.

4. *They favor physical rather than mental tasks.* Physical tasks require less cognitive labor than mental tasks, like verbal responses to conflict.

5. *They are self-centered.* They are indifferent or insensitive to the needs of other people, though they are generally not intentionally cruel or antisocial.

6. *They have a volatile temperament.* They are quick to anger and to express that anger.

Self-control theorists claim further that these characteristics are stable traits—or criminal propensities—that do not change substantially over time.[127] The impulsive, explosive 10-year-old grows into the impulsive, explosive 40-year-old. The opportunities for self-interested force or fraud may change as one ages, but the disposition does not, according to the theorists. The theory posits that there is *persistent heterogeneity*: There are differences (heterogeneity) across individuals' levels of self-control, and these differences continue over time (are persistent).

Gottfredson and Hirschi argue that the causes of low self-control are "negative," or due to the *absence* of learning rather than the presentation of it.[128] Children require no training in order to develop low self-control. Rather, the theorists regard weak impulse control as our innate state, which can only be remedied through monitoring, recognition of misbehavior, and intervention by caregivers early in childhood. All people require proper socialization to prevent the continuation of our natural self-serving impulsivity. And this must occur by around ages 8 to 10, when one's self-control becomes cemented, according to Gottfredson and Hirschi.

Analogous Behaviors and Criminal Versatility

Gottfredson and Hirschi argue that their theory is universal, that it is "meant to explain all crime, at all times, and, for that matter, many forms of behavior that are not sanctioned [punished] by the state" (p. 116).[129] They call these nonsanctioned forms of behavior analogous behaviors. Analogous behaviors are noncriminal actions that, like crime, are manifestations of low self-control. They include excessive drinking, smoking, gambling, getting into accidents, failing to wear a seatbelt, and engaging in high-risk sexual practices. Crime and analogous behaviors tend to co-occur because they have a shared cause.[130] There is nothing precious about crime in self-control theory. It is one of many types of risky, short-sighted, self-interested actions.

And what of other well-established predictors of criminal behavior, like having crime-involved friends, failing to finish high school, and having a spotty employment history? Self-control theorists regard these correlates as spurious, or noncausally related to crime.[131] The association between dropping out and illegal behavior? Both variables are being driven by the same underlying cause: low self-control. Dropping out, gang involvement, and employment failures are just another set of analogous behaviors in the self-control perspective. Self-control is *the* cause of crime, according to the theorists. Table 8.2 presents the empirical state of this and other self-control theory claims.

Analogous behavior fits with the notion of versatility in criminology. Versatility occurs when an individual engages in many different types of crime. Think of it as a "jack of all trades" phenomenon. When versatile, a burglar is not *just* a burglar; the person is also a drunk driver, an abusive partner, and an occasional drug trafficker. Self-control theorists rely on the many studies that find evidence of versatility in making a case for their explanation.[132] Even some offender types assumed to be narrowly focused on one kind of crime are, in fact, varied in their illicit conduct. For example, a study of 225 people convicted of federal sex offenses diagnosed as sexual sadists (i.e., people who "derive sexual excitement from the physical or psychological suffering of other people") found evidence of spillover into nonsexual crime.[133] The sexually sadistic sample had extensive nonsexual criminal histories that included nonsexual murders and aggravated assaults, burglaries, and many traffic violations.

In contrast, some explanations of crime assume criminal specialization, which is when an individual engages only in a single type of crime. When specializing, a burglar is just a burglar. Studies of adults who commit crime demonstrate that some offense types are often the domain of specialists, including some forms of fraud, certain sexual offenses, and "pure" arson.[134] It is a mistake, though, to frame the versatility-specialization distinction in zero-sum, or all-or-nothing, terms. It makes more sense to think of these as ends of a spectrum with many degrees in between.[135] Criminologists identify patterns of specialization (or "themes"), such as repeat homicide, even among criminal careers dotted with a variety of offenses.[136]

Evaluating Self-Control Theory

Gottfredson and Hirschi's book *A General Theory of Crime* has been cited by subsequent researchers over 14,000 times! It is safe to say that the theory has been thoroughly tested. It has also been thoroughly critiqued. The loudest critiques pertain to the concept of self-control, itself, and its measurement. Skeptics argue that the theory is tautological.[137] An explanation is tautological when a cause and an outcome are indistinguishable from one another. In other words, it relies on circular logic. How do

TABLE 8.2 ■ Summary of self-control theory: Claims vs. evidence

Claim	Type of evidence	Is it supported empirically?
Self-control predicts crime and deviance.	Published studies and meta-analyses	+
Parenting causes self-control.	Survey research; behavioral genetic designs	+/-
People who commit crime exhibit versatility rather than specialization.	Studies that examine degrees of specialization among select offending types	+
Self-control is relatively stable over time.	Longitudinal studies of patterns in self-control over time	+
Self-control is a general (or universal) theory.	Studies of various crime types (e.g., white-collar crime) and of various groups (e.g., by sex, race, or age)	+/-
Self-control is *the* cause of crime.	Studies measuring the proportion of variance in crime explained while controlling for other factors	-

Note: + mostly supported; - not generally supported; +/- mixed support

Source: Adapted from Rocque, M., & Piquero, A. (2019). Self-control theory: Theoretical and research issues. In M. Krohn, N. Hendrix, G. P. Hall, & A. Lizotte (Eds.), *Handbook on crime and deviance* (pp. 131-144). Cham, Switzerland: Springer.

you know someone has low self-control? They engage in crime. Why do they engage in crime? Low self-control. Around and around the circular logic goes, critics claim. For their part, Gottfredson and Hirschi regard claims of tautology as compliments.[138] The theory is *so good* at explaining crime, they counter, that low self-control and law-breaking are nearly synonymous.

The age-crime curve presents a potential problem for the theory, which claims that low self-control remains fixed as we age.[139] Crime declines precipitously following its peak in the late teens. This is true of analogous behaviors, as well. For example, of the male drivers killed in car accidents between the ages of 15 and 24, nearly one out of three were speeding—or behaving recklessly—at the time of the crash, with the proportion declining for each subsequent age group, as depicted in Figure 8.6. How can the theory reconcile this empirical incompatibility? Gottfredson and Hirschi warn criminologists not to "confuse change in crime (which declines with age) with change in tendency to commit crime (which may not change at all)" (p.137).[140] They make three specific arguments. First, they state that the age-crime curve is universal; it exists in all places and time periods. Second, they argue that the predictors of crime are the same across age groups. Third, they maintain that no criminological explanation accounts for the age-crime curve; it is inexplicable.[141] Therefore, they claim, they do not *need* to explain the age-crime curve.

Critics take aim at the theory's claim that self-control is set in stone by age 10 and stable as one grows older, and not just because people desist from crime with age.[142] As it turns out, risk-taking and impulsivity follow distinct trajectories over the life course.[143] Does this mean that the marshmallow experiments—the inspiration for Gottfredson and Hirschi's ideas—were wrong? Quite the opposite. Walter Mischel and others warn against interpreting the marshmallow studies as evidence of the immutability of self-control. In one interview, he asserted, "That iconic story is upside-down wrongthat your future is in a marshmallow—because it isn't."[144] In his final book before he died, Mischel argued forcefully that internal restraint can be developed in adulthood, a claim that runs counter to self-control theory.[145] Moreover, Mischel notes, the real lesson from the marshmallow experiments is that some children are provided strategies and reasons to delay gratification. Less-lucky children learn early on that adults cannot be taken at their word, that "the only guaranteed treats are the ones you have already swallowed" (p. 110).[146] In other words, what looks like low self-control is, in fact, rational behavior.

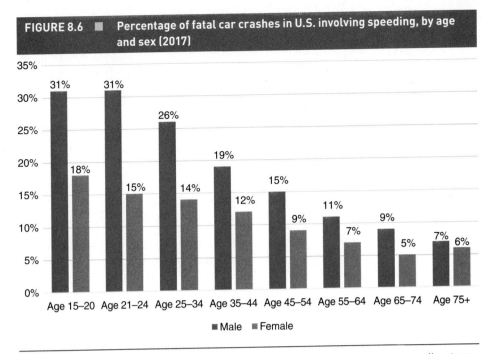

FIGURE 8.6 ■ Percentage of fatal car crashes in U.S. involving speeding, by age and sex (2017)

Source: National Highway Traffic Safety Administration, U.S. Department of Transportation. https://crashstats. nhtsa.dot.gov/Api/Public/ViewPublication/812687

Gottfredson and Hirschi's initial ideas about criminal opportunities also drew the ire of skeptics. How can they explain why some commit robbery and others commit wire fraud, or why there are peaks and valleys over the course of a criminal career? Differences in opportunities, so said the theorists. But, in the words of one critic,

> *Admittedly, those without fingers will find it difficult to pick pockets and those without jobs will be unable to violate anti-trust laws. But the opportunity to steal, rape, and murder seems virtually ubiquitous: It is about as unproblematic as the ability to smoke or overeat.* (p. 42)[147]

In other words, occasions for crime are everywhere. Therefore, it is an unsatisfactory argument that desistance from crime—or any other variation in behavior—among those with low self-control is a function of opportunities. Gottfredson and Hirschi heard this critique loud and clear, later conceding the ubiquity of opportunity.[148]

CHAPTER SUMMARY

LO 8.1   Differentiate between formal, informal, direct, and indirect control.

Formal control comes from those with the official capacity to enforce codified rules, resulting in formal sanctions (e.g., imprisonment), whereas informal control originates from unwritten social rules, resulting in informal sanctions (e.g., gossip or disapproval). Direct control occurs when the source of control is physically present, whereas indirect control happens when the source of control is psychologically present. All four are types of social control.

LO 8.2   Describe the four elements of the social bond in social control theory.

Attachment refers to emotionally close relationships to prosocial others. Commitment refers to the investment of time and energy in the pursuit of goals. Together, attachment and commitment create stakes in conformity. Involvement is about the amount of time spent in conventional activities. Belief pertains to the idea that the law is morally valid.

LO 8.3 Identify central tenets of the age-graded theory of informal social control, including concepts from life-course criminology.

The theory explains life-course patterns in crime—age of onset, escalation, persistence, and desistance—by noting that sources of informal controls change with age. Weak social bonds pile up in a pattern of cumulative disadvantage over time, but institutional turning points can promote desistance.

LO 8.4 Examine the main ideas in social disorganization theory, including collective efficacy.

Social disorganization is a structural-level theory of neighborhood crime rates. Characteristics like poverty and unemployment, physical dilapidation, residential mobility, and cultural heterogeneity predict crime rates because they foster social disorganization, which limits the capacity of communities to control crime. Specifically, disorganized neighborhoods lack collective efficacy, or an orientation towards collective problem-solving action.

LO 8.5 Contrast self-control theory with other control perspectives in criminology.

Self-control theory shares the assumption that people are naturally self-interested, but it rejects the notion that external controls are the primary cause of conformity. Instead, weak internal restraint is presented as the source of crime: impulsivity, risk-taking, emotional volatility, low tolerance for complex cognitive tasks. Weak social bonds, crime, and analogous behaviors (e.g., drinking, smoking, and gambling) share a common cause: low self-control.

ENGAGED DISCUSSION

1. Come up with an example of a time when direct control prevented you from violating a rule you wanted to violate. What was the source of that direct control?

2. How might Hirschi's social control theory explain the empirical finding that teenage employment (20+ hours/week) increases criminal involvement?

3. List three sources of informal social control in your life right now. How are they different from the sources of control when you were 10 years old? How will they be different in 20 years?

4. What social disorganization theory claims could you test using Google Street View along with data on crime rates? What parts of the theory could not be evaluated using Google Street View?

5. Come up with one type of crime that fits Gottfredson and Hirschi's description of crime and one type of crime that does not. What is it about that second type of crime that fails to align with their description?

KEY TERMS

Age of onset (p. 201)

Agency (p. 203)

Analogous behaviors (p. 217)

Attachment (p. 198)

Belief (p. 199)

Collective efficacy (p. 207)

Commitment (p. 199)

Criminal careers (p. 201)

Cultural heterogeneity (p. 207)

Desistance (p. 201)

Direct control (p. 197)

Escalation (p. 201)

Formal control (p. 197)

Indirect control (p. 198)

Informal control (p. 197)

Involvement (p. 199)

Life-course criminology (p. 201)

Persistence (p. 201)

Residential mobility (p. 206)

Self-control (p. 198)

Social capital (p. 208)

Social control (p. 197)

Social disorganization (p. 207)

Social ecology (p. 204)

Specialization (p. 217)

Stakes in conformity (p. 199)

Turning points (p. 202)

Versatility (p. 217)

9 LEARNING AND SUBCULTURAL PERSPECTIVES

LEARNING OBJECTIVES	
9.1	Describe how learning theories differ from other perspectives in criminology.
9.2	Explain the central tenets of differential association theory.
9.3	Identify how social learning theory elaborates on differential association theory.
9.4	Differentiate between subcultural perspectives in criminology.
9.5	Make connections between the drift perspective and techniques of neutralization.

Tracey Bogle served a 16-year prison sentence for auto theft, armed robbery, kidnapping, and sexual assault. Before that, he had spent time in Oregon's most secure juvenile facility, having been caught stealing semi trucks with his older brother, at one point ramming a truck through the side of a gun store and making off with a load of stolen firearms. Tracey and his brother weren't outcasts in the Bogle family. They fit right in among the 60 members of their extended family who had served time in prison, jail, juvenile detention, or had been under some form of community supervision. "What you are raised with, you grow to become," he observed. "If I had been raised in a family of doctors, I'd probably be a doctor. But I was raised in a family of outlaws who hated the law."[1]

The Bogle family criminal history stretched back generations. His grandparents made and sold moonshine during Prohibition. His father, nicknamed Rooster, committed frequent robberies and burglaries, assisted by Tracey's mother, who would drive the getaway car. "Rooster hated toys and sports, and the only fun thing to him was stealing," Tracey reported to the author of *In My Father's House*, a book on his family's multigenerational criminal history, "so he took us out with him to burglarize our neighbors' homes, or steal their cows and chickens, or take their Social Security checks out of their mailboxes." Rooster would bring young Tracey and his brothers to look at the prison near their home in Salem, Oregon, telling them, "When you grow up, this is where you are going to live." His sons heard a dare, not a warning. All the Bogle children—six boys and three girls—eventually spent time in prison.[2]

Judge Albin Norblad, an Oregon judge all too familiar with the Bogle family, believed that long prison terms for the Bogles were akin to throwing taxpayer money to the wind. The otherwise law-and-order judge argued instead for "something to separate Bogle family members so they will not keep reinfecting themselves." Judge Norblad, in talking of "reinfection," shared Tracey Bogle's belief that the family's criminality was a contagion. They would continue to train one another in criminal skills, commit crimes together, egg one another on, and teach younger family members to follow in their footsteps. Tracey Bogle and Judge Norblad understood the family's criminality, first and foremost, as learned behavior.

WHAT ARE LEARNING PERSPECTIVES?

Have you ever heard the saying "the apple doesn't fall far from the tree"? Did your parents or other adults in your life warn you to avoid "bad influences" or "bad apples" when you were young? Apple metaphors aside, the idea that we adopt the attitudes, behaviors, and dispositions of those close to us is as common to criminologists as it is to anxious parents. Learning perspectives see criminal activity as the product of an informal education with crime-involved others. Our peers, our parents, our siblings, our coworkers, our romantic partners—anyone in our lives—has the capacity to model norm-violating conduct, instill values that celebrate or tolerate violence, or teach us the ropes of breaking the law and getting away with it.

Remember the three factors present in theories of crime—motivation, control, and situational opportunities? Learning theories are primarily about motivation. They are about how people acquire norms and values that say committing crime is acceptable, motivating them to act. Learning theories highlight socialization. Socialization is the process by which we learn customs, norms, values, and beliefs. It is through socialization that we learn what is expected of us in particular groups (e.g., with our grandparents versus with our peers) or in specific situations (e.g., at a party versus in class). Primary socialization happens early in life, from birth through childhood. It is followed by secondary socialization, which continues through adulthood. Those responsible for socialization are called agents of socialization. Agents of primary socialization include parents, older siblings, caregivers, and teachers, and agents of secondary socialization include coworkers, college classmates, and romantic partners.

In learning theories, people are not assumed to be naturally inclined towards law-breaking, as is assumed in control perspectives (see Chapter 8). Instead, we must be taught. According to learning theories, we are born a blank slate, or *tabula rasa*, ready to be filled in with whatever cultural lessons we are exposed to through primary socialization. Built into this idea is the assumption of value conflict (versus value consensus), or the notion that there are multiple, competing versions of morality. Some versions say, "cheating is good and acceptable." Some say, "cheating is bad and never acceptable." Still others say, "cheating is generally bad and unacceptable but it's fine under certain circumstances." You may substitute "killing," "stealing," or any rule-breaking action for "cheating." Whether a person engages in crime depends on the version of morality they are socialized into, either early in life (primary socialization) or later on (secondary socialization).

Notice the use of the statement "whether *a person* engages in crime" in the previous paragraph. That is because learning theories are individual-level perspectives. Learning theorists explain why some individuals engage in crime and others do not, rather than why crime rates vary across regions, time periods, or demographic groups. In other words, learning theories explain individual-level variation in crime. They locate the source of offending in characteristics that differ between people, like their exposure to crime-involved friends or family, rather than in characteristics of societies (e.g., wealth inequality) or communities (e.g., neighborhood trust).

SUTHERLAND'S DIFFERENTIAL ASSOCIATION THEORY

The earliest statement of the learning perspective in criminology came from Edwin Sutherland, in 1939, in his book *Principles of Criminology*.[3] Sutherland had studied professional thieves in the 1930s, noting that amateur thieves learned the tricks of the trade from experienced mentors. During an early probationary period, apprentice thieves acquired the strategies, attitudes, interpersonal connections, and "larceny sense" required for criminal success. Like other occupations, professional thievery was characterized by specialization (as in shoplifting or pickpocketing), careful planning, congenial relationships with others in the same line of work, and adherence to an established code of ethics.[4] These observations contributed to Sutherland's vision of crime as learned behavior.

Gang prevention programs, like the one at this boxing club, seek to prevent the learning of pro-crime attitudes and behaviors by offering young people alternative activities and access to prosocial mentors.

Jamie Lusch/Mail Tribune via AP

The idea that people are socialized into crime is hardly novel today. We can thank Sutherland for that. Prior to differential association theory, many scholars studying individual criminality regarded criminals as abnormal, or different from "regular" people, by virtue of physiology or intellect. Sutherland's theory instead suggested that criminals and law-abiders are separated only by the lessons they learn: An ordinary person exposed to criminal family members and friends will adopt pro-crime attitudes and actions in the same way that they would become conventional if they only ever interacted with law-abiding people.

Nine Propositions of Differential Association Theory

Sutherland laid out his learning perspective in a series of nine claims, or propositions. Together, the propositions establish criminal behavior as the result of differential association, or relationships and interactions with people who support the learning of criminal attitudes and behaviors. People differ in law-violating behavior, the theory states, because they differ in their associations, as seen in the nine differential association theory propositions:

1. *Criminal behavior, like all behavior, is learned.* This statement was a rejection of perspectives, popular at the time, that treated criminality as innate or part of someone's essential character. Sutherland dismissed the idea that people who commit crime are different kinds of people than those who obey the law. In his view, all of us may become criminal if we are taught to be criminal.

2. *Criminal behavior is learned through interaction with others.* Like any behavior (taking turns, reading, having table manners), criminal behavior cannot be learned without communication between people. It is direct interactions with significant others—parents, siblings, friends, romantic partners—that matter, not learning through TV, movies, or other media.

3. *Learning of criminal behavior usually happens in intimate personal relationships and groups.* These relationships are the "associations" in differential association theory. The stronger, or more intimate, the relationships (or associations) are, the more readily crime is learned. Therefore, associations with family members and close friends are more influential than associations with neighbors, coworkers, and acquaintances.

4. *Learning of criminal behavior includes learning criminal skills, motivations, rationalizations, justifications, and pro-crime attitudes.* The content of what is learned is logistical (strategies for successful commission of crime), cognitive (thinking-based), and dispositional (attitudes about law-breaking). Attitudes, motivations, rationalizations, and justifications that support law-breaking are called definitions favorable to crime. For example, the belief that "stealing is fine as long as you only steal from big corporations" is a definition favorable to crime. Anti-crime attitudes—like "stealing is always wrong"—are definitions *unfavorable* to crime.

5. *Learning of criminal behavior entails learning interpretations of legal codes.* Through interactions, people learn whether the law is morally right and ought to be respected or that it can be disregarded entirely. These learned interpretations of law are complementary to learned interpretations of criminal conduct. For example, the attitude that "using violence is acceptable if someone has humiliated you" is supported by the learned belief that laws prohibiting violence need not be followed.

6. *Criminal behavior is likely when learning of pro-crime attitudes outweighs the learning of anti-crime attitudes.* Individuals are exposed to many different attitudes from the various groups of people in their lives (remember that this is a conflict perspective!). They will be exposed to definitions favorable to crime *and* definitions unfavorable to crime. For example, maybe a person's mother sends the message that "you never take what isn't yours," but their coworkers skim cash from the register or let their friends take merchandise without paying for it, informing them that "everyone does it." This is the "differential" part of differential association theory—people are exposed to different attitudes about crime and interpretations

of the rightfulness of law, influencing their drive to commit crime. Some definitions will matter more than others in determining a person's attitudes and actions.

7. *Differential associations vary in frequency, duration, priority, and intensity.* Frequency, duration, priority, and intensity are called modalities in differential association theory. Associations that occur many times (high in frequency), for a long period (long in duration), happen earlier in life (have priority), and are emotionally close and important to the person (strong intensity) are more likely to influence behavior than infrequent, brief, later-occurring, and emotionally distant associations. This is why emotionally close relationships with older siblings influence our values and behavior more than short-lived associations with casual acquaintances.[5] We are exposed to siblings' values and behaviors more frequently, for longer durations of time, from an earlier point in life, and in the context of a close relationship, as seen in the Bogle family described in the chapter's introduction.

8. *The mechanisms through which crime is learned are the same as the mechanisms through which all behavior is learned.* The social psychological processes involved in learning conventional behaviors also pertain to the learning of crime. This is similar to the first proposition (*criminal behavior, like all behavior, is learned*), but here Sutherland is making a claim about the particular process by which learning takes place.

9. *Although criminal behavior expresses general needs and values, those needs and values do not explain criminal behavior, as noncriminal behavior is an expression of the same needs and values.* Money, status, relief from frustration, and happiness can be achieved through legal actions. For example, money can be made by working extra hours. Therefore, wanting to accumulate money, alone, cannot explain why people engage in money-generating crimes. This was a repudiation of strain theory ideas, which are described in depth in Chapter 10.

In short, differential association theory states that people learn criminal attitudes (called definitions favorable to crime) and offending skills through their interactions with others. If they are exposed to pro-crime definitions more frequently, over a longer duration of time, earlier in life than other definitions, and in the context of an emotionally close and important relationship, relative to anti-crime definitions, then criminal behavior is likely.

Necessary and Sufficient Causes of Crime

Sutherland argued that his theory incorporated both necessary and sufficient causes of crime.[6] A condition is necessary if it *must* be present for crime to take place. A condition is sufficient if it will produce the outcome, crime. Imagine I said to you, "I don't know why my car won't run. I just filled the gas tank!" This demonstrates a necessary but *insufficient* explanation for why cars run. Gasoline is necessary (no gas, no driving), but it isn't sufficient; other parts of the car—like the alternator and the fuel pump—need to work, too. According to differential association theory, there are three necessary causes of crime:

1. *The person has learned the requisite skills and techniques for committing crime.*

2. *The person has learned an excess of definitions favorable to crime over unfavorable to crime.*

3. *The person has the objective opportunity to carry out the crime.* (p. 127)[7]

Each necessary cause is, on its own, insufficient. A person can learn all the offending skills in the world—how to pick locks, how to steal and use someone's social security number without getting caught, how to use a weapon and hold it in an effectively threatening manner—but they are unlikely to act if they haven't also learned that the behavior is acceptable, justifiable, or easily rationalized. Likewise, a person can learn that a particular criminal act is perfectly normal as well as how to carry it out, but if they don't have the opportunity to do it, it will not happen. For example, a person can know how to drive (requisite skill) and believe that drunk driving is fine as long as they stay off the highway (definition favorable to drunk driving), but if they don't have a car, then the offense won't take place. According to Sutherland, the three necessary causes of crime, *together*, provide a sufficient explanation of criminal acts. In fact, he claims that his theory is falsifiable, or testable, because of this: If crime occurs without any of the three causes present, or if crime doesn't occur when all three are present, then the theory has been falsified, or shown to be incorrect.[8]

Example: Learning to Be a Car Thief

One way to find out about the criminal learning process is to ask people who engage in criminal offending to recount their experiences, starting with initiation. Auto theft, like burglary and drug selling, tends to be a "social crime," with few participants beginning their criminal careers committing the offense completely on their own. In qualitative interviews, car thieves recount how their first exposure to car theft came in the form of joyriding as a passenger in a stolen car in their early teens. Echoing Sutherland, the criminologists conducting the interviews noted,

> *The neighborhoods they grew up in were flush with opportunities to observe and interact with individuals bearing both the requisite attitudes and knowledge to initiate an individual into motor vehicle theft.* (p. 285)[9]

In other words, definitions favorable to car theft were abundant for these burgeoning thieves. But "requisite attitudes," alone, are insufficient. They also needed the requisite knowledge. Auto thieves describe how, as novice thieves, they had apprenticeship-like relationships with more-experienced criminals (or "technical advisers"). They would serve as lookouts or passengers while learning the skills necessary for successfully stealing cars, often graduating quickly from novice to equal participant. Asked how they got into auto theft, one respondent reported, "Well, hanging out with [a] couple older guys, you know, they showed me the ropes... [W]hat cars to target and what cars you can't steal... That's how I got into it... Just hanging out with older guys, they showed me" (p. 286).[10] The "ropes" include breaking down the steering column, tampering with or bypassing ignitions, checking for alarms, and determining the length of time a stolen vehicle can be displayed in public before detection. Plus, having developed "larceny sense," they learned to exploit "found" opportunities, as when a careless driver would leave their car running while they went into a gas station to buy a drink or have a conversation with the cashier.

In addition to their mentoring and co-offending relationships that foster pro-crime attitudes, many auto thieves report connections within a broader car theft disposal network. Making money from stealing cars requires a willing customer. "Chop shops," typically body repair shops that buy and sell stolen vehicles on the side, play an important role in the market for stolen cars, as do associates who facilitate street sales of stolen parts and accessories (like rims and speakers). Entry into these criminal networks requires establishing trusting relationships and compliance with a shared code of conduct, such as "no snitching." Consistent with Sutherland's propositions, auto thieves acquire crime-supportive attitudes and offending skills through interactions with friends and criminal mentors.

Toronto police officers identify stolen vehicles at a chop shop. Participation in the market for stolen vehicles as an auto thief requires criminal learning and access to disposal networks.

Lucas Oleniuk/Toronto Star/Getty Images

Evaluating Differential Association Theory

It is difficult to overstate the importance of differential association theory in altering the path of criminology. The effects of delinquent peers on adolescent crime are so well-established that any study that does not attempt to measure and control for them is regarded as fatally flawed. Criminal associations remain one of the strongest predictors of individual law-breaking.[11] Study after study bears this out. For example, criminologists find that peer groups transmit favorable norms about behaviors like prescription drug abuse (e.g., frequent illicit misuse of Xanax and Adderall) and dating violence. This is different from peer pressure. In the case of prescription drug abuse, participants enjoy the experience-enhancing qualities of normalized misuse rather than feeling pressured into doing something they don't want to do.[12] Aggressive peer groups normalize violence as a mechanism for expressing emotions and resolving conflicts in the case of dating violence.[13] In short, learning matters. But how much?

Critics of differential association are quick to remind us that correlation does not equal causation. What *looks* like a learning effect might be a selection effect. A selection effect occurs when those who already possess an outcome characteristic, like criminality, seek out—or select into—a predictor characteristic, like having crime-involved friends. This is a critique about temporal ordering, one of the three requirements for causation (correlation, temporal ordering, and nonspuriousness; see Chapter 1). Sutherland's theory states that learning always comes *before* criminal conduct. We now know this is only half of the story. Plenty of studies show that many people begin to break the law absent any criminal influences. Once they dip their toes in crime, they then seek out similarly criminal acquaintances who reinforce their pro-crime attitudes and share their questionable interests. This operates as a feedback loop: Criminal behavior leads to criminal peers who lead to more criminal behavior.[14] It's not that Sutherland's theory was wrong; it was just incomplete.

Critics of the theory also argue that differential association theory is a theory of *how*, not *why*: It explains the process by which people learn to be criminal but not why pro-crime attitudes emerge in the first place. If we want to understand why crime happens, or the etiology of crime, we must seek out the root causes of criminal norms. After all, they don't appear out of nowhere. As we will see, this is a major task of subcultural theories of crime, which are addressed later in this chapter.

Another critique focuses on the difficulties of testing Sutherland's theory. Most of us will encounter people who gleefully flout the law (definitions favorable to crime) and others who frown upon any straying from the straight and narrow (definitions unfavorable). But how do we determine the ratio of favorable to unfavorable definitions? We cannot just add up each interaction to obtain comparable and competing sums. Sutherland himself acknowledged that it's impossible to create such a formula. In fact, the overall vagueness of Sutherland's theory was a point of displeasure among criminologists who sought a more precise description of how the learning of crime occurs. Fortunately for them, a new learning theory came to supplant Sutherland's groundbreaking, if flawed, perspective. It is now called social learning theory.

AKERS'S SOCIAL LEARNING THEORY

Back in 1966, criminologists Robert Burgess and Ronald Akers were tinkering with differential association, reformulating the theory by fusing it with insights from behavioral psychology.[15] Initially, they called their new perspective "differential association-reinforcement theory," which is rather a mouthful. In the decades since, Akers refined and revised the theory to create what criminologists now call *social learning theory*. Social learning refers to the process of learning through observing and imitating others.

Of Sutherland's original nine propositions, the sixth was most important for social learning theory: Criminal behavior is likely when learning of pro-crime attitudes (definitions favorable to crime) outweighs the learning of anti-crime attitudes (definitions unfavorable to crime). This *is* the principle of differential association. Akers, along with Burgess initially, agreed. They, too, thought that we learn criminal norms and values in our associations with others and that we are exposed to different sets of norms and values that conflict with one another. But here is where they departed: Social learning theory would explain exactly *why* we internalize some messages about crime and discard others by looking to differential reinforcement, or operant conditioning.

Operant Conditioning

Let's take a break from criminology to cover some Psychology 101 territory. Behaviorism (also called behavioral psychology) is a field of psychology that focuses on how behaviors are acquired through a process of conditioning. Behaviorists argue that we learn—or are conditioned—through association. Through interactions with our environment, we come to associate certain experiences with certain behaviors. For example, if you burn your hand every time (or even just some of the time) you touch a hot stove, you will become conditioned to keep your hand away from the stove. Or, if your mother shows you extra affection each time you rat out your sibling for breaking the rules, you will become conditioned to always turn in your siblings. Social learning theorists are most interested in a type of conditioning called operant conditioning, made famous by psychologist B. F. Skinner. Operant conditioning emphasizes rewards, called reinforcement, and punishments. Consequences affect learning in operant conditioning: We learn to repeat behaviors associated with rewards (like mom's affection) and to avoid actions that elicit a punishing response (like a burnt hand).[16]

Reinforcement is a consequence that increases an action if presented immediately following the behavior (if it helps, remember that reinforcement and reward both start with the letter R). Behavioral psychologists discern between positive reinforcement and negative reinforcement. Both types increase behavior. The positive-negative distinction has to do with whether something desired is presented (positive reinforcement) or something undesired is removed (negative reinforcement). In other words, a negative reinforcement isn't negative because it's a bad thing; it's negative because something bad is taken away. For example, imagine a teenager who is being mercilessly bullied at school. One day, they violently attack their bully and, as a result, the bullying stops. In the future, any time someone teases them, they retaliate violently. That is an example of negative reinforcement. Something bad (the bullying) was taken away as a consequence of the violent behavior, conditioning them to resort to violence in future interactions.

Punishments, in contrast, are consequences that decrease behavior when presented immediately afterwards. Like reinforcement, punishment can be positive or negative. Both types decrease behavior. Positive punishment presents something aversive (or disliked), like physical violence or ridicule. Negative punishment decreases behavior by removing something favored, like money, a treasured friendship, or a job.

Four Principles of Social Learning

Social learning theory has four components, some rooted in Sutherland's ideas and others rooted in behavioral psychology:

1. *Differential association* – Social learning theory adopts Sutherland's sixth and seventh propositions: Crime is likely if exposure to pro-crime attitudes and criminal behavior outweighs exposure to anti-crime attitudes and conventional behavior; the likelihood of adopting one set of attitudes and behaviors over a competing set of attitudes and behaviors is determined by the modalities (frequency, duration, priority, and intensity).

2. *Definitions* – Similar to Sutherland's description, social learning theory depicts definitions as "values, orientations, and attitudes toward criminal/deviant or conforming behavior," which we use to evaluate certain actions as being "more right or wrong, good or bad, desirable or undesirable, justified or unjustified, appropriate or inappropriate, excusable or inexcusable" (p. 116).[17]

    Definitions favorable to crime can be either *positive* or *neutralizing*. Positive definitions are pro-crime attitudes (e.g., "it's cool to sell cocaine"). Neutralizing definitions, in contrast, don't see the criminal behavior as good but as acceptable, justifiable, or excusable under certain circumstances (e.g., "selling cocaine isn't good but it's all right to do if you only sell to your friends and you never sell to kids"). According to Akers, neutralizing definitions are much more common than positive definitions.[18]

Social learning theorists differentiate between *general* and *specific* definitions. General definitions are broad sets of beliefs that cover a wide range of behaviors. Beliefs like "honesty is the best policy" and "we should treat others as we wish to be treated" are general definitions that are unfavorable to crime. General pro-crime definitions include beliefs like "might makes right" and "always look out for number one." Specific definitions pertain to particular, or specific, criminal acts. A person can hold permissive attitudes towards theft (like the neutralizing belief that theft is acceptable if you only take low-cost items from big box stores) while also abhorring violence of any kind. Their specific definitions of theft (favorable) and violence (unfavorable) differ. Importantly, all definitions—whether positive, neutralizing, conventional, general, or specific—exist on a spectrum, with people internalizing them to greater and lesser degrees. Two people might hold the belief that "honesty is the best policy," but one holds firmly to that belief and the other only weakly.[19]

3. *Differential reinforcement and punishment* – Social learning theory argues that people adapt their behavior based on their perception, experience, and anticipation of rewards and punishments, consistent with operant conditioning principles. The frequency and value of rewards for an action are compared to the frequency and severity of punishment for the action. If the balance tips in favor of rewards, then the act is more likely. Positive and negative reinforcers and punishments condition conduct.

   Reinforcement and punishment can be *direct* or *vicarious*. It is either experienced by the person engaging in the act (direct) or an observer sees it happen to another person who is engaging in the act (vicarious). Imagine a 16-year-old whose friends are planning to break into a neighbor's apartment and are encouraging him to join in. Let's say he participates in the burglary and makes off with some cash, a gaming console, a couple bottles of liquor, and a closer relationship with his friends, all things that he values. He has experienced the rewards (or positive reinforcement) of his crime directly. If he hadn't joined in but he saw how his friends got to enjoy the spoils of their crime, then the positive reinforcement would be vicarious: He has learned that this behavior yields benefits by watching it happen to others.

   Social learning theorists acknowledge that reinforcers and punishments can be *social* or *nonsocial*.[20] Let's imagine that our teenage burglar is heaped with praise from his friends upon completing the act. He has gained their respect. That is social reinforcement. The word *social* refers to processes that occur between two or more people. Any consequence— rewarding or punishing—that plays out between individuals is social, including attaining status, being feared, receiving sexual attention, getting kicked out of someone's house, and evoking disapproval. Nonsocial consequences are internal and often physiological. The exciting, heart-pumping, adrenaline-rush feeling during a criminal act, the pleasurable sensation of getting away with "sneaky thrills," and the high (literal or figurative) of breaking the rules are nonsocial rewards.[21] People who engage in "edgework," or voluntary risk-taking, describe the pleasure of mastering and controlling their fears during emotionally intense activities, whether legal (like skydiving) or illegal (like armed robbery).[22] Of course, one person's pleasure may feel painful to another. Some people find the physiological sensations of risk-taking or illicit substance use to be nausea-inducing or otherwise intrinsically punishing.

4. *Imitation* – You are familiar with the final component of social learning theory if you've used the term *role model* before (a term coined by anomie theorist Robert Merton, in fact). In imitation, a person observes another's behavior and mimics it, as when a child emulates the violence of an abusive parent by harming younger siblings or classmates. Imitation is especially likely in scenarios involving vicarious positive reinforcement; not only has the learner observed the criminal action, but they have also witnessed its rewards. Imitation is most likely to take place at the initiation of a novel or new behavior.[23]

Gang members in El Paso showing off hand signs and tattoos. Members report joining the gang to gain respect among peers and protect themselves against other gangs. Respect and protection are social reinforcers.

Hector Mata/AFP/Getty Images

ENGAGED CRIMINOLOGY 9.1
Applying Learning Perspectives to Shoplifting

In this activity you will complete a questionnaire on shoplifting (theft from a retail establishment during business hours). Then you will apply concepts from learning perspectives to the questionnaire.

Complete the questionnaire:

Question 1: About how many of your friends do you think have engaged in shoplifting?

- None
- Just a few
- About half
- More than half
- All or nearly all

Question 2: I've been with a friend or family member when they've shoplifted and gotten away with it.

- No
- Yes

Question 3: I think it's OK to shoplift items if you don't have the money to pay for them.

- Strongly disagree
- Disagree
- Agree
- Strongly agree

Now apply concepts from differential association theory and social learning theory to the questionnaire.

1. Which question measured definitions favorable to shoplifting?
   a. Question 1
   b. Question 2
   c. Question 3

2. Which question measured *differential associations*?
  a. Question 1
  b. Question 2
  c. Question 3

3. Which question measured imitation (or vicarious social reinforcement)?
  a. Question 1
  b. Question 2
  c. Question 3

Intergenerational Transmission of Violence

Just as families pass down their holiday traditions and shared memories, so too can they pass down their more troubling qualities, including violence. The intergenerational transmission of violence, sometimes call the cycle of violence, refers to the empirical pattern in which children exposed to violence in the home—as victim, witness, or both—grow up to engage in violence or become victims of violence.[24] The *inter-* in intergenerational means "between," so any pattern that is intergenerational happens between generations, or from one generation (parents) to the next (children). Adults incarcerated for violent crimes, including child abuse and intimate partner violence, are far more likely to have personal histories of child maltreatment than are nonviolent adults.[25] It is important to recognize, though, that surviving a violent family environment doesn't automatically translate into adult criminality, even though it is a risk factor. Most survivors do *not* become violent adults. Many "break the cycle."[26]

But what about those who do not break the cycle? What causes violence to become cyclical? Social learning theory is the most frequently invoked explanation. Children imitate role models like parents and older siblings, play-acting and mimicking their behaviors. Plus, physical violence at home establishes violence of all kinds as normal and legitimate responses to frustrations (i.e., a definition favorable to violence). Criminologists also argue that children exposed to violent home environments develop aggressive behaviors that carry over to peer interactions at school. Rejected by their nonaggressive classmates, they form friendships with similarly combative children, modeling and reinforcing violence for one another.[27]

Can you think of explanations for the intergenerational transmission of violence that are not related to social learning? One possibility is that maltreated children form weak attachments to their abusive caregivers, causing them to develop a hostile view of the world and other people. Having been mistreated, they assume others will also treat them poorly and respond aggressively in ambiguous situations. Another argument is that exposure to toxic stress at home alters children's neurophysiological development. Witnessing or experiencing family violence—including constantly worrying about a parent's unpredictable moods—activates the "fight or flight" stress response. This can cause post-traumatic stress disorder (PTSD) and its behavioral symptoms of hypervigilance, irritability, hostility, and self-destructive behavior (e.g., substance abuse and aggression).[28] Behavioral geneticists argue for a third possibility in which parental violence does not, in fact, cause violence in the younger generation. Instead, they argue, parents and children share inherited genetic risk factors for antisocial behavior. Twin studies suggest that both genes and social environments are at play in the cycle of violence.[29]

Evaluating Social Learning Theory

Social learning is a key component of much criminal conduct, ranging from illicit substance abuse[30] to youth gang behavior[31] to digital piracy[32] to hate crime[33] to intimate partner violence.[34] This is one of its key strengths: It explains both minor adolescent delinquency *and* serious adult crime. It applies to property crimes, public-order crimes, *and* violence. It is one of the most empirically tested, supported, endorsed, and cited theories in criminology.[35] It also holds up across cultures rather than just explaining crime within the U.S. context.[36] And unlike its forebearer, differential association theory, the social learning perspective offers a more nuanced explanation for how learning operates, rooted in psychological principles of operant conditioning. Furthermore, these principles provide a roadmap for crime prevention and programs designed to rehabilitate offenders. Programs based on social learning ideas work by altering antisocial values and rationalizations that excuse criminal behavior, rewarding positive behaviors, and isolating law-breakers from their crime-involved friends and associates.[37]

Many critiques of differential association theory apply to social learning theory as well: Perhaps it's a "birds of a feather" effect (or a selection effect) rather than a learning effect. Plus, the theory tells us more about how criminal norms spread than why they exist in the first place. Early detractors argued that the basis of social learning theory's reinforcement claims—operant conditioning—was tautological, or relied on circular logic.[38] Their argument was that the predictor (reinforcement) and the outcome (criminal behavior) were inseparable: How do you know an act was reinforced? They continued to do it. Why did they continue to do it? Reinforcement! Each was offered as evidence of the other. Criminologists avoid this problem by ensuring they measure reinforcement and crime separately.

SUBCULTURAL PERSPECTIVES

Subcultures are cultural systems—comprised of norms, values, and beliefs—that are products of, but distinct from, the broader culture in which they are embedded. While some subcultures revolve around shared interests (like music subcultures, gaming subcultures, or cosplay) or occupations (like oil rig subcultures and military subcultures), others are a collective solution to shared structural problems. A common thread in all subcultures is that members share behavioral expectations, tied to values, that set them apart from the dominant culture. Delinquent and criminal subcultures offer solutions to shared structural problems that involve law-breaking. Their norms, values, and beliefs support or tolerate criminal conduct.

Consider, for example, prison subculture, sometimes called the convict code.[39] Incarcerated people occupy a shared position (relative to nonincarcerated people): They lack autonomy, the threat of violent confrontation is often present, personal belongings are scarce and may be coveted by others, and maintaining one's dignity is a struggle. The deprivations of prison life give rise to subcultures that fulfill unmet needs. Some subcultural adaptations support self-serving exploitation. For example, some incarcerated people learn to control scarce valued goods in order to exploit others or to use physical force to extract scarce goods from weaker individuals.[40] Even those who quietly do their time without using or harming their peers subscribe to the convict code in order to survive. The code dictates never snitching on one another, minding one's own business, being tough, and never getting too friendly with correctional officers.[41] Criminologists describe the degree to which people become embedded in prison habits and dispositions as prisonization: The more immersed they become in prison subculture, the greater the degree of prisonization, and the harder it is to adapt to life outside of prison.[42] These effects are evident in Liam Martin's ethnographic study of people recently released from prison, as observed in this excerpt:

> Guy Jordan felt awkward with people behind him, put paper on the toilet seat, and found himself taking staunch body postures without reason. He stood from the bench where we talked to demonstrate: no smile, feet firmly planted shoulder width apart, arms folded tightly across chest, hands tucked in armpits. "I would find myself doing the same mannerisms I had in jail," he said. "I'm on the street physically, but mentally, I'm still doing what I would be doing in there." (p. 679)[43]

Other examples of criminal subcultures include gang subcultures, substance use and trafficking subcultures, cybercrime subcultures, illicit sex work subcultures, violent extremist subcultures, and more. Each has its own behavioral norms, attitudes, dispositions, specialized knowledge, and styles of self-presentation, such as dress or posture.

Subcultural perspectives presume that norms and values are transmitted through a process of socialization, or learning (hence their inclusion in this chapter). Criminologists frequently look to structural conditions, however, to understand the *origins* and *content* of criminal subcultures. Learning perspectives, like differential association theory and social learning theory, explain how criminal norms and values spread from person to person, but they don't explain why criminal norms and values exist in the first place. Subcultural perspectives do.

Subcultural explanations hit the criminological scene in the mid-20th century. At that time, adolescent crime (called juvenile delinquency) captured the attention of researchers, especially youth gang delinquency. Unsurprisingly, then, most subcultural perspectives developed back then explained the emergence of lower-class boys' law-breaking. Even today, analyses of criminal (and crime-tolerant) sub-cultures tend to focus on the values and behaviors of the poor.

The prison code is a subcultural system that guides day-to-day life behind bars. The more an incarcerated person embraces the prison code, the greater the extent of prisonization.

Kevork Djansezian/Getty Images News/Getty Images

Miller's Focal Concerns Perspective

Walter Miller set out to describe the value system of impoverished communities in his classic 1958 paper "Lower Class Culture as a Generating Milieu of Gang Delinquency." He detailed six focal concerns, or value orientations, that emerged because of the conditions of daily life in poor communities. Miller did not see these focal concerns as an inversion of middle-class culture (as we will see in Cohen's status frustration view). Instead, they represented a unique cultural orientation that was a "long established, distinctively patterned tradition with an integrity of its own" (p. 5).[44] In other words, "lower class culture" had its own history and traditions that could be understood without reference to middle-class culture. Importantly, Miller asserted, these value orientations promoted illegal conduct among those deeply committed to them. Through a three-year-long research project with 21 "corner groups" (or gangs) in a "slum district" of a large city, including white and Black young people, both male and female, Miller identified the dimensions, or focal concerns, of what he called "lower-class culture":

- *Trouble* – "Getting into trouble" and "staying out of trouble" are major concerns. Those who engage in law-abiding behavior do so not because they are committed to legal norms, but to avoid the complicating consequences of "getting into trouble." Status is conferred based on avoiding trouble (e.g., a prospective boyfriend who doesn't get into trouble is prized), which is, itself, regarded as an achievement. For others, like gang-involved young people, getting into trouble confers prestige and achieves other goals, as well, like providing excitement (another focal concern).

- *Toughness* – Physical prowess, shows of masculinity, and bravery in the face of threats are emphasized. Boys and men are concerned with being "hard, fearless, undemonstrative, [and] skilled in physical combat" (p. 9). They reject anything regarded as effeminate, such as physical weakness or exercising caution, and homophobic violence and slurs are common. Expressions of affection for other men must be concealed as their opposite, such as aggressive roughhousing and joking.

- *Smartness* – This doesn't refer to academic intelligence. Rather, it's about the ability to think on one's feet and to obtain something highly valued "though a maximum use of mental agility and a minimum use of physical effort" (p. 10). Being smart means outsmarting other people (conning or hustling), using one's wits to make money or to dominate aggressively in conversation. Though both are valued, smartness is more revered than toughness.

- *Excitement* – The rhythm of daily life cycles between long periods of boring, routine repetition and short bursts of sought-out excitement. The quest for excitement—through drinking, gambling, fighting, and sexual conquest—is a feature of life among the corner groups Miller studied. The emotional thrills of excitement-seeking offset the boredom and passivity of day-to-day life.

- *Fate* – Feeling that their lives are subject to forces over which they exercise little control, luck is valued as the primary determinant of life's outcomes. One's fortunes feel fated, or due to destiny. What will be, will be. This is often accompanied by the sense that one's efforts to secure goals are futile; things will only work out if luck is on your side.

- *Autonomy* – Autonomy is the freedom to do what one pleases, free of external control, behavioral restrictions, and coercive authority. Resentment towards those who seek to control one's behavior is expressed through sentiments like "I'm gonna tell him he can take this job and shove it…" or "I don't need *nobody* to take care of me. I can take care of myself!" (p. 12)

Millers described how single-sex (all-male or all-female), same-age social groups serve as a central organizing feature in poor communities. He argues that these "corner groups" are the most important source of relationships and behavioral modeling in people's lives, especially for boys, owing to the absence or lack of involvement of fathers at home. As their primary reference group, the peer-based social group confers both belonging and status. Staying accepted within the group requires demonstrated commitment to the values of toughness, smartness, and excitement. Rising to the top of the pecking order, or status hierarchy, within one's group is secured through being the toughest, the smartest, and the most resistant to authority relative to the other members. Fighting, theft, drunkenness, illicit gambling, and various other delinquent offenses are effective ways of generating excitement and proving one's manliness and street smarts.

Some of Miller's ideas strike a contemporary reader as completely off-base. Chief among them is his claim that the vocal lower-class rejection of authority and thirst for autonomy conceals a quiet desire for being controlled. His evidence for this was the constant cycling of lower-class adolescents and adults through coercive institutions, such as mental hospitals, disciplinary schools, and jails and prisons. That they engage in behaviors that land them in these highly restrictive environments was interpreted as a desire to be controlled or "cared for," an idea roundly rejected by modern criminologists. Nonetheless, Miller's ideas about lower-class focal concerns persist, infusing contemporary studies of crime. In fact, Anderson's *Code of the Street*—possibly criminology's most important modern work on subculture, described later in the chapter—echoes many of Miller's assertions.

The earliest subcultural perspectives in criminology focused primarily on teenage boys' crime in low-income neighborhoods.

Corbis Historical/Getty Images

Cohen's Status Frustration Perspective

Around the same time as Miller was writing about lower-class focal concerns, Albert Cohen was describing the origins of working-class "delinquent subcultures" in his book aptly titled *Delinquent Boys*.[45] Like Miller, he was interested in the criminal conduct of boys and young men in economically distressed communities. Unlike Miller, he saw their subculture and the behavior it encouraged as a rejection of out-of-reach middle-class expectations.

Cohen asserted that lower-class boys want to be successful in the ways that middle-class culture defines success: They want to get a good job, make money, and have a nice house, a nice car, and nice clothing. But they face nearly insurmountable hurdles in achieving this goal due to class-based socialization and skill deficits. Their families are ill-equipped to prepare them for successfully navigating schools and workplaces with middle-class expectations. The way they speak, the way they interact with authority, and their inability to delay gratification means that they always seem to fall short. This produces status frustration, a feeling of deprivation, resentment, and hostility arising from unfavorable class comparisons. Astute readers will soon realize that Cohen's perspective incorporates anomie and strain theory principles, which are the focus of Chapter 10.[46]

The school is central in Cohen's view. This is where teachers—all of them college educated and middle class—set the standards that students are expected to meet. Impressing authority figures at school (and, later, at work) means behaving and presenting oneself according to middle-class norms. All children, regardless of their family's social class position, are evaluated based on a middle-class measuring rod. Those who cannot measure up experience status frustration. Cohen outlines three subcultural adaptions to the feelings of failure and frustration generated by middle-class rejection: (1) the corner boy, (2) the college boy, and (3) the delinquent boy.

Corner boys realize that they can't compete with their middle-class peers, so they retreat to the familiar world of their working-class friendship groups. They stay living in the neighborhoods where they grew up, take on low-skilled jobs, and have families of their own. Corner boys adapt their expectations to their circumstances. They are not criminally inclined, but they may engage in minor offenses, like truancy from school (when young) and illicit substance use.

College boys, in contrast, do not throw in the towel—or adapt their expectations—in the face of frustration. They remain committed to middle-class goals and values. College boys keep trying to measure up against the middle-class measuring rod despite the significant hurdles in their way. Cohen offers a pessimistic view of college boys, whom he sees as facing an impossible uphill battle to achieve a middle-class life, due to their significant academic, social, and linguistic disadvantages.

Delinquent boys, the focus of Cohen's book, engage in "non-utilitarian, malicious, and negativistic" behaviors. Their criminal acts are expressive rather than driven by economic need; they are a way of expressing resistance to middle-class values. Cohen argues that delinquent boys experience reaction formation, an ego-related psychological defense against status frustration. Recognizing that others reject them, they reject the very system in which they cannot compete. Confronted with their failures to succeed in the competition with better-equipped middle-class peers, delinquent boys invert middle-class respectability norms. If their teachers want them to be compliant and respectful, they will instead value defiance and hostility. Spurning the mainstream virtues of prudence and moderation, delinquent boys value immediate gratification. They live in the present rather than planning for the future. They pursue acts of short-run hedonism, or pleasure-seeking, rather than considering long-term consequences. And they buck against authorities who attempt to control them and their friends, including family members and school staff. Their responses to perceived slights are disproportionate and aggressive, consistent with reaction formation. They are protecting their sense of self. Delinquent boys are not inherently bad people; they are reacting to social conditions.

According to the status frustration perspective, reaction formation leads to non-utilitarian offending, like vandalism, as a rejection of unobtainable middle-class expectations.

Richard Baker/In Pictures/Getty Images

Cloward and Ohlin's Differential Opportunity Perspective

Criminologists Richard Cloward and L. E. Ohlin, contemporaries of Miller and Cohen, also sought to describe and uncover the subculture of crime-involved boys and young men in poor neighborhoods in their book *Delinquency and Opportunity*.[47] As the title suggests, they saw opportunities—for legitimate work *and* for crime—as central to the explanation of lower-class criminality. Cloward and Ohlin's argument can be summarized in a series of answers to the questions that drive their research.[48]

Question: *What is the underlying problem faced by those who join delinquent groups, or gangs?*

Answer: They are unable to attain the financial success to which they aspire through legal channels, like doing well in school and getting a good job. "Differential opportunity" is about the various types of opportunities available (or not available) in a community. This answer pertains to the absence of *legitimate* opportunities for success. You will see this idea again in Chapter 10, which discusses strain perspectives in criminology, some of which claim that barriers to conventional success compel individuals to commit crime.

Question: *How do potential delinquents think about this underlying problem?*

Answer: They feel alienated and resentful because the American ideology of egalitarianism says that anyone can achieve, but their experiences with class barriers tell them that this isn't true. As a result, they develop a sense of unjust deprivation, and they grow disillusioned with mainstream social norms whose legitimacy they question.

Question: *How do potential delinquents behave once they become disillusioned?*

Answer: They seek out a collective solution to their problem by banding together with others who are similarly alienated. Together, the group develops "a supporting structure of beliefs and values that provide advance justification for deviant conduct" (p. 132).[49] In other words, they form a close-knit peer group that encourages rule-breaking. Criminal acts follow.

Question: *How do collections of disillusioned adolescent boys turn into delinquent gangs?*

Answer: This is where *criminal* opportunities come in. Those who live in impoverished communities with established networks of adult thieves will have opportunities to learn larceny skills under the guidance of experienced criminals, and they will form gangs that steal. We can substitute other offenses based on what opportunities for criminal learning are available. For example, established opportunities for drug trafficking will translate into the formation of drug dealing gangs. However, many groups of alienated young people lack access to, or competence in, organized and lucrative criminal gang activity. Cloward and Ohlin identify three types of gangs that differ in terms of (a) the criminal opportunities available in their communities and (b) the kinds of crimes they commit.

1. *Criminal gangs* – In criminal gangs, younger people are recruited into established groups whose goal is to successfully operate a continuing criminal enterprise. Recruits take on an apprentice-type role with limited participation until they have learned how the group operates and have internalized the criminal world's values and attitudes. These gangs emerge in stably lower-class neighborhoods where there are organized illegitimate opportunities (e.g., drug trafficking opportunities) but few opportunities for legal success.

2. *Conflict gangs* – These gangs emerge in disorganized areas absent of both legitimate and illegitimate opportunities, where crime is "individualistic, unorganized, petty, poorly paid, and unprotected" (p. 73).[50] With few successful criminal adult role models to emulate and learn from (as in criminal gangs), young people adopt violence as the primary way to attain status and express their frustrations. Respect from peers and a positive self-image are secured through unpredictable violence and the reputation that follows.

3. *Retreatist gangs* – Lacking legitimate opportunities, retreatist gangs occupy the fringes of conventional society and spend their time getting high or finding their next high. They lack the skills of criminal gangs and they do not engage in the violence of conflict gangs. They see themselves as culturally and socially disconnected from the mainstream world. They may "hustle" to support their substance use, but they prefer to use manipulation, persuasion, or quick wits, rather than violence, to get what they seek.

Anderson's Code of the Street

Now let's fast-forward about 40 years. Research on criminal subcultures waned after the initial burst of interest in the mid-20th century but was resurrected with the publication of Elijah Anderson's modern classic *Code of the Street: Decency, Violence, and the Moral Life of the Inner City,* an ethnographic study of an economically marginalized and racially segregated community in Philadelphia.[51] Anderson described the code of the street as "a set of informal rules governing interpersonal public behavior, particularly violence" in urban neighborhoods where respect is in short supply, the threat of violence is ever-present, and residents are reluctant to turn to police and the courts for assistance (p. 33).[52] It is the result of decades of residential segregation, social exclusion, economic deprivation, and racial discrimination.

There are two cultural orientations in communities dominated by the code, *street* and *decent,* which are the terms used by residents. Street-oriented residents are wholeheartedly dedicated to the code. Street parents train their children in the code's values and enforce its behavioral requirements, such as by threatening to beat children who come home crying from a schoolyard fight from which they've backed down. Street-oriented parents, often overwhelmed by the stresses of poverty and parenthood, are quick to anger and impatient with others. Drug use and violent relationships are common experiences. These families are "profound casualties of the social and economic system," residing on the bottom of the social hierarchy within the neighborhood. Residents with a decency orientation regard them as bad people.[53]

Decent families, in comparison, are poor families scraping by, working hard, and making sacrifices to secure a better future for themselves and their children. They are what some call the "working poor." They do not buy into the code of the street, yet they must educate their children in how to navigate public spaces where the code is king. Most residents are decent or are at least make their best attempts to be decent. Nevertheless, the street-oriented set the rules of interaction by which everyone must abide even though they are outnumbered by residents with a decency orientation.

The code of the street has four main characteristics: respect, reputation, violence, and victimization. Respect forms the foundation of the code. Being respected—and never disrespected—is the primary currency in public interaction. Respect is achieved and maintained through hyper-masculine shows of toughness, acts of violence, and opposition to authority.[54] Willingness to initiate violence and to retaliate against aggressors secures a person's reputation. The beliefs that "might makes right" and "respect is hard-won" run through the code. Small mistakes, like making eye contact for too long or brushing by someone on the street, can be cause for an altercation. There are nonviolent paths to respect, as well. Wearing expensive clothes and jewelry, having athletic prowess, and making money from drug sales can also establish reputation and garner respect.

Showing "nerve" and cultivating a reputation as someone who doesn't back down from a fight serves multiple functions for residents. First, it is an important source of self-worth for those who have few other ways to gain respect and status. Because respect is in short supply, the way to get respect is to take it away from another person. Second, it is defensive. Displaying weakness—or actions interpreted as weakness—opens a person up to further victimization in neighborhoods where "there are always people around looking for a fight" (p. 73).[55] Failing to retaliate against an insult, an assault, or a theft marks a person as a potential target.

Importantly, behaving in accordance with the code is not indicative of inferior morals or deviant socialization. Instead, the code is an "adaption to ... the persistent threat of violence that is present in some urban communities" (p. 304).[56] It is a survival strategy, or self-protection. Abiding by the code ensures a measure of safety irrespective of whether those enacting it are deeply committed to it or are personally disposed to physical aggression. Love it or hate it, avoiding violent confrontation, or being "messed with," requires adhering to the code of the street.

Criminologists have spent the past two decades studying the code of the street and its consequences in communities far beyond the Philadelphia neighborhood where Anderson conducted his original ethnographic research. Their studies confirm that individuals who have internalized the code's values are more likely to commit acts of violence.[57] But it turns out that subscribing to the code is poor protection against victimization, a presumed reason for establishing a reputation for toughness. In fact, those who embrace the code are victimized more than those who don't, and not just violent victimization. One reason is that they are out in public more; street-oriented people spend more time on the street, increasing their chances of insults, disputes, and being targeted for theft.[58]

Anti-violence community organizations like Stand Up to Violence seek to alter norms in neighborhoods with high rates of gun violence and provide aid to victims and their families.

Michael M. Santiago/Getty Images News/Getty Images

Evaluating Subcultural Perspectives

Subcultural perspectives like Anderson's code of the street have been game-changers in criminology. They make explicit connections between culture (norms and values), social structure (social institutions, public policies, the organization of opportunities, and large-scale inequalities), and individual action, providing a fuller understanding of criminal conduct and its allure. They fulfill the promise of the "criminological imagination."[59] Decades ago, sociologist C. Wright Mills, in his now-famous book *The Sociological Imagination,* argued that society ought to be viewed through a prism with three components: personal biography, social structure, and history.[60] Those who have a "sociological imagination" develop an awareness and understanding of the relationship between personal experience and the broader society. The **criminological imagination** applies this idea to crime: People's lives—including their criminal lives—must be understood within social and historical context.[61] Understanding youth gang subcultures in the U.S., for example, requires attention to public policies that transferred investment from urban centers to the suburbs, availability of educational and employment opportunities, mass incarceration, historical and contemporary patterns of racial segregation and wealth inequality, and other large-scale forces.

A major critique of the earliest subcultural theories is that they lacked a sufficient criminological imagination. Though they took seriously the social class position of delinquent boys and young men, the impact of structural racism and gender inequality was conspicuously absent. Skeptics also noted that these scholars tended to romanticize white working-class delinquency, which means that they glorified their harmful behaviors by offering an overly sympathetic picture of their lives.[62]

Critics of subcultural perspectives in criminology note that most are concerned primarily with the criminal actions of the poor, particularly boys and young men. This was especially true of the earliest explanations, like Miller's focal concerns and Cohen's status frustration perspectives. To be clear, plenty of ethnographers today study criminal subcultures that don't fit the standard "lower-class criminality" mold, but their goals are often descriptive rather than explanatory. For example, criminologists chronicle the online subcultures of crime-involved groups like Johns (men who purchase illicit sexual services)[63] and hackers who commit ideologically motivated attacks.[64] These studies are valuable, offering insight into the social rules governing illicit conduct, but they tend not to offer a unified theory of why those social rules came into being.

Some scholars of affluent criminal subcultures examine their subjects through the prism of the criminological imagination. For example, in *Dorm Room Dealers,* criminologists A. Rafik Mohamed and Erik Fritsvold describe the social world of white, affluent college campus drug dealers.[65] Their central question was: "Why do affluent college students, poised to embrace a series of legitimate avenues for upward mobility and success, choose to become drug dealers?" Through interviews with 50 campus drug sellers, they conclude that (1) dealing provides much-sought-after financial independence from parents, especially for those seeking "off the books" income to support their own substantial substance use; (2) college students can avoid the stigma of being a "drug dealer" by positioning themselves as "capitalists in training" (many, in fact, were business majors), who will give up their criminal conduct upon transitioning to the full-time labor force; and (3) as white college students from affluent families, their privileged position within racial and social class hierarchies renders them effectively invisible to law enforcement. In the authors' words, they are the "anti-targets" of the War on Drugs.

In sum, subcultural perspectives like those expressed in Cohen's status frustration ideas, Anderson's code of the street, and Mohamed and Fritzvold's ethnography of "dorm room dealers" portray human behavior with nuance and complexity. They accomplish this by linking individual action, social rules, and value orientations to conditions in the wider society, fulfilling the promise of the criminological imagination.

DRIFT AND NEUTRALIZATION

Few people are 100% criminal, seven days a week, 24 hours a day. Socialization doesn't always fully take, and subcultures don't shape the behavior of all participants at all times. Criminologist David Matza explored this idea in his theory of drift, which argues that young people drift between conforming behavior and law-breaking behavior across situations.[66] Crime-supportive subcultures may make the person feel like they are free from the moral chains of society, providing justifications for their misbehavior and imbuing them with an attitude that sources of authority are illegitimate, but these dispositions fail to fully overwrite their conventional values. Take, for example, Matza's observations of juvenile offenders[67]:

- They often show guilt or remorse over their law-breaking, which suggests they know these behaviors are wrong even in if the subculture says they are acceptable.

- They respect and admire conventional role models, like family members, teachers, or celebrities.

- They rule out certain people and places when selecting targets for their crimes, such as their neighbors and members of their ethnic in-group, suggesting that they understand these actions to be morally unacceptable.

- They engage in law-abiding conduct in addition to their offending, such as holding down a job at a grocery store or attending church.

Together, these observations portray law-breaking adolescents as neither fully conventional nor fully criminal. They are willing to break the law under certain circumstances, even though they understand criminal conduct to be bad behavior. If they aren't learning that crime is *good* from the subculture, what *are* they learning? They are learning to justify crime (before the act) and rationalize it (after the act). They are learning to adjust their thinking to resolve the tension of breaking laws that they believe in. They are learning that norms are "qualified guides" instead of "categorical imperatives" (p. 666).[68] In other words, they are learning techniques of neutralization.

Techniques of Neutralization

Have you ever done something that violated your own code of ethics, such as stealing, cheating on a partner, or cheating on a test? If you have, then you have probably also sought to minimize feelings of guilt or shame or tried to keep others from seeing you as a bad person. Perhaps you convinced yourself that you had no other choice, that you only did it because you had been drinking, or that it wasn't that big of a deal. You may have sought to justify or excuse your behavior.

Justifications are accounts of behavior that take full responsibility for an action but deny the wrongfulness of the act. An example of a justification would be an embezzler claiming that she deserved the money because her employer underpaid her. *Excuses* are accounts of behavior that accept the wrongfulness of an act while denying full responsibility. For example, another embezzler might claim that his coworkers pressured him to steal the money or that he needed the money to pay off debts and avoid bankruptcy.

Techniques of neutralization are the justifying and excusing strategies rule-breakers use to absolve themselves of guilt or shame, or to present themselves as nondeviant. They prevent people who commit criminal offenses from experiencing what social psychologists call cognitive dissonance. Cognitive dissonance is the discomfort people experience when their behavior and moral code do not align, or when they think one way and act another way. By invoking the techniques, a rule-breaker can maintain a sense that they are a good person while doing things they know to be unacceptable. Criminologists Sykes and Matza initially described five techniques:

1. *Denial of responsibility* – A person who has broken the law asserts they are not to blame. They may claim to be victims of circumstance or that the act was accidental or that they were subject to pressures beyond their control, such as alcohol intoxication or peer pressure. Denial of responsibility is a "master account" because it redefines the offender as not culpable, reducing both social stigma and the feeling that one has failed themselves morally.

2. *Denial of injury* – A person who has broken the law claims they've done nothing wrong because the act produced minimal or no harm or because they did not intend to inflict harm. This is a common technique among those who engage in victimless offenses, such as substance use, as well as among those who can frame their behavior as victimless, even if other people are affected, such as white-collar fraudsters, joyriding auto thieves, and workplace pilferers.

3. *Denial of victim* – A person who has broken the law acknowledges that their actions are harmful but refuses to acknowledge a legitimate victim. This can happen in two ways: (1) The person claims that the victim deserved what happened, such as in cases of retaliatory violence, or (2) the victim is unknown, abstract, or otherwise absent, such as in cases of cybercrime that involve no interactions with the victim or even knowledge of the names of the victims. In the former, the victim is denied status as a victim ("they had it coming"). In the latter, the victim is not visible and therefore is less of a burden on one's conscience.

4. *Condemning the condemners* – A person who has broken the law directs attention to those who judge them rather than their own behavior, claiming that those who condemn their actions have no right to do so because they are "hypocrites, deviants in disguise, or impelled by personal spite" (p. 668).[69] This is like saying, "I may be bad, but they [police, politicians, judges, etc.] are worse!"

5. *Appeal to higher loyalties* – A person who has broken the law claims that the act was necessary to meet the moral obligations of a group even if it means violating another set of rules, such as laws. There are multiple, competing loyalties in the one's life—to obey the law, to help friends, to assist coworkers, and so on. In this claim, the person who commits a crime states that the loyalties to one group (as to one's friends or to one's children) are more important—or higher—than the duty to obey the law.[70]

Additional techniques, offered after Sykes and Matza put forth the initial five, include the following:

1. *Metaphor of the ledger* – A person who has broken the law sees their criminal conduct as compensated for by their good deeds. They treat good and bad behavior as two columns on a ledger, adding up to the sum of their person. They point to all the good that they have done (such as being a good worker, being a good parent or spouse, or giving to charity) as evidence that their wrongful actions do not make them a bad person.

2. *Everybody does it/no one cares* – These complementary techniques position the law-breaking behavior as aligned with social values. "How wrong can it be," they ask, "if lots of people do the same thing as me and no one speaks up?" This combination of techniques is common to people who engage in minor offenses that go unpunished, such as underage substance use and restaurant employees pocketing small amounts of cash for orders they did not ring up.[71]

3. *Claim of inevitability* – This neutralization positions the person's unlawful behavior as irrelevant to the outcome. They argue that it was going to happen anyway, freeing them from the burden of responsibility for what occurred. This is observed among participants in crimes against humanity, who see themselves as minor actors in a violent drama that was already underway.[72]

4. *Selective social comparison* – People who have broken the law compare themselves favorably to others who have engaged in more serious offending. They acknowledge having done something bad but minimize their deviance by arguing that others are worse. *Condemning the condemners* can be understood as a subtype of selective social comparison.

Criminologists hear these techniques of neutralization across a people who commit a vast array of offenses, ranging from petty thieves to perpetrators of honor killings and genocide. See if you can spot the technique of neutralization used in the following accounts from the methamphetamine seller, the identity fraudster, the restaurant embezzler, and the genocide perpetrator:

Methamphetamine seller: "I didn't really feel bad about it 'cause I wasn't pushing my product on kids. I wasn't pushing my product on anybody that didn't want to do it, and everybody that touched my shit was of grown age... God gave us all free will. I didn't force anybody to do anything. Everybody came to me" (p. 20).[73]

Restaurant embezzler: "I think people can justify it saying they got stiffed on a table, or they didn't make any money or any great tips... like the company owes them because the customers aren't tipping what they're supposed to... even bartending, you see people not ringing in drinks and keeping the cash, I have never heard of anyone not doing it, which is sad" (p. 501).[74]

Identity fraudster: "I mean, like, real identity theft, man I can't do that. Intentionally screw someone over—it's not right to me. So I couldn't do that. But corporations, banks, police departments, the government? Oh, yeah, let's go get 'em. Because that's the way they treat you, you know what I'm saying. If they done screwed me over, screw them!" (p. 50).[75]

Genocide perpetrator: 'The one who did something really wrong was the person who told us to kill the Tutsi [victims of the 1994 Rwandan genocide]" (p. 51).[76]

Criminologists note a pattern of "stealing a little a lot" among restaurant staff who successfully neutralize their deviance. The small amounts stolen permit them to deny injury.

RyanJLane/E+/Getty Images

ENGAGED CRIMINOLOGY 9.2

Identifying Techniques of Neutralization

In this activity, you will read real-life college students' explanations of their criminal conduct and identify the technique of neutralization present in each one.

1. In one or two sentences, explain which technique of neutralization is present in this college student's account of drunk driving.

   Drunk driving: *"I was with a girl. We went to a party. She was significantly smaller than me yet had as much to drink as me, and I was feeling it. Which means God only know how drunk she was. I wasn't about to let her drive so I took her home, though tipsy. I wasn't comfortable doing so, but I felt that it needed to be done."*

2. In one or two sentences, explain which technique of neutralization is present in this college student's account of theft.

   Theft: *"I was bored and hungry with my buddy so we went to [grocery store]. I forgot my wallet, so I said, 'screw it' and walked out with a rotisserie chicken… I would never steal from a small locally owned store, but places like [grocery store] are making so much money selling us crap overpriced, I have no remorse for taking a Kit Kat or a pie every once in a while."*

CHAPTER SUMMARY

LO 9.1 Describe how learning theories differ from other perspectives in criminology.

Learning theories are individual-level perspectives that focus on how people are socialized into crime. They assume there are multiple competing versions of morality in society (conflict assumption) and that people are not born naturally inclined towards crime. Learning theories highlight processes in the development of criminal motivation rather than breakdowns in control.

LO 9.2 Explain the central tenets of differential association theory.

Differential association theory states that pro-crime attitudes, rationalizations, justifications, offending skills, and interpretations of legal codes are learned in interactions with others, in the same way that all learning occurs. Definitions favorable to crime outweigh unfavorable definitions if learned frequently and over a long duration, and if they are presented earlier in life and in the context of an emotionally close relationship.

LO 9.3 Identify how social learning theory elaborates on differential association theory.

Social learning theory fuses differential association theory with operant conditioning principles—differential reinforcement and punishment—from behavioral psychology. It also acknowledges the role of imitation on entry into crime. Social learning theory offers a more nuanced explanation of how the learning process operates.

LO 9.4 Differentiate between subcultural perspectives in criminology.

Subcultural perspectives explain why some groups develop norms and values that support crime. Miller described six value orientations, called focal concerns, that take hold in impoverished communities. Cohen states that lower-class boys' status frustration leads to a subcultural adaptation that inverts middle-class norms. Cloward and Ohlin argue that structured opportunities—both legitimate and criminal—determine the form that subcultures take. Anderson suggests that a "code of the street" emerges in economically marginalized communities where respect is in short supply.

LO 9.5 Make connections between the drift perspective and techniques of neutralization.

The drift perspective asserts that most law violators drift between criminality and conformity. They are willing to break the law under certain circumstances even though they understand crime to be wrong. They use techniques of neutralization so that they can maintain a "good" identity despite their "bad" behavior, including denying responsibility, denying injury, denying the victim, condemning the condemners, and appealing to higher loyalties, among others.

ENGAGED DISCUSSION

1. Which agents of socialization do you believe have the greatest impact on criminal learning, and why?

2. Do you agree with Sutherland that interactions with family and close friends produce much more criminal learning than TV, movies, or other media? Why or why not?

3. Come up with one type of criminal activity that involves neither imitation nor the learning of pro-crime attitudes in interactions with others. Can social learning theory still explain it?

4. Why do you think subcultural perspectives tend to focus on crimes of the poor? In what ways are crimes of the wealthy, like white-collar offending, supported by subcultural values?

5. Think of a time when you violated your own moral code. Did you use any of the techniques of neutralization? Which one(s)?

KEY TERMS

Code of the street (p. 238)
Cognitive dissonance (p. 241)
Convict code (p. 233)
Criminological imagination (p. 239)
Definitions favorable to crime (p. 225)
Differential association (p. 225)
Drift (p. 240)
Duration (p. 226)
Focal concerns (p. 234)
Frequency (p. 226)
Intensity (p. 226)
Intergenerational transmission of violence (p. 232)

Middle-class measuring rod (p. 236)
Modalities (p. 226)
Operant conditioning (p. 229)
Priority (p. 226)
Prisonization (p. 233)
Reaction formation (p. 236)
Reinforcement (p. 229)
Selection effect (p. 228)
Social learning (p. 228)
Status frustration (p. 236)
Subculture (p. 233)
Techniques of neutralization (p. 241)

ONly 19, Alone ON The
Street !!!
Just Trying To Survive!
$20 Get's Me A Bed At A
Hostel AND OFF the Street 2Nite
ANY Help Is A blessing!
Thankyou + Godbless

10 STRAIN PERSPECTIVES

LEARNING OBJECTIVES	
10.1	Explain Durkheim's contribution to strain perspectives in criminology.
10.2	Describe Merton's modes of adaptation and how they relate to his anomie theory.
10.3	Explain the central tenets of institutional anomie theory.
10.4	Identify the primary claims of general strain theory.

People stolen from me before. I guess that's why I got into it. My car got stolen, you know what I'm saying? When I first got into this, like I was mad, and I wanted revenge and I've been stealing cars ever since. (Quote from auto thief [Chernbonneau & Jacobs, 2015, p. 481])[1]

I couldn't go home. My mom beat me when she found out I liked girls... If they made me go back home, I might be dead. I'd rather take my chance sleeping in my car. (Quote from formerly homeless transgender youth [McCandless 2017, p. 564])[2]

It was my way of getting even. You know, teachers were saying and doing all this nasty shit, and I wasn't going to put up with that anymore... I guess I was trying to protect my dignity... To them I was like shit. Just because you're Puerto Rican or Latino, they treat you like dirt. (Quote from a delinquent youth [Padilla, 2003, p. 245])[3]

Shoplifting became a part of my way of life... I couldn't pay the bills; I was by myself and I had a drug habit. So I thought, where do I go from here? Being a heroin addict it was quick money; [because] I was always fearful of being sick. (Quote from a shoplifter [Caputo & King, 2015, p. 52])[4]

When I would get kicked out or run away from home I had to have some way to pay for food or help with rent for a friend. (Quote from a sex worker [Bucher, Manasse, & Milton, 2015, p. 443])[5]

What is the common thread that runs through these accounts? Each person was mired in stress. The stress of victimization, of parental rejection, of teacher mistreatment, of addiction, and of poverty. They found themselves in impossible situations: without a place to stay, lacking support, and denied dignity. And each person sought to deal with that stress through means regarded by law as criminal or delinquent—stealing cars, running away, fighting, shoplifting, or exchanging sex for money. Strain perspectives in criminology looks to stressors—individual stressors like family rejection and societal stressors like inequality—as the catalysts for criminal conduct.

Strain perspectives in criminology train their lenses on the stresses or pressures that induce criminality. Recall that criminological explanations invoke three factors: (1) motivation to commit crime, (2) controls that prevent crime, and (3) situational opportunities for committing crime. Strain theorists are concerned primarily with motivations for crime, assuming that people are compelled into crime by social conditions. Unlike learning theorists, the focus of Chapter 9, who also locate the causes of criminal motivation, strain theorists do not assume that people who commit crime necessarily hold favorable attitudes about their wrongdoing (though they might). Instead, strain thinkers see law-breakers as responding to negative situations or conditions.

The type of stresses and pressures examined differ by perspective. Structural (or macro-level) strain theories are concerned with abnormal societal conditions that create pressures for criminal behavior. Structural strain theorists examine variation in crime rates, such as state or national crime rates, rather than individual behavior, and they center on the concept of anomie. Individual (or micro-level) strain theories, in contrast, focus on the consequences of personal stresses for individual criminal conduct. This chapter addresses three of the most prominent strain perspectives in criminology: (1) Merton's anomie theory, (2) Messner and Rosenfeld's institutional anomie theory, and (3) Agnew's general strain theory.

DURKHEIM AND THE ORIGINS OF ANOMIE

The year is 1893. A book—not by a criminologist and not about crime—is published, and it will introduce a concept that will form the basis of the strain perspective in criminology. That book is called *The Division of Labor in Society,* by French sociologist Émile Durkheim, and the concept is anomie.

The Division of Labor in Society details Durkheim's ideas about the consequences wrought by quick and extreme transformations in the economic, political, and social structures of human societies. He was concerned specifically about the change in social relations sparked by the Industrial Revolution in Europe (it was 1893, after all, and Durkheim was French). Going back generations upon generations, people had lived in small communities surrounded by neighbors who shared their ways of life—the same daily routines, the same agricultural labor, the same supernatural beliefs. He called these mechanical societies. People's shared ways of life bound them together, Durkheim contended, and created a **collective consciousness** ("the totality of beliefs and sentiments common to the average members of a society")that produced conformity to strongly held community norms and values.[6] Solidarity—think of this as "in-it-togetherness"—was strong in mechanical societies.

As societies modernized, work become more specialized. There used to be mostly just farmers and now there were plumbers, clerks, nurses, machinists, cleaners, bankers, and so on. A complex division of labor emerged. Community members no longer shared daily routines and ways of life. The collective consciousness weakened. But Durkheim was an optimist, and he argued that people's reliance on one another in a complex division of labor would bring forth a new form of solidarity, which he called organic solidarity.

Durkheim was not a criminologist. His ideas about divisions of labor and solidarity were not criminological ideas. But in writing about them, Durkheim introduced the concept of anomie, and the anomie concept only makes sense once we first comprehend Durkheim's other ideas about human societies. Durkheim used the term *anomie* to describe a social condition in which the norms and values that once defined a society begin to break down and disappear, as they did in modernizing societies.

Durkheimian anomie occurs when there is a "widespread lack of commitment to shared values, standards, and rules needed to regulate the behaviors and aspirations of individuals."[7] Simply put, for Durkheim, anomie is a state of normlessness. It is a temporary state, though, he wrote, as new norms and values will emerge to supplant the old ones.[8] According to Durkheim, society serves to regulate human expectations and desires. Under conditions of anomie, society

The boys and girls employed by this textile factory in Fall River, Massachusetts, in January 1912 had lives unlike those of their forebearers. Durkheim believed that industrialization produced anomic conditions.

loses its grip on people. The old norms fail to keep their expectations and desires in check. Periods of massive economic, political, and social upheaval produce all forms of social problems, including crime, even when the upheaval is generally regarded as a good thing for society, as in periods of astronomical economic growth.

Durkheim's ideas about anomie, crafted more than a century ago, receive empirical support even today. For example, researchers who examine the transition from communist to democratic regimes in Eastern Europe in the post–Cold War era find that anomie proliferated during these sociopolitical shifts. Furthermore, anomie was felt more acutely by individuals with precarious economic and social positions, including people who are young, unemployed, single, lower class, and have less savings.[9]

MERTON'S ANOMIE THEORY

The year is now 1938. Robert K. Merton, a criminologist, has just published his landmark article "Social Structure and Anomie," which borrows and revises Durkheim's concept of anomie. But let's establish the context before diving into the arguments presented in his article. It is the 1930s in the United States. The country is years into the Great Depression. Murder rates, suicide rates, and unemployment have soared. Decades of immigration have transformed American cities, as has the Great Migration of Black Americans seeking work in northern cities and escaping the racial violence of the South. Many criminologists of the era—nearly all of them white men from rural areas—looked around the cities they had moved to in pursuing their educations (like Chicago, Philadelphia, and Boston) and saw cultural clashes and dysfunction: "As they looked voyeuristically into these 'bad' areas, they did not see diversity and elements of patterned behavior, but rather perceived teeming ghettos in the throes of social disorganization" (p. 14).[10] Merton, himself raised in a "benign slum" of Philadelphia, rejected their slum-based theories that located the root of crime in social conditions of impoverished neighborhoods. It wasn't the slum that created crime, according to Merton's anomie theory. It was the broader, mainstream society that spawned criminality. He believed that "conformity to conventional values can be criminogenic."[11]

Culture Structure and Anomie

Merton argued that all human societies have two types of structures, or systems of organization: culture structure and social structure. Culture structure is the organization of norms in a society. Two types of norms mattered most for crime in Merton's theory: (1) norms that regulate cultural goals and (2) norms that regulate the means for achieving cultural goals. The first type tells people what they ought to want. The second type tells them the acceptable ways of getting what they are told they ought to want.

How might a society define success? In other words, what are a society's cultural goals? Money is an obvious answer given our cultural context. But stopping there indicates a failure of imagination. What about having a large family to carry on your legacy? Or attaining spiritual enlightenment? Living a life of service to others? All societies define success in some way, and they grant respect accordingly. Merton was writing about the U.S.'s emphasis on monetary success, so let's concentrate on that cultural goal. What are some socially permissible means for achieving monetary success? Of course, one strategy is to complete education and work hard at a job that offers a decent wage. An additional method is to invest wisely in the stock market. Inheritance is another possibility if one is so lucky. Winning the state lottery is another legitimate, though infinitesimally unlikely, path to financial success. There are also socially *unacceptable*—but technically efficient!—ways to achieve the success that we are all told we ought to strive for. Here are just a few examples: burglary, embezzlement, human trafficking, bank robbery, manufacture and distribution of illicit substances, extortion, insider trading, and fraud.

Crime is unlikely when the norms that tell us how to behave are emphasized and internalized just as strongly as norms that dictate what success looks like. That is a society in equilibrium, Merton told us.[12] People strive to "make it," but they also adhere to the rules (or the "regulatory norms and moral imperatives") even though crime might be the more expedient choice. Stealing is, after all, faster and easier than slogging through a 50-hour work week. In the equilibrium scenario, success is determined both by "making it" *and* by following the rules.

If all societies were in equilibrium, the story (and theory) would end there. We might also never have had the famous quote from Merton:

> *A cardinal American virtue, "ambition," promotes a cardinal American vice, "deviant behavior."*[13]

How does virtue become vice? Anomie is the first ingredient. Recall that Durkheim used the term *anomie* to refer to normlessness, or a state that occurs when old norms and values disintegrate, particularly during times of rapid social change. That is *not* what Merton meant by anomie. Not quite, at least. For Merton, anomie is a very specific type of normlessness.

Mertonian anomie is a social condition in which there is disequilibrium in the culture structure: The norms regulating cultural success goals are emphasized more than the norms regulating the means to achieving success, as depicted in Figure 10.1. Note that anomie is a characteristic of societies, not of individuals. The phrase "the ends justify the means" captures the essence of Mertonian anomie. It is a "success at any cost" ideal. Ambition (virtue) leads to crime (vice) in societies that grant greater social esteem to the affluent cheater than the poor rule-follower. And evidence from cross-national research bears this out: Homicide rates are higher in anomic nations than those with greater cultural equilibrium.[14] There is another ingredient that, in combination with anomie, transforms virtue: a highly unequal social structure.

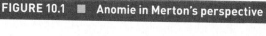

FIGURE 10.1 ■ Anomie in Merton's perspective

Merton described anomie as a discrepancy or imbalance in society between emphasis on success goals and emphasis on the appropriate means to achieve them.

Social Structure

American culture, Merton asserted in 1938, puts impoverished residents of the slum—along with once-prosperous individuals left destitute by the vagaries of financial markets—in an impossible position. They were encouraged, as are all Americans, to strive for economic success and to measure their personal value by their affluence. Emphasizing wealth, in and of itself, is not a problem, but it becomes a problem when a significant portion of the society cannot achieve it using legitimate channels like full-time employment. And if there are already anomic conditions? Crime will skyrocket, according to Merton. **Social structure** is the organization of people in a society, relative to one another. A related term is **social stratification**: a hierarchical organization of people or groups in a society. In a highly unequal, economically stratified social structure, some people are very wealthy while others remain penniless, with limited opportunities for upward mobility (moving up in social class position). Yet all are held to the same cultural expectations regarding ambition and success. They are measured using the same cultural standards. As Merton puts it,

> *The cultural demands made on persons in this situation are incompatible. On the one hand, they are asked to orient their conduct toward the prospect of accumulating wealth and on the other, they are largely denied effective opportunities to do so institutionally.*[15]

According to Merton's anomie theory, crime will run rampant when a "success at any cost" or "ends justify the means" cultural system comes together with a social structure that renders a large segment of the population unable to acquire wealth through legal work.

The distinction between absolute deprivation and relative deprivation is salient here. Absolute deprivation refers to conditions of objective poverty, as when a person cannot afford food or housing. They are deprived of wealth or material possessions; perception is irrelevant. **Relative deprivation**, in contrast, occurs when a group or a person compares themselves to a reference group (like their neighbors, coworkers, or people higher up in the social class hierarchy) and perceives themselves as unjustly disadvantaged.[16] They feel deprived in comparison to others. It is a subjective deprivation, though it may be accompanied by objectively impoverished conditions. Merton had little use for absolute deprivation in his theory. He pointed to low crime rates in low-income nations as evidence. Instead, he saw relative deprivation as predictive of crime.[17] It is not just being poor that causes crime for Merton. It is the seeing that others have more than you while being told you should be just as successful as they are. The evidence continues to be in Merton's favor on this point. For example, criminologists find that relative deprivation has a stronger impact on profit-motivated crimes like drug trafficking in nations that strongly embrace material success goals.[18]

Merton's anomie theory is also called *classical strain theory* or *structural strain theory*. It is classical because it is the original statement of a strain perspective in criminology. It is structural because Merton devotes most of his attention to macro-level functions and failings of societies. Crime, for Merton, is a "normal reaction of normal people to abnormal conditions."[19] If the people are normal, then it is the *society* that is pathological. But societies don't commit crime. People do. Merton explains how individuals respond to anomic societal conditions in his description of modes of adaptation.

Modes of Adaptation

Anomie is a societal condition, but not all individuals living in anomic societies engage in crime. Merton offers that people differ in their responses to anomie, with five possible adaptations: (1) conformity, (2) ritualism, (3) innovation, (4) retreatism, and (5) rebellion. Remember that there are two sets of norms that matter most in anomie theory: norms regulating cultural success goals (the emphasis on "making it") and norms regulating the means to achieving success (the emphasis on following the institutionalized rules). People can accept these norms, meaning that they internalize them and live according to them. Or they can reject them, meaning that they are not constrained by them. In addition, they might move beyond just rejecting them and attempt to replace them. **Modes of adaptation** are the various ways that individuals adapt to anomic societal conditions. As observed in Table 10.1, the modes of adaptation are defined by the combination of accepting, rejecting, and replacing these norms.

TABLE 10.1 ■ Modes of Adaptation From Merton's Anomie Theory

		Institutionalized means of achieving goals		
		Accept	Reject	Replace
Cultural success goals	Accept	Conformity	Innovation	
	Reject	Ritualism	Retreatism	
	Replace			Rebellion

Two of the adaptations are noncriminal: conformity and ritualism. **Conformity** occurs when an individual is committed to pursuing material success and they also adhere to the rules. The society may be in disequilibrium, but the conformist is not. They go to school, they go to work, they try to become successful the legitimate way. They have internalized all the messages. **Ritualism** is also marked by rule-following, but the ritualist doesn't buy into the aspiration to wealth, likely because they know it's not in their future. (Why pursue something that will never happen? You'll only make yourself miserable!) So why follow the rules at all? The ritualist is content enough to make ends meet, to work for the sake of the ritual or its intrinsic rewards.

The other three adaptations—innovation, retreatism, and rebellion—are more conducive to criminality, especially innovation. **Innovation** is the individual expression of anomic disequilibrium. The innovator is unrestrained by the rules in their pursuit of making a dollar. They develop new, creative (and illegal) methods for acquiring money because they are freed from the constraints of law and moral imperatives. Insurance fraudsters and auto thieves are examples of innovators. **Retreatism** involves rejection of both sets of norms, though it is not necessarily a criminal adaptation. They are interested in neither "making it" nor leading conventional lives. Doomsday preppers who opt to live "off the grid" and prepare for apocalyptic end times by stockpiling food and weapons fit into the retreatist mold, as do substance abusers who attempt to numb the despair of anomic conditions, at least temporarily.

Rebellion is the most complex adaptation. Like the retreatist, the rebel spurns society's messages about success and how to get it. Unlike the retreatist, the rebel attempts to replace the norms with their own ideals. To create their own vision of society. Unbound by the laws of conventional society, rebels feel justified in taking illegal steps to manifest their vision. Domestic terrorists, like those discussed in Chapter 4, are rebels in Merton's theory, as are cult leaders like Jim Jones, leader of the People's Temple, who led (and forced) his followers to die by mass suicide as a "revolutionary act,"[20] and Shoko Asahara, leader of Aum Shinrikyo, who orchestrated the 1995 Tokyo subway sarin nerve gas attack.[21]

Anna Sorokin, convicted in 2019 of grand larceny for defrauding banks, hotels, and wealthy acquaintances by posing as a German heiress, is an example of an innovator, one of Merton's modes of adaptation.

AP Photo/Richard Drew

ENGAGED CRIMINOLOGY 10.1

Applying Merton's Theory to Poverty in U.S. Cities

In this activity, you will examine the living wage, per capita income, and poverty rate in several U.S. cities. Review the definitions of the terms to ensure that you interpret the information correctly. You will then apply Merton's ideas to what you discover.

Living wage	Minimum income necessary for a worker to meet their basic needs but to provide no more than basic needs. Does not include enough income for savings, investments, or "extras" (e.g., pre-prepared meals, entertainment, travel). Varies based on size of household and local cost of living. Indicates cost of living.
Per capita income	The average income per person (including adults and children) in the population. It is calculated by dividing the total income of a group by the total population of that group.
Poverty rate	Percentage of persons with incomes less than the federal poverty threshold ($21,960 for a family of three in 2021).

TABLE 10.2 ■ Living Wage for a Family of Three (One Adult and Two Children), Per Capita Income, and Poverty Rate of Select U.S. Cities			
City	Living wage for family of three (one adult and two children)	Per capita income	Poverty rate
Boulder, CO	$48.72	$44,942	20.4%
Flint, MI	$40.43	$17,086	38.8%
Alexandria, VA	$48.99	$62,679	10.3%

Sources: Massachusetts Institute of Technology. (2021) *Living wage calculator.* https://livingwage.mit.edu/; United States Census Bureau. (2021). *QuickFacts.* https://www.census.gov/quickfacts/fact/table/US/PST045221

Answer the following questions:

1. Which one of the three cities do you expect to have the highest rate of robbery based on Merton's theory?

2. In one or two sentences, explain your answer using at least one key term from the section on Merton's theory (e.g., anomie, social structure, relative deprivation, and the four modes of adaptation).

3. Were you (and Merton) right? Examine the robbery rates (number of robberies per 100,000 people in the population) of the three cities in 2020 to see if your predictions were correct: Boulder, CO (21.77 robberies per 100,000); Flint, MI (102.15 robberies per 100,000); Alexandria, VA (52.71 robberies per 100,000).

Evaluating Anomie Theory

Merton's theory is one of the most enduring perspectives in criminology. His ideas about strain and anomie have inspired modern versions, like Messner and Rosenfeld's institutional anomie theory and Agnew's general strain theory, also described in this chapter. Those more contemporary criminologists address the questions left unanswered by Merton's perspective. For example, Merton's theory provides little insight into why some individuals become innovators while others become retreatists or ritualists. The theory also fails to explain the specific offense types that people commit. Why does one person innovate by engaging in armed robbery whereas another person commits online romance fraud (i.e., pretending to be a suitor to extract funds from an unsuspecting romance-seeker)? Moreover, it assumes that all members of society subscribe to the same values and have the same goals, which is patently untrue.[22] It is, at its core, a macro-level perspective that gives insufficient attention to individual-level factors and variation.

Recall from Chapter 5 that criminological explanations must be able to account for established correlates of crime. The age-crime curve is one such pattern. Yet Merton's theory cannot explain why criminal conduct peaks in the late teenage years and early 20s and then drops off. We would expect crime to increase throughout early adulthood if being thwarted in achieving financial goals is the primary driver of crime. This is clearly not the case. The aspirations of teenagers and people in their early 20s, who are disproportionately involved in crime, tend to lean towards immediate social status goals rather than long-term economic goals.[23]

Critics also point out that Merton is wrong about unemployment and crime, or at least he is not right anymore. Merton's theory suggests that unemployment, especially widespread unemployment, would cause an upsurge in crime rates. This may have been the case during the Great Depression, when Merton was writing, but that no longer appears to be true. Studies of the impact of the Great Recession (2007-2009) on crime identify no such link, even when investigating the groups and places (e.g., communities with many foreclosures) most impacted by the economic downturn.[24]

MESSNER AND ROSENFELD'S INSTITUTIONAL ANOMIE THEORY

Fast-forward to 1995. American criminologists Steven Messner and Richard Rosenfeld pick up where Merton left off. Again, let's set the context. In 1995, the U.S. is just starting to see the reversal of several decades of increasing and sustained high crime rates, but it will be years of continual decline before other criminologists dub it the "great crime decline."[25] Crime is still pervasive in the first half of the 1990s despite a booming economy. The U.S. economy is enjoying robust growth—more jobs, less unemployment, increasing wages, low inflation, higher productivity—and it will continue to grow throughout the decade. Messner and Rosenfeld questioned why an economically advanced nation like the U.S. would have so much crime, especially when other economically advanced nations were far safer.

First, they observed that the U.S. had a very high homicide rate compared to otherwise similar nations in Europe, Asia, and Oceania, and this was only partially due to easy gun access. Figure 10.2 shows how the U.S. continues to be a homicide outlier. Second, they remark on the "unrestrained and dangerous character" of U.S. crime (p. 22).[26] When it comes to property crimes, the U.S. looked, and continues to look, a lot like other nations. The big differences emerge only at the more extreme, violent end of offending. For example, the robbery rate in the U.S. is consistently (if only slightly) lower than in France and the United Kingdom. However, robberies in the U.S. are far more likely to involve firearms, injury, and death. They also contend that the massive scale of incarceration in the U.S.—well underway by 1995 and cresting in 2010[27]—masks the true extent of criminality in America. Recall from Chapter 1 that about 1 out of 100 working-age adults in the U.S. are currently in local jails, state prison, or federal prison.[28] Mass incarceration suppresses counts because crimes occurring in prisons and jails are not represented in official rates. In short, the U.S. has a lot of serious crime for a wealthy nation. Messner and Rosenfeld ask: What is it about the culture and structure of countries, the U.S. among them, that either boosts or suppresses crime?

Messner and Rosenfeld lay out their answer to that question in their book *Crime and the American Dream*, which describes **institutional anomie theory**.[29] Like Merton, their intellectual predecessor, they used the United States as a case study for exploring the cultural and structural predictors of national crime rates. They, too, are macro-level criminologists. Also like Merton, they argue that mainstream values can both nourish (ambition!) and poison (vice!), leading to a "success by any means necessary" culture that supports law-breaking. So how are they different from Merton? They believe Merton falls short by giving all his attention to stratification (an unequal class structure that leaves many unable to attain success legally) when describing social structure.[30] Messner and Rosenfeld bring a new focus into the anomie perspective: social institutions. This is why their theory is called *institutional* anomie theory.

Culture: American Dream Values

In 2019, an FBI sting operation (code named Operation Varsity Blues) revealed a scandal in higher education admissions. Thirty-three wealthy parents, famous actresses Lori Loughlin and Felicity Huffman among them, were charged with racketeering and other crimes.[31] The parents had allegedly been paying William Singer, an admissions consultant, to bribe college coaches at elite universities to grant their

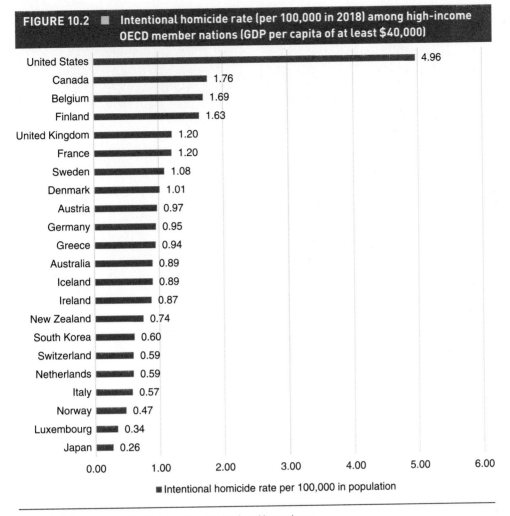

FIGURE 10.2 ■ Intentional homicide rate (per 100,000 in 2018) among high-income OECD member nations (GDP per capita of at least $40,000)

United States	4.96
Canada	1.76
Belgium	1.69
Finland	1.63
United Kingdom	1.20
France	1.20
Sweden	1.08
Denmark	1.01
Austria	0.97
Germany	0.95
Greece	0.94
Australia	0.89
Iceland	0.89
Ireland	0.87
New Zealand	0.74
South Korea	0.60
Switzerland	0.59
Netherlands	0.59
Italy	0.57
Norway	0.47
Luxembourg	0.34
Japan	0.26

■ Intentional homicide rate per 100,000 in population

Notes: 2017 data presented for Belgium, New Zealand, and Luxembourg

Source: UN Office on Drugs and Crime's International Homicide Statistics Database (2017). *Intentional homicides (per 100,000 people) – OECD members.* The World Bank Data. https://data.worldbank.org/indicator/VC.IHR.PSRC.P5?locations=OE. Licensed CC BY-4.0.

children recruitment slots (in some cases, applicants' athletic profiles were falsified entirely; they had never played the sport). Test administrators also accepted bribes, with SAT and ACT proctors paid to alter incorrect answers. In other cases, stand-ins took the college entrance exams for the students. The bribes amounted to an estimated $25 million between 2011 and 2019.[32]

The college admissions scandal drew media attention, in part, because of the involvement of high-profile actresses. Other instances of academic fraud garner much less public scrutiny. For example, degree mills are scam universities, sometimes supported by scam accrediting institutions, that sell bogus degrees for a fee without providing any education or requiring any course work. Consider the case of Colby Nolan, recipient of an MBA (master of business administration degree) from Trinity Southern University in Dallas in 2004; Nolan received his MBA after completing his bachelor's degree at Trinity Southern University, where his transcripts reported his 3.5 GPA. Colby Nolan was a Pennsylvania deputy attorney general's housecat.[33] The deputy attorney general applied on behalf of his cat to get an inside look at the scam. Of course, the Internet makes fake universities hard to pull off in the U.S. these days. Other options for unscrupulous students—or "students"—include hiring people to write their papers (even their PhD dissertations!) or take their online courses.[34] Some go the inexpensive route of just plain lying about having a degree with the hope that no one checks or notices the fraud. This route proved disastrous for Amy Robertson, former principal of Pittsburg High School in Kansas. Robertson resigned in 2017 after a group of student reporters unearthed evidence that she had lied about her multiple degrees.[35]

Actress Felicity Huffman, observed here leaving federal court in Boston, was charged in the 2019 college admissions scandal.

AP Photos/Charles Krupa, File

Parents bribing coaches and SAT proctors. Fake MBAs for sale. Students paying strangers to take their online courses. Principals lying about having degrees. That there are people willing to lie, cheat, and buy their way to success is unsurprising. That there are enough of them to fuel a massive global industry of paper-writers, online course takers, and scam universities (to say nothing of the market for cheating-detection software) is more interesting from an institutional anomie perspective. Institutional anomie theory states that four cultural values make "success at any cost" or "the ends justify the means" transgressions like academic fraud more acceptable.

In the 1930s version of anomie theory, Merton stated that an overemphasis on material success was at the root of American culture and American crime. Institutional anomie theory offers a more nuanced vision of American ideals and anomic culture. These values characterize the American Dream, the "rags-to-riches" ideal, according to Messner and Rosenfeld. [36] Each value contains a bright side and a dark side. None is exclusively good nor exclusively bad.

1. **Achievement** – The emphasis on accumulating successes, or to make something of oneself. On the bright side, this value inspires ambition. It is the source of entrepreneurship and innovation. But it also fosters the mentality that "it's not how you play the game, it's whether you win or lose."

2. **Individualism** – Cultural commitment to individual autonomy and rights is a hallmark of the American ideal. Combined with achievement, though, it casts people as competitors in the pursuit of success. Not only must one "make it," they must make it on their own. And if they fail to make it on their own, the blame rests solely on the individual.

3. **Universalism** – The ideal of individual achievement applies to all members of society, regardless of social class or background. It is universal. This value underlies democracy and is a source of pride: No one is chained to the circumstances of their birth. Since expectations for individual success apply equally to all, those who can never quite seem to escape the chains of poverty or come out on top are evaluated as failures. After all, success is open to everyone.

4. **Monetary fetishism** – Money is the metric of success. Money as an incentive for hard work keeps the economy going. But fetishizing money—desiring money simply for money's

sake—is conducive to crime. Wanting more just to have more is different than wanting money for particular purchases, donations, or trusts. It is open-ended. There is never a point at which one can say, "I am done" or "that's enough."

Though Messner and Rosenfeld use the term *American Dream*, the values they identify are not specific to the United States. The U.S. does not have a monopoly on a marketized mentality, or a psychological disposition towards egoistic self-interest borne of anomic culture.[37] In fact, these four values are embraced globally, albeit to varying degrees. Throughout the world, people with marketized mentalities have internalized the values of achievement, individualism, universalism, and monetary fetishism.

Structure: Institutional Imbalance

Social institutions are necessary subsystems that support society's survival. They serve the basic functions of society. Family, polity (government), religion, education, and the economy are but a few examples (see Figure 10.3 for more examples). The people who comprise these institutions will come and go, but the institutions will endure, though their form may change. For example, the institution of family will continue long after you, your parents, your siblings, and your children are gone, just as it continues to exist now even though your great-great-great-great-grandparents are long deceased. They endure because they fulfill essential needs of societies. What needs of human societies are met by these institutions? Table 10.3 provides examples for family, polity, and religion. See if you can come up with examples for education and economy.

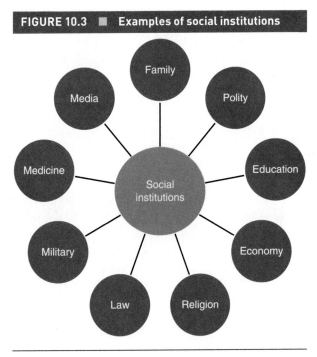

FIGURE 10.3 ■ Examples of social institutions

Social institutions are subsystems that serve the basic functions of a society.

Noneconomic institutions like family, polity, religion, and education provide important prosocial functions that constrain crime. Adolescent law-breaking is reduced when young people have strong bonds to supportive parents who can monitor their whereabouts.[38] Community trust increases when citizens participate in local governance, and law-breaking is reduced when governments provide a strong safety net for families in crisis.[39] Crime is abated when everyone has access to high-quality education throughout their lives.[40] Religious communities discourage law-breaking and provide social supports that buoy people through difficult times.[41] In sum, these noneconomic institutions encourage us to look out for one another in ways that reduce crime.

TABLE 10.3 ■ Select social institutions and their functions	
Social institution	**Needs of human societies that are fulfilled**
Family	Caring for children and elders; reproduction; social support
Polity	Protecting citizens; mobilizing resources to address collective problems
Religion	Search for meaning in life; providing community
Education	*Come up with your own examples*
Economy	*Come up with your own examples*

The market economy has important functions, as well, but encouraging people to look out for one another is not one of them. This isn't a problem, though, if the other institutions are strong such that there is a balance of power among the institutions in society. Institutions are dependent upon one another. For example, the economy cannot function if families don't socialize and care for children, nor can it function if schools don't educate the people who will become workers. And none of this can happen without some form of social order, which is the formal duty of polity. For societies to "work," institutions must be coordinated. But therein lies a problem! The demands of one institution often conflict with the demands of another.[42] You are familiar with this conflict if you have ever found yourself needing to care for a sick child during a workday.

Societies experience institutional imbalance if one institution overshadows the others—if it determines how all other institutions operate. Messner and Rosenfeld characterize the U.S. as suffering from economic dominance, a form of institutional imbalance. They describe the difference between *market economies* (capitalist nations that also have strong noneconomic institutions) and *market societies* (capitalist nations in which the economy dominates all other institutions). Market economies can maintain low crime rates, they contend, due to decommodification, or policies that free people to make choices that are, at least in principle, not constrained by market forces, such as having children, pursuing higher education, or serving in local government.[43] Unemployment insurance, paid sick leave, paid maternity and paternity leave policies, universal health care, and government-funded child care and college education are examples of decommodified policies. In nations with these policies, services—like medical care, daycare, and higher education—are not treated as commodities purchased by individual consumers within a market, hence the term *decommodification* (the prefix *de-* means "off" or "from").

In contrast, they write, market societies engender law-breaking because noneconomic institutions become weakened and unable to keep crime in check when the economy dominates. Economic dominance is observed in three ways:

- *Accommodation* – Noneconomic institutions must accommodate the needs of the economy when conflicts emerge. For example, families must alter their routines and schedules to meet the demands of the workplace. Schools prepare workers, not thinkers (and if they teach socioemotional skills, it is because employers demand them, not because they make for a healthier, happier populace).

- *Penetration* – The language and logic of economic efficiency permeate all other institutions. Families "manage" the household, "downsize" when moving, and "outsource" domestic labor. High schools receive corporate sponsorships to pay for sports equipment and other materials, and students are frequently reminded that school is "their job." Colleges see grade inflation as instructors' employment is tied to student evaluations of performance. Politicians campaign on their ability to run the government "like a business."

- *Devaluation* – Noneconomic roles (like parent, caregiver, mentor, and volunteer) are less valued than economic roles (like worker). And activity within noneconomic institutions—charitable work, caring for older parents, raising children, serving on a PTA or town council—is regarded as less important than paid labor. Social esteem is determined by the amount of money generated rather than the social value produced. For example, hedge fund managers are respected more than kindergarten teachers, even though teachers provide an essential social good.

According to institutional anomie theory, the result is that social institutions responsible for social support and social control are less able to perform their unique functions successfully. Furthermore, institutional imbalance also supports an anomic culture that overemphasizes the individual pursuit of money. The result is that crime abounds.

Of course, economic dominance is not the only form that institutional imbalance can take. The theory suggests that corruption runs rampant when polity is the dominant institution. When family or religion dominate other institutions, "crimes in defense of the moral order" result, such as violence against those who engage in sexual relations in nonmarital, extramarital, or same-sex contexts. All institutional imbalance is criminogenic.

The claims of institutional anomie theory are supported somewhat by evidence from cross-national studies. Criminologists use data from the World Values Survey, the World Health Organization, the World Bank, the United Nations, and other international agencies to examine whether anomic cultures and institutional imbalance increase nation-level crime rates[44] and crime-justifying attitudes.[45] Economic dominance typically predicts crime or pro-crime beliefs in these studies. Other criminologists find support for the theory when examining whether people who have internalized the four values (achievement, individualism, universalism, and monetary fetishism), or who have marketized mentalities, are more likely to commit or justify crime.[46] These studies find, perhaps unsurprisingly, that materialistic people who hold an "every man for himself" attitude tend to have few qualms about circumventing the law. In one study, a criminologist using U.S. survey data found that TV viewing operates as a conduit for individualistic and materialistic messages such that greater TV consumption leads to greater adherence to American Dream ideals, and, in turn, more involvement in "crimes of economic attainment" (e.g., stealing, selling drugs, and credit or debit card fraud).[47]

Evaluating Institutional Anomie Theory

Institutional anomie theory offers a sophisticated update to Merton's anomie theory. Its focus on social institutions challenges us to consider how national policies that appear unrelated to crime (like parental leave policies and educational policies) may, in fact, matter a great deal for crime rates. Its description of anomic culture prompts us to recognize the darker side of a culture of individual achievement. Despite its many strengths, though, the theory has its weak spots.

Like other macro-level perspectives, institutional anomie theory struggles to account for individual differences. Why are some people more apt to espouse values of egoistic self-interest and violate the law than others, even though they live in the same nation where they are exposed to the same anomic culture and institutional imbalances? For example, the gender gap in crime presents a puzzle for institutional anomie theory. Women, men, and people who don't fit neatly into binary gender categories live in the same nations but commit crime at different rates. How can the theory explain this? One explanation is that ideals of rugged individualism and self-interest are experienced and interpreted differently by women than men, and that women are also more embedded in institutions that buffer against criminality, like family and religion.[48] It can be argued that, as a macro-level perspective, institutional anomie theory does not have to account for person-to-person or even group-level variation because its guiding research question is not about individuals or groups but nations or states. *Who* commits crime is less important than the fact that many more people commit crime in one nation relative to another nation.

AGNEW'S GENERAL STRAIN THEORY

In 1998, researchers published the results of a groundbreaking study on health determinants. They studied more than 17,000 middle-aged adults to learn what negative social experiences in childhood—called adverse childhood experiences (ACEs)—predicted medical problems later in life, including cancer, heart disease, chronic lung disease, high blood pressure, skeletal fractures, liver disease, and early death.[49] Trauma, it turns out, mattered a great deal for health, even when controlling for the impact of harmful behaviors like smoking, drinking, and drug use. The study pointed to several types of traumatic childhood experiences that were especially predictive of poor health when experienced at high levels between birth and age 17:

- Experiencing violence, abuse, or neglect

- Witnessing violence in the home

- Having a family member attempt or die by suicide

- Having a household member who misuses drugs or alcohol

- Having a household member with serious mental health problems

- Experiencing instability due to parental separation or incarceration of household members

In the years that followed, other researchers examined the impact of these childhood traumas on mental health and social behaviors, finding that a high magnitude of ACEs increases the risk of depression, anxiety, post-traumatic stress disorder (PTSD), insomnia, eating disorders, substance abuse, and suicide attempts.[50] According to the Centers for Disease Control and Prevention (CDC):

> *ACEs and associated conditions, such as living in under-resourced or racially segregated neighborhoods, frequently moving, and experiencing food insecurity, can cause toxic stress (extended or prolonged stress). Toxic stress from ACEs can change brain development and affect such things as attention, decision-making, learning, and response to stress.*[51]

Criminal decision-making is one type of decision-making affected by the toxic stress of childhood trauma, especially when it comes to violence.[52] The phrase "hurt people hurt people" can be readily invoked when considering the trauma-offending link among young people.[53] Maltreated and traumatized children are overrepresented among incarcerated children and adolescents, and histories of trauma are similarly abundant among imprisoned adults. About 9 out of 10 young people in the juvenile justice system have experienced at least one ACE, and 3 out of 10 meet the threshold for PTSD as a result of chronic exposure to ACEs.[54] In the words of one group of criminologists, "trauma changes everything."[55]

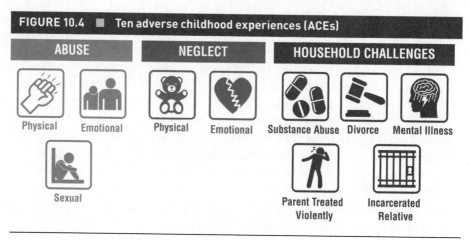

FIGURE 10.4 ■ Ten adverse childhood experiences (ACEs)

ABUSE — Physical, Emotional, Sexual

NEGLECT — Physical, Emotional

HOUSEHOLD CHALLENGES — Substance Abuse, Divorce, Mental Illness, Parent Treated Violently, Incarcerated Relative

Source: Centers for Disease Control and Prevention. (2021). *Adverse Childhood Experiences Prevention Strategy.* National Center for Injury Prevention and Control, Centers for Disease Control and Prevention. https://www.cdc.gov/injury/pdfs/priority/ACEs-Strategic-Plan_Final_508.pdf

The ACEs study was not a criminological undertaking, yet its results align with a criminological perspective called general strain theory. **General strain theory (GST)** is an individual-level theory of crime that emphasizes that stress is criminogenic (or is a risk factor for crime). This perspective, first developed by criminologist Robert Agnew, suggests that crime is a form of coping, a "corrective action" that allows individuals faced with overwhelming, accumulating stresses (or strains) to deal with their negative emotions, like anger, disappointment, and fear.[56] Especially anger. More so than sadness or worry, anger is an externalizing emotion that compels people to act. The theory's basic premise can be boiled down to three statements: (1) Strains are events and conditions that we don't like, (2) strains produce negative emotions (anger being most salient for crime), and (3) some people cope with strains and negative emotions through crime. Strains don't always lead to criminal coping in GST, though. Some kinds of strains are particularly criminogenic (see Types of Strain), and some individuals are better-equipped than others to deal with negative emotions in constructive, noncriminal ways (see When Is Criminal Coping Likely?).

It may be odd to think of crime as coping. After all, breaking the law usually introduces a whole new host of stresses, especially if caught and punished. But, in the moment, behavior that is illegal can provide a release. There are three ways it does this. First, crime can reduce or allow a person to escape from the strain itself, even if only temporarily. Any money-generating crime—larceny, fraud, robbery, drug trafficking, burglary—can momentarily reduce the stress of relentless financial need. And teenagers live on the streets and engage in crimes of survival (such as shoplifting, trespassing, or exchanging sex for necessities like food) to escape hostile and abusive homes.[57] Second, crime allows people to get revenge against people who have wronged them (or a more vulnerable target). Assaults and homicides involving acquaintances or strangers in public settings frequently begin with a verbal insult issued in front of an audience of onlookers.[58] Angry motorists threaten one another or, if the driver is not present, do physical damage to the car (keying the door or puncturing a tire, for instance). If the supposed wrongdoer cannot be attacked, the stressed-out person might unleash their anger on someone more vulnerable or accessible, like their child or spouse. Third, criminal conduct—illicit substance use, especially—can help to dull strain-induced negative emotions.

Types of Strain

To understand GST, we must start with the most basic element of the theory: strain. Agnew describes three basic types of strain:

1. *Failure to achieve positively valued goals* – Think about your own goals. What do you want right now in life? Perhaps you want to complete college, get a job that pays enough so you don't need to worry about bills, form meaningful romantic relationships, or buy a car. You probably want to be treated fairly and with dignity. Those are all positively valued goals (or things we want or need). People become stressed when they are unable to achieve them, especially when this happens repeatedly. Agnew explains that there are three forms of failing to achieve positively valued goals:
   - *Aspirations vs. expectations* – In this version, the person really wants (or needs) to achieve their goals, but they do not actually *expect* to achieve them. Realizing that one's aspirations are likely to be dashed is a source of strain and creates feelings of defeat, sadness, anger, and frustration.
   - *Expectations vs. achievements* – In some cases, the person truly believes that they will get what they want or need, but reality does not deliver. Their actual achievements fall short of what they thought would happen, a frustrating and demoralizing experience.
   - *Idealized justice vs. injustice* – Most people have a strong desire to be treated fairly. Idealized justice is what would happen in a perfectly fair world. Their vision of what is right and fair is violated when people experience injustice (unfair treatment or conditions), and that can generate a sense of indignation or outrage.

2. *Removal of positively valued stimuli* – Now think about the things in your life that you hold dear. What would cause you distress if it were to be lost or taken away? Your mother? Your home? Your child? Your job? Your place in college? Simply put, removal of positively valued stimuli is losing something good.

3. *Presentation of negatively valued stimuli* – Consider the kinds of treatment or experiences that would upset you, perhaps to the point of lashing out at others or trying to drown out the bad

feelings with maladaptive behaviors. Being berated by your boss? Seeing your family fighting? Getting cyberbullied? Being injured in a car accident through no fault of your own? These are examples of noxious or negatively valued stimuli.[59]

Strains come in a variety of forms, many of them unlikely to lead to criminal coping. For example, final exams cause stress, but it's not the kind of stress that usually leads to crime. Why not? For one thing, students who care about their academic performance and standing stress out about final exams, and highly invested students have a lot to lose if they break the law. Also, final exams might keep a student up at night, but they don't violate their sense of justice (though a bad grade might), and the stress of exams is temporary. Plus, there is little to be gained from crime when final exams are the source of stress (one deviant but not criminal exception is cheating or lying to avoid taking the exam).

Strains are most criminogenic when they (1) are perceived as unjust, an experience particularly likely to lead to anger and, therefore, pressure for the corrective action of crime; (2) are high in magnitude and long in duration such that the stress is severe and overwhelming, as in the toxic stress of ACEs; (3) are associated with low social control, which means that the strain weakens emotional attachments or investments in conventional life; and (4) provide an incentive for rule-breaking behavior because the strain can be resolved through crime.

What kinds of experiences do you believe are universally (or nearly universally) stressful? Here is a possible list: being evicted from an apartment with nowhere else to go, being beaten up by a loved one, being unable to afford food and other necessities. These are objective strains. They are events or conditions that most people dislike.[60] The stress of eviction, being victimized, and going hungry does not depend on the person's perspective. Many strains aren't objectively stressful, though. Rather, they are subjective strains. The end of a romantic relationship, the loss of a job, and the death of a grandparent are experienced as major crises by some individuals but are not particularly upsetting to others. Their subjective evaluation determines whether it is truly a strain and, thus, whether it might lead to criminal coping. For example, recall the mass murderers Elliot Rodger and Alec Minassian from Chapter 3. Both men were angry about their romantic failings, and they blamed women for denying them sex to which they felt entitled. Most people, of course, do not perceive romantic rejection as so unjust and severe a stressor that they become enraged and commit mass violence. Their criminogenic strain was subjective rather than objective.

Strains can be direct, vicarious, or anticipated. Thus far, nearly all the strains described in this chapter have been direct strains. They happen to the strained individual, personally (e.g., *they* lost their job or *they* lost custody of their children). Imagine a scenario, though, where witnessing others enduring harms causes strain, such as watching a close friend suffer from illness or abuse. That is vicarious strain, or strain experienced through another person. We don't need to experience bad things personally, or directly, to feel the anger, frustration, and other emotional states that give rise to illicit coping. In direct and vicarious strain, the stressful events or conditions have occurred already, either to the strained person (direct) or to people they care about (vicarious). In anticipated strain, the stressful events or conditions are predicted, and that prediction—or expectation that bad things are coming down the line—is the source of upset.

When Is Criminal Coping Likely?

Until now, the focus of this section of the chapter has been strain—the forms it takes and the kinds that ignite anger and criminal behavior, as depicted in Figure 10.5. Now let's talk about people. Many people weather infuriating chronic, toxic stresses without resorting to criminal coping. General strain theory outlines several factors that differentiate the strained law-breaker from the strained law-abider.

Strained law-breakers tend to have *poorer coping skills* (e.g., help-seeking, finding distractions, and learning to reinterpret adversity). Also, they are less likely to have the social skills required to deal with difficulties in prosocial ways. In addition, they have *fewer social supports* to lean on—fewer (noncriminal) friends, trusted teachers or coworkers, neighbors, religious figures, family members, and so on. Plus, the costs of crime are low for them, meaning that they have *low social control*. They have little to lose in the way of relationships to people or investments in work, school, or other facets of conventional life. They are also more likely to have *criminal associates and hold pro-crime beliefs*. Crime-involved friends encourage criminal responses and may convince the strained person that they can "get away" with law-breaking.

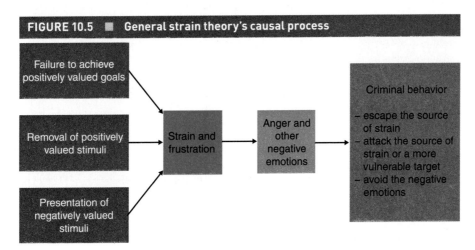

FIGURE 10.5 ■ General strain theory's causal process

Example: Legal Debt as Strain

If I had to design a system that was intended to keep people addicted, I'd design exactly the system that we have right now… I'd attack people, and ostracize them… The more you stress people, the more they're going to use. The more you de-stress people, the less they're going to use. So to create a system where you ostracize and marginalize and criminalize people, and force them to live in poverty with disease, you are basically guaranteeing they will stay at it. (Addiction specialist Dr. Gabor Maté, quoted in *Chasing the Scream*[61])

If the cause of so much law-breaking is strain, then our solutions to crime are, in fact, major contributors to it. Any system that increases poverty, impedes positive social connections (e.g., through work or relationships), and fosters despair is a criminogenic system. That is the point in Dr. Maté's quote about substance abuse. Legal debt is one way that criminal justice involvement creates strains that general strain theory identifies as likely to lead to future offending.

Legal debts accrue from court fees, surcharges, community supervision fees (i.e., paying to be on probation), jail and prison fees (including pay-to-stay fees that charge jail inmates for each day they are incarcerated), fines, restitution, and other legal financial obligations that act as "invisible punishments" as part of the U.S.'s offender-funded justice model.[62] These monetary sanctions are mostly supplementary; they are in addition to other forms of punishment rather than a replacement for them.[63] And the burdens they create are shared by the families of justice-involved persons, as they provide personal loans, places to stay, and other supports for indebted loved ones.

People who fail to pay their legal debts risk additional fees for late payments, accumulating interest, loss of their driver's licenses, incarceration, and a poor credit rating that can cost them educational, housing, and other opportunities. A debt that starts at $1,347 (the median for a felony conviction in Washington State in one seminal study) can quickly balloon to $11,471 just five years later (the median assessed amount five years later in the Washington State study) due to interest and additional fees.[64]

Figure 10.6 depicts the median ($5,349) and distribution of monetary sanctions in Alabama between 2005 and 2011. The values do not include interest owed. Importantly, these costs are shouldered by most justice-involved persons—about 85% of them, according to Bureau of Justice Statistics data and other sources[65]—across a wide range of convicted persons, ranging from low-level misdemeanants to former felons exiting prison. Most are in arrears, which means they are not making payments on time.[66] In fact, about one in five jail incarcerations are for failure to pay legal financial obligations rather than new criminal activity or other violations.[67]

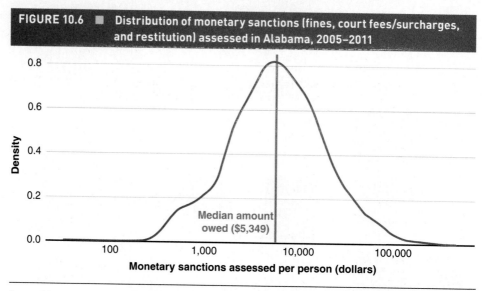

FIGURE 10.6 ■ Distribution of monetary sanctions (fines, court fees/surcharges, and restitution) assessed in Alabama, 2005–2011

Source: Adapted from Meredith, M., & Morse, M. (2017). Discretionary disenfranchisement: The case of legal financial obligations. *Journal of Legal Studies, 46*(2), 309–38. https://www.sas.upenn.edu/~marcmere/workingpapers/DiscretionaryLFOs.pdf

Criminologists who study legal debt conduct qualitative and mixed-methods studies to find out how owing money has mattered in the lives of people who owe it. The following four examples are typical of the patterns they observe in their interviews.

Well, I've been a fisherman for a long time, and I've been a laborer, and now I'm truck driving. I can't do it [truck driving] no more. Because the state took my license away. I'm in noncompliance because I can't pay. [68]

I got my Section 8 *voucher… If I [got] a one-bedroom apartment, my part would only be $216 a month, but I don't have $216 a month. Cause I gotta pay $50 a month on the LFOs [legal financial obligations]. If I did pay the $216, I couldn't feed myself, I couldn't pay LFOs and utilities. So I gotta stay in this shelter.* [69]

You're just making minimum wage, and they [the state] just take in half of that. And then the first thing you say is, "How am I supposed to survive?" or "How am I supposed to meet the obligations when everything I make, you take?" Then you want me to stay positive.… But the more I try to be good, the more you take the necessary things I need to be good. It's like you're putting me in a Catch-22 here. You know, I go to work every day … I can't even pay the rent. Like what do I do? Get another job? If I get another job, it [the state] just takes more. So I still don't meet the obligation that I'm demanded to meet. [70]

Well I was paying $20 until I lost my job and I decided to just cut and run on these people, and then they caught up with me, and I just—he wanted me to send $20 or $40 a month—I said, "[DOC officer's name], the money's not there!" So I'm on the run again. [71]

The quotes reveal the many ways that legal debt exacerbates strains that can be resolved through crime: loss of work, loss of housing, and incentives to go "on the run." Criminologists document how, like the final quoted person, those with criminal records often engage in system avoidance, or "avoiding institutions that keep formal records (i.e., put them 'in the system')." [72] Avoiding the system means forgoing legal work, schooling, banks, medical facilities when sick or injured, and more. Record-keeping institutions form the backbone of conventional life. Plus, individuals with legal debt also report greater stress and poorer mental health, including feelings of being overwhelmed and a sense of hopelessness; they also report increased substance use, just as Dr. Maté would predict. [73]

Criminologists are just now beginning to study the costs of debt for recidivism (or re-offending). Their findings will speak to questions of whether criminal justice policies are undermining their stated goal of deterring further criminal conduct. While some older studies found that owing restitution (payments to those harmed by one's criminal conduct) reduces re-offending,[74] more recent examinations of fees and fines identify the opposite effect.[75] For example, one study of juveniles involved in the justice system found that financial penalties increase re-offending two years later.[76] Plus, the more money owed, the higher the likelihood of subsequent law-breaking.

Example: Racism as Strain

Strain theorists have long argued that criminologists should pay attention to the specific types of strain faced by social status groups, including racial and ethnic groups.[77] Understanding racial patterns in offending, they write, requires understanding the unique social position of people of color in America. Part of that unique social position includes the far-reaching impacts of generations of systemic exclusion, segregation, and discrimination. Another term for this is **systemic racism**, which refers to how racial inequality is built into the ordinary operations of institutions—including laws, policies, and practices—rather than just in one-on-one interactions.[78]

One example of systemic racism is found in mortgage lending. The federal Fair Housing Act of 1968 prohibited racial discrimination by lending agencies. This banned practices like redlining, a "state-sponsored system of segregation" in which the federal agencies, local governments, and the private sector refused to back or provide loans to prospective buyers in Black communities; they were already shut out of white communities by restrictive racial covenants and discriminatory real estate practices.[79] Nonetheless, racial inequality has persisted in mortgage lending in the years since the passage of the Fair Housing Act. The Federal Reserve and Department of Justice, in an analysis of 31 million records, found distinct race- and ethnicity-based patterns of home loan denials even when controlling for income, neighborhood characteristics, and loan amount (other, smaller studies expand the number of factors controlled for, yielding the same results). Black loan applicants faced the greatest hurdles, especially in southern cities, followed by Latino applicants.[80] Some of the disparity is due to proprietary credit scores, which are produced by algorithms acknowledged by credit scoring agencies as having a racially discriminatory effect.[81]

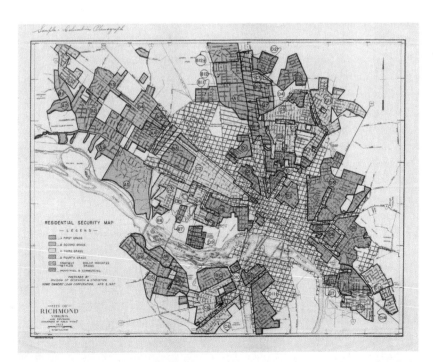

This Home Owners' Loan Corporation (HOLC) map from Richmond, Virginia, designated Black-majority neighborhoods, color-coded red, as too risky for new home loans. HOLC Created Redlined Maps for the Federal Home Loan Bank Board.

Records of the Federal Home Loan Bank Board, Readline map for Richmond, Va. ca. 1935

Systemic racism in mortgage lending matters because home ownership is the primary source of wealth for most Americans. The racial gap in homeownership, depicted in Figure 10.6, contributes to the racial wealth gap in the United States. In 2019, the typical, or median, white family had a net worth of about $184,000, which was eight times greater than the net worth of a typical Black family ($23,000).[82] The white-Latino wealth gap was also large in 2019, with a median net worth of $38,000 for Latino families.[83] Racial wealth gaps are not a simple reflection of income differences, though income divides on the basis of race and ethnicity continue despite narrowing of educational gaps.[84] In fact, the Black-white wealth gap persists even for individuals with the *exact same* education and yearly income.[85] It only disappears for those on the bottommost rung of the income ladder (the bottom 20%, or quintile), and that's only because *everyone* has zero or negative assets (i.e., debt). In the words of one author, "racism eats wealth for breakfast."[86]

Wealth matters more than income in determining life circumstances of adults and their children. People with assets accrued have a cushion in the case of an employment, medical, or family crisis. And parents pass on the benefits of wealth to children through spending and transfers (gifting them money or leaving inheritance). They can afford to move to and live in safe communities with high-quality schools,[87] they can subsidize a college education and pay for the experiences that increase college readiness,[88] or they can contribute to a down payment for a new home.[89] Their children begin their adult lives with less debt and more security.[90] In short, wealth buys options.

What does this have to do with strain and crime? Systemic racism creates long-lasting economic burdens. It increases the risk of exposure to violence and harmful social environments by eliminating options for housing, for schooling, and for work.[91] Barriers to homeownership and wealth acquisition represent only a portion of its toll. The earlier section on legal debt speaks to another major contributor: the criminal justice system. Chapter 11 addresses racially disproportionate school discipline as an additional source of stress. In sum, systemic racism creates strains that general strain theory highlights as most salient: unjust, high in magnitude, and creating incentives for illicit coping.[92]

Black, Latino, and Native Americans, overall, experience a greater *quantity* of strains due to systemic racism, including financial strains. Criminologists also note the importance of racially and ethnically specific strains, or strains that are unique to Black, Latino, and Native Americans, as well as other groups.[93] This is a difference in *quality,* or form, of strain. Specifically, experiencing racial discrimination is a distinct source of strain for non-white Americans. Face-to-face discrimination— "verbal, nonverbal, and environmental indignities that relay hostile and derogatory messages"—exacts an emotional toll.[94] It includes overt, intended mistreatment (like a person yelling a racial slur from a passing vehicle) as well as mundane slights and putdowns that invoke stereotypes and demean one's racial identity, regardless of intent (like being followed by store employees).

Criminologists studying Native American and Canadian First Nations youth living on reservations/reserves found a link between perceived mistreatment and involvement in aggressive delinquency.[95] This was attributed to the anger and depression brought on by discrimination. A similar outcome was identified in a study of racially diverse middle-schoolers: Black students who recounted frequent experiences of being disrespected, called names, and treated as dangerous or unintelligent were at an increased risk of juvenile delinquency. Plus, experiencing discrimination amplified the criminogenic effects of other strains for these adolescents. [96] Discrimination is, in the authors' words, a "mundane extreme environmental stress."

Subjective perceptions of discrimination are particularly important, according to the general strain perspective. This is borne out in a study on white people's perceptions of anti-white bias, anger, and crime.[97] Despite clear evidence that, overall, white Americans endure less racial discrimination than Black Americans,[98] a sizeable minority of white people report that white Americans have it worse than Black Americans when it comes to race-based mistreatment. For instance, a 2019 Pew Research poll found that 8% of respondents believe that white people face a lot or some discrimination while Black people face only a little or no discrimination.[99] This group tends to perceive racial progress as a zero-sum process wherein non-white gains translate into white losses.[100] In one study of young white people, criminologists found that perceptions of anti-white bias strongly predicted serious felony-level offending, particularly among young men, and that this link was exacerbated by anger.[101] They referred to this as "whitelash," a play on the term *backlash*.

ENGAGED CRIMINOLOGY 10.2
Seeing Strain Theories in Quotes

In this activity, you will select one quote from a provided list and identify which strain perspective—Merton's anomie theory, Messner and Rosenfeld's institutional anomie theory, Agnew's general strain theory—most aligns with the sentiment of the quote.

- Quote #1: *"Every society has the criminals it deserves."* –Alexandre Lacassagne

- Quote #2: *"Pacin' going upstate's my destination; Handcuffed in back of a bus, forty of us; Life as a shorty shouldn't be so rough; But as the world turns I learned life is hell; Living in the world no different from a cell; Everyday I escape from Jakes givin' chase, sellin' base' Smokin' bones in the staircase; Though I don't know why I chose to smoke sess; I guess that's the time when I'm not depressed"* –Wu-Tang Clan (lyrics from C.R.E.A.M.)

- Quote #3: *"It's called the American Dream because you have to be asleep to believe it."* –George Carlin

- Quote #4: *"How vainly shall we endeavor to repress crime by our barbarous punishment of the poorer class of criminals so long as children are reared in the brutalizing influences of poverty, so long as the bite of want drives men to crime."* –Henry George

Answer the following questions:

1. Which quote did you select? Identify it by its number (e.g., Quote #2).

2. Which strain perspective (Merton's anomie theory, Messner and Rosenfeld's institutional anomie theory, or Agnew's general strain theory) most aligns with your selected quote, and why? Use a key term from the theory in your answer.

Evaluating General Strain Theory

General strain theory surpasses many other criminological explanations in its scope (the number of crime types it can explain) and empirical validity (the degree to which it is supported by evidence). The theory offers a broad, comprehensive explanation for individual offending that incorporates insights from many perspectives in criminology. While criminal motivation is its primary focus, the theory also centers on controls that prevent offending and acknowledges the impact of situational opportunities in determining how people cope with strains. Agnew is not a purist. He welcomes other criminological perspectives, and, if they are empirically valid, he builds them into general strain theory.

General strain theory's critics take aim at the theory's breadth.[102] They argue that testing the theory with data requires the inclusion of too many variables, rendering it difficult to examine empirically. Plus, they write, researchers are bound to find support for the theory because they include so many variables in their analyses (in other words, throw enough at the wall and something will stick). Essentially, the critique is that the theory is too thorough. Critics also contend that the concept of strain is vague, and that anything can be interpreted as strain.[103] Agnew responded to this critique by outlining the types of strain that are most criminogenic.[104] Less explored in the theory are the reasons that some people are more prone than others to interpret experiences as subjectively stressful. However, Agnew's latest installment mentions negative emotionality (temperament marked by intensely sad or angry emotional responses) and weak self-control as potential factors.[105]

CHAPTER SUMMARY

LO 10.1   Explain Durkheim's contribution to strain perspectives in criminology.

Durkheim developed the concept of anomie, which he described as a state in which old norms break down and fail to regulate behavior, leading to crime and other societal dysfunctions, especially during periods of rapid social change. Structural strain theories, like Merton's anomie theory and Messner and Rosenfeld's institutional anomie theory, adopt and transform Durkheim's ideas about anomie to explain why some societies have more crime than others.

LO 10.2 Describe Merton's modes of adaptation and how they relate to his anomie theory.

Merton identified five adaptations to anomic conditions, or a state in which norms regulating cultural success goals are emphasized more than the norms regulating the means to achieving success. These included conformity (accept goal/accept means), ritualism (reject goal/accept means), innovation (accept goal/reject means), retreatism (reject goal/reject means), and rebellion (reject and replace goal and means). Innovation is most associated with criminal conduct, but retreatism and rebellion can also result in law-breaking.

LO 10.3 Explain the central tenets of institutional anomie theory.

Institutional anomie theory, a structural level perspective on nation- or state-level crime, posits that the values of achievement, individualism, universalism, and monetary fetishism can contribute to a criminogenic "success at any cost" anomic culture. Crime is especially likely when the economy comes to dominate other social institutions, a form of institutional imbalance that undermines the social support and social control functions of noneconomic institutions.

LO 10.4 Identify the primary claims of general strain theory.

General strain theory, an individual-level perspective, claims that crime is a form of coping with strains or stressors by allowing strained persons to escape the strain, avoid the negative feelings it produces, or attack its source or a more vulnerable target. Strains are especially likely to be criminogenic when they are perceived as unjust, are high in magnitude, weaken social control, and produce incentives for criminal coping. Anger is regarded as the most salient emotion for crime.

ENGAGED DISCUSSION

1. Come up with an example of a character from a TV show, movie, or book who was driven to criminality by stressful conditions. Was their stress presented as personal (specific to them), caused by abnormal societal conditions, or both?

2. Evaluate the scope of Merton's anomie theory: What kinds of crimes *cannot* be explained by his theory? Why can't they?

3. Would you stay in college if earning a degree did not improve your employment and earning prospects? Imagine that college were free. Does that change your answer? What do these questions and your answers have to do with institutional anomie theory?

4. How would a general strain theorist explain the gender gap in violent crime (the much higher rates of criminal violence among men and boys than women and girls)? Come up with two ways they might explain it.

KEY TERMS

Achievement (p. 256)

Collective consciousness (p. 248)

Conformity (p. 252)

Culture structure (p. 249)

Decommodification (p. 258)

Durkheimian anomie (p. 248)

General strain theory (GST) (p. 261)

Individualism (p. 256)

Innovation (p. 252)

Institutional anomie theory (p. 255)

Institutional imbalance (p. 258)

Legal debt (p. 263)

Marketized mentality (p. 257)

Mertonian anomie (p. 250)

Modes of adaptation (p. 251)

Monetary fetishism (p. 256)

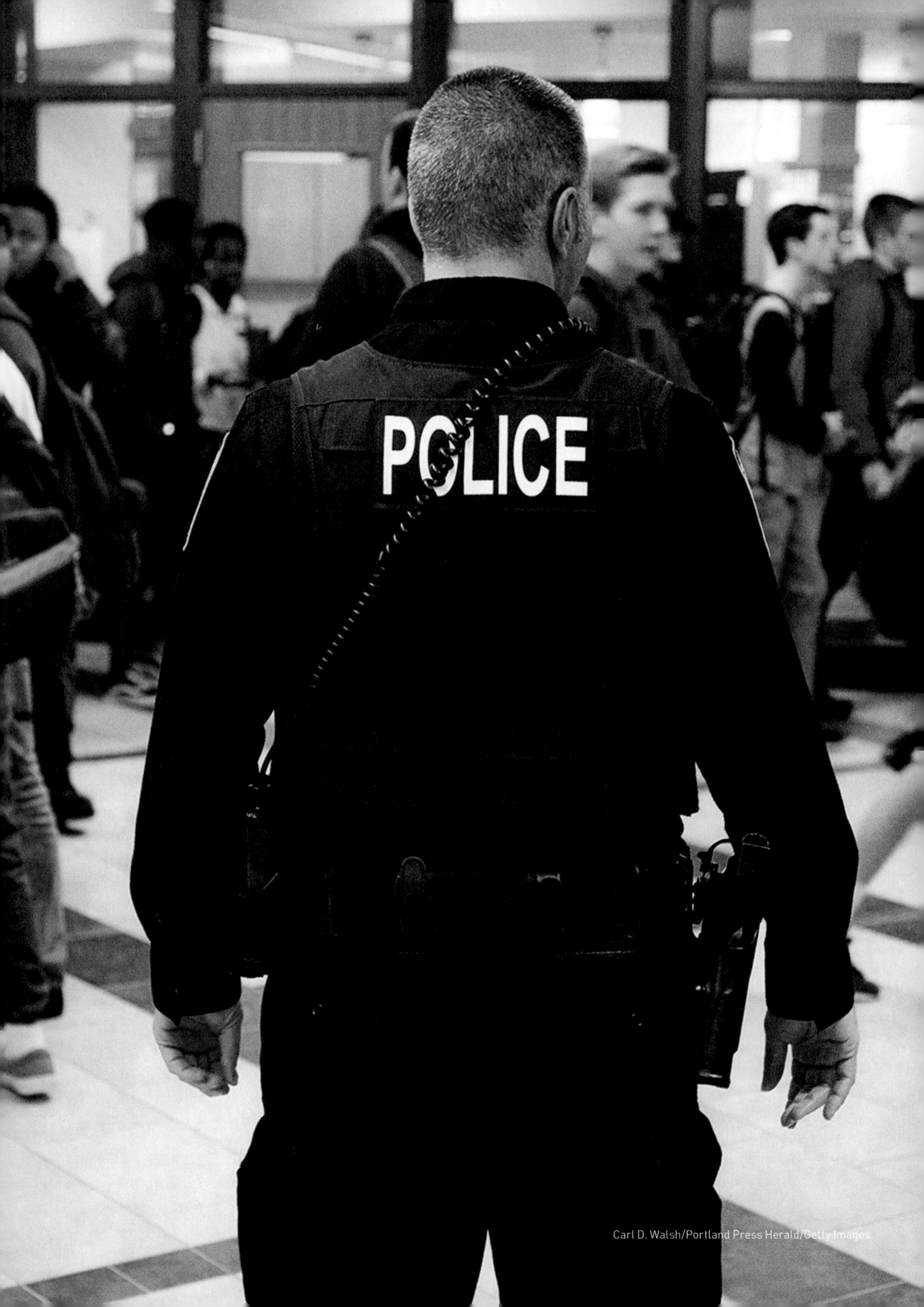

Carl D. Walsh/Portland Press Herald/Getty Images

11 LABELING AND DEFIANCE

LEARNING OBJECTIVES

11.1 Summarize labeling theory's central concepts.

11.2 Describe the causes of the school-to-prison pipeline.

11.3 Identify the effects of a criminal record.

11.4 Explain the primary claims of defiance theory and differentiate it from labeling theory.

She [teacher] had my father and, like, one time we were sitting in class and she got really upset with me and said I'm going to be like my father... Right now he's in jail and she said I'm going to be like him. And after that—she was like one of my favorite teachers—but after that, every time I look at her, I'm like, she doesn't like me. She thinks negative about me. She thinks I'm going to be nothing. (Tyrel, p. 186)

One of the administrators, he looked at my paper [and said], "Oh, so you came from Brig [alternative school]. What did you do to go to Brig?" I told him, fighting. "Oh, so you're a fighter," he said, and I said, "No, I'm not a fighter." He said, "Well, it says on your record that you're a fighter. And I said, "Well I'm not. That was just that one time." Then he would always see me in the hallway and he told another teacher, "Oh, we have a Mike Tyson [famous boxer] here. (Jayda, p. 190)

It [getting suspended] makes people feel like they can't do nothing with their life. They just drop out. I went to an alternative school, ain't nobody gonna want to take me. If you write Brig [alternative school] on your thing, the schools you went to, they look up your record... you might not even get into college. People hear that you been to Brig, they gonna doubt you. (Rayquan, p. 186)

I used to feel worthless... because teachers used to tell me that and junk. Like when you feel bad already and they tell you that you need to do this or you ain't going to be nothing. You going to be like a gang member. You going to be in jail or dead. That makes you feel worse. And I think that's what makes kids drop out of school faster and start gangs and stuff. That's why a lot of young kids like my age don't care. They just want to make money and all this other dumb things. Just to prove a point that they aren't worthless. (Damian, p. 188)

These quotes come from high school students interviewed by sociologist Marsha Weissman for her book *Prelude to Prison: Student Perspectives on School Suspension.*[1] The students understand intuitively how stigma operates. How a person can be marked as "bad" and that label becomes a stain that won't wash out. It taints how others treat them ("Oh, we have a Mike Tyson here") and what they expect of them ("She ... said I'm going to be like my father"). It makes them feel worthless, like a nobody, like they "can't do nothing with their life."

Criminologists would interpret these students' accounts through the lens of labeling theory, a perspective that claims that people are transformed by the labels that are attached to them by the people and institutions (like school) that order their daily lives. Damian's observation that kids start gangs and do "other dumb things" to prove that they aren't worthless also fits with defiance theory, which asserts that punishment and stigma can backfire, causing righteous defiance of the rules in an effort to escape shame. This chapter addresses the multiple ways that stigmatizing labels become a "prelude to prison."

LABELING THEORY

Labeling theory argues that labels—like felon, deviant, sex offender, juvenile delinquent, or trouble-maker—have powerful effects on self-concept, life circumstances, and future behavior. It is a "societal reaction" explanation of crime (and other norm-violating behaviors) because it locates the root of chronic offending in other people's responses to rule-breakers.[2] Therefore, labeling theory is an interactionist perspective (see Chapter 1); people are "criminals" or "deviants" *because* they are regarded as criminals or deviants in social interactions.

Labeling theory grew out of symbolic interactionism in sociology. Symbolic interactionism claims that the way people make sense of their social worlds is by exchanging meaning through language and symbols. The meanings themselves are the result of social interaction. For example, a dress is understood as feminine attire, even though there is nothing intrinsically "female" about a piece of sewn fabric; people only regard dresses as feminine because their interactions sustain the gendered meaning of dresses. People believe dresses are feminine and act based on this belief (e.g., buying dresses for daughters rather than sons, making assumptions about the gender identities of persons wearing dresses). Through interactions, people come to ascribe meaning to all manner of objects, people, locations, and interactions—a "nice" neighborhood versus a "bad" neighborhood, "ugly" people versus "beautiful" people, "normal" behavior versus "deviant" behavior, and so on. Symbolic interactionists argue that we ought to examine how people experience the social world, including how their interactions create—and are the result of—interpretations that are attached people, objects, and places.

Labeling theory emphasizes the power of definitions. Who is defined, or labeled, as deviant (including the label of "criminal") is the result of a social process in which others react as though the person is deviant. Although deviant labeling may be related to rule-violating behavior, it is the *reaction* rather than the behavior itself that produces the label of deviant. Following this logic, no actual rule-violating behavior is necessary for the deviant label to be applied.[3] For example, a child is labeled as a trouble-maker because adults react to the child as though they are a problem; the child would not receive the negative label (troublemaker) if the adults reacted differently (e.g., "This is a child who needs extra support"). The social reaction is what matters. Deviance is in the eye of the beholder. Labeling theorist Howard Becker put it this way:

> Deviance is not a quality of the act the person commits, but rather a consequence of the application by others of rules and sanctions to an "offender." The deviant is one to whom that label has successfully been applied; deviant behavior is behavior that people so label. (p. 9)

Labels have the power to transform people. In labeling perspective, the person who is treated as deviant becomes deviant. Labeling theory relies on the logic of the Thomas theorem: "If men [*sic*] define situations as real, they are real in their consequences" (p. 572).[4] Franklin Tannenbaum, an early labeling theorist, referred to this as the "dramatization of evil."[5] Tannenbaum's focus was on youth behavior. He argued that police reactions to the ordinary rule-breaking behaviors of adolescents construct them as deviant or "bad." The social interplay of the adolescent and the police (the drama) is what creates the "evil," not the act itself. For instance, imagine two friends who get into an argument at school that leads to shoving and then punches being thrown. Are these just teenagers blowing off steam or are they criminals committing assault? It depends on whether they end up in the principal's office or the backseat of a police cruiser. And where they end up depends on how school authorities and the police already view them. "Good kids" get the principal's office, "bad kids" get the police cruiser.[6]

Deviant labeling, thus, operates as a kind of *self-fulfilling prophecy*. By defining a situation or person in a particular way (e.g., as dangerous or criminal), people set into motion a series of future circumstances—like heightened police scrutiny and arrest—that shapes the labeled person into the image that others have of them.[7] The definition makes it so.

Primary Versus Secondary Deviance

Edwin Lemert elaborated on Tannenbaum's ideas, discerning between primary and secondary deviance.[8] **Primary deviance** is rule-breaking that individuals engage in in the absence of a deviant label. They do not regard themselves as deviant, nor—so far—do others. Primary deviance is ordinary, and most of it goes undetected. But sometimes it is identified and reacted to as deviant. Further rule-breaking behavior that occurs *as a result of a deviant label* is called **secondary deviance**. In labeling theory, the label itself causes an increase in deviant or criminal conduct. This process is called deviance amplification. Labeling theory explains secondary deviance, or deviance amplification.

To illustrate, let's imagine there are two people attending a party. Both get behind the wheel after drinking too much. Both cause an accident involving another driver who is badly injured. Person A drives away from the scene and is not caught. Person B cannot drive away from the scene because his car was badly damaged in the collision. Person B is arrested and ultimately pleads guilty to felony DUI with injury. As a result, person B is sentenced to 12 months in state prison and now has a felony record. The drunk driving that led to the label of "felon" for person B (and didn't for person A) was primary deviance. According to the labeling perspective, the felon label will increase the risk that person B will go on to engage in other criminal acts, or secondary deviance. Person A, in comparison, avoided a deviant label that would increase her likelihood of future rule-breaking.[9]

Deviant Labels and Stigma

The label of felon in the drunk driving example is a formal label. **Formal labels** are labels applied by an authority, such as the state (e.g., felon, delinquent, sex offender), the military (e.g., dishonorably discharged), a school (e.g., truant), or a medical facility (e.g., HIV positive). Formal labels are official. Because they are documented by recognized authorities, formal labels are difficult to shed and have important consequences for obtaining resources, such as jobs and housing. **Informal labels**, in contrast, occur when a person has been deemed deviant by family members, teachers, coworkers, neighbors, or members of the public. Informal labels are unofficial, yet they still affect how people are treated.

Both formal and informal labels can be stigmatizing. **Stigma** is a mark of disgrace, and interactions that communicate that one is disgraced, dishonorable, or otherwise deviant are stigmatizing. Once labeled a criminal, others believe that the stigmatized person is unable to "act as a moral being and therefore might break other important rules" (p. 34).[10] Any rule-breaking—in the past and in the future—is interpreted as evidence of the labeled person's "essential criminal nature" (p. 180).[11] They *are* their stigma.

In some instances, the deviant label—or spoiled identity—becomes a **master status**, or the primary status by which others interact with a person. In the case of a deviant master status, the "negative images attached to the deviant label ... override other attributes a person might have" (p. 180).[12] Master statuses are sticky; they adhere to the person no matter the situation or context of interaction. Labels such as "sex offender" or "murderer" are particularly likely to become master statuses because of the extent of the stigma assigned to them.[13]

"Sex offender" is a formal label that confers stigma and often acts as a master status.

Miami Herald/Tribune News Service/Getty Images

Reflected Appraisals and Role Engulfment

The stigmatizing reactions of both official authorities and everyday people matter for secondary deviance because they can alter self-concept (through reflected appraisals) and produce role engulfment. In reflected appraisals, people form a sense of self based on others' opinions of them, or what they believe to be others' opinions of them.[14] They think they are what other people tell them they are. It helps to consider what is meant by the words "reflected" and "appraisals." Appraising is assessing or determining the value of something. When people appraise others negatively or in stigmatizing ways—interacting with them as though they are a "problem," "crazy," "stupid," or "bad"—it is like they are holding up a mirror, showing the person who they are. The labeled person then reflects back the negative image they have seen in the mirror.

Role engulfment occurs when the deviant role takes over people's other social roles. This happens because people relate to them according to their "spoiled identity."[15] They become immersed in (or engulfed by) the deviant role. Role engulfment entails processes of (1) social exclusion, (2) social withdrawal, and (3) involvement in deviant subcultures. Imagine a person who has just been released from prison after serving time for a violent offense. Others may—to the extent that they know about the spoiled identity—relate to them based on their "former inmate" or "violent criminal" status, including property owners who won't rent to them, employers who won't hire them, and people who won't date them. In other words, they are denied access to conventional social life—to housing, to jobs, to relationships. That is social exclusion.

Anticipating that others will devalue, distrust, and reject them, a labeled person may avoid interactions with "normal" (non-labeled) people. The person in our example may not even apply for the job in the first place, expecting to be turned away and wishing to avoid the embarrassment and discomfort of the interaction. Sociologist of stigma, Erving Goffman, noted that "the anticipation of such contacts can … lead normals and the stigmatized to arrange life so as to avoid them" (p. 13).[16] That is social withdrawal.

For the labeled person who is socially excluded or socially withdrawn, the only source of companionship and support often comes from other labeled persons. The labeled person may seek out, or find themselves a part of, a deviant subculture that celebrates or at least tolerates spoiled identities. When conventional society rejects, a community of similarly labeled others offers acceptance.

Labeling, Social Location, and Discrimination

Social location, which refers to where one resides in a system of social stratification or inequality, is central in the labeling perspective. The power to define others as deviant and to resist having the label applied to oneself is linked to social position. Those with greater power—for example, politicians, professionals, and other members of the upper-middle and upper classes—are better able to resist deviant labeling, even when their behavior does not differ from that of the less-powerful "deviant." This can be seen clearly by comparing the results of two criminological works.

In his book *Human Targets*, Victor Rios describes the daily lives and interactions of low-income Latinx teenagers in a southern California city.[17] The teenagers deal with stigmatization, humiliation, and harassment by adult authority figures like teachers, school administrators, and police who presume they are "bad kids," gang members, and criminals. And they shift their identities and performance of self across settings in response to how they are regarded. The teenagers—marginalized economically, educationally, and racially and ethnically—understand from a young age that they are defined as a problem. One 16-year-old respondent who had been expelled for fighting described the labeling this way:

> I think they [teachers] feel that like white kids are like better… like Mexican kids are, I guess, like gang-related and I think they think they're like bad influences, and they think we're not like smart. They think that like white kids are… smart, and they're like good kids, they're like good influences… You could tell how the teachers are like how they look at you before you even start dressing different. (p. 18)[18]

Rios notes that labeling adolescents as "criminals" and "bad influences" creates a self-fulfilling prophecy. Degrading interactions with authority figures drive the youths in Rios's study to adopt negative identities, rejecting school and propelling them towards criminal activity. For example, one 16-year-old respondent reported his reaction to an incident in which he was assumed to be a bad student because he is Mexican:

> *I felt like shit, so I just skip school. Go to a friend's house, help my parents with work, do drugs, fucking just go look for fights, go to Beach Street. Just anything rather than school. I hate school.* (p. 18)[19]

Sociologist Michael Salinas examines a different group of young people: 25 mostly white, "conventional" British drug dealers in their mid-20s, whom he calls "the Lads." Unlike the teenagers in *Human Targets*, the young men in Salinas's study—aptly titled "The Unusual Suspects"—are "unpoliced and unpunished" (p. 239).[20] The Lads grew up in stable families with a range of incomes, engaged in extensive petty delinquency (mostly undetected) during adolescence, and went on to earn university degrees, start legal businesses, and hold down professional jobs while trafficking (wholesaling, brokering, importing, and exporting) cocaine, cannabis, ketamine, and MDMA on the side. In their conventional lives, they are financial advisors, human resource managers, small business owners, and graduate students. They are regarded as upstanding citizens, and they experience no negative consequences of their law-breaking behavior. The Lads see their drug trafficking as profit-generating entrepreneurship secondary to their professional lives, and they view themselves "as part of an aspiring and upwardly mobile working class," not as criminals (p. 231).[21] Their privileges of wealth, race, and place enable them to resist detection and stigmatizing labeling.

What if the Lads were to be caught and punished? Salinas contends that a formal label (which none had, in fact, experienced) would be unlikely to consign the Lads to the lowest rung of the social hierarchy:

> *It may be the case that The Lads were merely one arrest or custody term away from being like those marginalized agents [poor, incarcerated young men involved in "street crime"] ... Yet, they were each privy to a range of protective features that would have likely lessened the collateral consequences of a drug conviction, including having vocational or academic qualifications, work experience, and supportive parents who could provide stable housing if needed.* (p. 238)

In other words, a formal label would likely prove less detrimental to the Lads because they are well-positioned socially.

Rios's and Salinas's qualitative results match what labeling theorists write about stereotypes, discrimination, and the risk of being labeled. Stereotypes are overgeneralized and oversimplified beliefs about members of a group, such that all members are assumed to share particular characteristics. Discrimination is unequal treatment of individuals or groups based on actual or perceived traits (e.g., race, socioeconomic status, age, or disability), often fueled by stereotypes. The labeling process contributes to stereotyping and discrimination. For example, patients labeled as addicts report stigmatizing encounters with hospital staff who presume that they are drug-seeking, dishonest, and taking the spot of a more deserving patient—even when seeking treatment for medical problems unrelated to their substance use.[22]

Labeling is also an outcome of unequal treatment. Consider, for example, the formal label that comes with an arrest and conviction for marijuana possession (in states where possession remains illegal, as well as in the federal system). Marijuana possession arrest rates are 3.6 times higher for Black persons in the U.S. than white persons, despite nearly identical rates of use; the gap is much larger in some states than others (e.g., 2.4 times greater in Arkansas versus 9.4 times greater in Kentucky).[23] Plus, racial disparities in arrests—and formal labels—persist in states with marijuana decriminalization and legalization.[24] The drivers of these inequalities include heightened police attention to and stops of people in majority-Black neighborhoods as well as police stops of Black persons regardless of community characteristics.[25] In other words, racial profiling of places and individuals produces inequality in criminal labels not attributable to differences in substance possession.

Howard Becker refers to those labeled as deviant or criminal despite the absence of any actual deviant or criminal behavior as the "falsely accused."[26] Marginalized, or relatively powerless, members of society are at greatest risk of being falsely accused. As Table 11.1 notes, Becker described those who engage in deviance or crime as "pure deviants," as the label is a true reflection of their actions. The British drug dealers in the "The Unusual Suspects" were what Becker called "secret deviants," because they avoided detection and labeling. Conformists, in contrast, do not engage in deviant behavior and are not labeled (we might also conceive of conformists as "pure nondeviants").

TABLE 11.1 ■ Becker's Typology of Deviance

	Deviant behavior	Conforming behavior
Labeled deviant	Pure deviant	Falsely accused
Not labeled deviant	Secret deviant	Conformist

ENGAGED CRIMINOLOGY 11.1
Criminal Activities Checklist

This activity is designed to get you thinking about experiences with labeling—or lack thereof. Examine the list of activities. Put a mental checkmark next to each one you have participated in at least once (when at least age 14). Only count an act one time even if you have engaged in it multiple times. *Your instructor will not ask you to submit your checklist responses.* When you are done, you will add up the total number of checkmarks to obtain a value between 0 and 22, which you and your classmates will submit anonymously to observe the total distribution for the whole class.

1. _____ Gave someone a broken nose, black eye, or other injury during a fight

2. _____ Attempted, unsuccessfully, to cause physical injury to another person (e.g., by hitting, kicking, throwing objects)

3. _____ Intentionally damaged the property of another without their consent and the damage is less than $500

4. _____ Entered a "No Trespass" area without the owner's permission

5. _____ Entered and remained in another person's home, car, or place of business without that person's permission

6. _____ Shoplifted minor articles; items worth less than $500 total

7. _____ Kept lost or mislaid money or property (e.g., lost wallet)

8. _____ Received, disposed of, or retained property that you knew or believed was stolen

9. _____ Performed, offered, or consented to, an act of sexual intercourse for money, or paid money for sexual services where such transactions are not legal

10. _____ Disseminated content to anyone (via text, social media) that would be considered obscene by a majority of your community members

11. _____ Used electronic communications (phone, text, email, or social media) repeatedly to threaten, terrify, harass, or embarrass another person

12. _____ If you were 18 years of age or older and had sex with someone who was between the ages of 13 and 16

13. _____ Urinated in public

14. _____ Made a bet for money on the final result of any game

15. _____ Lied to a police officer

16. _____	Drove in such a way that could have been considered in reckless disregard of others
17. _____	Driven after you've had enough to drink to register .08 (alcohol concentration) when 21 or older
18. _____	Driven after you've had any alcohol to drink when age 20 or younger
18. _____	Purchased or been in possession of prescription medication (e.g., Adderall, Xanax) not prescribed to you
19. _____	Purchased or been in possession of less than one ounce of marijuana where illegal for anyone or for a person your age
20. _____	Purchased or been in possession of less than one ounce of cocaine, MDMA/ecstasy, hallucinogenic mushrooms, LSD, or other narcotics
21. _____	Have, under the age of 21, been in possession of alcohol
22. _____	Other act(s) you knew to be illegal

Total number of checkmarks = _____

Answer the following questions:

1. Examine the distribution for the class, including the average score. What can you conclude about college students' involvement in criminal activities?

2. In one or two sentences, apply at least one key term from labeling theory to your observations during this exercise. (Keys terms include primary deviance, secondary deviance, stigma, master status, role engulfment, reflected appraisals, falsely accused, secret deviance, and social location.)

Source: Adapted from Woodall, D. (2017). Interrupting constructions of a criminalized other through a revised criminal activities checklist classroom exercise. *Teaching Sociology, 45*(2), 161-167.

Example: Sex Offender Residence Restrictions

Sex offender residence restrictions, which more than half of U.S. states have on the books, limit where people who have been convicted of sex offenses can live. They typically specify a certain distance—typically ranging from 500 to 2,000 feet—from areas where children congregate, such as schools, daycares, churches, youth centers, playgrounds, or bus stops.[27] Some state restrictions, like Alabama's, apply to people convicted of any sex offense; others, like Indiana's, apply only to certain people convicted of sex offenses, usually those with minor victims. The purpose of residence restrictions is social exclusion above and beyond the exclusion generated by a felony record. Georgia House Majority Leader Jerry Keen, who cosponsored the residence restriction bill passed into Georgia law, made this goal explicit, stating:

> *My intent personally is to make it so onerous on those that are convicted of these offenses that when they are paroled and when they are released, they will want to move to another state.*[28]

Social exclusion is especially apparent in Miami-Dade County, Florida, where strict residence restrictions make it nearly impossible for people convicted of sex offenses to live anywhere in the county. In fact, only 0.05% of residences in the county are outside restricted zones, though even this sliver of available locations is largely inaccessible due to property costs and unwilling landlords.[29] People convicted of sex offenses are also barred from using homeless shelters in Miami-Dade County.[30] The law has resulted in the emergence of "sex offender colonies," comprised of tents and makeshift cardboard structures. They are found in areas not meant for human habitation, like under the Julia Tuttle Causeway (a highway) and in an industrial zone near the Miami International Airport. Colony residents, like many homeless populations, are often forced to relocate.[31]

Concepts from labeling theory help us to understand sex offender residence restrictions and their consequences, intended or otherwise. The master status of "sex offender," a formal label, transforms social interactions (e.g., with potential landlords and employers), even after a prison or probation term has ended. Residence restrictions create legal barriers to conventional life, like finding an apartment or a job, which contributes to role engulfment through social exclusion and social withdrawal. Sex offender communities, like the encampment under the highway, offer acceptance when everyone else regards the person as a social pariah (i.e., involvement in a deviant subculture).

Sex offender laws are, according to their proponents, intended to reduce recidivism by limiting interactions between convicted persons and children. Labeling theory, in contrast, suggests that the sex offender label might, in fact, lead to greater recidivism, or secondary deviance. Which is correct? Researchers conclude, first, that residence restrictions do not make children any safer, nor do they have the potential to do so.[32] There are a number of reasons. One is that residence restrictions only apply to detected and convicted persons (a small proportion of all who commit these crimes). Second, the restrictions do little to prevent the most common types of sex offenses against children (i.e., crimes committed within homes by family members, acquaintances, neighbors, and others known to the child).[33] Sex offender laws do, however, increase conditions that make future law-breaking more likely.[34] Specifically, they increase joblessness, homelessness, and frequent moves.[35] When people convicted of sex offenses are able to access housing, it tends to be in socially disorganized, crime-prone communities.[36] The general ineffectiveness of sexual offender residence restrictions in reducing recidivism leads criminologists to conclude that the laws are largely symbolic, or that their purpose is to "express societal disdain for sex offenders and mandate the physical manifestation of that disdain through exclusion" (p. 231).[37] In other words, to label.

SCHOOL-TO-PRISON PIPELINE

Between the first day of kindergarten and graduation day 13 years later, U.S. children spend roughly 15,000 hours in school, about a quarter of their waking hours. Unsurprisingly, then, school is an essential site of children's "socialization, social sorting, and social control" (p. 150).[38] Schools can shape young people in prosocial ways, building valuable skills, fostering social bonds, and granting credentials that open doors to future opportunities. Schools can also prime students for prison when they are a source of stigmatizing labeling, criminalization, deviant identity formation, and rejection. Students most vulnerable to these harms—children of color, children with disabilities, children who attend resource-poor schools—may end up in the school-to-prison pipeline.

The school-to-prison pipeline describes "the policies and practices that push our nation's school children ... out of the classrooms and into the juvenile and criminal justice system" (p. 1).[39] The pipeline metaphor captures the idea that there is a flow of people from one institution (school) to another (juvenile or adult criminal legal system). Researchers describe mass incarceration—the massive growth in the size of the incarcerated population in the U.S. over the past several decades—as the result of parallel moves towards greater punitiveness in criminal justice and in educational settings.[40] As the criminal legal system became more extreme in handling rule violators, so, too, did schools.

Some argue that the pipeline metaphor doesn't adequately capture the complexities of a system that is more akin to a "web of intertwined, punitive threads" than a pipeline (p. 31).[41] Criminologists describe two major shifts in school policies and practices—or punitive threads—that push students, and especially low-income students of color and students with disabilities, into the juvenile and adult criminal legal systems: (1) exclusionary discipline and (2) policing in schools.[42]

Exclusionary Discipline

Exclusionary discipline refers to school disciplinary practices that push students out of, or exclude them from, the normal classroom setting. Suspensions and expulsions are types of exclusionary discipline, as are transfers to alternative schools. Students who have been expelled or transferred for disciplinary reasons frequently end up in alternative educational settings (i.e., schools specifically for chronically disruptive or failing students), where academic standards are low and dropout rates are high.[43] Exclusionary discipline increases the chances that a young person will end up in the criminal legal system.[44]

Zero-tolerance policies were a major driver of the rise in exclusionary discipline. These policies proscribe harsh responses—usually out-of-school suspension or expulsion on the first offense—to student rule violations regardless of the contexts in which they occurred. For example, under zero-tolerance policies, the punishment is the same for a student who brings a knife to school to threaten classmates as it is for a student who brings a knife to school for self-protection because they were violently attacked on their walk home from school the week before.

When first adopted in the 1990s, zero-tolerance policies applied primarily to serious instances of school violence, aligning with federal regulations laid out in the Gun Free Schools Act of 1994.[45] Soon after, in the wake of the 1999 Columbine school shooting, states and localities extended zero-tolerance policies to all manner of school infractions, including nonviolent and noncriminal acts (e.g., smoking cigarettes or fighting). By the 2000s, zero-tolerance policies "became a practice of doling out mandatory, pre-determined punishments for disruptive students who violated school rules, regardless of mitigating circumstances" (p. 62).[46] Suspensions and expulsions shot up, and schools began referring students to law enforcement for arrest.[47]

How much did exclusionary discipline increase? Between 1974 and 2000, a period of increasingly punitive school policies, the rate of out-of-school suspensions increased more than 80%.[48] The suspension rate has remained high since then, with about 2 million high school students suspended each year, though it has decreased somewhat in recent years as school districts have scaled back their reliance on zero-tolerance policies.[49] One way to examine the exclusionary effect of out-of-school suspensions is to calculate the numbers of instructional days lost. An analysis of the U.S. Department of Education's Civil Rights Data Collection showed that U.S. students lost more than 11 million days of school due to suspensions in a single academic year, or 23 instructional days lost per 100 students.[50]

There is a large racial gap in suspensions and exclusions in the United States. Black male students are the most likely to be suspended, with a suspension rate that is three times greater than that for white male students. The racial gap is even larger for female students, with Black female students suspended at a rate that is six times that of white female students.[51] The number of lost days of instruction also varies by race, as well as by disability status. As seen in Figure 11.1, the greatest losses were observed for Black students, who lost 4.7 times as many days as white students (66 days vs. 14 days per 100 students), and Native American and Pacific Islander students (31 and 30 days vs. 14 days per 100 students). Students with disabilities lost more than twice the instructional days of students without disabilities (44 days vs. 20 days per 100 students).

You may be imagining a surly 16-year-old when thinking about suspensions and expulsions. Yet exclusionary discipline, including racial disciplinary gaps, begins much earlier, observed even in preschool.[52] This has prompted some scholars to use the expression "cradle-to-prison pipeline."[53] Prekindergarten children experience "soft suspension" and "soft expulsion," which are informal mechanisms for excluding young children whose developmentally typical behavior (e.g., biting, tantrums, noncompliance) is labeled as problematic. Soft suspension occurs when parents are frequently called to pick up their children early due to behavioral issues. If this occurs many times, it can lead to soft expulsion as parents can no longer risk missing work for early pickups. Soft expulsion also occurs when parents are told that their children are "not a good fit" for the early childhood program or that the program can "no longer support" their children.[54] Children experiencing trauma in the home, such as domestic violence or parental substance abuse, are at heightened risk of being suspended and expelled from preschools,[55] as are children with disabilities.[56]

Racial gaps in suspension and expulsion are observed at every age, from preschool to senior year, and they grow wider as children get older.[57] Black students and Native American students, in particular, and Latinx students to a lesser extent, are referred to the principal's office, suspended, and expelled at higher rates than white and Asian students.[58] Of course, it is possible that differences in discipline reflect differences in school misconduct. Importantly, though, these higher rates are not explained away by dissimilarity in misbehavior. Researchers find that racial and ethnic gaps persist even when controlling for student fighting, substance use, cheating, and attitudes towards rule-breaking.[59]

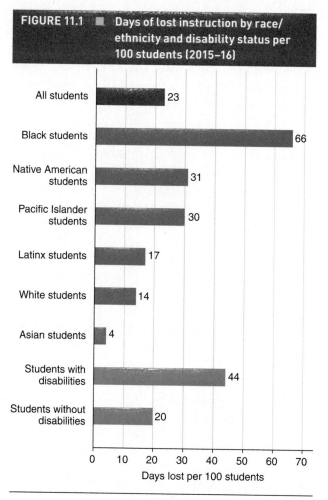

FIGURE 11.1 ■ Days of lost instruction by race/ethnicity and disability status per 100 students (2015–16)

Days lost per 100 students

- All students: 23
- Black students: 66
- Native American students: 31
- Pacific Islander students: 30
- Latinx students: 17
- White students: 14
- Asian students: 4
- Students with disabilities: 44
- Students without disabilities: 20

Source: Losen, D., & Whitaker, A. (2018). *11 million days lost: Race, discipline, and safety at U.S. public schools* (Part 1). American Civil Liberties Union, Center for Civil Rights Remedies. https://www.aclu.org/sites/default/files/field_document/final_11-million-days_ucla_aclu.pdf

Demonstrators holding signs that read "End the Preschool to Prison Pipeline" and "Black Families Matter" at a protest in Brooklyn, NY, in June 2020

Erik McGregor/LightRocket/Getty Images

Criminologists and education scholars offer alternative explanations for the racial gaps in suspension and expulsion, with most studies focused on the Black-white gap. The first explanation centers on teachers. Teachers' perceptions of students, formed in elementary school, follow students as they move on to middle and high school. These perceptions are racially conditioned, with teachers evaluating minor misbehavior—like talking back, dress code violations, and disruptive behavior—as more threatening, and therefore warranting an office referral, when the student is Black.[60] Teachers who have internalized stereotypes of Black students as "threatening or dangerous may react more quickly to relatively minor threats to authority, especially if fears are paired with a misunderstanding of cultural norms of social interaction" (p. 12).[61] This effect disappears when Black students have Black teachers.[62]

The second explanation focuses on school context. Black, Native American, and Latinx students are more likely than white students to be concentrated in highly punitive schools that employ zero-tolerance policies.[63] For example, in a study of Indiana schools, researchers found that suspension rates increase along with the proportion of students in a school district who are Black, as seen in Figure 11.2.[64] This finding is in line with the **minority threat hypothesis**, which states that a dominant group's social control efforts increase as the proportion of minority group members goes up.[65] Similarly, a study in Arizona found that schools with higher rates of Black, Native American, and Latinx students are less likely to use mild and restorative discipline, such as referring students to intervention programs, though they didn't find support for the minority threat hypothesis when examining suspensions and expulsions.[66] In sum, the racial composition of schools predicts how students are disciplined, though not uniformly across locations.

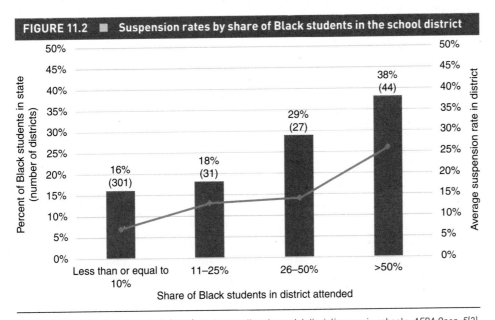

FIGURE 11.2 ■ Suspension rates by share of Black students in the school district

Source: Gopalan, M., & Nelson, A. A. (2019). Understanding the racial discipline gap in schools. *AERA Open, 5*(2), 1-26.

Notes: Number of school districts are in parentheses. Left-hand Y-axis and percentages depict the share of Black students in Indiana who attend school in each district type (e.g., 38% of Black students attend school district in which >50% of students are Black). The right-hand Y-axis and line graph display the average suspension rates in each district type (e.g., >25% of students in districts that are majority-Black are suspended annually).

Exclusionary discipline is criminogenic. Students who are suspended or expelled are substantially more likely than other students to be arrested and incarcerated.[67] It is possible, of course, that the correlation between exclusionary discipline and legal system involvement is spurious, or noncausal. Perhaps suspended teenagers and arrested 20-somethings are drawn from the same high-risk pool of rule-breakers (called selection effects). Yet studies reveal that suspended and expelled students are more likely to be arrested when compared to similarly behaved peers who avoided getting caught and punished.[68] Another possibility is that the school infraction is what triggered the arrest in the first place. Though this is certainly the case for some arrested youth, examinations of the timing of school discipline and arrests reveal that this does not drive the correlation between exclusionary discipline and legal system involvement.[69] In other words, the relationship is causal.

So *why* is it causal? What is it about getting suspended or expelled that propels young people towards (greater) criminal involvement? There are several mechanisms at work, each linked to exclusion. For one thing, suspended and expelled young people spend time away from school, unsupervised.[70] More importantly, though, exclusionary discipline attaches stigmatizing labels to "problem students," including official documentation in school records and informal labels that influence treatment by school administrators, teachers, parents, and other students.[71] And suspended and expelled students are well-aware of how others perceive them (as seen in the chapter's introductory quotes). After interviewing suspended and alternative school students for her book *Prelude to Prison*, sociologist Marsha Weissman concluded:

> The experience of public punishment sends powerful messages to youth about their value, about humiliation, and degradation, invading their sense of worth. The suspension process conveys a clear sense of how other authoritative entities see them. (p. 183)[72]

The experience of rejection and "dismissal of [their] essential humanity" leaves punished students feeling like others are waiting for them to make a mistake and it severs their bond to school (p. 183).[73] It is little surprise, then, that dropout rates—a predictor of arrest and incarceration—are much higher for students who have been suspended.[74] Students who are discouraged from continuing to attend school as a result of exclusionary and biased disciplinary practices are "pushouts," a term that more accurately captures the process leading up to school-leaving.[75] Plus, even if they stay enrolled, they face rejection by conventional peers, turning instead to delinquent friendship groups for acceptance.[76] In sum, exclusionary discipline acts as a negative turning point in the life course.[77]

Police in Schools

In 1976, police were stationed in only 1% of U.S. schools.[78] By 2016, 48% of U.S. schools had police present in the school at least once per week, and the percentage rose to 65% among high schools.[79] The National Association of School Resource Officers describes three main roles of police officers who work in schools, called school resource officers (SROs): (1) educator (e.g., informing students about transportation safety and alcohol and drug risks); (2) informal counselor (e.g., building rapport with students, having an "open-door" policy for those seeking help, and making social service referrals); and (3) law enforcer (e.g., patrolling the school, issuing citations, and making arrests).

Does police presence in schools heighten the risk of student arrest? There are several possibilities. If police have a deterrent effect on in-school crime, then their presence could, in theory, reduce arrests. Alternatively, their presence might increase arrests as teachers and school administrators hand over responsibility for school discipline to law enforcement.[80] Analyses of nationally representative data from schools with and without SROs (and before and after the introduction of SROs) reveal that police presence, generally, boosts student arrests, with the largest effects observed for Black students and boys.[81] This matters because students who are arrested are less likely than other, similar students (who avoided arrest) to graduate high school.[82] They are also more likely to go on to be arrested and incarcerated in adulthood.[83]

Recent criminological research tells a more nuanced story about the impact of police in schools. It turns out that not all police presence leads to greater punitiveness. School administrators and SROs vary in their attitudes towards the "get-tough" approach—some embrace it while others are more support-oriented (e.g., favoring counseling over arrest). When police and the schools they work in adopt the same approach, they tend to achieve their shared goal of punitiveness or support. But sometimes they are not aligned. When support-oriented SROs work in punishment-focused schools, they prevent school administrators from pushing students into the justice system.[84] In short, police presence, on average, increases student arrests, but this need not always be the case.

Alternative Approaches

Zero-tolerance policies were, in part, a reaction to high-profile instances of serious violent crime at schools. Mass shootings, like those at Marjory Stoneman Douglas High School (Parkland, FL) and

Santa Fe High School (Santa Fe, TX), both in 2018, continue to compel politicians and school boards to "double down on zero tolerance" and policing in schools despite calls for reform.[85] The school-to-prison pipeline is a consequence of these punitive, exclusionary practices, especially when implemented in schools that are disproportionately Black and Latinx.[86] Yet, the mass violence in Florida, Texas, and elsewhere is a stark reminder that some students pose a serious threat to their classmates. School threat assessments are an alternative to zero-tolerance policies that permit identification of "high-risk" students in need of intervention.

Students are referred for threat assessments if they threaten violence or engage in threatening acts, such as bringing weapons to school. The goals of threat assessments are to determine the seriousness of the threat (i.e., Do they intend to commit violence, or are they blowing off steam?) and to resolve student conflicts peacefully.[87] Threat assessment teams are comprised of school administrators, mental health professionals, and SROs who interview the student, witnesses, and others to get a full picture of the circumstances leading up to the threat or the act. The outcomes of an assessment can be disciplinary (suspension or expulsion) or nondisciplinary, such as a referral for mental health counseling.[88] If zero-tolerance policies are a sledgehammer (knocking down all in their path), school threat assessments are a scalpel. Their goal is to reserve exclusionary discipline, when deemed appropriate, for only the most serious cases.

Let's switch up the metaphor. One-size-fits-all discipline (like zero-tolerance) casts a wide net that captures many more guppies than sharks. School threat assessments seek to weed out the sharks—or potential sharks. But how should schools respond to the rule violators who don't pose a serious public safety threat (the guppies)? Some school systems have piloted programs that treat student misbehavior as an indicator of need rather than badness. One such diversion program is the Safety Net Collaborative in Cambridge, Massachusetts. Diversion programs move people out of—or divert them away from—the criminal legal system and into programs that can meet their needs, thereby attending to the underlying causes of their law-breaking.[89] Cambridge youth who engage in nonviolent offending, either in school or in the community, are eligible for diversion through the Safety Net Collaborative. They are assigned a Youth Resource Officer (YRO) who works with the school and the student's family to create a diversion plan, linking them to services (including mental health services, family and foster family support, and mentoring programs) and setting expectations for reparation to the community or victims through mediation, community service, or restitution. As a result, community juvenile arrests in Cambridge decreased by half.[90]

Diversion programs like the one in Cambridge adopt a restorative justice approach, which is rooted in the idea that justice requires more than just punishing rule violators (see Chapter 13 for more on restorative justice). Instead, justice is achieved when harms to victims, offenders, and communities are repaired. As one scholar describes it,

A restorative philosophy emphasizes problem-solving approaches to discipline, attends to the social/emotional as well as the physical/intellectual needs of students, recognizes the importance of the group to establish and practice agreed-upon norms and rules, and emphasizes prevention and early restorative intervention to create safe learning environments. (p. 10)[91]

EFFECTS OF A CRIMINAL RECORD

Criminal records are common in the United States. By 2018, there were 112,450,300 individual offender arrest records on file with police, which is more than double the number 20 years prior.[92] The true number of people with arrest records is somewhat lower than 112,450,300 as some individuals have arrest records in more than one state and the tally includes some people who are now deceased. However, even if we eliminate 10 million individual records to obtain a more conservative estimate, more than 3 in 10 people in the U.S. have an arrest history, as do 4 in 10 people age 18 and older (though some people with arrest records are under age 18). For perspective, the proportion of adults (age 25 and older) in the U.S. who have a bachelor's degree falls between these values (37.5% in 2020).[93] By 2010, 20 million people in the U.S. had a felony conviction under their belts, or 1 in 12 adults in the population.[94] By 2019, that number had risen to an estimated 24 million people, still representing roughly 8% of adults (or 1 in 12 adults) in the U.S.[95]

Criminal records apply stigmatizing labels that follow people as they search for jobs, look for housing, make plans to return to school, and—depending on the state—head to the voting booth. Some of these impediments are formalized, with state and federal laws or corporate policies preventing access to persons with felony records. These are called collateral consequences.

Collateral consequences are "legal and regulatory restrictions that limit or prohibit people convicted of crimes from accessing employment, business and occupational licensing, housing, voting, education, and other rights, benefits, and opportunities."[96] Some collateral consequences serve essential public safety functions, such as preventing people with violent felony records from purchasing firearms and prohibiting people with child abuse convictions from working with children. Others lack an apparent legitimate public safety purpose, such as the loss of or inability to obtain a cosmetology or commercial fishing license for persons with prior convictions for drug possession.

Other effects of criminal records operate informally, with individual decision-makers, such as rental property managers and business owners, simply favoring applicants with clean records. In these cases, decision-makers act as gatekeepers who use their discretion in identifying quality candidates. Criminal records may become known to gatekeepers through required disclosure on applications, through online background checks, or both.[97]

Criminal records influence decisions—for example, to hire or rent to someone—because they communicate, or are presumed to communicate, something about a person's character, particularly when little else is known about them. They are a type of credential. Sociologists distinguish between positive and negative credentials. Positive credentials are formalized accomplishments or markers that improve life circumstances, such as a high school diploma, college degree, or an occupational license.[98] They provide "proof of ability or trustworthiness" (p. 37).[99] People with negative credentials, in contrast, are "institutionally branded" as untrustworthy, irresponsible, or dangerous. They are "deeply discredited" (p. 3).[100] A criminal record is a formalized negative credential; other examples include bankruptcy or a dishonorable discharge from the military.

You may wonder: What goes in a criminal record? Any formally recorded criminal history. This includes arrests (regardless of whether the person was convicted) and convictions (misdemeanors and felonies), as well as charges pending or dismissed. Criminal records are maintained by law enforcement agencies, and these data are widely available to the public and employers—for free or for a fee—through third-party providers (i.e., background check companies).[101] Some formalized rules apply only to felony convictions, such as state voting restrictions. Minor criminal record details, like misdemeanor arrests without conviction, can influence outcomes when decision-makers are able to exercise discretion.[102]

Derek Hobbs, who has a criminal record, struggled to find employment before participating in the innovative West Philadelphia Skills Initiative (WPSI), which provided training and matched him with a job in his local community.

Dominick Reuter/AFP/Getty Images

Criminal Records and Employment

Tyrone Williams and Matthew O'Brien, both 30-year-old high school graduates living in Columbus, Ohio, are applying for entry-level jobs, including jobs at restaurants, hotels, call centers, and retail establishments. The men have identical work histories. Both have a year-old felony drug conviction. They have each applied to about 100 positions. Except Tyrone Williams and Matthew O'Brien don't exist. They are characters created by a researcher for an experimental study.[103] The job openings were real. The applications and résumés were real—or so it appeared to the hiring managers. The callbacks and job offers were real (few as they were). And there were other versions of Tyrone Williams and Matthew O'Brien. These alternate men had either no criminal record or a year-old misdemeanor drug conviction—everything else about them was the same. Only two characteristics differed across the fictional applicants: (1) their criminal record status (none, misdemeanor drug conviction, felony drug conviction) and (2) their race, as it is likely to be interpreted based on their names.

Experimental studies like this one allow criminologists to determine the impact of a criminal record on hiring, as well as whether criminal records are more or less detrimental based on the applicant's race or ethnicity. Their results help policymakers understand the need for reforms that improve outcomes not just for applicants with criminal records but for the public at large. After all, gainful employment is essential for reducing recidivism, which makes everyone safer.[104] The massive scale of criminal records among the U.S. population transforms this concern from a private trouble into a public issue.

Figure 11.3 displays the results of the Tyrone Williams/Matthew O'Brien study. The findings are consistent with the results from research conducted in other regions of the country.[105] Some studies, like the one described earlier, are correspondence tests, involving online or mailed applications. Others are audit studies in which matched pairs of people (played by actors) apply for jobs in person.[106] Together, these experiments tell a cohesive story about the effects of criminal records on the search for employment, including the following:

- A criminal record weakens job prospects significantly.[107]

- The more serious the criminal record is, the more detrimental its impact is—felonies, convictions, and violent histories are more ruinous than misdemeanors, arrests, and drug histories.[108]

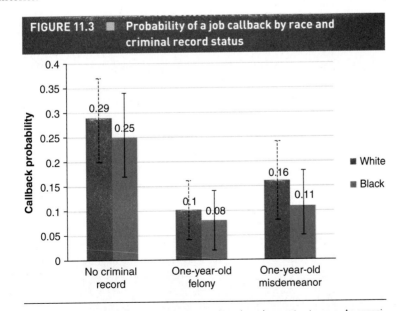

FIGURE 11.3 ■ Probability of a job callback by race and criminal record status

Source: Leasure, P. (2019). Misdemeanor records and employment outcomes: An experimental study. Crime & Delinquency, 65(13), 1850-1872.

- Black and Latinx applicants receive fewer callbacks than white applicants, such that Black applicants with criminal records are the least likely to make it to the next stage of hiring and white applicants without a criminal record are the most likely to hear back from prospective employers.[109] Racial gaps at the initial callback stage tend to be smaller when applications are submitted online.[110]

- Positive credentials, like a favorable letter from a previous employer, can counter the stigma of a criminal record in hiring.[111]

- Applicants with criminal records fare better when they have the opportunity to build rapport with hiring managers by interacting with them in person.[112]

Occupational licensing bans are an additional barrier to employment for people with criminal records. Many occupations—from barber to tree trimmer to real estate agent—require licenses. Nearly one in four jobs in the U.S. requires an occupational license. Licensing requirements are intended to protect consumers' health and safety by creating hurdles to employment, including training, testing, and required fees for licensure.[113] Licensing laws vary from state to state, with some state laws explicitly barring employment for people with criminal records. In other cases, licensing authorities are granted the power to deny license applicants because they have a criminal record, in accordance with a "moral character" requirement.[114]

Criminal Records, Housing, and Education

People with criminal records who wish to improve their job prospects through higher education may find themselves shut out at higher rates than other applicants.[115] Put differently, a negative credential (criminal record) creates barriers to obtaining a positive credential (college degree). Over 70% of U.S. colleges require criminal background disclosure as part of their application process. Those who indicate having a criminal record on their application are typically prompted to submit additional documentation, such as a written explanation of the incident, copies of police or court records, or letters from probation officers.[116]

In a rare experimental audit study using matched pairs (real people with real academic records), criminologists found that college applicants who indicated a prior low-level felony conviction on their applications were rejected at about three times the rate of matched applicants with a clean record, even though the study was designed to make the record-having applicants more attractive to admissions officials (higher GPAs and/or ACT scores).[117] Unlike employment studies, their results did not show differences based on the applicant's race. More experimental studies are needed before criminologists can reach conclusions about the full impact of a criminal record on college admissions.

Criminologists who study housing access also use experiments. The recipients of the experimental applications are landlords or property management companies. Housing experiments demonstrate the long reach of a criminal record, with felony convictions creating the greatest barriers to securing a rental home. As Figure 11.4 shows, even felonies from a decade earlier impact property managers' decisions to consider rental applicants.

People applying for federally subsidized housing, including public housing and voucher programs (for use in the private rental market), can be denied based on their criminal records—or the records of other people in their households. Since 2015, the federal government has advised public housing authorities (PHAs) against blanket rejections of applicants with criminal records, with exceptions for some offenses, including sex offenses and prior evictions for drug-related criminal activity within the past three years.[118] Instead, the U.S. Department of Housing and Urban Development (HUD) instructs PHAs to consider the severity of the crime, how long ago it occurred, and evidence of rehabilitative efforts in the intervening time.[119]

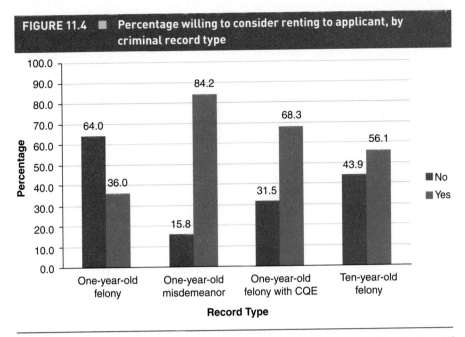

FIGURE 11.4 ■ Percentage willing to consider renting to applicant, by criminal record type

Source: Leasure, P., & Martin, T. (2017). Criminal records and housing: An experimental study. *Journal of Experimental Criminology, 13*(4), 527-535.

Note: CQE is Ohio's Certificate of Qualification for Employment, issued by the Court of Common Pleas to qualified applicants with criminal convictions who would otherwise be barred from certain occupations.

Felony Disenfranchisement

Criminal records can be barriers to full participation in civic life due to felony disenfranchisement. **Felony disenfranchisement** is the practice, set by state law, of preventing people who have been convicted of felonies from voting in elections. Barring incarcerated people from voting is practiced in countries around the world, yet the U.S. is unique in prohibiting non-incarcerated people from voting, including lifelong bans—at least in some states.[120]

Felony disenfranchisement policies exist on a spectrum. States like Maine and Vermont, which impose no felony restrictions on voting, are on one end of the spectrum. States like Kentucky and Virginia, which permanently rescind the right to vote following any felony conviction, are on the other end of the spectrum. Most states fall somewhere between these extremes.[121]

As of 2020, approximately 5.17 million people were disenfranchised because of a felony record, representing a 15% decline from 2016 (6.11 million) but a massive increase since before the prison boom (e.g., 1.17 million in 1976). One out of every 44 adults in the U.S. is unable to vote due to a felony conviction, or 2.27% of the adult population. Only one-quarter of those disenfranchised persons are currently incarcerated. More than two-fifths (43%) are post-sentence (i.e., finished a sentence of probation or incarceration in the past), 22% are on felony probation, and 10% are on parole.[122] Most have convictions for nonviolent crimes.[123] Figures 11.5 and 11.6 display rates of felony disenfranchisement by state and race/ethnicity.

Proponents of felony disenfranchisement argue that people convicted of felonies have forfeited their right to vote by violating the social contract.[124] They suggest that "those who do not follow the law should not benefit from the privilege of making the law" (p. 298).[125] They see voting as a privilege rather than a right of citizenship. In addition, they note that these laws are consistent with the 14th amendment to the U.S. Constitution, which permits the right to vote to be "abridged" due to "participation in rebellion, or other crime."[126]

Opponents argue that participation in the democratic process is a right rather than a privilege, and one that, if removed, should be reinstated once a person has paid their debt to society. They see restoring the right to vote, called re-enfranchisement, as essential for reintegration into community life.[127] Further, they note that felony disenfranchisement laws, though race-neutral in language, disproportionately deprive Black Americans of the right to vote, due to racial disparities in criminal justice processioning that persist even when differences in criminal offending are taken into account.[128] In fact, criminologists observe that the likelihood of a state having laws disenfranchising people with prior felony convictions increases as the share of the prison population that is Black increases.[129]

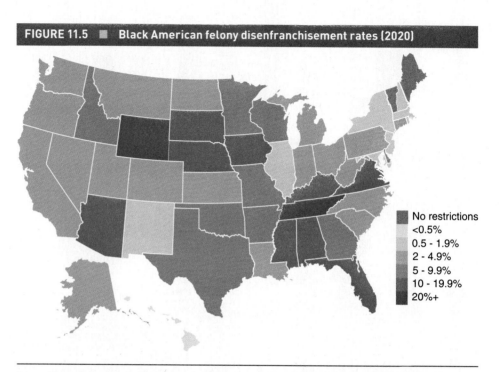

FIGURE 11.5 ■ Black American felony disenfranchisement rates (2020)

No restrictions
<0.5%
0.5 - 1.9%
2 - 4.9%
5 - 9.9%
10 - 19.9%
20%+

Source: Uggen, C., Larson, R., Shannon, S., & Pulido-Nava, A. (2020, October). *Locked out 2020: Estimates of people denied voting rights due to a felony conviction.* Washington DC: The Sentencing Project. Copyright © 2020 by The Sentencing Project.

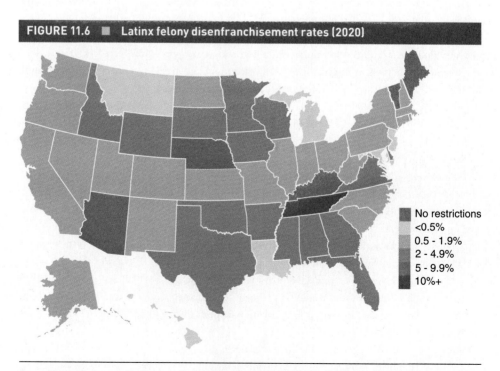

FIGURE 11.6 ■ Latinx felony disenfranchisement rates (2020)

No restrictions
<0.5%
0.5 - 1.9%
2 - 4.9%
5 - 9.9%
10%+

Source: Uggen, C., Larson, R., Shannon, S., & Pulido-Nava, A. (2020, October). *Locked out 2020: Estimates of people denied voting rights due to a felony conviction.* Washington DC: The Sentencing Project. Copyright © 2020 by The Sentencing Project.

Policy Reforms: Reducing the Impact of Criminal Records

Many policymakers recognize that the "eternal criminal record" harms individuals and communities by erecting hurdles to conventional life, affecting a broad swath of the American public.[130] Their proposed and enacted reforms aim to improve lives while also ensuring public safety. They usually focus on reducing collateral consequences for people with low-level or nonviolent records, especially when there is evidence of personal redemption, typically indicated by numbers of crime-free years since conviction.

Public opinion is in the reformers' corner. For example, opinion research shows that the U.S. public favors policies that make it possible for reformed people to clear their records (called expungement).[131] And a large majority oppose private online companies publishing arrest records.[132] Three main areas of reform are: (1) expungement, (2) certificates of relief, and (3) ban-the-box policies.

Expungement

How can a person with a criminal record shed the stigma and get a fresh start? One option may be expungement. Expungement, also called expunction, is the process of having one's record of arrest or convictions sealed or destroyed. The rules vary from state to state but, generally speaking, expungement is available primarily to people with misdemeanor records who have completed their sentence or probation, or who obtain a Certificate of Actual Innocence because charges were dropped or they were found not guilty.[133] Once expunged, criminal records no longer have to be disclosed. If a prospective employer or landlord asks if an applicant has even been convicted of a crime, they can lawfully answer "no."

Expungement provides a clean slate. At least, it's supposed to. But even those with expunged records find that they can be haunted by online records of past arrests or convictions. There are few truly fresh starts in the age of Google.

You may be part of the 15% of Americans who searched online for a person's criminal record in the past year.[134] If you did, you most likely found yourself on the website of a private company that obtains data through wholesalers who have bought the data in bulk from courts or government agencies. These third-party providers of criminal background data are part of a $4 billion industry.[135] The problem? Their data are static. They are not updated to reflect changes in a person's case. Charges are dropped and records sealed through expungement without any alterations to private databases.

Criminologist Sarah Lageson, an expert on online criminal records, uses the term digital punishment to refer to the stigmatizing effects of the online mugshots, arrest records, and inaccurate data that flood the private online market.[136] Despite the damning digital trail, however, there is some evidence that employment rates and earnings increase for people whose records have been cleared through expungement.[137]

Code for America Team Symonne Singleton (left), Zak Auerbach (middle), and Laura Kogler (right) worked on identifying every marijuana-related conviction eligible for expungement under California's Proposition 64.

San Francisco Chronicle/Hearst Newspapers via Getty Images/Contributor

Certificates of Relief

Some states offer certificates of relief (also called certificates of rehabilitation), which are documents that help people with criminal records access employment and housing.[138] They are issued through court order to individuals who meet eligibility requirements, such as having no more than a specified number of convictions and having no felony convictions above a certain level of severity. Certificate applicants are typically required to submit evidence of remorse and "good character," including work history, treatment program participation, family caregiving, and community service.[139] Judges decide who is granted the certificate, and not all applicants receive one.

Certificates of relief "demonstrate rehabilitation, remove automatic licensing bars, protect employers from negligent hiring claims, and help decision-makers make better-informed decisions about hiring individuals with criminal records" (p. 1067).[140] Unlike expungement, certificates of relief do not seal the person's criminal record. Instead, they act as a positive credential that says "it's safe to hire this person despite their record."

Do certificates of relief actually provide relief? Initial evidence suggests that they improve hiring outcomes, but only for white applicants. For example, an experimental study involving Black and white applicants showed that white applicants with a certificate of relief fared as well as white applicants without a criminal record, but Black applicants with a certificate relief fared just as poorly as Black applicants with a criminal record and no certificate, as observed in Figure 11.7.[141] In other words, certificates of relief do not overcome the persistent harms of racial discrimination.

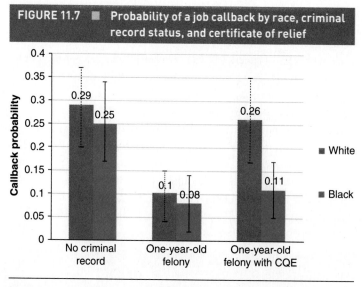

FIGURE 11.7 ■ Probability of a job callback by race, criminal record status, and certificate of relief

Source: Leasure, P., & Andersen, T. S. (2020). Race, criminal records, and certificates of relief: An experimental pilot study. *Deviant Behavior, 41*(9), 1065-1083.

Note: CQE is Ohio's Certificate of Qualification for Employment (i.e., certificate of relief).

Ban-the-Box Policies

Many job applications have a criminal history question. Applicants must check a box if they have any prior convictions or, in some cases, arrests. Reformers in the "ban-the-box" movement call for removing these checkboxes on job applications.[142] They acknowledge that some individuals should be prohibited from working in particular environments (e.g., those who have sexually abused children should be prevented from working with children), and they do not wish to deny employers the right to ask about or check criminal backgrounds. They argue, though, that eliminating applicants at the initial application phase is a problem, as many criminal records are years or decades old and have no bearing on the applicant's ability to perform the job well. By banning the box, they claim, the 1-in-12 Americans with felony conviction records (and the tens of millions more with arrest histories) will not be rejected before having the opportunity to explain their record and demonstrate their worthiness as an employee.

Hawaii was the first state to enact a ban-the-box (BTB) policy, in 1998. Since then, and primarily in the past decade, another 35 states as well the District of Columbia and more than 150 cities and counties have adopted BTB laws.[143] Ban-the-box policies, where enacted, primarily target hiring in the public sector (or private companies that contract with the public sector) rather than hiring in the private market. In addition, some large companies—like Walmart, Target, and Starbucks—have voluntarily adopted BTB in their hiring. In these states and companies, applicants can still be rejected on the basis of a criminal record, but this occurs after the initial application stage, and therefore after the applicant has been individually assessed on characteristics like work experience and relevant skills. This big question is: Does it work? The answer is a half-hearted "maybe" or "only for some people." Studies of employment rates before and after the implementation of BTB policies reveal contradictory results.[144]

Banning the box has unintended consequences. In the absence of criminal record information on applications, some employers engage in **statistical discrimination** in which they rely on "easily identifiable traits like race, gender, and age to infer the likelihood of criminal behavior in the face of limited information" (p. 170).[145] Specifically, employers who eliminate the criminal background checkbox discriminate against Black male applicants (regardless of whether they have a criminal record) on the assumption that they are more likely to have a prior felony conviction.[146] In an experimental study involving roughly 15,000 job applications, researchers found that the Black-white gap in callbacks was significantly larger at companies that banned the box. Prior to removing the checkbox, white applicants received 7% more callbacks than comparable Black applicants; after BTB, the gap grew to 43%. They concluded that "employers are relying on exaggerated impressions of real-world racial differences in felony conviction rates," or stereotypes (p. 191).[147]

DEFIANCE, PROCEDURAL JUSTICE, AND LEGAL CYNICISM

Imagine you are riding your bike back to your apartment after class. The street looks dangerous. The cars are driving fast and recklessly, and there is no shoulder or bike lane. The sidewalk, however, is wide and smooth and there are few pedestrians about. You make the reasonable decision to ride on the sidewalk—just until you make it to a safer stretch of road. You are about three minutes into your ride when a police officer stops you. They issue you a ticket for riding your bike on the sidewalk, lecture you about road safety, and pat you down, asking if you have any drugs or weapons on you. Across the street, you see a few other bicyclists on the sidewalk pass by without comment from the ticket-issuing officer. You also see cars continuing to speed by, far in excess of the speed limit; one even runs a red light. Yet you are the only one being stopped.

How would you feel in that scenario? Probably angry or upset. Indignant, even. And why is that? A big part of it is the unfairness of the punishment: Why are you being punished for something harmless? Why are you being ticketed and searched when others, some who have committed far more serious infractions, get a pass? If this has happened before—you get stopped for minor infractions when everyone else is left alone—the sense of injustice will be even stronger. You might even feel a moral obligation to defy the no-bikes-on-the-sidewalk rule in the future, or other rules like it. It's not that the label of "law violator" has turned you into a law violator by altering your self-concept or limiting your opportunities to get ahead. Rather, you no longer feel bound by the rules of an unjust or illegitimate authority. You are defiant.

Consider this quote from a gang-associated Latino respondent called Francisco in a qualitative study by criminologists Victor Rios, Greg Prieto, and Jonathan Ibarra:

> *Oh si? Ay fool, serio [seriously], but like the pigs right here, like if they see any homies or anything you know like riding their bikes on the sidewalk ... like I got pulled over just for riding my bike on the sidewalk. And then, they see like other fuckin' people, they see white people riding on the fucking sidewalk. But they only stop us. At least a fuckin' ticket or something. They just wanna get us pulled over, just to get info on us and get us caught up... they have us tracked like dogs with dog collars"* (p. 68)[148]

Francisco describes feeling like he is being treated like an animal—that he is tracked like a dog. And he sees that he and his friends are the only ones incurring police attention—white bicyclists don't get stopped. Just them. He understands these stops as a pre-text for questioning them, for discovering their assumed criminal activity. The result is feelings of "indignity and violation" and seeing police as adversaries.[149] To be sure, Francisco and his friends have been labeled as gang members and criminals, but this quote suggests a different process at work than just labeling. It suggests a process of defiance.

Defiance Theory

Labeling theory states that punishment increases criminal offending. This is opposite the prediction of deterrence theory, which claims that punishment reduces crime. In truth, sanctions produce a variety of effects, sometimes deterring and sometimes increasing crime.[150] Criminologist Lawrence Sherman offers an alternative view, defiance theory, which explains why some people respond to sanctions and labels with law-breaking and others do not.

Defiance theory states that punishment and stigma—when it is perceived as unjust—can lead to rule-breaking. In other words, punishment can backfire.[151] Sherman describes defiance as "the net increase in the prevalence, incidence, or seriousness of future offending against a sanctioning community caused by a proud, shameless reaction to the administration of a criminal sanction" (p. 459).[152] What is called secondary deviance in labeling theory is called defiance in Sherman's theory, though the perspectives offer different explanations for why punishment backfires.

Causes of Defiance

Sherman describes several conditions necessary for producing defiant responses to sanctions, including formal criminal justice penalties (like citation, arrest, or incarceration) and other types of sanctions (like expulsion, getting fired, or being treated disrespectfully). The following are causes of defiance:

1. *The person defines the sanction as unfair or the sanctioning agent as disrespectful.* Punishments that are discriminatory, arbitrary, or out-of-proportion tend to be perceived as unjust. The person might recognize that they have done wrong and that punishment would be warranted, but defiance is likely when the sanction is seen as unreasonable. In addition, a fair punishment meted out disrespectfully also incurs defiance. When this occurs, the punishing authority, like police or school administrators, lose their legitimacy in the eyes of the sanctioned person. This is an issue of procedural justice. Procedural justice is the perception that agents of social control—for example, police, judges, or teachers—treat people fairly and equitably.[153] Procedural justice is evident when authorities are "perceived to be *trustworthy*, are seen to be acting with *neutrality*, when they treat people with *respect and dignity*, and when they allow people the opportunity to participate and express their viewpoints (i.e. *voice*) before decisions are made" (p. 358, emphasis in original).[154] Procedural *injustice*—or belief that the criminal legal system and its representatives treat people unfairly—alters legitimacy perceptions. Legitimacy perceptions are beliefs about the moral authority of rule-setters and rule-enforcers.

2. *The person has a weak bond to the community and sanctioning agents.* Informal bonds, like close relationships and school and work commitments, become the last line of defense against rule-breaking when formal rules lose their legitimacy. Even if a sanction is unfair and provokes indignation, a strongly bonded person won't risk their relationships and investments by getting into even more trouble. Also, if a person is strongly bonded to the sanctioning agent (e.g., a suspended student who is committed to school success and attached to teachers), then they are likely to feel shame that keeps them from escalating their rule-violating behavior.

3. *The person views the punishment as stigmatizing, but they reject the shame caused by the sanction.* Defiance theory acknowledges shame and pride as "master emotions" that propel people towards certain behaviors.[155] People with strong social bonds may feel a deep shame when

punished and labeled, as they have let others and themselves down. They accept the shame and mend their ways. But consider the person with few social bonds or supports. They, too, feel the sting of stigma. But they are isolated and rejected, and so they reject the shame that others seek to compel in them. They become self-righteously angry in the face of punishment, and proud to be separate from the community that punishes them. They get caught in a shame/rage spiral in which "rage is a protective measure against shame, a way of rejecting the shame, and a defense against a perceived attack."[156] Rage certainly feels better than impotence. Hatred, resentment, and violence become a shield.

In sum, defiance theory tells us that punishment backfires when it is experienced as unfair and stigmatizing, particularly by a person with weak bonds. When this happens, the rules and the people who enforce them lose their legitimacy (think back, for example, to Francisco's reference to police as "pigs"). Efforts to shame the offender are met with rage and defiance, a form of self-protection. Defiance is another way of saying crime (as in defying the law) or other types of rule-breaking, like school infractions.

Research on school punishment provides support for defiance theory. When students are punished harshly for minor violations, they become more—not less—defiant of the rules. Why? Because their punishment is perceived as out-of-proportion and therefore unjust. And being suspended or expelled, especially when it is seen as unfair, weakens or severs bonds to school. This effect is especially noteworthy among students of color, who are disproportionately referred to the office and suspended for minor misbehavior (see section on Exclusionary Discipline earlier).[157]

A study of prisoner defiance in Australia similarly demonstrates how fairness perceptions influence conduct. Researchers found that people who are incarcerated are more likely to comply with the rules administered and enforced by prison staff when they perceive a high degree of procedural justice. Procedural justice perceptions included incarcerated people's ratings of the staff as respectful, trustworthy, neutral in their decision-making, and willing to let inmates voice their positions.[158]

Types of Defiance

There is more than one way to defy the rules. Sherman describes four ways that we can distinguish forms of defiance: (1) direct versus displaced defiance, (2) specific versus general defiance, (3) concealed versus identifiable defiance, and (4) active versus passive defiance.

Let's start with direct versus indirect defiance. Direct defiance occurs when a sanctioned person aims their defiant actions at the particular individual who has treated them unfairly. For example, imagine a high school student who falls asleep in class because they were kept awake all night by fighting parents. Their teacher, seeing them dozing off, accuses them of being "lazy as usual" and assigns detention. The student, feeling righteous indignation, screams "F*** off!" at the teacher. That is direct defiance. In displaced defiance, defiant actions target people other than the specific person who has punished them unjustly, including those "belonging to and representing the same group."[159] For example, the sleepy student might aim their hostilities at other teachers in the school. Sherman gives the example of domestic abusers who, following an arrest, turn their violent anger at police against their partners and others in the community.[160]

Now let's distinguish between specific and general defiance. Specific defiance is an individual reaction to an unfair sanction. The tired student and the arrested abuser (both individuals) engaged in specific defiance in the earlier examples. General defiance is a collective reaction of a group to unfair punishment of a group member. A prison riot in reaction to abuse of a fellow incarcerated person would fall into this category.

The distinction between concealed and identifiable defiance is exactly what the terms imply. Offenders engage in concealed defiance when they attempt to hide (or conceal) their behavior, as by fleeing the scene. In contrast, identifiable defiance occurs when they seek to attract attention to their defiance. Examples include a suicide-bomber who records a statement before their crime, a mass shooter who leaves behind a manifesto, or an insurrectionist who posts photos of their crimes on social media.

The examples of defiance presented in the chapter so far are of active defiance, or defiance that requires action (e.g., yelling expletives, assaulting people, murder). Defiance can also be passive—or withholding of action. If the rules require a person to *do something,* then defiance looks like the absence of that action. Think of a motorcyclist who defies a helmet law by refusing to wear one. Or an angry tenant who refuses to leave when the sheriff's deputy shows up to enforce an eviction. Or a person who purposefully goes limp when ordered by police to stand up, get in a vehicle, or otherwise move.

People who stormed the Capitol on January 6, 2021, engaged in criminal acts, including unlawful entry, assault, and weapons violations. Their actions were identifiable, active criminal defiance of an authority they perceived as illegitimate.

AP Photo/zz/STRF/STAR MAX/IPx

Legal Cynicism

Defiance is one outcome of procedural injustice. Legal cynicism is another. **Legal cynicism** is a "cultural orientation in which the law and the agents of its enforcement are viewed as illegitimate, unresponsive, and ill-equipped to ensure public safety" (p. 443).[161] Legal cynicism flourishes when people believe the police and other representatives of the criminal legal system use unfair and disrespectful methods, or when they are ineffective at preventing crime.[162] Under these conditions, the law itself is no longer binding. The rules of an unjust system lose their legitimacy.[163] Indeed, one set of criminologists measured individuals' levels of legal cynicism by asking them whether they agreed with statements such as the following:

- "Laws are made to be broken."

- "It's okay to do anything you want as long as you don't hurt anyone."

- "To make money, there are no right or wrong ways anymore, only easy ways and hard ways."

- "Fighting between friends or within family is nobody else's business."[164]

Each statement gets at the relevance (or, more accurately, irrelevance) of law in everyday life. The more that people agree that "laws are meant to be broken" and that fighting is "nobody else's business," the more cynical they are. More recently, researchers have considered alternative measures, finding that there are three distinct dimensions of legal cynicism captured by various statements put to respondents. These include (1) legal antipathy, or "feelings of disdain toward laws and those who follow them"; (2) legal corruption, or "the belief that societal elites shape laws to serve their interests over the wellbeing of

TABLE 11.2 ■ Measures in Gifford and Reisig's three-dimensional legal cynicism scale	
Dimension of legal cynicism	**Statement**
Legal antipathy	"People who always follow the law are suckers."
	"It is fun to break the law and get away with it."
	"Sometimes you need to ignore the law and do what you want to do."
	"It's all right to break the law if you don't get caught."
	"To get ahead, you have to do some things that are not right."
	"It is all right to get around the law if you can get away with it."
	"Suckers deserve to be taken advantage of."
Legal corruption	"The law does not protect my interests."
	"Laws are usually bad."
	"The law is rotten to the core."
Low legal legitimacy (reversed)	"Nearly all laws deserve our respect."
	"There is never an excuse for breaking the law."
	"People should always obey the law even if it interferes with their personal ambition."
	"Society would be a better place if all laws were enforced."
	"I try to obey the law, even if it goes against what I think is right."

Source: Adapted from Gifford, F. E., & Reisig, M. D. (2019). A multidimensional model of legal cynicism. *Law and Human Behavior, 43*(4), 383-396.

others"; and (3) low legal legitimacy, or "reduced willingness to accept the rightfulness of legal prohibitions" (p. 384).[165] Table 11.2 presents measures of these forms of legal cynicism.

Legal cynicism matters for how people behave, including the likelihood that they will obey the law, comply with law enforcement, and report crime to authorities.[166] After all, in the legal cynic's perspective, it makes little sense to follow unjust rules or laws enforced by an illegitimate authority. Why, the legal cynic might ask, should I cooperate with or aid authorities who regard me with contempt? Besides, the thinking goes, they will do little to help the situation anyway. This view of the legal system is found to be greatest in impoverished communities with high concentrations of formerly incarcerated people and where adverse police encounters are common, particularly when those encounters are perceived as racially biased.[167] Survey research shows that Black and Latinx persons, men, single people, and those with limited economic resources and prior experiences with violent victimization are most likely to espouse legal cynicism.[168]

Legal cynicism might sound a lot like defiance to you. That makes sense, because both emerge from experiences—individually or collectively—with unfair treatment by people with the power to punish and label. And both involve the rejection of those in authority. In fact, legal cynicism may allow people to "den[y] the shameful aspects of sanctioning and instead place blame on the law itself" (p. 287).[169] In other words, legal cynicism is part of the defiance process. Yet not all legal cynics will engage in defiant acts (or passive defiance). Legal cynicism is a cultural viewpoint, or an orientation towards law-related norms, that can be held regardless of one's actions. A person can feel disdainful towards the law and unwilling to accept the law's rightfulness without, in fact, violating any laws. Defiance, in contrast, is behavior.

ENGAGED CRIMINOLOGY 11.2

Are You a Legal Cynic?

For this activity, you will complete a short survey that measures your level of legal cynicism. You will then consider the causes and consequences of your views.

Complete the Survey

Read the following statements. Indicate whether you agree or disagree with each statement. For questions 1 through 10, use the following:

1 = Strongly disagree, 2 = Disagree, 3 = Neither agree nor disagree, 4 = Agree, 5 = Strongly agree

1. People who always follow the law are suckers. _____

2. It is fun to break the law and get away with it. _____

3. Sometimes you need to ignore the law and do what you want to do. _____

4. It's all right to break the law if you don't get caught. _____

5. To get ahead, you have to do some things that are not right. _____

6. It is all right to get around the law if you can get away with it. _____

7. Suckers deserve to be taken advantage of. _____

8. The law does not protect my interests. _____

9. Laws are usually bad. _____

10. The law is rotten to the core. _____

For questions 11 through 15, use the following (opposite of the previous rating scale):

1 = Strongly agree, 2 = Agree, 3 = Neither agree nor disagree, 4 = Disagree, 5 = Strongly disagree

11. Nearly all laws deserve our respect. _____

12. There is never an excuse for breaking the law. _____

13. People should always obey the law even if it interferes with their personal ambition. _____

14. Society would be a better place if all laws were enforced. _____

15. I try to obey the law, even if it goes against what I think is right. _____

Now add up your scores. Your summed value should be between 15 and 75. _____

The closer your value is to 75, the higher your level of legal cynicism is.

- A score of 15-30 indicates a low level of legal cynicism.
- A score of 31-59 falls in the middle (neither high nor low).
- A score of 60-75 indicates a high level of legal cynicism.

Reflect on your level of legal cynicism and answer the following questions:

1. Why do you think you have this view of the law? What are its origins?

2. Do you think your view of the law makes you more likely to break the law? Why or why not?

CHAPTER SUMMARY

LO 11.1 Summarize labeling theory's central concepts.

Labeling theory is a symbolic interactionist perspective that argues that stigmatizing labels, both formal and informal, increase the likelihood of future law-breaking, called secondary deviance. This is because they alter self-concept (reflected appraisals) and lead to role engulfment through social exclusion, social withdrawal, and involvement in a deviant subculture that embraces or tolerates the labeled person's spoiled identity.

LO 11.2   Describe the causes of the school-to-prison pipeline.

The practices and policies that push children out of schools and into the criminal legal system include zero-tolerance policies and exclusionary disciplinary practices (suspension and expulsion), which disconnect students from school. The presence of law enforcement in schools increases the likelihood of arrest and interaction with the juvenile justice system.

LO 11.3   Identify the effects of a criminal record.

Criminal records impact hiring, access to housing, college admission, and—in some states—the right to vote, called felony disenfranchisement. Restrictions that prevent people with criminal records from accessing jobs, housing, schooling, and voting are called collateral consequences. Collateral consequences affect many people in the U.S., with roughly 1 in 12 adults having a felony conviction record.

LO 11.4   Explain the primary claims of defiance theory and differentiate it from labeling theory.

Like labeling theory, defiance theory claims that punishment can backfire, causing more crime. Unlike labeling theory, defiance theory argues that sanctions and labels cause crime (called defiance) when they are perceived as unfair and stigmatizing, bonds to society are weak, and the person shields themselves from shame with defiant rage.

ENGAGED DISCUSSION

1. Come up with an example of a deviant label. Is it formal or informal? Is it likely to become a master status—why or why not?

2. Using a key term from the chapter, identify one way that labeling theory applies to the school-to-prison pipeline.

3. This chapter addresses four areas of life affected by criminal records: employment, education, housing, and voting. What is an additional area of life that may be negatively impacted by criminal records?

4. Think of a time that you experienced procedural injustice. Did you become defiant in response? Why or why not?

KEY TERMS

Collateral consequences (p. 284)

Defiance (p. 292)

Digital punishment (p. 289)

Discrimination (p. 275)

Diversion programs (p. 283)

Exclusionary discipline (p. 278)

Expungement (p. 289)

Felony disenfranchisement (p. 287)

Formal labels (p. 273)

Informal labels (p. 273)

Legal cynicism (p. 294)

Legitimacy perceptions (p. 292)

Master status (p. 273)

Minority threat hypothesis (p. 281)

Negative credentials (p. 284)

Primary deviance (p. 273)

Procedural justice (p. 292)

Reflected appraisals (p. 274)

Role engulfment (p. 274)

School threat assessment (p. 283)

School-to-prison pipeline (p. 278)

Secondary deviance (p. 273)

Social location (p. 274)

Statistical discrimination (p. 291)

Stereotypes (p. 275)

Stigma (p. 273)

Symbolic interactionism (p. 272)

Zero-tolerance policies (p. 279)

12 WHAT IS VICTIMOLOGY?

LEARNING OBJECTIVES

12.1 Trace the origins and evolution of victimology.

12.2 Identify common patterns in criminal victimization.

12.3 Describe the consequences of criminal victimization.

12.4 Outline the history and impact of the victims' rights movement.

Lisa Montgomery was executed by lethal injection in the early hours of January 13, 2021. She was the first woman on federal death row to be executed since 1953.[1] The murder that put her on death row shocks the senses. In 2004, Lisa Montgomery posed online as a potential customer interested in purchasing a puppy from a Missouri woman who operated a dog-breeding business with her husband: 23-year-old Bobbie Jo Stinnett, who was eight months pregnant with her first child. Montgomery told Stinnett that she, too, was pregnant and the women connected online over their impending motherhood. But Montgomery was not pregnant. When she arrived at Stinnett's home, supposedly to collect the puppy, she attacked the young woman, strangling her until she lost consciousness. She then used a kitchen knife to cut into Stinnett's uterus, at which point Stinnett regained consciousness. A struggle ensued and Montgomery asphyxiated Stinnett until she was dead. She removed the newborn, who survived, and returned home, attempting (unsuccessfully) to pass the child off as her own.[2] She confessed to the murder and kidnapping soon afterwards.

There is little doubt that Lisa Montgomery was deeply disturbed. An investigation into her history—not presented at sentencing—reveals a life derailed by persistent and brutal violent victimization and its psychological fallout. Post-conviction court documents containing interviews with over 450 family members, teachers, neighbors, and others chronicle the abuse Montgomery endured since babyhood (be forewarned that these descriptions are disturbing): Her mother would duct tape her mouth to silence her so frequently that she learned not to cry, she was viciously beaten regularly, her stepfather sexually abused her starting at age 13 and invited groups of friends over to rape her, and her mother trafficked her for sex to get money to pay bills. Montgomery married at 18 and her husband continued the pattern of sadistic abuse.[3] Court documents describe how many adults in her life knew about the abuse but did little to intervene. By adulthood, Montgomery had experienced 9 out of 10 adverse childhood experiences, suffered from brain damage and dysfunction, and had severe mental health conditions, including complex post-traumatic stress disorder.[4]

What Lisa Montgomery did to Bobbie Jo Stinnett was an outlier to established patterns in victimology in that she was a woman killing another woman. And a stranger, at that. That is incredibly unusual, as is homicide by asphyxiation. At the same time, all that was done to Lisa Montgomery in the years leading up to her crime is a textbook example of what victimologists know to be true: Most people who commit violent offenses have histories of trauma. Victims of family violence often endure repeat victimization. The psychological costs of recurring victimization are profound and can be criminogenic. The greatest threats to children's safety are the trusted adults in their lives.

Bobbie Jo Stinnett's mother, Becky Harper, read a prepared statement in Kansas City, M.O., alongside Stinnett's husband, Zeb Stinnett (right), following the conviction and death sentence of Stinnett's murderer, Lisa M. Montgomery.

THE STUDY OF VICTIMIZATION

Victimology, the scientific study of criminal victimization, is a subfield within criminology. Criminology's focus is the making of laws, the breaking of laws, and reactions to law-breaking, with most attention going to the criminal offender. Victimology shifts attention to the victim: (1) victims' participation in the making of laws (e.g., through the victims' rights movement; (2) the nature, extent, and causes of victimization (the "how much?" and "why?" questions); and (3) reactions to victimization, including the reactions of media, the public, the criminal justice system, and victims themselves.

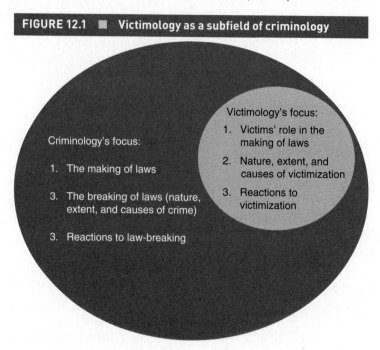

FIGURE 12.1 ■ Victimology as a subfield of criminology

Criminology's focus:

1. The making of laws

3. The breaking of laws (nature, extent, and causes of crime)

3. Reactions to law-breaking

Victimology's focus:

1. Victims' role in the making of laws

2. Nature, extent, and causes of victimization

3. Reactions to victimization

The Early Years: Victim Typologies and Victim Precipitation

The scientific study of people who commit crimes first emerged with the positivist school of the 19th century, and it has continued since then. The scientific study of victims has a far shorter history. The word *victimology* and the notion that victims ought to be a subject of study was born in the 1940s. The first victimologists sought to organize victims into typologies, or types of victims.[5] Their organizational schemes reveal a less-than-sympathetic view of their research subjects. The research question guiding early victimologists was "What role do victims play in their victimization?" Their typologies sorted victims based on the magnitude of the victim's contribution to the criminal event. To their thinking, explaining crime required understanding the characteristics and actions of both offender *and* victim.

The first victimologists developed the concept of victim precipitation to describe the victim's level of blameworthiness. The verb *precipitate* means to cause something to happen (typically a bad thing), and a precipitating factor is an action or characteristic that brings about an outcome. Victim precipitation, therefore, occurs when the victim contributes to or causes their own victimization.[6]

There are two forms of victim precipitation: (1) victim facilitation and (2) victim provocation. Victim facilitation assigns the least amount of blame to the victim; victim provocation assigns the most. Victim facilitation occurs when a victim makes victimization easier for the offender through their own actions, even though that was not their intention. Think of the person who runs into a convenience store with their empty car still running or the student who leaves their laptop unattended while using the library bathroom. Of course, the car and laptop thieves should not steal. They—not the victims—are responsible for the crimes. But the victims inadvertently facilitated the offenses by presenting an easy opportunity, which is why they were targeted instead of more cautious drivers and students.

Victim provocation occurs when a victim instigates, or provokes, the criminal event. It would not have occurred were it not for the victim's actions. Consider a case in which a would-be burglar is injured by an armed homeowner acting in self-defense. The victim of violence—the intruder—provoked their victimization by being the first to act in the sequence of events. They brought the victimization upon themselves by instigating the interaction with the homeowner.

Hans von Hentig and the Criminal-Victim Dyad

German criminologist Hans von Hentig developed the first victim typology that identified precipitating factors.[7] Von Hentig had devoted much of his career to figuring out why some individuals were strongly predisposed to crime. In other words, he had asked: What makes a criminal a criminal? He then began to ponder: What makes a victim a victim? Are there traits that predispose some individuals to victimization? He believed that determining a victim's propensity to become a victim requires analysis of the *criminal-victim dyad,* or the dynamics of interaction between the offender and the victim. Understanding crime requires looking beyond just the outcome of the event, von Hentig wrote. The person who ends up injured is often revealed to be the aggressor initially. Sometimes the person who throws the first punch ends up as the victim of homicide. He called this victim the *agent provocateur* in his 1948 book *The Criminal and His Victim.*[8] They have actively provoked the victimization through their behavior.

Von Hentig studied the dynamics of interaction between offender and victim, which he called the criminal-victim dyad.

Paul Bradbury/OJO Images/Getty Images

Von Hentig acknowledged that many victims do not contribute to their victimization through action. Instead, he argued that they have a predisposition to become victims due to characteristics beyond their control. They are susceptible or vulnerable to victimization. Their contribution is passive rather than active. He was not blaming them for their victimization, per se. Rather, he saw these traits as determinants of victimization, or predictive variables. His victim typology included 13 types, as seen in Table 12.1. The language reflects the time period in which von Hentig was working.

TABLE 12.1 ■ Hans von Hentig's victim typology	
Victim type	**What it means**
The young	Infants and children
The female	Girls and women
The old	Persons of advanced age
The mentally defective and deranged	Persons with profound intellectual disabilities, mental illness, and/or substance abuse
Immigrants	Foreigners unaccustomed to the culture
Minorities	Persons of color and ethnic groups that experience social exclusion
Dull normals	Persons with low intelligence

(Continued)

TABLE 12.1 ■ Hans von Hentig's victim typology (*Continued*)	
Victim type	**What it means**
The depressed	Persons suffering from psychological problems
The acquisitive	Greedy persons seeking quick gains
The wanton	Sexually promiscuous persons
The lonesome and the heartbroken	Widows, widowers, and other persons in mourning
The tormentor	Persons who are abusive
The blocked, exempted, or fighting	Victims of blackmail, extortion, or scams

Source: Adapted from von Hentig, H. (1948). *The criminal and his victim: Studies in the sociology of crime.* New Haven, CT: Yale University Press.

Benjamin Mendelsohn and the Guilty Victim

Around the same time, attorney Benjamin Mendelsohn—the first to use the term *victimology*—offered his own version of a victim typology, this time much more explicitly addressing the blameworthiness of victims. In his work as an attorney, Mendelsohn had administered detailed questionnaires to victims, witnesses, and bystanders to establish the dynamics of interaction between offenders and their victims. Like many criminologists after him, Mendelsohn noted that most criminal-victim pairs had an established interpersonal connection prior to the criminal event. He created a six-category classification system based on the results of the questionnaires.[9] His purpose was to differentiate levels of victim culpability based on legal considerations. After all, he was an attorney. Figure 12.2 displays five of Mendelsohn's victim types in a continuum ranging from *completely innocent victim* (least blameworthy) to *most guilty victim* (most blameworthy). The greater the role of the victim's actions in bringing about the harm, the greater their culpability. And culpable victims mean less-blameworthy offenders. The sixth type, the *imaginary victim*, doesn't fit on the continuum because this person is not, in fact, a victim at all. An imaginary victim falsely claims to be a victim when no crime has taken place.

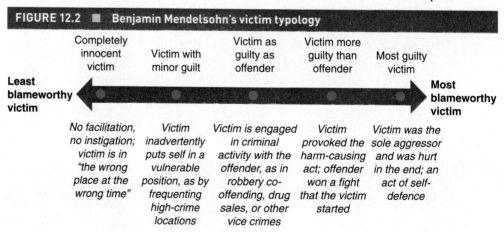

FIGURE 12.2 ■ Benjamin Mendelsohn's victim typology

Marvin Wolfgang and the Homicide Drama

Criminologist Marvin Wolfgang, the first to use the phrase "victim precipitation," thrust the study of victim behavior into the spotlight with this groundbreaking study of homicide. For his 1958 book *Patterns in Criminal Homicide,* Wolfgang studied every reported homicide that happened in Philadelphia between 1948 and 1952.[10] There were 588 of them. He was most interested in the "homicide drama." Think of the homicide event as a play. Who are the main characters, and what are their motivations? What is their relationship to one another? What is the setting (e.g., a bedroom, a bar, a roadway)? What is the main conflict of the drama, and what are they doing as it unfolds? These are the questions Wolfgang answered with the Philadelphia data. He found that 26% of the homicide dramas he studied (150 out of 588) were victim-precipitated killings.

Wolfgang offered a restrictive definition of victim-precipitated homicide based solely on the victim as the initial physical aggressor:

> *The role of the victim is characterized by his having been the first in the homicide drama to use physical force against his subsequent slayer... the first to show and use a deadly weapon, to strike a blow in an altercation.*[11]

In Wolfgang's view, a victim who hurls insults or cheats the offender out of money does not precipitate the homicide even if their actions incite violence. Victim precipitation requires a violent victim, typically with an offender acting in self-defense or retaliation.

Wolfgang went a step further and asked: How are victim-precipitated murders different from other murders (besides the victim's initial violence)? His analysis revealed a disproportionate amount of victim precipitation among homicides involving stabbing, alcohol use, female offenders with male victims, intimate partner killings, and victims with criminal records. These characteristics are abundant in the real-life examples from Wolfgang's data:

> *A husband accused his wife of giving money to another man, and while she was making breakfast, he attacked her with a milk bottle, then a brick, and finally a piece of concrete block. Having had a butcher knife in hand, she stabbed him during the fight.*

> *A victim became incensed when his eventual slayer asked for money which the victim owed him. The victim grabbed a hatchet and started in the direction of his creditor, who pulled out a knife and stabbed him.*

> *During a lover's quarrel, the male (victim) hit his mistress and threw a can of kerosene at her. She retaliated by throwing the liquid on him, and then tossed a lighted match in his direction. He died from the burns.*[12]

Menachim Amir, Sexual Violence, and Victim-Blaming

The victim precipitation concept was dealt a death blow when criminologist Menachim Amir applied it to rape in the late 1960s. Amir abandoned Wolfgang's restrictive version of victim precipitation based on the victim's physical aggression. Instead, he proposed that nonviolent victim behavior, either active or passive, could precipitate sexual assault. For Amir, active precipitation includes agreeing to a drink or riding in a car with a stranger. He described "fail[ing] to react strongly enough to sexual suggestions and overtures" as passive precipitation. Using crude language and gestures, having a "bad" reputation, and wearing revealing clothing are additional precipitating factors, according to Amir. He argued that these factors, when interpreted as sexual interest by perpetrators, make potential victims "candidates for the event."[13] In his analysis of 646 rapes, he described 19% of them as victim precipitated. In his view of victim precipitation, it seemed to critics, a sociable woman in a bar was equivalent to a hatchet-wielding attacker killed in self-defense (as in Wolfgang's example).

Amir's ideas about victim-precipitated rape were controversial but hardly new. They reflected rape narratives (also called rape myths) that minimized the blameworthiness assigned to perpetrators by suggesting that victims "ask for it" by bucking the conventions of modest femininity. "Good girls," so the reasoning went, "don't get raped."[14] The scenarios that Amir characterized as victim-precipitated were those that didn't fit the "real rape" stereotype. According to this stereotype, rapes are only "real"—that is, the assailant is only solely to blame—if it is a stranger attack involving overwhelming physical force, extreme resistance by a female victim, serious injury and torn clothing, and immediate reporting to police.[15] In other words, the monster jumping from the bushes or sneaking in through a second-story window with a knife. Ideas about "real rape" and victims "asking for it" are called rape *myths* because they are false beliefs.[16]

In an odd twist, Amir's research also exposed several widely accepted beliefs about rape as empirically false. For example, he found that about three-quarters of rapes were planned by perpetrators (*not crimes of passion*). He also found that in almost 9 out of 10 rapes, the offender(s) subdued the victim using coercion rather than physical violence. Furthermore, he argued that courts should not consider the absence of physical resistance as evidence of consent. Amir called upon courts to acknowledge that terror causes many victims to freeze.[17]

When Amir was writing in the 1960s and early 1970s, rape myths were widely accepted by perpetrators, law enforcement, attorneys, judges, juries, and victims who were encouraged to blame themselves.[18] And they continue to shape public and criminal justice responses to sexual violence today.[19] For example, rape trial observation studies detail how defense attorneys appeal to juries' prejudices by using "bad girl" narratives to call victims' credibility into question.[20] Despite the pervasiveness of rape myths, the criminological response to Amir's victim precipitation claims was mostly a loud rejection. In the words of two criminologists, "the concept [victim-precipitated rape] merely converts sexist rationalization into a causal explanation" that should be abandoned.[21] The discipline ultimately proved uninterested in granting legitimacy to victim-blaming.

Anti-rape demonstrators protesting victim-blaming in Dhaka, Bangladesh, in January 2021, following the multiple-perpetrator rape and murder of 17-year-old Aurna Amin.

Mamunur Rashid/NurPhoto/Getty Images

Escaping a Victim-Blaming Past

The victim precipitation model had been all but abandoned by the 1990s. Its critics listed several concerns that prompted its expulsion, including that (1) victim precipitation thinking encourages victim-blaming when responsibility lies with the offender, and (2) the victim precipitation model offers insufficient insight about how to predict or prevent crime.[22] Furthermore, critics argued that victim precipitation reflected an ideology that places all blame for social problems on individuals rather than on the structural causes of crime. As a result, the existing social, political, and economic orders remained unquestioned and unchanged.[23] We end up with victim-blaming instead of system-naming. To illustrate, imagine that household burglaries have increased in your town due to the opioid crisis. In a victim precipitation approach, unlit front porches or unlocked back doors are the cause. A more system-focused approach would instead point to inadequate substance abuse treatment options, drug market conditions, and economic circumstances that breed despair. Locking your doors might protect *your* house, but it is not a solution to the problem.

Victim precipitation lives on in criminology to some extent, though it is applied primarily to homicide. These studies follow Wolfgang's lead, defining victim-precipitated killings as "incidents in which a physical attack by the victim provokes the offender's lethal attack."[24] Their results are strikingly like Wolfgang's findings from the 1950s. For example, homicide dramas with female offenders and male victims are particularly likely to be victim-precipitated; many are women who kill their abusers.[25] Escalating conflicts are also apt to produce male-on-male victim-precipitated homicide; these disputes often arise over drug transactions or slights to one's masculine status.[26]

The notion of a *completely innocent victim*, or the absence of any victim precipitation, endures in the criminological concept of the ideal victim. An **ideal victim** is a victim regarded as worthy of sympathy and compassion (by juries, by media, by the public), or as a legitimate victim, because they possess certain characteristics. The ideal victim is blameless, engaged in virtuous activity at the time of the crime, and weak or vulnerable (e.g., a child victim).[27] In cases of sexual violence, the ideal victim is targeted by a stranger and actively resists the attack, as in the "real rape" stereotype.[28] Criminologists today study how offenders with non-ideal victims, such as sex workers, substance-dependent persons, and crime-involved victims receive more lenient criminal penalties.[29] Unlike early victimologists, criminologists today do not claim that ideal victims are less blameworthy than non-ideal victims. Rather, they shine a spotlight on the public's *perceptions* of victims as precursors to injustice.[30]

Victim precipitation's popularity as a research subject has been eclipsed by present-day focus on (1) identifying empirical patterns in victimization, including the extent of victimization and its correlates; (2) addressing individual and societal consequences of victimization; (3) developing theories of victimization that consider structural predictors instead of just victim behavior; and (4) examining the growing role of the victim in criminal justice processes.

PATTERNS IN VICTIMIZATION

How likely are you to be a victim of homicide? Of armed robbery? What about identity fraud or losing your savings in an investment scam? Perhaps some of these have already happened to you. Your probability of becoming a victim depends on where you live, your demographic profile, the economic circumstances of the surrounding community, the year it happens to be, and more. For instance, a 55-year-old woman living in the wealthy upper east side of Manhattan in 2015 was far less likely to become a victim of violent crime than a 20-year-old man living in the South Bronx in 1992.[31] Their risks are reversed, however, when it comes to being targeted for identity fraud and investment scams.[32, 33] Demographic, spatial (geographic), and temporal (time-based) trends are three types of empirical patterns that victimologists study. When it comes to establishing the nature and extent of victimization, researchers ask:

- How much victimization is happening (by location, time period, type of crime)?

- Who is most vulnerable to various forms of victimization?

- What is the nature of the victim-offender relationship?

- Are the predictors of victimization distinct from the predictors of criminal behavior?

- What factors increase the risk of recurrent victimization?

Measuring Victimization

Victimologists rely on victims' official and unofficial reports to answer the "How much?" question. Official statistics from law enforcement, such as the National Incident-Based Reporting System (NIBRS), only include crimes reported to police (see Chapter 2 for more on this). That's a problem. Official statistics give us decent data on homicide and motor vehicle theft, but they suffer from a large dark figure for most other offenses. According to the National Crime Victimization Survey (NCVS), only 40.2% of violent victimizations were reported to law enforcement in 2020.[34] Even the most serious violence—attacks with weapons and/or injury—saw reporting rates hovering around half. Property crimes fared even worse, with only one-third of victims reporting these offenses in 2020.[35]

The NCVS proves a much better source of victimization data than official statistics, as it contains criminal events that were never reported to police. Nevertheless, victimologists must contend with a few limitations. First, the NCVS is restricted to respondents age 12 and older. Researchers interested in measuring the extent of child victimization must look elsewhere, such as the National Child Abuse and Neglect Data System, which includes data from Child Protective Services (CPS).[36] Second, the NCVS only provides U.S. data, though victimologists wanting to compare patterns across countries—called cross-national research—can look to the International Crime Victims Survey (ICVS) instead.[37] Third, the NCVS permits analysis of only demographic (e.g., age, sex, and race/ethnicity of victim) and household (e.g., residential location, income) trends. It doesn't tell us much about victims' lifestyles and daily routines that might expose them to risky situations.[38] Fortunately, other surveys and ethnographic studies provide this insight.

What kinds of victimization happen the most in the U.S.? You might think it is violent crime if you watch courtroom dramas on TV. In fact, there are many more cases of property crime victimization than violent victimization, theft most especially. This is true regardless of the data source we use. For example, Table 12.2 shows that there were about 1.8 victims of property crime (approximately 4.24 million people) in 2020 for every 1 victim of violence (approximately 2.35 million people) in that year, according to NIBRS data from participating law enforcement agencies. NCVS data, which includes crimes not reported to police, shows a similar pattern despite differences in how the data are collected and the types of offenses reported, as found in Table 12.3. In the NCVS, property victimizations (approximately 12.09 million) outnumbered violent victimizations (approximately 4.56 million) by more than 2.6 to 1. Most property offenses tallied in both sources were larceny/theft.

Note a few things when comparing the extent of victimization using NIBRS (police data) and NCVS (victimization survey) data. First, NIBRS includes more types of offenses than the NCVS, so the categories "violent crimes" and "property crimes" are not entirely equivalent across sources. For example, NIBRS includes victims of human trafficking and kidnapping/abduction in its count of victims of violent crimes, but the NCVS does not. NIBRS also counts homicide victims, who are omitted from the NCVS because homicide victims don't complete surveys. You might expect that the numbers would be larger in the NIBRS data because more offense types are included, but you would be wrong. That's because of the second point: The NCVS values are estimates based on nationally representative survey data whereas NIBRS data come from participating police agencies. No report to a participating police agency or the police agency doesn't participate in NIBRS? No NIBRS data. Now it should make sense that we see far higher counts in the NCVS, like the 4.56 million violent victimizations in the NCVS versus the 2.35 million victims of violence in the NIBRS count. Nonetheless, the overall pattern is markedly alike across data sources: Property crime victimization dwarfs violent victimization.

TABLE 12.2 ■ Number of victims by crime type in the National Incident-Based Reporting System (NIBRS), 2020

Type of crime	Number of victims
Violent crimes	**2,352,943**
Assault offenses	2,063,412
Homicide offenses	11,815
Human trafficking offenses	1,576
Kidnapping/abduction	31,216
Robbery	117,663
Sex offenses	127,261
Property crimes	**4,244,451**
Arson	18,219
Bribery	463
Burglary/breaking and entering	467,235

Type of crime	Number of victims
Counterfeiting/forgery	51,187
Destruction/damage/vandalism	845,368
Embezzlement	5,452
Extortion/blackmail	9,294
Fraud offenses	588,383
Larceny/theft offenses	1,811,008
Motor vehicle theft	381,071
Stolen property offenses	66,771
Total	**8,950,337**

Source: Federal Bureau of Investigation. (2021). *Victims, adult and juvenile age category, by offense category, 2020* [Data set]. Crime Data Explorer. https://crime-data-explorer.app.cloud.gov/pages/downloads

Note: Table only includes data provided by the 9,880 law enforcement agencies (LEAs) reporting to NIBRS, covering a population of 177,522,400, or about 54% of the U.S. population. Victims in multiple-offense incidents are counted in more than one category.

TABLE 12.3 ■ Number of victimizations by crime type in the National Crime Victimization Survey (NCVS), 2020

Type of crime	Number of victimizations
Violent crimes	**4,558,154**
Rape/sexual assault	319,948
Robbery	437,258
Aggravated assault	812,182
Simple assault	2,988,767
Property crimes	**12,085,165**
Motor vehicle theft	545,807
Other theft	9,798,106
Burglary	1,210,638
Trespassing	530,614
Total	**16,643,319**

Source: U.S. Department of Justice. (2021). *Number of victimizations by crime type, 2020.* https://ncvs.bjs.ojp.gov/single-year-comparison/crimeType

Official crime statistics undercount white-collar victimization. For that information, we must look to alternative sources like victimization surveys designed specifically to measure white-collar crime as well as agencies like the Federal Trade Commission (FTC). Their results expose the pervasiveness of white-collar (and gray-collar) harms. The most recent report from the FTC on mass-market consumer fraud found that 15.9% of U.S. adults—about 40 million people—were victims of some form of consumer fraud.[39] And that count only includes people who were taken in by the fraud, rather than the number of people targeted by fraudsters. More than twice as many people were victims of consumer fraud than there were victimizations involving *all* property crimes reported in the NCVS that year.[40] Figure 12.3 displays the scale of consumer fraud victimization, broken down by type.

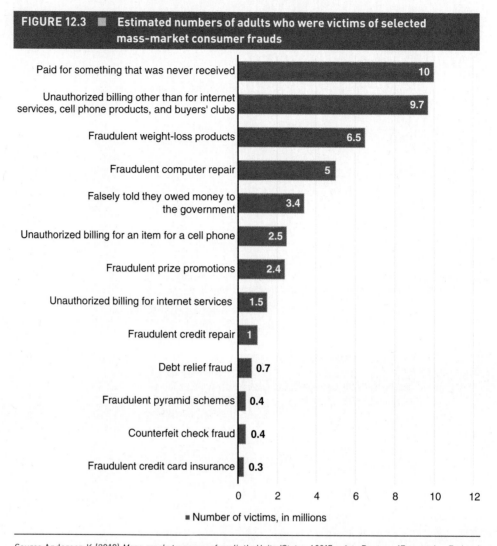

FIGURE 12.3 ■ Estimated numbers of adults who were victims of selected mass-market consumer frauds

Category	Number of victims, in millions
Paid for something that was never received	10
Unauthorized billing other than for internet services, cell phone products, and buyers' clubs	9.7
Fraudulent weight-loss products	6.5
Fraudulent computer repair	5
Falsely told they owed money to the government	3.4
Unauthorized billing for an item for a cell phone	2.5
Fraudulent prize promotions	2.4
Unauthorized billing for internet services	1.5
Fraudulent credit repair	1
Debt relief fraud	0.7
Fraudulent pyramid schemes	0.4
Counterfeit check fraud	0.4
Fraudulent credit card insurance	0.3

■ Number of victims, in millions

Source: Anderson, K. (2019). *Mass-market consumer fraud in the United States: A 2017 update.* Bureau of Economics, Federal Trade Commission. https://www.ftc.gov/reports/mass-market-consumer-fraud-united-states-2017-update

Note: Counts only include persons who fell victim to the frauds (e.g., purchased fraudulent products or paid unauthorized bills).

People injured by corporate and occupational crimes are "neglected victims" in criminology, though victimologists seek to change this.[41] They face a formidable task. Compared to street crimes, white-collar offenses are likely to go undetected, unreported, and unprosecuted. Victims may not even be aware that they have been victimized. For example, they may think an unnecessary surgery was essential, or they may not realize that they have been cheated by a service provider. Even more challenging, corporate crimes like illegal dumping of toxic waste and price-fixing have diffuse effects. They don't target individual victims; their harms are shouldered by many.

Correlates of Victimization

Victimologists ask: Who is most vulnerable to victimization? The statistical predictors, or correlates, of victimization depend on the offense under investigation. For example, the predictors of rape and sexual assault victimization differ from the predictors of homicide victimization. Nonetheless, victimization surveys point researchers towards a portrait of a *typical victim* of non-elite crimes like assault, rape, robbery, burglary, larceny, and motor vehicle theft. Official sources give insight into the typical victim of homicide. Such descriptions paint with broad strokes. Consider, for example, that there are many types of homicide. The typical victim of a domestic homicide is older and more likely to be female than the typical victim of other homicides, who are overwhelmingly young and male.[42] In fact, men and boys outnumber women and girls as victims of most forms of serious violence perpetrated by people who are not intimate partners. For example, as shown in Figure 12.4, nearly four out of five homicide victims between 2016 and 2020 were male (and this count includes domestic homicides).[43] The one noteworthy exception is rape and sexual assault, for which the sex gap was reversed and considerably wider; about 9 out of 10 victims of reported rapes and sexual assaults were female.[44]

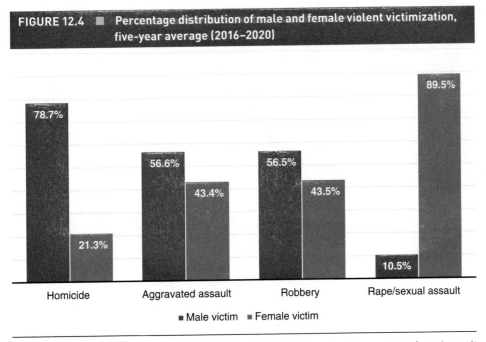

FIGURE 12.4 ■ Percentage distribution of male and female violent victimization, five-year average (2016–2020)

Sources: Homicide data from FBI's Uniform Crime Reports; Aggravated assault, robbery, and rape/sexual assault data from the U.S. Department of Justice, National Crime Victimization Survey ("Number of victimizations by crime type by sex, 2020").

Note: Height of bars indicates percentage, *not* counts or rates of victimization.

Astute observers will notice that the sex gaps in victimization match the sex gaps in offending, as described in Chapter 5, apart from rape/sexual assault. Men and boys are overrepresented among perpetrators of aggravated assaults, robberies, and homicides, just as they are overrepresented among victims, though offender sex gaps tend to be larger than victimization sex gaps. Other demographic correlates of violent victimization mirror offending patterns, as well. Take the age-crime curve. Risk of violent victimization declines with age just as offending drops off. The highest rates of violent victimization occur between ages 18 and 24, as found in Table 12.4. Elder abuse is a significant risk for older adults, and it is underreported in victimization surveys.[45] Nonetheless, it remains clear that violent victimization trends downward with age after peaking in the late teens and early 20s.

Table 12.4 displays a rudimentary breakdown of violent victimization rates by race and ethnicity, showing that white/non-Hispanic people, on average, experience the lowest rate of victimization relative to other groups. However, the NCVS uses broad categories that obscure important distinctions. The "other" category includes any person who does not identify as white, Black, or Hispanic. That is a lot of people! The resulting rate combines demographic groups with very low violent victimization rates, such as Asian persons (also a broad category), and groups with worryingly high rates of violent victimization, such as Native Americans.[46]

TABLE 12.4 ■ Serious violent victimization rates per 1,000 persons age 12 and older, five-year averages (2016–2020)	
Victim characteristic	Rate of victimization per 1,000 persons age 12 and older
Age	
12 to 14	6.7
15 to 17	10.6
18 to 20	16.5
21 to 24	13.6
25 to 34	10.0
35 to 49	7.1
50 to 64	5.0
65 or older	1.7
Race/ethnicity	
White (non-Hispanic)	6.6
Black (non-Hispanic)	7.9
Other non-Hispanic identity or multiracial	7.2
Hispanic/Latino	8.3
Household income	
Less than $7,500	26.8
$7,500 to $14,999	18.6
$15,000 to $24,999	11.5
$25,000 to $34,999	9.1
$35,000 to $49,999	7.4
$50,000 to $74,999	6.0
$75,000 or more	4.3
Marital status	
Never married	11.2
Married	3.1
Widowed	3.9
Divorced	11.0
Separated	19.1
Sex	
Male	6.9
Female	7.4

Source: Bureau of Justice Statistics. National Crime Victimization Survey (NCVS) Dashboard (N-DASH) Tool at www.bjs.gov.

Note: Serious violent victimization in the NCVS includes aggravated assault, rape/sexual assault, and robbery. Includes threatened, attempted, and completed offenses. Does not include homicide.

ENGAGED CRIMINOLOGY 12.1

Evaluating Victim Images

In this activity you will examine stock photos of crime victims to determine whether they accurately represent empirical patterns in victimization.

Examine the Photos

These four photos are representative of stock photos found in a typical online search for "crime victims." Examine them.

Karen Moskowitz/The Image Bank/Getty Images

Yuri_Arcurs/E+/Getty Images

Silvia Turra/EyeEm/Getty Images

LEREXIS/Moment/Getty Images

Identify characteristics of the typical victim in these images.

1. What gender, race/ethnicity, and age are depicted most frequently among the victims in the stock photos?

2. Does the representation of victims in stock photos accurately reflect those most likely to become victims of crime? (See Table 12.4)

3. Why do you think the creators of these stock photos chose to depict victims in these ways?

Rates of serious violent victimization (aggravated assault, robbery, and rape/sexual assault) are mostly similar across racial and ethnic groups, according to Table 12.4, but the nature of violence differs somewhat. Black victims report higher rates of firearm-related victimization—more than two out of five victimizations reported by Black respondents (or 42.8%) involved a perpetrator armed with a gun in 2020.[46] The corresponding proportions were 22.6% for non-Hispanic white victimization, 10.8% for Hispanic/Latino victimization, and 5.5% for all others in 2020. The use of weapons during a violent encounter increases the risk of serious injury or death when those weapons are used (rather than just brandished), and exposure to gun violence—whether experienced directly or witnessed—has lasting traumatic effects on victims and communities.[47, 48]

We must look beyond the NCVS to learn about the correlates of homicide victimization. The FBI's Supplementary Homicide Reports and the Centers for Disease Control (CDC), which report causes of death, give us a glimpse of the demographic groups at greatest risk of lethal victimization. Black men suffer the highest rates of homicide victimization in the U.S., and the risk of being killed is greatest in early adulthood (see Table 12.4). The FBI reports that more than half of homicide victims in 2019 were Black even though Black persons comprised only 13.4% of the U.S. population that year (8,839 out of 16,425 homicides, as seen in Table 12.5). This troubling pattern was driven mostly by violence against Black men. Black men, alone, comprise 46.4% of *all* homicide victims (7,614 out of 16,425 victims) despite representing only about 7% of people in the U.S.[49] Among women, Black and Indigenous women (i.e., Native American and Alaska Native) have the highest rates of murder victimization. Death certificate data from the CDC reveal these concerning patterns, as well.[50]

TABLE 12.5 ■ Number of homicide victims, by race and sex, 2019				
	Sex of victim			
Race of victim	Male	Female	Unknown	Total
White	4,743	2,066	2	6,811
Black	7,614	1,222	4	8,839
Native American or Alaska Native	135	61	0	196
Asian, Native Hawaiian, or Pacific Islander	195	103	2	300
Unknown	184	68	27	279
Total	12,870	3,520	35	16,425

Source: Federal Bureau of Investigation. *Supplementary homicide reports 1980–2019* [Machine-readable data files]. https://www.ojjdp.gov/ojstatbb/ezashr/

Students often ask: How many of these homicides are police killings? Analyses of the Fatal Encounters database, which tracks police-involved deaths, suggest that about 8% of adult men's homicides between 2012 and 2018 were the result of non-accidental police killings by gun shot, asphyxiation, beating, a chemical agent, or other method; vehicular collisions were excluded (official police statistics put the percentage closer to 4%).[51] This proportion does not tell us how many of these homicides were justifiable (necessary to prevent greater harm during the course of a felony). The risk of being killed by police was about three times higher for Black men (1.9 to 2.4 deaths per 100,000) than for white men (0.6 to 0.7 per 100,000) during the years of the analysis, with Latino men's risk falling in between (0.8 to 1.2 per 100,000). During the same time period, an annual average of 48 law enforcement officers were killed in the line of duty.[52]

Many correlates of victimization have little to do with individual demographics. Instead, they are about the kinds of places that people live, work, attend school, and socialize. For example, medical staff, security workers, and police personnel are more likely than others to encounter people in crisis, which increases their risk of violent victimization.[53] Living in an economically distressed neighborhood with schools that struggle to retain students until graduation amplifies the probability of being targeted for household burglary[54] and aggravated assault.[55] Importantly, subcultural norms that value toughness, autonomy, respect, and a "might makes right" attitude emerge when social institutions (e.g., education system and government) fail to meet the needs of struggling communities and violence flourishes.[56] Adherents to this code of conduct (or "code of the street") must "watch their back, gain respect, use violence, and not back down from confrontations" in order to avoid victimization while maintaining status (p. 1).[57]

Demographic correlates of victimization like race, ethnicity, and household poverty matter *because* they are so strongly linked to geography due to histories of residential and economic segregation in the U.S.[58] Living in or near areas of concentrated poverty, or areas where many people are poor, is a strong predictor of the types of victimization that most people fear: homicides, robberies, household break-ins, gun-related assaults, and other non-elite offenses.[59] And the harmful consequences of extreme poverty—crime and victimization, concentrated incarceration, health problems, poor-performing schools—impact *all* residents, even those who are not low-income (though the effects are most acute for the lowest-income residents).[60] Black and Native American children in the U.S. are about seven times as likely than white children to grow up in a community marked by extreme poverty, where more than 30% of the surrounding households live below the poverty line.[61] Exposure to extreme poverty was nearly five times higher for Hispanic/Latino children than for white children. These patterns are not simply a reflection of individual income. Low-income Native American and Black families are far more likely to live in extremely disadvantaged areas than white families that are *equally* poor.[62] The result is differing levels of exposure to conditions ripe for victimization. In other words, victimization patterns are a consequence of pervasive inequalities.

The Victim-Offender Relationship

In the 1980s and 1990s, parents in the U.S. were gripped by fears of child abductions committed by strangers. High-profile kidnappings and murders of children like Adam Walsh and Polly Klaas contributed to the nation's growing anxiety. Six-year-old Adam Walsh was murdered after being abducted from a Sears department store in 1981; his father, John Walsh, would later become the host of the TV show *America's Most Wanted*. Polly Klaas was murdered after being kidnapped at knifepoint during a slumber party by repeat criminal Richard Allen Davis in 1993. The era of "stranger danger" was underway.[63] Children were instructed not to talk to strangers and certainly to never take anything from them. Stranger abductions and stranger murders happen. They happened to Adam Walsh and Polly Klaas. But just how common *is* stranger violence? Who poses a greater threat to children (and adults)—the nefarious stranger or the trusted friend or relative? This is a question about victim-offender relationships.

Some crimes are committed by complete strangers—the anonymous bicycle thief, the mugger, or the faceless fraudster calling with an offer too good to be true. Other times, the wrongdoer is someone close, like a family member, an ex-spouse, a coworker, or a friend. Victimologists track patterns in victim-offender relationships, asking questions such as the following:

- How likely are we to even *know* the relationship between the victim and offender?

- What kinds of victim-offender relationships are most common among various types of crimes?

Let's begin with the first question. Establishing the victim-offender relationship requires that we know (1) who the victim is and (2) who the offender is. The latter proves trickier than the former. Recall that direct-contact crimes are those in which the offender and victim come together in time and place. They are in direct contact, as in violent crimes like robbery or assault. Victim-offender relationships are easier to identify in direct-contact crimes, many of which are violent crimes.[64] Even if the victim does not know *who* the attacker was, they can identify them as a stranger versus a non-stranger. A non-stranger is an "offender who is either related to, well known to, or casually acquainted with the victim," according to the Bureau of Justice Statistics.[65] As a result, most data on victim-offender relationships—from police statistics and victimization surveys—pertain to violent crimes.

What about property crimes like larceny/theft, fraud, and burglary? It is possible to determine the relationship if the victim sees the offender or knows who committed the crime (e.g., if they know the credit card thief was their child). Another possibility is that law enforcement identifies the offender. However, the proportion of unknown offenders—not to be confused with "stranger" offenders—is large for property crimes because so many are non-direct-contact offenses that go unsolved. The NCVS only reports victim-offender relationships for direct-contact crimes, including personal theft (but not household theft), for this reason.[66] NIBRS only reports these relationships for crimes in which the offender has been identified by law enforcement.[67]

Now we can move on to the second question: What kinds of victim-offender relationships are most common among various types of crimes? Most data sources designate known relationships as one of the following:

1. *Intimates* – Current or former spouses, boyfriends, girlfriends, or romantic partners.

2. *Other relatives* – Parents, stepparents, children, stepchildren, brothers, sisters, and other relatives; does not include spouses or other romantic partners.

3. *Well known/casual acquaintances* – Current or former friends, roommates, classmates, neighbors, coworkers, and other known nonrelatives/non-intimates.

4. *Strangers* – Anyone not previously known to the victim.

Figure 12.5 displays victim-offender relationships for aggravated assault, simple assault, rape/sexual assault, and robbery. Rape/sexual assault was the most likely to be committed by someone known to the victim; 29.8% of victims reported that the person who sexually assaulted them was a current or former intimate partner and 35.3% reported a well-known or casual acquaintance. About two-fifths of aggravated assault and simple assault victims report that they were attacked by an acquaintance or current or former intimate partner. Robbery victims were the most likely of the four types to be targeted by a stranger (50.4%), yet you may be surprised to learn that nearly 40% of robbery victims were attacked by intimates, relatives, or acquaintances (8.7%, 12.1%, and 19.1%, respectively).

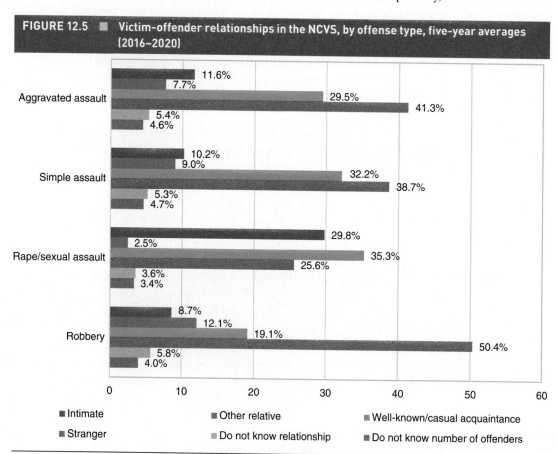

FIGURE 12.5 ■ **Victim-offender relationships in the NCVS, by offense type, five-year averages (2016–2020)**

Source: Bureau of Justice Statistics. National Crime Victimization Survey (NCVS) Dashboard (N-DASH) Tool at www.bjs.gov.

Note: Values represent percentages, not victimization rates; percentages total to 100% for each offense category.

Victim-offender relationships in homicides are the stuff of crime fiction. Television detectives examine the extent and type of injury done to a murder victim and instantly pronounce the likely relationship between the perpetrator and their target. And there is certainly evidence that victim-offender relationships are correlated with the mode of attack (e.g., spouses, lovers, and exes are especially likely to wound their victim's face with an object found in the home).[68] In many shows, the murderer is a serial killer, a terrifying stranger lurking in the shadows or beneath the façade of normalcy. In other words, stranger danger. But how common *are* stranger murders? Not very, according to the FBI's Supplementary Homicide Report. Among homicides for which the victim-offender relationship is known (i.e., cases for which an offender has been identified and the relationship determined), only about one in five were committed by strangers in 2020 (though the proportion may be higher if stranger homicide assailants are less likely to be identified).[69] Two-fifths of murder victims were killed by casual acquaintances, friends, neighbors, and coworkers. The remaining murder victims were killed by a current or former spouse, romantic partner, or family member. These are called domestic homicides.[70] Intimate partner homicides—domestic homicides committed by spouses, romantic partners, and exes—prove less newsworthy than other murders despite their relative frequency: Media outlets report them less prominently, the news stories are shorter, and they are less likely to include images than are stories about other kinds of homicide.[71]

Stranger danger is also about abductions. Of the 24,284 kidnappings/abductions reported by NIBRS in 2019, less than 10% were committed by strangers (another 10% are listed as having at least one offender whose relationship to the victim is unknown). According to these police data, 8 out of 10 kidnapping victims are abducted by family members (usually in a custody dispute, when the victims are minors) or another person known to the victim, acting either alone or with help from others.[72] Most abduction victims are adults; there were 3.7 adult abduction victims for every one child victim in 2019.[73] The number of *children* abducted by strangers falls between 100 and 300 children each year.[74] Studies consistently show that the greatest threats to children's safety—whether abductions, assaults, sexual violence, or homicides—are family members and other people they know well.[75] These days, child safety organizations have scrapped the "stranger danger" message in favor of more nuanced messaging about safe help-seeking and signs of untrustworthy adult behavior, such as telling children to keep secrets.[76]

Victim-Offender Overlap

Many people think of victims and people who commit crimes as mutually exclusive categories. The reality is more complicated. Incarcerated populations, much more so than the general public, have extensive histories of victimization in childhood and beyond, especially incarcerated women and girls.[77] When it comes to non-elite crimes, victims and people who commit offenses, as groups, share many demographic and behavioral characteristics.[78] They are statistically more likely than non-victims and non-offenders to be young, low-income, and living in distressed communities. They also are more apt to have low self-control, mental health challenges, and a high-risk lifestyle such as excessive substance use.[79] An additional commonality is exposure to traumatic experiences in childhood.[80] **Victim-offender overlap** refers to the relationship between, or co-occurrence of, victimization and criminal offending.

Of course, many victims have no history of criminal conduct, nor do they fit the mold for the "typical" victim or offender. Law violators are more likely to have been victims than the reverse.[81] This is especially true of property crime victims. Plus, many people who commit offenses have avoided becoming targets of others' misdeeds. Therefore, criminologists suggest we consider three categories:

1. Victims – Persons with no histories of criminal conduct (i.e., pure victims).

2. Offenders – Crime-involved persons with no histories of victimization (i.e., pure offenders).

3. Victim-offenders – Persons who switch between criminal conduct and victimization.[82]

We can think of victim-offenders as occupying the overlap in a Venn diagram of victims and offenders. The overlap is especially large for violent crimes like homicide and aggravated assault. The

Cyntoia Brown, a 16-year-old sex trafficked minor (seen here as an adult in 2018), was sentenced to 51 years in prison (later commuted to 15 years) in 2004 for murdering 43-year-old Johnny Allen, who had solicited her for sex. Brown's story is one of victim-offender overlap.

Lacy Atkins / The Tennessean via AP, Pool

Venn diagram looks nearly like a circle (complete overlap) for homicides linked to criminal conduct, such as drug-related killings.[83] Criminologists describe crime-involved lifestyles—involvement in drug trafficking, possessing and distributing illegal firearms, operating illicit businesses, and so on—as **victimogenic**. Victimogenic conditions are risk factors for victimization.

Think about the reasons that criminal lifestyles are victimogenic. First, it may be an issue of proximity.[84] Being surrounded by crime-involved (and armed) acquaintances increases the chances of becoming a target eventually. Second, imagine a cheated customer or a disgruntled business partner of an illegal gun distributor. They can't remedy the problem by submitting a complaint to the Better Business Bureau or filing a civil suit, and they aren't going to ask for police assistance. Violent retaliation or "self-help justice" is more likely when legal options for dispute resolution are unavailable.[85] As many illicit businesses move online, however, the strategies for settling disagreements are less likely to turn people who commit offenses into victims. For example, wronged parties in drug cryptomarkets (i.e., drug trafficking on the dark web) resolve disputes by damaging the wrongdoer's reputation in public posts, using third-party interventions by platform administrators, and threatening to expose the vendor or buyer as a scammer.[86] Third, offenders select victims who are unlikely to report the crime. This is evident in ethnographic studies of armed robbers. For instance, the armed robbers interviewed for Randol Contreras's book *The Stickup Kids* targeted drug traffickers; in turn, the drug robbers were vulnerable to robbery victimization by others who had heard of their recent windfall.[87]

Recurring Victimization

Recurring victimization happens when a person or place experiences multiple instances of victimization, either the same form on repeat or multiple types spread out over time. Think of it as serial victimization, or the victim equivalent of recidivism. For example, prior burglary victimization is a strong predictor of future burglary victimization, at least for the first few months or so after a break-in, with the same burglar returning to the initial site.[88] Recurring victimization is called **repeat victimization** if the same offense happens over and over. **Polyvictimization**, another type of recurring victimization, refers to multiple *forms* of victimization happening to one person (*poly-* means many).

An example helps illustrate. Homelessness is a victimogenic condition that accelerates repeat victimization and polyvictimization. Experiencing violence is a common pathway to temporary and chronic homelessness. In fact, domestic violence is the primary reason women and their children become home-less,[89] and more than four out of five unaccompanied homeless youth (on their own without family) screen positive for histories of child physical or sexual abuse.[90] Victims of family violence typically experi-ence repeat victimization—they are subjected to the same form of violence over and over.[91] Homelessness then increases the risk of additional forms of criminal harm. Over half of homeless young people report being robbed, beaten, stolen from, or sexually assaulted after becoming unhoused.[92] In other words, they experience polyvictimization. Available sleeping arrangements—shelters, couch-surfing with acquain-tances or near-strangers, sleeping in cars or in public areas—reduce privacy, autonomy, and the capacity to avoid those who seek to do harm.[93] Exchanging sex for necessities, or "survival sex," exposes individuals to even greater risk of physical violence,[94] as does hard drug use.[95] Trauma begets trauma.

CONSEQUENCES OF VICTIMIZATION

Victims of crime endure multiple forms of suffering, including death, physical injury, loss of property and income, psychological burdens, and fearfulness that reorders daily life. Their families and com-munities must shoulder these problems, as well. Furthermore, all of society pays in a literal sense (e.g., the costliness of operating the criminal legal system and purchasing home security measures) and figu-ratively, as the threat of crime fuels collective anxiety. This section addresses the costs to individual victims and the broader communities they inhabit.

Physical and Economic Consequences

Death due to homicide is the most extreme form of physical suffering, but there are other bodily costs of violent crime. The NCVS estimates that there were approximately 1.16 million violent victimiza-tions involving injury in 2020, with 793,753 violent events resulting in victims receiving medical treat-ment for their injuries.[96] Data from emergency departments at hospitals suggest an even greater extent of violence-related injury. The National Hospital Ambulatory Medical Care Survey indicates about 1.7 million annual emergency room visits for assault.[97] Even this higher value is likely an underestimation of the true need for medical assistance. Some victims, particularly victims of family violence, neither report the crime nor seek out necessary medical help.[98]

The economic toll of crime on victims covers a range of costs: property lost or damaged during the crime, the cost of medical treatment and funeral expenses, loss of income (due to injury, psycho-logical distress, or participation in the criminal justice process), and more. The FBI reports the average amount of value stolen by type of offense: $1,797 stolen in the average robbery, $2,661 stolen in the average burglary, $1,162 stolen in the average larceny-theft (non–motor vehicle), and $8,886 stolen in the average motor vehicle theft.[99] Factor in the 243,600 robberies, 1,035,314 burglaries, 4,606,324 larcenies, and 810,400 motor vehicle thefts reported in 2020 and you will quickly discover the astro-nomical direct costs to victims.[100]

The financial losses for victims of white-collar crimes are far steeper than for street crimes.[101] The Association of Certified Fraud Examiners estimates that businesses lose 5% of their total revenue to employee fraud, or about $800 million annually in the U.S.[102] The Internal Revenue Service (IRS) reports an average annual loss of $441 billion due to tax evasion.[103] And even though the median loss for individual victims of consumer frauds is only $100, the massive scale of victimization puts the col-lective loss around $4 billion annually.[104]

Our collective response to crime—the criminal legal system—is expensive, as well. It costs tax-payers about $300 billion annually to cover the costs of law enforcement ($142.5 billion); prisons, jails, probation, and parole ($88.5 billion); and the judicial and legal system ($64.7 billion).[105] Plus, individual households incur the expenses of anticipating crime: home security systems and measures, secure parking lot fees, insurance fees, and the costs of moving to safer neighborhoods. Crime is costly.

Psychological and Behavioral Consequences

The most enduring harms of victimization are often psychological. Victims report experiencing depression, loss of self-esteem, and anxiety in the aftermath of a crime.[106] They also describe increased alcohol and drug use as a coping strategy.[107] For example, a study of cyberstalking victims found that three-quarters of victims suffer negative psychological impacts of being stalked online, including difficulty concentrating, nightmares or trouble sleeping, loss of interest in their daily activities, eating problems or disorders, increased drinking, and isolating themselves from friends and family.[108] Identity theft victims report feeling anxious, angry, violated, and vulnerable.[109] Robbery victims recount significant emotional distress and maladaptive coping (e.g., substance use), and they frequently alter their daily routines for fear of repeat victimization.[110] Some researchers argue that chronic intimate partner victimization can produce a psychological consequence called learned helplessness.[111] **Learned helplessness** is a neurological adaption in which a victim becomes passive and numb, having learned that resisting mistreatment is pointless and will not change the outcom. Others contend that this is an instinctive neurological "freeze" response rather than something that is learned.[112]

Post-traumatic stress disorder (PTSD), a trauma response typically associated with war, is well-documented among victims of violent crimes, including robbery,[113] rape and sexual assault,[114] stalking,[115] and intimate partner violence.[116] PTSD is a psychiatric diagnosis for which several criteria must be met, according to the American Psychiatric Association's *Diagnostic and Statistical Manual of Mental Disorders (DSM-V)*. These critieria include the following:

1. Exposure to actual or threatened death, serious injury, or sexual violence.

2. Presence of one or more intrusive symptoms associated with the traumatic event(s) (e.g., recurrent, involuntary, and intrusive memories of the traumatic event; recurrent distressing dreams; dissociative reactions).

3. Persistent avoidance of stimuli associated with the traumatic event(s) (e.g., avoiding people, places, activities, and objects associated with the trauma).

4. Negative alterations in cognitions and mood associated with the traumatic event(s) (e.g., persistent feelings of fear or shame, distorted beliefs about the cause of the trauma).

5. Marked alterations in arousal and reactivity associated with the traumatic event(s) (e.g., exaggerated startle response, concentration problems, hypervigilance, sleep disturbance, and irritability).[117]

A diagnosis of PTSD requires that symptoms persist for at least one month and produce significant distress and impairment. Though most research focuses on violent crime and PTSD, there is evidence that property crime victimization can also lead to PTSD symptoms. For example, researchers found that two out of five burglary victims meet the criteria for PTSD at a severe level.[118]

The traumatic consequences of victimization extend beyond immediate victims and their families. The threat of violence in high-crime neighborhoods puts residents on high alert, activating the body's stress response system in ways that undermine well-being.[119] The specter of violence forces people into a state of hypervigilance, impairing executive functions like memory, concentration, and impulse control.[120] Criminologists find that a recent homicide in the local community profoundly reduces children's performance on cognitive tests, as if they have lost two years of schooling.[121] "Local violence does not make children less intelligent," writes researcher Patrick Sharkey. "Rather, it occupies their minds" (p. 87).[122]

Memorial for homicide victim Reuben Lewis in Concordia Park in Oakland, CA, in February 2021. Homicides like Lewis's have profound effects on children's well-being in neighborhoods where they occur.

Jane Tyska/Digital First Media/East Bay Times/Getty Image

Fear of Crime

How worried are you about being robbed when walking alone in your neighborhood after dark? Very worried? Not worried at all? An answer of "very worried" suggests a greater level of fearfulness. Fear of crime is emotional and subjective; two people within the same household can feel different levels of fear.[123] How likely are you to become a victim of a robbery in the next 12 months? Very likely? Not likely at all? An answer of "not likely at all" implies a low level of perceived risk of victimization. It is entirely possible to answer "very worried" and "not likely at all" (or the inverse), because fear of crime is distinct from perceived risk.[124] Notice that both—fear of crime and perceived risk—are about perception rather than the objective likelihood of harm. This explains, in part, why the public's fear of crime remains relatively stable even when victimization rates plummet.[125]

Fear of crime generates anxiety and alters the behavior of direct victims of crime, those geographically near to crime, and even those who are unlikely to become its target. The consequences of fearfulness can be significant. For example, researchers studied crime locations and ninth-graders' school transportation routes in Baltimore, finding that students missed more school days when getting public transportation to school meant they had to walk through or wait in high-violence areas. Frequent absences are a precursor to low achievement scores and dropping out. In the authors' words, "every day these students must weigh the incremental benefit of one more day at school against the possibility of real physical injury or death on the way to school."[126]

The fearful ninth-graders were engaging in avoidant behaviors. Avoidant behavior is one type of precautionary measure taken by those who fear victimization. As its name suggests, it involves avoiding feared locations or situations. Other precautionary measures include protective behaviors, like owning or carrying a weapon or pepper spray, installing home security measures, or learning self-defense.[127] Avoidant and protective behaviors constrain the worried person's routines.

The absentee ninth-graders' precautionary measures, though detrimental academically, were quite reasonable. They avoided locations that posed a serious threat to their safety. Their fears were justified. This is not the case for all who are fearful, however. Victimologists observe that people with relatively low odds of becoming victims often express higher levels of fear than people who are at much greater risk. This pattern is called a fear-of-crime paradox. The two primary fear-of-crime paradoxes pertain to gender and age: (1) Women are much more fearful of crime than men even though men and women are at about equal risk of nonlethal victimization and men are at a much greater risk of lethal victimization than women, and (2) older people feel less safe and take more precautions against crime than younger people despite younger people's much higher chances of being victimized.[128]

Victimologists offer several explanations for fear-of-crime paradoxes, each supported somewhat by evidence. First, the gender paradox reflects women's greater sense of vulnerability to crime due to believing themselves to be physically smaller or weaker than potential male assailants.[129] This is also the go-to explanation for the age-based paradox: People feel more vulnerable as their bodies age and their health declines.[130] Second, there is evidence that women's fear of crime is, in fact, fear of sexual assault, or the worry that all crimes can lead to rape. This is called the *shadow hypothesis*: Fear of sexual assault casts a shadow on all other fears.[131] Third, some argue that women's greater fears are warranted; it's just that violence against women is hidden from view, as in the case of unreported intimate partner violence, sexual assault, and stalking.[132] The final explanation is that women are socialized to think they are potential victims who should constantly be on guard, whereas men are socialized to view expressions of fear as feminine and weak.[133] In this view, men may fear crime as much as or more than women, but they are less likely to say so.

ENGAGED CRIMINOLOGY 12.2

Reflecting on Fear of Crime

This reflection exercise asks you to think about your constrained behaviors and fear of crime. Use the table to do the following:

- Make a list of actions you take (or actions you avoid) to reduce your chances of becoming a victim of crime. Include three in the table.

- Identify whether each behavior on your list is an avoidant behavior or a protective behavior.

- Identify which criminal offense(s) each behavior seeks to reduce.

Constraining behaviors (list three)	Avoidant or protective?	Criminal offense you seek to reduce with each constraining behavior?

Questions for discussion or individual reflection:

1. Why do you think you fear these crimes the most? (If you don't fear them most, why do you take actions to avoid them?)

2. What crimes *don't* you fear or take actions to avoid, and why?

CRIME VICTIMS' RIGHTS

Over the course of nine days in 2018, 204 victims of Larry Nassar, a former physician at Michigan State University, provided heart-wrenching statements about the traumatic consequences of sexual abuse they suffered while being treated by Nassar, many as young children.[134] Nassar was ultimately sentenced to life in prison. The victims' accounts were not witness testimony. They were victim-impact statements given during Nassar's sentencing. Granting victims a voice in the courtroom, not as witnesses but as *victims impacted by crimes*, began in the 1980s. The first legislation providing this right to victims was passed in 1982 in California, following the high-profile advocacy efforts of Doris Tate, the mother of actor Sharon Tate, who was murdered by Charles Manson's followers in 1969.[135] Crime victims today have access to rights and services that did not exist a half-century ago due to the accomplishments of victims' rights advocates like Doris Tate. Achievements of the victims' rights movement include, but are not limited to the following:

- Victims can give victim-impact statements in court and at parole hearings, as in the Nassar case. **Victim-impact statements** are oral (live, audio, or video) or written accounts provided to judges, juries, or parole boards by victims or family members of deceased victims. They describe the effects of the crime on the victim's life, typically with the purpose of achieving an emotional recovery (or "closure") and to influence sentencing and parole decisions.[136] They are distinct from witness testimony. It is still unclear whether these statements do, in fact, impact legal decision-making in typical (i.e., non–death penalty) criminal cases, as most research focuses on capital trials.[137]

- Victims can access restitution and compensation funds to cover the costs of victimization-related medical bills, lost wages, damaged or lost property, insurance deductibles, crime-scene clean-up costs, and expenses arising from involvement in the criminal justice process, such as child care or travel costs. The expenses covered vary state to state. Court-ordered payments from convicted offenders supply **restitution** funds whereas the government provides compensation funds when certain criteria are met by the victim, such as reporting the offense within a specified time frame and cooperating with the investigation and prosecution.[138]

- Victims of sex offenses are protected by rape shield laws, which restrict use of victims' sexual histories in sexual assault cases. Prior to these laws, victims' sexual pasts could be used to attack their credibility or suggest that the victim had consented. Fear of humiliation and sexual stereotyping discouraged victims from coming forward or participating in the legal process.[139] Rape shield laws in some states also restrict the admissibility of the victim's clothing to instances when it can demonstrate absence or presence of a struggle or bodily fluids. Under such laws, clothing cannot be used to indicate consent or that the victim was "asking" for the offender's sexual attention.[140]

- Child victims are often permitted to testify without the accused person present. Instead, they may make in-court appearances using closed-circuit television or video-recorded depositions. Their privacy may also be protected with courtroom closure procedures (i.e., not open to the public).[141] These rights of child victims are especially important in child abuse criminal trials.

Hazem Mohammed's was one of 90 victim- impact statements at the August 2020 trial of Brenton Tarrant, a white supremacist who committed mass murder at a mosque in Christchurch, New Zealand.

John Kirk-Anderson/POOL/AFP/Getty Images

Prior to these and other achievements, many victims and their family members felt mistreated by a criminal justice system that seemed to protect the rights of defendants instead of the rights of victims. They complained of a second victimization inflicted by an insensitive system that denied them dignity and a voice in criminal justice proceedings.[142] It was victims' and their families' anger and grassroots advocacy—with support from various political camps with vastly different agendas—that produced the victims' rights legislation we see today.

History of the Victims' Rights Movement

The history of the victims' right movement, which began in the 1960s but picked up steam in the 1970s and 1980s, is an unusual coupling of conservativism and feminism. Between 1961 and 1966, the Supreme Court made a series of decisions that strengthened crime defendants' rights, sometimes called the "criminal procedure revolution."[143] Outcomes included the exclusionary rule (which prevented the use of evidence obtained from warrantless searches), Miranda warnings (police notification of suspects' rights, as you've likely heard on TV: "You have the right to remain silent…"), and the provision of court-appointed attorneys for defendants unable to afford them. Conservative politicians, recognizing that a law-and-order platform appealed to (mostly white) voters shaken by the unrest of the civil rights and anti-war movements, seized upon the Court's rulings as evidence of an imbalance of power between the dangerous criminal minority and the law-abiding, victimized majority.[144] In 1970, Vice President Spiro Agnew claimed that "the rights of the accused have become more important than the rights of victims in our courtrooms."[145] "Restore the balance" became the central theme of the victims' rights movement.

The practical goals of conservative reformers—ensuring victims' rights—aligned with the goals of women's rights advocates, even if their ideological purposes did not. Rather than adopt a law-and-order agenda set on countering the expansion of defendants' due process (or criminal procedure) rights, feminist reformers were concerned with the powerlessness of women victims within the criminal justice process.[145] Up through the 1970s, domestic violence was frequently treated as a private family affair rather than as criminal assault. Husbands could not be convicted of raping their wives (marital rape laws didn't exist in all U.S. states until 1993). And sexual assault victims were routinely disbelieved and humiliated in the courtroom. Women's rights advocates—seeking to advance the cause of victim-impact statements, rape shield laws, and mandatory arrest policies for domestic abusers—adopted conservatives' victims' rights language.

The first federal victims' rights legislation became law in 1982. The Victim and Witness Protection Act of 1982 enhanced the role of victims in criminal proceedings through victim-impact statements. It included protections by enforcing steep penalties for those who intimidate, harass, or retaliate against victims. It also expanded victim restitution.[146] The federal Crime Control Act of 1990 broadened victims' procedural rights. Now victims had the right to be informed of court dates and times, to attend court proceedings, to communicate with the prosecutor, and to be notified when an offender's detention status changes (e.g., from incarceration to parole).[147] It also granted a slate of rights specific to child victims. The 1994 omnibus Violent Crime Control and Law Enforcement Act further extended victims' rights regarding speaking at sentencing hearings, increased funding for local victims' services, and made restitution mandatory for specified criminal case types (e.g., sexual assault).[148] States followed suit, expanding the rights and services available to victims of crimes. The subsequent years saw even greater gains with the passage of victims' bills of rights.

Protesters hold up childhood photos of clergy sexual abuse victims in Philadelphia in March 2011.

AP Photo/Matt Rourke

Victims' Bill of Rights

The Crime Victims' Rights Act, enacted in 2004, lists the rights afforded to victims of federal crimes and authorizes federal funding to support victims in accessing their rights.[149] It is also known as a victims' bill of rights. These rights include the following:

1. The right to be reasonably protected from the accused.

2. The right to reasonable, accurate, and timely notice of any public court proceeding, or any parole proceeding, involving the crime or of any release or escape of the accused.

3. The right not to be excluded from any such public court proceeding, unless the court, after receiving clear and convincing evidence, determines that testimony by the victim would be materially altered if the victim heard other testimony at that proceeding.

4. The right to be reasonably heard at any public proceeding in the district court involving release, plea, sentencing, or any parole proceeding.

5. The reasonable right to confer with the attorney for the Government in the case.

6. The right to full and timely restitution as provided in law.

7. The right to proceedings free from unreasonable delay.

8. The right to be treated with fairness and with respect for the victim's dignity and privacy.

9. The right to be informed in a timely manner of any plea bargain or deferred prosecution agreement.

10. The right to be informed of the rights under this section and the services described in section 503(c) of the Victims' Rights and Restitution Act of 1990 (42 U.S.C. 10607(c)) and provided contact information for the Office of the Victims' Rights Ombudsman of the Department of Justice.[150]

Remember, though, that each state has its own criminal justice system and most defendants in the U.S. end up in state courts rather than federal courts. Every U.S. state has its own version of a victims' bill of rights, many of them amendments to state constitutions (some are called Marsy's Law). Other victims' bills of rights are statutory rather than constitutional. Statutes are laws passed by legislatures, whereas constitutional amendments are put to voters through ballot initiatives (states vary in their amendment procedures; there is no one-size-fits-all model).

Controversy in Victims' Rights Legislation

You might assume that victims' rights laws are uncontroversial. After all, their most ardent advocates spanned the political spectrum from die-hard law-and-order conservatives to the liberal women's movement. But you would be wrong. Legal scholars critique the restoring-the-balance narrative that treats the rights of defendants and the rights of victims as equivalent and competing. These critics are quick to point out that the rights of the accused, enshrined in the U.S. Constitution, are protections against the fearsome power of a government that can strip them of life, liberty, and property (recall that the prosecutor represents the government, not the victims). Victims, in contrast, face no such threat from the government.[151]

Many critiques of victim involvement in criminal proceedings—a crowning achievement of the victims' rights movement—focus on issues of justice. For example, Judge Match, the judge in Oklahoma City bomber Timothy McVeigh's criminal trial, allowed victims to *either* watch the trial or speak at the sentencing, but not both, as watching the trial might taint their testimony. He argued that this was not a matter of denying victims' rights but of "the integrity of the process by which defendants are judged and the evidence is judged."[152]

Victim-impact statements have been the focus of contentious debate. Supreme Court justice Thurgood Marshall wrote in a dissenting opinion in *Payne v. Tennessee* (1991), the first Supreme Court ruling to uphold victim-impact statements in capital cases, that they "draw the jury's attention away from the character of the defendant and the circumstances of the crime to such illicit considerations as the eloquence with which family members express their grief and the status of the victim in the community."[153] Critics ask: Is it justice to punish the murder of a well-loved middle-class stay-at-home mother more harshly than the murder of a drug-addicted teenager who has run away from their latest foster care placement? And they point to research showing that victim-impact statements in death penalty cases arouse anger in jurors who then pay attention only to evidence that confirms their anger and disregard evidence that favors the defendant.[154]

CHAPTER SUMMARY

LO 12.1   Trace the origins and evolution of victimology.

Victimology, the scientific study of criminal victimization, began in the 1940s. Early victimologists developed victim typologies and the concept of victim precipitation, seeking to determine the victim's level of blame in the criminal event. The victim-blaming approach was supplanted by contemporary victimologists' focus on measuring victimization as well as identifying and explaining its predictors and consequences.

LO 12.2   Identify common patterns in criminal victimization.

Police data and victimization surveys indicate that the extent of property crime victimization surpasses violent victimization. Correlates of victimization include demographic, community, and lifestyle factors. Victims of violence are more likely than other victims to know the perpetrator (victim-offender relationship). Many offenders have also been victims (victim-offender overlap), and many victims experience repeat and polyvictimization.

LO 12.3   Describe the consequences of criminal victimization.

Consequences of victimization include physical costs (i.e., injury and death), economic costs (e.g., property lost or damaged, lost wages, costs of criminal justice system), psychological effects (e.g., anxiety, depression, post-traumatic stress disorder), and fear of crime. Consequences are borne by direct victims, family members, and broader communities.

LO 12.4   Outline the history and impact of the victims' rights movement.

The victims' rights movement originated with the advocacy efforts of crime victims, conservative politicians, and feminists. They have fought for victims to have a voice in criminal cases and access to compensation, services, and information. Their achievements are listed in federal and state victims' bills of rights.

ENGAGED DISCUSSION

1.   Which of Mendelsohn's victim types describe victim facilitation? Which describe victim provocation?

2.   Thefts comprise a much larger share of all victimizations in the National Crime Victimization Survey (NCVS) than in National Incident-Based Reporting System (NIBRS) data. Use what you know about these two data sources to devise an explanation.

3.   Which crime types do you fear the most, and why? Which consequences of victimization (e.g., injury, property loss, psychological trauma) do you fear the most, and why?

4.   Should victim-impact statements be allowed in court? Make a case for or against them, or both.

KEY TERMS

Avoidant behavior (p. 319)

Fear-of-crime paradox (p. 319)

Ideal victim (p. 305)

Learned helplessness (p. 318)

Polyvictimization (p. 316)

Post-traumatic stress disorder (PTSD) (p. 318)

Protective behavior (p. 319)

Recurring victimization (p. 316)

Repeat victimization (p. 316)

Restitution (p. 320)

Victim facilitation (p. 300)

Victim-impact statements (p. 320)

Victim-offender overlap (p. 315)

Victimogenic (p. 316)

Victimology (p. 300)

Victim precipitation (p. 300)

Victim provocation (p. 301)

Victims' bill of rights (p. 322)

13

THEORIES OF PUNISHMENT

LEARNING OBJECTIVES

13.1 Describe how retributive principles inform sentencing guidelines.

13.2 Distinguish between specific, general, partial, and marginal deterrence.

13.3 Contrast incapacitation with retribution and deterrence.

13.4 Explain how problem-solving courts are rooted in the rehabilitation ideal.

13.5 Identify the primary principles and strategies of restorative justice.

Mike Anderson was 22 years old when he joined a companion in robbing a Burger King manager of $2,000 in Missouri in 1999. The gun used in the robbery was never located. Anderson insisted to police that it was a BB gun held by his codefendant whose idea it was to commit the robbery spontaneously on that August night in 1999. However, police found a brochure advertising a firearm in Anderson's home, which was presented to the court as evidence that he possessed and used a gun during the robbery. Mike Anderson was convicted in 2000 and sentenced to 13 years in prison.[1]

As is common, Anderson was released on bond prior to serving his sentence, during which time he was appealing his conviction (the conviction was upheld). Due to a clerical error, though, his bond was never revoked. That means no one showed up to bring him to prison, and no warrant was issued for his arrest. The Missouri Department of Corrections mistakenly thought Anderson was already incarcerated. Anderson filed another appeal in 2004, stating in the very first line that he was not in prison. Moreover, his home address was listed in several places throughout the appeal filing. Still, the Department of Corrections failed to realize their error.[2]

The Department of Corrections only figured out the mistake in 2013, when Anderson was scheduled for release from prison. They couldn't release an inmate who was never incarcerated in the first place! A warrant was issued for Anderson's arrest. He was to be imprisoned for 13 years ... 13 years after the fact.

In the years between his conviction and 2013, Mike Anderson quietly went on with his life. He got married, had children, and began a construction business. He didn't hide from police: He renewed his driver's license, filed his taxes, registered his business in his name. He didn't leave town, either. In fact, at the time of his arrest in 2013, he was living just two blocks away from the address the courts last had on record for him. He led an ordinary, law-abiding life. He had no further offenses—not even a speeding ticket.

The victim of his robbery struggled a great deal in the aftermath of the crime: He quit his job, become isolated, and grew paranoid and fearful. Nonetheless, when he became aware of the mix-up 13 years later, he didn't demand Anderson's incarceration. Instead, upon learning about how Anderson had built a conventional life for himself and his family, he publicly stated that he forgave Anderson and believed he should be released from prison.[3]

Upstanding citizen or not, the state of Missouri determined that Mike Anderson still owed them 13 years for his crime. He was imprisoned in 2013 to serve his full sentence. After one year, though, a judge ruled that he was to be released with his 13 years free counting as "time served." The judge announced: "I believe that continuing to [incarcerate you] serves no purpose... I think it would be a waste of taxpayer dollars. I think it would unnecessarily punish an obviously rehabilitated man."[4]

Should Mike Anderson have been required to stay in prison for the full 13 years? Should he have been incarcerated at all once the error was discovered? And do you think his pristine record since his conviction should have mattered? Your answers depend on what you see as the goal of criminal punishment.

When people violate criminal laws, there is, by definition, a legal response. The form of that legal response depends on prevailing ideas about the purpose of punishment. Do we punish law-breakers because they "deserve it"? Because the threat of punishment is the last line of defense against all-out mayhem? Or simply to cage wrongdoers so that they cannot harm the rest of us? Maybe we want to use legal responses to encourage or compel people to get help for the problems that led them down the criminal path. These are some of the approaches that shape formal reactions to law-breaking.

The title of this chapter should perhaps be "How Do We Respond to Crime?" instead of "Theories of Punishment." Though all responses to crime entail consequences for the law violator, some are more punitive, or punishment-focused, than others. In fact, the five dominant perspectives on how the law ought to respond to crime fall into two broad categories: (1) the punishment response and (2) the social welfare response.[5] Punishment responses center primarily on the person who has violated the law, and include retribution, deterrence, and incapacitation. Rehabilitation and restoration are social welfare responses, which aim to use legal consequences to improve conditions that lead to, or result from, criminal conduct.

Elements of retribution, deterrence, incapacitation, and rehabilitation infuse the current U.S. criminal legal system. This chapter presents examples of how these approaches inform specific legal policies and practices, including sentencing guidelines, capital punishment, risk assessment algorithms, and problem-solving courts. The fifth approach, restoration (also called restorative justice), is an alternative to the typical criminal justice response.

RETRIBUTION

You are familiar with the concept of **retribution** if you have ever heard "an eye for an eye." This is the notion that the punishment must fit the crime, or that the harms caused by a criminal offense require an equivalent amount of harm be done to the offender. The offender must feel the pain they have caused. Retribution is about getting even, though it is not about getting revenge—instead, it is evening out the harms using punishment. If someone gets their "just deserts," then retribution has been achieved. The "just" in just deserts refers to what is fair, and the "deserts" refers to what is deserved. Retributive punishments are fair and deserved, and they are deserved because the offender used their free will to break the law. Three principles form the basis of the retributive perspective:

1. People who commit serious crimes morally deserve to suffer a punishment proportionate to their offense.

2. Intentionally punishing the innocent or imposing disproportionately severe punishments on law-breakers is morally unacceptable.

3. When the state or another legitimate punisher exacts a deserved punishment, that is an intrinsically moral good, irrespective of other benefits that it might produce.

The first two principles highlight just deserts and proportionality as the foundations of retribution. The third principle tells us that the goal of retribution is *not* to reduce crime or to increase public safety. Punishment is the point—it is an end in and of itself (a moral good!). Retribution, therefore, is nonutilitarian, as punishment does not serve some other purpose.

Retribution is evident in the U.S. criminal legal system. For example, consider the differences in punishments inflicted on people who have committed minor misdemeanors versus serious felonies. Though criminal legal systems vary state to state, all U.S. states differentiate between levels of crime seriousness, with the most extreme punishments (life in prison or capital punishment, where applicable) reserved for the most serious crimes. For example, in Indiana, felonies are organized into Levels 1 through 6, and murder, which has its own level (Level 1 felonies are punishable by prison terms between 20 and 50 years; Level 6 felonies result in prison terms between 6 months and 2½ years).[6] Level 1 felonies include serious violent offenses like attempted murder and aggravated rape. Level 6 felonies include crimes that are minor in comparison, like possession of methamphetamine, theft, and failure to register as a sex offender.

Also consider the public outcry over extreme punishments for people convicted of drug-related offenses. For instance, in 1994, 24-year-old Kemba Smith was sentenced to 24.5 years in federal prison for conspiring to participate in her boyfriend's crack cocaine distribution activities.[7] Her crime was holding money; she had neither possessed nor distributed the illicit substance. Smith stated that she was fearful of refusing to assist her boyfriend, who was physically abusive.[8] She had no prior criminal record. Smith's family launched a campaign to draw attention to the injustice of her punishment, ultimately resulting in President Clinton granting her clemency nearly seven years into her sentence. The movement to free Kemba Smith relied on the logic of retributivism. Her supporters claimed that her punishment violated a principle of retributive justice: Imposing disproportionately severe punishments on law-breakers is morally unacceptable. They argued that her punishment was neither just nor deserved. Similar arguments are made today about long prison sentences for cannabis trafficking crimes, especially when sentences are being served in states where cannabis has been legalized.[9]

Kemba Smith in the fourth year of her mandatory 24.5-year sentence for a first-time non-violent drug offense. (She received a presidential pardon after seven years.) Her sentence sparked national outrage as a violation of retributive principles of justice.

Karjean Levine/Archive Photos/Getty Images

Sentencing Guidelines

A person is convicted of second-degree forcible rape (i.e., used physical force without a deadly weapon or inflicting serious injury, or committed the act against a mentally or physically incapacitated victim). How long should that person's prison sentence be? Should it depend on whether this is their first or their fifth conviction? Should it matter whether they expressed remorse? What about whether they were a ringleader, prompting others to also harm the victim? Should it depend on whether they happened to be assigned a particularly lenient or punitive judge? Should it matter whether the convicted person is college educated?

Until about 40 years ago, there were few limits on judges' sentencing decisions. For example, if a crime was "punishable by up to 25 years in prison," a judge could sentence a convicted person to 2 years or 25 years. It was up to the judge. Indeterminate sentencing was also the norm in the U.S. at this time. In indeterminate sentencing, judges sentenced convicted persons to a range of months or years (e.g., "5 to 12 years"), with the person's release date determined by a parole board. It was "indeterminate" in that sentence lengths were not predetermined. And the sentence range was up to the individual judge, who had a great deal of discretion.[10] This approach allowed judges and corrections officials to consider the individual characteristics of convicted persons and make decisions based on evidence of rehabilitation and their unique public safety risks. Plus, prisoners could secure early release by accruing "good time" credit, intended to encourage rule-abiding behavior while incarcerated.[11]

By the 1970s, though, critics from across the political spectrum were demanding reform.[12] Critics on the right protested that indeterminate sentencing was "coddling criminals" and violating the principle of retribution: People convicted of crimes were not receiving their deserved punishments because parole boards were releasing them. They desired "truth in sentencing," meaning that offenders would be required to remain in prison for the entirety (or close to the entirety) of their sentenced term. Critics on the left argued that judges' and parole boards' racial (and other) biases and reliance on stereotypes produced unjust differences in sentence lengths across demographic groups. Critics of all political stripes took aim at the problems of inconsistency in sentences. Why, they asked, should two people who committed the exact same crime receive two starkly different sentences?

Reformers hoped that structured sentencing would eliminate unwarranted disparities in punishment. If a disparity, or difference, in sentencing is due solely to legally relevant factors (like the extent of injury or loss to the victim, the use of a deadly weapon, and evidence of premeditation), then it is a warranted disparity. It is an unwarranted disparity if the difference is due to extralegal factors, which are characteristics that are legally irrelevant, like race, ethnicity, sex, social class, and physical attractiveness. Inter-judge disparities (differences in average sentences across judges) and regional disparities (differences in average sentences across regions within the same state) are other examples of unwarranted disparities that reformers intended to remedy.

Determinate sentencing was a proposed solution. In determinate sentencing, the length of a prison term is a set number of months or years. Rather than sentence an offender to a range of months or years, with their eventual release date yet to be determined, sentencing judges issue a specific sentence (e.g., 78 months). But determinate sentencing alone cannot fix the problem of unwarranted disparities and disproportionate sentences. Reformers looked to structured sentencing, or sentencing guidelines, to achieve consistency and proportionality.

Sentencing guidelines, typically created by state sentencing commissions (a legislative body), are sets of standards—usually presented in a grid format, as in Table 13.1—that aim to achieve equivalent sentences across offenders who have committed similar crimes and have similar criminal histories. Minnesota was the first state to adopt sentencing guidelines in 1980. Many states followed suit, and the federal system enacted guidelines in 1987. Though no two sentencing guideline systems are the same, all provide judges with narrow sentence ranges based on the seriousness of the crime, the offender's criminal history, and factors that either mitigate (reduce) or aggravate (increase) the recommended sentence. Table 13.2 presents examples of mitigating and aggravating factors taken into consideration in sentencing.

Sentencing guidelines were established to achieve uniformity (across convicted persons and across judges) and proportionality, with the time fitting the crime. Their goal is retributive. Yet critics argue that they fall short of this ideal, especially when they impose lengthy mandatory minimum sentences, which are rigid and formulaic.[13] Sentencing guidelines are usually nonmandatory recommendations, with judges able to depart from the suggested (or presumptive) sentence if they determine a more lenient or severe punishment to be justified. Mandatory minimum sentences, in contrast, are required. They set the lowest possible sentence that a person can receive for a particular offense, such as the federal five-year minimum sentence for possessing 100 grams of heroin.[14] Even if the judge believes the sentence is too long, they cannot use their discretion to grant a shorter term. Their hands are tied.

TABLE 13.1 ■ Pennsylvania sentencing guidelines for Level 5 offenses

Level	OGS	Example Offenses	Print Record Score							REVOC	AGG/MIT
			0	**1**	**2**	**3**	**4**	**5**	**RFEL**		
Level 5 State Incar	14	Murder 3 Inchoate Murder (SBI) Rape (victim <13 years)	72-SL	84-SL	96-SL	120-SL	168-SL	192-SL	204-SL	SL	~/-12
	13	Inchoate Murder (no SBI) Weapons Mass Destr-Use PWID Cocaine (>1,000 g)	60-78	66-84	72-90	78-96	84-102	96-114	108-126	240	+/- 12
	12	Rape-Forcible Compulsion IDSI-Forcible Compulsion Robbery-Inflicts SBI	48-66	54-72	60-78	66-84	72-90	84-102	96-114	120	+/- 12
	11	Agg Assault-Cause SBI Voluntary Manslaughter Sexual Assault PWID Cocaine (100-1,000 g)	36-54 BC	42-60	48-66	54-72	60-78	72-90	84-102	120	+/- 12
	10	Kidnapping Agg Indecent Assault F2 Arson-Person in Building Hom by Vehicle-DUI & Work Zone PWID Cocaine (50- <100 g)	22-36 BC	30-42 BC	36-48 BC	42-54	48-60	60-72	72-84	120	+/- 12
	9	Sexual Exploitation of Children Robbery-Commit/Threat F1/F2 Burglary-Home/Person Present Arson-No Person in Building	12-24 BC	18-30 BC	24-36 BC	30-42 BC	36-48 BC	48-60	60-72	120	+/- 12

Note: OGS = Offense gravity score; SL = Statutory limit (longest minimum sentence); REFEL = Repeat felony 1 and felony 2 offender category; REVOC = Repeat violent offender category; AGG/MIT = Aggravating/Mitigating; BC = Boot camp

Source: Pennsylvania General Assembly. § 303.16(a). Basic sentencing matrix (7th edition amendment). https://sentencing.umn.edu/sites/sentencing.umn.edu/files/pennsylvania_basic_sentencing_matrix_2018.pdf

An example of mandatory minimums is found in Virginia's sentencing guidelines, which obligate judges to impose minimum sentences across a vast array of criminal charges. For example, if a person is convicted of using a gun in the commission of a felony, they will receive a mandatory three-year sentence for the first offense and a five-year sentence for any subsequent gun offense. Let's say they are convicted of committing three robberies with a firearm. Judges are required to sentence them to 13 years in prison just for the gun charges, with additional sentencing for the three robberies.[15]

A consequence of inflexible sentencing policies is that discretion is taken away from the judge and transferred to the prosecutor. The prosecutor decides what charges to pursue and what plea deals to offer.[16] Because they know the sentence that will be handed down in advance, they can use that information to alter the charges to obtain a desired outcome (e.g., pursuing lower-level charges to ensure a more reasonable, shorter sentence). They can also use the threat of a long mandatory sentence to extract guilty pleas from defendants who want to avoid the possibility of extreme punishments.[17]

TABLE 13.2 ■ Examples of aggravating and mitigating factors that influence sentence lengths		
Type of factor	**Example**	**What it means**
Aggravating factor *Supports upward departure from the default sentence (longer sentence)*	Prior convictions	Has a criminal history, as in habitual offender laws
	Vulnerable victim	Victim was very young, very old, or had a physical, mental, or intellectual disability
	Leadership role	Was a ringleader and/or induced others to participate in the offense
	Weapon	Used or was armed with a deadly weapon during the offense
Mitigating factor *Supports downward departure from the default sentence (shorter sentence)*	First-time offender	Had no prior convictions
	Victim culpability	Victim was a voluntary participant in, or consented to, the defendant's conduct
	Minor role	Was a passive participant or played a peripheral role in the offense
	Substantial assistance	Testified for the prosecution in the prosecution of another person's felony, or aided in their apprehension

DETERRENCE

You are familiar with the concept of deterrence if you have already read Chapter 6. Remember the classical school of criminology, which included 18th century scholars like Cesare Beccaria and Jeremy Bentham? Here is a refresher: During the Enlightenment era, utilitarianism (the notion that law should produce the greatest overall good for society) rose in prominence, as did the idea that people are rational actors with free will to choose how they will behave. Thus, classical school thinkers called for legal systems that provided swift, certain, and proportional punishments for those who commit crimes, thereby ensuring that people decide it makes more sense to follow the law than to break it.

Why would people decide it makes more sense to follow the law than to break it? Because they are presumed to rationally calculate the costs and benefits of crime and its alternative (conformity to law). If the costs of crime (punishment) outweigh the benefits (like easy money, social status, or expression of outrage), they will choose to abide by the law. In this view, punishment assures that "crime doesn't pay" because the costs of offending exceed its rewards. In other words, punishment deters. Deterrence is an approach that seeks to reduce crime by altering the costs and benefits associated with offending.

Classical school scholars established three features of punishment as necessary for deterrence: (1) certainty of punishment, (2) severity of punishment, and (3) celerity or swiftness of punishment. In deterrence theory, the state's punitive reaction to crime must be sufficiently certain and (proportionately) severe to deter, and it must happen quickly after the crime, to discourage would-be law violators—at least some of them. These three factors continue to shape thinking about deterrence, with certainty remaining the most important element.

Astute readers will note that deterrence *and* retribution highlight proportionality. Yet proportionality serves a different purpose for retribution than for deterrence. Retributivists demand proportionality to ensure that wrongdoers get what they deserve—and getting what you deserve is the point. In deterrence, proportionality is necessary for punishing people enough to prevent them from continuing to offend while avoiding excess suffering. Utilitarianism's goal is to reduce overall suffering, with crime and punishment both operating as sources of suffering.

Types of Deterrence: Specific, General, Marginal, and Partial

Deterrence has several audiences in mind. The first audience is the punished individual. Specific deterrence occurs when a punished person alters their future behavior due to fear of additional sanctions. The *specific* criminal has been deterred by the *experience* of punishment. They have been "scared straight." The second audience is the broader community. The public, who observes the costs of crime to people who violate the law, is similarly less likely to commit crime for fear that they, too, will be punished. This is general deterrence: The *general* public is deterred through the *threat* of punishment.[18]

Marginal deterrence refers to the differences—or margins—between the deterrent capacities of various punishments. It is based on the principle that more severe offenses require more severe sanctions. In theory, the margins grow larger with greater differences in the severity of one punishment relative to another. For example, deterrence thinkers would expect a significant marginal difference between the effects of life in prison versus a year of probation.

The principle of marginal deterrence leads to the conclusion that people will opt to commit more extreme offenses if punishments are not graduated or scaled by seriousness. Consider what would happen if the punishment for first-degree aggravated rape were the same as the punishment for murder. The marginal deterrence principle tells us that rapists would have no disincentive to kill their victims. Similar issues were at the center of *Coker v. Georgia* (1977), in which the U.S. Supreme Court ruled that the death penalty was disproportionately severe, and therefore unconstitutional, in non-homicide cases of rape with adult victims.[19] Though the justices did not appeal to marginal deterrence in their decision, their ruling aligns with the concept.

Deterrence can be somewhat effective without leading to perfect conformity to the law. Imagine a scenario in which an armed robber considers shooting their victim. Knowing that injuring or killing a victim with a firearm will lead to a much more severe penalty, they leave the victim otherwise unharmed. Or perhaps they strike the victim with a gun rather than shooting them. Some deterrence occurred: They did not shoot the victim because the potential costs were too great. This is called partial deterrence, which is when a deterred individual still commits crime but opts for a less serious offense.

Understanding the distinction between marginal deterrence and partial deterrence is tricky. Think of it this way: Marginal deterrence is about *differences in punishment* that produce varying levels of specific or general deterrence. Partial deterrence, in contrast, is about *differences in behavior* produced by a single punishment (i.e., without the punishment, the offender would have committed a more harmful act).

Does Deterrence Work?

Deterrence—both specific and general—is one of the guiding principles of the U.S. criminal legal system. But does it work? In a thorough review of decades of deterrence research, criminologist Daniel Nagin offered a list of conclusions[20]:

- Certainty of punishment, rather than length or severity of sentences, is deterrence's driving force. Visibility of police increases the perception that the risk of punishment is high, creating a deterrent effect.

- Certainty of apprehension is the type of certainty that most matters for specific deterrence, as compared to certainty of prosecution, certainty of conviction, or certainty of receiving a particular punishment.

- Making long prison sentences even longer adds no general deterrence value. Therefore, general deterrence cannot be used to rationalize the high costs (monetary and social) that excessive punishments exact on society.

- Prison and jail provide no added specific deterrence effect relative to noncustodial punishments like probation ("noncustodial" refers to not being in the state's custody).

In short, some types of deterrence efforts work (increasing perceived certainty of getting caught) while others do not (increasing severity of punishments). Further, criminologists who study perceptions of certainty identify tipping points at which deterrence kicks in. In other words, the anticipated risk of getting caught must reach a certain threshold—usually a 30-40% chance of apprehension—for deterrence to occur.[21]

Perceptions of sanction risks are the true deterrent, regardless of what the *real* risks are. There is a disconnect between actual probabilities of punishment and people's beliefs about the likelihood of punishment (the "dirty little secret of deterrence").[22] To illustrate, think about your own answers to the following questions: (1) What is the likelihood that you would be caught if you attempted to shoplift at a local department store? One in 100? One in 10? 50-50? (2) If you were caught shoplifting $1,000 worth of merchandise, how likely is it that you would be criminally charged? If charged, how likely is it that you would be charged with a felony versus a misdemeanor? And what penalty are you likely to incur? Your perception of each likelihood is unlikely to perfectly—or even just barely—match the actual probabilities. What keeps the crime-inclined from becoming the crime-involved is their *beliefs* about the risks.

Focused Deterrence

Deterrence proponents call for strategies that increase the certainty of punishment *and* heighten would-be law violators' awareness that they will be punished. That is, they try to increase both the perception and reality of punishment, bringing them into alignment. One example of a perception-focused approach is called focused deterrence, in which law enforcement select a specific crime problem on which to focus, like street drug sales or youth homicide. It begins with identifying the core group of individuals committing most of the offenses. Police then implement special enforcement strategies aimed at the key participants and the contexts in which they commit their crimes, making it difficult for the target population to "get away with it." Unlike sweeping policing tactics that aggressively target large swaths of the population, these strategies are narrowly aimed at a small group of individuals known to be deeply involved in the targeted offense. Importantly, focused deterrence that alters perceptions about apprehension risk, in which police

> Communicat[e] directly and repeatedly with the targeted criminal population to inform them of the heightened scrutiny they are being subjected to, what acts or "triggering events" (such as shootings) will get special attention, what increased enforcement and sanctions will follow, and what they can do to avoid increased attention. This message is often disseminated during a "forum," "offender notification meeting," or "call-in," in which offenders are invited or directed (usually because they are on probation or parole) to attend these face-to-face meetings with law enforcement, social service providers, and representatives from the community. (p. 209)[23]

Capital Punishment

Proponents of capital punishment make several arguments in favor of the death penalty, including incapacitation (eliminating dangerous people) and retribution (requiring "an eye for an eye"). However, advocates' most frequently invoked justification for state executions is deterrence, or the notion that capital punishment is necessary to prevent people from committing murder.[24] But does the death penalty deter?

Before digging into the empirical research on capital punishment and deterrence, let's address the type of deterrence under consideration. If capital punishment were to deter, it would not produce specific deterrence. That's because the person experiencing the punishment is dead. They might not commit any crimes in the future, but it's not due to a change in the relative costs and benefits of crime! Death penalty supporters make arguments about general deterrence, or how the threat of execution prevents would-be murderers from following through.

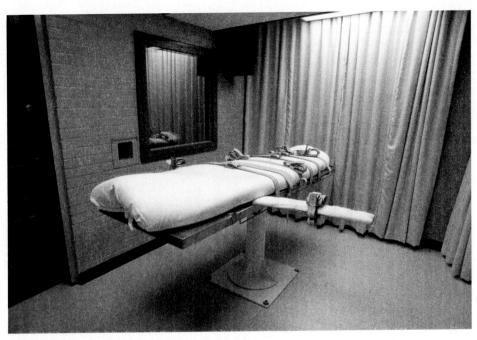

Lethal injection room at Huntsville Unit Prison in Texas. Proponents of capital punishment claim it is a necessary deterrent, though there is little contemporary evidence supporting this claim.

Greg Smith/CORBIS/Corbis/Getty Images

In a highly influential 1975 study, Isaac Ehrlich reported that each execution prevented between seven and eight homicides.[25] Capital punishment was on heavy rotation in the news cycle in the 1970s in the U.S. In *Furman v. Georgia* (1972), the U.S. Supreme Court ruled that capital punishment was unconstitutional in its current form because states applied it in an "arbitrary and capricious" manner, particularly regarding race.[26] This resulted in a moratorium (or pause), during which time capital punishment was not permitted. The moratorium ended in 1976, with the *Gregg v. Georgia* decision.[27] The Court allowed the death penalty to be reinstated but placed restrictions on the circumstances in which it can be applied, including prohibiting mandatory death sentences. Two years later, in 1978, the National Research Council published a report that detailed the methodological problems with Ehrlich's study.[28] Over the next several decades, capital punishment research became more methodologically sophisticated yet the answer to "Does the death penalty deter?" remains elusive.[29]

It would be unethical to conduct experimental research on the death penalty's impact, so we must rely on observational research. Let's begin with some observations of homicide trends in places with and without the death penalty. Figure 13.1 displays these patterns. Back in 1992, New York and Texas had similar (high) murder rates. Texas reacted by escalating the use of the death penalty.[30] New York, in contrast, had no executions between 1992 and 2003. Texas's homicide rate declined by 49.6% between 1992 and 2003. You might conclude that Texas's death penalty prevented murder—that is, until you realize that New York's homicide rate dropped by 62.9% during those years. Lots of factors contribute to homicide trends, but capital punishment does not appear to be one of them.

Why wouldn't the death penalty deter? After all, execution is the most severe penalty available. Contemporary scholars remind us, though, that capital sentences and executions are incredibly rare, even for capital-eligible convictions (when a person commits a crime that *could* result in a death sentence) and even in states like Texas and Florida, which use the death penalty more than other states.[31] Consider, for instance, that there were 22 executions in 2019 and 17 executions in 2020 in the U.S.[32] For scale, compare these values to the 100 people who were injured by lightning strikes in 2019![33] Capital punishment is exceedingly unusual despite 27 states having capital punishment on the books and despite the extent of homicide in the U.S. (there were 305,340 known homicides between 2000 and 2020).[34]

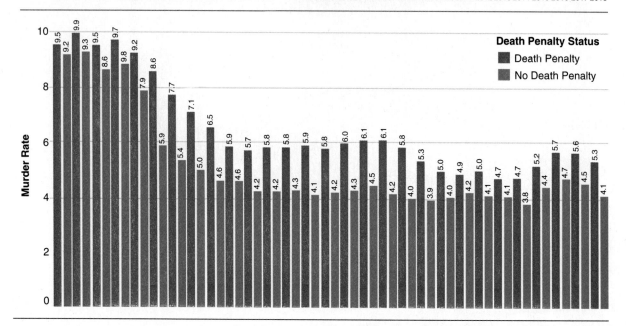

FIGURE 13.1 ■ **Murder rates in death penalty and non–death penalty states, 1990–2018**

Source: Death Penalty Information Center. (2019). *Murder rate of death penalty states compared to non–death penalty states.* https://deathpenaltyinfo.org/facts-and-research/murder-rates/murder-rate-of-death-penalty-states-compared-to-non-death-penalty-states

As we know, though, perception of punishment's certainty is more important than its actual certainty. Maybe it doesn't matter that there were only 17 executions in 2020. If people *believe* that they will face the death penalty if they commit murder, then perhaps that is all that is necessary to deter. It is more complicated still. Most people do not require the threat of *any* punishment to keep them from committing murder. For most, it is simply unthinkable. The only people who require deterrence are those with a proclivity for lethal violence. Yet there is scarcely any research on the perceptions of this population of potential murderers.[35] In short, we don't know if the death penalty deters those it is intended to deter because nearly all studies rely on aggregate homicide rates.

Deterrence researchers also warn us that the real question is not "Does the death penalty deter homicide?" but "Does the death penalty deter homicide to a greater extent than other available sanctions, like life in prison?" Notice that the second question is about marginal deterrence, or whether capital punishment is marginally more effective than life in prison.[36] Unfortunately, there is not sufficient research to settle this matter, either. We do observe, however, that the typical alternative to a death sentence—a life sentence without the possibility of parole, or "death by incarceration"—fails to produce a deterrent effect relative to life sentences with the possibility of parole. In other words, dying in prison (by causes other than execution) has no greater utility than a sentence that may one day end.[37]

INCAPACITATION

Prison serves an **incapacitation** function by removing people from society, either for a set amount of time or indefinitely. While confined to prison (or to home with electronic monitoring, an institution, or to any other restricted setting), the person is unable to offend against nonconfined persons. Incapacitation is not about getting one's deserved consequences (like retribution) or altering people's decisions to commit crime (like deterrence). Incapacitation is more basic: Lock them up and they *can't* commit more crimes—at least not against people in free society. It is about denying the punished person the opportunity to offend. Proponents of incapacitation aren't concerned with *why* offenders committed their crimes. Instead, they view them as dangerous creatures—predators—whose inherent nature is taken for granted and unlikely to change. Public safety, therefore, requires that they be locked up, away from society.

There are two forms of incapacitation policies: (1) collective incapacitation and (2) selective incapacitation. In **collective incapacitation**, large groups of convicted persons are uniformly incarcerated or institutionalized. Their personal characteristics—including their individual likelihoods of reoffending—are not considered. *Everyone* who commits the offense is locked away for a set period of time to ensure the safety of the community. It is a blanket policy that applies to all law-breakers, which makes it collective. Mass incarceration is, in part, due to collective incapacitation policies like mandatory minimums, which lengthened sentences for all convicted persons. **Selective incapacitation**, in contrast, targets "habitual offenders" (or "career criminals") and those who pose the greatest threat to the community. In other words, it reserves the "lock them up" approach, or lengthy sentences, solely for those considered most dangerous and likely to reoffend.[38]

Does incapacitation work? It depends on what we mean by "work." It is undeniable that people who are incarcerated are (mostly) unable to commit crimes against people outside of the prison setting while they are locked up. A repeat liquor store robber is not robbing any liquor stores in prison, after all. Yet caging people in the aggregate—that is, incapacitating people who violate the law on a large scale—produces substantial diminishing returns for public safety. In other words, locking up additional people will produce smaller and smaller effects on crime rates if there are already many people already incarcerated.[39] Plus, collective incapacitation can become criminogenic.

Incapacitation confronts two challenges. First, its logical end point is the construction and filling of more and more prisons. Because most offenders have some risk of recidivism, the conclusion reached by a judge with an incapacitation mindset is "Better safe than sorry; better send this one to prison" (p. 11).[40] There are costs to imprisoning large segments of the population on a massive scale, including costs to incarcerated people and their families as well as to the wider community. Prisons are expensive to build, staff, and operate—to the tune of $80 billion per year.[41] And there are steep opportunity costs associated with the buildup of prisons. Opportunity costs are the opportunities lost when money or efforts are put elsewhere. Choosing one course of action (like building 30 new prisons) means forgoing another course of action. When money is spent on one thing, it cannot be spent on another. Funds that go toward the prison construction and operations are funds that will not go towards education, treatment programs, or early prevention–focused initiatives.

The incapacitation approach's second limitation is that it doesn't tell us what to do about the approximately 600,000 people exiting prison each year, most of whom have served two to three years in prison.[42] Perhaps incapacitation works while people are behind bars (to the extent that they cannot commit crimes out in society), but if "locking them up" is all we do, then the likelihood of formerly

Josue Torres-Rubio stands in the solitary confinement cell where he spends 23 hours of each day, at the Washington Corrections Center in Shelton, WA. Solitary confinement is an example of incapacitation within an incapacitating institution (jail or prison).

AP Photo/Ted S. Warren

incarcerated people successfully reentering society—finding a place to live, getting paid work, meeting obligations to family, staying law-abiding—is slim. Ironically, incapacitation, with its sole focus on caging offenders, ends up making us less safe by worsening criminality.[43]

Life Sentences

One in seven people in prison in the U.S. is serving a life sentence.[44] In fact, the number of lifers in U.S. prisons (more than 200,000 people) is greater than the *total* number of people in U.S. prisons in the 1970s. This number includes people serving life sentences without parole, life with the possibility of parole, and virtual life sentences (50 years or more), as well as people on death row. Life sentences and capital punishment are incapacitating punishments, presumably reserved for the most dangerous and incorrigible individuals who are beyond the possibility of redemption.

There are several pathways to spending the rest of one's life, and therefore one's death, in prison in the U.S. The most obvious entry point is the commission of a serious, usually violent, crime like murder (though nearly 4,000 people are serving life terms for drug-related offenses, with about two-fifths of them in federal prison).[45] Another pathway to life in prison—or lifelong incapacitation—is three-strikes laws. These are policies that impose lengthy mandatory minimums for a third felony conviction, regardless of the circumstances of the third crime. The language of these laws comes from baseball: three strikes (three felonies), and you're out (life sentence). Three-strikes laws are a type of habitual offender law, though not all habitual offender laws automatically result in life sentences. Habitual offender laws lead judges to impose stiffer sentences on persons with multiple prior felony convictions. The goal of three-strikes laws is selective incapacitation: People who repeatedly commit felonies are selected for perpetual incarceration.

Douglas Walker, seen with his attorney (left), was sentenced to life in prison in 2018 under California's three-strikes law following a conviction for assaulting his girlfriend. Walker, who participated in the robbery-homicide of Kimber Reynolds in 1992, was the inspiration for California's three-strikes law.

Pablo Lopez/The Fresno Bee via AP

Risk Assessments

Selective incapacitation requires identification of the most dangerous, or riskiest, defendants or convicted persons. Courtroom decision-makers, like judges, rely on risk assessments to help them single out high-risk individuals for incapacitation, such as pretrial detention or longer sentences. The goal of any **risk assessment** is to determine the likelihood that a person will commit crime in the future, especially serious crime, as well as whether they will fail to appear for a court date. They are predictive tools.

Risk assessments have been used in the U.S. legal system for over a century.[46] Early risk assessments were *clinical* assessments conducted by psychologists, probation officers, social workers, and others with expertise. *Actuarial* risk assessments, which provide numeric risk scores based on static statistical models, grew in prominence in the 1970s and 1980s. Over the past few decades, *algorithmic* risk assessments (a sophisticated type of actuarial tool) have replaced older versions. This modern type of risk assessment involves computer programs that calculate risk scores based on complex statistical models or machine learning. The individual defendant's data are entered into the risk assessment tool, and the algorithm determines their risk score—usually "low," "medium," or "high."

Imagine you want to predict whether a person is likely to commit a serious violent crime in the future. What characteristics would you include in your predictive tool? Many algorithmic risk assessment tools are proprietary (privately owned), which means that their "secret sauce" is not publicly available. However, some share their ingredients with the public. Factors used in predictive analytics include variables identified as criminogenic by criminologists and supported by empirical evidence. These include prior arrests and convictions, history of violence, age at first arrest, substance abuse, history of noncompliance with probation or parole, residential stability, employment status, education level, expulsion history, level of family support, and age.[47] Some tools include defendants' responses on questionnaires administered by court or corrections officials while others omit questionnaire data.

Risk assessment algorithms have mostly been used—and therefore studied—in pretrial release decisions. Judges choose whether to detain or release (on bail or personal recognizance) defendants prior to trial. They must consider whether the defendant is a safety risk. They want to avoid a scenario in which, for example, a defendant facing stalking and domestic violence charges murders his ex-girlfriend while released on bond. Risk scores—including risk scores tailored to particular types of offending, like domestic violence—can inform these decisions, with judges limiting pretrial detention to "high-risk" defendants.[48] Across many studies, pretrial risk assessments show a high degree of predictive validity. This means that the algorithm accurately forecasts future behavior at a level that makes it a helpful tool for judges.[49]

Risk scores are also used in higher-stakes post-conviction decisions, like sentencing and parole determinations. Often, this means that "low-risk" convicted persons are diverted into reduced or alternative sentences, such as probation or community service instead of prison time.[50] Risk assessments are, in fact, seen as a tool for reducing mass incarceration by flagging people who are unlikely to reoffend or cause harm to the community. Conversely, risk assessments can lead "high-risk" persons to be sentenced to prison and kept there longer than others who have committed the same crimes. As per the decision in *Loomis v. Wisconsin* (2016), release decisions cannot be determined solely by risk scores.[51] And risk assessments are advisory rather than mandated. In other words, they can be disregarded if other information is more compelling.

Algorithmic risk assessments appear to remove the problem of human judgment, including biases. Indeed, according to some studies, algorithms outperform human judges in predicting which persons released on bail will show up for their court dates.[52] However, skeptics warn that algorithms, as human creations, are not, in fact, free of human judgment:

Algorithms are designed by humans, run on computers that humans built, trained on data that humans collect, and evaluated based on how well they reflect human priorities and values.[53]

Importantly, the human element of algorithms can lead to disparate outcomes. For example, an analysis of a federal post-conviction risk assessment tool found that Black defendants receive higher risk scores than white defendants. This difference was due almost exclusively to racial variation in criminal records; Black defendants were more likely to have prior arrests and convictions.[54] Risk assessment critics worry that racial inequalities in criminal justice processing—like the likelihood of accruing an arrest history due to heavy policing of majority-Black communities—will be compounded by algorithms that inaccurately flag Black defendants as "high risk."[55] Those championing algorithmic risk assessments counter that criminal histories are already built into pretrial detention and sentencing decisions. They also contend that decisions about risk levels will be made either way, either by a human or a computer—and the computer is less likely to discriminate. In other words, they argue that algorithms reduce racial bias rather than widen it. More research is needed to determine if they are correct.[56]

Civil Confinement

Incapacitation is all about confinement. Prison is usually the type of confinement that people mean when talking about incapacitation. However, imprisonment is not the only way that the state confines those who have broken the law. **Civil confinement** is a form of involuntary commitment imposed on some individuals who been convicted of sexual offenses in the U.S., with civil confinement beginning after a prison sentence has been completed.

A series of high-profile, appalling sex offenses in the 1980s and 1990s spurred the creation of "sexually violent predator" (SVP) laws, which enabled states to house individuals identified as "sexually violent predators" or "sexually dangerous persons" indefinitely within prison-like psychiatric facilities. Across the 20 states with SVP laws and the federal system, the review procedures vary widely, and more than half allow civil confinement of people who committed their offenses as juveniles. Because the confinement is civil instead of criminal, constitutional protections regarding double jeopardy (being prosecuted twice for the same offense) and due process (respect for legal rights in criminal proceedings) do not apply.[57]

In general, civil confinement statutes apply to a narrow set of individuals who commit sex offenses. Civil confinement can only be used if the prosecutor can prove that the defendant (1) has a sex offense conviction or charge, (2) has a mental disorder or mental abnormality that impairs their ability to control sexual impulses and predisposes them to sexually violent offending, and (3) is likely to commit sexual offenses in the future.[58] Risk assessments, like those described in the previous section, are used to determine the risk that a person will commit sex offenses once released from prison.[59] About 5,400 people in the U.S. are currently civilly committed under SVP laws.[60]

TABLE 13.3 ■ Theories of punishment				
Approach	**Purpose**	**Utilitarian**	**Focus**	**Policies**
Retribution	Get even	No	Crime	Determinate sentencing
	Do justice			
Deterrence		Yes	Crime	Mandatory sentences
				Abolish parole
(1) General	Scare the public straight		Crime	High levels of imprisonment
				Long prison sentences
(2) Specific	Scare offenders straight		Crime	Intensive supervision
				Scared-straight programs
Incapacitation		Yes	Both	Imprisonment
(1) Collective	Imprison all offenders		Criminal	Mass incarceration
(2) Selective	Imprison high-rate offenders		Criminal	Incarcerate career criminals
Rehabilitation	Reform offender	Yes		Treatment programs
				Probation and parole
				Juvenile justice system
Restoration	Reduce harm to offender, victim, and community	Yes	Criminal	Sentencing conferences
				Restitution
				Offender reintegration

Source: Cullen, F. T., & Jonson, C. L. (2017). *Correctional theory: Context and consequences.* Thousand Oaks, CA: SAGE.

The stated purpose of civil confinement for people convicted of sex offenses is to safeguard the public by teaching confined individuals how to control their sexual impulses through therapy. Yet in practice, these laws achieve incapacitation rather than rehabilitation. Most who are civilly confined will remain confined for life. For example, at Avenel, a special treatment unit for "sexually violent predators" in New Jersey, only 15% of individuals committed to the program have ever been released.[61]

ENGAGED CRIMINOLOGY 13.1

Analyzing Aging Lifers

In this activity, you will analyze data on prisoners age 55 and older who are serving life sentences (with the possibility of parole). The data in Figure 13.2 come from Georgia, where 26% of people serving life sentences are age 55 or older (the national average is 30%). The blue bars depict the number of people age 55 and older (on Y-axis) who have served each number of years (on X-axis) on their life sentence in Georgia. For example, we can see that 47 prisoners age 55 and older have been in prison for 20 years (yellow bar).

FIGURE 13.2 ■	Time served among persons 55 and older serving life with parole in Georgia

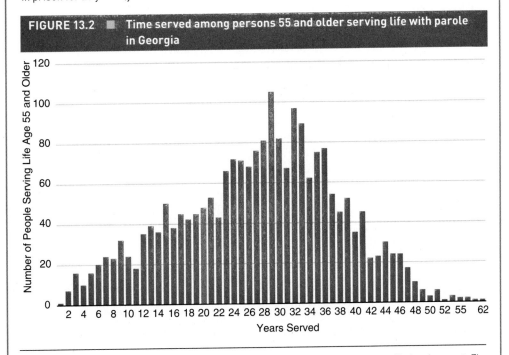

Source: Nellis, A. (2021, February 17). *No end in sight: America's enduring reliance on life imprisonment.* The Sentencing Project. https://www.sentencingproject.org/publications/no-end-in-sight-americas-enduring-reliance-on-life-imprisonment/. Copyright © 2021 by The Sentencing Project

Using the data in the figure, answer the following questions:

1. What are the <u>three</u> most common numbers of years served among lifers age 55 and older in Georgia?

2. In one or two sentences, explain whether you think incarcerating older people (in their 60s, 70s, and 80s) who committed crimes in their teens and 20s achieves the goal of incapacitation.

   ● If so, explain how this achieves the goal of incapacitation.
   ● If not, do you think they ought to be released—why or why not?

REHABILITATION

Rehabilitation is about identifying and improving the behaviors, attitudes, traits, and conditions that contribute to individuals' offending, thereby reducing future criminal behavior. Rehabilitation doesn't deny that people make choices, but it rejects the idea of pure free will. Instead, it regards choices as shaped by individual and social risk factors. Making "good choices" is a greater challenge for some people than others due to factors like addiction, psychosis, impulsive temperament, PTSD, or internalization of antisocial values. Corrections scholars Cullen and Jonson describe rehabilitation as

> a planned correctional intervention that targets for change internal and/or social criminogenic factors with the goal of reducing recidivism and, where possible, of improving other aspects of an offender's life. (p. 295)[62]

Let's examine each aspect of the definition. First, rehabilitation is the task of the correctional system (i.e., prisons, jails, and probation). In other words, the criminal legal system should assist offenders in changing and not expect punishments alone to induce law-abiding behavior. Second, it addresses internal and social factors that make crime more likely. These might include mental health challenges, substance use problems, homelessness, joblessness, problematic peer networks, or educational deficits. Third, the rehabilitated person's life also improves in ways unrelated to criminal conduct when they receive effective rehabilitation, such as better physical health and healthier relationships. Moreover, improving the lives of people who have committed crimes in the past improves the lives of all people by boosting public safety. Rehabilitation is a utilitarian goal.

Rehabilitation adopts a medical model. In this view, crime is seen as a symptom of an underlying condition. The symptoms cannot be improved without accurate diagnosis of the condition. Some diagnoses are actual diagnostic categories (e.g., substance use disorder) while others are not (e.g., exposure to crime-involved associates). Once diagnosed, correctional treatment is prescribed to address the condition, or "cure the underlying ailment" (p. 174).[63] This model calls for individualized treatment, with a person's unique constellation of needs determining their course of treatment.

Nothing Works?

One of the earliest and most notorious prisons in the United States was Eastern State Penitentiary, which is now a famous Philadelphia tourist attraction. Like other prisons of the 19th century, Eastern State was a *penitentiary*, a word deriving from *penitence*, referring to remorseful sinners who regret their actions. Reform schools, another name for juvenile prisons, also emerged during the 19th century. The language of penitence and reform draws attention to the early purpose of punishment in the United States: reforming the moral character of the sinner or wayward youth.[64] This was a stark departure from the gallows and pillories of an earlier era. By 1900, the Progressive Era of punishment was underway, and transforming transgressors into moral law-abiders was its main focus. The rehabilitation ideal was born.[65] Rehabilitation dominated corrections from the turn of the 20th century until the early 1970s.

The tide began to turn in the 1970s, with criminologists, politicians, and the public growing increasingly skeptical of rehabilitation. The target of their ire was states' misuse of discretion. Remember indeterminate sentencing, wherein convicted people were sentenced to a range of months or years, with parole boards determining when they were ready for release (see Sentencing Guidelines section)? That system of individualized punishments was created with rehabilitation in mind, and it required judges and parole boards to exercise discretion. Critics charged that they abused their decision-making power, either by going easy on vicious predators (on the political right) or by discriminating against poor people and people of color (on the political left).[66]

The retreat from rehabilitation was nearly assured following the 1974 publication of the Martinson Report, which established the "nothing works" doctrine.[67] Martinson's essay was a summary of a study that reviewed 231 correctional program evaluations produced between 1945 and 1967. He surmised, *"With few and isolated exceptions, the rehabilitative efforts that have been reported so far have had no appreciable effect on recidivism"* (p. 25, emphasis in original).[68] Though Martinson never used the phrase "nothing works" in his article, that was the insinuation.

The Martinson Report was like an accelerant poured on a fire that was already building. It provided evidence that rehabilitation should be scrapped—and that retribution, deterrence, and incapacitation (all punitive approaches) should dominate. It also transformed the debate.[69] Early on, critics argued that abuse of discretion as the problem. After the Martinson Report, critics argued that rehabilitation, itself, was the problem because it didn't work. This was a more damning argument because who on earth would support a system—abused or not—built on a faulty principle? The shattering of rehabilitation's reputation ushered in the era of tough-on-crime policies and mass incarceration.

Criminologists have since challenged the "nothing works" narrative. Even during the 1970s, criminologists disagreed with Martinson's conclusion. The studies included in the review were so ineptly designed, skeptics argued, that it was impossible to reach conclusions about the programs they claimed to evaluate. Moreover, rehabilitative programs in the 1940s, 1950s, and 1960s were poorly implemented by untrained prison staff. Martinson detractors asked: Was it any wonder if they didn't work? The solution shouldn't be putting rehabilitation out with the garbage, according to the critics. Instead, the goal ought to be improving rehabilitation programs and ensuring that they are administered competently.[70]

After decades of punitive policies and prison expansion, rehabilitation has crept back in. The past several decades witnessed the rise of "evidence-based corrections," or making informed decisions about correctional policies based on scientific research, nearly all of it with recidivism as the outcome under investigation.[71] And contemporary scientific research shows that some types of rehabilitation work far better than punishment alone, including vocational education, cognitive skills programs, community drug treatment, and problem-solving courts. Effective rehabilitation programs share characteristics such as the following:

- They include interventions that target cognitive or behavioral skills.

- They integrate a human services component, such as housing assistance and counseling.

- They are multimodal, which means multiple challenges are addressed simultaneously, such as substance dependency and mental illness.

- They focus on positive individual change, with cognitive transformation as a prerequisite for benefitting from opportunities, like work or educational opportunities.[72]

Problem-Solving Courts

The rehabilitation ideal is at the heart of problem-solving courts. Problem-solving courts are specialty courts that only handle cases involving defendants who share a common challenge (or problem).[73] They provide incentives and supports to assist in rehabilitation. Mental health courts, drug courts, veterans' courts, DUI courts, and domestic violence courts are a few examples of problem-solving courts.

Problem-solving courts are grounded in therapeutic jurisprudence, an approach whose goal is to improve the emotional and psychological health of people ensnared in the legal system. Unlike traditional courts, problem-solving courts "do not focus on establishing guilt and the appropriate punitive response, but instead attempt to leverage the authority of the court to have a positive effect on the defendant's wellbeing" (p. 231).[74] They aim to slow the "revolving door" of people entering the legal system due to conditions like untreated mental illness, alcohol and drug dependency, and homelessness.[75] A mental health court judge described the varied goals of the court this way:

> We want this person to be better, not only … altruistically – I am a person and I want to see people do better in their lives, but also from a systemic point of view, if they are doing better, they are not committing new crimes. They are not creating victims, causing resource drains, etc. (p. 32)[76]

The modern problem-solving court movement began with the creation of the first drug court in Dade County, Florida, in 1989. During the peak years of the War on Drugs, Dade County—like other counties throughout the U.S.—was inundated with people with low-level drug charges and convictions who were being warehoused in overcrowded jails and prisons. In Dade County, people with drug-related charges and histories of substance abuse could be (voluntarily) diverted to a separate court designed to address substance abuse. The Dade County drug court became a model for other

Jamie Cline (right), recovering from a 10-year heroin addiction, smiles as she greets a defense attorney during a drug court session in Thurston County Superior Court, in Olympia, WA, in December 2019. Drug courts are a type of rehabilitation-focused problem-solving court.

AP Photo/Elaine Thompson

jurisdictions. There were over 4,300 problem-solving courts, including more than 3,000 drug courts, in the U.S. a quarter-century later.[77]

Problem-solving courts share key components. First, they are voluntary, and participants can opt out at any time, which means they will transfer to the traditional criminal court system. Second, they are non-adversarial. In the traditional system, the prosecution and defense are adversaries, making opposing arguments. In contrast, teams work collaboratively to create individualized treatment plans in speciality courts. These teams include judges, prosecutors, defense counsel, and treatment providers. Third, they employ non-incarceration incentives and punishments. The goal is to keep people out of prison. Fourth, they require participation in treatment or services, such as cognitive-behavioral treatment, parenting classes, and housing assistance. Participants are closely monitored to ensure accountability and compliance.[78]

Some problem-solving courts are pre-adjudication, which means that criminal charges are pending until completion of (or failure to complete) the court's requirements. In post-adjudication courts, participation occurs after a guilty plea or conviction. In either model, successful completion of the court's program can result in reduced or dismissed charges (if pre-adjudication) or a cleared record (if post-adjudication). Repeated noncompliance with requirements—like treatment, drug testing, employment, and showing up for court dates—leads to termination from the program and a return to criminal court.

Only some defendants are eligible for specialty court participation. For example, many mental health courts require a diagnosis of mental illness that is severe and chronic—for example, schizophrenia or bipolar disorder.[79] Only veterans are eligible for veterans' courts, and, in most cases, only people with multiple DUIs are eligible for DUI courts.[80] Plus, speciality courts impose restrictions on the types of cases that are eligible. Some only accept misdemeanor cases while others take only felony cases. Some limit the kinds of felonies that are eligible, such as only accepting people charged with or convicted of nonviolent felonies.[81]

Do problem-solving courts work? By "work," researchers usually mean "reduce recidivism." In general, the answer is yes, though programs differ in their effectiveness. DUI courts produce modest reductions in rearrest rates. Adult drug courts, on average, also yield modest improvements (8-14% reductions in rearrests within two years), though high-quality programs have reductions between 35% and 80%. Mental health courts also show substantial decreases in rearrests. Importantly, the beneficial effects of these specialty courts persist several years after people complete the programs.[82]

There is another way problem-solving courts work. They save money. The criminal legal system is expensive. Operating courtrooms, jailing people, paying police officers, attorneys and judges, and corrections staff—all of it costs money. Interventions that reduce rearrests and incarceration save money. We can measure cost-effectiveness by answering the question: How much money do we save for every dollar invested? A comprehensive governmental study showed that adult drug courts save $2 to $4 for every $1 invested (a 200-400% return on investment). DUI courts save about $2 for every $1 invested. Unfortunately, despite their effectiveness, mental health courts do not recoup their investment because their services are so costly.[83]

ENGAGED CRIMINOLOGY 13.2

Applying Theories of Punishment to Mike Anderson's Case

In this activity, you will apply chapter concepts of retribution, deterrence, incapacitation, and rehabilitation in deciding the appropriate punishment for Mike Anderson, the man at the center of a real-life criminal justice mix-up described at the start of the chapter. You will answer the question "What should have happened to Mike Anderson once the error was discovered in 2013?" from multiple perspectives.

1
Don't incarcerate him

10
Incarcerate him for full 13 years sentenced

Answer the following questions:

1. What do *you* think should have happened to Mike Anderson? Indicate your position on a scale of 1 to 10, where 1 means "don't incarcerate him" and 10 means "incarcerate him for the full 13 years."

2. What scores (1 to 10) would you give if you were concerned only with (a) retribution, (b) specific deterrence, (c) incapacitation, or (d) rehabilitation?

3. Which perspective (retribution, deterrence, incapacitation, or rehabilitation) most fits your answer about what should have happened to Mike Anderson?

Source: Adapted from Zito, R. (2020). Identifying problems in the criminal justice system. In K. Korgen, M. Trautner, & M. Atkinson (Eds.), *Social problems in action*. Thousand Oaks, CA: SAGE.

RESTORATION

I asked him why he abused me. He said he picked me because I was the youngest sibling and therefore the easiest to manipulate. He said he didn't choose [to form a relationship with] my mum so he could get to us children, it just happened. I also asked him if he understood that my anorexia was caused by what he'd done to me. He told me he'd deliberately blanked it out so he didn't have to admit to himself that it was his fault.

It was really important to me to let him know that while he'd affected the first 30 years of my life, I wasn't going to let him ruin the next 30…

He got very emotional and had to leave the room – he said he couldn't understand why I'd want to forgive him. I told him it was because I didn't want to carry around what he'd done to me anymore. I'd moved on, and forgiving him was for me, not for him.

I wanted an apology, and I got one. An apology is one word, but it's a massive thing. I'm not as angry anymore – that's lifted. And hearing him say that it was all his fault was massive. I didn't believe that until I heard it from him, and no one else would have been able to convince me.[84]

The quote above comes from Laura Coel, a British woman who participated in a restorative justice conference with her formerly incarcerated stepfather. The meeting had been arranged by the UK's National Probation Service at her request. Conferences like this one are the centerpiece of restorative justice.

Restorative justice seeks to reduce harms by setting things right after one has done wrong. In this view, crime is a violation against people (victims and the community), and it is a violation against relationships between the person who has caused harm, the victim, and the community. In turn, violations create obligations to right the wrong. The restorative goal is not simply to punish. Instead,

Restorative justice aims to reestablish the balance that has been offset as a result of a crime by involving the primary stakeholders (i.e. victim, offender, and the affected community) in the decision-making process of how best to restore this balance. The focus is on healing as opposed to punishment. Other important principles of restorative justice include offender accountability for wrongdoing, respect for all participants, and the centrality of the victim throughout the process. (p. 2)[85]

The restorative approach is rooted in three principles. First, it acknowledges that crime produces harm and views repairing that harm as the proper purpose of justice responses to crime. Second, it states that individuals who are most affected by the crime (e.g., victims, people who commit offenses, and family members of both parties) should have the opportunity to participate in its resolution. They should also be able to decline participation if that is their choice. Third, it sees maintaining order as the state's responsibility while building peace is seen as the community's responsibility. In fact, restorative justice is a response to crime supported by "peacemaking criminology."[86]

Though restorative justice aims to reduce future criminal conduct by transforming people who have committed crimes, its primary intention is to address the harms of prior crimes, like the harm done to Laura Coel by her stepfather. In this sense, it is a utilitarian approach. But how does it achieve these goals? The form differs depending on the program and type of crime addressed (e.g., adolescent property destruction vs. dating violence vs. homicide). Nonetheless, a common thread is the use of face-to-face meetings, or conferences, that bring together people who have committed offenses, victims or proxies for victims (if the victim is unwilling or unable to participate), others affected by the crime (such as parents of the victim), support persons (such as a friend of the victim), and trained facilitators. The conferences are organized around the harmed person's needs. In general, restorative justice conferences involve the following steps:

1. The victim or the person who harmed them decides they want a restorative justice conference. If the criminal case is still working its way through the courts, they must wait until it is complete.

2. If both parties consent to the conference, a trained facilitator will meet with each party separately to prepare them and discuss what they wish to express during the conference. The facilitator ensures that the person who committed the offense understands that the conference requires accepting responsibility, and they will not give the go-ahead for the conference unless they are confident it is safe for the victim.

3. During the conference, the facilitators establish ground rules, such as not interrupting one another and being able to take breaks or stop the conference at any time. These are structured settings for facilitated dialogue, not free-for-alls. Facilitators will take turns asking the person who committed the offense and the victim questions like, "How did you feel at the time?" and "Who was affected by the incident?" The conversation will be geared towards addressing the

impacts of the crime. In some cases, it may also involve an outcome agreement, approved by both parties, that establishes steps the wrongdoer will take to make things right.

4. In the days following the conference, facilitators check in with participants to discuss whether they got what they wanted from the conference.[87]

Reintegrative Shaming

The theory of reintegrative shaming provides the theoretical rationale for restorative justice. It explains *why* restorative justice conferences ought to be more effective than typical criminal legal system responses to crime. As the name implies, the reintegrative shaming perspective treats shame as central to understanding crime. According to John Braithwaite, who developed the theory, communities will have less crime if they send messages about crime's shamefulness in effective ways. In contrast, crime will proliferate where crime is not understood and experienced as a source of shame:

> *They will have a lot of violence if violent behaviour is not shameful, high rates of rape if rape is something men can brag about, endemic white-collar crime if business people think law-breaking is clever rather than shameful.* (p. 1)[88]

In this theory, shame is elicited by expressing disapproval or condemnation with the purpose of causing remorse.[89] Shame is not just an emotional reaction to letting oneself down by acting against one's own standards (that is guilt); rather, it is an emotional reaction to violating collective standards. It is the feeling that one has done something wrong. Shame is similar to embarrassment but with a moral dimension. There are two primary ways that communities express to law-breakers that their behavior is shameful: (1) reintegrative shaming and (2) stigmatization. Both communicate disapproval of crime. But only of them—reintegrative shaming—keeps people from breaking the law, in this view.

Reintegrative shaming reduces crime by separating the act from the actor. It regards the person who violates the law as a redeemable person who has done a bad thing. The focus of shame is the "bad thing" rather than the person's character. Instead of using shame to sever the wrongdoer from the community, or to tell them they are evil, reintegrative shaming tries to bring the wrongdoer back into the community (rather like "hate the sin, love the sinner"). This approach has the following features:

- Disapproval of the criminal act is expressed in a way that is respectful of the person.

- The person is not labeled as evil or bad, and a crime-related label does not become a master status.

- Shaming ends with forgiveness, typically through a ceremony that communicates reintegration into the community.

Rather than cast out the law-breaker, reintegrative shaming is a welcoming back once the person has accepted the shamefulness of their act. This can be accomplished through restorative justice conferences. Because the offender feels that they have been treated as a worthwhile human being, they are less likely to reject those who disapprove of them and are, therefore, less likely to transgress once again. They have been effectively shamed.

Contrast this with stigmatization. Stigmatization shames the person rather than just the act. It applies a sticky label of "bad," "evil," or "criminal" that follows the person through life. Stigmatizing disapproval is communicated with disrespect for the individual. It leads to humiliation and unresolved, persistent feelings of shame. The result is disintegrative shaming, in which the connection between the wrongdoer and the disapproving community disintegrates or breaks down. They feel alienated and justified in violating the rules imposed by a scornful, rejecting community. They have not been effectively shamed. In fact, they respond with shameless pride. Crime becomes *more* likely, consistent with the defiance perspective (see Chapter 11).

Example: Common Justice

Common Justice is an "alternative-to-incarceration and victim-service program ... that focuses on violent felonies in the adult courts," including robbery and assault.[90] The organization works mostly with young people (ages 16 to 26) in Brooklyn and the Bronx who have committed violent crimes. Common Justice relies on a restorative justice model to hold perpetrators accountable, reduce crime, and heal victims and communities. The organization calls for a move away from reliance on incarceration as the sole response to violence, arguing that prison is ineffective beyond incapacitation:

Eric Small, an inmate at the Columbia Correctional Institution in Portage, WI, received his diploma as part of a graduation ceremony for prisoners who completed a 25-session restorative justice program.

AP Photo/Wisconsin State Journal, Kyle McDaniel

We cannot incarcerate our way out of violence. That is in part because incarceration is an inadequate and often counterproductive tool to transform those who have committed violence or protect those who have been harmed. It is neither the most effective way to change people nor the most effective way to keep people safe. Its standing in society is based largely on its role in protecting people from violence and those who commit it, but as a violence intervention strategy, it fails to deliver the outcomes all people deserve—at great human and financial cost. Increasingly, this message is being sounded not only by justice reformers, but by crime survivors themselves. (p. 2)[91]

Crime victims contacted by Common Justice—over 90% of them—overwhelmingly opt for their intervention program instead of sending the person who harmed them to prison.[92] Why would they do this? They want to have a voice and to regain a sense of control by talking directly to the perpetrator, holding them accountable. And they don't want the person who hurt them to hurt them or anyone else ever again. Moreover, they live in communities buckling under the strain of mass incarceration, so they know firsthand how unlikely it is that imprisonment will reform the person who committed the crime or make anyone safer once they return from prison.[93] Many Common Justice crime victims express a burning desire for revenge, but they understand that the Common Justice model is more likely to be effective. Said one victim: "If he can't be gone forever, I'd rather he be changed."[94]

The Common Justice model uses "restorative justice circles," or conferences. Circles provide victims the opportunity to ask the perpetrator questions that have nagged at them since the attack, such as:

Why did you do it? Why did you choose me? What, if anything, could I have done to stop you? Did you think I did something to you? Did you think I was someone else? Was that a real gun? Were you really prepared to shoot me? Did you feel bad at the time? Do you feel bad now? What would you have done if I had fought back? What happened to you? Did you think you could get away with this?

Crime survivors also have their voices heard, expressing the pain the perpetrator caused and how they feel about it. The purpose is to heal the trauma of victimization as well as to force the person who committed the offense to appreciate fully the consequences of their behavior. Together, the circle participants establish "circle agreements." Circle agreements are obligations that the person who committed the crime must meet, such as paying restitution (e.g., paying back money stolen), completing community service, and regularly attending school or work. They also must participate in 12- to 15-month intensive violence intervention classes, with program staff monitoring compliance with the circle agreement. Fewer than 10% of individuals who go through the Common Justice process are arrested for a new crime before completing the program.[95]

CHAPTER SUMMARY

LO13.1 Describe how retributive principles inform sentencing guidelines.

Retribution is the idea that the punishment must fit the crime. Just and proportional punishment is the goal. Sentencing guidelines seek to achieve just and proportional sentences by setting recommended levels of punishment dependent upon crime seriousness, criminal history, and aggravating or mitigating factors.

LO13.2 Distinguish between specific, general, partial, and marginal deterrence.

Deterrence is the utilitarian approach of using punishment to alter the rational cost-benefit calculation of would-be offenders. Specific deterrence is achieved when punished law-breakers are deterred, whereas general deterrence occurs when onlookers are deterred. If the deterred individual still commits crime but opts for a less serious offense, partial deterrence has taken place. Marginal deterrence refers to the differences in deterrent capacity of various punishments.

LO13.3 Contrast incapacitation with retribution and deterrence.

Retribution is about getting one's deserved consequences; it is not about reducing crime. Deterrence is about reducing crime by altering the costs associated with crime. Incapacitation also seeks to reduce crime, but it proposes achieving this by incarcerating people, thereby denying them opportunities to commit crime. Collective incapacitation is applied to all, while selective incapacitation is reserved for high-rate or particularly dangerous law-breakers.

LO13.4 Explain how problem-solving courts are rooted in the rehabilitation ideal.

Problem-solving courts handle cases involving offenders who share a common challenge (or problem). Examples include drug courts, mental health courts, DUI courts, and veterans' courts. They use the power of the court to incentivize and support rehabilitation, including participation in treatment, counseling, and social services (e.g., housing assistance).

LO13.5 Identify the primary principles and strategies of restorative justice.

Restorative justice seeks to repair the harm produced by crime, encourages offender accountability, and welcomes individuals most impacted by crime to participate in its resolution. Its goal is to restore individuals, relationships, and communities rather than to punish, and it takes theoretical guidance from reintegrative shaming. Restorative justice conferences are a primary strategy for enacting these principles.

ENGAGED DISCUSSION

1. What is more important to you—making sure criminals "get what they deserve" (retribution) or reducing crime (even if they don't "get what they deserve")?

2. Think of a time in your life when you were tempted to violate a rule but were ultimately deterred. Was general deterrence or specific deterrence at work?

3. Imagine you are designing a risk assessment tool that will be used to identity high-risk individuals for selective incapacitation. What factors will you include, and why? What factors will you exclude, and why?

4. Drug courts, mental health courts, veterans' courts, DUI courts, and domestic violence courts are problem-solving courts. Come up with an idea for another type of problem-solving court. What is the problem it addresses?

5. For what kinds of crimes or criminal offenders would restorative justice conferences be ineffective, and why?

KEY TERMS

Civil confinement (p. 340)
Collective incapacitation (p. 337)
Determinate sentencing (p. 330)
Disintegrative shaming (p. 347)
Focused deterrence (p. 334)
General deterrence (p. 333)
Habitual offender law (p. 338)
Incapacitation (p. 336)
Indeterminate sentencing (p. 330)
Mandatory minimum sentences (p. 330)
Marginal deterrence (p. 333)
Partial deterrence (p. 333)
Problem-solving courts (p. 343)

Rehabilitation (p. 342)
Reintegrative shaming (p. 347)
Restorative justice (p. 346)
Retribution (p. 328)
Risk assessment (p. 339)
Selective incapacitation (p. 337)
Sentencing guidelines (p. 330)
Specific deterrence (p. 333)
Therapeutic jurisprudence (p. 343)
Three-strikes laws (p. 338)
Unwarranted disparity (p. 330)
Warranted disparity (p. 330)

14 PLACE-BASED APPROACHES TO PREVENTING CRIME

On January 1, 2014, at 8:00 a.m., Sean Azzariti, an Iraq War veteran who campaigned for recreational marijuana legalization in Colorado, made the symbolic "first purchase" at a Denver cannabis dispensary called the 3D Cannabis Center (*cannabis* is another term for marijuana). "We did it!" he exclaimed after purchasing an eighth of an ounce of a cannabis strain called Bubba Kush and marijuana-infused candies, which, he told reporters, helped ease the symptoms of his PTSD. Behind Azzariti were thousands of customers who had lined up—some for hours—to legally purchase marijuana at one of the city's many newly opened cannabis businesses. As with many other recreational dispensaries, 3D Cannabis Center had formerly operated as a medical marijuana business (medical marijuana has been legal in Colorado since 2000). Its former name was Denver's Discrete Dispensary, which reflected an earlier era in which marijuana purchasing and use were secretive, something to hide.[1] The name was outdated by 2014.

In 2012, Colorado voters approved Amendment 64, which legalized recreational marijuana. The new law established guidelines for personal use of cannabis as well as individual and commercial cultivation, manufacturing, transporting, and retail sales. In essence, marijuana was to be regulated much the same way that the state regulated alcohol. These regulations included restrictions based on age (must be at least 21 years old), licensing requirements for cannabis businesses (e.g., cultivation facilities, testing sites, and retail establishments), and provisions for how tax revenue is to be used.[2]

Mason Tvert, a spokesperson for the pro-legalization Marijuana Policy Project and codirector of the Amendment 64 campaign stated, "Making marijuana legal for adults is not an experiment. Prohibition was the experiment, and the results were abysmal."[3] And while 54% of Colorado voters in 2012 agreed with Tvert that it was high time to change the law (pun intended), not all were convinced. More than half of Colorado's municipalities have chosen to prohibit the retail sale of recreational cannabis within city limits, including Colorado's second-largest city, Colorado Springs.[4] Their reasons include possible social harms of legalization, including underage use and crime.

Opponents of cannabis legalization—and those in favor of legalization but opposed to the opening of dispensaries in their communities—argue that dispensaries increase crime in nearby neighborhoods. In 2012, the sheriff in Douglas County, Colorado, cautioned the public: "Expect more crime, more kids using marijuana, and pot for sale everywhere."[5] In California, which was also early to legalize recreational marijuana, the state's Police Chiefs Association's task force on marijuana dispensaries put it plainly (prior to legalization): "Marijuana dispensaries bring in the criminal element and attract loiterers."[6] Critics name the cash-only nature of recreational marijuana businesses (due to federal laws that criminalize cannabis) as a cause for concern. The influx of customers and other outsiders (including those engaged in "cannabis tourism"), along with many people carrying cash or cannabis, has the potential to generate robberies, burglaries, assaults, and other offenses, opponents argue. Are they correct, though? Environmental criminologists offer some insight.

ENVIRONMENTAL CRIMINOLOGY

Ask any real estate agent the three most important things to consider when selecting a home and they will tell you: "location, location, location." Ask any criminologist the three most important things to consider when studying crime and you're likely to hear some combination of motivation, control, and opportunity. But there are many ways to approach motivation, control, and opportunity. Often, they are treated as characteristics of individuals or groups—some *people* or *groups of people* are more motivated to commit crime, are less controlled, and have access to more opportunities to violate the law than others. Environmental criminologists see motivation, control, and opportunity as characteristics of places—some *locations* generate more motivation, exert less control, or provide more ample opportunities for crime than others. One might even say that environmental criminologists agree with real estate agents. What matters for both is "location, location, location."

Environmental criminology is a type of criminology that analyzes variation in crime and victimization across places. While other criminologists study the *social* distribution of crime (variation across individuals or social groups), environmental criminologists explore the *spatial*, or ecological, distribution of crime.[7] Environmental criminologists examine

> crime, criminality, and victimization as they relate, first, to particular places, and secondly, to the way individuals and organizations shape their activities spatially, and in doing so are in turn influenced by place-based or spatial factors. (p. 620)[8]

In other words, environmental criminologists study not only where crime occurs but also what it is about some places that causes crime—or its absence.

The environmental perspective may sound familiar. The cartographic approach pioneered by André-Michel Guerry and Adolphe Quetelet in 19th century France (see Chapter 6), the social ecology of the Chicago school, and social disorganization theory (see Chapter 8) all focus on the spatial distribution of crime. This chapter, however, will address environmental perspectives designed with criminal event characteristics and crime prevention efforts in mind. Rather than concern themselves with background predictors (or "distal factors") like economic disadvantage, family dysfunction, or school failure, environmental criminologists train their lens on the foreground of crime, or the moment in which would-be law violators become actual law violators. They examine the situations in which criminal events take place. The empirical study of crime situations is sometimes called crime science.[9]

The Environmental Approach to Crime Prevention

Imagine how you might prevent crime before it occurs. If you were to follow the logic of traditional criminological theories—like social control, social learning, or strain theories—your aim would be to change people or the broader social forces that influence them. Your focus would be on "risk factors," such as crime-involved peers, school difficulties, neighborhood violence, or lack of coping resources.[10] Whether it's training in emotional regulation, treatment for substance use disorders, or youth mentoring programs, crime prevention efforts typically set out to fix underlying pathologies that lead to criminal behavior. And legal system responses to crime, both punitive (like deterrence) and social welfare–focused (like rehabilitation), seek to transform the individual and the decisions they make (see Chapter 13). Environmental criminology suggests a different way of preventing crime, that is, by changing the environment instead of changing the person.

You are familiar with the notion of modifying the environment to reduce crime if you have ever locked your front door or removed belongings from the backseat of a car. In taking these measures, you increased the effort required (locked door) or minimized the opportunity (removing belongings) for crime. Place-based approaches to crime prevention are more complex than just locking a door, yet they are based on similar ideas—they alter offender decision-making in specific locations by minimizing opportunities for crime or removing features of the environment that might prompt crime.

This chapter addresses four perspectives on crime prevention rooted in the place-based approach: (1) routine activities theory, (2) the broken windows theory, (3) crime prevention through environmental design, and (4) situational crime prevention. To understand each, we must first answer some questions common to all environmental explanations: What, exactly, are they trying to prevent? And how do environmental criminologists figure out where crime occurs and whether crime prevention efforts are effective?

Criminal Events Versus Criminality

Environmental criminology is about crime, *not* criminality. More precisely, environmental criminology is about criminal events: Why do criminal events concentrate in certain places? What situational factors increase the odds that certain types of criminal events will take place? A robbery at 112 N. Main St. at 3:32 a.m. on a Saturday morning is a criminal event. A 911 call about an intimate partner assault at a motel located near exit 145 off Interstate-40 marks another criminal event. Criminal events are acts, or occurrences. When we speak of crime incidence rates (see Chapter 2), we are speaking of criminal events. Environmental criminologists examine not just how many criminal events occur but also where, specifically, they occur.

Criminality, in contrast, is a property of individuals. It tells us about their propensity to commit crime, or their disposition towards crime. The more motivated a person is to break the law and the more frequently they follow these impulses, the greater their level of criminality. Many traditional theories of crime are, in fact, theories of criminality. They answer the question: Why do (or don't) people commit crime? Environmental criminologists instead ask: Why do some places have more (or fewer) criminal events than others? They figure that solving the problem of criminality is far too complex—and likely impossible. Solving the problem of criminal events, however, is a reachable goal. It's much easier to change the features of a place than to change a person's character, according to environmental criminologists. Thus, the answer to the question "What, exactly, are they trying to prevent?" is crime—not criminals.

Spatial Analysis in Environmental Criminology

Think about the kinds of data you would require if you wished to examine the geographic locations of criminal events, also called spatial analysis. You have some idea of how this process begins if you've ever dropped a pin while using a GPS mapping app. Environmental criminologists use something called geo-coding to mark crime locations. Geo-coding converts text-based location descriptions, like "112 N. Main St., Springfield, Illinois" into coordinates that can be mapped and analyzed statistically.[11] In criminology, those location descriptions are usually of criminal events, but they can also be businesses, victim residences, or other places.

Spatial analysis requires accurate location data. That usually comes from police calls for service (911 calls) or official data on crime incidents, like NIBRS data. You may recall from Chapter 2 that police data are plagued by the dark figure of crime, or crime that never becomes known to law enforcement due to nonreporting or the absence of a victim. For this reason, researchers are most confident when their spatial analyses examine offenses with smaller dark figures, like homicide.[12]

Spatial studies of crime reveal that criminal events are overwhelmingly concentrated in very small units of geographic space, called micro-places.[13] Micro-places include intersections, street segments, and specific addresses. Criminologists offer the "5-50 rule" to describe crime concentration in micro-places: About 5% of micro-places are responsible for 50% of street crimes (p. 446).[14] For example, researchers observe the following:

- 50% of crimes occurred at 4.5% of street segments in Seattle over a 14-year period.[15]

- 50% of shootings took place at less than 3% of intersections and street segments over a 29-year period in Boston[16]; 50% of Boston robberies occurred at about 8.1% of intersections and street segments (100% of Boston robberies occurred at just 12% of the city's micro-places).[17]

- 50% of crimes in a Minnesota suburb (Brooklyn Park) over a 15-year period took place at 2% of street segments.[18]

- 50% of robberies and thefts occurred at 3.66% of street segments in Campinas, Brazil, over a three-year period.[19]

- 50% of assaults, burglaries, robberies, larcenies, and motor vehicle thefts over a 16-year period in Vancouver, British Columbia, Canada, occurred at 3.25% to 4.35% of street segments.[20]

These results are so consistent across time periods, nations, and crime types that criminologists assert that there is a **law of crime concentration at places**.[21] Another term for these high-activity crime locations is hotspots (see Chapter 5).[22] Figure 14.1 presents a visual depiction of the law of crime concentration, showing how a small number of street segments have extremely high rates of sexual assault (at least as reported to law enforcement). And the inverse is also observed: There appear to be "crime-free" places. For example, another study of crime in Vancouver found that 40% of street segments in the city experienced no crimes at all over a span of 16 years.[23]

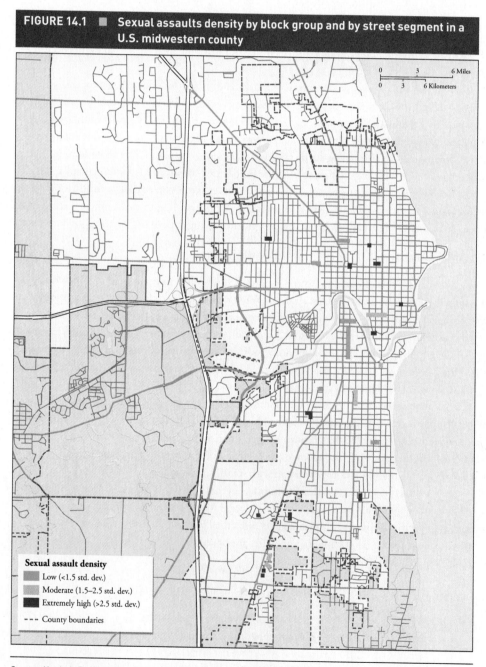

FIGURE 14.1 ■ Sexual assaults density by block group and by street segment in a U.S. midwestern county

Sexual assault density
- Low (<1.5 std. dev.)
- Moderate (1.5–2.5 std. dev.)
- Extremely high (>2.5 std. dev.)
- - - - County boundaries

Source: Konkel, R. H., Hafemeister, A. J., & Daigle, L. E. (2019). The effects of risky places, motivated offenders, and social disorganization on sexual victimization: A microgeographic- and neighborhood-level examination. *Journal of Interpersonal Violence.*

Micro-places also include types of businesses, called "micro place-based institutions." Bars, night-clubs, liquor stores, gas stations, motels, pawn shops, and marijuana dispensaries are a few examples of micro-places that criminologists analyze spatially. Just as crime concentrates on some streets, it also concentrates around some kinds of venues. Alcohol outlets, in particular, are found to increase interpersonal, direct-contact crimes like assault and robbery. You might jump to the conclusion that this is the result of on-premises drinking—that people become intoxicated and either commit crimes or become vulnerable to victimization. Yet the alcohol outlet effect holds for retailers that sell alcohol that is consumed elsewhere, including liquor stores and convenience stores that sell alcohol.[24]

The criminogenic effects of micro place-based institutions like bars and liquor stores are felt not just in the immediate area surrounding the business, but also in adjacent neighborhoods. Criminologists call these **spillover effects** (also called spatial diffusion of crime). The crime has spilled over, or spread, into the surrounding area.[25]

Crime often concentrates in red light districts, which are micro-places (stretches of road) where many adult entertainment businesses are located, like "the block," which is Baltimore's red light district.

Photo by Steelplug/Wikimedia Creative Commons

Crime Generators and Crime Attractors

Why do some micro-places become crime hotspots? They might be crime generators. **Crime generators** are locations that are easily accessed by large groups of people who use the space for noncriminal reasons. They may be places with lots of foot traffic or areas where people congregate. They create (or generate) occasions for crime by bringing together many people in one place, some of whom will inevitably be motivated to commit crime and will take advantage of easy opportunities to victimize others. Shopping districts, bus stations, and high schools are examples of crime generators.[26]

Micro-places also become crime hotspots if they are crime attractors. **Crime attractors** are locations that appeal to (or attract) people wishing to commit criminal offenses. They do this by supplying vulnerable victims or desirable targets, such as items to steal or structures to burglarize.[27] Businesses that rely on cash transactions are especially attractive for this reason. Bars, gas stations, pawn shops, and check-cashing businesses are examples of crime attractors. Locations where illegal markets operate—like markets for illicit commercial sex, drug dealing, gambling, of the sale of stolen goods—are also crime attractors beyond the criminal activity of the market itself. That's because these are largely cash-based enterprises whose participants are typically unwilling to report victimization to police.[28]

Check-cashing businesses and payday lenders are a kind of micro place-based institution studied by environmental criminologists.

Robert Lachman/Los Angeles Times/Getty Images

Example: Marijuana Dispensaries and the Spatial Distribution of Crime

The chapter began with a description of Colorado's burgeoning cannabis industry. Recall that some cities, such as Colorado Springs, opted to prohibit recreational cannabis businesses entirely. Even cities that embraced legalized marijuana, like Denver, had detractors concerned with the impact of dispensaries on local crime rates. Enough time has passed since the first dispensary openings in 2014. Now environmental criminologists can weigh in on whether recreational cannabis dispensaries do, in fact, operate as crime generators or crime attractors. Figure 14.2 displays the distribution of recreational and medical marijuana dispensaries in Denver.

FIGURE 14.2 ■ Map of marijuana dispensaries in Denver, Colorado, 2014–2016

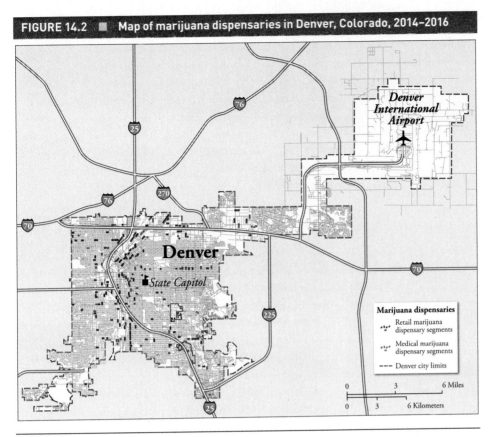

Source: Adapted from Connealy, N., Piza, E., & Hatten, D. (2020). The criminogenic effect of marijuana dispensaries in Denver, Colorado: A microsynthetic control quasi-experiment and cost-benefit analysis. *Justice Evaluation Journal, 3*(1), 69-93.

Environmental criminologists use spatial analysis to determine whether dispensary openings are followed by changes in the frequency of various types of criminal events. It's possible that changes aren't due to dispensaries, though, but to general crime rate fluctuations. To solve this problem, they compare dispensary areas to otherwise similar communities that didn't have a dispensary opening.[29] Their studies mimic experiments with treatment groups (dispensary) and control groups (no dispensary).

One set of researchers found that dispensary openings in Denver, Colorado, didn't increase violent crime, drug offenses, or general disorder in surrounding areas. But it wasn't all good news: Property crimes rose by about 18%.[30] This result fits with some critics' arguments about dispensaries as crime attractors due to their cash-only business model. Other criminologists found that openings of recreational marijuana dispensaries across Colorado (not just Denver) are associated with increases—though weak—in criminal events in the neighborhoods surrounding each new dispensary, with the exception of homicide and auto theft.[31] They conclude that this is a function of increased foot traffic and an increase in marijuana-specific offenses (e.g., public use, underage possession, and traffic-related use/possession). Cannabis businesses, they conclude, pull in "the criminal element," including those who commit smash-and-grab burglaries of dispensaries. Most studies find that medical marijuana dispensaries, in contrast to recreational dispensaries, have minimal effects on crime.[32]

BROKEN WINDOWS

The year is 1982. An article is published in the magazine *The Atlantic,* penned by criminologist George Kelling and political scientist James Q. Wilson. It's title is "Broken Windows."[33] In that article, Kelling and Wilson proposed an idea that would strike a chord with politicians, law enforcement, and the public, all of whom were frustrated by the rising tide of violent crime (U.S. crime rates shot up during the 1970s and 1980s). Their idea was simple: Broken windows—or any other signs of disorder—lead to serious crime.

Broken Windows Theory

The broken windows theory holds that neighborhood disorder sends a message that no one will intervene if the law is broken. The message is received by the criminally inclined, like drug dealers, violent Johns, muggers, and burglars. It is also received by law-abiding residents who retreat fearfully into their homes or move away. Residents keep their mouths shut when they encounter troubling behavior—like drug sales out in the open, people injecting heroin in public, or drunk teenagers harassing passersby—for fear of violent reprisals. The unspoken rule is "don't get involved." The problems spiral. In the logic of broken windows, unrepaired windows and broken streetlights lead to loitering teenagers and graffiti, which lead to aggressive panhandlers and squatters, which lead to open-air drug markets and street prostitution, which lead to shootings and robberies. As Kelling and Wilson argued,

> *Disorder and crime are usually inextricably linked, in a kind of developmental sequence... If a window in a building is broken and is left unrepaired, all the rest of the windows will soon be broken.*[34]

There are several forms of disorder that signal an area is "an unmanaged space where danger might lurk" (p. 55).[35] Graffiti tags, abandoned or unkempt properties, litter and overflowing waste receptacles, discarded drug paraphernalia like needles, physical traces of homelessness like makeshift structures and shopping carts, and broken windows are examples of physical disorder. Physical disorder refers to the environmental artifacts of disorder—it is the refuse of disorderly behavior.

Social disorder is behavioral. It is actions that are regarded as nuisances by most residents, visitors, business owners, and police. Examples include public intoxication, public urination, aggressive panhandling, street harassment, turnstile jumping, and the behaviors of people experiencing symptoms of psychosis in public. A related term, incivilities, refers to norm violations that show a lack of respect or concern for other members of the community, such as blasting loud music at night, leaving a vehicle double-parked, or dumping garbage in neighbors' yards. According to Kelling and Wilson, disorderly people are the source of fears that catapult neighborhoods towards serious crime:

> *Many citizens, of course, are primarily frightened by crime, especially crime involving a sudden, violent attack by a stranger. This risk is very real... in many large cities. But we tend to overlook another source of fear—the fear of being bothered by disorderly people. Not violent people, nor, necessarily, criminals, but disreputable or obstreperous or unpredictable people: panhandlers, drunks, addicts, rowdy teenagers, prostitutes, loiterers, the mentally disturbed.*[36]

According to Kelling and Wilson, signs of physical and social disorder lead to serious crime even when disorderly people, themselves, aren't particularly criminal. They offer two reasons. First, their presence invites serious offenders who see that "anything goes" in the neighborhood. "If nobody does anything about the public defecation," the serious offender might think, "then nobody is going to do anything about me robbing this drunk person." Second, their presence discourages prosocial behaviors that prevent crime, like neighbors getting involved when they witness unacceptable conduct. Disorderly places become "vulnerable to criminal invasion."[37]

Broken Windows Policing

Few criminological ideas have had greater influence on criminal justice policy—or been more controversial—than the broken windows theory. It became the philosophical basis for policing in many U.S. cities, most notably in New York City, beginning in the 1990s.[38] One of the earliest efforts at broken windows policing is found in New York City's "quality-of-life" initiative within the transit system, cracking down on turnstile jumpers in subway stations. Following broken windows logic, seeing people breaking the rules by evading the fare caused other riders to feel unsafe—it sent the message that "anything goes" in the subway. As part of the initiative, police issued 30% more summonses and made 80% more arrests for turnstile jumping.[39] The initiative spread to other forms of disorder, including unsolicited window washing, panhandling, leaving property on public roadways, public urination, street vending without a permit, unreasonable noise, and public alcohol consumption.[40]

Proponents of broken windows policing, also called order-maintenance policing, maintain that police can disrupt the disorder-to-crime process by cracking down on low-level disorderly behavior.

These overdose awareness day murals are displayed in Vancouver's downtown Eastside, which has high rates of public drug use and overdose, visible homelessness, vandalism, and other forms of disorder.

Darryl Dyck/The Canadian Press via AP

They believe a zero-tolerance approach to minor disorder is the key to preventing serious crime. This may take the form of ticketing or making misdemeanor arrests for drug possession, public intoxication, obstructing pedestrian traffic, jaywalking, sleeping on a park bench, or loitering. Other options are "move-along orders" for which police instruct disorderly persons, such as people experiencing homelessness, to leave without issuing a citation.[41]

Broken Windows, Broken Lives?

On July 17, 2014, police stopped Eric Garner after he had been seen selling single cigarettes, called "loosies," on a Staten Island street in New York. The arresting officer put Garner, a 43-year-old Black man, in a chokehold, a tactic prohibited by the NYPD, ultimately killing him. Garner's death at the hands of law enforcement raised serious questions about broken windows policing—especially concerns about policing in communities of color.[42]

Critics of broken windows policing recognize disorder as a real problem for community members, but they argue that some police tactics used to address it—like the heavy-handed order-maintenance policing that ended in Mr. Garner's death—create an even worse problem. They point to overpolicing of low-income communities of color characterized by frequent stops, searches, misdemeanor arrests, and citations for minor offenses, like selling "loosies."[43] These tactics, they argue, strain relationships between residents and police, and they burden poor residents with fines, court dates, and fees for minor violations that go unpoliced in middle- and higher-income neighborhoods. Criminologist Issa Kohler-Hausmann calls this "procedural hassle."[44]

As misdemeanor citations and arrests increased under the guise of maintaining order, more and more ordinary people found themselves caught up in the criminal legal system. Throughout the 1980s, before broken windows policing, about one in four misdemeanor arrests in New York City were of people with prior felony convictions. By the 2010s, two decades into broken windows policing, only about one in ten (12%) had a felony record—even though the number of people with felony records, in general, was much higher in the 2010s relative to the 1980s.[45] Researchers noted a pattern of mass misdemeanors that seemed to parallel mass incarceration (though most misdemeanants are not sentenced to jails or prisons).[46] Prosecutors and judges saw that their caseloads increasingly included, in their words, "junk" cases—like public urination, putting feet up on a subway seat, not having ID when being stopped for jaywalking—during the surge of broken windows policing.[47]

Protesters criticizing broken windows policing point to the rise of misdemeanor citations and arrests disproportionately borne by communities of color.

AP Photo/Bebeto Matthews

Skeptics also note that disorder is in the eye of the beholder.[48] For instance, is a group of teenagers hanging out on the sidewalk disorderly? What about a 43-year-old Black man selling loose cigarettes? It's subjective. And perceptions are shaped by biases, particularly racial biases. Criminologists Robert Sampson and Stephen Raudenbush studied the disconnect between objective markers of disorder and perceptions of disorder, finding that predominantly Black and poor neighborhoods are perceived by observers of all races as more disorderly, even when controlling for actual neighborhood conditions.[49] Plus, what is seen as an arrest- or ticket-worthy offense by police may not be the fear-inducing disorder that concerns residents.[50] And resentments build when behaviors of Black, Latinx, and American Indian persons are particularly likely to be perceived and treated as disorderly by police.[51]

Even one of the creators of the broken windows theory, George Kelling, took aim at those who use his theory as a basis for mass misdemeanor arrests for trivial behaviors. When interviewed for a *Frontline* documentary, Kelling summed up his reaction to the misapplication of his ideas with two words: "Oh sh*t."[52] "A lot of sins have been committed in the name of 'broken windows,'" Kelling wrote. The sins to which he was referring were aggressive police stops for behaviors like jaywalking or selling "loosies." Kelling argued that reliance on misdemeanor arrests does not, in fact, fit with the vision of broken windows, which is about partnering with communities to restore order:

> *Broken windows policing is a highly discretionary set of activities that seeks the least intrusive means of solving a problem—whether that problem is street prostitution, drug dealing in a park, graffiti, abandoned buildings, or actions such as public drunkenness. Moreover, depending on the problem, good broken windows policing seeks partners to address it: social workers, city code enforcers, business improvement district staff, teachers, medical personnel, clergy, and others. The goal is to reduce the level of disorder in public spaces so that citizens feel safe, are able to use them, and businesses thrive. Arrest of an offender is supposed to be a last resort—not the first.[53]*

Addressing Physical Disorder

What are some ways a city can reduce disorder without resorting to citations and arrests? The broken windows view of crime prevention extends beyond just policing. In fact, some of the earliest applications of the theory involved rapid cleanup of graffiti and seat repair in New York City subways.[54] Other efforts to reduce physical disorder include fixing broken streetlights and the creation of greenspace, which entails adding planned and orderly vegetation to urban spaces. This is sometimes called "cleaning and greening," and it includes strategies like replacing vacant lots with grassy areas or community gardens, as well as planting trees or shrubs along walkways.[55] Well-maintained greenspace signals that the area is cared for and managed, whereas barren space signals neglect and abandonment.[56]

Increasing greenspace is a form of blight abatement. **Blight** refers to something that has a damaging or spoiling effect. Physical disorder is a form of blight, and it includes boarded-up structures (like houses, storefronts, or warehouses), abandoned vehicles, and empty lots. Blight abatement involves the removal or repair of physical disorder, as when replacing condemned buildings with small parks. Other times it means covering up unsightly spaces, as with community mural projects.

An example of blight abatement is found in the New Orleans program Fight the Blight.[57] Hurricane Katrina ravaged New Orleans in 2005, with some of its most devastating effects on low-income neighborhoods where residents often lacked the money needed to rebuild. Many walked away from their homes, which had been left uninhabitable by the flooding. The massive increase in abandoned and rotting structures, along with overgrown vacant lots, exacerbated a blight problem that New Orleans was already battling even before the hurricane hit.[58] A decade later, between January 2014 and September 2016, housing inspectors noted 154,000 building code violations on fewer than 5,000 land parcels in New Orleans.[59] Flight the Blight targeted this problem by providing routine mowing of overgrown lots (recorded on the property owner's tax bill) for six targeted neighborhoods.

Experimental studies of blight abatement programs, like Fight the Blight, show that reducing physical disorder can, in fact, prevent some forms of crime in the nearby area. The New Orleans program reduced drug violations surrounding the maintained lots.[60] The researchers speculate that the remediated lots communicate that the area is managed by people who will take note of illegal activity. A similar program in Philadelphia that improved 5,112 abandoned buildings and vacant lots reduced firearm violence substantially. Gun violence decreased by 39% in and around abandoned structures that were fixed up. Vacant lot remediation resulted in a smaller reduction of just 5%.[61]

Demolition of condemned buildings is also sometimes found to reduce firearm violence, consistent with the broken windows view. For example, a study of Detroit's demolition program found that neighborhoods with six or more abandoned houses removed saw an 11% reduction in firearm assaults in the ensuing years.[62] Of course, broken window thinkers would question what happened to those lots *after* the structures were demolished—were the lots turned into attractive greenspace or were they empty and neglected? The Detroit program researchers suggest that the effect would have been greater had the post-demolition treatment been better. It's not enough to remove blight if another version of blight is left in its place.

A project engineer stands in front of construction in a new community in Highland Park, Michigan, where vacant lots are being transformed into desirable living space.

Virginia Lozano/Detroit News via AP

ENGAGED CRIMINOLOGY 14.1
Broken Windows Word Association

Word association is the spontaneous production of other words in response to a given word. For example, if I said "scary," you might respond "nightmare," because the words *scary* and *nightmare* are connected in your mind. This activity presents you with a list of words for word association. Here is the catch: You will participate in this word association as a broken windows theorist. Respond as you think a broken windows thinker would respond. Your word responses do not need to be key terms.

Here Are Your Words:

1. Fear Your word: _____
2. Order Your word: _____
3. Litter Your word: _____
4. Community Your word: _____
5. Arrest Your word: _____

Why Those Words?

In two or three sentences, explain why you chose the words you selected. Why do they fit the broken windows perspective?

ROUTINE ACTIVITIES THEORY

The year is 1979. Nearly 35 years have passed since the end of World War II. The fortunes of most people improved in the postwar decades: Poverty and unemployment declined, graduation rates and median incomes went up. These were the macro-level predictors that criminologists usually reached for. The motivation for crime *should* have gone down. Yet crimes like robbery and burglary increased. The creators of routine activities theory, Lawrence Cohen and Marcus Felson, thought most criminologists were looking in the wrong place. The explanation lies not in changes to motivation, they charged, but in changes to peoples' daily routines (or routine activities) during those years.[63] People's lifestyles looked a lot different in 1979 than in 1952—just as they look different now relative to 1979.

Pause to think about your own daily routines. What time do you usually wake up and go to bed? Do you leave your home to attend school during the day? Does your job require that you are out in public after dark? Daily routines differ in how much they expose people to conditions conducive to victimization. And routine activities theory is about patterns in victimization.

To illustrate, imagine two people. Let's call them Lara and Marc. Lara works a 9-to-5 job from her home office, after which she spends her evenings caring for her two young children. When she must go into her employer's main office, she drives. Marc, who lives alone, works the night shift at a hospital. He relies on buses and the subway to get to and from work, though he walks when he misses the bus. Who is more likely to become a victim of robbery, Lara or Marc? What about burglary? Routine activities theorists would point to Marc. He is vulnerable to robbery while walking to or waiting for public transportation, whereas Lara is safe at home or in her car. Plus, Marc's home is empty while he works, making it a more attractive target for burglars, while Lara's home is occupied most of the time.

Now think about how daily routines, in general, have changed over time. Even back in 1979, criminologists observed major transformations in the structure of day-to-day life. People were delaying marriage and going to college at higher rates, which meant more young people living alone or with roommates, away from their parents and free of the responsibilities of child care. Women were entering the paid labor force in record numbers, which meant that households were left unattended during daytime hours. At the same time, consumer goods were becoming smaller and easier to transport. As the fortunes of ordinary people improved, they had more valuable belongings to take. Opportunities for crime abounded.[64]

Three Elements Necessary for Crime

The primary claim of routine activities theory (also called routine activity theory) is that victimization occurs when three things come together in time and space[65]:

1. Motivated offenders,

2. Suitable targets or victims, and

3. Absence of capable guardianship.

A *motivated offender* is exactly what it sounds like: a person who will commit crime if the opportunity arises. But all the motivation in the world won't lead to crime if there is nothing ripe for the taking (or assaulting or destroying). A *suitable target* is a person, place, or thing that is desirable and readily available for victimization. It is also called an attractive target. A restaurant employee carrying a full bank deposit bag is a more suitable (or attractive) target for robbery than a restaurant employee on a smoke break. An unlocked car filled with recently purchased store merchandise is a more suitable target for theft than an empty, locked vehicle. A person with a high credit score is more suitable target for identity fraud than a person with a low credit score.

Routine activities researchers offer several acronyms that capture the characteristics of highly suitable targets for crime. One is VIVA, which stands for value, inertia, visibility, and access.[66] *Value* is straightforward—the higher the value, the more attractive the target or victim. For example, one might expect that a brand new BMW to be more attractive to an auto thief than a 1998 Toyota Camry. Value can be either real, as in monetary value (like in the BMW example), or symbolic, as when the target or victim is meaningful to the offender or confers status. *Inertia* refers to the ability to move the target, or the amount of effort it would take to commit the crime. Impediments or obstacles make a target less suitable. Burglars frequently steal cash, small electronics, and prescription drugs, but they rarely take refrigerators.[67] *Visibility* is about how exposed the target is to the offender—can they see it? A glass case filled with valuable jewelry is a more attractive target than a safe with the same contents. This is also true due to *access,* the fourth element of VIVA. The design of the setting and the placement of the target will determine its attractiveness. Inaccessibility—due, for example, to the presence of door staff, effective locks, credit freezes, and cybersecurity measures—renders a target or victim unsuitable.

Another acronym (shared by situational crime prevention) is CRAVED—concealable, removable, available, valuable, enjoyable, and disposable. These characteristics pertain specifically to the suitability of hot products, or frequently stolen items.[68] There are obvious overlaps with the VIVA acronym: Value and valuable, access and available, inertia and removable. But CRAVED adds additional features, including the ability of the offender to hide their criminal activity (concealable), the level of pleasure the offender anticipates getting from the act (enjoyable), and—in the case of markets for stolen items or identities—the ease with which they can be sold or exchanged in an underground market (disposable).[69]

The third element must be present or, more accurately, *absent* for the motivated offender to take advantage of the attractive target: capable guardianship. Capable guardians are physically or symbolically present to prevent the crime, whether they intend to or not.[70] For example, a police officer, security guard, neighbor, or passerby may be physically present, deterring the individual who is motivated to commit an offense. Closed-circuit cameras in stores and home security systems mean that guardians are symbolically present. Routine activities thinkers assume that motivated offenders are rational and therefore sensitive to the risks presented by guardianship.

Unlike other theories of crime, including control theories, routine activities theory is not *about* people who commit crime. They are a necessary part of the equation (no motivated offender, no crime), but they are not the central explanatory factor. Crime doesn't increase and decrease because of changes in motivation, in this perspective. The driving force is changes in the actions of ordinary people going about their daily lives. Another term for these people is "potential victims." Victimization rates climb when large segments of the population change how they live their lives in such a way that they become suitable targets for people motivated to commit crimes in the absence of capable guardians. This is a theory of victimization, *not* criminal offending. It could just as easily appear in Chapter 12 (What Is Victimology?).

You may bristle at routine activities theory's focus on victims' behaviors in explaining their victimization. Is this victim-blaming? It isn't. The theory does not assign *responsibility* to victims. Rather, it points to *vulnerabilities*. And it links those vulnerabilities to large-scale social conditions rather that reducing them to poor decision-making. For example, the fact that many more people work from home these days isn't due to their better choices, but to technological advances and the shift to an information economy.

Contemporary routine activities scholars have expanded their focus beyond temporal trends, or changes over time. They also draw on the three elements—motivated offenders, suitable targets, and absence of capable guardianship—to understand demographic and spatial patterns in victimization. For instance, they suggest that young and single people are victims of violence and personal theft more than older and married people because they lead higher-risk lifestyles; namely, they have a nighttime social life.[71] They also designate some geographic areas as hotspots for victimization due to problems with guardianship, such as poorly lit parking lots or dark alleys.[72]

The Routine Activities Perspective on Crime Prevention

In the routine activities view, preventing crime requires changes to target and victim suitability as well as to guardianship. Targets and victims can be made less appealing to offenders through target hardening. Target hardening involves reducing the ease with which targets or victims can be accessed. Examples include tamper-proof packaging, window locks, and online credit freezes. We use target hardening to prevent against online victimization when we implement two-factor authentication, opt for highly restrictive privacy settings, and use antivirus software.[73] Even traveling in pairs or groups to reduce the risk of victimization is considered a form of target hardening.

Improving guardianship requires the work of controllers. *Controllers* are responsible for supervising or managing targets, places, or people who might commit offenses. There are three types of controllers: (1) *guardians,* who supervise potential targets or victims (e.g., museum staff); (2) *place managers,* who oversee locations, including online locations, to secure them against intruders (e.g., security guards and cybersecurity professionals); and (3) *handlers,* who look after people who might engage in illegal conduct to keep them out of trouble (e.g., bouncers).[74]

Ideas about target hardening and controllers are elaborated in situational crime prevention (SCP), covered in the final section of the chapter. In fact, routine activities theory and situational crime prevention are often presented simultaneously, as SCP strategies are the on-the-ground application of routine activities ideas on how to prevent crime.[75] Routine activities is the theory, and situational crime prevention is the practice. Keep reading to the end of the chapter to learn about the full scope of crime prevention measures inspired by routine activities thinking.

Evaluating Routine Activities Theory

Routine activities theory has remained popular for more than 40 years, owing to its continued empirical support and its practical applications to crime prevention. It has been applied to many forms of criminal victimization, with recent examinations extending beyond the street crimes for which it was developed. For example, criminologists find that the likelihood of cybercrime victimization—phishing, cyberstalking, cyberthreats, malware, consumer fraud—corresponds to target attractiveness and weaknesses in knowledge of online risks and protective measures (i.e., capable guardianship).[76] It also applies to elder fraud. Elder fraudsters prey on older persons by first cultivating their trust, such as a scammer masquerading as an investment advisor, estate planner, or housekeeper. Victims of elder fraud lack the capable guardianship that other older persons possess: They are especially likely to be childless, socially isolated (without friends), and to suffer from cognitive decline.[77] As a result, they have neither the personal faculties to recognize the fraud nor the family and friends to step in and protect them.

The theory has its critics despite its empirical validity. Critics take aim at the theory's sole emphasis on how "legitimate" routines drive patterns in victimization.[78] Recognizing that victims and people who violate the law are often drawn from the same group (called victim-offender overlap; see Chapter

13), they argue for greater attention to risky, victimogenic lifestyles. "It is not simply going outside of the house that matters," critics assert, "but it is instead the differential risks associated with *what one is actually doing outside*—such as planting flowers in a garden versus selling drugs on a street corner— that influence one's susceptibility to victimization" (p. 104).[79] This criticism responds to criminologists' practice of measuring routine activities as "time spent away from home" or "time spent online." In other words, behavior matters.

Personal dispositions matter also, critics write, but routine activities theory neglects this possibility. For example, they argue that people with low self-control self-select into risky situations that make them suitable targets for people motivated to offend.[80] Other criticisms of routine activities theory are common to all theories that focus on situational opportunities. The loudest of these is the accusation that the theory ignores criminal motivation and the root causes of criminality.

ENGAGED CRIMINOLOGY 14.2
Applying Routine Activities Theory to the COVID-19 Pandemic

This activity asks you to imagine what a routine activities theorist would predict about the effect of pandemic lockdown on robbery. Recall that robbery is a violent crime that involves taking (or attempting to take) something of value from another person by force or threat of force.

The figure below depicts three possible patterns in robbery victimization rates (options A, B, and C) over time: before lockdown (pre-pandemic), during lockdown, when lockdown restrictions were relaxed, and after the lockdown ended.

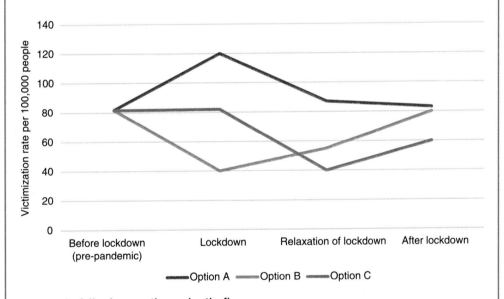

Answer the following questions using the figure:

1. Which option (A, B, or C) best depicts what a routine activities theorist would predict regarding the effect of a pandemic lockdown on robbery?

2. In one or two sentences, explain why a routine activities theorist would make the prediction you chose. Include at least two of the following terms in your answer: attractive targets, capable guardianship, motivated offenders, target hardening.

ENVIRONMENTAL DESIGN AND SITUATIONAL CRIME PREVENTION

What if the solution to crime and the fear it provokes is not found in policing or punishment but, rather, in the built environment? Crime prevention through environmental design (CPTED) and situational crime prevention suggest that we can thwart would-be law breakers by designing spaces—apartment buildings, outdoor areas, businesses, and online spaces—to reduce opportunities for crime. This is different from the physical disorder remediation favored by broken windows theorists. Rather than just reduce criminogenic physical environments like abandoned homes, CPTED and situational crime prevention use design to reduce crime and disorder before they even occur. In this approach, crime prevention isn't just for criminal justice professionals' it is also the task of architects, city planners, and designers.

Crime Prevention Through Environmental Design (CPTED)

Crime prevention through environmental design (CPTED) is an approach to crime prevention that claims the design of physical spaces can encourage or discourage crime. Physical spaces include structures, landscaping, and outdoor environments. CPTED hit the criminological scene in the early 1970s following the publication of two books: Jane Jacob's *The Death and Life of Great American Cities*[81] and Oscar Newman's *Defensible Space*.[82] Jacobs and Newman were not criminologists. They weren't even social scientists. Jacobs was an advocate for humane urban planning, and Newman was an architect and city planner who argued that other architects and city planners could design and build public and private spaces that safeguard communities from crime. The notion that design features and site layout can alter behavior was picked up by criminologists who, to this day, study situational opportunities for crime.[83]

Defensible space is any area—like a neighborhood, office, house, park, or hotel—that deters crime by virtue of its design features. The three design features that matter most in CPTED are (1) territoriality, (2) surveillance, and (3) symbolic barriers. *Territoriality* is the demarcation of ownership. Can a person entering the space tell if it belongs to anyone? Is it clear who has responsibility for the space? Hedges, fences, gates, and signs communicate ownership and establish territorial boundaries. *Surveillance* refers to the ability to monitor the activities taking place in an area. This need not be formal surveillance, as with cameras and security guards. Often the goal is natural surveillance, or the capacity of the public to observe activity, or "eyes on the street."[84] Design features that increase natural surveillance (or the risk of an informal audience) include outdoor lighting, low landscaping, sidewalks that increase pedestrian foot traffic, and windows that look out onto public walkways. All increase bystander visibility. *Symbolic barriers,* unlike the built barriers of territoriality, are objects that convey or symbolize ownership. For example, lawn furniture, picnic tables, and potted plants communicate that an area is managed and maintained.

Creating defensible space is, in part, a project in creating boundaries between public spaces and private spaces. CPTED thinkers differentiate between private space, semi-private space, semi-public space, and fully public space. It is access, not ownership, that marks a location as private versus public. For instance, a privately owned shopping mall functions as a public space, and a public elementary school is at least semi-private because access is restricted to students and staff. Private spaces are more defensible than public spaces because of the ease with which intruders can be recognized.[85] Because they are open to all, public spaces require natural surveillance to thwart bad behavior.

Some city planners attempt to prevent crime by designing *permeable space*. Unlike defensible space, which attempts to clearly mark the boundaries between public and private, permeable space integrates public and private land uses. One example is combining residential and retail areas with the goal of enhancing natural surveillance. The intent is for residents to walk more, observing their surroundings as they go about their lives. Despite the popularity of permeable design, the evidence on whether it prevents crime is mixed, and largely dependent on the type of crime examined.[86]

Crime prevention through environmental design is based on the logic that "if offenders [think] that they can be observed (even if they are not), they may be less likely to offend, given the increased potential for intervention, apprehension, and prosecution" (p. 163).[87] This effect is seen quite clearly in Jacob and Cherbonneau's qualitative study of carjackers.[88] The active carjackers they interviewed described three offending strategies that responded to natural surveillance, or "publicity management" (p. 44). First, they seek out secluded settings to commit their crimes free from prying eyes. Second, if isolation isn't an option, they commit their crimes with incredible speed, completing them before bystanders become "wise" to what is happening; this approach requires an unobstructed escape. Third, if neither seclusion nor speed is possible, they exploit bystander indifference: They choose settings where natural surveillance is weak because the audience is unwilling to get involved. Though CPTED can do little to fix bystander apathy, it does point to several environmental changes that could prevent carjacking, including improved surveillance and visibility in parking garages and exits that hinder easy getaways, like parking lot boom gates.

In the decades since it was first articulated, CPTED has remained popular with city planners and architects, but it has mostly been supplanted by situational crime prevention in criminology. Situational crime prevention builds on CPTED ideas about territoriality and surveillance, identifying even more strategies for preventing criminal events.

Boom gates, or barrier gates, are a design feature that increase the risk of detection for offenses like auto theft and burglary.

iStockphoto.com/Ratchat

Situational Crime Prevention

Ronald Clarke, one of the main contributors to the development of situational crime prevention, claims that criminologists often mistake the problem of explaining "crime" with the problem of explaining "the criminal." Instead, he argues, we can predict and prevent criminal acts without addressing people who violate the law at all. What we need to focus on is the features of situations—the places, products, procedures, and services—that produce and reduce crime by either increasing deterrence or minimizing motivation.

Situational crime prevention thinkers first ask: What happens in the moment (or situation) when people decide to, for example, rob a jewelry store, solicit minors online for sexual images, commit accounting fraud, or drive recklessly through a school zone? Second, they ask: How can we design spaces (physical or online), products, procedures, and services to prevent people from choosing to violate the law?

Situational crime prevention isn't quite a theory of crime causation—at least not in the way that other criminological theories purport to explain crime.[89] For example, control, strain, and learning theories claim to explain many kinds of crime; they are "general theories" of crime. **Situational crime prevention** is more like a series of tactics, with each series of tactics specific to a particular offense that occurs in a particular place at a particular time. Nonetheless, situational crime prevention is guided by criminological theory, including rational choice theory (see Chapter 7), routine activities theory, and neutralization theory (see Chapter 9).[90] And regardless of the particular offense, location, and time under investigation, the situational crime prevention approach is rooted in four basic assumptions[91]:

1. *Crime results from the interaction between individual disposition and situation.* Disposition is another word for motivation or criminal propensity. Crime, however, is an act or event. Propensity alone cannot explain why a person engages in one criminal act instead of another. Rather, criminal acts happen when a person with a criminal disposition finds themselves in a situation conducive to crime.

2. *Perpetrators choose to commit crime.* Background factors, like poverty or discrimination, might predict criminal motivation, but they don't explain the choice to commit particular criminal acts. Why commit armed robbery on this street corner instead of bank robbery at that bank branch? Preventing crime requires understanding the circumstances in which individuals predisposed to commit crime decide *not* to commit crime.

3. *Opportunity is an important cause of crime.* People who commit crimes don't break the law every minute of every day. They must have the opportunity to commit crime, or access to desirable goods or vulnerable victims without risk of detection. Traditional theories of crime acknowledge that opportunity matters, but it usually gets relegated to the back burner, with motivation or control treated as most important. Situational crime prevention reverses this. Understanding specific criminal events (vs. criminality) draws attention to opportunities specific to the situation, the location, and the target or victim.

4. *Situational elements can stimulate crime.* Situations can create motivation just as much as they provide opportunities. That is, motivation can be externally prompted rather than simply the result of internal pressures. These are called "provocations" in situational crime prevention. For example, high-conflict situations provoke aggression and motivation for assault.

Recall the law of crime concentration at places, or the 5-50 rule. Environmental criminologists observe how some micro-places, like streets, intersections, or businesses, become hotspots of particular types of crime. Situational crime prevention aims to improve minor disorder (like littering and vandalism) and prevent threats to public safety (like robbery and assault) in areas of crime concentration by altering criminal opportunities and incentives. And it achieves this without relying on law enforcement or the criminal legal system. Instead, it is implemented by organizations and agencies like transit systems, hospitals, schools, business districts, entertainment centers, and more.[92]

Situational crime prevention strategies achieve five goals; they (1) increase the effort required to commit the crime, (2) increase the risks associated with committing the crime, (3) reduce the rewards of the crime, (4) reduce provocations or features that stimulate criminal motivation, and (5) remove excuses for crime.[93] Notice that the first three goals are about deterrence or altering the perceived balance of rule-breaking's costs and benefits. Table 14.1 displays 25 situational crime prevention strategies that achieve these goals; each is accompanied by an example.

The type of situational crime prevention strategies adopted depends on the particular offense of concern. If the primary problem at a sports arena is drunk fans assaulting supporters of the opposing team, then the recommended strategies will focus on preventing excess consumption of alcohol, blocking access to opposing fans, and minimizing conflict. If graffiti is a pressing concern for a community, prevention techniques will center on blocking youth access to spray paint, increasing natural surveillance, and quickly removing graffiti when it appears. Crime prevention strategies will look very different in a hospital attempting to reduce theft of prescription painkillers than in a subway station seeking to curb sexual assaults.

Situational crime prevention strategies are supported by years of empirical evidence.[94] Most studies of these strategies involve quasi-experimental designs that are able to tease out the causal effect of the intervention. In one review of more than 200 studies, nearly three-quarters showed a quick decline in crime following implementation, leaving little doubt about the source of the reduction.[95] Some reviews focus on specific types of situational crime prevention strategies. For example,

TABLE 14.1 ■ Five mechanisms and 25 techniques of situational crime prevention, with examples				
Increase the effort	**Increase the risks**	**Reduce the rewards**	**Reduce provocations**	**Remove excuses**
Target hardening	Extend guardianship	Conceal targets	Reduce frustrations and stress	Set rules
Example:	*Example:*	*Example:*	*Example:*	*Example:*
Credit freezes	Leave signs of occupancy	Unmarked armored trucks	Efficient lines	Harassment codes
Control access	Assist natural surveillance	Remove targets	Avoid disputes	Post instructions
Example:	*Example:*	*Example:*	*Example:*	*Example:*
Electronic card access for buildings	Improved street lighting	Replacing cash transactions with online payment systems	Fixed fares for ridesharing services	"No trespassing" signs
Screen exits	Reduce anonymity	Identify property	Reduce temptation and arousal	Alert conscience
Example:	*Example:*	*Example:*	*Example:*	*Example:*
Electronic merchandise tags	Taxi or ridesharing ID displays	"This property is managed by" signs	Controls on violent pornography	Roadside speed display boards
Deflect offenders	Use place managers	Disrupt markets	Neutralize peer pressure	Assist compliance
Example:	*Example:*	*Example:*	*Example:*	*Example:*
Disperse bars	Parking lot attendants and CCTV cameras	Monitor online markets for illicit products and services	"Friends don't let friends drive drunk" messaging	Litter receptacles
Control tools/weapons	Strengthen formal surveillance	Deny benefits	Discourage imitation	Control drugs and alcohol
Example:	*Example:*	*Example:*	*Example:*	*Example:*
"Smart" guns	*Security guards*	Rapid graffiti cleaning	Censor details of modus operandi	Server intervention programs

Source: Adapted from Cornish, D. B., & Clarke, R. V. (2003). Opportunities, precipitators and criminal decisions: A reply to Wortley's critique of situational crime prevention. In M. J. Smith & D. B. Cornish (Eds.), *Theory for practice in situational crime prevention, Crime Prevention Studies* (Vol. 16, pp. 41-96). Monsey, NY: Criminal Justice Press.

a meta-analysis (statistical analysis of many studies) of the impact of closed-circuit television surveillance (CCTV) found a significant decrease in crime across many studies, especially for parking lot and residential crime.[96]

The "Dark Side" of Crime Prevention?

Crime prevention through environmental design (CPTED) and situational crime prevention offer popular, low-cost solutions to problems that plague communities the world over. Indeed, the United Nations recommends CPTED principles in their reports on enhancing urban safety throughout the rapidly urbanizing world.[97] However, crime prevention strategies have a "dark side" that their supporters must acknowledge.[98] These include excessive target hardening, hostile architecture, and exclusionary design that reduce quality of life and enforce social segregation.

CPTED-inspired design frequently works by keeping out "undesirable" or "unwanted" populations from public spaces. This is achieved through hostile (or defensive) architecture, such as barriers surrounding hot air vents, underpass areas with installed floor studs or spikes, and benches with dividers to prevent lying down. These designs harden targets and deny benefits. They are aimed at populations that are visibly homeless though they also impact housed residents who wish to rest in public spaces or access warm air while standing outside on a cold night. Other examples of hostile design include water sprinklers and high-pitched sound devices designed to repel young loiterers, as well as blue lights in restrooms to prevent intravenous drug use.[99]

Critics argue that hostile strategies make public areas less accommodating for everyone. They further assert that hostile design—along with gated communities and other territoriality-reinforcing design—sorts public settings into spaces for the wealthy and spaces for the poor. Moreover, they argue that overimplementation of defensive space (e.g., barbed wire, barred windows, high walls, aggressive guard dogs) can create a "fortress society" that is "annoying, frustrating, ugly, and even threatening or oppressive" (p. 84).[100]

Floor studs on ledges, window sills, stairway edges, and underpasses are a target-hardening strategy.

Jansos/Alamy Stock Photo

Another "dark side" of place-based crime prevention is the creation of "offensive space." Offensive space happens when offenders use CPTED principles to conceal their law-breaking.[101] In other words, they use principles of territoriality, natural surveillance, and target hardening to design spaces where criminal activity can be hidden from the prying eyes of residents or law enforcement. Just as gated communities use high fencing, staffed access points, and mechanical (e.g., solid doors and deadbolt locks) and technological (e.g., cameras) additions to buildings to keep out undesirable populations, so too do organized groups attempting to conceal criminal activities like drug distribution or human trafficking.[102]

Displacement and Diffusion

Skeptics suggest that situational crime prevention strategies might not eliminate crime at all. Rather, people who violate the law might just alter their behavior so they can carry on committing crime. This is called **displacement**, or the "relocation of a crime from one place, time, target, offense, tactic, or offender to another as a result of some crime-prevention initiative" (p. 1333).[103] Rather than act as a vacuum, critics assert, prevention strategies may act as a broom, moving the dust (or crime) around. There are several types of displacement that might undermine place-based crime prevention efforts.[104]

- *Spatial displacement* – Crime averted in one micro-place (e.g., street segment, intersection, business, public area) transfers to another micro-place. For example, effective theft-prevention strategies in one hardware store might lead to more theft in the hardware store up the road. This also applies to online spaces, as when digital drug markets move from one platform to another.[105]

- *Temporal displacement* – Prevention tactics that are time-specific result in law-breaking moving to a different time of day. For example, if a business district employs more security guards in the evening hours, then criminal activity will shift to the morning or afternoon hours.

- *Offense displacement* – One type of crime is supplanted by another type of crime. Consider a scenario in which prevention strategies targeted at disrupting drug markets lead would-be dealers to instead engage in the online sale of stolen store merchandise. The offense has changed, but the individual is still committing criminal acts.

- *Target displacement* – People who commit crime opt for a different type of target or victim because access to the original target or victim has been curtailed, typically because of target hardening. For example, if a department store begins keeping designer purses in a locked glass case, shoplifters might opt to steal high-end cosmetics instead. The offense (theft) is the same, but the item targeted has changed.

- *Tactical displacement* – When one method of committing crime is made difficult, people change tacks, committing the same crime using different strategies. For example, with the rise of online security measures, organized crime groups increasingly rely on corrupt public officials to gain access to protected information.[106]

An additional type, *offender displacement,* is not, in fact, displacement at all, as it doesn't involve people changing their behavior in response to reduced opportunities. Instead, it is more like offender *replacement*—new individuals take the place of old individuals who have been deterred or incapacitated, as by arrest or imprisonment.[107] Offender displacement is of greatest concern for income-generating crimes involving underground markets. In this logic, targeting particular groups of law-breakers may be ineffective because there is a line of willing participants waiting to step in and fulfill the demand for illicit substances, stolen goods, commercial sex, and more.

Diffusion, while real, is not as large a problem as might be feared when it comes to well-designed place-based crime prevention. In fact, a diffusion of benefits is observed as much as—or even more so—than displacement.[108] A diffusion of benefits happens when the benefits of crime prevention efforts spread out to locations or targets that did not receive the intervention. This is also called a "halo effect"—the positive effects of a crime reduction strategy radiate out, like a halo.

CHAPTER SUMMARY

LO 14.1 Differentiate environmental criminology from traditional criminological approaches.

Environmental criminology is about variation in crime across places (spatial distribution), rather than variation across individuals or groups (social distribution). Environmental perspectives focus on opportunity, control, and motivation as characteristics of places instead of people. The outcome of interest is criminal events, not criminality.

LO 14.2 Describe how the broken windows theory has impacted crime prevention efforts.

The broken windows theory states that signs of physical and social disorder send a message that no one will intervene if the law is broken. This leads to more serious crime, as fearful residents retreat from public life. Crime prevention efforts guided by the perspective include order-maintenance policing, scrutinized for its role in producing mass misdemeanor arrests and citations of poor persons of color, and blight abatement, which remedies physical disorder.

LO 14.3 Summarize the central tenets of routine activities theory.

Victimization occurs when three things converge: motivated offenders, suitable targets, and absence of capable guardianship. Victimization rates (over time, across geographic locations, or among groups) go up when targets become more attractive and guardianship is weakened. In this perspective, preventing victimization requires reducing the suitability of targets and victims as well as increasing effective guardianship. It does not seek to alter offender motivation.

LO 14.4 Explain the strategies offered by CPTED and situational crime prevention.

CPTED suggests the creation of defensible space, designed with territoriality, natural surveillance, and symbolic barriers in mind. Situational crime prevention builds on CPTED, offering tactics that increase efforts and risks of crime (e.g., target hardening and controlling access) and reduces crime's rewards, provocations, and excuses (e.g., disrupting markets, denying benefits, and alerting conscience).

ENGAGED DISCUSSION

1. Come up with an example of one criminogenic micro place-based institution (other than the examples provided in the chapter). Is it a crime attractor, a crime generator, or both?

2. Which do you think is easier to fix—physical disorder or social disorder? Why?

3. What is one way that patterns of daily routines changed over the past decade? What kind of victimization has that change reduced or increased?

4. Think of one type of crime for which situational crime prevention would be ineffective. Why would it not work for that type of crime?

KEY TERMS

Attractive target (p. 365)
Blight (p. 363)
Broken windows (p. 360)
Capable guardianship (p. 365)
Crime attractors (p. 358)
Crime generators (p. 357)
Crime prevention through environmental design (p. 369)
Crime science (p. 354)
Criminality (p. 355)
Defensible space (p. 368)
Diffusion of benefits (p. 373)
Displacement (p. 372)
Environmental criminology (p. 354)

5-50 rule (p. 356)
Hot products (p. 365)
Incivilities (p. 360)
Law of crime concentration at places (p. 356)
Micro-places (p. 355)
Natural surveillance (p. 368)
Order-maintenance policing (p. 360)
Physical disorder (p. 360)
Routine activities theory (p. 364)
Situational crime prevention (p. 369)
Social disorder (p. 360)
Spatial analysis (p. 355)
Spillover effect (p. 358)
Target hardening (p. 366)

GLOSSARY

Absolutism: The idea that some acts or conditions are objectively, inherently deviant or wrong regardless of public sentiment or response.

Achievement: In institutional anomie theory, a cultural element of the American Dream that emphasizes accumulating successes and making something of oneself.

Age of onset: The life-course period at which a person begins engaging in criminal behavior.

Age-crime curve: Inverted-J shaped pattern depicting how criminal behavior rises sharply in the teenage years, peaks in late teens and early 20s, and then gradually declines thereafter.

Agency: An individual's capacity to make context-specific choices.

Analogous behaviors: Noncriminal actions that, like crime, are manifestations of low self-control.

Applied research: Type of research that aims to solve practical problems by focusing on real-world settings.

Arson: Unlawful and intentional burning of someone else's or one's own property.

Atavistic stigmata: Lombroso's idea that physiological traits could indicate atavism (reversion to an earlier evolutionary stage) and alert observers to a person's innate criminality.

Attachment: Emotional closeness to and affection for others and institutions; one of the four elements of the social bond in Hirschi's social control theory.

Attractive target: A person, place, or thing that is desirable and readily available for victimization.

Avoidant behavior: Precautionary measures taken to avoid exposure to criminal victimization.

Basic research: Type of research that investigates the foundational principles, including theory testing.

Behavioral genetics: In biosocial criminology, the field of study devoted to determining the extent of genetic heritability in predicting aggression and law-breaking.

Belief: Ideas about the moral validity of the law, which support a conventional orientation; one of the four elements of the social bond in Hirschi's social control theory.

Big data: A large data set too complex for traditional data analysis software and containing information from networked devices or any Internet activity.

Biosocial criminology: Contemporary school of criminological thought that analyzes the ways that biological factors and social factors interact to produce criminal behavior.

Blight: Physical conditions that have a damaging or spoiling effect on a neighborhood, such as boarded-up structures, abandoned vehicles, and empty lots.

Bounded rationality: The idea that consideration of various courses of action are limited, or bounded, by the actor's abilities and knowledge.

Broken windows: Perspective that neighborhood disorder leads to more serious crime because it sends a message that no one will intervene if the law is broken.

Brutalization effect: The argument that brutal punishments cause the public to behave inhumanely against one another because they become accustomed to savagery.

Burglary: Unlawful entry into a structure without permission in order to commit certain forms of crime, such as theft, assault, rape, or arson.

Capable guardianship: People who are physically or symbolically present to prevent crime, regardless of whether they intend to prevent it.

Cartographic approach: Criminological method, first developed in the 19th century, of using maps to show the spatial distribution of crime and other social problems.

Chivalry hypothesis: An explanation of the gender gap in crime that claims police treat women more leniently than they treat men.

Civil confinement: A form of involuntary commitment imposed on some individuals who been convicted of sexual offenses, with confinement beginning after a prison sentence has been completed.

Civil law: Type of law that deals with disputes between parties, including persons, businesses, or other entities.

Classical school: School of criminological thought that emerged in mid-18th century Europe and adopted Enlightenment ideas about human nature and society.

Clearance rate: The proportion of known offenses that are cleared or closed by either arrest or exceptional means.

Code of the street: Norms of public interaction, especially violence, in urban neighborhoods where respect is in short supply, violence is a common threat, and residents are reluctant to call police for assistance, as described in Anderson's subcultural perspective.

Cognitive dissonance: Discomfort people experience when their behavior and moral code do not align, or when they think one way and act another way.

Collateral consequences: Restrictions that limit or prevent people with criminal records from accessing rights and opportunities, including employment, occupational licensing, housing, voting, and education.

Collective consciousness: In Durkheim's anomie perspective, the beliefs and sentiments that are shared among typical members of a society and produce conformity to strongly held community norms and values.

Collective efficacy: A community's orientation towards collective problem-solving action said to reduce crime in social disorganization theory.

Collective incapacitation: Type of incapacitation in which large groups of convicted persons are uniformly incarcerated, institutionalized, or otherwise confined.

Commitment: Investments in prosocial activities that influence the calculation of the costs of law violation for future goals; one of the four elements of the social bond in Hirschi's social control theory.

Conflict perspective: Perspective that assumes that law reflects the interests of those who are most powerful in society.

Conformity: In Merton's anomie theory, a mode of adaption in which an individual is committed to pursuing societal success goals and adheres to the institutionalized rules regarding how to achieve success.

Consensus perspective: Perspective that assumes that laws reflect general agreement in society about what is and is not acceptable behavior.

Convict code: Prison subculture that results from the conditions of prison life and emphasizes never snitching, minding one's business, being tough, never getting too friendly with correctional officers.

Co-offending: Commission of crime by two or more people.

Corporate crime: A type of white-collar crime committed by business entities, or individuals acting on behalf of business entities, for organizational gain.

Correlates of crime: Variables that are statistically associated with criminal behavior or crime rates, which may or may not be causally related to crime.

Corruption: Criminal actions and abuses of power by persons in positions of authority for personal gain.

Crime attractors: Locations that supply vulnerable victims or desirable targets, attracting people who wish to commit criminal offenses.

Crime generators: Locations that are easily accessed by large groups of people who use the space for noncriminal reasons, creating occasions for crime by bringing together many people in one place.

Crime hotspots: The small percentage of places responsible for the majority of crime in a geographic location.

Crime prevention through environmental design: An approach to crime prevention that claims the design of physical space (including structures, landscaping, and outdoor environments) can encourage or discourage crime.

Crime rate: Ratio of the number of crimes occurring in a location to the size of that location's population.

Crime science: The empirical study of crime event characteristics.

Crime typologies: Organizational tools for grouping together criminals or criminal offenses that have common characteristics.

Criminal anthropology: The 19th century practice of offender profiling based on physical features.

Criminal careers: Developmental trajectories of law-breaking, from onset to cessation of crime, that characterize an individual's life course.

Criminal enterprise: Legal and illegal businesses and hierarchical organizations that engage in an ongoing pattern of illicit activity.

Criminal justice system: The institutions and agencies, including policing, courts, and corrections, that are responsible for apprehending, prosecuting, defending, sentencing, imprisoning, and supervising individuals who are suspected, charged with, and convicted of criminal offenses.

Criminal law: Type of law that deals with individuals who commit punishable offenses against the state or federal government.

Criminality: A property of individuals indicating their propensity to commit crime, or their disposition towards crime.

Criminogenic: Term that describes conditions that cause crime.

Criminological imagination: Awareness and appreciation of how people's lives, including their criminal behavior and victimization, must be understood within social and historical context.

Criminology: The scientific study of the characteristics of, extent of, causes of, and responses to crime and victimization.

Critical race criminology: Critical school of criminological thought that addresses the relationship between race/ethnicity, racism, and power in the creation of crime and society's response to it.

Cross-sectional: Describes surveys or other research designs that collect data at only one point in time.

Cultural heterogeneity: Condition in which many different subcultures, including ethnic or linguistic subcultures, comprise a neighborhood; one of the characteristics of crime-prone communities in social disorganization theory.

Culture structure: The organization of norms in a society, including norms that regulate cultural goals and norms that regulate the means for achieving cultural goals, as described in Merton's anomie theory.

Cybercrime: Any criminal action that is facilitated using a computer and network, or a crime that targets a computer or network.

Dark figure of crime: Unreported and undiscovered crime that does not become known to officials.

Decommodification: Policies in market economies that support institutional balance by freeing people to make choices that are not constrained by market forces, such as having children, pursuing higher education, or serving in local government.

Defensible space: Any area (like a neighborhood, office, house, park, or hotel) that deters crime by virtue of its design features.

Defiance: A proud and shameless reaction to a penalty that is administered disrespectfully or perceived as unfair, thereby increasing the likelihood or seriousness of future rule violation.

Definitions favorable to crime: Attitudes, motivations, rationalizations, and justifications that support law-breaking.

Demonic perspective: Earliest explanation of crime in human societies in which perpetrators were viewed as either tempted by or possessed by evil forces.

Descriptive research: Research that describes the extent and characteristics of crime.

Desistance: Reduction in the frequency or severity of criminal conduct over the life course, including termination of a criminal career.

Determinate sentencing: Form of sentencing in which the length of a term of incarceration is a set number of months or years.

Determinism: The premise that human behavior is caused, or determined, by forces external to the individual will.

Deterrence: The idea that crime can be reduced by altering the costs and benefits associated with offending.

Deviance: Violations of social norms, including violations of folkways, mores, and laws.

Differential association: Sutherland's idea that people differ in their criminal behavior because they differ in their relationships and interactions with people who support the learning of criminal attitudes and behaviors.

Diffusion of benefits: Pattern in which the benefits of crime prevention efforts spread out to locations or targets that did not receive the intervention.

Digital punishment: The stigmatizing effects of the online mugshots, arrest records, and inaccurate data that flood the private online market for criminal records.

Direct control: Form of social control in which the source of control restrains behavior by being physically present.

Direct-contact crime: Crime in which the perpetrator and the victim are in the same place and time at the moment of the offense.

Discounting: A source of bounded rationality in which crime becomes a rational choice because the actor weighs immediate rewards of crime more heavily than future costs of punishment.

Discrimination: Unequal treatment of individuals or groups based on actual or perceived traits.

Disintegrative shaming: A stigmatizing form of shaming that communicates disapproval and disrespect for the individual, causing humiliation and persistent feelings of shame, ultimately increasing criminal behavior.

Disparity: An inequality or a difference that is unfair.

Displacement: Pattern in which a crime prevention strategy results in the movement of a crime from one place, target, time, offense, tactic, or offender to another.

Diversion programs: Programs that move people out of the criminal legal system and into alternative programs that address the underlying causes of their law-breaking.

Domestic terrorism: "Violent, criminal acts committed by individuals and/or groups to further ideological goals stemming from domestic influences, such as those of a political, religious, social, racial, or environmental nature," as defined by the FBI.

Double consciousness: Du Bois's description of Black Americans' sense of having a dual self, or a "two-ness," wrought by oppression and devaluation.

Drift: Matza's idea that people drift between conforming behavior and law-breaking behavior across situations, rather than being fully committed to either orientation.

Duration: The longer a person is exposed to a pro-crime definition, the more likely they are to internalize it and act on it; one of the modalities in differential association theory.

Durkheimian anomie: A state of normlessness resulting from a breakdown in shared values, standards, and rules that govern the behaviors and aspirations of members of a society.

Ecological patterns: Crime patterns across space, or geographic location, including variation across neighborhoods, cities, states, and nations.

Economic marginalization hypothesis: An explanation of the shrinking gender gap that locates women's growing economic hardships relative to men's economic hardships as the source of the narrowing gap.

Economic model of crime: Perspective that views crime as the result of a rational decision-making process in which potential offenders weigh the probable costs of crime against its potential benefits.

Enlightenment: Eighteenth-century period that transformed politics, science, and philosophy by emphasizing humans' free will and their capacity for rationality.

Entrepreneurial crime: Profit-generating crimes that rely on illegal methods for generating financial proceeds through an organized criminal business (also called enterprise crime).

Environmental criminology: Subfield of criminology that analyzes variation in crime and victimization across places.

Escalation: A period of increasing frequency and severity of criminal conduct.

Ethnography: The qualitative study of groups of people in their natural setting, usually over an extended period of time and involving participant observation.

Etiology: The study of causes.

Eugenics: The unscientific and racially biased study and practice of controlling reproduction to improve the human race.

Exclusionary discipline: School disciplinary practices that push students out of, or exclude them from, the normal classroom setting, including suspension and expulsion.

Experiment: A quantitative method in which a researcher manipulates a condition to observe if it causes a change in an outcome, typically involving random assignment to experimental and control groups.

Explanatory research: Research that explains patterns in and identifies causes of crime, victimization, and punishment.

Expressive crimes: Crimes committed as an expression of negative feelings, such as anger or frustration, often spontaneously.

Expungement: The process of having one's record of arrest or convictions sealed or destroyed (also called expunction).

Fear-of-crime paradox: Observation that people with relatively low odds of becoming victims often express higher levels of fear than people who at much greater risk of victimization.

Felonies: Serious offenses that carry the possibility of a prison sentence of a year or longer.

Felony disenfranchisement: The practice, set by state law, of preventing people who have been convicted of felonies from voting in elections.

Feminist criminology: Critical school of criminological thought that calls for greater attention to the role of gender in crime and criminal justice experiences.

5-50 rule: Observation that about 5% of micro-places are responsible for about 50% of street crimes.

Focal concerns: Value orientations that resulted from the conditions of daily life in poor communities, in Miller's focal concerns perspective.

Focused deterrence: A law enforcement strategy that attempts to deter specific offenses committed by a target population by increasing the risk of apprehension.

Folkways: Taken-for-granted social rules that govern everyday behavior.

Foreground: The dynamics of the crime situation in the moment when the offense takes place.

Forensics: Scientific techniques used in the detection of crime or in legal processes.

Formal control: Form of social control in which one is compelled to conform by the state or others with the official capacity to enforce codified rules.

Formal labels: Official labels applied and documented by a record-keeping authority, such as the state, the military, a school, or a medical facility.

Fraud: A type of theft in which victims are deceived into giving money or property to perpetrators, including white-collar perpetrators, who have misrepresented facts.

Frequency: The more often a person is exposed to a pro-crime definition, the more likely they are to internalize it and act on it; one of the modalities in differential association theory.

Gangs: According to the FBI definition, gangs are organizations, associations, or groups of at least three people that exist for the purpose of engaging in illegal activity and have an identifying name, sign, or symbol.

Gender gap: Term that describes the higher rates of criminal offending, especially violent offending, among men and boys relative to women and girls.

Gender performance: The acting out of masculinity or femininity for social audience, as when boys perform masculinity by taking risks, drinking to excess, and physically dominating rivals.

Gene-environment interaction: The interplay of genetic traits and the social environment in predicting criminal conduct.

General deterrence: Type of deterrence in which the public is less likely to commit crime because they have observed the costs of crime to punished offenders.

General strain theory (GST): Individual-level theory of crime that locates the causes of criminal conduct in stressors that provoke strong negative emotions.

Green crimes: Actions of people and institutions, including governments and corporations, that cause ecological destruction and harmful disruptions to ecosystems, negatively affecting humans and nonhuman animals.

Green criminology: Critical school of criminological thought that focuses on criminal and legal-but-detrimental harms to the environment that negatively impact ecosystems, humans, and nonhuman animals (also called green crimes).

Habitual offender law: Policies that impose longer sentences for persons convicted of multiple felonies; three-strikes laws are one type.

Hacking: Accessing a computer system without authorization with the intent to commit crime.

Hard determinism: A form of determinism that disregards agency and free will.

Harm principle: Position that only that which causes harm to other people, such as physical injury, violations of privacy, or monetary loss, can justify criminalization.

Hate/bias crime: A violent or property crime motivated, either partially or entirely, by the perpetrator's bias against a race, religion, disability, sexual orientation, ethnicity, gender, gender identity, or other protected class.

Hedonistic calculus: The notion that people weigh potential pleasures against potential pains, rationally selecting the course of action that produces the greatest satisfaction with the least discomfort.

Heteronormativity: The belief that heterosexuality is the default sexual orientation and the assumption that all people are heterosexual; queer criminologists challenge heteronormativity in criminology.

Historical materialism: Radical perspective that views societies' political and legal structures as determined by the mode of production, or the way societies develop and produce material goods.

Homicide: Any intentional and unlawful killing of a person by another person.

Hot products: Frequently stolen items, typically because they are some combination of concealable, removable, available, valuable, enjoyable, and easily disposable.

Ideal victim: Victim regarded as worthy of sympathy and compassion (by juries, by media, by the public), or as a legitimate victim, because they possess characteristics that cause others to consider them blameless.

Ideologically motivated crime: Crime that is used to express or further a worldview.

Immigrant paradox: The finding that immigrants engage in less crime than native-born people despite their higher levels of social disadvantage.

Immigrant revitalization hypothesis: An explanation for the crime-reducing effects of immigration that focuses on how immigrants' dense social ties, entrepreneurship, and economic and residential activity improves community life in economically distressed areas.

Incapacitation: Principle that punishment can be used to reduce crime by confining people so they do not have the opportunity to offend against those who are not confined.

Incidence: The occurrence or frequency of criminal events.

Incivilities: Norm violations that show a lack of respect or concern for other members of the community.

In-depth interviews: Probing interviews of study participants, ranging from unstructured free-flow interviews to highly structured interviews with predetermined questions.

Indeterminate sentencing: Form of sentencing in which the convicted person is sentenced to a range of months or years, with the person's release date determined by a parole board.

Indirect control: Form of social control in which the source of control is psychologically present rather than physically present.

Individualism: In institutional anomie theory, a cultural element of the American Dream that emphasizes individual autonomy in the pursuit of success or making it on one's own.

Informal control: Form of social control that originates from unwritten social rules rather than laws, including fear of embarrassment, disapproval, or letting others down.

Informal labels: Unofficial labels applied to a person who has been deemed deviant by other people, including family members, teachers, co-workers, neighbors, or members of the public.

Infractions: Petty violations typically of ordinances, municipal codes, or administrative regulations rather than criminal codes.

Innovation: In Merton's anomie theory, a mode of adaption in which an individual is committed to pursuing societal success goals but rejects the institutionalized rules regarding how to achieve success, favoring expedient but illegal methods.

Institutional anomie theory: Structural-level theory of crime that regards high national crime rates as due to cultural commitment to material success and institutional imbalance characterized by economic dominance.

Institutional imbalance: Societal condition in which one social institution dominates all other social institutions, determining how they operate; economic dominance is the primary type in institutional anomie theory.

Institutional Review Board (IRB): Board that examines researchers' proposed procedures to ensure that they follow certain guidelines that protect the people being studied.

Instrumental crimes: Crimes committed to achieve desired goals, such as financial rewards or status benefits.

Intensity: The more emotionally close one is to the person from whom they are learning a pro-crime definition, the more likely they are to internalize it and act on it; one of the modalities in differential association theory.

Intergenerational transmission of violence: Empirical pattern in which children exposed to violence in the home grow up to engage in violence or become victims of violence (also called cycle of violence).

International terrorism: "Violent, criminal acts committed by individuals and/or groups who are inspired by, or associated with, designated foreign terrorist organizations or nations (state-sponsored)," as defined by the FBI.

Intersectionality: The notion that people's overlapping identities shape the disadvantages and privileges they experience; a central component of feminist criminology.

Involvement: Time spent in conventional activities; one of the four elements of the social bond in Hirschi's social control theory.

Jails: Short-term holding facilities that house individuals who have been arrested, are awaiting case disposition, are awaiting sentencing, or are completing a short sentence for a misdemeanor or low-level felony.

Larceny: The unlawful appropriation of personal property belonging to an individual or business with the intention of permanently depriving them of it.

Law of crime concentration at places: Term referring to the persistent observation of criminal events clustering in a small number of micro-places (or 5-50 rule), as observed across time periods, nations, and crime types.

Laws: Social rules that have been formally codified by a governing authority, such as the state or federal government.

Learned helplessness: Neurological adaption in which a victim becomes passive and numb, having learned that resisting mistreatment is pointless and will not change the outcome.

Left realism: An ideological view that locates the root causes of crime in social structures, or the unequal organization of groups in society.

Legal cynicism: A cultural orientation in which the criminal legal system and its representatives are seen as illegitimate and ineffective, such that the law loses its legitimacy or is regarded with disdain.

Legal debt: Financial debts that accrue from court fees, surcharges, community supervision fees, jail and prison fees, fines, restitution, and other legal financial obligations, acting as invisible punishments in the criminal legal system.

Legitimacy perceptions: Beliefs about the moral authority of rule-setters and rule-enforcers.

Level of analysis: The scale or size of our research focus, ranging from the individual (or micro) level to the structural (or macro) level.

Liberation hypothesis: An explanation of the shrinking gender gap that claims that growing gender equality in social roles produced greater gender equality in criminal behavior.

Life-course criminology: Subfield of criminology focused on within-individual patterns of law-breaking over the life course, including age of onset, escalation, persistence, and desistance.

Lone wolf terrorists: Individuals who become radicalized and commit terrorist attacks on their own.

Longitudinal: Describes surveys or other research designs that collect data at multiple points in time, including panel studies and trend studies.

Mala in se: Crimes regarded as morally wrong irrespective of whether they are prohibited by law.

Mala prohibita: Crimes regarded as wrong because they are against the law, not because they are inherently immoral.

Mandatory minimum sentences: A sentencing standard that requires courts to impose a prison term of a minimum specified length for select offenses, regardless of the circumstances.

Manslaughter: Homicide in which an offender kills another person without malice aforethought or premeditation.

Marginal deterrence: The principle that more severe offenses require more severe sanctions to deter because people will opt to commit more extreme offenses if punishments are not scaled by seriousness.

Marketized mentality: In institutional anomie theory, a psychological disposition towards egoistic self-interest caused by anomic culture.

Mass incarceration: Term describing the high rate of incarceration in the United States in both historical and cross-national perspective.

Mass murder: Homicide in which an offender kills several victims, usually four or more, in a single incident or during a brief crime spree.

Master status: The primary status by which others interact with a person.

Mertonian anomie: A social condition in which there is disequilibrium in the culture structure, with norms regulating cultural success goals emphasized more than norms regulating the means to achieving success.

Micro-places: Very small units of geographic space, including intersections, street segments, and specific addresses.

Middle-class measuring rod: Middle-class norms used as a baseline for evaluating behavior of everyone regardless of their social class position, as described in Cohen's status frustration perspective.

Minority threat hypothesis: Hypothesis that a dominant group's social control efforts increase as the proportion of minority group members goes up.

Misdemeanors: Lower-level offenses with penalties that include fines, community service, probation, and jail terms of under one year.

Modalities: Characteristics of exposures to definitions favorable to crime said by differential association theory to increase the likelihood of criminal learning (include frequency, duration, priority, and intensity).

Modes of adaptation: In Merton's anomie theory, the various ways that individuals adapt to anomic societal conditions, including conformity, ritualism, innovation, retreatism, and rebellion.

Molecular genetics: In biosocial criminology, the field of study involving the identification of specific genes that may be correlated with antisocial behavior.

Monetary fetishism: In institutional anomie theory, a cultural element of the American Dream that emphasizes money as the metric of success.

Moral entrepreneur: A person who attempts to alter social norms, including laws, to bring them into alignment with their own moral worldview.

Moral statistics: Term coined by Guerry to describe the use of quantitative methods, or statistics, to analyze social behaviors.

Mores: Serious social rules that have a moral dimension.

Murder: Homicide involving malice aforethought, or the purposeful intent to kill or seriously injure the victim.

National Crime Victimization Survey (NCVS): A nationally representative, household-based survey that collects data on household and personal victimization of people age 12 and older in the U.S.

National Incident-Based Reporting System (NIBRS): Source of official U.S. crime data, reported by the Federal Bureau of Investigation, providing detailed information on crime incidents, including characteristics of offenses, known offenders, arrestees, and victims.

Natural experiment: An experiment-like method in which naturally occurring conditions mimic the random assignment to experimental and control groups that occurs in experiments.

Natural surveillance: The capacity of the public to observe activity, or "eyes on the street."

Negative credentials: Formalized records, including criminal records, that mark a person as untrustworthy, irresponsible, or dangerous in interactions with others who evaluate their character, such as prospective employers.

Neoclassical criminology: Contemporary school of criminological thought that adopts classical school principles of utility maximization, rationality, and deterrence.

Neurocriminology: A subdiscipline of biosocial criminology concerned with the anatomy, physiology, and chemistry of the brain.

Occupational crime: A type of white-collar crime committed for personal gain in the context of a legitimate occupation that involves exploiting opportunities for crime provided by one's occupation.

Operant conditioning: In social learning, a type of conditioning that emphasizes reinforcement and punishment.

Order-maintenance policing: Type of policing that emphasizes reducing crime by cracking down on low-level disorderly behaviors (also called broken windows policing).

Organized crime: A profit-oriented criminal enterprise that provides in-demand illicit goods and services, has a hierarchical structure, and is maintained through threats, violence, monopoly control, and/or corruption.

Panopticon: Bentham's prison design that ensures control by enabling a single guard to observe all inmates simultaneously.

Partial deterrence: Type of deterrence in which a deterred individual still commits crime but opts for a less serious offense.

Patriarchy: A social system in which men dominate women and masculinity is believed to be superior to femininity.

Persistence: Continuation of criminal behavior over several life course periods.

Physical disorder: The environmental artifacts of disorder, or the refuse of disorderly behavior, such as litter, discarded needles, and graffiti.

Policy change hypothesis: An explanation of the shrinking gender gap that claims that changes in arrest policies and charging decisions led to more women becoming involved in the criminal legal system.

Policy research: A type of explanatory research that studies the impact of policy changes, including changes in laws and practices, on crime and other outcomes.

Polyvictimization: A type of recurring victimization in which multiple forms of victimization happen to one person.

Population: All the people or other research units that are the focus of the research and from which a sample is drawn.

Positivism: A doctrine claiming that society is ordered, measurable, and can be understood objectively through research.

Positivist school: Nineteenth-century school of thought that emphasized empirical research and saw the root causes of crime as internal and external forces outside of the individual's control.

Post-traumatic stress disorder (PTSD): A psychiatric diagnosis frequently experienced by crime victims in which exposure to trauma causes symptoms such as intrusive memories, persistent avoidance of trauma-associated places or activities, sleep disturbances, and hypervigilance.

Prevalence: The proportion of a population that engages in or is a victim of crime.

Primary deviance: Rule-breaking behavior that individuals engage in in the absence of a deviant label.

Priority: The earlier in life a person is exposed to a pro-crime definition, the more likely they are to internalize it and act on it; one of the modalities in differential association theory.

Prisonization: The process in which incarcerated persons become embedded in prison habits and dispositions.

Prisons: Correctional institutions that house individuals convicted of felonies at the state or federal level.

Problem-solving courts: Specialty courts, rooted in the rehabilitation ideal, that only handle qualifying cases involving defendants who share a common challenge, such as substance dependency or mental illness.

Procedural justice: The perception that agents of social control treat people fairly and equitably, or that legal processes are just.

Procedural law: Area of criminal law that pertains to the procedures or processes that occur in a criminal case.

Property crime: Crime in which the objective is to take or do damage to property without consent of its rightful owner.

Proportionality: The severity of punishment is proportional to the severity of the crime

Protective behavior: Actions taken by those who fear victimization to safeguard oneself or one's property, such as carrying a weapon, installing home security measures, or learning self-defense.

Public-order crime: Unlawful actions that impede societal functioning or violate moral sentiments of a community or a powerful segment of the community.

Queer criminology: Critical school of criminological thought that brings LGBTQ (lesbian, gay, bisexual, transgender, and queer) issues and perspectives into the study of crime, victimization, and criminal punishment.

Racial disproportionality: In criminology, a pattern in which a racial group's representation in crime or victimization statistics is not equal to their representation in the general population.

Racial invariance hypothesis: The argument that the causes of crime are the same for all people, regardless of race or ethnicity.

Radical criminology: Critical school of criminological thought that critiques the capitalist state's overcriminalization of the poor and its failure to address harmful actions of the powerful.

Radicalization: Process whereby beliefs, feelings, and actions become more extreme in ways that justify violence against out-groups and require sacrifice in defense of the in-group.

Rape: According to the current FBI definition, rape is "penetration, no matter how slight, of the vagina or anus with any body part or object, or oral penetration by a sex organ of another person, without the consent of the victim."

Rational choice theory: Neoclassical theory that assumes humans use their free will to make the rational choice to break or abide by the law.

Reaction formation: An ego-related psychological defense against status frustration in which the frustrated person rejects the system in which they cannot compete.

Rebellion: In Merton's anomie theory, a mode of adaption in which an individual rejects societal success goals and institutionalized rules while also attempting to replace the old societal norms with their own ideals, sometimes through illegal actions.

Recurring victimization: Situation in which a person or place experiences multiple instances of victimization, either the same form over and over or multiple types spread out over time.

Reflected appraisals: Process in which people form a sense of self based on others' opinions of them, or what they believe to be others' opinions of them.

Rehabilitation: Principle that emphasizes identifying and improving the behaviors, attitudes, traits, and conditions that contribute to individuals' offending in an effort to reduce future criminal behavior.

Reinforcement: A consequence that increases an action through presentation of something valued (positive reinforcement) or removal of something undesired (negative reinforcement).

Reintegrative shaming: Type of shaming that reduces crime by separating the act from the actor and welcoming the wrongdoer back into the community once they have accepted the shamefulness of their act.

Relative deprivation: Occurs when a group or a person compares themselves to a better-off reference group and perceives themselves as disadvantaged unjustly.

Relativism: The idea that the deviance or wrongfulness of an act or condition depends upon the response to it, as determined by cultural and historical context.

Repeat victimization: A type of recurring victimization in which the same offense happens over and over.

Residential mobility: The frequency with which residents move or change housing; one of the characteristics of crime-prone communities in social disorganization theory.

Restitution: Court-ordered payment by convicted persons used to cover the costs of victimization-related medical bills, lost wages, damaged or lost property, insurance deductibles, crime-scene clean-up costs, and expenses arising from involvement in the criminal justice process.

Restorative justice: Principle that emphasizes repairing harm and healing people and communities after a crime has occurred through a process of reconciliation.

Retreatism: In Merton's anomie theory, a mode of adaption in which an individual rejects societal success goals and the institutionalized rules regarding how to achieve success.

Retribution: The idea that the punishment must fit the crime, or that the harms caused by a criminal offense require an equivalent amount of harm be done to the offender.

Right realism: An ideological view that disregards structural contexts of people's lives as root causes of crime and instead places all attention on the individual and their choices.

Risk assessment: Predictive tool used to determine the likelihood that a person will engage in some future behavior, such as failing to appear for a court date or committing a violent crime.

Ritualism: In Merton's anomie theory, a mode of adaption in which an individual adheres to the institutionalized rules regarding how to achieve success but rejects societal success goals.

Robbery: Violent crime in which an offender takes or attempts to take something of value from another person using force, the threat of force, or putting the victim in a state of fear.

Role engulfment: Process in which a deviant role takes over people's other social roles due to social exclusion, social withdrawal, and/or involvement in a deviant subculture.

Routine activities theory: Theory that claims that victimization occurs when people's daily routines increase the likelihood that motivated offenders and suitable targets come together in the absence of capable guardianship.

Sample: A subset of a population of interest, preferably representative of that population, that is selected for inclusion in research.

Satisficing: A source of bounded rationality in which actors make the best decisions possible with the information available.

School threat assessment: Assessments by teams of school administrators, mental health professionals, and school resource officers aimed at identifying students at a high risk of committing violence for the purpose of early intervention.

School-to-prison pipeline: Term used to describe the policies and practices that push children out of schools and into the juvenile or adult criminal legal system.

Secondary deviance: Rule-breaking behavior that occurs as a result of a deviant label.

Selection effect: Occurs when those who already possess an outcome characteristic, like criminality, seek out or select into a predictor characteristic, like having crime-involved friends.

Selective incapacitation: Type of incapacitation that targets high-rate offenders and those who pose the greatest threat to the community for incarceration or institutionalization.

Self-control: Internal control of impulses, which is regulated by one's conscience and exercised from within rather than through a social process.

Sensation-seeking hypothesis: Biosocial claim that people with low resting heart rates engage in higher rates of crime because they require greater stimulation to experience arousal of the autonomic nervous system.

Sentencing guidelines: Sets of standards, typically created by sentencing commissions and presented in a grid format, that aim to achieve equivalent sentences across persons who have committed similar crimes and have similar criminal histories.

Serial murder: Homicide in which an offender kills multiple victims over three or more incidents with a cooling off period between each act.

Sexual assault: Broad category that includes multiple forms of nonconsensual sexual contact, such as groping, rubbing, unwanted kissing, forcing a victim to touch an offender in a sexual manner, child sexual abuse, and rape.

Situational crime prevention: An approach to crime prevention that offers offense-specific tactics that increase the required effort and risks of crime, reduce the rewards of and features that provoke crime, and remove excuses for crime.

Social capital: Social relationships, including ties to neighbors and institutional gatekeepers, that operate as resources for reducing crime in social disorganization theory.

Social contract: The notion that people submit to society's laws with the guarantee that a common authority will protect them from others who violate those laws.

Social control: The processes by which conformity to social norms is regulated, encouraged, and enforced.

Social disorder: Actions regarded as nuisances by most residents, visitors, business owners, and police, such as public intoxication, public urination, and aggressive panhandling.

Social disorganization: A characteristic of high-crime communities in which residents are unable to realize shared values or effectively address shared problems.

Social ecology: The study of relationships of people to one another and their physical surroundings.

Social institutions: Necessary subsystems that support society's survival, including family, education, polity, religion, and the economy.

Social learning: The process of learning through observing and imitating others.

Social location: Where one resides in a system of social stratification or inequality.

Social physics: Term coined by Quetelet to describe the application of statistical principles to the study of social behavior, including crime (same meaning as *moral statistics*).

Social stratification: A hierarchical organization of people or groups in a society.

Social structure: The organization of people in a society, relative to one another; an important element of Merton's anomie theory.

Sociology: The scientific study of society, including how individuals both shape and are shaped by society.

Soft determinism: A form of determinism that views people as enacting free will within constraints set by biological, psychological, or environmental forces.

Spatial analysis: Empirical study of the geographic locations of criminal events, offender or victim residences, or other crime-relevant locations.

Specialization: When criminal offenders engage only in, or specialize in, particular crime types.

Specific deterrence: Type of deterrence in which a punished person alters their future behavior due to fear of additional sanctions.

Spillover effect: Patterns in which crime spreads, or spills over, from a high-crime area into an adjacent area.

Stakes in conformity: Valued relationships or investments that would be jeopardized if the bonded person does not follow the law; refers to the attachment and commitment elements of the social bond.

State crime: Acts or inactions by state actors committed on behalf of the state that break the law (domestic or interactional), violate human rights, and/or produce systematic harms.

State-corporate crime: State crime in which governments and corporations, acting together to achieve shared goals, produce significant harm.

Statistical discrimination: Discrimination that occurs when decision-makers with limited information rely on easily identifiable traits like race to conclude whether someone is likely to have a criminal record or engage in crime.

Status frustration: A feeling of deprivation, resentment, and hostility arising from unfavorable class comparisons.

Stereotypes: Overgeneralized and oversimplified beliefs about members of a group, with all members assumed to share particular characteristics.

Stigma: A mark of disgrace communicated through social interaction.

Subculture: Cultural systems that are products of, but distinct from, the broader culture in which they are embedded.

Substantive law: Area of criminal law that pertains to what is criminal and what punishments are associated with given offenses.

Symbolic interactionism: Sociological perspective that claims the way people make sense of their social worlds is by exchanging meaning through language and symbols.

System avoidance: Practice in which people with warrants or criminal records avoid institutions that keep formal records, including schools, hospitals, and banks.

Systemic racism: Refers to how racial inequality is built into the ordinary operations of institutions, including laws, policies, and practices, rather than operating solely in one-on-one interactions.

Target hardening: Measures taken to reduce the ease with which targets or victims can be accessed by motivated offenders.

Techniques of neutralization: Justifying and excusing strategies offenders use to absolve themselves of guilt or shame, or to present themselves as nondeviant.

Temporal patterns: Time-based patterns in crime, including variation across times of day, day of the week, months, years, and historical eras.

Theory: An abstract explanation composed of proposed relationships between two or more concepts.

Therapeutic jurisprudence: An approach whose goal is to improve the emotional and psychological health of people ensnared in the legal system.

Three-strikes laws: Policies that impose a lengthy mandatory minimum sentence (often a life sentence) for a third felony conviction, regardless of the circumstances of the third crime.

Transnational organized crime: Organized crime that operates across national boundaries by exploiting systems of international commerce and communication.

Triangulation: The process of relying on several data sources or research methods to gain a more complete and accurate understanding of a research topic.

Turning points: Life changes that link a person to institutional sources of informal control, leading to desistance.

Uniform Crime Reporting (UCR) program: Longest running source of official U.S. crime data provided by police and reported by the Federal Bureau of Investigation.

Universalism: In institutional anomie theory, a cultural element of the American Dream in which expectations for individual achievement apply equally to all members of society.

Unobtrusive research: Research that does not intrude into the lives of research participants, including physical trace analysis, analysis of available data, content analysis, and covert observation.

Unwarranted disparity: A difference in criminal justice outcomes that is due to extralegal factors, which are characteristics that are legally irrelevant, like race, ethnicity, social class, and physical attractiveness.

Utilitarianism: The idea that law is correct if it produces the greatest overall good, or happiness, for society.

Versatility: When people who commit crime engage in many different types of crime.

Victim facilitation: Form of victim precipitation in which a victim makes victimization easier for the offender through their own actions, even though that was not their intention.

Victim precipitation: Situation in which a victim contributes to or causes their own victimization.

Victim provocation: Form of victim precipitation in which a victim instigates, or provokes, the criminal event, as in cases of self-defense.

Victim-impact statements: Oral or written accounts of the harmful effects of victimization on victims and their families, which are provided to judges, juries, or parole boards by victims or family members of victims during criminal justice hearings.

Victimless crime: Crime in which there is no aggrieved or injured party, such as drug or gambling offenses.

Victim-offender overlap: The co-occurrence of criminal offending and criminal victimization.

Victimogenic: Conditions that increase the risk of criminal victimization.

Victimology: The scientific study of criminal victimization; victimology is a subfield of criminology.

Victims' bill of rights: Federal and state lists of the rights afforded to crime victims, including but not limited to the right to notice of court or parole proceedings, protection from the accused, the right to be heard at public proceedings regarding release decisions, and the right to restitution.

Violent crime: Crime in which an offender harms or threatens to harm a victim.

Warranted disparity: A difference in criminal justice outcomes between individuals or groups that is due solely to legally relevant factors, such as extent of injury or use of a deadly weapon.

White-collar crime: Unlawful acts committed for personal gain (occupational crime) or organizational gain (corporate crime) by individuals of respectable social status, involving violations of trust and typically occurring in the course of legitimate workplace activity.

Zero-tolerance policies: Policies that proscribe consistent, harsh responses to rule violators regardless of the context and regardless of whether it is a first offense.

NOTES

CHAPTER 1

1. WHO Timeline—COVID-19. (April 27, 2020). Retrieved May 22, 2020, from https://www.who.int/news-room/detail/27-04-2020-who-timeline---covid-19

2. Farrell, G., & Tilley, N. (April 2, 2020). Coronavirus: How crime changes during a lockdown. *The Conversation.* Retrieved from https://theconversation.com/coronavirus-how-crime-changes-during-a-lockdown-134948

3. Atkinson, M., & Korgen, K. (Eds.). (2018). *Sociology in action.* Thousand Oaks, CA: SAGE.

4. Cook, P. J. (2018). Gun markets. *Annual Review of Criminology, 1*(1), 359–377. doi:10.1146/annurev-criminol-032317-092149

5. Bhavsar, V., & Bhugra, D. (2018). Violence towards people with mental illness: Assessment, risk factors, and management. *Psychiatry and Clinical Neurosciences, 72*(11), 811–820.

6. Beckley, A. L., Caspi, A., Broadbent, J., Harrington, H., Houts, R. M., Poulton, R., . . . Moffitt, T. E. (2018). Association of childhood blood lead levels with criminal offending. *JAMA Pediatrics, 172*(2), 166–173.

7. Sutherland, E. H. (1924). *Criminology.* Philadelphia, PA: JB Lippincott.

8. Wearing of masks, hoods, etc., on public property. North Carolina § 14-12.8 (1953, c. 1193, s. 7.).

9. *Ku Klux Klan.* (n.d.). Southern Poverty Law Center. Retrieved May 26, 2020, from https://www.splcenter.org/fighting-hate/extremist-files/ideology/ku-klux-klan

10. COVID-19 Time Sensitive Matters, 019-STfzp-47A [v.3], General Assembly of North Carolina (2020). Retrieved May 26, 2020, from https://ncleg.gov/documentsites/committees/house2019-199/Continuity%20of%20State%20Operations%20Working%20Group/4-23-20/2019-STfzp-47A%20v3.pdf

11. Exec. Order No. 121. Stay at home order and strategic directions for North Carolina in response to increasing Covid-19 cases (2020). Retrieved from https://governor.nc.gov/documents/executive-order-no-121

12. Smith, A. (April 21, 2020). *Hundreds gather in North Carolina and Missouri to protest stay-at-home orders.* NBC News. Retrieved from https://www.nbcnews.com/politics/politics-news/hundreds-gather-north-carolina-missouri-protest-stay-home-orders-n1188936

13. Department of Justice, U.S. Attorney's Office, Central District of California. (2020, May 22). *Hollywood executive arrested on federal fraud charges that allege he pocketed money from COVID-19 relief program.* Retrieved from https://www.justice.gov/usao-cdca/pr/hollywood-executive-arrested-federal-fraud-charges-allege-he-pocketed-money-covid-19

14. Department of Justice, U.S. Attorney's Office, Southern District of New York. (2020, May 26). *New Jersey man arrested for $45 million scheme to defraud and price gouge New York City during COVID-19 pandemic.* Retrieved from https://www.justice.gov/usao-sdny/pr/new-jersey-man-arrested-45-million-scheme-defraud-and-price-gouge-new-york-city-during

15. Department of Justice, U.S. Attorney's Office, District of Columbia. (2020, April 10). *Georgia man arrested for attempting to defraud the Department of Veterans Affairs in a multimillion-dollar COVID-19 scam.* Retrieved from https://www.justice.gov/usao-dc/pr/georgia-man-arrested-attempting-defraud-department-veterans-affairs-multimillion-dollar

16. Kaptein, M., & Van Helvoort, M. (2019). A model of neutralization techniques. *Deviant Behavior, 40,* 1260–1285.

17. Gottschalk, P. (2020). *The convenience of white-collar crime in business.* New York, NY: Springer.

18. Gottfredson, M., & Hirschi T. (1990). *A general theory of crime.* Palo Alto, CA: Stanford University Press.

19. Hövermann, A., & Messner, S. (2019). Institutional anomie theory across nation states. In H. Pontell (Ed.), *Oxford research encyclopedia of criminology and criminal justice.* New York, NY: Oxford University Press.

20. Tilley, N., Farrell, G., & Clarke, R V. (2015). Target suitability and the crime drop. In M. Andresen & G. Farrell (Eds.), *Routine activities and the criminal act* (pp. 59–76). London, UK: Palgrave.

21. Worden, R. (2015). The "causes" of police brutality: Theory and evidence on police use of force. In E. R. Maguire & D. E. Duffee (Eds.), *Criminal justice theory: Explaining the nature and behavior of criminal justice* (pp. 149–204). Milton Park, UK: Routledge

22. Messerschmidt, J. W. (2012). *Gender, heterosexuality, and youth violence.* Lanham, MD: Rowman & Littlefield.

23. Burch, A. (April 1, 2020). Coronavirus misbehavior. When was licking a toilet ever a good idea? *The New York Times.* Retrieved from https://www.nytimes.com/2020/04/01/us/coronavirus-terrorist-threat-felony.html

24. Fausset, R. (May 22, 2020). What we know about the shooting death of Ahmaud Arbery. *The New York Times.* Retrieved from https://www.nytimes.com/article/ahmaud-arbery-shooting-georgia.html

25. Oppel, R. A., Jr. (May 30, 2020). Here is what you need to know about Breonna Taylor's death. *The New York Times.* Retrieved from https://www.nytimes.com/article/breonna-taylor-police.html

26. Lovan, D. (2020, September 15). *"Say her name": City to pay $12 M to Breonna Taylor's family.* Associated Press. Retrieved from https://apnews.com/article

/shootings-police-us-news-ap-top-news-racial-injustice-42df1f3ebea59ff20a309b8fe04619df

27. Nagin, D. S. (2013). Deterrence: A review of the evidence by a criminologist for economists. *Annual Review of Economics, 5*, 83–105.

28. Roman, J. K. (2013). *Race, justifiable homicide, and stand your ground laws: Analysis of FBI supplementary homicide report data.* Urban Institute.

29. Ridgeway, G. (2020). The role of individual officer characteristics in police shootings. *ANNALS of the American Academy of Political and Social Science, 687,* 58–66.

30. Steidley, T., & Ramey, D. M. (2019). Police militarization in the United States. *Sociology Compass,13*(4), 1–16.

31. Wagner, P., & Bertram, W. (January 16, 2020). What percent of the U.S. is incarcerated? (And other ways to measure mass incarceration). *Prison Policy Initiative.* Retrieved from https://www.prisonpolicy.org/blog/2020/01/16/percent-incarcerated/

32. HB 123/SB 838. Nonpayment of wages; cause of action, penalties. *Virginia's Legislative Information System.* Retrieved from https://lis.virginia.gov/cgi-bin/legp604.exe?ses=201&typ=bil&val=sb838

33. Lee, J. J., & Smith, A. (2019). Regulating wage theft. *Washington Law Review, 94,* 759–822.

34. Durkheim, E. (1895/1982). *The rules of sociological method.* Glencoe, IL: Free Press.

35. Garland, D. (2013). Punishment and social solidarity. In J. Simon & R. Sparks (Eds.), *The SAGE handbook of punishment and society* (pp. 23–39). London, UK: SAGE.

36. Durkheim, E. (1895/1982). *The rules of sociological method.* Glencoe, IL: Free Press.

37. Bae, J. Y., Anderson, E., Silver, D., & Macinko, J. (2014). Child passenger safety laws in the United States, 1978–2010: Policy diffusion in the absence of strong federal intervention. *Social Science & Medicine, 100,* 30–37.

38. Hundley, T. (2015, February 3). *Southeast Asia: Death rides a moto.* Pulitzer Center. Retrieved from https://pulitzercenter.org/reporting/southeast-asia-death-rides-moto

39. Mill, J. S. (1859). *On liberty.* Oxford, UK: Oxford University.

40. Lawrence v. Texas, 539 U.S. 558 (2003).

41. Thomas, C., & Hepburn, J. (1983). *Crime, criminal law, and criminology.* Dubuque, IA: Wm. Brown.

42. Morris, A. (2012, November 13). Hunter Moore – The most hated man on the Internet. *Rolling Stone.* Retrieved from https://www.rollingstone.com/culture/culture-news/hunter-moore-the-most-hated-man-on-the-internet-184668/

43. Wolfgang, M. E., Figlio, R. M., Tracy, P. E., & Singer, S. I. (1985). *The National Survey of Crime Severity* (pp. vi–x). Washington, DC: U.S. Department of Justice.

44. People of the State of California v. Brock Allen Turner, No. H043709 (California 2015).

45. Animal: Cruelty; Sales; Animal enterprise protection. Florida Title XLVI, Chapter 828.123 (2019). Retrieved from http://www.leg.state.fl.us/statutes/index.cfm?App_mode=Display_Statute&Search_String=&URL=0800-0899/0828/Sections/0828.122.html

46. Franklin v. Peterson, Civil No. 14-1467 (D. Minnesota 2016).

47. Voltaire. (1771). Rights. *Questions sur l'Encyclopédie.*

48. Reiman, J., & Leighton, P. (2020). *The rich get richer and the poor get prison* (12th ed.). New York, NY: Routledge.

49. Lewd and lascivious cohabitation. Virginia § 18.2-345 (Code 1950, 18.1-193; 1960, c. 358; 1975, cc. 14, 15).

50. Barton, R. (October 4, 2017). Understanding the so-called "Twinkie Defense." *The Crime Report.* Retrieved from https://thecrimereport.org/2017/10/04/understanding-the-so-called-twinkie-defense/

51. Sugar consumption worldwide in 2019/2020, by leading country (in million metric tons). *Statista.* Retrieved from https://www.statista.com/statistics/496002/sugar-consumption-worldwide/

52. Suglia, S. F., Solnick, S., & Hemenway, D. (2013). Soft drinks consumption is associated with behavior problems in 5-year-olds. *Journal of Pediatrics, 163*(5), 1323–1328.

53. Tcherni-Buzzeo, M. (2019). The "great American crime decline": Possible explanations. In M. D. Krohn, A. Lizotte, & G. P. Hall (Eds.), *Handbook on crime and deviance* (pp. 309–335). New York, NY: Springer.

54. Wildeman, C. (2020). The intergenerational transmission of criminal justice contact. *Annual Review of Criminology, 3,* 217–244.

55. Demir, M., & Kule, A. (2020). The effect of body-worn cameras on satisfaction and general perceptions of police: Findings from a quasi-randomized controlled trial. *European Journal of Criminology,* 1–24.

56. Bernstein, N. (2014). *Burning down the house: The end of juvenile prison.* New York, NY: New Press.

57. Kaasa, S. O., Vidal, S., Meadows, K., Foster, M., & Lowe, N. (2019). Kentucky juvenile justice reform evaluation: Implementation evaluation report. Retrieved from http://www.ncjrs.gov/App/publications/abstract.aspx?ID=277702

58. Rios, V. M., Prieto, G., & Ibarra, J. M. (2020). *Mano suave-mano dura*: Legitimacy policing and Latino stop-and-frisk. *American Sociological Review, 85,* 58–75.

59. Lehmann, P. S. (2020). Race, ethnicity, crime type, and the sentencing of violent felony offenders. *Crime & Delinquency, 66,* 770–805.

60. National Organization for Human Services. (n.d.). *What is human services?* Retrieved from https://www.nationalhumanservices.org/what-is-human-services

61. Crime Lab. (n.d.). Retrieved from https://urbanlabs.uchicago.edu/labs/crime

62. Hendrix, J., & Young, A. (April 26, 2018). *Sexual assault kit processing: Policies and resources needed for improved efficiency.* RTI International. Retrieved from https://www.rti.org/insights/sexual-assault-kit-processing-policies-and-resources-needed-improved-efficiency

CHAPTER 2

1. McCarthy, J. (2020, November 13). *Perceptions of increased U.S. crime at highest since 1993.* Gallup Poll. Retrieved from https://news.gallup.com/poll/323996/perceptions-increased-crime-highest-1993.aspx

2. Roberts, J. (2018). *Public opinion, crime, and criminal justice.* New York, NY: Routledge.

3. Rader, N. (2017). Fear of crime. In H. Pontell (Ed.), *Oxford research encyclopedias: Criminology and criminal justice.* New York, NY: Oxford University Press.

4. Lee, M. (2013). *Inventing fear of crime: Criminology and the politics of anxiety.* New York, NY: Routledge.

5. Zeoli, A. M., McCourt, A., Buggs, S., Frattaroli, S., Lilley, D., & Webster, D. W. (2018). Analysis of the strength of legal firearms restrictions for perpetrators of domestic violence and their associations with intimate partner homicide. *American Journal of Epidemiology, 187,* 2365–2371.

6. Zeoli, A. M., & Paruk, J. K. (2020). Potential to prevent mass shootings through domestic violence firearm restrictions. *Criminology & Public Policy, 19,* 129–145.

7. Heap, V., & Waters, J. (2019). *Mixed methods in criminology.* New York, NY: Routledge.

8. Caulfield, L., & Hill, J. (2018). *Criminological skills and research for beginners: A student's guide.* New York, NY: Routledge.

9. Porter, L. C., De Biasi, A., Mitchell, S., Curtis, A., & Jefferis, E. (2019). Understanding the criminogenic properties of vacant housing: A mixed methods approach. *Journal of Research in Crime and Delinquency, 56,* 378–411.

10. Benson, M. L., & Simpson, S. S. (2014). *Understanding white-collar crime: An opportunity perspective.* New York, NY: Routledge.

11. Howell, J. C., & Griffiths, E. (2018). *Gangs in America's communities.* Thousand Oaks, CA: SAGE.

12. Gaston, S. (2019). Enforcing race: A neighborhood-level explanation of black–white differences in drug arrests. *Crime & Delinquency, 65,* 499–526.

13. Hanrath, L., & Font, S. (2020). Gender disparity in Pennsylvania child abuse and neglect sentencing outcomes. *Crime & Delinquency, 66,* 1703–1728.

14. Federal Bureau of Investigation, Criminal Justice Information Services Division. (2018). *About UCR.* Retrieved from https://ucr.fbi.gov/crime-in-the-u.s/2018/crime-in-the-u.s.-2018

15. Strom, K. J., & Smith, E. L. (2017). The future of crime data: The case for the National Incident-Based Reporting System (NIBRS) as a primary data source for policy evaluation and crime analysis. *Criminology & Public Policy, 16,* 1027–1048.

16. Dahl, P. P. (2017). Uniform Crime Reports. In C. J. Schreck (Ed.), *Encyclopedia of juvenile delinquency and justice.* New York, NY: Wiley-Blackwell.

17. Strom, K. J., & Smith, E. L. (2017). The future of crime data: The case for the National Incident-Based Reporting System (NIBRS) as a primary data source for policy evaluation and crime analysis. *Criminology & Public Policy, 16,* 1027–1048.

18. Federal Bureau of Investigation. (2018). Aggravated assault—Crime in the United States. Retrieved from https://ucr.fbi.gov/crime-in-the-u.s/2018/crime-in-the-u.s.-2018/topic-pages/aggravated-assault

19. Strom, K. J., & Smith, E. L. (2017). The future of crime data: The case for the National Incident-Based Reporting System (NIBRS) as a primary data source for policy evaluation and crime analysis. *Criminology & Public Policy, 16,* 1027–1048.

20. Federal Bureau of Investigation. *Crime in the United States, 2020.* Washington, DC: U.S. Department of Justice.

21. Prison Rape Elimination Act of 2003. Pub. L. No. 108-79, 117 Stat. 972 (2003).

22. National Archive of Criminal Justice Data. (n.d.). *Resource guide: National Crime Victimization Survey.* Retrieved from https://www.icpsr.umich.edu/web/pages/NACJD/NCVS/index.html

23. Bureau of Justice Statistics. (n.d.). *Data collection: National Crime Victimization Survey (NCVS).* Retrieved from https://www.bjs.gov/index.cfm?ty=dcdetail&iid=245

24. Langton, L., Planty, M., & Lynch, J. P. (2017). Second major redesign of the National Crime Victimization Survey (NCVS). *Criminology & Public Policy, 16,* 1049.

25. Salkind, N. J. (2010). *Encyclopedia of research design* (Vols. 1-0). Thousand Oaks, CA: SAGE. doi:10.4135/9781412961288

26. Karstedt, S. (2015). Charting Europe's moral economies: Citizens, consumers and the crimes of everyday life. In J. van Erp, W. Huisman, & G. Vande Walle (Eds.), *The Routledge handbook of white-collar and corporate crime in Europe* (pp. 79–110). New York, NY: Routledge.

27. National Survey on Drug Use and Health. (n.d.). *What is the NSDUH?* Retrieved from https://nsduhweb.rti.org/respweb/homepage.cfm

28. Griffin, V. W., & Evans, M. (2021). The duality of stigmatization: An examination of differences in collateral consequences for black and white sex offenders. *Justice Quarterly, 38,* 1019–1046.

29. Ferri, R. (2020). The benefits of live court date reminder phone calls during pretrial case processing. *Journal of Experimental Criminology, 18,* 1–21.

30. Kirk, D. S., & Wakefield, S. (2018). Collateral consequences of punishment: A critical review and path forward. *Annual Review of Criminology, 1,* 171–194.

31. DeWitt, S. E., & Denver, M. (2020). Criminal records, positive employment credentials, and race. *Journal of Research in Crime and Delinquency, 57,* 333–368.

32. Harding, D. J., Morenoff, J. D., Nguyen, A. P., & Bushway, S. D. (2018). Imprisonment and labor market outcomes: Evidence from a natural experiment. *American Journal of Sociology, 124,* 49–110.

33. Jacobs, B. A., & Cherbonneau, M. (2017). Nerve management and crime accomplishment. *Journal of Research in Crime and Delinquency, 54,* 617–638.

34. Dickinson, T. (2020). Identity, situational elements, and responses to drug debt. *Journal of Research in Crime and Delinquency, 57,* 66–104.

35. Rios, V. M., Prieto, G., & Ibarra, J. M. (2020). *Mano suave-mano dura*: Legitimacy policing and Latino stop-and-frisk. *American Sociological Review, 85,* 58–75.

36. Trejbalová, T., Monaghan, H., Kennedy, M. A., Decker, M. R., & Cimino, A. N. (2021). Detention experiences of commercial sexual exploitation survivors. *Feminist Criminology,16,* 73–90.

37. Wincup, E. (2017). *Criminological research: Understanding qualitative methods.* Thousand Oaks, CA: SAGE.

38. Topalli, V., Dickinson, T., & Jacques, S. (2020). Learning from criminals: Active offender research for criminology. *Annual Review of Criminology, 3,* 189–215.

39. Haney, L. (2018). Incarcerated fatherhood: The entanglements of child support debt and mass imprisonment. *American Journal of Sociology, 124,* 1–48.

40. Boeri, M., & Shukla, R. K. (Eds.). (2019). *Inside ethnography: Researchers reflect on the challenges of reaching hidden populations.* Berkeley: University of California Press.

41. Wincup, E. (2017). *Criminological research: Understanding qualitative methods.* Thousand Oaks, CA: SAGE.

42. Webb, E. J., Campbell, D. T., Schwartz, R. D., & Sechrest, L. (1999). *Unobtrusive measures* (Vol. 2). Thousand Oaks, CA: SAGE.

43. Wheeler, A. P. (2018). The effect of 311 calls for service on crime in DC at microplaces. *Crime & Delinquency, 64,* 1882–1903.

44. Boessen, A., & Chamberlain, A. W. (2017). Neighborhood crime, the housing crisis, and geographic space: Disentangling the consequences of foreclosure and vacancy. *Journal of Urban Affairs, 39,* 1122–1137.

45. Kort-Butler, L. (2016). Content analysis in the study of crime, media, and popular culture. In *Oxford research encyclopedia: Criminology and criminal justice.* New York, NY: Oxford University Press.

46. Collins, R. E. (2016)."'Beauty and bullets": A content analysis of female offenders and victims in four Canadian newspapers. *Journal of Sociology, 52,* 296–310.

47. Pruitt, M. V. (2018). "Just a Gigolo": Differences in advertisements of male-for-female and male-for-male online escorts. *Deviant Behavior, 39,* 64–79.

48. Nolasco Braaten, C., & Vaughn, M. S. (2021). Convenience theory of cryptocurrency crime: A content analysis of US Federal Court decisions. *Deviant Behavior, 42,* 958–978.

49. Park, S. M., Kim, J. L., Park, H., Kim, Y., & Cuadrado, M. (2021). Social constructions of racial images in introductory criminal justice and criminology textbooks: A content analysis. *Race Ethnicity and Education, 24,* 842–855.

50. Melendez, M. S., Lichtenstein, B., & Dolliver, M. J. (2016). Mothers of mass murderers: Exploring public blame for the mothers of school shooters through an application of courtesy stigma to the Columbine and Newtown tragedies. *Deviant Behavior, 37,* 525–536.

51. Lindegaard, M. R., & Bernasco, W. (2018). Lessons learned from crime caught on camera. *Journal of Research in Crime and Delinquency, 55,* 155–186.

52. Willits, D. W., & Makin, D. A. (2018). Show me what happened: Analyzing use of force through analysis of body-worn camera footage. *Journal of Research in Crime and Delinquency, 55,* 51–77.

53. Williams, M. L., Burnap, P., & Sloan, L. (2017). Crime sensing with big data: The affordances and limitations of using open-source communications to estimate crime patterns. *British Journal of Criminology, 57,* 320–340.

54. Hipp, J. R., Bates, C., Lichman, M., & Smyth, P. (2019). Using social media to measure temporal ambient population: Does it help explain local crime rates? *Justice Quarterly, 36,* 718–748.

55. Lynch, J. (2018). Not even our own facts: Criminology in the era of big data. *Criminology, 56,* 437–454.

56. Williams, M. L., Burnap, P., & Sloan, L. (2017). Crime sensing with big data: The affordances and limitations of using open-source communications to estimate crime patterns. *British Journal of Criminology, 57,* 320–340.

57. Maxfield, M. G., & Babbie, E. R. (2014). *Research methods for criminal justice and criminology.* New York, NY: Cengage Learning.

CHAPTER 3

1. Patterson, R. (October 6, 2006). The organ grinder. *New York Magazine.* Retrieved from https://nymag.com/news/features /22326/

2. Penalties: Classification of felonies. Wisconsin Chapter 939.50 (2020). Retrieved from https://docs.legis.wisconsin .gov/statutes/statutes/939/IV/50

3. Possession of controlled substances. Ohio Title 29 Chapter 2925 (2019). Retrieved from http://codes.ohio.gov/ orc/2925.11

4. Trafficking in controlled substances: Schedule II substances. Nevada NRS 453.3395 (2020). Retrieved from https: //www.leg.state.nv.us/nrs/nrs-453.html#NRS453Sec339

5. U.S. Department of Justice. (2017). *Drugs of abuse: A DEA enforcement guide.* Drug Enforcement Administration. Retrieved from https://www.dea.gov/sites/default/files/dru g_of_abuse.pdf

6. Monk, J. (August 22, 2012). Man pleads guilty to cutting off acquaintance's hand for insurance money. *The State.* Retrieved from https://www.thestate.com/latest-news/arti cle14408531.html

7. Jacobs, B. A., & Wright, R. (2008). Moralistic street robbery. *Crime & Delinquency, 54*(4), 511–531.

8. *"She will kill again": Father of road rage victim angry over Lowell woman's sentence.* CBS Boston. Retrieved from https://bost on.cbslocal.com/2019/11/01/lowell-road-rage-graciela-paulino-marc-devoue-sentencing/

9. Diamond, D. (July 29, 2019). Children dying in hot cars: A tragedy that can be prevented. *The Conversation.* Retrieved from https://theconversation.com/children-dying-in-hot-cars-a-tragedy-that-can-be-prevented-60909

10. The U.S. non-gun homicide rate was calculated as follows: 4,150 non-gun homicides + 860 homicides with an unknown weapon (23% of the 3,740 homicides with an unknown weapon) = 5,010 homicides/population of 329.5 million multiplied by 100,000 = 1.52.

11. Associated Press. (April 24, 2018). Toronto van attack suspect held on 10 counts of murder; portrait of "socially awkward" man emerges. *Los Angeles Times*. Retrieved from https://www.latimes.com/world/la-fg-canada-toronto-van-attack-20180424-story.html

12. Fox, J. A., Levin, J., & Fridel, E. E. (2019). *Extreme killing: Understanding serial and mass murder*. Thousand Oaks, CA: SAGE.

13. Blair, J., & Schweit, K. (2014). *A study of active shooter incidents in the United States between 2000 and 2013*. Washington, DC: U.S. Department of Justice.

14. Murray, J. L. (2017). The transcendent fantasy in mass killers. *Deviant Behavior, 38*, 1172–1185.

15. Marganski, A. J. (2019). Making a murderer: The importance of gender and violence against women in mass murder events. *Sociology Compass, 13*, 1–15.

16. Kalish, R., & Kimmel, M. (2010). Suicide by mass murder: Masculinity, aggrieved entitlement, and rampage school shootings. *Health Sociology Review, 19*, 451–464.

17. Krause, W., & Richardson, D. (2015). *Mass murder with firearms: Incidents and victims, 1999-2013*. Congressional Research Service. Retrieved from https://fas.org/sgp/crs/misc/R44126.pdf

18. Gun Violence Archive. Retrieved from https://www.gunviolencearchive.org/

19. Federal Bureau of Investigation. (2018). Table 1. Crime in the United States: By volume and rate per 100,000 inhabitants, 1999-2018. *Crime in the United States, 2018*. Retrieved from https://ucr.fbi.gov/crime-in-the-u.s/2018/crime-in-the-u.s.-2018/topic-pages/tables/table-1

20. Schildkraut, J., Elsass, H. J., & Meredith, K. (2018). Mass shootings and the media: Why all events are not created equal. *Journal of Crime and Justice, 41*(3), 223–243.

21. Zezima, K., & Dewan, S. (2010, February 17). New look at killing of brother of professor. *The New York Times*. Retrieved from https://www.nytimes.com/2010/02/17/us/17alabama.html

22. Yardley, E., & Wilson, D. (2016). In search of the "angels of death": Conceptualizing the contemporary nurse healthcare serial killer. *Journal of Investigative Psychology and Offender Profiling, 13*, 39–55.

23. Holmes, R., & Holmes, S. (1998). *Serial murder* (2nd ed.). Thousand Oaks, CA: SAGE.

24. Wiest, J. (2019). *Creating cultural monsters: Serial murder in America*. Baton Rouge, FL: CRC Press.

25. Federal Bureau of Investigation. (n.d.). *Serial murder: Multidisciplinary perspectives for investigators*. Behavioral Analysis Unit, National Center for the Analysis of Violent Crime. Retrieved from https://www.fbi.gov/stats-services/publications/serial-murder

26. Aamodt, M. G. Leary, T., & Southard, L. (2020). *Radford/FGCU annual report on serial killer statistics: 2020*. Radford, VA: Radford University.

27. Ohlheiser, A. (2017, October 19). The woman behind "Me Too" knew the power of the phrase when she created it—10 years ago. *The Washington Post*. Retrieved from https://www.washingtonpost.com/news/the-intersect/wp/2017/10/19/the-woman-behind-me-too-knew-the-power-of-the-phrase-when-she-created-it-10-years-ago/

28. Iles, I. A., Waks, L., Atwell Seate, A., Hundal, S., & Irions, A. (2018). The unintended consequences of rape disclosure: The effects of disclosure content, listener gender, and year in college on listener's reactions. *Journal of Interpersonal Violence*, 1–27.

29. Cohn, A. M., Zinzow, H. M., Resnick, H. S., & Kilpatrick, D. G. (2013). Correlates of reasons for not reporting rape to police: Results from a national telephone household probability sample of women with forcible or drug-or-alcohol facilitated/incapacitated rape. *Journal of Interpersonal Violence, 28*, 455–473.

30. Langton, L., Berzofsky, M., Krebs, C. P., & Smiley-McDonald, H. (2012). *Victimizations not reported to the police, 2006-2010*. Washington, DC: U.S. Department of Justice, Office of Justice Programs, Bureau of Justice Statistics.

31. Weiss, K. G. (2010). Too ashamed to report: Deconstructing the shame of sexual victimization. *Feminist Criminology, 5*, 286–310.

32. Hahn, C. K., Hahn, A. M., Gaster, S., & Quevillon, R. (2020). Predictors of college students' likelihood to report hypothetical rape: Rape myth acceptance, perceived barriers to reporting, and self-efficacy. *Ethics & Behavior, 30*, 45–62.

33. Venema, R. M. (2016). Police officer schema of sexual assault reports: Real rape, ambiguous cases, and false reports. *Journal of Interpersonal Violence, 31*, 872–899.

34. Morabito, M. S., Pattavina, A., & Williams, L. M. (2019). It all just piles up: Challenges to victim credibility accumulate to influence sexual assault case processing. *Journal of Interpersonal Violence, 34*, 3151–3170.

35. U.S. Department of Justice, Federal Bureau of Investigation. (n.d.). *UCR offense descriptions*. Retrieved from https://www.bjs.gov/ucrdata/offenses.cfm

36. Federal Bureau of Investigation. (2013). Uniform Crime Reporting program changes definition of rape. *Crime in the United States, 2013*. Retrieved from https://ucr.fbi.gov/crime-in-the-u.s/2013/crime-in-the-u.s.-2013/rape-addendum/rape_addendum_final

37. Truman, J., & Langton, L. (September, 2014). *Criminal victimization, 2013*. U.S. Department of Justice, Office of Justice Statistics. Retrieved from https://www.bjs.gov/content/pub/pdf/cv13.pdf

38. Bureau of Justice Statistics. (Number of rape/sexual assaults by victim-offender relationship, 2015-2019). Generated using the NCVS Victimization Analysis Tool (NVAT) at www.bjs.gov. (November 5, 2021).

39. Wilson, L. C., & Miller, K. E. (2016). Meta-analysis of the prevalence of unacknowledged rape. *Trauma, Violence, & Abuse, 17*, 149–159.

40. Cook, S., Cortina, L., & Koss, M. (2018, September 20). What's the difference between sexual abuse, sexual assault, sexual harassment and rape? *The Conversation*. Retrieved from https://theconversation

.com/whats-the-difference-between-sexual-abuse-sexual-assault-sexual-harassment-and-rape-88218

41. Cook, S., Cortina, L., & Koss, M. (2018, September 20). What's the difference between sexual abuse, sexual assault, sexual harassment and rape? *The Conversation*. Retrieved from https://theconversation.com/whats-the-difference-between-sexual-abuse-sexual-assault-sexual-harassment-and-rape-88218

42. Equal Employment Opportunity Commission. (n.d.). Facts about sexual harassment. Retrieved from https://www.eeoc.gov/publications/facts-about-sexual-harassment

43. Federal Bureau of Investigation. (2021). *Robbery offense characteristics: Type of weapon involved by offense, 2016-2020* [Data set]. Crime Data Explorer. https://crime-data-explorer.fr.cloud.gov/pages/explorer/crime/crime-trend

44. Federal Bureau of Investigation. (2021). *Robbery offense characteristics: Location type* [Data set]. Crime Data Explorer. https://crime-data-explorer.fr.cloud.gov/pages/explorer/crime/crime-trend

45. Matthews, R. (2012). *Armed robbery*. New York, NY: Routledge.

46. GoFundMe—Paying it forward. (2017, November 22). *Internet Archive: Wayback machine*. Retrieved from https://web.archive.org/web/20171122015618/https://www.gofundme.com/hvv4r-paying-it-forward

47. *Johnny Bobbitt: Two admit GoFundMe hoax about homeless man.* (2019, March 6). BBC News. Retrieved from https://www.bbc.com/news/world-us-canada-47475561

48. Federal Bureau of Investigation. (2018). *Crime in the United States, 2018.* Retrieved from https://ucr.fbi.gov/crime-in-the-u.s/2018/crime-in-the-u.s.-2018/topic-pages/larceny-theft

49. Why I steal. (September 27, 2017). *Death, Sex, & Money*. Retrieved from https://www.wnycstudios.org/podcasts/deathsexmoney/episodes/why-i-steal-death-sex-money

50. Cameron, M. O. (1964). *The booster and the snitch: Department store shoplifting.* New York, NY: Macmillan.

51. Tarallo, M. (2019, September 1). *Shoplifting, Inc.* Security Management. Retrieved from https://www.asisonline.org/security-management-magazine/articles/2019/09/shoplifting-inc/

52. French, L. A. (2013). Shoplifting. In J. I. Ross (Ed.), *Encyclopedia of street crime in America* (pp. 376–378). Thousand Oaks, CA: SAGE.

53. Why I steal (transcript). (September 27, 2017). *Death, Sex, & Money*. Retrieved from https://www.wnycstudios.org/podcasts/deathsexmoney/episodes/why-i-steal-death-sex-money

54. Cameron, M. O. (1964). *The booster and the snitch: Department store shoplifting.* New York, NY: Macmillan.

55. Bennett, T. (2011). Residential burglary. In B. Huebner (Ed.), *Oxford bibliographies in criminology*. New York, NY: Oxford University Press.

56. Federal Bureau of Investigation. (2018). *Burglary*. Retrieved from https://ucr.fbi.gov/crime-in-the-u.s/2018/crime-in-the-u.s.-2018/topic-pages/burglary

57. Mawby, R. I. (2014). Commercial burglary. In M. Gill (Ed.), *The handbook of security* (pp. 279–301). New York, NY: Springer.

58. Lister, S. C., & Wall, D. S. (2006). Deconstructing distraction burglary: An ageist offence? In A. Wahidin & M. Cain (Eds.), *Ageing, crime, and society* (pp. 107–123). Cullompton, UK: Willang. Available at SSRN: https://ssrn.com/abstract=1085050

59. Fox, B. H., & Farrington, D. P. (2016). Is the development of offenders related to crime scene behaviors for burglary? *International Journal of Offender Therapy and Comparative Criminology, 60,* 1897–1927.

60. Pedneault, A., Beauregard, E., Harris, D. A., & Knight, R. A. (2015). Rationally irrational: The case of sexual burglary. *Sexual Abuse, 27,* 376–397.

61. Treaster, J. B. (June 12, 1975). 8 Landlords and associates are indicted in Bronx fires. *The New York Times*. Retrieved from https://www.nytimes.com/1975/06/12/archives/8-landlords-and-associates-are-indicted-in-bronx-fires-8-indicted.html

62. Jacobson, M., & Kasinitz, P. (1986, November 15). Burning the Bronx for profit. *The Nation*.

63. Mahler, J. (2006). *Ladies and gentlemen, the Bronx is burning.* New York, NY: Farrar, Straus, & Giroux.

64. Irizarry, V. V., Hildebran, G., & Allen, J. S. (Directors). (2019, November 4). *Decade of fire* [Film]. PBS Independent Lens.

65. Garner, B. A. (2019). *Black's law dictionary* (11th ed.). Toronto, Ontario: Thomson Reuters.

66. Grubb, J. A., & Nobles, M. R. (2016). A spatiotemporal analysis of arson. *Journal of Research in Crime and Delinquency, 53,* 66–92.

67. Icove, D., & Hargrove, T. (2014, September 22). *Project Arson: Uncovering the true arson rate in the United States* [Paper presentation]. International Symposium on Fire Investigation Science and Technology, College Park, MD.

68. Federal Bureau of Investigation. (2018). Table 25. Percent of offenses cleared by arrest or exceptional means. *Crime in the United States, 2018.* Retrieved from https://ucr.fbi.gov/crime-in-the-u.s/2018/crime-in-the-u.s.-2018/topic-pages/tables/table-25

69. Barrowcliffe, E. R., & Gannon, T. A. (2016). Comparing the psychological characteristics of un-apprehended firesetters and non-firesetters living in the UK. *Psychology, Crime & Law, 22,* 382–404.

70. Wulf, T., & Meier, R. (2015). Public order crimes. In B. Huebner (Ed.), *Oxford bibliographies in criminology*. New York, NY: Oxford University Press.

71. Colby, I. (2011). Runaway and throwaway youth: Time for policy changes and public responsibility. *Journal of Applied Research on Children, 2,* 1–11.

72. Robinson, T. (2019). No right to rest: Police enforcement patterns and quality of life consequences of the criminalization of homelessness. *Urban Affairs Review, 55,* 41–73.

73. Zito, R. (2018). Identifying deviant behavior. In K. Korgen & M. Atkinson (Eds.), *Sociology in action* (pp. 99–119). Thousand Oaks, CA: SAGE.

74. Mothers Against Drunk Driving. (n.d.). *The mission.* Retrieved from https://www.madd.org/#

75. Centers for Disease Controls and Prevention. (n.d.). *Opioid overdose.* Retrieved from https://www.cdc.gov/drugoverdose/index.html

76. Musto, D. F. (1999). *The American disease: Origins of narcotic control.* New York, NY: Oxford University Press.

77. Anslinger, H. (July 1937). Marijuana: Assassin of youth. *The American Magazine,* 24.

78. Williams, E. H. (1914, February 8). Negro cocaine "fiends" are a new Southern menace. *The New York Times.* Retrieved from https://www.nytimes.com/1914/02/08/archives/negro-cocaine-fiends-are-a-new-southern-menace-murder-and-insanity.html

79. Provine, D. M. (2008). *Unequal under law: Race in the war on drugs.* Chicago, IL: University of Chicago Press.

80. U.S. Department of Justice, Office of Juvenile Justice and Delinquency Prevention. (2018). *Statistical briefing book.* Retrieved from https://www.ojjdp.gov/ojstatbb/crime/ucr.asp?table_in=1

81. Goldstein, P. J. (1985). The drugs/violence nexus: A tripartite conceptual framework. *Journal of Drug Issues, 15,* 493–506.

82. Reuter, P. (2016). On the multiple sources of violence in drug markets. *Criminology & Public Policy, 15,* 877–883.

83. Kammersgaard, T. (2019). Harm reduction policing: From drug law enforcement to protection. *Contemporary Drug Problems, 46,* 345–362.

84. Ringdal, N. J. (2007). *Love for sale: A world history of prostitution.* New York, NY: Grove Press.

85. Smith, M., & Mac, J. (2018). *Revolting prostitutes: The fight for sex workers' rights.* New York, NY: Verso.

86. U.S. Department of Justice. (n.d.). *Citizen's guide to U.S. obscenity law.* Retrieved from https://www.justice.gov/criminal-ceos/citizens-guide-us-federal-law-obscenity

87. Federal Bureau of Investigation. (2018). *Offense definitions.* Retrieved from https://ucr.fbi.gov/crime-in-the-u.s/2018/crime-in-the-u.s.-2018/topic-pages/offense-definitions

88. Preble, K., Magruder, K., & Cimino, A. N. (2019). "It's like being an electrician, you're gonna get shocked": Differences in the perceived risks of indoor and outdoor sex work and its impact on exiting. *Victims & Offenders, 14,* 625–646.

89. McCutcheon, J. C., Mustaine, E. E., & Tewksbury, R. (2016). Working the stroll: Prostitutes, pimps, and johns. *Deviant Behavior, 37,* 1449–1458.

90. Chicago Alliance Against Sexual Exploitation. (2020). *Policing and enforcement of prostitution laws in Chicago.* Retrieved from https://www.caase.org/wp-content/uploads/2020/05/Report-PEOPL-Jan20-v1.3-WithAppx.pdf

91. U.S. Department of Homeland Security. (n.d.). *What is human trafficking?* Retrieved from https://www.dhs.gov/blue-campaign/what-human-trafficking

92. Hickle, K., & Roe-Sepowitz, D. (2017). "Curiosity and a pimp": Exploring sex trafficking victimization in experiences of entering sex trade industry work among participants in a prostitution diversion program. *Women & Criminal Justice, 27,* 122–138.

93. Meshelemiah, J. C. A. (2019). Criminal provisions for human trafficking: Rankings, state grades, and challenges. *HSOA Journal of Forensic, Legal & Investigative Sciences, 5,* 1–8.

CHAPTER 4

1. Speights, D., Downs, D., & Raz, A. (2018, October 31). Research: Retail theft and loss prevention analytics. *Loss Prevention Magazine.* Retrieved from https://lossprevention media.com/retail-theft-loss-prevention-analytics/

2. Pomorski, C. (May 2, 2018). The baby formula crime ring. *The New York Times Magazine.* Retrieved from https://www.nytimes.com/interactive/2018/05/02/magazine/money-issue-baby-formula-crime-ring.html

3. Clay, A., & Phillips, K. M. (2015). *The misfit economy: Lessons in creativity from pirates, hackers, gangsters, and other informal entrepreneurs.* New York, NY: Simon & Schuster.

4. Associated Press. (June 4, 2005). *Powdered baby formula goes behind the counter.* NBC News. Retrieved from http://www.nbcnews.com/id/8088953/ns/health-childrens_health/t/powdered-baby-formula-goes-behind-counter/#.X0eOh4t7k2w

5. Poovey, B. (April 2, 2005). Baby formula among growing criminal cargo traveling by interstate. *My Plainview.* Retrieved from https://www.myplainview.com/news/article/Baby-formula-among-growing-criminal-cargo-8489788.php

6. Heywood, A. (2017). *Political ideologies: An introduction.* London, UK: Palgrave Macmillan.

7. Sutherland, E. H. (1940). White-collar criminality. *American Sociological Review, 5,* 1–12.

8. Sutherland, E. H. (1949). *White collar crime.* New York, NY: Dryden Press.

9. Helmkamp, J., Ball, R., & Townshend, K. (1996). *Definitional dilemma: Can and should there be a universal definition of white-collar crime?* Morgantown, WV: National White-Collar Crime Center Training and Research Institute.

10. Simpson, S. (2013). White-collar crime: A review of recent developments and promising directions for future research. *Annual Review of Sociology, 39,* 309–331.

11. Benson, M. L., & Chio, H. L. (2019). Who commits occupational crimes? In M. Rorie & C. Wellford (Eds.), *The handbook of white-collar crime* (pp. 95–112). New York, NY: Wiley-Blackwell.

12. Ramamoorti, S. (2019). Fraud. In R. Morgan (Ed.), *SAGE encyclopedia of criminal psychology.* Thousand Oaks, CA: SAGE.

13. Holtfreter, K. (2005). Is occupational fraud "typical" white-collar crime? A comparison of individual and organizational characteristics. *Journal of Criminal Justice, 33*(4), 353–365.

14. Association of Certified Fraud Examiners. (2020). *Report to the nations: 2020 global study on occupational fraud and abuse.* Retrieved from https://www.acfe.com/report-to-the-nations/2020/

15. Association of Certified Fraud Examiners. (2020). *Report to the nations: 2020 global study on occupational fraud and*

abuse. Retrieved from https://www.acfe.com/report-to-the-nations/2020/

16. Centers for Disease Control and Prevention. (n.d.). *Multistate outbreak of Salmonella typhimurium infections linked to peanut butter, 2008-2009* (final update). Retrieved from https://www.cdc.gov/salmonella/2009/peanut-butter-2008-2009.html

17. Department of Justice, Office of Public Affairs. (2015, September 21). *Former peanut company president receives largest criminal sentence in food safety case; two others also sentenced for their roles in salmonella-tainted peanut product outbreak* [Press release]. Retrieved from https://www.justice.gov/opa/pr/former-peanut-company-president-receives-largest-criminal-sentence-food-safety-case-two

18. Sherman Anti-Trust Act (July 2, 1890). Enrolled Acts and Resolutions of Congress, 1789-1992; General Records of the United States Government; Record Group 11; National Archives.

19. U.S. Department of Justice. (n.d.). *Price fixing, bid rigging, and market allocation schemes: What they are and what to look for.* Retrieved from https://www.justice.gov/atr/price-fixing-bid-rigging-and-market-allocation-schemes

20. U.S. Department of Justice. (n.d.). *Price fixing, bid rigging, and market allocation schemes: What they are and what to look for.* Retrieved from https://www.justice.gov/atr/price-fixing-bid-rigging-and-market-allocation-schemes

21. Payne, B. (2016). *White-collar crime: The essentials.* Thousand Oaks, CA: SAGE.

22. Heilpern, W. (2016, March 31). 18 false advertising scandals that cost some brands millions. *Business Insider.* Retrieved from https://www.businessinsider.com/false-advertising-scandals-2016-3

23. United States v. Arif, No. 17-1597 (1st Cir. 2018). Retrieved from https://law.justia.com/cases/federal/appellate-courts/ca1/17-1597/17-1597-2018-07-18.html

24. Croall, H. (2009). White collar crime, consumers, and victimization. *Crime, Law, and Social Change, 51*(1), 127–146.

25. U.S. Food and Drug Administration. (2017, January 18). *Owner of major online colored contact lens business sentenced to 46 months in prison in largest-ever scheme to import and sell counterfeit and misbranded contact lenses prosecuted in the United States* [Press release]. Retrieved from https://www.fda.gov/inspections-compliance-enforcement-and-criminal-investigations/press-releases/january-18-2017-owner-major-online-colored-contact-lens-business-sentenced-46-months-prison-largest

26. Payne, B. (2016). *White-collar crime: The essentials.* Thousand Oaks, CA: SAGE.

27. Cullen, F. T., Cavender, G., Maakestad, W. J., & Benson, M. L. (2014). *Corporate crime under attack: The fight to criminalize business violence.* New York, NY: Routledge.

28. U.S. Department of Justice. (2016, April 6). *Blankenship sentenced to a year in federal prison. U.S. Attorney's Office, Southern District of West Virginia* [Press release]. Retrieved from https://www.justice.gov/usao-sdwv/pr/blankenship-sentenced-year-federal-prison

29. U.S. Department of Justice. (2015, May 14). *Duke Energy subsidiaries plead guilty and sentenced to pay $102 million for Clean Water Act crimes. Office of Public Affairs.* Retrieved from https://www.justice.gov/opa/pr/duke-energy-subsidiaries-plead-guilty-and-sentenced-pay-102-million-clean-water-act-crimes

30. U.S. Environmental Protection Agency. (2017). *2017 Major criminal cases.* Retrieved from https://www.epa.gov/enforcement/2017-major-criminal-cases

31. U.S. Department of Justice, U.S. Attorney's Office, District of Colorado. (2014, January 28). Statements regarding the sentencing of Eric and Ryan Jensen. Retrieved from https://www.justice.gov/usao-co/pr/statements-regarding-sentencing-eric-and-ryan-jensen

32. Retrieved from https://www.reuters.com/legal/government/former-bumble-bee-ceo-loses-appeal-price-fixing-conviction-2021-07-07/

33. Retrieved from https://www.justice.gov/opa/pr/detroit-area-doctor-sentenced-45-years-prison-providing-medically-unnecessary-chemotherapy

34. Retrieved from https://www.gq.com/story/smilin-bob-enzyte-steve-warshak-male-enhancement

35. Hébert, J., Bittle, S., & Tombs, S. (2019). Obscuring corporate violence: Corporate manslaughter in action. *Howard Journal of Crime and Justice, 58*(4), 554–579.

36. Bureau of Labor Statistics (2020, December 16). *National census of fatal occupational injuries – 2019.* U.S. Department of Labor. Retrieved from https://www.bls.gov/news.release/pdf/cfoi.pdf

37. Bureau of Labor Statistics (2020, November 4). *Employer-reported workplace injuries and illnesses – 2019.* U.S. Department of Labor. Retrieved from https://www.bls.gov/news.release/archives/osh_11042020.pdf

38. Tombs, S. (1999). Health and safety crimes: (In)visibility and the problems of "knowing." In P. Davies (Ed.), *Invisible crimes* (pp. 77–104). London, UK: Palgrave Macmillan.

39. Bal, B. S., & Brenner, L. H. (2016). The law and social values: Medical necessity and criminal prosecution. *Clinical Orthopaedics and Related Research, 474*(4), 887–891.

40. Garrett, B. L. (2020). Wrongful convictions. *Annual Review of Criminology, 3*, 245–259.

41. National Registry of Exonerations. (2020). *Exonerations in 2019.* Retrieved from http://www.law.umich.edu/special/exoneration/Documents/Exonerations_in_2019.pdf

42. National Registry of Exonerations. (n.d.). *Conviction integrity units.* Retrieved from https://www.law.umich.edu/special/exoneration/Pages/Conviction-Integrity-Units.aspx

43. Weber, M. (1919). *Politics as a vocation.* Retrieved from https://web.archive.org/web/20130319092642/http://anthropos-lab.net/wp/wp-content/uploads/2011/12/Weber-Politics-as-a-Vocation.pdf

44. MacManus, T. (2020). State crime. In H. Pontell (Ed.), *Oxford research encyclopedia of criminology and criminal justice* (Online). Oxford, UK: Oxford University Press.

45. United Nations. (n.d.). *Genocide.* Office on Genocide Prevention and the Responsibility to Protect. Retrieved from https://www.un.org/en/genocideprevention/genocide.shtml

46. Green, P., MacManus, T., & de la Cour Venning, A. (2018). *Genocide achieved, genocide continues: Myanmar's annihilation of the Rohingya.* International State Crime Initiative. Retrieved from http://statecrime.org/data/2018/04/ISCI-Rohingya-Report-II-PUBLISHED-VERSION-revised-compressed.pdf

47. Rothe, D. L. (2020). Moving beyond abstract typologies? Overview of state and state-corporate crime. *Journal of White Collar and Corporate Crime, 1*(1), 7–15.

48. Albanese, J. (2015). *Organized crime: From the mob to transnational organized crime, seventh edition.* New York, NY: Routledge.

49. Howell, J. (2015). *The history of street gangs in the United States: Their origins and transformations.* Lanham, MD: Lexington Books.

50. Cressey, D. R. (1969). *Theft of the nation: The structure and operations of organized crime in America.* New York, NY: Harper and Row.

51. Albanese, J. (2015). *Organized crime: From the mob to transnational organized crime, seventh edition.* New York, NY: Routledge.

52. Albanese, J. (2015). *Organized crime: From the mob to transnational organized crim,* (7th ed.). New York, NY: Routledge.

53. United Nations Office of Drugs and Crime. (2010). *The globalization of crime – A transnational organized crime threat assessment.* Vienna: UNODC. Retrieved from https://www.unodc.org/documents/data-and-analysis/tocta/1.The-threat-transnational-organized-crime.pdf

54. Albanese, J., & Reichel, P. (2014). Introduction. In J. Albanese & P. Reichel (Eds.), *Transnational organized crime: An overview from six continents* (pp. 1–6). Thousand Oaks, CA: SAGE.

55. Van Dijk, J., & Spapens, T. (2014). Transnational organized crime networks across the world. In J. Albanese & P. Reichel (Eds.), *Transnational organized crime: An overview from six continents* (pp. 7–28). Thousand Oaks, CA: SAGE.

56. Van Dijk, J., & Spapens, T. (2014). Transnational organized crime networks across the world. In J. Albanese & P. Reichel (Eds.), *Transnational organized crime: An overview from six continents* (pp. 7–28). Thousand Oaks, CA: SAGE.

57. INTERPOL. (2020, November 20). INTERPOL marks a decade of tackling serious organized environmental crime. Retrieved from https://www.interpol.int/en/News-and-Events/News/2020/INTERPOL-marks-a-decade-of-tackling-serious-organized-environmental-crime

58. Rucevska, I., Nelleman, C., Isarin, N., Yang, W., Liu, N., Yu, K., . . . Nilsen, R. (2015). *Waste crime - waste risks: Gaps in meeting the global waste challenge.A UNEP Rapid Response Assessment.* Norway: United Nations Environmental Programme.

59. Bisschop, L. (2016). Illegal trade in hazardous waste. In L. Elliott & W. Schaedla (Eds.), *Handbook of transnational environmental crime* (pp. 190–211). Northampton, MA: Edward Elgar.

60. Stickle, W., Hickman, S., & White, C. (2020). *Human trafficking: A comprehensive exploration of modern day slavery.* Thousand Oaks, CA: SAGE.

61. Preble, K. M. (2019). Under their "control": Perceptions of traffickers' power and coercion among international female trafficking survivors during exploitation. *Victims & Offenders, 14*(2), 199–221.

62. Bouche, V. (2017). *An empirical analysis of the intersection of organized crime and human trafficking in the United States.* National Criminal Justice Reference Service, Office of Justice Programs.

63. Goodey, J. (2008). Human trafficking: Sketchy data and policy responses. *Criminology & Criminal Justice, 8*(4), 421–442.

64. International Labour Organization. (2014). *Profits and poverty: The economics of forced labor.* Retrieved from http://ilo.org/global/publications/ilo-bookstore/order-online/books/WCMS_243391/lang--en/index.htm

65. Campana, P. (2020). Human smuggling: Structure and mechanisms. *Crime and Justice, 49*(1), 471–519.

66. Stickle, W., Hickman, S., & White, C. (2020). *Human trafficking: A comprehensive exploration of modern day slavery.* Thousand Oaks, CA: SAGE.

67. May, C. (2017, March). *Transnational crime and the developing world.* Global Financial Integrity. Retrieved from http://www.gfintegrity.org/wp-content/uploads/2017/03/Transnational_Crime-final.pdf

68. Williams, L., & McKnight, E. (2014). The real impact of counterfeit medications. *U.S. Pharmacist, 39*(6), 44–46.

69. United Nations Office of Drugs and Crime. *Counterfeit products trafficking.* Retrieved from https://www.unodc.org/e4j/en/organized-crime/module-3/key-issues/counterfeit-products-trafficking.html

70. Federal Bureau of Investigation. (n.d.). *Transnational organized crime.* Retrieved from https://www.fbi.gov/investigate/organized-crime#Glossary-of%20Terms

71. Federal Bureau of Investigation. (n.d.). *Most wanted: Tomas Alberto Roque Espinoza.* Retrieved from https://www.fbi.gov/wanted/cei/tomas-alberto-roque

72. Federal Bureau of Investigation. (n.d.). *Most wanted: Fausto Isidro Meza Flores.* Retrieved from https://www.fbi.gov/wanted/cei/fausto-isidro-meza-flores

73. Federal Bureau of Investigation. (n.d.). *Most wanted: Gerard L. Trice, Jr.* Retrieved from https://www.fbi.gov/wanted/cei/gerard-l.-trice-jr

74. Federal Bureau of Investigation. (n.d.). *Most wanted: Criminal enterprise investigations.* Retrieved from https://www.fbi.gov/wanted/cei

75. U.S Food and Drug Administration. (2018, April 4). *Fences indicted in multi-million dollar, multi-state criminal theft operations.* Office of Criminal Investigations. Retrieved from https://www.fda.gov/inspections-compliance-enforcement-and-criminal-investigations/press-releases/april-4-2018-fences-indicted-multi-million-dollar-multi-state-criminal-theft-operations

76. Paoli, L. & Vander Beken, T. (2014). Organized crime: A contested concept. In L. Paoli (Ed.), *The Oxford handbook of organized crime* (pp. 13–31). New York, NY: Oxford University Press.

77. Hagan, F. E. (2006). "Organized Crime" and "organized crime": Indeterminate problems of definition. *Trends in Organized Crime, 9*(4), 127–137.

78. Decker, S., & Pyrooz, D. (2015). Street gangs, terrorists, drug smugglers, and organized crime. In S. Decker & D. Pyrooz (Eds.), *The handbook of gangs* (pp. 294–308). Hoboken, NJ: John Wiley & Sons.

79. National Gang Center. (2020, July). *Highlights of gang-related legislation.* Retrieved from https://www.nationalgangcenter.gov/Legislation/Highlights

80. National Institute of Justice. (2011, October 27). *What is a gang? Definitions.* Retrieved from https://nij.ojp.gov/topics/articles/what-gang-definitions#note2

81. Howell, J. C., & Griffiths, E. (2019). *Gangs in America's communities* (3rd ed.). Thousand Oaks, CA: SAGE.

82. U.S. Department of Justice. (2020, December 10). *40 charged in largest federal racketeering conspiracy in South Carolina history.* Office of Public Affairs. Retrieved from https://www.justice.gov/opa/pr/40-charged-largest-federal-racketeering-conspiracy-south-carolina-history

83. Barrett, B. (2018, August 19). How to protect yourself against a SIM swap attack. *Wired Magazine.* Retrieved from https://www.wired.com/story/sim-swap-attack-defend-phone/

84. Francheschi-Bicchierai, L. (2018, July 17). The SIM hijackers. *Motherboard: Tech by Vice.* Retrieved from https://www.vice.com/en_us/article/vbqax3/hackers-sim-swapping-steal-phone-numbers-instagram-bitcoin

85. Maimon, D., & Louderback, E. R. (2019). Cyber-dependent crimes: An interdisciplinary review. *Annual Review of Criminology, 2,* 191–216.

86. Seebruck, R. (2015). A typology of hackers: Classifying cyber malfeasance using a weighted arc circumplex model. *Digital Investigation, 14,* 36–45.

87. Maimon, D., & Louderback, E. R. (2019). Cyber-dependent crimes: An interdisciplinary review. *Annual Review of Criminology, 2,* 191–216.

88. Holt, T. J. (2017). On the value of honeypots to produce policy recommendations. *Criminology & Public Policy, 16,* 737–745.

89. NCA. (2016). *NCA strategic cyber industry group cybercrime assessment 2016.* National Crime Agency, Strategic Cybercrime Industry Group, London. Retrieved from https://www.nationalcrimeagency.gov.uk/who-we-are/publications/357-cyber-crime-assessment-2016/file

90. Romagna, M. (2020). Hacktivism: Conceptualization, techniques, and historical overview. In T. Holt & A. Bossler (Eds.), *Palgrave handbook of international cybercrime and cyberdeviance* (pp. 743–769). London, UK: Palgrave Macmillan.

91. Decker, E. (2019). Full count? Crime rate swings, cybercrime misses and why we don't really know the score. *Journal of National Security Law & Policy, 10,* 583–604.

92. Federal Bureau of Investigation. (2020, February 11). *2019 Internet crime report.* Retrieved from https://pdf.ic3.gov/2019_IC3Report.pdf

93. Reinhart, R.J. (2018, December 10). *One in four Americans have experienced cybercrime.* Gallup. Retrieved from https://news.gallup.com/poll/245336/one-four-americans-experienced-cybercrime.aspx

94. Anderson, R., Barton, C., Bölme, R., Clayton, R., Ganán, C., Grasso, T., . . . Vasek, M. (2019). Measuring the changing cost of cybercrime. Presented at the 2019 Workshop on the Economics of Information Security, Boston, U.S., June 3-4, 2019.

95. Ward, P. R., Lord, R., & Navratil, L. (October 27, 2018). 29 federal charges filed against shooting suspect Robert Bowers—Social posts attributed to suspect may provide clues. *Pittsburgh Post-Gazette.* Retrieved from https://www.post-gazette.com/news/crime-courts/2018/10/27/squirrel-hill-synagogue-shooting-suspect-pittsburgh-mass-officers-victims-casualties/stories/201810270072

96. Belew, K. (August 4, 2019). The right way to understand white nationalist terrorism. *The New York Times.* Retrieved from https://www.nytimes.com/2019/08/04/opinion/el-paso-terrorism.html?searchResultPosition=28

97. Federal Bureau of Investigation. (n.d.). *Hate crimes.* Retrieved from https://www.fbi.gov/investigate/civil-rights/hate-crimes

98. Stotzer, R. L., & Sabagala, A. P. (2020). "Message" crimes: Understanding the community impacts of bias crime. In R. J. Sternberg (Ed.), *Perspectives on hate: How it originates, develops, manifests, and spreads* (pp. 251–276). American Psychological Association. doi:10.1037/0000180-012

99. Meli, L. (2014). Hate crime and punishment: Why typical punishment does not fit the crime. *University of Illinois Law Review, 2014,* 921–966.

100. The Matthew Shepard and James Byrd, Jr., Hate Crimes Prevention Act of 2009, Pub. L. No. 111-83, 18 U.S.C. § 249 (2009). https://www.justice.gov/crt/matthew-shepard-and-james-byrd-jr-hate-crimes-prevention-act-2009-0

101. U.S. Department of Justice. (n.d.). *Federal laws and statutes.* Retrieved from https://www.justice.gov/hatecrimes/laws-and-policies

102. Kena, G., & Thompson, A. (2021, September). *Hate crime victimization, 2005-2019.* Washington, DC: U.S. Department of Justice. Retrieved from https://bjs.ojp.gov/library/publications/hate-crime-victimization-2005-2019

103. Federal Bureau of Investigation. Hate crime. *Uniform Crime Reports.* Retrieved from https://ucr.fbi.gov/hate-crime

104. Pezzella, F. S., Fetzer, M. D., & Keller, T. (2019). The dark figure of hate crime underreporting. *American Behavioral Scientist,* 1–24.

105. Chakraborti, N. (2018). Responding to hate crime: Escalating problems, continued failings. *Criminology & Criminal Justice, 18*(4), 387–404.

106. Haas, S. M., Nolan, J. J., Turley, E., & Stump, J. (2011). *Assessing the validity of hate crime reporting: An analysis of NIBRS data.* Charleston, WV: Criminal Justice Statistical Analysis Center.

107. McDevitt, J., & Iwama, J. A. (2016). Challenges in measuring and understanding hate crime. In B. Huebner & T. Bynum (Eds.), *The handbook of measurement issues in criminology*

and criminal justice (pp. 131–156). Malden, MA: John Wiley & Sons.

108. WHAM-TV. (June 20, 2015). *FBI director: Charleston shooting not terrorism.* Retrieved from https://web.archive.org/web/20150628135934/http://13wham.com/news/features/nation-news/stories/fbi-director-charleston-shooting-not-terrorism-3408.shtml

109. Federal Bureau of Investigation. (n.d.). *Terrorism.* Retrieved from https://www.fbi.gov/investigate/terrorism

110. 18 U.S. Code § 2331. Definitions. Terrorism. Retrieved from https://www.law.cornell.edu/uscode/text/18/2331

111. Deloughery, K., King, R. D., & Asal, V. (2012). Close cousins or distant relatives? The relationship between terrorism and hate crime. *Crime & Delinquency, 58*(5), 663–688.

112. Groll, E. (June 18, 2015). Was the Charleston massacre an act of terrorism? *Foreign Policy.* Retrieved from https://foreignpolicy.com/2015/06/18/was-the-charleston-massacre-an-act-of-terrorism/

113. Jenkins, B. M. (2009). In G. Lester, Social acceptability of domestic intelligence. In B. Jackson (Ed.), *The challenge of domestic intelligence in a free society.* Santa Monica, CA: RAND Corporation.

114. Mills, C. E., Freilich, J. D., & Chermak, S. M. (2017). Extreme hatred: revisiting the hate crime and terrorism relationship to determine whether they are "close cousins" or "distant relatives." *Crime & Delinquency, 63*, 1191–1223.

115. Anders Behring Breivik: The indictment. (2012, April 16). *The Guardian.* Retrieved from https://www.theguardian.com/world/2012/apr/16/anders-behring-breivik-indictment

116. Seierstad, Å. (2015). *One of us: The story of Anders Breivik and the massacre in Norway.* New York, NY: Macmillan.

117. Schuurman, B., Lindekilde, L., Malthaner, S., O'Connor, F., Gill, P., & Bouhana, N. (2019). End of the lone wolf: The typology that should not have been. *Studies in Conflict & Terrorism, 42*(8), 771–778.

118. Schuurman, B., Lindekilde, L., Malthaner, S., O'Connor, F., Gill, P., & Bouhana, N. (2019). End of the lone wolf: The typology that should not have been. *Studies in Conflict & Terrorism, 42*(8), 771–778.

119. Schuurman, B., Bakker, E., Gill, P., & Bouhana, N. (2018). Lone actor terrorist attack planning and preparation: A data-driven analysis. *Journal of Forensic Sciences, 63*(4), 1191–1200.

120. McCauley, C., & Moskalenko, S. (2008). Mechanisms of political radicalization: Pathways toward terrorism. *Terrorism and Political Violence, 20*, 415–433.

121. National Consortium for the Study of Terrorism and Responses to Terrorism. (n.d.). *Profiles of individual radicalization in the United States (PIRUS).* Retrieved from https://www.start.umd.edu/data-tools/profiles-individual-radicalization-united-states-pirus

122. National Consortium for the Study of Terrorism and Responses to Terrorism. (n.d.). *PIRUS – Frequently asked questions.* Retrieved from https://www.start.umd.edu/pirus-frequently-asked-questions#q7

123. Moghaddam, F. M. (2005). The staircase to terrorism: A psychological exploration. *American Psychologist, 60*(2), 161–169.

124. Fiske, A. P., & Rai, T. S. (2014). *Virtuous violence: Hurting and killing to create, sustain, end, and honor social relationships.* Cambridge, UK: Cambridge University Press.

125. Borum, R. (2017). The etiology of radicalization. In G. LaFree & G. Freilich (Eds.), *The handbook of the criminology of terrorism* (pp. 17–32). Malden, MA: John Wiley & Sons.

126. Saiya, N. (2020). Confronting apocalyptic terrorism: Lessons from France and Japan. *Studies in Conflict & Terrorism, 43*(9), 775–795.

127. Borum, R. (2017). The etiology of radicalization. In G. LaFree & G. Freilich (Eds.), *The handbook of the criminology of terrorism* (pp. 17–32). Malden, MA: John Wiley & Sons.

128. McCauley, C., & Moskalenko, S. (2017). Understanding political radicalization: The two-pyramids model. *American Psychologist, 72*(3), 205.

CHAPTER 5

1. Feng, Z. (2021, March 18). *Atlanta shootings: Suspect charged with murder as victims identified.* BBC News. Retrieved from https://www.bbc.com/news/world-us-canada-56433181

2. Holcombe, M., Yan, H., & Vera, A. (2021, March 19). *Victims of the spa shootings highlight the vulnerability of working-class Asian women as more Asian Americans get attacked.* CNN. Retrieved from https://www.cnn.com/2021/03/18/us/metro-atlanta-shootings-thursday/index.html

3. Sun-Times Wire. (2021, March 16). Duo charged with attempted murder, carjacking in Lawndale. *Chicago Sun Times.* Retrieved from https://chicago.suntimes.com/crime/2021/3/16/22335196/duo-charged-attempted-murder-carjacking-lawndale

4. Cullotta, K., & Sobol, R. (2021, March 17). Bail denied for two men charged with attempted murder, carjacking in attacks minutes apart in Lawndale neighborhood. *Chicago Tribune.* Retrieved from https://www.chicagotribune.com/news/breaking/ct-attempted-murder-carjacking-charges-20210317-tx2imztpebcu3j65j5hxqdsk5y-story.html

5. Young, M. (2021, March 13). Arrest made in fatal drive-by shooting in Bradenton. The murder suspect is 15. *Bradenton Herald.* Retrieved from https://www.bradenton.com/news/local/crime/article249920288.html

6. Shaw, A. (2021, March 17). Second teenager arrested in fatal Bradenton shooting of Antonio Aguirre. *Herald Tribune.* Retrieved from https://www.heraldtribune.com/story/news/crime/2021/03/17/second-15-year-old-arrested-fatal-bradenton-shooting-police-report/4730299001/

7. Associated Press. (2021, March 12). *Mesa police arrest suspect in theft of car with boy inside.* Retrieved from https://apnews.com/article/arrests-mesa-kidnapping-theft-c7f5de9f8ae4347ff358bf7e416e5393

8. Goodman, J. (2021, March 12). Weeklong search leads to arrest of Mesa man accused of stealing car with child inside. *AZ Family.* Retrieved from https://www.azfamily.com/news/weeklong-search-leads-to-arrest-of-mesa-man-accused-of-stealing-car-with-child-inside/article_d9fae682-8365-11eb-85a6-432827798645.html

9. Mallicoat, S. (2019). *Women, gender, and crime.* Thousand Oaks, CA: SAGE.

10. Cunneen, C., & Tauri, J. M. (2019). Indigenous peoples, criminology, and criminal justice. *Annual Review of Criminology, 2,* 359–381.

11. Nielsen, M. O. (2019). *Native Americans, crime, and justice.* New York, NY: Routledge.

12. Wilson, S., & Kordenbrock, M. (2019, April 14). Native American homicide rates are soaring, but causes aren't clear due to inconsistent data. *Billings Gazette.* Retrieved from https://billingsgazette.com /news/state-and-regional/mmiw/native-american-homicide-rates-are-soaring-but-causes-aren-t-clear-due -to-inconsistent-data/article_cd39d5e5-0bae-5f6d-9da5-99 4e3e8bdbd6.html

13. Maguire, M., & McVie, S. (2017). Crime data and criminal statistics: A critical reflection. In A. Liebling, L. McAra, & S. Maruna (Eds.), *Oxford handbook of criminology* (pp. 163–189). Oxford, UK: Oxford University Press.

14. Slocum, L. A., Huebner, B. M., Greene, C., & Rosenfeld, R. (2020). Enforcement trends in the city of St. Louis from 2007 to 2017: Exploring variability in arrests and criminal summonses over time and across communities. *Journal of Community Psychology, 48*(1), 36–67.

15. Kohler-Hausmann, I. (2018). *Misdemeanorland: Criminal courts and social control in an age of broken windows policing.* Princeton, NJ: Princeton University Press.

16. Britt, C. L. (2019). Age and crime. In D. Farrington, A. Piquero, & L. Kazemian (Eds.), *The Oxford handbook of developmental and life-course criminology* (pp. 13–33). Oxford, UK: Oxford University Press.

17. Steffensmeier, D., Zhong, H., & Lu, Y. (2017). Age and its relation to crime in Taiwan and the United States: Invariant, or does cultural context matter? *Criminology, 55*(2), 377–404.

18. Loeber, R., & Farrington, D. (2018). Age-crime curve. In G. Bruinsma & D. Weisburd (Eds.), *Encyclopedia of criminology and criminal justice* (pp. 12–18). New York, NY: Springer.

19. Fabio, A., Tu, L. C., Loeber, R., & Cohen, J. (2011). Neighborhood socioeconomic disadvantage and the shape of the age–crime curve. *American Journal of Public Health, 101*(S1), S325–S332.

20. DeCamp, W., & Zaykowski, H. (2015). Developmental victimology: Estimating group victimization trajectories in the age–victimization curve. *International Review of Victimology, 21*(3), 255–272.

21. Bersani, B. E., & Doherty, E. E. (2018). Desistance from offending in the twenty-first century. *Annual Review of Criminology, 1,* 311–334.

22. Moffitt, T. (2018). Male antisocial behaviour in adolescence and beyond. *Nature Human Behaviour, 2*(3), 177–186.

23. Steinberg, L. (2017). Adolescent brain science and juvenile justice policymaking. *Psychology, Public Policy, and Law, 23*(4), 410–420.

24. Do, K. T., Prinstein, M. J., & Telzer, E. H. (2020). Neurobiological susceptibility to peer influence in adolescence. In K. C. Kadosh (Ed.), *The Oxford handbook of developmental cognitive neuroscience.* Oxford, UK: Oxford University Press.

25. Mizel, M. L., & Abrams, L. S. (2018). What I'd tell my 16-year-old self: Criminal desistance, young adults, and psychosocial maturation. *International Journal of Offender Therapy and Comparative Criminology, 62*(10), 3038–3057.

26. Stolzenberg, L., & D'Alessio, S. J. (2008). Co-offending and the age-crime curve. *Journal of Research in Crime and Delinquency, 45*(1), 65–86.

27. Federal Bureau of Investigation. (2020). *Homicide offender vs. victim demographics* [Data set]. Crime Data Explorer. Retrieved from https://crime-data-explorer.fr.cloud.gov/pa ges/explorer/crime/crime-trend

28. Krohn, M. D., Curry, J. P., & Nelson-Kilger, S. (1983). Is chivalry dead? An analysis of changes in police dispositions of males and females. *Criminology, 21*(3), 417–437.

29. Visher, C. A. (1983). Gender, police arrest decisions, and notions of chivalry. *Criminology, 21*(1), 5–28.

30. Wagner, B. M. (2019). Chivalry and arrests. In F. Bernat & K. Frailing (Eds.), *The encyclopedia of women and crime.* Hoboken, NJ: John Wiley & Sons.

31. Javaid, A. (2020). *Violence in everyday life: Power, gender and sexuality.* London, UK: Zed Books.

32. Messerschmidt, J. W. (2018). *Masculinities and crime: A quarter century of theory and research.* Lanham, MD: Rowman & Littlefield.

33. Belknap, J. (2020). *The invisible woman: Gender, crime, and justice.* Thousand Oaks, CA: SAGE.

34. Jones, N. (2009). *Between good and ghetto: African American girls and inner-city violence.* New Brunswick, NJ: Rutgers University Press.

35. Schwartz, J., & Steffensmeier, D. (2017). Gendered opportunities and risk preferences for offending across the life course. *Journal of Developmental and Life-Course Criminology, 3*(2), 126–150.

36. Britton, D. M., Jacobsen, S. K., & Howard, G. E. (2017). *The gender of crime.* Lanham, MD: Rowman & Littlefield.

37. Lauritsen, J. L., Heimer, K., & Lynch, J. P. (2009). Trends in the gender gap in violent offending: New evidence from the National Crime Victimization Survey. *Criminology, 47*(2), 361–399.

38. Wang, T. (2021). Mismatched liberation theory: A comparative method to explain increasing female crime share in the United States. *Feminist Criminology, 16*(5), 1–36.

39. Estrada, F., Bäckman, O., & Nilsson, A. (2016). The darker side of equality? The declining gender gap in crime: Historical trends and an enhanced analysis of staggered birth cohorts. *British Journal of Criminology, 56*(6), 1272–1290.

40. U.S. Census Bureau. (2020, September 15). Income and poverty in the United States: 2019. Table B-1. People in poverty by selected characteristics: 2018 and 2019. Retrieved from https://www.census.gov/library/publications/2020/demo/ p60-270.html

41. U.S. Census Bureau. (2020, September 15). Income and poverty in the United States: 2019. Table B-2. Families and

people in poverty by type of family: 2018 and 2019. Retrieved from https://www.census.gov/library/publications/2020/demo/p60-270.html

42. Roth, J. J., & King, L. L. (2019). Sex-based predictors of male and female property crime arrest rates: Disadvantage and drug use. *Women & Criminal Justice, 29*(2), 112–127.

43. Vaughan, T. J., Pollock, J., & Vandiver, D. M. (2015). Sex differences in arrest for juvenile assaults. *Violence and Gender, 2*(1), 24–34.

44. Estrada, F., Bäckman, O., & Nilsson, A. (2016). The darker side of equality? The declining gender gap in crime: Historical trends and an enhanced analysis of staggered birth cohorts. *British Journal of Criminology, 56*(6), 1272–1290.

45. Sharkey, P., Besbris, M., & Friedson, M. (2016). Poverty and crime. In D. Brady & L. Burton (Eds.), *The Oxford handbook of the social science of poverty* (pp. 623–636). Oxford, UK: Oxford University Press.

46. Payne, B. K. (2016). *White-collar crime: The essentials.* Thousand Oaks, CA: SAGE.

47. Schauer, P. (Ed.) (2018). *Homelessness and street crime.* New York, NY: Greenhaven Press.

48. Clarke, R., & Felson, M. (2017). Introduction: Criminology, routine activity, and rational choice. In R. Lambert (Ed.), *Routine activity and rational choice* (Vol. 5). New York, NY: Taylor & Francis.

49. Foley, C. F. (2011). Welfare payments and crime. *Review of Economics and Statistics, 93*(1), 97–112.

50. Duck, W. (2015). *No way out: Precarious living in the shadow of poverty and drug dealing.* Chicago, IL: University of Chicago Press.

51. Billings, S., & Hoekstra, M. (2019). *Schools, neighborhoods, and the long-run effect of crime-prone peers* (Working Paper No. 25730). National Bureau of Economic Research. Retrieved from https://papers.ssrn.com/sol3/papers.cfm?abstract_id=3368020

52. Ha, Y., Thomas, M. M., Byrne, T., & Miller, D. P. (2020). Patterns of multiple instability among low-income families with children. *Social Service Review, 94*(1), 129–168.

53. Bosick, S. J., & Fomby, P. (2018). Family instability in childhood and criminal offending during the transition into adulthood. *American Behavioral Scientist, 62*(11), 1483–1504.

54. Sharkey, P., Besbris, M., & Friedson, M. (2016). Poverty and crime. In D. Brady & L. Burton (Eds.), *The Oxford handbook of the social science of poverty* (pp. 623–636). Oxford, UK: Oxford University Press.

55. Hipp, J. R., & Yates, D. K. (2011). Ghettos, thresholds, and crime: Does concentrated poverty really have an accelerating increasing effect on crime? *Criminology, 49*(4), 955–990.

56. Sharkey, P., Besbris, M., & Friedson, M. (2016). Poverty and crime. In D. Brady & L. Burton (Eds.), *The Oxford handbook of the social science of poverty* (pp. 623–636). Oxford, UK: Oxford University Press.

57. Hirschfield, P. J. (2018). Schools and crime. *Annual Review of Criminology, 1*, 149–169.

58. Morris, M. (2016). *Pushout: The criminalization of Black girls in schools.* New York, NY: New Press.

59. Ewert, S., Sykes, B. L., & Pettit, B. (2014). The degree of disadvantage: Incarceration and inequality in education. *ANNALS of the American Academy of Political and Social Science, 651*(1), 24–43.

60. Ewert, S., Sykes, B. L., & Pettit, B. (2014). The degree of disadvantage: Incarceration and inequality in education. *ANNALS of the American Academy of Political and Social Science, 651*(1), 24–43.

61. Pettit, B., & Western, B. (2004). Mass imprisonment and the life course: Race and class inequality in US incarceration. *American Sociological Review, 69*(2), 151–169

62. Sweeten, G., Bushway, S. D., & Paternoster, R. (2009). Does dropping out of school mean dropping into delinquency? *Criminology, 47*(1), 47–91.

63. Savolainen, J., Hughes, L. A., Mason, W. A., Hurtig, T. M., Ebeling, H., Moilanen, I. K., Kivivuori, J., & Taanila, A. M. (2012). Antisocial propensity, adolescent school outcomes, and the risk of criminal conviction. *Journal of Research on Adolescence, 22*(1), 54–64.

64. Sweeten, G., Bushway, S. D., & Paternoster, R. (2009). Does dropping out of school mean dropping into delinquency? *Criminology, 47*(1), 47–91.

65. Na, C. (2017). The consequences of school dropout among serious adolescent offenders: More offending? More arrest? Both? *Journal of Research in Crime and Delinquency, 54*(1), 78–110.

66. Dennison, C. R. (2020). Dropping out of college and dropping into crime. *Justice Quarterly*, 1–27.

67. Barnes, J. C. (2018). A constructivist view of race in modern criminology. *Journal of Criminal Justice, 59*, 81–86.

68. Zuberi, T., & Bonilla-Silva, E. (Eds.). (2008). *White logic, white methods: Racism and methodology.* Lanham, MD: Rowman & Littlefield.

69. Martinez-Cola, M., with, English, R., Min, J., Peraza, J., Tambah, J., & Yebuah, C. (2018). When pedagogy is painful: Teaching in tumultuous times. *Teaching Sociology, 46*(2), 97–111.

70. Beck, A. (2021, January). *Statistical brief: Race and ethnicity of violent crime offenders and arrestees, 2018.* Washington, DC: U.S. Department of Justice.

71. U.S. Census Bureau. (2021, August 12). *Race and ethnicity in the United States: 2010 census and 2020 census.* Retrieved from https://www.census.gov/library/visualizations/interactive/race-and-ethnicity-in-the-united-state-2010-and-2020-census.html

72. Frey, W. (2019, June 24). *Less than half of US children under 15 are white, census shows.* Brookings Institution. Retrieved from https://www.brookings.edu/research/less-than-half-of-us-children-under-15-are-white-census-shows/

73. Frey, W. (2021, July 1). The nation is diversifying even faster than predicted, according to new census data. Brookings Institution. Retrieved from https://www.brookings.edu/research/new-census-data-shows-the-nation-is-diversifying-even-faster-than-predicted/

74. U.S. Census Bureau. (2020, June). *Population and housing using estimates: Population distribution in the United States in 2019, by generation.* Retrieved from https://www.census.gov/

75. Unnever, J. D., Barnes, J. C., & Cullen, F. T. (2016). The racial invariance thesis revisited: Testing an African American theory of offending. *Journal of Contemporary Criminal Justice, 32*(1), 7–26.

76. Unnever, J. D., & Gabbidon, S. L. (2011). *A theory of African American offending: Race, racism, and crime.* New York, NY: Routledge.

77. Brown, J. A. (2016). Running on fear: Immigration, race and crime framings in contemporary GOP presidential debate discourse. *Critical Criminology, 24*(3), 315–331.

78. Gallup. (2017, June 28). *Americans more positive about effects of immigration.* Retrieved from https://news.gallup.com/poll/213146/americans-positive-effects-immigration.aspx

79. Ousey, G. C., & Kubrin, C. E. (2018). Immigration and crime: Assessing a contentious issue. *Annual Review of Criminology, 1*, 63–84.

80. Ousey, G. C., & Kubrin, C. E. (2018). Immigration and crime: Assessing a contentious issue. *Annual Review of Criminology, 1*, 63–84.

81. Ferraro, V. (2016). Immigration and crime in the new destinations, 2000–2007: A test of the disorganizing effect of migration. *Journal of Quantitative Criminology, 32*(1), 23–45.

82. Sampson, R. J. (2017). Immigration and the new social transformation of the American city. In D. Vitiello & T. Sugrue (Eds.), *Immigration and metropolitan revitalization in the United States* (pp. 11–24). Philadelphia: University of Pennsylvania Press.

83. Shihadeh, E. S., & Barranco, R. E. (2010). Latino employment and Black violence: The unintended consequence of U.S. immigration policy. *Social Forces, 88*(3), 1393–1420.

84. Gunadi, C. (2021). On the association between undocumented immigration and crime in the United States. *Oxford Economic Papers, 73*(1), 200–224.

85. Light, M. T., & Miller, T. (2018). Does undocumented immigration increase violent crime? *Criminology, 56*(2), 370–401.

86. Light, M. T., Miller, T., & Kelly, B. C. (2017). Undocumented immigration, drug problems, and driving under the influence in the United States, 1990–2014. *American Journal of Public Health, 107*(9), 1448–1454.

87. Martinez, R., Jr. (2010). Economic conditions and racial/ethnic variations in violence: Immigration, the Latino paradox, and future research. *Criminology & Public Policy, 9*, 707–714.

88. Rima, D., Yerbol, A., Batyrbek, S., Orynbassar, T., & Beaver, K. M. (2019). Examining the potential association between immigration and criminal involvement using a nationally representative and longitudinal sample of youth. *Journal of Interpersonal Violence, 36*, 1–21.

89. Chouhy, C. (2018). Segmented assimilation and crime: Rethinking the relationship between assimilation and crime. In H. V. Miller & A. Peguero (Eds.), *Routledge handbook on immigration and crime.* New York, NY: Routledge.

90. Froyum, C. (2020). Understanding institutions: Family. In K. Korgen & M. Atkinson (Eds.), *Sociology in action.* Thousand Oaks, CA: SAGE.

91. Farrington, D. P. (2011). Families and crime. In J. Wilson & J. Petersilia (Eds.), *Crime and public policy* (pp. 130–157). Oxford, UK: Oxford University Press.

92. Livingston, G. (2018, April 27). *About one-third of U.S. children are living with an unmarried parent.* Pew Research Center. Retrieved from https://www.pewresearch.org/fact-tank/2018/04/27/about-one-third-of-u-s-children-are-living-with-an-unmarried-parent/

93. Livingston, G. (2018, April 25). *The changing profile of unmarried parents.* Pew Research Center. Retrieved from https://www.pewresearch.org/social-trends/2018/04/25/the-changing-profile-of-unmarried-parents/

94. Hadfield, K., Amos, M., Ungar, M., Gosselin, J., & Ganong, L. (2018). Do changes to family structure affect child and family outcomes? A systematic review of the instability hypothesis. *Journal of Family Theory & Review, 10*(1), 87–110.

95. Barnhart, S., & Maguire-Jack, K. (2016). Single mothers in their communities: The mediating role of parenting stress and depression between social cohesion, social control and child maltreatment. *Children and Youth Services Review, 70*, 37–45.

96. Mackler, J. S., Kelleher, R. T., Shanahan, L., Calkins, S. D., Keane, S. P., & O'Brien, M. (2015). Parenting stress, parental reactions, and externalizing behavior from ages 4 to 10. *Journal of Marriage and Family, 77*(2), 388–406.

97. Gottman, J. M. (2014). *What predicts divorce? The relationship between marital processes and marital outcomes.* New York, NY: Psychology Press.

98. van Dijk, R., van der Valk, I. E., Deković, M., & Branje, S. J. (2020). A meta-analysis on interparental conflict, parenting, and child adjustment in divorced families: Examining mediation using meta-analytic structural equation models. *Clinical Psychology Review, 79*, 101861.

99. Jensen, T. M., & Lippold, M. A. (2018). Patterns of stepfamily relationship quality and adolescents' short-term and long-term adjustment. *Journal of Family Psychology, 32*(8), 1130.

100. Pinquart, M. (2017). Associations of parenting dimensions and styles with externalizing problems of children and adolescents: An updated meta-analysis. *Developmental Psychology, 53*(5), 873.

101. Nguyen, H., & Loughran, T. A. (2018). On the measurement and identification of turning points in criminology. *Annual Review of Criminology, 1*, 335–358.

102. Barnes, J. C., Golden, K., Mancini, C., Boutwell, B. B., Beaver, K. M., & Diamond, B. (2014). Marriage and involvement in crime: A consideration of reciprocal effects in a nationally representative sample. *Justice Quarterly, 31*(2), 229–256.

103. Giordano, P. C., Seffrin, P. M., Manning, W. D., & Longmore, M. A. (2011). Parenthood and crime: The role of wantedness, relationships with partners, and SES. *Journal of Criminal Justice, 39*(5), 405–416.

104. Pyrooz, D. C., McGloin, J. M., & Decker, S. H. (2017). Parenthood as a turning point in the life course for male and female gang members: A study of within-individual changes in gang membership and criminal behavior. *Criminology, 55*(4), 869–899.

105. Ziegler, J. A., Kuhl, D. C., Swisher, R. R., & Chavez, J. M. (2017). Parenthood residency status and criminal desistance across neighborhood contexts. *Deviant Behavior, 38*(1), 17–33.

106. Hayslip Jr, B., Fruhauf, C. A., & Dolbin-MacNab, M. L. (2019). Grandparents raising grandchildren: What have we learned over the past decade? *The Gerontologist, 59*(3), e152–e163.

107. Chung, H. L., & Steinberg, L. (2006). Relations between neighborhood factors, parenting behaviors, peer deviance, and delinquency among serious juvenile offenders. *Developmental Psychology, 42*(2), 319–331.

108. Abdullah, A., Emery, C. R., & Jordan, L. P. (2020). Neighbourhood collective efficacy and protective effects on child maltreatment: A systematic literature review. *Health & Social Care in the Community, 28*(6), 1863–1883.

109. Gillespie, L. K. (2015). Family disorganization and crime. In W. Jennings (Ed.), *The encyclopedia of crime and punishment* (pp. 1–4). New York, NY: John Wiley & Sons.

110. Pew Research Center. (2020, June 11). *Unemployment rose higher in three months of COVID-19 than it did in two years of the Great Recession.* Retrieved from https://www.pewresearch.org/fact-tank/2020/06/11/unemployment-rose-higher-in-three-months-of-covid-19-than-it-did-in-two-years-of-the-great-recession/

111. Alegretto, S., & Pitts, S. (2010). *The Great Recession, jobless recoveries, and Black workers.* Joint Center for Political and Economic Studies. Retrieved from https://laborcenter.berkeley.edu/pdf/2010/the-great-recession.pdf

112. Pew Research Center. (2020, June 11). *Unemployment rose higher in three months of COVID-19 than it did in two years of the Great Recession.* Retrieved from https://www.pewresearch.org/fact-tank/2020/06/11/unemployment-rose-higher-in-three-months-of-covid-19-than-it-did-in-two-years-of-the-great-recession/

113. Cunningham, E. (2018, April). Great Recession, great recovery? Trends from the Current Population Survey. *Monthly Labor Review,* U.S. Bureau of Labor Statistics. Retrieved from https://www.bls.gov/opub/mlr/2018/article/great-recession-great-recovery.htm

114. Ghosh, P. K. (2018). The short-run effects of the great recession on crime. *Journal of Economics, Race, and Policy, 1*(2), 92–111.

115. Uggen, C. (2012). *Crime and the Great Recession.* Stanford, CA: Stanford Center on Poverty and Inequality.

116. Cantor, D., & Land, K. C. (1985). Unemployment and crime rates in the post-World War II United States: A theoretical and empirical analysis. *American Sociological Review, 50*(3), 317–332.

117. Kleck, G., & Jackson, D. (2016). What kind of joblessness affects crime? A national case–control study of serious property crime. *Journal of Quantitative Criminology, 32*(4), 489–513.

118. Siwach, G. (2018). Unemployment shocks for individuals on the margin: Exploring recidivism effects. *Labour Economics, 52,* 231–244.

119. Schneider, D., Harknett, K., & McLanahan, S. (2016). Intimate partner violence in the great recession. *Demography, 53*(2), 471–505.

120. Dollar, C. B., Donnelly, E. A., & Parker, K. F. (2019). Joblessness, poverty, and neighborhood crime: Testing Wilson's assertions of jobless poverty. *Social Currents, 6*(4), 343–360.

121. Chalfin, A., & McCrary, J. (2018). Are U.S. cities under-policed? Theory and evidence. *Review of Economics and Statistics, 100*(1), 167–186.

122. Kirk, D. S., & Wakefield, S. (2018). Collateral consequences of punishment: A critical review and path forward. *Annual Review of Criminology, 1,* 171–194.

123. Shannon, S. K., Uggen, C., Schnittker, J., Thompson, M., Wakefield, S., & Massoglia, M. (2017). The growth, scope, and spatial distribution of people with felony records in the United States, 1948–2010. *Demography, 54*(5), 1795–1818.

124. Rose, E. (2018). *The effects of job loss on crime: Evidence from administrative data.* University of Chicago. Retrieved from SSRN 2991317: https://ssrn.com/abstract=2991317

125. Rosenfeld, R. (2018). Studying crime trends: Normal science and exogenous shocks. *Criminology, 56*(1), 5–26.

126. Rosenfeld, R., & Levin, A. (2016). Acquisitive crime and inflation in the United States: 1960–2012. *Journal of Quantitative Criminology, 32*(3), 427–447.

127. Zuckerman, P. (2020). *Society without God: What the least religious nations can tell us about contentment.* New York: NYU Press.

128. Lipka, M., & Wormald, B. (2016, February 29). *How religious is your state?* Pew Research Center. Retrieved from https://www.pewresearch.org/fact-tank/2016/02/29/how-religious-is-your-state/?state=alabama

129. Sumter, M., Wood, F., Whitaker, I., & Berger-Hill, D. (2018). Religion and crime studies: Assessing what has been learned. *Religions, 9*(6), 193.

130. Jang, S. J. (2019). Religiosity, crime, and drug use among juvenile offenders: A latent growth modeling approach. *Journal of Quantitative Criminology, 35*(1), 27–60.

131. Sturgis, P. W., & Baller, R. D. (2012). Religiosity and deviance: An examination of the moral community and antiasceticism hypotheses among U.S. adults. *Journal for the Scientific Study of Religion, 51*(4), 809–820.

132. Jang, S. J., Johnson, B. R., Hays, J., Hallett, M., & Duwe, G. (2018). Religion and misconduct in "Angola" prison: Conversion, congregational participation, religiosity, and self-identities. *Justice Quarterly, 35*(3), 412–442.

133. Perrin, C., Blagden, N., Winder, B., & Norman, C. (2018). Religion and desistance: Working with sexual and violent offenders. In K. Kerley (Ed.), *Finding freedom in confinement: The role of religion in prison life* (pp. 24–42). Santa Barbara, CA: ABC-CLIO.

134. Johnson, B., & Jang, S. (2010). Crime and religion: Assessing the role of the faith factor. In R. Rosenfeld, K. Quinet, & C. Garcia, (Eds.), *Contemporary issues in criminological theory and research: The role of social institutions* (pp. 117–149). Belmont, CA: Wadsworth.

135. Guo, S. (2020). Developmental patterns of religiosity in relation to criminal trajectories among serious offenders moving from adolescence to young adult. *Crime & Delinquency, 67,* 1–31.

136. Jang, S. J., & Johnson, B. R. (2017). Religion, spirituality, and desistance from crime. In A. Blokland & A. van der Geest (Eds.), *International handbook of criminal careers and life-course criminology* (pp. 74–86). New York, NY: Routledge.

137. Hallett, M., & McCoy, J. S. (2015). Religiously motivated desistance: An exploratory study. *International Journal of Offender Therapy and Comparative Criminology, 59*(8), 855–872.

138. Schroeder, R. D., Broadus, E. J., & Bradley, C. (2018). Religiosity and crime revisited: Accounting for non-believers. *Deviant Behavior, 39*(5), 632–647.

139. Koch, J. R., & Ramirez, I. L. (2010). Religiosity, Christian fundamentalism, and intimate partner violence among U.S. college students. *Review of Religious Research, 51*, 402–410.

140. Rodriguez, C. M., & Henderson, R. C. (2010). Who spares the rod? Religious orientation, social conformity, and child abuse potential. *Child Abuse & Neglect, 34*(2), 84–94.

141. Beller, J., Kröger, C., & Hosser, D. (2019). Disentangling honor-based violence and religion: The differential influence of individual and social religious practices and fundamentalism on support for honor killings in a cross-national sample of Muslims. *Journal of Interpersonal Violence, 36*(19–20), 1–20.

142. Beller, J., Kröger, C., & Hosser, D. (2019). Disentangling honor-based violence and religion: The differential influence of individual and social religious practices and fundamentalism on support for honor killings in a cross-national sample of Muslims. *Journal of Interpersonal Violence, 36*(19–20), 1–20.

143. Federal Bureau of Investigation. (2019). Table 23: Offense analysis. *Crime in the United States, 2019.* Retrieved from https://ucr.fbi.gov/crime-in-the-u.s/2019/crime-in-the-u.s.-2019/tables/table-23

144. Hewitt, A. N., Andresen, M. A., Beauregard, E., & Brantingham, P. L. (2020). Dangerous times? A routine activities examination of the temporal patterns of sexual offenses over time. *Justice Quarterly*, 1–21.

145. Andresen, M. A., & Malleson, N. (2015). Intra-week spatial-temporal patterns of crime. *Crime Science, 4*(1), 1–11.

146. Tompson, L., & Townsley, M. (2010). (Looking) back to the future: Using space-time patterns to better predict the location of street crime. *International Journal of Police Science & Management, 12*(1), 23–40.

147. Felson, M., & Poulsen, E. (2003). Simple indicators of crime by time of day. *International Journal of Forecasting, 19*(4), 595–601.

148. Andresen, M. A., & Malleson, N. (2013). Crime seasonality and its variations across space. *Applied Geography, 43*, 25–35.

149. Andresen, M. A., & Malleson, N. (2015). Intra-week spatial-temporal patterns of crime. *Crime Science, 4*(1), 1–11.

150. Ceccato, V., & Uittenbogaard, A. C. (2014). Space–time dynamics of crime in transport nodes. *Annals of the Association of American Geographers, 104*(1), 131–150.

151. Andresen, M. A., & Malleson, N. (2013). Crime seasonality and its variations across space. *Applied Geography, 43*, 25–35.

152. Tcherni-Buzzeo, M. (2019). The "great American crime decline": Possible explanations. In M. Krohn, N. Hendrix, G. P. Hall, & A. Lizotte (Eds.), *Handbook on crime and deviance* (pp. 309–335). Cham, Switzerland: Springer.

153. Rosenfeld, R., Abt, T., & Lopez, E. (2021). *Pandemic, social unrest, and crime in U.S. cities: 2020 year-end update.* Washington, DC: Council on Criminal Justice.

154. Phillips, J. A. (2006). The relationship between age structure and homicide rates in the United States, 1970 to 1999. *Journal of Research in Crime and Delinquency, 43*(3), 230–260.

155. McCall, P. L., Land, K. C., & Parker, K. F. (2010). An empirical assessment of what we know about structural covariates of homicide rates: A return to a classic 20 years later. *Homicide Studies, 14*(3), 219–243.

156. McDowall, D. (1991). Firearm availability and homicide rates in Detroit, 1951–1986. *Social Forces, 69*(4), 1085–1101.

157. Farrell, G. (2013). Five tests for a theory of the crime drop. *Crime Science, 2*(1), 1–8.

158. Tcherni-Buzzeo, M. (2019). The "great American crime decline": Possible explanations. In M. Krohn, N. Hendrix, G. P. Hall, & A. Lizotte (Eds.), *Handbook on crime and deviance* (pp. 309–335). Cham, Switzerland: Springer.

159. Federal Bureau of Investigation. (2020). *Trends of violent crime from 2010 to 2020, by state* [Data set]. Crime Data Explorer. Retrieved from https://crime-data-explorer.fr.cloud.gov/pages/explorer/crime/crime-trend

160. Federal Bureau of Investigation. (2020). *Trends of violent crime from 2010 to 2020, by state and police department (Oakland Police Department and Long Beach Police Department)* [Data set]. Crime Data Explorer. Retrieved from https://crime-data-explorer.fr.cloud.gov/pages/explorer/crime/crime-trend

161. Thomas, S. A., Medaris, D. C., & Tuttle, C. R. (2018). Southern culture and aggravated assault: Exploring the generality of the Southern culture of violence. *Sociological Spectrum, 38*(2), 103–116.

162. Lee, M. R., Bankston, W. B., Hayes, T. C., & Thomas, S. A. (2007). Revisiting the southern culture of violence. *Sociological Quarterly, 48*(2), 253–275.

163. Miller, J. M. (2014). Southern subculture of violence theory. In J. M. Mitchell (Ed.), *The encyclopedia of theoretical criminology.* New York, NY: John Wiley & Sons.

164. Thomas, S. A., Medaris, D. C., & Tuttle, C. R. (2018). Southern culture and aggravated assault: Exploring the generality of the Southern culture of violence. *Sociological Spectrum, 38*(2), 103–116.

165. Nesbitt, R., & Cohen, D. (2018). *Culture of honor: The psychology of violence in the South.* New York, NY: Routledge.

166. Lee, M. R., Bankston, W. B., Hayes, T. C., & Thomas, S. A. (2007). Revisiting the southern culture of violence. *Sociological Quarterly, 48*(2), 253–275.

167. Lee, M. R., & Ousey, G. C. (2011). Reconsidering the culture and violence connection: Strategies of action in the rural South. *Journal of Interpersonal Violence, 26*(5), 899–929.

168. Rose, M. R., & Ellison, C. G. (2016). Violence as honorable? Racial and ethnic differences in attitudes toward violence. *Crime & Delinquency, 62*(6), 800–820.

169. Andersen, M., & Hodgkinson, T. (2019). Place-based data, methods, and analysis: Past, present, and future. In M. Krohn, N. Hendrix, G. P. Hall, & A. Lizotte (Eds.), *Handbook on crime and deviance.* Cham, Switzerland: Springer.

170. Weisburd, D., & Wire, S. (2018). Crime hot spots. In H. Pontell (Ed.), *Oxford encyclopedia of criminology and criminal justice* (pp. 1–15). Oxford, UK: Oxford University Press.

171. Wilcox, P., & Eck, J. E. (2011). Criminology of the unpopular: Implications for policy aimed at payday lending facilities. *Criminology & Public Policy, 10*, 473–482.

172. Weisburd, D., Eck, J., Braga, A., Telep, C., Cave, B., Bowers, K., . . . Yang, l. -M. (2016). *Place matters: Criminology for the twenty-first century.* Cambridge, UK: Cambridge University Press.

173. Wheeler, A. P., Worden, R. E., & McLean, S. J. (2016). Replicating group-based trajectory models of crime at micro-places in Albany, NY. *Journal of Quantitative Criminology, 32*(4), 589–612.

174. Topalli, V., Dickinson, T., & Jacques, S. (2020). Learning from criminals: Active offender research for criminology. *Annual Review of Criminology, 3*, 189–215.

175. Katz, J. (1988). *Seductions of crime: Moral and sensual attractions in doing evil.* New York, NY: Basic Books.

176. Carrington, P. (2018). Co-offending. In G. Bruinsma & D. Weisburd (Eds.), *Encyclopedia of criminology and criminal justice.* New York, NY: Springer.

177. Beck, A. (2021). *Race and ethnicity of violent crime offenders and arrestees, 2018.* Bureau of Justice Statistics. Retrieved from https://www.bjs.gov/content/pub/pdf/revcoa18.pdf

178. Lantz, B. (2020). Co-offending group composition and violence: The impact of sex, age, and group size on co-offending violence. *Crime & Delinquency, 66*(1), 93–122.

179. McGloin, J. M., & Rowan, Z. R. (2015). A threshold model of collective crime. *Criminology, 53*(3), 484–512.

180. McGloin, J. M., & Thomas, K. J. (2016). Incentives for collective deviance: Group size and changes in perceived risk, cost, and reward. *Criminology, 54*(3), 459–486.

181. Tillyer, M. S., & Tillyer, R. (2015). Maybe I should do this alone: A comparison of solo and co-offending robbery outcomes. *Justice Quarterly, 32*(6), 1064–1088.

182. Carrington, P. (2018). Co-offending. In G. Bruinsma & D. Weisburd (Eds.), *Encyclopedia of criminology and criminal justice.* New York, NY: Springer.

183. Bichler, G., Malm, A., & Enriquez, J. (2014). Magnetic facilities: Identifying the convergence settings of juvenile delinquents. *Crime & Delinquency, 60*(7), 971–998.

184. Zimring, F. E., & Laqueur, H. (2015). Kids, groups, and crime: In defense of conventional wisdom. *Journal of Research in Crime and Delinquency, 52*(3), 403–413.

185. Oudekerk, B., & Morgan, R. (2016). *Special report: Co-offending among adolescents in violent victimizations, 2004-2013.* Bureau of Justice Statistics. Retrieved from https://www.bjs.gov/content/pub/pdf/caavv0413.pdf

186. Zimring, F. E., & Laqueur, H. (2015). Kids, groups, and crime: In defense of conventional wisdom. *Journal of Research in Crime and Delinquency, 52*(3), 403–413.

187. Carrington, P. J. (2009). Co-offending and the development of the delinquent career. *Criminology, 47*(4), 1295–1329.

188. Warr, M. (2002). *Companions in crime: The social aspects of criminal conduct.* Cambridge, UK: Cambridge University Press.

189. McGloin, M., & Nguyen, H. (2012). It was my idea: Considering the instigation of co-offending. *Criminology, 50*(2), 463–494.

190. Weerman, F. (2018). Theories of co-offending. In G. Bruinsma & D. Weisburd (Eds.), *Encyclopedia of criminology and criminal justice* (pp. 5173–5184). New York, NY: Springer.

191. Bureau of Justice Statistics. (Number of violent crimes excluding simple assaults by weapon category and injury, 2019). Generated using the NCVS Victimization Analysis Tool. Retrieved March 25, 2021, from www.bjs.gov.

192. Planty, M., & Truman, J. L. (2013). *Firearm violence,1993–2011* (Bureau of Justice Statistics Report No. NCJ 241730). Washington, DC: U.S. Department of Justice.

193. Braga, A. A., Griffiths, E., Sheppard, K., & Douglas, S. (2020). Firearm instrumentality: Do guns make violent situations more lethal? *Annual Review of Criminology, 4*, 147–164.

194. Bureau of Justice Statistics. (Number of aggravated assaults by weapon category and injury, 2019). Generated using the NCVS Victimization Analysis Tool. Retrieved March 25, 2021, from www.bjs.gov.

195. Braga, A. A., Griffiths, E., Sheppard, K., & Douglas, S. (2020). Firearm instrumentality: Do guns make violent situations more lethal? *Annual Review of Criminology, 4*, 147–164.

196. Cook, P. J. (2018). Gun markets. *Annual Review of Criminology, 1*, 359–377.

197. Weaver, G. S., Wittekind, J. E. C., Huff-Corzine, L., Corzine, J., Petee, T. A., & Jarvis, J. P. (2004). Violent encounters: A criminal event analysis of lethal and nonlethal outcomes. *Journal of Contemporary Criminal Justice, 20*(4), 348–368.

198. Felson, R. B., & Messner, S. F. (1996). To kill or not to kill? Lethal outcomes in injurious attacks. *Criminology, 34*(4), 519–545.

199. Braga, A. A., Griffiths, E., Sheppard, K., & Douglas, S. (2020). Firearm instrumentality: Do guns make violent situations more lethal? *Annual Review of Criminology, 4*, 147–164.

200. Pelletier, K. R., & Pizarro, J. M. (2019). Homicides and weapons: Examining the covariates of weapon choice. *Homicide Studies, 23*(1), 41–63.

201. Pizarro, J. M., Holt, K., & Pelletier, K. R. (2019). An examination of the situated transactions of firearm homicides. *Journal of Behavioral Medicine, 42*(4), 613–625.

202. Pizarro, J. M., Holt, K., & Pelletier, K. R. (2019). An examination of the situated transactions of firearm homicides. *Journal of Behavioral Medicine, 42*(4), 613–625.

203. Topalli, V., & Wright, R. (2013). Affect and the dynamic foreground of predatory street crime. In J. van Gelder, H. Elfers, D. Reynald, & D. Nagin (Eds.), *Affect and cognition in criminal decision-making* (pp. 42–57). New York, NY: Routledge.

204. Pierce, M., Hayhurst, K., Bird, S. M., Hickman, M., Seddon, T., Dunn, G., & Millar, T. (2017). Insights into the link between drug use and criminality: Lifetime offending of

criminally-active opiate users. *Drug and Alcohol Dependence, 179*, 309–316.

205. White, H. R. (2016). Substance use and crime. In K. Sher (Ed.), *The Oxford handbook of substance use and substance use disorders* (pp. 347–378). Oxford, UK: Oxford University Press.

206. Rand, M., Sabol, W., Sinclair, M., & Snyder, H. (2010). *Alcohol and crime: Data from 2002 to 2008.* Washington, DC: Bureau of Justice Statistics.

207. Exum, M. L., Austin, L. A., & Franklin, J. D. (2017). The effect of alcohol and arousal on criminal decision making. In W. Bernasco, J. van Gelder, & H. Elfers (Eds.), *The Oxford handbook of offender decision making* (pp. 445–459). Oxford, UK: Oxford University Press.

208. Rand, M., Sabol, W., Sinclair, M., & Snyder, H. (2010). *Alcohol and crime: Data from 2002 to 2008.* Washington, DC: Bureau of Justice Statistics.

209. Kuhns, J. B., Exum, M. L., Clodfelter, T. A., & Bottia, M. C. (2014). The prevalence of alcohol-involved homicide offending: A meta-analytic review. *Homicide Studies, 18*(3), 251–270.

210. Exum, M. L., Austin, L. A., & Franklin, J. D. (2017). The effect of alcohol and arousal on criminal decision making. In W. Bernasco, J. van Gelder, & H. Elfers (Eds.), *The Oxford handbook of offender decision making* (pp. 445–459). Oxford, UK: Oxford University Press.

211. Gutwinski, S., Heinz, A., & Heinz, A. (2018). Alcohol-related aggression and violence. In A. Beech, A. Carter, R. Mann, & P. Rotshtein (Eds.), *The Wiley Blackwell handbook of forensic neuroscience, I and II* (pp. 455–480). New York, NY: Wiley Blackwell.

CHAPTER 6

1. Tyree, E. (2019, January 30). *Warrants: Roommates talked about their problems with others before gruesome murder.* ABC 13 News. Retrieved from https://wset.com/news/local/warrants-roommates-talked-about-their-problems-with-others-before-gruesome-murder

2. Gangloff, M. (2019, October 7). Luisa Cutting pleads guilty to Radford murder of Alexa Cannon; sentenced to 20 years. *The Roanoke Times.* Retrieved from https://roanoke.com/news/local/luisa-cutting-pleads-guilty-to-radford-murder-of-alexa-cannon-sentenced-to-20-years/article_aa5b3284-409e-51cd-bde6-2073d51cd69a.html

3. Associated Press. (2019, October 7). Virginia woman admits to fatally stabbing roommate. *U.S. News and World Report.* Retrieved from https://www.usnews.com/news/best-states/virginia/articles/2019-10-07/radford-student-pleads-guilty-to-fatally-stabbing-roommate

4. Greenstone, G. (2010). The history of bloodletting. *British Columbia Medical Journal, 52*, 12–14.

5. Hartley, L. P. (1953). *The go-between.* London, UK: Hamish Hamilton.

6. Berger, P. (1967). *The sacred canopy.* Garden City, NJ: Doubleday.

7. Einstadter, W. J., & Henry, S. (2006). *Criminological theory: An analysis of its underlying assumptions.* New York, NY: Rowman & Littlefield.

8. Pfohl, S. J. (1994). *Images of deviance and social control: A sociological history.* New York, NY: McGraw-Hill.

9. Huff, C. R. (2008). Historical explanations of crime: From demons to politics. In C. Kubrin, G. Bridges, J. Weis, & R. Crutchfield (Eds.), *Crime: Readings* (pp. 10–22). Thousand Oaks, CA: SAGE.

10. Erikson, K. T. (1966). *Wayward Puritans: A study in the sociology of deviance.* New York, NY: Wiley.

11. Mixon, F. G., Jr. (2015). *Public choice economics and the Salem witchcraft hysteria.* New York, NY: Palgrave Macmillan.

12. Pfohl, S. J. (1994). *Images of deviance and social control: A sociological history.* New York, NY: McGraw-Hill.

13. Kerr, M. H., Forsyth, R. D., & Plyley, M. J. (1992). Cold water and hot iron: Trial by ordeal in England. *Journal of Interdisciplinary History, 22*(4), 573–595.

14. Largo, M. (2014). *The big, bad book of botany: The world's most fascinating flora.* New York, NY: William Morrow.

15. Tyson, P. (2000). *The eighth continent: Life, death, and discovery in the lost world of Madagascar.* New York, NY: William Morrow.

16. Pfohl, S. J. (1994). *Images of deviance and social control: A sociological history.* New York, NY: McGraw-Hill.

17. Newman, G. (1978). *The punishment response.* Philadelphia, PA: Lippincott.

18. Peters, E. (2018). *Torture.* Philadelphia: University of Pennsylvania Press.

19. Groebner, V. (1995). Losing face, saving face: Noses and honour in the late Medieval town. *History Workshop Journal, 40*, 1–15.

20. Pinker, S. (2011). *The better angels of our nature: The decline of violence in history and its causes.* London, UK: Penguin UK.

21. Mavroforou, A., Malizos, K., Karachalios, T., Chatzitheofilou, K., & Giannoukas, A. D. (2014). Punitive limb amputation. *Clinical Orthopaedics and Related Research, 472*(10), 3102–3106.

22. Bessler, J. (2017). *The death penalty as torture: From the dark ages to abolition.* Durham, NC: Carolina Academic Press.

23. Innes, B. (2012). *The history of torture.* London, UK: Amber Books.

24. Scott, G. R. (2009). *The history of torture throughout the ages.* New York, NY: Routledge.

25. Gatrell, V. A. (1996). *The hanging tree: Execution and the English people 1770-1868.* Oxford, UK: Oxford University Press.

26. King, P., & Ward, R. (2015). Rethinking the Bloody Code in eighteenth-century Britain: Capital punishment at the centre and on the periphery. *Past & Present, 228*(1), 159–205.

27. Walliss, J. (2018). *The Bloody Code in England and Wales, 1760-1830.* Basingstoke, UK: Palgrave Macmillan.

28. Pfohl, S. J. (1994). *Images of deviance and social control: A sociological history*. New York, NY: McGraw-Hill.

29. Newman, G. (1978). *The punishment response*. Philadelphia, PA: Lippincott.

30. Preyer, K. (1982). Penal measures in the American colonies: An overview. *American Journal of Legal History, 26*(4), 326–353.

31. Newman, G. (1978). *The punishment response*. Philadelphia, PA: Lippincott.

32. O'Gorman, F. (1997). *The long eighteenth century: British political and social history, 1688-1832*. London, UK: St. Martin's Press.

33. Kavka, G. S. (1983). Hobbes's war of all against all. *Ethics, 93*(2), 291–310.

34. Hobbes, T. (Ed.) (1651). Chapter XIII: Of the natural condition of mankind as concerning their felicity and misery. In *Leviathan or the matter, forme and power of a common wealth ecclesiasticall and civil*. Cambridge, UK: University of Cambridge Press.

35. Tibbetts, S. G. (2019). *Criminological theory: The essentials*. Thousand Oaks, CA: SAGE.

36. Elahi, M. (2005). *What is the social contract?* The Sophia Project: Philosophy Archives. Retrieved from http://www.sophia-project.org/philosophy-archives.html

37. Tuckness, A. (2020). Locke's political philosophy. In E. N. Zalta (Ed.), *The Stanford encyclopedia of philosophy*. Retrieved from https://plato.stanford.edu/archives/spr2020/entries/locke-political/

38. Newman, G. (1978). *The punishment response*. Philadelphia, PA: Lippincott.

39. Haist, M. (2008). Deterrence in a sea of just deserts: Are utilitarian goals achievable in a world of limiting retributivism? *Journal of Criminal Law & Criminology, 99*, 789–822.

40. Unger, M., Crete, J., & Pavlich, G. (2018). Criminal entryways in the writing of Cesare Beccaria. In R. A. Triplett (Ed.), *The handbook of the history and philosophy of criminology* (pp. 17–31). New York, NY: John Wiley & Sons.

41. Bruinsma, G. B. (2018). Classical theory: The emergence of deterrence theory in the age of enlightenment. In D. S. Nagin, F. T. Cullen, & C. L. Jonson (Eds.), *Deterrence, choice, and crime: Vol. 23. Contemporary perspectives*. New York, NY: Routledge.

42. Harcourt, B. E. (2013). *Beccaria's "On crimes and punishments": A mirror on the history of the foundations of modern criminal law* (Coase-Sandor Institute for Law & Economics Working Paper No. 648). Retrieved from https://chicagounbound.uchicago.edu/cgi/viewcontent.cgi?article=1633&context=law_and_economics

43. Maestro, M. (1973). A pioneer for the abolition of capital punishment: Cesare Beccaria. *Journal of the History of Ideas, 34*(3), 463–468.

44. Beccaria, C. (1764/1775). *An essay on crimes and punishments, translated from the Italian; with a commentary attributed to Mons. de Voltaire, translated from the French*. London, UK: K. Newberry.

45. Beccaria, C., & Bellamy, R. (Ed.) (1764/1995). *Beccaria: 'On crimes and punishments' and other writings* (R. Davis, Trans.). Cambridge, UK: University of Cambridge Press.

46. U.S. Sentencing Commission. (2019, October). *Mandatory minimum penalties for drug offenses in the federal criminal justice system*. Retrieved from https://www.ussc.gov/sites/default/files/pdf/research-and-publications/research-publications/2017/20171025_Drug-Mand-Min.pdf

47. U.S. Sentencing Commission. (2020). *Quick facts: Mandatory minimum penalties*. Retrieved from https://www.ussc.gov/sites/default/files/pdf/research-and-publications/quick-facts/Quick_Facts_Mand_Mins_FY19.pdf

48. Price, M. (2019). Weaponizing justice: Mandatory minimums, the trial penalty, and the purposes of punishment. *Federal Sentencing Reporter, 31*(4–5), 309–315.

49. Luna, E. (Ed.). (2017). Mandatory minimums. In *Reforming criminal justice: Vol. 4. Punishment, incarceration, and release* (pp. 117–146). Phoenix: Arizona State University.

50. Nagin, D. S. (2013). Deterrence in the twenty-first century. *Crime and justice, 42*(1), 199–263.

51. Coker v. Georgia, 433 U.S. 584 (1977).

52. Solem v. Helm, 463 U.S. 277 (1983).

53. Tonry, M. (2018). An honest politician's guide to deterrence: Certainty, severity, celerity, and parsimony. In D. Nagin, F. Cullen, & C. L. Jonson (Eds.), *Deterrence, choice, and crime: Contemporary perspectives* (Vol. 23). New York, NY: Routledge.

54. Weisburd, D., Einat, T., & Kowalski, M. (2008). The miracle of the cells: An experimental study of interventions to increase payment of court-ordered financial obligations. *Criminology & Public Policy, 7*(1), 9–36.

55. Pogarsky, G., & Loughran, T. A. (2016). The policy-to-perceptions link in deterrence: Time to retire the clearance rate. *Criminology & Public Policy, 15*, 777.

56. Woodward, V. (2017). Hedonistic calculus. In K. R. Kerley (Ed.), *The encyclopedia of corrections*. New York, NY: John Wiley & Sons.

57. Bentham, J. (2011/1789). An introduction to the principles and morals of legislation. In M. Tonry (Ed.), *Why punish? How much?* (pp. 51–70). New York, NY: Oxford University Press.

58. Bentham, J. (2011/1789). An introduction to the principles and morals of legislation. In M. Tonry (Ed.), *Why punish? How much?* (pp. 51–70). New York, NY: Oxford University Press.

59. Foucault, M. (1995). *Discipline and punish: The birth of the prison*. New York, NY: Vintage Books.

60. Kenis, P., Kruyen, P. M., Baaijens, J., & Barneveld, P. (2010). The prison of the future? An evaluation of an innovative prison design in the Netherlands. *The Prison Journal, 90*(3), 313–330.

61. Abrutyn, S. (2017). Positivism. In L. Spillman (Ed.), *Oxford bibliographies in sociology*. New York, NY: Oxford University Press.

62. Walsh, A., & Ellis, L. (2006). *Criminology: An interdisciplinary approach*. Thousand Oaks, CA: SAGE.

63. Agnew, R. (1995). Determinism, indeterminism, and crime: An empirical exploration. *Criminology, 33*(1), 83–109.

64. Walsh, A., & Wright, J. P. (2015). Biosocial criminology and its discontents: A critical realist philosophical analysis. *Criminal Justice Studies, 28*(1), 124–140.

65. Garofalo, R. (1885). *Criminologia: Studio sul delitto, sulle sue cause e sui mezzi di repressione.* Torino, Italy: Fratelli Bocca.

66. Moore, K., & Lux, J. (2010). Eugenics and crime: Early American positivism. In F. Cullen & P. Wilcox (Eds.), *Encyclopedia of criminological theory* (pp. 305–308). Thousand Oaks, CA: SAGE.

67. Gould, S. J., & Gold, S. J. (1996). *The mismeasure of man.* New York, NY: Norton.

68. Rafter, N., Posick, C., & Rocque, M. (2016). *The criminal brain: Understanding biological theories of crime* (2nd ed.). New York: NYU Press.

69. Spitzka, E. A. (1907). A study of the brains of six eminent scientists and scholars belonging to the American Anthropometric Society: Together with a description of the skull of Professor Ed Cope (Vol. 21). *American Philosophical Society, 21*, 175–308.

70. Rafter, N. (2005). The murderous Dutch fiddler: Criminology, history and the problem of phrenology. *Theoretical Criminology, 9*(1), 65–96.

71. Rafter, N. (2005). The murderous Dutch fiddler: Criminology, history and the problem of phrenology. *Theoretical Criminology, 9*(1), 65–96.

72. Lombroso, C. (1876/2006). *Criminal man.* Durham, NC: Duke University Press.

73. Darwin, C. (1859). *On the origin of species.* London, UK: John Murray.

74. Bannister, R. (2010). *Social Darwinism: Science and myth in Anglo-American social thought.* Philadelphia, PA: Temple University Press.

75. Horn, D. (2015). *The criminal body: Lombroso and the anatomy of deviance.* New York, NY: Routledge.

76. Lombroso, C. (1876/2006). *Criminal man.* Durham, NC: Duke University Press

77. Woodruff, R. (1921). A classification of the causes of crime. *Journal of the American Institute of Criminal Law and Criminology, 12*(1), 105–109.

78. Lombroso, C. (1911). *Criminal man, according to the classification of Cesare Lombroso Briefly summarised by his daughter, Gina Lombroso Ferrero, with an introduction by Cesare Lombroso.* New York, NY: Putnam.

79. Knepper, P. (2018). Laughing at Lombroso: Positivism and criminal anthropology in historical perspective. In R. A. Triplett (Ed.), *The handbook of the history and philosophy of criminology* (pp. 51–66). New York, NY: John Wiley & Sons.

80. Ciliberti, R., Monza, F., De Stefano, F., & Licata, M. (2018). The trial of the skull studied by the founder of criminal anthropology: The war of the Lombroso Museum. *Journal of Forensic and Legal Medicine, 59*, 13–15.

81. Lombroso, C. (1876/2006). *Criminal man.* Durham, NC: Duke University Press.

82. Gibson, M. (2013). Cesare Lombroso, prison science, and penal policy. In P. Knepper & P. J. Ystehede (Eds.), *The Cesare Lombroso handbook* (pp. 30–46). New York, NY: Routledge.

83. Gatti, U., & Verde, A. (2012). Cesare Lombroso: Methodological ambiguities and brilliant intuitions. *International Journal of Law and Psychiatry, 35*(1), 19–26.

84. Zola, E. (1889). Intervista in the newspaper *La Tribuna.* Reproduced in Cronaca del Manicomio provinciale di Pavia in Voghera, 9 nn. 10-11, 12.

85. Lombroso, C. (1896/2006). Edition 5. In *Criminal man* (M. Gibson & N. H. Rafter, Trans.). Durham, NC: Duke University Press.

86. Gatti, U., & Verde, A. (2012). Cesare Lombroso: Methodological ambiguities and brilliant intuitions. *International Journal of Law and Psychiatry, 35*(1), 19–26.

87. Speranza, G. C. (1901). Lombroso in science and fiction. *Green Bag, 13*, 475–477.

88. Whibley, C. (1909). Science, real and false—Lombroso's method. *Blackwood's Magazine, 186*(December), 843–850.

89. Goring, C. (1913). *The English convict: A statistical study.* London, UK: His Majesty's Stationary Office.

90. Knepper, P. (2018). Laughing at Lombroso: Positivism and criminal anthropology in historical perspective. In R. A. Triplett (Ed.), *The handbook of the history and philosophy of criminology* (pp. 51–66). New York, NY: John Wiley & Sons.

91. Goring, C. (1919). *The English convict.* London, UK: HMSO.

92. DeLisi, M. (2013). Revisiting Lombroso. In F. T. Cullen & P. Wilcox (Eds.), *The Oxford handbook of criminological theory* (pp. 5–21). Oxford, UK: Oxford University Press.

93. Rafter, N. (2008). Criminology's darkest hour: Biocriminology in Nazi Germany. *Australian & New Zealand Journal of Criminology, 41*(2), 287–306.

94. Mazzarello, P. (2011). Cesare Lombroso: An anthropologist between evolution and degeneration. *Functional Neurology, 26*(2), 97.

95. Musumeci, E. (2013). New natural born killers? The legacy of Lombroso in neuroscience and the law. In P. Knepper & P. J. Ystehede (Eds.), *The Cesare Lombroso handbook* (pp. 131–146). New York, NY: Routledge.

96. Gatti, U., & Verde, A. (2012). Cesare Lombroso: Methodological ambiguities and brilliant intuitions. *International Journal of Law and Psychiatry, 35*(1), 19–26.

97. Flannigan, K., Pei, J., Stewart, M., & Johnson, A. (2018). Fetal alcohol spectrum disorder and the criminal justice system: A systematic literature review. *International Journal of Law and Psychiatry, 57*, 42–52.

98. Lombroso, C., & Ferrero, G. (1895). *The female offender.* New York, NY: D. Appleton.

99. Calafato, T. (2017). The similarities between Lombroso's theories on political crime and contemporary terrorism issues. *Behavioral Sciences of Terrorism and Political Aggression, 9*(2), 78–105.

100. Lombroso, C. (1888). *Palimsesti del carcere: Raccolta unicamente destinate agli uomini di scienza.* Turin, Italy: Bocca.

101. Quetelet, A. (1835). *Sur l'homme et le développement de ses facultés, ou Essai de physique sociale* (Vol. 2). Paris, France: Bachelier.

102. Andresen, M. (2020). *Environmental criminology: Evolution, theory, and practice.* New York, NY: Routledge.

103. Guerry, A. (1833). *A translation of Andre-Michel Guerry's essay on the moral statistics of France: A sociological report to the French Academy of Science* (H. P. Whitt & V. W. Reinking, Eds. & Trans.). Lewiston, NY: Edwin Mellen Press.

104. Friendly, M. (2007). A. M. Guerry's "Moral statistics of France": Challenges for multivariable spatial analysis. *Statistical Science, 22,* 368–399.

105. Guerry, A. (1833). *A translation of Andre-Michel Guerry's essay on the moral statistics of France: A sociological report to the French Academy of Science* (H. P. Whitt & V. W. Reinking, Eds. & Trans.). Lewiston, NY: Edwin Mellen Press.

106. Quetelet, L. A. J. (1835/1842). *A treatise on man and the development of his faculties.* Edinburgh, UK: Robert and William Chambers.

107. Donnelly, K. (2015). *Adolphe Quetelet, social physics and the average men of science, 1796–1874.* New York, NY: Routledge.

108. Weisburd, D., Bruinsma, G. J., & Bernasco, W. (2009). Units of analysis in geographic criminology: Historical development, critical issues, and open questions. In D. Weisburd, W. Bernasco, & G. Bruinsma (Eds.), *Putting crime in its place* (pp. 3–31). New York, NY: Springer.

109. Beirne, P. (1987). Adolphe Quetelet and the origins of positivist criminology. *American Journal of Sociology, 92*(5), 1140–1169.

110. Jahoda, G. (2015). Quetelet and the emergence of the behavioral sciences. *SpringerPlus, 4*(1), 1–10.

111. Beirne, P. (1987). Adolphe Quetelet and the origins of positivist criminology. *American Journal of Sociology, 92*(5), 1140–1169.

112. Weisburd, D., Bruinsma, G. J., & Bernasco, W. (2009). Units of analysis in geographic criminology: Historical development, critical issues, and open questions. In D. Weisburd, W. Bernasco, & G. Bruinsma (Eds.), *Putting crime in its place* (pp. 3–31). New York, NY: Springer.

113. Gabbidon, S. L. (2016). *W. E. B. Du Bois on crime and justice: Laying the foundations of sociological criminology.* New York, NY: Routledge.

114. Du Bois, W. E. B. (1896). *The suppression of the African slave-trade to the United States of America, 1638-1870.* New York, NY: Longmans, Green.

115. Du Bois, W. E. B. (1904/2016). *The souls of Black folk.* Mineola, NY: Dover.

116. Du Bois, W. E. B. (1897, August). Strivings of the Negro people. *Atlantic.* Retrieved from https://www.theatlantic.com/magazine/archive/1897/08/strivings-of-the-negro-people/305446/

117. Gabbidon, S. L. (2019). Pioneering Black criminology: W. E. B. Du Bois and *The Philadelphia Negro.* In J. D. Unnever, S. L. Gabbidon, & C. Chouhy (Eds.), *Building a Black criminology: Race, theory, and crime* (pp. 29–44). New York, NY: Routledge.

118. Gabbidon, S. L. (2016). *W. E. B. Du Bois on crime and justice: Laying the foundations of sociological criminology.* New York, NY: Routledge.

119. Gabbidon, S. L. (2019). Pioneering Black criminology: W. E. B. Du Bois and *The Philadelphia Negro.* In J. D. Unnever, S. L. Gabbidon, and C. Chouhy (Eds.), *Building a Black criminology: Race, theory, and crime* (pp. 29–44). New York, NY: Routledge.

120. Du Bois, W. E. B. (1899, May). The Negro and crime. *The Independent, 51,* 1355–1357.

121. Seguin, C., & Rigby, D. (2019). National crimes: A new national data set of lynchings in the United States, 1883 to 1941. *Socius, 5,* 1–9.

122. Equal Justice Initiative. (2017). *Lynching in America: Confronting the legacy of racial terror* (3rd ed.). Retrieved from https://lynchinginamerica.eji.org/report/

123. Du Bois, W. E. B. (1996). *The Philadelphia Negro: A social study.* Philadelphia: University of Pennsylvania Press. (Original work published 1899)

124. Du Bois, W. E. B. (1996). *The Philadelphia Negro: A social study.* Philadelphia: University of Pennsylvania Press. (Original work published 1899)

125. Gabbidon, S. L. (2019). Pioneering Black criminology: W. E. B. Du Bois and *The Philadelphia Negro.* In J. D. Unnever, S. L. Gabbidon, & C. Chouhy (Eds.), *Building a Black criminology: Race, theory, and crime* (pp. 29–44). New York, NY: Routledge.

126. Du Bois, W. E. B. (1996). *The Philadelphia Negro: A social study.* Philadelphia: University of Pennsylvania Press. (Original work published 1899)

127. Wolfgang, M. E., Figlio, R. M., & Sellin, T. (1972). *Delinquency in a birth cohort.* Chicago, IL: University of Chicago Press.

128. Morris, A. (2017). *The scholar denied: W. E. B. Du Bois and the birth of modern sociology.* Berkeley: University of California Press.

129. Gabbidon, S. L. (2016). *W. E. B. Du Bois on crime and justice: Laying the foundations of sociological criminology.* New York, NY: Routledge.

CHAPTER 7

1. Eligon, J., Arango, T., Dewan, S., & Bogel-Burroughs, N. (2021, April 20). Derek Chauvin verdict brings a rare rebuke of police conduct. *The New York Times.* Retrieved from https://www.nytimes.com/2021/04/20/us/george-floyd-chauvin-verdict.html

2. Kateron, A., Bell, J., Shabazz, R., & Simmons, R. (2021, April 20). Why this trial was different: Experts react to the guilty verdict for Derek Chauvin. *The Conversation.* Retrieved from https://theconversation.com/why-this-trial-was-different-experts-react-to-guilty-verdict-for-derek-chauvin-159420

3. Buchanan, L., Bui, Q., & Patel, J. K. (2020, July 3). Black Lives Matter may be the largest movement in U.S. history. *The New York Times.* Retrieved from https://www.nytimes.com/interactive/2020/07/03/us/george-floyd-protests-crowd-size.html

4. Hattery, A., & Smith, E. (2021). *Policing Black bodies: How Black lives are surveilled and how to work for change* (updated edition). Lanham, MD: Rowman & Littlefield.

5. Vitale, A. S. (2017). *The end of policing.* New York, NY: Verso Books.

6. Thompson, C. (2015, March 31). *Public shamings.* The Marshall Project. Retrieved from https://www.themarshallp roject.org/2015/03/31/public-shamings

7. Thompson, C. (2015, March 31). *Public shamings.* The Marshall Project. Retrieved from https://www.themarshallp roject.org/2015/03/31/public-shamings

8. Collins, M. E., & Loughran, T. A. (2017). Rational choice theory, heuristics, and biases. In W. Bernasco, J. van Gelder, & H. Elffers (Eds.), *The Oxford handbook of offender decision-making* (online). New York, NY: Oxford University Press.

9. Natarajan, M. (2016). Introduction. In M. Natarajan (Ed.), *Crime opportunity theories: Routine activity, rational choice, and their variants* (pp. xiiv–xxxvi). New York, NY: Routledge.

10. Jacobs, B. A., & Wright, R. (2010). Bounded rationality, retaliation, and the spread of urban violence. *Journal of Interpersonal Violence, 25*(10), 1739–1766.

11. Pickett, J. T., & Roche, S. P. (2016). Arrested development: Misguided directions in deterrence theory and policy. *Criminology & Public Policy, 15*(3), 727–751.

12. Van Gelder, J. L. (2017). Dual-process models of criminal decision making. In W. Bernasco, J. van Gelder, & H. Elffers (Eds.), *The Oxford handbook of offender decision-making* (pp. 166–80). New York, NY: Oxford University Press.

13. Mamayek, C., Paternoster, R., & Loughran, T. (2017). Temporal discounting, present orientation, and criminal deterrence. In W. Bernasco, J. van Gelder, & H. Elffers (Eds.), *The Oxford handbook of offender decision-making* (pp. 209–227). New York, NY: Oxford University Press.

14. Jacobs, B. A., & Wright, R. (2010). Bounded rationality, retaliation, and the spread of urban violence. *Journal of Interpersonal Violence, 25*(10), 1739–1766.

15. Pedneault, A., Beauregard, E., Harris, D. A., & Knight, R. A. (2017). Myopic decision making: An examination of crime decisions and their outcomes in sexual crimes. *Journal of Criminal Justice, 50*, 1–11.

16. Matthews, R. (2014). *Realist criminology.* Cham, Switzerland: Springer.

17. Rocque, M., & Posick, C. (2017). Paradigm shift or normal science? The future of (biosocial) criminology. *Theoretical Criminology, 21*(3), 288–303.

18. Wright, J. P., Beaver, K. M., Gajos, J. M., & Sacarellos, C. (2017). Three strikes and you're out: A short but modern history of biosocial criminology. In R. Triplett (Ed.), *The handbook of the history and philosophy of criminology* (pp. 237–254). New York, NY: Wiley Blackwell.

19. Rafter, N. (2008). Criminology's darkest hour: Biocriminology in Nazi Germany. *Australian & New Zealand Journal of Criminology, 41*(2), 287–306.

20. Rocque, M., & Posick, C. (2017). Paradigm shift or normal science? The future of (biosocial) criminology. *Theoretical Criminology, 21*(3), 288–303.

21. Gajos, J. M., Fagan, A. A., & Beaver, K. M. (2016). Use of genetically informed evidence-based prevention science to understand and prevent crime and related behavioral disorders. *Criminology & Public Policy, 15*(3), 683–701.

22. Belsky, J., Zhang, X., & Sayler, K. (2021). Differential susceptibility 2.0: Are the same children affected by different experiences and exposures? *Development and Psychopathology,* 1–9.

23. Barnes, J. C., Boutwell, B., & Beaver, K. (2016). Contemporary biosocial criminology: A systematic review of the literature, 2000-2012. In A. Piquero (Ed.), *The handbook of criminological theory* (pp. 75–99). New York, NY: John Wiley & Sons.

24. Barnes, J. C., Boutwell, B., & Beaver, K. (2016). Contemporary biosocial criminology: A systematic review of the literature, 2000-2012. In A. Piquero (Ed.), *The handbook of criminological theory* (pp. 75–99). New York, NY: John Wiley & Sons.

25. Grotzinger, A. D., Mann, F. D., Patterson, M. W., Tackett, J. L., Tucker-Drob, E. M., & Harden, K. P. (2018). Hair and salivary testosterone, hair cortisol, and externalizing behaviors in adolescents. *Psychological Science, 29*, 688–699.

26. Barnes, J. C., Boutwell, B., & Beaver, K. (2016). Contemporary biosocial criminology: A systematic review of the literature, 2000-2012. In A. Piquero (Ed.), *The handbook of criminological theory* (pp. 75–99). New York, NY: John Wiley & Sons.

27. Carré, J. M., & Archer, J. (2018). Testosterone and human behavior: The role of individual and contextual variables. *Current Opinion in Psychology, 19*, 149–153.

28. Carré, J. M., & Olmstead, N. A. (2015). Social neuroendocrinology of human aggression: Examining the role of competition-induced testosterone dynamics. *Neuroscience, 286*, 171–186.

29. Portnoy, J., & Farrington, D. P. (2015). Resting heart rate and antisocial behavior: An updated systematic review and meta-analysis. *Aggression and Violent Behavior, 22*, 33–45.

30. Choy, O., Portnoy, J., Raine, A., Remmel, R. J., Schug, R., Tuvblad, C., & Yang, Y. (2018). Biosocial influences on offending across the life course. In D. Farrington, A. Piquero, & L. Kazemian (Eds.), *The Oxford handbook of developmental and life-course criminology* (pp. 325–351). New York, NY: Oxford University Press.

31. Cauffman, E., Steinberg, L., & Piquero, A. R. (2005). Psychological, neuropsychological and physiological correlates of serious antisocial behavior in adolescence: The role of self-control. *Criminology, 43*(1), 133–176.

32. Koegl, C. J., Farrington, D. P., & Raine, A. (2018). The relationship between low resting heart rate, systolic blood pressure and antisocial behavior in incarcerated males. *Journal of Criminal Justice, 55*, 88–95.

33. Armstrong, T. A., Boisvert, D., Flores, S., Symonds, M., & Gangitano, D. (2017). Heart rate, serotonin transporter linked polymorphic region (5-HTTLPR) genotype, and violence in an incarcerated sample. *Journal of Criminal Justice, 51*, 1–8.

34. Piquero, N. L., Ling, S., Raine, A., & Piquero, A. R. (2019). Heart rate fails to predict white collar crime. *American Journal of Criminal Justice, 45*, 1–14.

35. Raine, A. (2014). *The anatomy of violence: The biological roots of crime*. New York, NY: Vintage.

36. Hammerton, G., Heron, J., Mahedy, L., Maughan, B., Hickman, M., & Murray, J. (2018). Low resting heart rate, sensation seeking and the course of antisocial behaviour across adolescence and young adulthood. *Psychological Medicine, 48*(13), 2194–2201.

37. Portnoy, J., Raine, A., Rudo-Hutt, A. S., Gao, Y., & Monk, K. (2020). Heart rate reactivity, neighborhood disadvantage, and antisocial behavior. *Crime & Delinquency, 66*(10), 1392–1418.

38. Fuqua, L. M. (2019, November 10). Identical twins connected by DNA and murder – True crime. *Medium.* Retrieved from https://medium.com/true-crime-addiction/identical-twins-connected-by-dna-and-murder-true-crime-6e22df2b84e5

39. Barnes, J. C., Boutwell, B., & Beaver, K. (2016). Contemporary biosocial criminology: A systematic review of the literature, 2000-2012. In A. Piquero (Ed.), *The handbook of criminological theory* (pp. 75–99). New York, NY: John Wiley & Sons.

40. Barnes, J. C., Wright, J. P., Boutwell, B. B., Schwartz, J. A., Connolly, E. J., Nedelec, J. L., & Beaver, K. M. (2014). Demonstrating the validity of twin research in criminology. *Criminology, 52*(4), 588–626.

41. Polderman, T. J., Benyamin, B., De Leeuw, C. A., Sullivan, P. F., Van Bochoven, A., Visscher, P. M., & Posthuma, D. (2015). Meta-analysis of the heritability of human traits based on fifty years of twin studies. *Nature Genetics, 47*(7), 702–709.

42. Knoblach, R. A., Schwartz, J. A., McBride, M., & Beaver, K. M. (2020). The association between genetic predisposition and parental socialization: An examination of gene-environment correlations using an adoption-based design. *International Journal of Offender Therapy and Comparative Criminology, 64*(2–3), 187–209.

43. Burt, C. H., & Simons, R. L. (2014). Pulling back the curtain on heritability studies: Biosocial criminology in the postgenomic era. *Criminology, 52*(2), 223–262.

44. Lewontin, R. C., Rose, S., & Kamin, L. J. (1984). *Not in our genes: Biology, ideology, and human nature*. New York, NY: Pantheon Books.

45. Barnes, J. C., Boutwell, B., & Beaver, K. (2016). Contemporary biosocial criminology: A systematic review of the literature, 2000-2012. In A. Piquero (Ed.), *The handbook of criminological theory* (pp. 75–99). New York, NY: John Wiley & Sons.

46. Holland, N., & DeLisi, M. (2014). The warrior gene: MAOA genotype and antisocial behavior in males. In M. DeLisi & M. Vaughn (Eds.), *The Routledge international handbook of biosocial criminology* (online) (pp. 179–189). New York, NY: Routledge.

47. Ficks, C. A., & Waldman, I. D. (2014). Candidate genes for aggression and antisocial behavior: A meta-analysis of association studies of the 5HTTLPR and MAOA-uVNTR. *Behavioral Genetics, 44*(5), 1–18.

48. Hollerbach, P., Johansson, A., Ventus, D., Jern, P., Neumann, C. S., Westberg, L., . . . Mokros, A. (2018). Main and interaction effects of childhood trauma and the MAOA uVNTR polymorphism on psychopathy. *Psychoneuroendocrinology, 95*, 106–112.

49. Guo, G., Roettger, M. E., & Shih, J. C. (2007). Contributions of the DAT1 and DRD2 genes to serious and violent delinquency among adolescents and young adults. *Human Genetics, 121*(1), 125–136.

50. Gajos, J. M., Fagan, A. A., & Beaver, K. M. (2016). Use of genetically informed evidence-based prevention science to understand and prevent crime and related behavioral disorders. *Criminology & Public Policy, 15*(3), 683–701.

51. Caspi, A., McClay, J., Moffitt, T. E., Mill, J., Martin, J., Craig, I. W., . . . Poulton, R. (2002). Role of genotype in the cycle of violence in maltreated children. *Science, 297*(5582), 851–854.

52. Davis, K. (2017). *The brain defense: Murder in Manhattan and the dawn of neuroscience in America's courtrooms*. New York, NY: Penguin Press.

53. Concannon, D. (2019). *Neurocriminology: Forensic and legal applications, public policy implications*. Boca Raton, FL: CRC Press.

54. Fallin, M., Whooley, O., & Barker, K. K. (2019). Criminalizing the brain: Neurocriminology and the production of strategic ignorance. *BioSocieties, 14*(3), 438–462.

55. Glenn, A. L., & Raine, A. (2014). Neurocriminology: Implications for the punishment, prediction and prevention of criminal behaviour. *Nature Reviews Neuroscience, 15*(1), 54–63.

56. Teicher, M. H., & Samson, J. A. (2016). Annual research review: Enduring neurobiological effects of childhood abuse and neglect. *Journal of Child Psychology and Psychiatry, 57*(3), 241–266.

57. Schwartz, J., Wright, E. M., Spohn, R., Campagna, M., Steiner, B., & Epinger, E. (2021, March 12). *Changes in jail admissions before and after traumatic brain injury.* Retrieved from https://doi.org/10.31235/osf.io/x34kr

58. Sampson, R., & Winter, A. (2018). Poisoned development: Assessing childhood lead exposure as a cause of crime in a birth cohort followed through adolescence. *Criminology, 56*(2), 269–301.

59. Wright, J. P., Dietrich, K. N., Ris, M. D., Hornung, R. W., Wessel, S. D., Lanphear, B. P., . . . Rae, M. N. (2008). Association of prenatal and childhood blood lead concentrations with criminal arrests in early adulthood. *PLoS Medicine, 5*(5), e101.

60. Barnes, J. C., Boutwell, B., & Beaver, K. (2016). Contemporary biosocial criminology: A systematic review of the literature, 2000-2012. In A. Piquero (Ed.), *The handbook of criminological theory* (pp. 75–99). New York, NY: John Wiley & Sons.

61. Jansen, A., Mous, S., White, T., Posthuma, D., & Polderman, T. (2015). What twin studies tell us about the heritability of brain development, morphology, and function: A review. *Neuropsychology Review, 25*, 27–46.

62. Schwartz, J. A., Walsh, A., & Beaver, K. M. (2019). The biosocial perspective: A brief overview and potential contributions to criminological theory. In M. Krohn, N. Hendrix, G. Penly Hall, & A. Lizotte (Eds.), *Handbook on crime and deviance* (pp. 89–111). Cham, Switzerland: Springer.

63. Raine, A. (2019). The neuromoral theory of antisocial, violent, and psychopathic behavior. *Psychiatry Research, 277*, 64–69.

64. Glenn, A. L., & Raine, A. (2014). Neurocriminology: Implications for the punishment, prediction and prevention of criminal behaviour. *Nature Reviews Neuroscience, 15*(1), 54–63.

65. Yang, Y., & Raine, A. (2009). Prefrontal structural and functional brain imaging findings in antisocial, violent, and psychopathic individuals: A meta-analysis. *Psychiatry Research, 174*, 81–88.

66. Raine, A. (2019). The neuromoral theory of antisocial, violent, and psychopathic behavior. *Psychiatry Research, 277*, 64–69.

67. Raine, A. (2014). *The anatomy of violence: The biological roots of crime.* New York, NY: Vintage.

68. Pujol, J., Harrison, B. J., Contreras-Rodriguez, O., & Cardoner, N. (2019). The contribution of brain imaging to the understanding of psychopathy. *Psychological Medicine, 49*(1), 20–31.

69. Vaughn, M. G. (2016). Policy implications of biosocial criminology: Toward a renewed commitment to prevention science. *Criminology & Public Policy, 15*, 703.

70. Gajos, J. M., Fagan, A. A., & Beaver, K. M. (2016). Use of genetically informed evidence-based prevention science to understand and prevent crime and related behavioral disorders. *Criminology & Public Policy, 15*(3), 683–701.

71. Brody, G. H., Beach, S. R., Philibert, R. A., Chen, Y. F., & Murry, V. M. (2009). Prevention effects moderate the association of 5-HTTLPR and youth risk behavior initiation: Gene x environment hypotheses tested via a randomized prevention design. *Child Development, 80*(3), 645–661.

72. Vaughn, M. G. (2016). Policy implications of biosocial criminology: Toward a renewed commitment to prevention science. *Criminology & Public Policy, 15*, 703.

73. Vaughn, M. G. (2016). Policy implications of biosocial criminology: Toward a renewed commitment to prevention science. *Criminology & Public Policy, 15*, 703.

74. Dye, H. (2018). The impact and long-term effects of childhood trauma. *Journal of Human Behavior in the Social Environment, 28*(3), 381–392.

75. Centers for Disease Control and Prevention. (2016). *Preventing child abuse and neglect: A technical package for policy, norm, and programmatic activities.* Division of Violence Prevention. Retrieved from https://www.cdc.gov/violenceprevention/pdf/CAN-Prevention-Technical-Package.pdf

76. National Law Center on Homelessness and Poverty. (2018). *Tent city, USA: The growth of America's homeless encampments and how communities are responding.* Retrieved from https://nlchp.org/wp-content/uploads/2018/10/Tent_City_USA_2017.pdf

77. Aykanian, A., & Fogel, S. J. (2019). The criminalization of homelessness. In H. Larkin, A. Aykanian, & C. Streeter (Eds.), *Homelessness prevention and intervention in social work* (pp. 185–205). Cham, Switzerland: Springer.

78. Dum, C. P., Norris, R. J., & Weng, K. (2017). Punishing benevolence: The criminalization of homeless feeding as an act of state harm. *Critical Criminology, 25*(4), 483–506.

79. National Law Center on Homelessness and Poverty. (2018). *Tent city, USA: The growth of America's homeless encampments and how communities are responding.* Retrieved from https://nlchp.org/wp-content/uploads/2018/10/Tent_City_USA_2017.pdf

80. Stuart, F. (2016). *Down, out, and under arrest: Policing and everyday life in skid row.* Chicago, IL: University of Chicago Press.

81. Schwartz, M., & DeKeseredy, W. (2014). Critical criminology. In J. Albanese (Ed.), *Encyclopedia of criminology and criminal justice* (online). New York, NY: Wiley.

82. Weis, V. V. (2017). *Marxism and criminology: A history of criminal selectivity.* Leiden, Netherlands: Brill.

83. Quinney, R. (1975). Crime control in capitalist society: A critical philosophy of legal order. In *Critical criminology* (pp. 181–203). New York, NY: Routledge.

84. Reiman, J., & Leighton, P. (2020). *The rich get richer and the poor get prison.* New York, NY: Routledge.

85. Marx, K. (1867/1906). *Capital: A critique of political economy.* New York, NY: Charles H. Kerr.

86. Weiss, R., & Weiss, R. (2015). Capitalism as a criminogenic society: Conflict and radical theories of crime. In M. Lanier & S. Henry (Eds.), *Essential criminology.* Nashville, TN: Westview.

87. Matthews, R. (2012). Marxist criminology. In M. Dragiewicz & W. DeKeseredy (Eds.), *Routledge handbook of critical criminology* (pp. 93–104). New York, NY: Routledge.

88. Lynch, M. (2018). Conflict and crime: Marx, Engels, Marxist/radical criminology and the explanation of crime. In R. Triplett (Ed.), *The handbook of the history and philosophy of criminology* (pp. 84–101). Hoboken, NJ: Wiley Blackwell.

89. Chambliss, W. J. (1988). *Exploring criminology.* New York, NY: Macmillan.

90. Engels, F. (1845/1958). *The condition of the working class in England.* Oxford, UK: Blackwell.

91. Quinney, R. (1977). *Class, state, and crime: On the theory and practice of criminal justice.* New York, NY: David McKay.

92. Quinney, R. (1977). *Class, state, and crime: On the theory and practice of criminal justice.* New York, NY: David McKay.

93. Quinney, R. (1977). *Class, state, and crime: On the theory and practice of criminal justice.* New York, NY: David McKay.

94. Chambliss, W. J. (1975). Toward a political economy of crime. *Theory and Society, 2*(1), 149–170.

95. The Sentencing Project. (2021, March 3). *Private prisons in the United States.* Retrieved from https://www.sentencingproject.org/publications/private-prisons-united-states/

96. Human Rights Watch. (2018). *"Set up to fail": The impact of offender-funded private probation on the poor.* Retrieved from https://www.hrw.org/report/2018/02/21/set-fail/impact-offender-funded-private-probation-poor

97. Eisen, L. B. (2017). *Inside private prisons: An American dilemma in the age of mass incarceration.* New York, NY: Columbia University Press.

98. Spitzer, S. (1975). Toward a Marxian theory of deviance. *Social Problems, 22*(5), 638–651.

99. Snedker, K., & McKinney, J. (2018, June 5). Four myths about homelessness: Voices from a tent city. *The Conversation.* Retrieved from https://theconversation.com/four-myths-about-homelessness-voices-from-a-tent-city-96943

100. Marx, K., & Engels, F. (2012). *The communist manifesto.* New Haven, CT: Yale University Press.

101. Friedrichs, D. (2018). Critical criminology and the critique of domination, inequality, and injustice. In H. Pontell (Ed.), *Oxford research encyclopedia of criminology and criminal justice* (online). Oxford, UK: Oxford University Press.

102. Reiman, J., & Leighton, P. (2020). *The rich get richer and the poor get prison.* New York, NY: Routledge.

103. Matthews, R (2010). Realist criminology revisited. In E. McLaughlin & T. Newburn (Eds.), *The SAGE handbook of criminological theory* (pp. 193–209). Thousand Oaks, CA: SAGE.

104. Madfis, E., & Cohen, J. (2016). Critical criminologies of the present and future: Left realism, left idealism, and what's left in between. *Social Justice, 43*(4), 1–21.

105. Britton, D. M., Jacobsen, S. K., & Howard, G. E. (2017). *The gender of crime.* New York, NY: Rowman & Littlefield.

106. Potter, H. (2015). *Intersectionality and criminology: Disrupting and revolutionizing studies of crime.* New York, NY: Routledge.

107. Cook, K. J. (2016). Has criminology awakened from its "androcentric slumber"? *Feminist Criminology, 11*(4), 334–353.

108. Daly, K., & Chesney-Lind, M. (1988). Feminism and criminology. *Justice Quarterly, 5,* 497–538.

109. Hughes, L. A. (2005). The representation of females in criminological research. *Women & Criminal Justice, 16*(1–2), 1–28.

110. Kahle, L., Rosenbaum, J., & King, S. (2018). Examining the intersections of gender and sexual orientation within the discipline: A case for feminist and queer criminology. In R. Martinez, J. Stowell, & M. Hollis (Eds.), *The handbook of race, ethnicity, crime, and justice* (pp. 303–326). New York, NY: Wiley.

111. Kahle, L., Rosenbaum, J., & King, S. (2018). Examining the intersections of gender and sexual orientation within the discipline: A case for feminist and queer criminology. In R. Martinez, J. Stowell, & M. Hollis (Eds.), *The handbook of race, ethnicity, crime, and justice* (pp. 303–326). New York, NY: Wiley.

112. Renzetti, C. M. (2018). Feminist perspectives. In M. Dragiewicz & W. DeKeseredy (Eds.), *Routledge handbook of critical criminology* (pp. 74–82). New York, NY: Routledge.

113. Britton, D. M., Jacobsen, S. K., & Howard, G. E. (2017). *The gender of crime.* New York, NY: Rowman & Littlefield.

114. Renzetti, C. M. (2018). Feminist perspectives. In M. Dragiewicz & W. DeKeseredy (Eds.), *Routledge handbook of critical criminology* (pp. 74–82). New York, NY: Routledge.

115. Connor, R. A., Glick, P., & Fiske, S. T. (2017). Ambivalent sexism in the twenty-first century. In C. Sibley & F. Barlow (Eds.), *Cambridge handbook of the psychology of prejudice* (pp. 295–320). Cambridge, UK: Cambridge University Press.

116. Scaptura, M. N., & Boyle, K. M. (2020). Masculinity threat, "incel" traits, and violent fantasies among heterosexual men in the United States. *Feminist Criminology, 15*(3), 278–298.

117. Connor, R. A., Glick, P., & Fiske, S. T. (2017). Ambivalent sexism in the twenty-first century. In C. Sibley & F. Barlow (Eds.), *Cambridge handbook of the psychology of prejudice* (pp. 295–320). Cambridge, UK: Cambridge University Press.

118. Cutroni, L., & Anderson, J. (2021). Lady injustice: The moderating effect of ambivalent sexism in a mock case of intimate partner homicide. *Criminal Justice and Behavior, 48*(3), 373–390.

119. Renzetti, C. M. (2018). Feminist perspectives. In M. Dragiewicz & W. DeKeseredy (Eds.), *Routledge handbook of critical criminology* (pp. 74–82). New York, NY: Routledge.

120. Chesney-Lind, M., & Morash, M. (2013). Transformative feminist criminology: A critical re-thinking of a discipline. *Critical Criminology, 21*(3), 287–304.

121. Renzetti, C. M. (2018). Feminist perspectives. In M. Dragiewicz & W. DeKeseredy (Eds.), *Routledge handbook of critical criminology* (pp. 74–82). New York, NY: Routledge.

122. Goodmark, L. (2018). Innovative criminal justice responses to intimate partner violence. In C. M. Renzetti, J. L. Edleson, & R. K. Bergen (Eds.), *Sourcebook on violence against women* (3rd ed., pp. 253–270). Thousand Oaks, CA: SAGE.

123. Richie, B. E. (2012). *Arrested justice: Black women, violence, and America's prison nation.* New York, NY: New York University Press.

124. National Network to End Domestic Violence. (2021). Violence Against Women Act. Retrieved from https://nnedv.org/content/violence-against-women-act/

125. Cabage, L. N. (2019). Prison programming for females. In N. Rafter (Ed.), *The encyclopedia of women and crime* (online). New York, NY: Wiley.

126. Sue, K. (2019). *Getting wrecked: Women, incarceration, and the American opioid crisis.* Berkeley: University of California Press.

127. Phillips, N. D., & Chagnon, N. (2020). "Six months is a joke": Carceral feminism and penal populism in the wake of the Stanford sexual assault case. *Feminist Criminology, 15*(1), 47–69.

128. Levenson, J., & Ackerman, A. (2016, July 19). The Stanford rape case: Maybe we're having the wrong conversation? *Psychology Today.* Retrieved from https://www.psychologytoday.com/us/blog/the-guest-room/201607/the-stanford-rape-case

129. Pali, B. (2017). Towards integrative frameworks for addressing sexual violence: Feminist, abolitionist, social harm, and restorative perspectives. In E. Zinsstag, & M. Keenan (Eds.), *Restorative responses to sexual violence: Legal, social and therapeutic dimensions* (pp. 28–43). New York, NY: Taylor & Francis.

130. Kahle, L., Rosenbaum, J., & King, S. (2018). Examining the intersections of gender and sexual orientation within the discipline: A case for feminist and queer criminology. In R. Martinez, J. Stowell, & M. Hollis (Eds.), *The handbook of*

race, ethnicity, crime, and justice (pp. 303–326). New York, NY: Wiley.

131. Buist, C., Lenning, E., & Ball, M. (2018). Queer criminology. In M. Dragiewicz & W. DeKeseredy (Eds.), *Routledge handbook of critical criminology* (pp. 96–106). New York, NY: Routledge.

132. American Civil Liberties Union. (n.d.). *Why sodomy laws matter.* Retrieved from https://www.aclu.org/other/why-sodomy-laws-matter

133. Human Right Watch. (n.d.). *#Outlawed: "The love that dare not speak its name."* Retrieved from http://internap.hrw.org/features/features/lgbt_laws/index-june15.html#type-of-laws

134. Alexander, M. (2010). *The new Jim Crow: Mass incarceration in the age of colorblindness.* New York: NYU Press.

135. GLAAD. (2017, April). *Debunking the "bathroom bill" myth—Accurate reporting on nondiscrimination: A guide for journalists.* Retrieved from https://www.glaad.org/sites/default/files/Debunking_the_Bathroom_Bill_Myth_2017.pdf

136. James, S. E., Herman, J. L., Rankin, S., Keisling, M., Mottet, L., & Anafi, M. (2016). *The report of the 2015 U.S. transgender survey.* Washington, DC: National Center for Transgender Equality.

137. Lenning, E., Brightman, S., & Buist, C. L. (2021). The trifecta of violence: A socio-historical comparison of lynching and violence against transgender women. *Critical Criminology, 29*(1), 151–172.

138. Kutateladze, B. L. (2021). Acting "straight": Socio-behavioral consequences of anti-queer hate crime victimization. *Justice Quarterly*, 1–23.

139. Walters, M. A., Paterson, J., Brown, R., & McDonnell, L. (2020). Hate crimes against trans people: Assessing emotions, behaviors, and attitudes toward criminal justice agencies. *Journal of Interpersonal Violence, 35*(21–22), 4583–4613.

140. Robinson, B. A. (2020). *Coming out to the streets: LGBTQ youth experiencing homelessness.* Berkeley: University of California Press.

141. Brown, J. A., & Jenness, V. (2020). LGBT people in prison: Management strategies, human rights violations, and political mobilization. In H. Pontell (Ed.), *Oxford research encyclopedia of criminology and criminal justice* (online). Oxford, UK: Oxford University Press.

142. Buist, C., & Lenning, E. (2016). *Queer criminology.* London, UK: Routledge.

143. Buist, C., Lenning, E., & Ball, M. (2018). Queer criminology. In M. Dragiewicz & W. DeKeseredy (Eds.), *Routledge handbook of critical criminology* (pp. 96–106). New York, NY: Routledge.

144. Hastings, A., Browne, A., Kall, K., & DiZerega, M. (2015, April). *Keeping vulnerable populations safe under PREA: Alternative strategies to the use of segregation in prisons and jails.* Washington, DC: National PREA Justice Center.

145. Ross, L. (2020). Frameworks of critical race theory. In H. Pontell (Ed.), *Oxford research encyclopedia of criminology and criminal justice* (online). Oxford, UK: Oxford University Press.

146. Patel, T., & Tyrer, D. (2011). *Race, crime, and resistance.* Thousand Oaks, CA: SAGE.

147. Delgado, R., & Stefancic, J. (2010). *Critical race theory: An introduction.* New York, NY: NYU Press.

148. Ross, L. (2020). Frameworks of critical race theory. In H. Pontell (Ed.), *Oxford research encyclopedia of criminology and criminal justice* (online). Oxford, UK: Oxford University Press.

149. Delgado, R., & Stefancic, J. (2010). *Critical race theory: An introduction.* New York: NYU Press.

150. Gabbidon, S., & Greene, H. (2019). *Race and crime* (5th ed.). Thousand Oaks, CA: SAGE.

151. Netherland, J., & Hansen, H. (2017). White opioids: Pharmaceutical race and the war on drugs that wasn't. *BioSocieties, 12*(2), 217–238.

152. Johnson, D. (2019). Foreword. In I. Chettiar & P. Raghavan (Eds.), *Ending mass incarceration: Ideas from today's leaders.* New York: Brennan Center for Justice at the New York School of Law.

153. Alexander, M. (2010). *The new Jim Crow: Mass incarceration in the age of colorblindness.* New York, NY: New Press.

154. Netherland, J., & Hansen, H. (2017). White opioids: Pharmaceutical race and the war on drugs that wasn't. *BioSocieties, 12*(2), 217–238.

155. Provine, D. M. (2011). Race and inequality in the war on drugs. *Annual Review of Law and Social Science, 7,* 41–60.

156. Light, M. T. (2021). The declining significance of race in criminal sentencing: Evidence from U.S. federal courts. *Social Forces,* 1–32.

157. Gabbidon, S., & Greene, H. (2019). Race and crime (5th ed.). Thousand Oaks, CA: SAGE.

158. Alexander, M. (2010). *The new Jim Crow: Mass incarceration in the age of colorblindness.* New York, NY: New Press.

159. Beirne, P., & South, N. (2013). Introduction: Approaching green criminology. In P. Beirne & N. South (Eds.), *Issues in green criminology* (pp. xiii–xxii). New York, NY: Routledge.

160. Lynch, M. J., Long, M. A., Stretesky, P. B., & Barrett, K. L. (2017). *Green criminology: Crime, justice, and the environment.* Berkeley: University of California Press.

161. Brisman, A., & South, N. (2019). Green criminology and environmental crimes and harms. *Sociology Compass, 13*(1), e12650.

162. Lynch, M. J., Long, M. A., Stretesky, P. B., & Barrett, K. L. (2017). *Green criminology: Crime, justice, and the environment.* Berkeley: University of California Press.

163. White, R., & Heckenberg, D. (2014). *Green criminology: An introduction to the study of environmental harm.* Abingdon, UK: Routledge.

164. Brisman, A., & South, N. (2019). Green criminology and environmental crimes and harms. *Sociology Compass, 13*(1), e12650.

165. Lynch, M. J., Long, M. A., Stretesky, P. B., & Barrett, K. L. (2017). *Green criminology: Crime, justice, and the environment.* Berkeley: University of California Press.

166. Lynch, M. J. (2020). Green criminology and environmental crime: Criminology that matters in the age of global ecological collapse. *Journal of White Collar and Corporate Crime, 1*(1), 50–61.

167. White, R. (2017). Introduction. In R. White (Ed.), *Transnational environmental crime* (pp. xiii–xxix). Abingdon, UK: Routledge.

CHAPTER 8

1. Oppmann, P. (2010, July 22). *Court records reveal troubled childhood of "barefoot bandit."* CNN. Retrieved from https://www.cnn.com/2010/CRIME/07/22/barefoot.bandit.profile/index.html

2. Department of Justice, U.S. Attorney's Office, Western District of Washington. (2012, January 27). *Camano Island man sentenced to 78 months in prison for multi-state crime spree.* Retrieved from https://www.justice.gov/archive/usao/waw/press/2012/jan/harris.html

3. Yardley, W. (2010, July 12). Barefoot run ends in Bahamas. *The New York Times.* Retrieved from https://www.nytimes.com/2010/07/13/us/13barefoot.html?searchResultPosition=7

4. Oppmann, P. (2010, July 22). *Court records reveal troubled childhood of "barefoot bandit."* CNN. Retrieved from https://www.cnn.com/2010/CRIME/07/22/barefoot.bandit.profile/index.html

5. Dahl, J. (2010, December 15). *Report: "Barefoot Bandit" Colton Harris-Moore endured abuse, family dysfunction before crime spree.* CBS News. Retrieved from https://www.cbsnews.com/news/report-barefoot-bandit-colton-harris-moore-endured-abuse-family-dysfunction-before-crime-spree/

6. Kersten, J. (2010, May 13). The airplane thief. *Rolling Stone Magazine.* Retrieved from https://www.rollingstone.com/culture/culture-news/the-airplane-thief-244878/

7. Oppmann, P. (2010, July 22). *Court records reveal troubled childhood of "barefoot bandit."* CNN. Retrieved from https://www.cnn.com/2010/CRIME/07/22/barefoot.bandit.profile/index.html

8. Adler, R. (2011, September 8). Colton Harris-Moore psychiatric evaluation. *Internet Archive.* Retrieved from https://archive.org/stream/274832-colton-harris-moore-psychological-evaluation/274832-colton-harris-moore-psychological-evaluation_djvu.txt

9. Adler, R. (2011, September 8). Colton Harris-Moore psychiatric evaluation. *Internet Archive.* Retrieved from https://archive.org/stream/274832-colton-harris-moore-psychological-evaluation/274832-colton-harris-moore-psychological-evaluation_djvu.txt

10. Cullen, F. T., Wilcox, P., Sampson, R. J., & Dooley, B. D. (Eds.) (2015). *Challenging criminological theory: The legacy of Ruth Rosner Kornhauser.* Piscataway, NJ: Transaction Publishers.

11. Hirschi, T. (1969). *Causes of delinquency.* Berkeley: University of California Press.

12. Costello, B. J., & Laub, J. H. (2020). Social control theory: The legacy of Travis Hirschi's Causes of delinquency. *Annual Review of Criminology, 3,* 21–41.

13. Ward, J. T. (2019). Developmental and life-course theories of crime and deviance. In M. Krohn, N. Hendrix, G. P. Hall, & A. Lizotte (Eds.), *Handbook on crime and deviance* (pp. 283–308). Cham, Switzerland: Springer.

14. Nagin, D. S., & Sampson, R. J. (2019). The real gold standard: Measuring counterfactual worlds that matter most to social science and policy. *Annual Review of Criminology, 2,* 123–145.

15. Hardie, B. (2019). Why monitoring doesn't always matter: The interaction of personal propensity with physical and psychological parental presence in a situational explanation of adolescent offending. *Deviant Behavior,* 1–24.

16. Hirschi, T. (1969). *Causes of delinquency.* Berkeley: University of California Press.

17. Hirschi, T. (1969). *Causes of delinquency.* Berkeley: University of California Press.

18. Hoeve, M., Stams, G. J. J., Van der Put, C. E., Dubas, J. S., Van der Laan, P. H., & Gerris, J. R. (2012). A meta-analysis of attachment to parents and delinquency. *Journal of Abnormal Child Psychology, 40,* 771–785.

19. Costello, B. J., & Laub, J. H. (2020). Social control theory: The legacy of Travis Hirschi's *Causes of Delinquency. Annual Review of Criminology, 3,* 21–41.

20. Ishoy, G. A. (2017). Exploring morality as a mediator of the association between parenting practices and violent and property offending among a sample of juvenile delinquents. *Crime & Delinquency, 63,* 113–136.

21. Staff, J., Osgood, D. W., Schulenberg, J. E., Bachman, J. G., & Messersmith, E. E. (2010). Explaining the relationship between employment and juvenile delinquency. *Criminology, 48,* 1101–1131.

22. Gibbons, D. C. (1994). *Talking about crime and criminals: Problems and issues in theory development in criminology.* Englewood Cliffs, NJ: Prentice Hall.

23. Mills, C. E., Freilich, J. D., Chermak, S. M., Holt, T. J., & LaFree, G. (2019). Social learning and social control in the off-and online pathways to hate crime and terrorist violence. *Studies in Conflict & Terrorism,* 1–29.

24. Gottschalk, P. (2020). *Case studies of executive deviance: A theory of business convenience.* Northampton, MA: Edward Elgar.

25. van Onna, J. H., & Denkers, A. J. (2019). Social bonds and white-collar crime: A two-study assessment of informal social controls in white-collar offenders. *Deviant Behavior, 40,* 1206–1225.

26. Hirschi, T. (1969). *Causes of delinquency.* Berkeley: University of California Press.

27. McGloin, J. M., & Thomas, K. J. (2019). Peer influence and delinquency. *Annual Review of Criminology, 2,* 241–264.

28. Buist, K. L. (2010). Sibling relationship quality and adolescent delinquency: A latent growth curve approach. *Journal of Family Psychology, 24,* 400–410.

29. Meisel, S. N., & Colder, C. R. (2019). Dyadic and group-level positive friendship characteristics and susceptibility to perceived delinquent peer substance use. *Journal of Early Adolescence, 39,* 477–498.

30. Boman, J. H., Krohn, M. D., Gibson, C. L., & Stogner, J. M. (2012). Investigating friendship quality: An exploration of self-control and social control theories' friendship hypotheses. *Journal of Youth and Adolescence, 41,* 1526–1540.

31. Hirschi, T. (1969). *Causes of delinquency.* Berkeley: University of California Press.

32. Ward, J. T. (2019). Developmental and life-course theories of crime and deviance. In M. Krohn, N. Hendrix, G. P. Hall, & A. Lizotte (Eds.), *Handbook on crime and deviance* (pp. 283–308). Cham, Switzerland: Springer.

33. Ellis, L., Farrington, D. P., & Hoskin, A. W. (2019). *Handbook of crime correlates.* Cambridge, MA: Academic Press.

34. Laub, J. H., & Sampson, R. J. (2003). *Shared beginnings, divergent lives: Delinquent boys to age 70.* Cambridge, MA: Harvard University Press.

35. Sampson, R. J., & Laub, J. H. (2016). Turning points and the future of life-course criminology: Reflections on the 1986 criminal careers report. *Journal of Research in Crime and Delinquency, 53,* 321–335.

36. Farrington, D. (2017). *Integrated developmental and life-course theories of offending.* New York, NY: Routledge.

37. El Sayed, S. A., Pacheco, D. F., & Morris, R. G. (2016). The link between onset age and adult offending: The role of developmental profiles. *Deviant Behavior, 37,* 989–1002.

38. Liu, J., Francis, B., & Soothill, K. (2011). A longitudinal study of escalation in crime seriousness. *Journal of Quantitative Criminology, 27,* 175–196.

39. Ouellet, F. (2019). Stop and go: Explaining the timing of intermittency in criminal careers. *Crime & Delinquency, 65,* 630–656.

40. Bersani, B. E., & Doherty, E. E. (2018). Desistance from offending in the twenty-first century. *Annual Review of Criminology, 1,* 311–334.

41. Sampson, R. J., & Laub, J. H. (2017). A general age-graded theory of crime: Lessons learned and the future of life-course criminology. In D. Farrington (Ed.), *Integrated developmental and life-course theories of offending* (pp. 165–182). New York, NY: Routledge.

42. Sampson, R. J., & Laub, J. H. (2016). Turning points and the future of life-course criminology: Reflections on the 1986 criminal careers report. *Journal of Research in Crime and Delinquency, 53,* 321–335.

43. Laub, J. H., & Sampson, R. J. (2003). *Shared beginnings, divergent lives: Delinquent boys to age 70.* Cambridge, MA: Harvard University Press.

44. Nguyen, H., & Loughran, T. A. (2018). On the measurement and identification of turning points in criminology. *Annual Review of Criminology, 1,* 335–358.

45. Healy, D. (2017). *The dynamics of desistance: Charting pathways through change.* New York, NY: Taylor & Francis.

46. Mitchell, O., Landers, M., & Morales, M. (2018). The contingent effects of fatherhood on offending. *American Journal of Criminal Justice, 43,* 603–626.

47. Dupéré, V., Leventhal, T., Dion, E., Crosnoe, R., Archambault, I., & Janosz, M. (2015). Stressors and turning points in high school and dropout: A stress process, life course framework. *Review of Educational Research, 85,* 591–629.

48. Weijers, I. (2020). The role of partners and parents in young persistent offenders' struggles to desist from crime. *European Journal of Probation, 12,* 112–128.

49. Laub, J., Rowan, Z., & Sampson, R. (2019). The age-graded theory of informal social control. In D. Farrington, L. Kazemian, & A. Piquero (Eds.), *The Oxford handbook of developmental and life-course criminology* (pp. 295–322). New York, NY: Oxford University Press.

50. Laub, J., Rowan, Z., & Sampson, R. (2019). The age-graded theory of informal social control. In D. Farrington, L. Kazemian, & A. Piquero (Eds.), *The Oxford handbook of developmental and life-course criminology* (pp. 295–322). New York, NY: Oxford University Press.

51. Bottoms, A. (2006). Desistance, social bonds, and human agency: A theoretical exploration. In P. H. Wikström & R. J. Sampson (Eds.), *The explanation of crime: Context, mechanisms and development* (pp. 243–290). Cambridge, UK: Cambridge University Press.

52. Nextdoor. (n.d.). *About us.* Retrieved from https://about.nextdoor.com/

53. Nextdoor. (n.d.). *Tap into Nextdoor.* Retrieved from https://nextdoor.com/

54. Kubrin, C. E., & Wo, J. C. (2016). Social disorganization theory's greatest challenge: Linking structural characteristics to crime in socially disorganized communities. In A. Piquero (Ed.), *The handbook of criminological theory* (pp. 121–136). New York, NY: Wiley Blackwell.

55. Bernard, T. J., Snipes, J. B., & Gerould, A. L. (2010). *Vold's theoretical criminology* (6th ed.). New York, NY: Oxford University Press.

56. Gaines, L. K., & Kappeler, V. E. (2014). *Policing in America.* New York, NY: Routledge.

57. Steverson, L. (2008). *Policing in America: A reference handbook.* Santa Barbara, CA: ABC-CLIO.

58. Chicago Department of Development and Planning. (1976). *The people of Chicago: Who we are and who we have been: Census data on foreign born, foreign stock, and race, 1837-1970.* Chicago, IL: City of Chicago.

59. Du Bois, W. E. B. (1996). *The Philadelphia negro: A social study.* Philadelphia: University of Pennsylvania Press. (Original work published 1899)

60. Park, R. E., & Burgess, E. W. (1925). The growth of the city: An introduction to a research project. In R. E. Park, E. W. Burgess, & R. D. McKenzie (Eds.), *The city* (Chap. 2). Chicago, IL: University of Chicago Press.

61. Shaw, C. R., & McKay, H. D. (1942). *Juvenile delinquency and urban areas.* Chicago, IL: University of Chicago Press.

62. Kubrin, C., & Mioduszewski, M. (2019). Social disorganization theory: Past, present, and future. In M. Krohn, N. Hendrix, G. P. Hall, & A. Lizotte (Eds.), *Handbook on crime and deviance* (pp. 197–211). Cham, Switzerland: Springer.

63. Kubrin, C. E., & Wo, J. C. (2016). Social disorganization theory's greatest challenge: Linking structural characteristics to crime in socially disorganized communities. In A. Piquero (Ed.), *The handbook of criminological theory* (pp. 121–136). New York, NY: Wiley Blackwell.

64. Kubrin, C., & Mioduszewski, M. (2019). Social disorganization theory: Past, present, and future. In M. Krohn, N. Hendrix, G. P. Hall, & A. Lizotte (Eds.), *Handbook on crime and deviance* (pp. 197–211). Cham, Switzerland: Springer.

65. Brunton-Smith, I., Sturgis, P., & Leckie, G. (2018). How collective is collective efficacy? The importance of consensus in judgments about community cohesion and willingness to intervene. *Criminology, 56,* 608–637.

66. Wickes, R., Hipp, J., Sargeant, E., & Mazerolle, L. (2017). Neighborhood social ties and shared expectations for informal social control: Do they influence informal social control actions? *Journal of Quantitative Criminology, 33,* 101–129.

67. Kubrin, C. E., & Wo, J. C. (2016). Social disorganization theory's greatest challenge: Linking structural characteristics to crime in socially disorganized communities. In A. Piquero (Ed.), *The handbook of criminological theory* (pp. 121–136). New York, NY: Wiley Blackwell.

68. Sharkey, P., Torrats-Espinosa, G., & Takyar, D. (2017). Community and the crime decline: The causal effect of local nonprofits on violent crime. *American Sociological Review, 82,* 1214–1240.

69. Bursik, R. J., Jr., & Grasmick, H. G. (1993). *Neighborhoods and crime.* New York, NY: Lexington Books.

70. National Archive of Criminal Justice Data. (n.d.). *Resource guide: Project on human development in Chicago neighborhoods.* Retrieved from https://www.icpsr.umich.edu/web/pages/NACJD/guides/phdcn/index.html

71. Becker, J. H. (2019). Within-neighborhood dynamics: Disadvantage, collective efficacy, and homicide rates in Chicago. *Social Problems, 66,* 428–447.

72. Morenoff, J. D., Sampson, R. J., & Raudenbush, S. W. (2001). Neighborhood inequality, collective efficacy, and the spatial dynamics of urban violence. *Criminology, 39,* 517–558.

73. Melo, S. N. D., Andresen, M. A., & Matias, L. F. (2017). Geography of crime in a Brazilian context: An application of social disorganization theory. *Urban Geography, 38,* 1550–1572.

74. Cho, S., Lee, Y. H., & Harper, S. B. (2020). Testing the systemic model of social disorganization theory in South Korean neighborhoods: A latent class growth analysis approach to specifying pathways to homicide. *Homicide Studies,* 1–25.

75. Danielsson, P. (2019). Collective efficacy and violent crime in suburban housing estates. *European Journal of Criminology,* 1–21.

76. He, D., & Messner, S. F. (2020). Social disorganization theory in contemporary China: A review of the evidence and directions for future research. *Asian Journal of Criminology, 15,* 1–24.

77. Prison Policy Initiative. (2020). *Mass incarceration: The whole pie, 2020.* Retrieved from https://www.prisonpolicy.org/reports/pie2020.html

78. Kirk, D. S. (2019). Where the other 1 percent live: An examination of changes in the spatial concentration of the formerly incarcerated. *RSF: The Russell Sage Foundation Journal of the Social Sciences, 5,* 255–274.

79. Simes, J. T. (2018). Place and punishment: The spatial context of mass incarceration. *Journal of Quantitative Criminology, 34,* 513–533.

80. National Research Council. (2014). The growth of incarceration in the United States: Exploring causes and consequences. Washington, DC: National Academies Press. Retrieved from https://doi.org/10.17226/18613

81. Clear, T. R., Rose, D. R., Waring, E., & Scully, K. (2003). Coercive mobility and crime: A preliminary examination of concentrated incarceration and social disorganization. *Justice Quarterly, 20,* 33–64.

82. Rose, D. R., & Clear, T. R. (1998). Incarceration, social capital, and crime: Implications for social disorganization theory. *Criminology, 36,* 441–480.

83. Kirk, D. S., & Matsuda, M. (2011). Legal cynicism, collective efficacy, and the ecology of arrest. *Criminology, 49,* 443–472.

84. Kirk, D. S. (2016). Prisoner reentry and the reproduction of legal cynicism. *Social Problems, 63,* 222–243.

85. Wilson, W. J. (2012). *The truly disadvantaged: The inner city, the underclass, and public policy.* Chicago, IL: University of Chicago Press.

86. Raleigh, E., & Galster, G. (2015). Neighborhood disinvestment, abandonment, and crime dynamics. *Journal of Urban Affairs, 37,* 367–396.

87. Kennedy, M., & Leonard, P. (2001). *Dealing with neighborhood change: A primer on gentrification and policy changes.* Discussion paper prepared for the Brookings Institution Center on Urban and Metropolitan Policy. Retrieved from https://www.brookings.edu/wp-content/uploads/2016/06/gentrification.pdf

88. Frey, W. (2020, May 26). *American cities saw uneven growth last decade, new census data show.* Brookings Institution. Retrieved from https://www.brookings.edu/research/new-census-data-show-an-uneven-decade-of-growth-for-us-cities/

89. MacDonald, J. M., & Stokes, R. J. (2020). Gentrification, land use, and crime. *Annual Review of Criminology, 3,* 121–138.

90. The Uprooted Project. (n.d.). *Understanding gentrification and displacement.* University of Texas at Austin. Retrieved from https://sites.utexas.edu/gentrificationproject/understanding-gentrification-and-displacement/

91. Barton, M. S., Valasik, M. A., Brault, E., & Tita, G. (2020). "Gentefication" in the barrio: Examining the relationship between gentrification and homicide in East Los Angeles. *Crime & Delinquency, 66,* 1888–1913.

92. Gibbons, J., Barton, M. S., & Reling, T. T. (2020). Do gentrifying neighbourhoods have less community? Evidence from Philadelphia. *Urban Studies, 57,* 1143–1163.

93. Barton, M. S. (2016). Gentrification and violent crime in New York City. *Crime & Delinquency, 62,* 1180–1202.

94. Doering, J. (2020). *Us versus them: Race, crime, and gentrification in Chicago neighborhoods.* New York, NY: Oxford University Press.

95. Zuk, M., Bierbaum, A. H., Chapple, K., Gorska, K., & Loukaitou-Sideris, A. (2018). Gentrification, displacement, and the role of public investment. *Journal of Planning Literature, 33,* 31–44.

96. Barton, M. S. (2016). Gentrification and violent crime in New York City. *Crime & Delinquency, 62,* 1180–1202.

97. Boggess, L. N., & Hipp, J. R. (2016). The spatial dimensions of gentrification and the consequences for neighborhood crime. *Justice Quarterly, 33*, 584–613.

98. Barton, M. S., Valasik, M. A., Brault, E., & Tita, G. (2020). "Gentefication" in the barrio: Examining the relationship between gentrification and homicide in East Los Angeles. *Crime & Delinquency, 66*, 1888–1913.

99. Papachristos, A. V., Smith, C. M., Scherer, M. L., & Fugiero, M. A. (2011). More coffee, less crime? The relationship between gentrification and neighborhood crime rates in Chicago, 1991 to 2005. *City & Community, 10*, 215–240.

100. Rogers, E., & Pridemore, W. (2016). Research on social disorganization theory and crime in rural communities. In J. Donnemeyer (Ed.), *The Routledge international handbook of rural criminology*. New York, NY: Routledge.

101. Singer, S. I., & Drakulich, K. (2019). Crime and safety in suburbia. *Annual Review of Criminology, 2*, 147–165.

102. Kang-Brown, J., & Subramanian, R. (2017). *Out of sight: The growth of jails in rural America*. Vera Institute of Justice. Retrieved from https://www.vera.org/downloads/publications/out-of-sight-growth-of-jails-rural-america.pdf

103. Kang-Brown, J., & Subramanian, R. (2017). *Out of sight: The growth of jails in rural America*. Vera Institute of Justice. Retrieved from https://www.vera.org/downloads/publications/out-of-sight-growth-of-jails-rural-america.pdf

104. Palombi, L. C., St Hill, C. A., Lipsky, M. S., Swanoski, M. T., & Lutfiyya, M. N. (2018). A scoping review of opioid misuse in the rural United States. *Annals of Epidemiology, 28*, 641–652.

105. Oppel, Jr., R. A. (2019, December 13). "A cesspool of a dungeon": The surging population in rural jails. *The New York Times*. Retrieved from https://www.nytimes.com/2019/12/13/us/rural-jails.html

106. Snowden, A. J., Stucky, T. D., & Pridemore, W. A. (2017). Alcohol outlets, social disorganization, and non-violent crimes in urban neighborhoods. *Journal of Crime and Justice, 40*, 430–445.

107. Ford, J. A., Sacra, S. A., & Yohros, A. (2017). Neighborhood characteristics and prescription drug misuse among adolescents: The importance of social disorganization and social capital. *International Journal of Drug Policy, 46*, 47–53.

108. Ward, K. C., Kirschner, E. E., & Thompson, A. J. (2018). Social disorganization and rural/urban crime rates: A county level comparison of contributing factors. *International Journal of Rural Criminology, 4*, 43–65.

109. Bouffard, L. A., & Muftić, L. R. (2006). The "rural Mystique": Social disorganization and violence beyond urban communities. *Western Criminology Review, 7*, 56–66.

110. Chilenski, S. M., Syvertsen, A. K., & Greenberg, M. T. (2015). Understanding the link between social organization and crime in rural communities. *Journal of Rural and Community Development, 10*, 109–127.

111. Lee, M. R., & Thomas, S. A. (2010). Civic community, population change, and violent crime in rural communities. *Journal of Research in Crime and Delinquency, 47*, 118–147.

112. Kaylen, M. T., & Pridemore, W. A. (2013). The association between social disorganization and rural violence is sensitive to the measurement of the dependent variable. *Criminal Justice Review, 38*, 169–189.

113. Bellair, P. (2017). Social disorganization theory. In H. Pontell (Ed.), *Oxford research encyclopedia of criminology and criminal justice*. New York, NY: Oxford University Press.

114. Liu, L. (2020). Family, parochial, and public levels of social control and recidivism: An extension of the systemic model of social disorganization. *Crime & Delinquency, 66*, 864–886.

115. Hart, T. C., & Waller, J. (2013). Neighborhood boundaries and structural determinants of social disorganization: Examining the validity of commonly used measures. *Western Criminology Review, 14*, 16–33.

116. Hipp, J. R., & Boessen, A. (2013). Egohoods as waves washing across the city: A new measure of "neighborhoods." *Criminology, 51*, 287–327.

117. Kubrin, C. E., & Weitzer, R. (2003). New directions in social disorganization theory. *Journal of Research in Crime and Delinquency, 40*, 374–402.

118. Porter, J. R., Rader, N. E., & Cossman, J. S. (2012). Social disorganization and neighborhood fear: Examining the intersection of individual, community, and county characteristics. *American Journal of Criminal Justice, 37*, 229–245.

119. Rogers, E., & Pridemore, W. (2016). Research on social disorganization theory and crime in rural communities. In J. Donnemeyer (Ed.), *The Routledge international handbook of rural criminology* (pp. 23–31). New York, NY: Routledge.

120. Singer, S. I., & Drakulich, K. (2019). Crime and safety in suburbia. *Annual Review of Criminology, 2*, 147–165.

121. Mischel, W., Ebbesen, E. B. (1970). Attention in delay of gratification. *Journal of Personality and Social Psychology, 16*, 329–337.

122. Mischel, W., Ebbesen, E. B., & Raskoff Zeiss, A. (1972). Cognitive and attentional mechanisms in delay of gratification. *Journal of Personality and Social Psychology, 21*, 204–218.

123. Shoda, Y., Mischel, W., & Peake, P. K. (1990). Predicting adolescent cognitive and self-regulatory competencies from preschool delay of gratification: Identifying diagnostic conditions. *Developmental Psychology, 26*, 978–986.

124. Casey, B. J., Somerville, L. H., Gotlib, I. H., Ayduk, O., Franklin, N. T., Askren, M. K., . . . Glover, G. (2011). Behavioral and neural correlates of delay of gratification 40 years later. *Proceedings of the National Academy of Sciences, 108*, 14,998–15,003.

125. Gottfredson, M., & Hirschi, T. (1990). *A general theory of crime*. Redwood City, CA: Stanford University Press.

126. Gottfredson, M., & Hirschi, T. (1990). *A general theory of crime*. Redwood City, CA: Stanford University Press.

127. Turner, M. G., & Piquero, A. R. (2002). The stability of self-control. *Journal of Criminal Justice, 30*, 457–471.

128. Gottfredson, M., & Hirschi, T. (1990). *A general theory of crime*. Redwood City, CA: Stanford University Press.

129. Gottfredson, M., & Hirschi, T. (1990). *A general theory of crime*. Redwood City, CA: Stanford University Press.

130. Paternoster, R., & Brame, R. (2000). On the association among self-control, crime, and analogous behaviors. *Criminology, 38*, 971–982.

131. Rocque, M., & Piquero, A. (2019). Self-control theory: Theoretical and research issues. In M. Krohn, N. Hendrix, G. P. Hall, & A. Lizotte (Eds.), *Handbook on crime and deviance* (pp. 131–144). Cham, Switzerland: Springer.

132. Mazerolle, P., & McPhedran, S. (2018). Specialization and versatility in offending. In D. Farrington, L. Kazemian, & A. Piquero (Eds.), *The Oxford handbook of developmental and life-course criminology* (pp. 49–69). New York, NY: Oxford University Press.

133. DeLisi, M., Drury, A., Elbert, M., Tahja, K., Caropreso, D., & Heinrichs, T. (2017). Sexual sadism and criminal versatility: Does sexual sadism spillover into nonsexual crimes? *Journal of Aggression, Conflict and Peace Research, 9*, 2–12.

134. Mazerolle, P., & McPhedran, S. (2018). Specialization and versatility in offending. In D. Farrington, L. Kazemian, & A. Piquero (Eds.), *The Oxford handbook of developmental and life-course criminology* (pp. 49–69). New York, NY: Oxford University Press.

135. DeLisi, M., Bunga, R., Heirigs, M. H., Erickson, J. H., & Hochstetler, A. (2019). The past is prologue: Criminal specialization continuity in the delinquent career. *Youth Violence and Juvenile Justice, 17*, 335–353.

136. DeLisi, M., Bunga, R., Heirigs, M. H., Erickson, J. H., & Hochstetler, A. (2019). The past is prologue: Criminal specialization continuity in the delinquent career. *Youth Violence and Juvenile Justice, 17*, 335–353.

137. Geis, G. (2000). On the absence of self-control as the basis for a general theory of crime: A critique. *Theoretical Criminology, 4*, 35–53.

138. Hirschi, T., & Gottfredson, M. (1993). Commentary: Testing the general theory of crime. *Journal of Research in Crime and Delinquency, 30*, 47–54.

139. Geis, G. (2000). On the absence of self-control as the basis for a general theory of crime: A critique. *Theoretical Criminology, 4*, 35–53.

140. Gottfredson, M., & Hirschi, T. (1990). *A general theory of crime.* Redwood City, CA: Stanford University Press.

141. Sweeten, G., Piquero, A. R., & Steinberg, L. (2013). Age and the explanation of crime, revisited. *Journal of Youth and Adolescence, 42*, 921–938.

142. Burt, C. H., Sweeten, G., & Simons, R. L. (2014). Self-control through emerging adulthood: Instability, multidimensionality, and criminological significance. *Criminology, 52*, 450–487.

143. Forrest, W., Hay, C., Widdowson, A. O., & Rocque, M. (2019). Development of impulsivity and risk-seeking: Implications for the dimensionality and stability of self-control. *Criminology, 57*, 512–543.

144. Spigel, A. (2016, June 24). The personality myth [Audio podcast episode]. In *Invisibilia*. NPR. Retrieved from https://www.npr.org/programs/invisibilia/482836315/the-personality-myth

145. Mischel, W. (2015). *The marshmallow test: Understanding self-control and how to master it.* London, UK: Transworld.

146. Kidd, C., Palmeri, H., & Aslin, R. N. (2013). Rational snacking: Young children's decision-making on the marshmallow task is moderated by beliefs about environmental reliability. *Cognition, 126*, 109–114.

147. Geis, G. (2000). On the absence of self-control as the basis for a general theory of crime: A critique. *Theoretical Criminology, 4*, 35–53.

148. Hirschi, T., & Gottfredson, M. (2008). Critiquing the critics: The authors respond. In E. Goode (Eds.), *Out of control: Assessing the general theory of crime* (pp. 217–231). Redwood City, CA: Stanford University Press.

CHAPTER 9

1. Butterfield, F. (2018, October 22). When crime is a family affair. *The Atlantic.* Retrieved from https://www.theatlantic.com/family/archive/2018/10/crime-runs-family/573394/

2. Butterfield, F. (2018). *In my father's house: A new view on how crime runs in families.* New York, NY: Knopf.

3. Sutherland, E. (1939). *Principles of criminology.* Philadelphia, PA: J. B. Lippincott.

4. Sutherland, E. (1937). *The professional thief.* Chicago, IL: University of Chicago Press.

5. Walters, G. D. (2018). Sibling delinquency as a risk factor for future offending: An exploratory analysis. *Youth Violence and Juvenile Justice, 16*(4), 343–357.

6. Jackson, E. F., Tittle, C. R., & Burke, M. J. (1986). Offense-specific models of the differential association process. *Social Problems, 33*(4), 335–356.

7. Matsueda, R. (2007). Differential association theory. In G. Ritzer (Ed.), *The Blackwell encyclopedia of sociology* (pp. 125–130). Malden, MA: Blackwell.

8. Matsueda, R. L. (1988). The current state of differential association theory. *Crime & Delinquency, 34*(3), 277–306.

9. Mullins, C. W., & Cherbonneau, M. G. (2011). Establishing connections: Gender, motor vehicle theft, and disposal networks. *Justice Quarterly, 28*(2), 278–302.

10. Mullins, C. W., & Cherbonneau, M. G. (2011). Establishing connections: Gender, motor vehicle theft, and disposal networks. *Justice Quarterly, 28*(2), 278–302.

11. McGloin, J. M., & Thomas, K. J. (2019). Peer influence and delinquency. *Annual Review of Criminology, 2*, 241–264.

12. Kelly, B. C., Vuolo, M., & Marin, A. C. (2017). Multiple dimensions of peer effects and deviance: The case of prescription drug misuse among young adults. *Socius, 3*, 1–18.

13. Ellis, W. E., Chung-Hall, J., & Dumas, T. M. (2013). The role of peer group aggression in predicting adolescent dating violence and relationship quality. *Journal of Youth and Adolescence, 42*(4), 487–499.

14. McGloin, J. M., & Thomas, K. J. (2019). Peer influence and delinquency. *Annual Review of Criminology, 2*, 241–264.

15. Burgess, R. L., & Akers, R. L. (1966). A differential association-reinforcement theory of criminal behavior. *Social Problems, 14*(2), 128–147.

16. Staddon, J. E. R., & Cerutti, D. T. (2003). Operant conditioning. *Annual Review of Psychology, 54*, 115–144.

17. Akers, R. L., & Jennings, W. (2019). The social learning theory of crime and deviance. In M. Krohn, N. Hendrix, G. P. Hall, & A. Lizotte (Eds.), *Handbook on crime and deviance* (pp. 113–129). Cham, Switzerland: Springer.

18. Akers, R. L., & Jennings, W. (2019). The social learning theory of crime and deviance. In M. Krohn, N. Hendrix, G. P. Hall, & A. Lizotte (Eds.), *Handbook on crime and deviance* (pp. 113–129). Cham, Switzerland: Springer.

19. Akers, R. L. (2011). *Social learning and social structure: A general theory of crime and deviance.* Piscataway, NJ: Transaction Publishers.

20. Brezina, T., & Piquero, A. R. (2017). Exploring the relationship between social and non-social reinforcement in the context of social learning theory. In G. Jensen (Ed.), *Social learning theory and the explanation of crime* (pp. 265–288). Abingdon, UK: Taylor & Francis.

21. Stevens, J., May, D., Rice, N., & Jarjoura, G. R. (2011). Nonsocial versus social reinforcers: Contrasting theoretical perspectives on repetitive serious delinquency and drug use. *Youth Violence and Juvenile Justice, 9*(4), 295–312.

22. Lyng, S. (2004). Crime, edgework and corporeal transaction. *Theoretical Criminology, 8*(3), 359–375.

23. Nicholson, J., & Higgins, G. E. (2017). Social structure social learning theory: Preventing crime and violence. In B. Teasdale & M. Bradley (Eds.), *Preventing crime and violence* (pp. 11–20). Cham, Switzerland: Springer.

24. Lünnemann, M. K. M., Van der Horst, F. C. P., Prinzie, P., Luijk, M. P. C. M., & Steketee, M. (2019). The intergenerational impact of trauma and family violence on parents and their children. *Child Abuse & Neglect, 96*, 1–12.

25. Debowska, A., & Boduszek, D. (2017). Child abuse and neglect profiles and their psychosocial consequences in a large sample of incarcerated males. *Child Abuse & Neglect, 65*, 266–277.

26. Widom, C. S., & Wilson, H. W. (2015). Intergenerational transmission of violence. In J. Lindert & I. Levav (Eds.), *Violence and mental health: Its manifold faces* (pp. 27–45). New York, NY: Springer.

27. Widom, C. S., & Wilson, H. W. (2015). Intergenerational transmission of violence. In J. Lindert & I. Levav (Eds.), *Violence and mental health: Its manifold faces* (pp. 27–45). New York, NY: Springer.

28. McCullough, K., & Ressler, K. J. (2018). Posttraumatic stress disorder: From neurobiology to cycles of violence: Integrating research, practice, and policy. In J. M. Fogler & R. Phelps (Eds.), *Trauma, autism, and neurodevelopmental disorders* (pp.19–54). Cham, Switzerland: Springer.

29. Widom, C. S. (2017). Long-term impact of childhood abuse and neglect on crime and violence. *Clinical Psychology: Science and Practice, 24*(2), 186–202.

30. Kruis, N. E., Seo, C., & Kim, B. (2020). Revisiting the empirical status of social learning theory on substance use: A systematic review and meta-analysis. *Substance Use & Misuse, 55*(4), 666–683.

31. Hashimi, S., Wakefield, S., & Apel, R. (2021). Sibling transmission of gang involvement. *Journal of Research in Crime and Delinquency, 58*, 1–38.

32. Morris, R. G., & Higgins, G. E. (2010). Criminological theory in the digital age: The case of social learning theory and digital piracy. *Journal of Criminal Justice, 38*(4), 470–480.

33. Mills, C. E., Freilich, J. D., Chermak, S. M., Holt, T. J., & LaFree, G. (2019). Social learning and social control in the off-and online pathways to hate crime and terrorist violence. *Studies in Conflict & Terrorism*, 1–29.

34. Cochran, J. K., Maskaly, J., Jones, S., & Sellers, C. S. (2017). Using structural equations to model Akers' social learning theory with data on intimate partner violence. *Crime & Delinquency, 63*(1), 39–60.

35. Ellis, L. Johnathon, A. C., & Walsh, A. (2008). Criminologists' opinions about causes and theories of crime and delinquency: A follow-up. *The Criminologist, 33* (May/June), 23–26.

36. Jensen, G. (Ed.). (2017). *Social learning theory and the explanation of crime.* New York, NY: Routledge.

37. Akers, R. L., & W. Jennings. (2019). The social learning theory of crime and deviance. In M. Krohn, N. Hendrix, G. P. Hall, & A. Lizotte (Eds.), *Handbook on crime and deviance* (pp. 113–129). Cham, Switzerland: Springer.

38. Akers, R. L. (2011). *Social learning and social structure: A general theory of crime and deviance.* Piscataway, NJ: Transaction Publishers.

39. Irwin, J., & Cressey, D. R. (1962). Thieves, convicts and the inmate culture. *Social Problems, 10*(2), 142–155.

40. Sykes, G. M. (1958/2007). *The society of captives: A study of a maximum security prison.* Princeton, NJ: Princeton University Press.

41. Kreager, D. A., & Kruttschnitt, C. (2018). Inmate society in the era of mass incarceration. *Annual Review of Criminology, 1*, 261–283.

42. Martin, L. (2018). "Free but still walking the yard": Prisonization and the problems of reentry. *Journal of Contemporary Ethnography, 47*(5), 671–694.

43. Martin, L. (2018). "Free but still walking the yard": Prisonization and the problems of reentry. *Journal of Contemporary Ethnography, 47*(5), 671–694.

44. Miller, W. B. (1958). Lower class culture as a generating milieu of gang delinquency. *Journal of Social Issues, 14*(3), 5–19.

45. Cohen, A. K. (1956). *Delinquent boys: The culture of the gang.* New York, NY: Macmillan.

46. Blackman, S. (2014). Subculture theory: An historical and contemporary assessment of the concept for understanding deviance. *Deviant Behavior, 35*(6), 496–512.

47. Cloward, R., & Ohlin, L. E. (1960). *Delinquency and opportunity.* New York, NY: Free Press.

48. Toby, J. (1961). Delinquency and opportunity. *The British Journal of Sociology, 12*(3), 282–289.

49. Cloward, R., & Ohlin, L. E. (1960). *Delinquency and opportunity.* New York, NY: Free Press.

50. Cloward, R., & Ohlin, L. E. (1960). *Delinquency and opportunity.* New York, NY: Free Press.

51. Anderson, E. (2000). *Code of the street: Decency, violence, and moral life of the inner city.* New York, NY: Norton.

52. Anderson, E. (2000). *Code of the street: Decency, violence, and moral life of the inner city.* New York, NY: Norton.

53. Intravia, J. (2020). The code of the street: Causes and consequences. In J. I. Ross (Ed.), *Routledge handbook of street culture* (pp. 219–228). Abingdon, UK: Routledge.

54. Mitchell, M. M., Fahmy, C., Pyrooz, D. C., & Decker, S. H. (2017). Criminal crews, codes, and contexts: Differences and similarities across the code of the street, convict code, street gangs, and prison gangs. *Deviant Behavior, 38*(10), 1197–1222.

55. Anderson, E. (2000). *Code of the street: Decency, violence, and moral life of the inner city.* New York, NY: Norton.

56. Brezina, T., Agnew, R., Cullen, F. T., & Wright, J. P. (2004). The code of the street: A quantitative assessment of Elijah Anderson's subculture of violence thesis and its contribution to youth violence research. *Youth Violence and Juvenile Justice, 2*(4), 303–328.

57. Erickson, J. H., Hochstetler, A., & Dorius, S. F. (2020). Code in transition? The evolution of code of the street adherence in adolescence. *Deviant Behavior, 41*(3), 1–19.

58. McNeeley, S., & Wilcox, P. (2015). Street codes, routine activities, neighbourhood context and victimization. *British Journal of Criminology, 55*(5), 921–943.

59. Yeomans, H. (2019). Historical context and the criminological imagination: Towards a three-dimensional criminology. *Criminology & Criminal Justice, 19*(4), 456–474.

60. Mills, C. W. (1959). *The sociological imagination.* Oxford, UK: Oxford University Press.

61. Frauley, J. (2017). For a refractive criminology: Against science machines and cheerful robots. In J. Frauley (Ed.), *C. Wright Mills and the criminological imagination: Prospects for creative inquiry* (pp. 21–58). London, UK: Routledge.

62. Carrabine, E. (2016). Changing fortunes: Criminology and the sociological condition. *Sociology, 50*(5), 847–862.

63. Blevins, K. R., & Holt, T. J. (2009). Examining the virtual subculture of Johns. *Journal of Contemporary Ethnography, 38*(5), 619–648.

64. Holt, T. J., Freilich, J. D., & Chermak, S. M. (2017). Exploring the subculture of ideologically motivated cyber-attackers. *Journal of Contemporary Criminal Justice, 33*(3), 212–233.

65. Jacques, S., & Wright, R. (2015). *Code of the suburb: Inside the world of young middle-class drug dealers.* Chicago, IL: University of Chicago Press.

66. Matza, D. (1968). *Becoming delinquent.* Englewood Cliffs, NJ: Prentice Hall.

67. Matza, D. (1964). *Delinquency and drift.* London, UK: Routledge.

68. Sykes, G., & Matza, D. 1957. Techniques of neutralization: A theory of delinquency. *American Sociological Review, 22,* 664–670.

69. Sykes, G., & Matza, D. 1957. Techniques of neutralization: A theory of delinquency. *American Sociological Review, 22,* 664–670.

70. Adapted from Zito, R. (2020). Identifying deviant behavior. In K. Korgen & M. Atkinson (Eds.), *Sociology in action* (2nd ed., pp. 99–119). Thousand Oaks, CA: SAGE.

71. Shigihara, A. M. (2013). It's only stealing a little a lot: Techniques of neutralization for theft among restaurant workers. *Deviant Behavior, 34*(6), 494–512.

72. Anderson, K. (2017). "Who was I to stop the killing?" Moral neutralization among Rwandan genocide perpetrators. *Journal of Perpetrator Research, 1*(1), 39–63.

73. Dickinson, T., & Jacques, S. (2019). Drug sellers' neutralizations of guiltless drug sales and avoidance of "drug dealer" identities. *International Journal of Drug Policy, 73,* 16–23.

74. Shigihara, A. M. (2013). It's only stealing a little a lot: Techniques of neutralization for theft among restaurant workers. *Deviant Behavior, 34*(6), 494–512.

75. Copes, H., & Vieraitis, L. (2012). *Identity thieves: Motives and methods.* Boston, MA: Northeastern University Press.

76. Anderson, K. (2017). "Who was I to stop the killing?" Moral neutralization among Rwandan genocide perpetrators. *Journal of Perpetrator Research, 1*(1), 39–63.

CHAPTER 10

1. Cherbonneau, M., & Jacobs, B. A. (2015). Retaliatory auto theft. *Journal of Contemporary Criminal Justice, 31,* 468–491.

2. McCandless, S. (2018). LGBT homeless youth and policing. *Public Integrity, 20,* 558–570.

3. Padilla, F. M. (2003). Becoming a gang member. In P. Cromwell (Ed.), *In their own words: Criminals on crime.* Los Angeles, CA: Roxbury.

4. Caputo, G. A., & King, A. (2015). Shoplifting by male and female drug users: Gender, agency, and work. *Criminal Justice Review, 40,* 47–66.

5. Bucher, J., Manasse, M., & Milton, J. (2015). Soliciting strain: Examining both sides of street prostitution through general strain theory. *Journal of Crime and Justice, 38,* 435–453.

6. Smith, K. S. (2014). *Émile Durkheim and the collective consciousness of society: A study in criminology* (Vol. 1). London: Anthem Press.

7. Bernburg, J. G. (2019). Anomie theory. In *Oxford research encyclopedia of criminology and criminal justice.* New York, NY: Oxford University Press.

8. Marks, S. R. (1974). Durkheim's theory of anomie. *American Journal of Sociology, 80,* 329–363.

9. Zhao, R., & Cao, L. (2010). Social change and anomie: A cross-national study. *Social Forces, 88,* 1209–1229.

10. Cullen, F. T., & Messner, S. F. (2007). The making of criminology revisited: An oral history of Merton's anomie paradigm. *Theoretical Criminology, 11,* 5–37.

11. Chamlin, M. B., & Sanders, B. A. (2013). Falsifying Merton's macro-level anomie theory of profit-motivated crime: A research note. *Deviant Behavior, 34,* 961–972.

12. Merton, R. K. (1938). Social structure and anomie. *American Sociological Review, 3*, 672–682.

13. Merton, R. K., & Merton, R. C. (1968). *Social theory and social structure*. New York, NY: Simon & Schuster.

14. Schaible, L. M., & Altheimer, I. (2016). Social structure, anomie, and national levels of homicide. *International Journal of Offender Therapy and Comparative Criminology, 60*, 936–963.

15. Merton, R. K. (1938). Social structure and anomie. *American Sociological Review, 3*, 672–682.

16. Burraston, B., McCutcheon, J. C., & Watts, S. J. (2018). Relative and absolute deprivation's relationship with violent crime in the United States: Testing an interaction effect between income inequality and disadvantage. *Crime & Delinquency, 64*, 542–560.

17. Webber, C. (2007). Revaluating relative deprivation theory. *Theoretical Criminology, 11*, 97–120.

18. Chamlin, M. B., & Sanders, B. A. (2013). Falsifying Merton's macro-level anomie theory of profit-motivated crime: A research note. *Deviant Behavior, 34*, 961–972.

19. Merton, R. K. (1938). Social structure and anomie. *American Sociological Review, 3*, 672–682.

20. Chidester, D. (2003). *Salvation and suicide. Jim Jones, the Peoples Temple, and Jonestown*. Bloomington: Indiana University Press.

21. Reader, I. (2002). Dramatic confrontations: Aum Shinrikyo against the world. In D. Bromley & J. G. Melton (Eds.), *Cults, religion, and violence* (pp. 189–208). Cambridge, UK: Cambridge University Press.

22. Messner, S. F., & Rosenfeld, R. (2012). *Crime and the American dream*. New York, NY: Cengage Learning.

23. Agnew, R. (1995). The contribution of social psychological strain theory to the explanation of crime and delinquency. In F. Adler & W. Laufer (Eds.), *The legacy of anomie theory: Advances in criminological theory* (Vol. 6, pp. 111–122). New Brunswick, NJ: Transaction Press.

24. Rosenfeld, R. (2014). Crime and the great recession: Introduction to the special issue. *Journal of Contemporary Criminal Justice, 30*, 4–6.

25. Zimring, F. (2006). *The great American crime decline*. New York, NY: Oxford University Press.

26. Messner, S. F., & Rosenfeld, R. (2012). *Crime and the American dream*. New York, NY: Cengage Learning.

27. Cullen, J. (2018, July 20). *The history of mass incarceration*. Brennan Center for Justice. Retrieved from https://www.brennancenter.org/our-work/analysis-opinion/history-mass-incarceration

28. Wagner, P., & Bertram, W. (2020, January 16). *What percent of the U.S. is incarcerated? (And other ways to measure mass incarceration)*. Northampton, MA: Prison Policy Initiative. Retrieved from https://www.prisonpolicy.org/blog/2020/01/16/percent-incarcerated/

29. Messner, S. F., & Rosenfeld, R. (2012). *Crime and the American dream*. New York, NY: Cengage Learning.

30. Messner, S. F., Rosenfeld, R., & Hövermann, A. (2019). Institutional anomie theory: An evolving research program. In M. Krohn, N. Hendrix, G. P. Hall, & A. Lizotte

(Eds.), *Handbook on crime and deviance* (pp. 161–177). Cham, Switzerland: Springer.

31. Kates, G. (2019, March 12). *Lori Loughlin and Felicity Huffman among dozens charged in college bribery scheme*. CBS News. Retrieved from https://www.cbsnews.com/news/college-admissions-scandal-bribery-cheating-today-felicity-huffman-arrested-fbi-2019-03-12/

32. Richer, A. D., & Binkley, C. (2019, March 12). *TV stars and coaches charged in college bribery scheme*. AP News. Retrieved from https://apnews.com/2450688f9e67435c8590e59a1b0e5b47

33. Associated Press. (2004, December 7). *School that awarded MBA to cat sued*. NBC News. Retrieved from http://www.nbcnews.com/id/6664906#.X1-s5lt7nb0

34. Wolverton, B. (2016, August 28). The new economy of cheating. *Chronicle of Higher Education*. Retrieved from https://www.chronicle.com/article/the-new-cheating-economy/

35. Hess, A. (2017, April 6). *These high school journalists uncovered a principal's resume lie*. CNBC. Retrieved from https://www.cnbc.com/2017/04/06/these-high-school-journalists-uncovered-a-principals-resume-lie.html

36. Bjerregaard, B. (2018). Institutional anomie theory. In G. Bruinsma & D. Weisburd (Eds.), *Encyclopedia of criminology and criminal justice*. New York, NY: Springer.

37. Hövermann, A., & Messner, S. F. (2019). Institutional imbalance, marketized mentality, and the justification of instrumental offenses: A cross-national application of institutional anomie theory. *Justice Quarterly, 38*, 1–26.

38. Costello, B. J., & Laub, J. H. (2020). Social control theory: The legacy of Travis Hirschi's *Causes of Delinquency. Annual Review of Criminology, 3*, 21–41.

39. Tuttle, J. (2018). Specifying the effect of social welfare expenditures on homicide and suicide: A cross-national, longitudinal examination of the stream analogy of lethal violence. *Justice Quarterly, 35*, 87–113.

40. Lochner, L. (2020). Education and crime. In S. Bradley & C. Green (Eds.), *The economics of education: A comprehensive overview* (pp. 109–117). Cambridge, MA: Academic Press.

41. Sumter, M., Wood, F., Whitaker, I., & Berger-Hill, D. (2018). Religion and crime studies: Assessing what has been learned. *Religions, 9*, 193.

42. Messner, S. F., Rosenfeld, R., & Hövermann, A. (2019). Institutional anomie theory: An evolving research program. In M. Krohn, N. Hendrix, G. P. Hall, & A. Lizotte (Eds.), *Handbook on crime and deviance* (pp. 161–177). Cham, Switzerland: Springer.

43. Messner, S. F., & Rosenfeld, R. (1997). Political restraint of the market and levels of criminal homicide: A cross-national application of institutional-anomie theory. *Social Forces, 75*, 1393–1416.

44. Fei, J., & Zakrzewski Jr, W. J. (2020). Institutional imbalance as a force of direction: The implication of institutional anomie theory in stream analogy of lethal violence. *The Sociological Quarterly, 62*, 1–26.

45. Zito, R. C. (2019). Institutional anomie and justification of morally dubious behavior and violence cross-nationally: A

multilevel examination. *Australian & New Zealand Journal of Criminology, 52,* 250–271.

46. Groß, E. M., Hövermann, A., & Messner, S. F. (2018). Marketized mentality, competitive/egoistic school culture, and delinquent attitudes and behavior: An application of institutional anomie theory. *Criminology, 56,* 333–369.

47. Rosenberger, J. S. (2016). Television consumption and institutional anomie theory. *Sociological Focus, 49,* 305–325.

48. Applin, S., & Messner, S. F. (2015). Her American dream: Bringing gender into institutional-anomie theory. *Feminist Criminology, 10,* 36–59.

49. Felitti, V. J., Anda, R. F., Nordenberg, D., Williamson, D. F., Spitz, A. M., Edwards, V., . . . Marks, J. S. (1998). Relationship of childhood abuse and household dysfunction to many of the leading causes of death in adults: The Adverse Childhood Experiences (ACE) study. *American Journal of Preventive Medicine, 14,* 245–258.

50. Merrick, M. T., Ports, K. A., Ford, D. C., Afifi, T. O., Gershoff, E. T., & Grogan-Kaylor, A. (2017). Unpacking the impact of adverse childhood experiences on adult mental health. *Child Abuse & Neglect, 69,* 10–19.

51. Centers for Disease Control and Prevention. (n.d.). *Preventing adverse childhood experiences.* Retrieved from https://www.cdc.gov/violenceprevention/acestudy/fastfact.html?CDC_AA_refVal=https%3A%2F%2Fwww.cdc.gov%2Fviolenceprevention%2Fchildabuseandneglect%2Faces%2Ffastfact.html

52. Fox, B. H., Perez, N., Cass, E., Baglivio, M. T., & Epps, N. (2015). Trauma changes everything: Examining the relationship between adverse childhood experiences and serious, violent and chronic juvenile offenders. *Child Abuse & Neglect, 46,* 163–173.

53. Bernstein, N. (2014). *Burning down the house: The end of juvenile incarceration.* New York, NY: New Press.

54. Dierkhising, C. B., Ko, S. J., Woods-Jaeger, B., Briggs, E. C., Lee, R., & Pynoos, R. S. (2013). Trauma histories among justice-involved youth: Findings from the National Child Traumatic Stress Network. *European Journal of Psychotraumatology, 4,* 1–12.

55. Fox, B. H., Perez, N., Cass, E., Baglivio, M. T., & Epps, N. (2015). Trauma changes everything: Examining the relationship between adverse childhood experiences and serious, violent and chronic juvenile offenders. *Child Abuse & Neglect, 46,* 163–173.

56. Agnew, R. (1992). Foundation for a general strain theory of crime and delinquency. *Criminology, 30,* 47–88.

57. Schauer, P. (Ed.). (2018). *Homelessness and street crime.* New York, NY: Greenhaven.

58. Brookman, F. (2015). Killer decisions: The role of cognition, affect and 'expertise' in homicide. *Aggression and Violent Behavior, 20,* 42–52.

59. Agnew, R. (2006). *Pressured into crime: An overview of general strain theory.* Los Angeles, CA: Roxbury.

60. Froggio, G., & Agnew, R. (2007). The relationship between crime and "objective" versus "subjective" strains. *Journal of Criminal Justice, 35,* 81–87.

61. Hari, J. (2015). *Chasing the scream: The first and last days of the war on drugs.* New York, NY: Bloomsbury.

62. Link, N. W. (2019). Criminal justice debt during the prisoner reintegration process: Who has it and how much? *Criminal Justice and Behavior, 46,* 154–172.

63. Beckett, K., & Harris, A. (2011). On cash and conviction: Monetary sanctions as misguided policy. *Criminology & Public Policy, 10,* 505–507.

64. Harris, A., Evans, H., & Beckett, K. (2010). Drawing blood from stones: Legal debt and social inequality in the contemporary United States. *American Journal of Sociology, 115,* 1753–1799.

65. Link, N. W. (2019). Criminal justice debt during the prisoner reintegration process: Who has it and how much? *Criminal Justice and Behavior, 46,* 154–172.

66. Harper, A., Ginapp, C., Bardelli, T., Grimshaw, A., Justen, M., Mohamedali, A., . . . Puglisi, L. (2020). Debt, incarceration, and re-entry: A scoping review. *American Journal of Criminal Justice, 46,* 1–29.

67. Liu, P., Nunn, R., & Shambaugh, J. (2019). *Nine facts about monetary sanctions in the criminal justice system. The Hamilton Project.* Washington, DC: Brookings Institution. Retrieved from https://www.brookings.edu/wp-content/uploads/2019/03/BailFacts_20190314.pdf

68. Harris, A., Evans, H., & Beckett, K. (2010). Drawing blood from stones: Legal debt and social inequality in the contemporary United States. *American Journal of Sociology, 115,* 1753–1799.

69. Harris, A., Evans, H., & Beckett, K. (2010). Drawing blood from stones: Legal debt and social inequality in the contemporary United States. *American Journal of Sociology, 115,* 1753–1799.

70. Pleggenkuhle, B. (2018). The financial cost of a criminal conviction: Context and consequences. *Criminal Justice and Behavior, 45,* 121–145.

71. Harris, A., Evans, H., & Beckett, K. (2010). Drawing blood from stones: Legal debt and social inequality in the contemporary United States. *American Journal of Sociology, 115,* 1753–1799.

72. Brayne, S. (2014). Surveillance and system avoidance: Criminal justice contact and institutional attachment. *American Sociological Review, 79,* 367–391.

73. Pleggenkuhle, B. (2018). The financial cost of a criminal conviction: Context and consequences. *Criminal Justice and Behavior, 45,* 121–145.

74. Ruback, R., Shaffer, J., Logue, M. (2004). The imposition and effects of restitution in four Pennsylvania counties: Effects of size of county and specialized collection units. *Crime & Delinquency, 50,* 168–188.

75. Martin, K. D., Sykes, B. L., Shannon, S., Edwards, F., & Harris, A. (2018). Monetary sanctions: Legal financial obligations in U.S. systems of justice. *Annual Review of Criminology, 1,* 471–495.

76. Piquero, A. R., & Jennings, W. G. (2017). Research note: Justice system-imposed financial penalties increase the likelihood of recidivism in a sample of adolescent offenders. *Youth Violence and Juvenile Justice, 15,* 325–340.

77. Kaufman, J. M., Rebellon, C. J., Thaxton, S., & Agnew, R. (2008). A general strain theory of racial differences in criminal offending. *Australian & New Zealand Journal of Criminology, 41,* 421–437.

78. O'Dowd, M. F. (2020, February 4). *Explainer: What is systemic racism and institutional racism?* Retrieved from https://theconversation.com/explainer-what-is-systemic-racism-and-institutional-racism-131152

79. Rothstein, R. (2017). *The color of law: A forgotten history of how our government segregated America.* New York, NY: Liveright.

80. Glantz, A., & Martinez, E. (2018, February 15). Kept out: For people of color, banks are shutting the door to homeownership [Audio podcast episode]. In *Reveal.* Center for Investigative Reporting. Retrieved from https://www.revealnews.org/article/for-people-of-color-banks-are-shutting-the-door-to-homeownership/

81. Rice, L., & Swesnik, D. (2013). Discriminatory effects of credit scoring on communities of color. *Suffolk University Law Review, 46,* 935–966.

82. Kent, A. H., & Ricketts, L. (2021, January 5). *Wealth gaps between White, Black and Hispanic families in 2019.* Federal Reserve Bank of St. Louis. Retrieved from https://www.stlouisfed.org/on-the-economy/2021/january/wealth-gaps-white-black-hispanic-families-2019

83. Kent, A. H., & Ricketts, L. (2021, January 5). *Wealth gaps between White, Black and Hispanic families in 2019.* Federal Reserve Bank of St. Louis. Retrieved from https://www.stlouisfed.org/on-the-economy/2021/january/wealth-gaps-white-black-hispanic-families-2019

84. Chetty, R., Hendren, N., Jones, M. R., & Porter, S. R. (2020). Race and economic opportunity in the United States: An intergenerational perspective. *Quarterly Journal of Economics, 135,* 711–783.

85. McIntosh, K., Moss, E., Nunn, R., & Shambaugh, J. (2020, February 27). *Examining the black-white racial gap.* Brookings Institution. Retrieved from https://www.brookings.edu/blog/up-front/2020/02/27/examining-the-black-white-wealth-gap/

86. Martin, C. E. (2019, April 23). Closing the racial wealth gap. *The New York Times.* Retrieved from https://www.nytimes.com/2019/04/23/opinion/closing-the-racial-wealth-gap.html

87. Krysan, M., & Crowder, K. (2017). *Cycle of segregation: Social processes and residential stratification.* New York, NY: Russell Sage Foundation.

88. Hotz, V. J., Wiemers, E., Rasmussen, J., & Koegel, K. M. (2018). *The role of parental wealth and income in financing children's college attendance and its consequences* (NBER Working Paper No. 25144). Retrieved from National Bureau of Economic Research website: https://www-nber-org.ezproxy.elon.edu/papers/w25144

89. Choi, J. H., Zhu, J., & Goodman, L. (2018, October). *Intergenerational homeownership: The impact of parental homeownership and wealth on young adults' tenure choices.* Urban Institute's Housing Finance Policy Center. Retrieved from https://www.urban.org/sites/default/files/publication/99251/intergenerational_homeownership_0.pdf

90. Dwyer, R. E. (2018). Credit, debt, and inequality. *Annual Review of Sociology, 44,* 237–261.

91. Sharkey, P. (2018). The long reach of violence: A broader perspective on data, theory, and evidence on the prevalence and consequences of exposure to violence. *Annual Review of Criminology, 1,* 85–102.

92. Kaufman, J. M., Rebellon, C. J., Thaxton, S., & Agnew, R. (2008). A general strain theory of racial differences in criminal offending. *Australian & New Zealand Journal of Criminology, 41,* 421–437.

93. Isom Scott, D. A., Whiting, S., & Grosholz, J. M. (2020). Examining and expanding Latinx general strain theory. *Race and Justice,* 1–25.

94. De Coster, S., & Thompson, M. S. (2017). Race and general strain theory: Microaggressions as mundane extreme environmental stresses. *Justice Quarterly, 34,* 903–930.

95. Hautala, D., & Sittner, K. (2019). Longitudinal mechanisms linking perceived racial discrimination to aggressive delinquency among North American Indigenous youth. *Journal of Research in Crime and Delinquency, 56,* 694–735.

96. De Coster, S., & Thompson, M. S. (2017). Race and general strain theory: Microaggressions as mundane extreme environmental stresses. *Justice Quarterly, 34,* 903–930.

97. Isom Scott, D. A., & Stevens Andersen, T. (2020). 'Whitelash?' status threat, anger, and white America: A general strain theory approach. *Journal of Crime and Justice,* 1–19.

98. Earle, M., & Hodson, G. (2020). Questioning white losses and anti-white discrimination in the United States. *Nature Human Behaviour, 4,* 160–168.

99. Jones, B. (2019, November 1). *Democrats far more likely than Republicans to see discrimination against blacks, not whites.* Pew Research Center. Retrieved from https://www.pewresearch.org/fact-tank/2019/11/01/democrats-far-more-likely-than-republicans-to-see-discrimination-against-blacks-not-whites/

100. Earle, M., & Hodson, G. (2020). Questioning white losses and anti-white discrimination in the United States. *Nature Human Behaviour, 4,* 160–168.

101. Isom Scott, D. A., & Stevens Andersen, T. (2020). 'Whitelash?' status threat, anger, and white America: A general strain theory approach. *Journal of Crime and Justice, 43,* 1–19.

102. Agnew, R. (2001). Building on the foundation of general strain theory: Specifying the types of strain most likely to lead to crime and delinquency. *Journal of Research in Crime & Delinquency, 4,* 319–362.

103. Jensen, F. G. (1995). Salvaging structure through strain: A theoretical and empirical critique. In F. Adler & W. Laufer (Eds.), *The legacy of anomie theory: Advances in criminological theory* (Vol. 6, pp. 139–158). New Brunswick, NJ: Transaction Press.

104. Agnew, R. (2001). Building on the foundation of general strain theory: Specifying the types of strain most likely to lead to crime and delinquency. *Journal of Research in Crime & Delinquency, 4,* 319–362.

105. Agnew, R. (2006). *Pressured into crime: An overview of general strain theory.* Los Angeles, CA: Roxbury.

CHAPTER 11

1. Weissman, M. (2015). *Prelude to prison: Student perspectives on school suspension.* Syracuse, NY: Syracuse University Press.

2. Crank, B. R. (2018). Accepting deviant identities: The impact of self-labeling on intentions to desist from crime. *Journal of Crime and Justice, 41*(2), 155–172.

3. Adapted from Zito, R. (2020). Identifying deviant behavior. In K. Korgen & M. Atkinson (Eds.), *Sociology in action* (2nd ed.). Thousand Oaks, CA: SAGE.

4. Thomas, W. I, & Thomas, D. (1928). *The child in America: Behavior problems and programs.* New York, NY: Knopf.

5. Tannenbaum, F. (1938). *Crime and community.* New York, NY: Columbia University Press.

6. Zito, R. (2020). Identifying deviant behavior. In K. Korgen & M. Atkinson (Eds.), *Sociology in action* (2nd ed.). Thousand Oaks, CA: SAGE.

7. Becker, H. (1963/1973). *Outsiders.* New York, NY: Free Press.

8. Lemert, E. (1951). *Social pathology: A systematic approach to the theory of sociopathic behavior.* New York, NY: McGraw-Hill.

9. Zito, R. (2020). Identifying deviant behavior. In K. Korgen & M. Atkinson (Eds.), *Sociology in action* (2nd ed.). Thousand Oaks, CA: SAGE.

10. Becker, H. (1963/1973). *Outsiders.* New York, NY: Free Press.

11. Bernburg, J. G. (2019). Labeling theory. In M. Krohn, N. Hendrix, G. P. Hall, & A. Lizotte (Eds.), *Handbook on crime and deviance* (pp. 179–196). Cham, Switzerland: Springer.

12. Bernburg, J. G. (2019). Labeling theory. In M. Krohn, N. Hendrix, G. P. Hall, & A. Lizotte (Eds.), *Handbook on crime and deviance* (pp. 179–196). Cham, Switzerland: Springer.

13. Denver, M., Pickett, J. T., & Bushway, S. D. (2017). The language of stigmatization and the mark of violence: Experimental evidence of the social construction and use of criminal record stigma. *Criminology, 55,* 664–690.

14. Matsueda, R. L. (1992). Reflected appraisals, parental labeling, and delinquency: Specifying a symbolic interactionist theory. *American Journal of Sociology, 97,* 1577–1611.

15. Goffman, E. (1963). *Stigma: Notes on the management of a spoiled identity.* New York, NY: Touchstone.

16. Goffman, E. (1963). *Stigma: Notes on the management of a spoiled identity.* New York, NY: Touchstone.

17. Rios, V. (2017). *Human targets: Schools, police, and the criminalization of Latino youth.* Berkeley: University of California Press.

18. Rios, V. (2017). *Human targets: Schools, police, and the criminalization of Latino youth.* Berkeley: University of California Press.

19. Rios, V. (2017). *Human targets: Schools, police, and the criminalization of Latino youth.* Berkeley: University of California Press.

20. Salinas, M. (2018). The unusual suspects: An educated, legitimately employed drug dealing network. *International Criminal Justice Review, 28*(3), 226–242.

21. Salinas, M. (2018). The unusual suspects: An educated, legitimately employed drug dealing network. *International Criminal Justice Review, 28*(3), 226–242.

22. Carusone, S. C., Guta, A., Robinson, S., Tan, D. H., Cooper, C., O'Leary, B., . . . Strike, C. (2019). "Maybe if I stop the drugs, then maybe they'd care?" Hospital care experiences of people who use drugs. *Harm Reduction Journal, 16*(1), 1–10.

23. American Civil Liberties Union. (2020). *A tale of two countries: Racially targeted arrests in the era of marijuana reform.* Retrieved from https://www.aclu.org/news/criminal-law-reform/a-tale-of-two-countries-racially-targeted-arrests-in-the-era-of-marijuana-reform/

24. Firth, C. L., Maher, J. E., Dilley, J. A., Darnell, A., & Lovrich, N. P. (2019). Did marijuana legalization in Washington State reduce racial disparities in adult marijuana arrests? *Substance Use & Misuse, 54*(9), 1582–1587.

25. Nguyen, H., & Reuter, P. (2012). How risky is marijuana possession? Considering the role of age, race, and gender. *Crime & Delinquency, 58*(6), 879–910.

26. Becker, H. (1963/1973). *Outsiders.* New York, NY: Free Press.

27. Williams, M. (2018). *The sex offender housing dilemma: Community activism, safety, and social justice.* New York, NY: NYU Press.

28. Pettys, D. (2005, September 28). *Republicans unveil first draft of proposed sex offender law.* Associated Press. Retrieved from https://accesswdun.com/article/2005/9/138606

29. Rabin, C. (2019, November 22). Miami-Dade uproots sex offender camp yet again. Does harsh law really make public safer? *Miami Herald.* Retrieved from https://www.miamiherald.com/news/local/crime/article237545129.html

30. Schwartzapfel, B., & Kassie, E. (2018, October 3). *Banished.* The Marshall Project. Retrieved from https://www.themarshallproject.org/2018/10/03/banished

31. Rabin, C. (2019, November 22). Miami-Dade uproots sex offender camp yet again. Does harsh law really make public safer? *Miami Herald.* Retrieved from https://www.miamiherald.com/news/local/crime/article237545129.html

32. Savage, J., & Windsor, C. (2018). Sex offender residence restrictions and sex crimes against children: A comprehensive review. *Aggression and Violent Behavior, 43,* 13–25.

33. Savage, J., & Windsor, C. (2018). Sex offender residence restrictions and sex crimes against children: A comprehensive review. *Aggression and Violent Behavior, 43,* 13–25.

34. Kilmer, A., & Leon, C. S. (2017). "'Nobody worries about our children": Unseen impacts of sex offender registration on families with school-age children and implications for desistance. *Criminal Justice Studies, 30*(2), 181–201.

35. Cann, D., & Isom Scott, D. A. (2020). Sex offender residence restrictions and homelessness: A critical look at South Carolina. *Criminal Justice Policy Review, 31*(8), 1119–1135.

36. Tewksbury, R., Mustaine, E. E., & Rolfe, S. (2016). Sex offender residential mobility and relegation: The collateral consequences continue. *American Journal of Criminal Justice, 41*(4), 852–866.

37. Williams, M., Comartin, E. B., & Lytle, R. D. (2020). The politics of symbolic laws: State resistance to the allure of sex offender residence restrictions. *Law & Policy, 42*(3), 209–235.

38. Hirschfield, P. J. (2018). Schools and crime. *Annual Review of Criminology*, 1, 149–169.

39. American Civil Liberties Union. (n.d.). *Locating the school-to-prison pipeline*. Washington, DC: Author.

40. Sykes, B. L., Piquero, A. R., Gioviano, J. P., & Pittman, N. (2015). The school-to-prison pipeline in America, 1972–2012. *Oxford handbooks online*. Retrieved from https://doi.org/10.1093/oxfordhb/9780199935383.013.110

41. Meiners, E. R. (2007). *Right to be hostile: Schools, prisons, and the making of public enemies*. New York, NY: Routledge.

42. Rocque, M., & Snellings, Q. (2018). The new disciplinology: Research, theory, and remaining puzzles on the school-to-prison pipeline. *Journal of Criminal Justice, 59*, 3–11.

43. Welsh, R. O. (2020). Overlooked exclusionary discipline: Examining placement in alternative schools, expulsions, and referrals to hearing in an urban district. *Educational Policy*, 1–37.

44. Novak, A. (2018). The association between experiences of exclusionary discipline and justice system contact: A systematic review. *Aggression and Violent Behavior, 40*, 73–82.

45. Kang-Brown, J., Trone, J., Fratello, J., & Daftary-Kapur, T. (2013, December 2013). *A generation later: What we've learned about zero tolerance in schools*. Vera Institute of Justice, Center on Youth Justice. Retrieved from https://www.vera.org/publications/a-generation-later-what-weve-learned-about-zero-tolerance-in-schools

46. Goldstein, N. E., Cole, L. M., Houck, M., Haney-Caron, E., Holliday, S. B., Kreimer, R., & Bethel, K. (2019). Dismantling the school-to-prison pipeline: The Philadelphia police school diversion program. *Children and Youth Services Review, 101*, 61–69.

47. Hirschfield, P. J. (2018). The role of schools in sustaining juvenile justice system inequality. *The Future of Children, 28*(1), 11–36.

48. Sykes, B. L., Piquero, A. R., Gioviano, J. P., & Pittman, N. (2015). The school-to-prison pipeline in America, 1972–2012. *Oxford handbooks online*. Retrieved from https://doi.org/10.1093/oxfordhb/9780199935383.013.110

49. Kamenetz, A. (2018, December 17). *Suspensions are down in U.S. schools but large racial gaps remain*. National Public Radio. Retrieved from https://www.npr.org/2018/12/17/677508707/suspensions-are-down-in-u-s-schools-but-large-racial-gaps-remain

50. Losen, D., & Whitaker, A. (n.d.). *11 million days lost: Race, discipline, and safety at U.S. public schools* (Part 1). American Civil Liberties Union, Center for Civil Rights Remedies. Retrieved from https://www.aclu.org/report/11-million-days-lost-race-discipline-and-safety-us-public-schools-part-1

51. Walker, B. L. T. (2020). "Loud, proud, and love a crowd": African American girls and school discipline practices. *Middle School Journal, 51*(1), 12–18.

52. Giordano, K., Vega, V., & Gubi, A. (2021). Expelled from childcare: Suspension and expulsion practices in one state's community childcare centers. *Early Childhood Education Journal, 50*, 1–10.

53. Edelman, M. W. (2007). The cradle to prison pipeline: An American health crisis. *Preventing Chronic Disease, 4*(3), A43.

54. Loomis, A., Davis, A., Cruden, G., Padilla, C., & Drazen, Y. (2021). Early childhood suspension and expulsion: A content analysis of state legislation. *Early Childhood Education Journal, 50*, 1–18.

55. Zeng, S., Corr, C. P., O'Grady, C., & Guan, Y. (2019). Adverse childhood experiences and preschool suspension expulsion: A population study. *Child Abuse & Neglect, 97*, 1–9.

56. Zeng, S., Pereira, B., Larson, A., Corr, C. P., O'Grady, C., & Stone-MacDonald, A. (2021). Preschool suspension and expulsion for young children with disabilities. *Exceptional Children, 87*(2), 199–216.

57. Gopalan, M., & Nelson, A. A. (2019). Understanding the racial discipline gap in schools. *AERA Open, 5*(2), 1–26.

58. Hirschfield, P. J. (2018). The role of schools in sustaining juvenile justice system inequality. *The Future of Children, 28*(1), 11–36.

59. Huang, F. L. (2018). Do Black students misbehave more? Investigating the differential involvement hypothesis and out-of-school suspensions. *Journal of Educational Research, 111*(3), 284–294.

60. Morris, E. W., & Perry, B. L. (2017). Girls behaving badly? Race, gender, and subjective evaluation in the discipline of African American girls. *Sociology of Education, 90*(2), 127–148.

61. Skiba, R. J. (2000). *Zero tolerance, zero evidence: An analysis of school disciplinary practice* (Policy research report). Terre Haute: Indiana Education Policy Center.

62. Lindsay, C. A., & Hart, C. M. (2017). Exposure to same-race teachers and student disciplinary outcomes for Black students in North Carolina. *Educational Evaluation and Policy Analysis, 39*(3), 485–510.

63. Hirschfield, P. J. (2018). The role of schools in sustaining juvenile justice system inequality. *The Future of Children, 28*(1), 11–36.

64. Gopalan, M., & Nelson, A. A. (2019). Understanding the racial discipline gap in schools. *AERA Open, 5*(2), 1–26.

65. Welch, K., & Payne, A. A. (2010). Racial threat and punitive school discipline. *Social Problems, 57*(1), 25–48.

66. Mitchell, M. M., Armstrong, G., & Armstrong, T. (2020). Disproportionate school disciplinary responses: An exploration of prisonization and minority threat hypothesis among black, Hispanic, and Native American students. *Criminal Justice Policy Review, 31*(1), 80–102.

67. Novak, A. (2018). The association between experiences of exclusionary discipline and justice system contact: A systematic review. *Aggression and Violent Behavior, 40*, 73–82.

68. Mowen, T. J., Brent, J. J., & Boman IV, J. H. (2020). The effect of school discipline on offending across time. *Justice Quarterly, 37*(4), 739–760.

69. Cuellar, A. E., & Markowitz, S. (2015). School suspension and the school-to-prison pipeline. *International Review of Law and Economics, 43*, 98–106.

70. Hirschfield, P. J. (2018). The role of schools in sustaining juvenile justice system inequality. *The Future of Children, 28*(1), 11–36.

71. Pesta, R. (2021). School punishment, deterrence, and race: A partial test of defiance theory. *Crime & Delinquency*, 1–32.

72. Weissman, M. (2015). *Prelude to prison: Student perspectives on school suspension.* Syracuse, NY: Syracuse University Press.

73. Weissman, M. (2015). *Prelude to prison: Student perspectives on school suspension.* Syracuse, NY: Syracuse University Press.

74. Pesta, R. (2018). Labeling and the differential impact of school discipline on negative life outcomes: Assessing ethno-racial variation in the school-to-prison pipeline. *Crime & Delinquency, 64*(11), 1489–1512.

75. Morris, M. (2016). *Pushout: The criminalization of Black girls in schools.* New York, NY: New Press.

76. Jacobsen, W. C. (2020). School punishment and interpersonal exclusion: Rejection, withdrawal, and separation from friends. *Criminology, 58*(1), 35–69.

77. Mowen, T. J., Brent, J. J., & Boman IV, J. H. (2020). The effect of school discipline on offending across time. *Justice Quarterly, 37*(4), 739–760.

78. National Institute of Education. (1978). *Safe school study.* Washington, DC: U.S. Department of Health, Education, and Welfare, National Institute of Education.

79. Musu-Gillette, L., Zhang, A., Wang, K., Zhang, J., Kemp, J., Diliberti, M., & Oudekerk, B. A. (2018). *Indicators of school crime and safety: 2017* (NCES 2018–036/NCJ 251413). Washington, DC: National Center for Education Statistics & Bureau of Justice Statistics.

80. Gottfredson, D. C., Crosse, S., Tang, Z., Bauer, E. L., Harmon, M. A., Hagen, C. A., & Greene, A. D. (2020). Effects of school resource officers on school crime and responses to school crime. *Criminology & Public Policy, 19*(3), 905–940.

81. Homer, E. M., & Fisher, B. W. (2020). Police in schools and student arrest rates across the United States: Examining differences by race, ethnicity, and gender. *Journal of School Violence, 19*(2), 192–204.

82. Kirk, D. S., & Wakefield, S. (2018). Collateral consequences of punishment: A critical review and path forward. *Annual Review of Criminology, 1*, 171–194.

83. Wiley, S. A., & Esbensen, F.-A. (2016). The effect of police contact: Does official intervention result in deviance amplification? *Crime & Delinquency, 62*(3), 283–307.

84. Brown, S. J., Mears, D. P., Collier, N. L., Montes, A. N., Pesta, G. B., & Siennick, S. E. (2020). Education versus punishment? Silo effects and the school-to-prison pipeline. *Journal of Research in Crime and Delinquency, 57*(4), 403–443.

85. Black, D. W. (2018, March 15). Zero tolerance discipline policies won't fix school shootings. *The Conversation.* Retrieved from https://theconversation.com/zero-tolerance-discipline-policies-wont-fix-school-shootings-93399

86. Rocque, M., & Snellings, Q. (2018). The new disciplinology: Research, theory, and remaining puzzles on the school-to-prison pipeline. *Journal of Criminal Justice, 59*, 3–11.

87. Maeng, J. L., Cornell, D., & Huang, F. (2020). Student threat assessment as an alternative to exclusionary discipline. *Journal of School Violence, 19*(3), 377–388.

88. Crepeau-Hobson, F., & Leech, N. (2020). Disciplinary and nondisciplinary outcomes of school-based threat assessment in Colorado schools. *School Psychology Review*, 1–10.

89. Goldstein, N. E., Cole, L. M., Houck, M., Haney-Caron, E., Holliday, S. B., Kreimer, R., & Bethel, K. (2019). Dismantling the school-to-prison pipeline: The Philadelphia police school diversion program. *Children and Youth Services Review, 101*, 61–69.

90. Barrett, J. G., & Janopaul-Naylor, E. (2016). Description of a collaborative community approach to impacting juvenile arrests. *Psychological Services, 13*(2), 133.

91. Riestenberg, N. (2007). The restorative recovery school: Countering chemical dependency. *Reclaiming Children & Youth, 16*(2), 21–23.

92. Goggins, B. R., & DeBacco, D. A. (2020, November 5). *Survey of state criminal history information systems: A criminal justice information policy report, 2018.* Washington, DC: U.S. Department of Justice, Bureau of Justice Statistics. Retrieved from https://www.ojp.gov/pdffiles1/bjs/grants/255651.pdf

93. U.S. Census Bureau. (2021, April). *Educational attainment in the United States: 2020.* Retrieved from https://www.census.gov/data/tables/2020/demo/educational-attainment/cps-detailed-tables.html

94. Shannon, S. K., Uggen, C., Schnittker, J., Thompson, M., Wakefield, S., & Massoglia, M. (2017). The growth, scope, and spatial distribution of people with felony records in the United States, 1948–2010. *Demography, 54*(5), 1795–1818.

95. Eberstadt, N. (2019, May 22). *America's invisible felon population: A blind spot in U.S. national statistics.* Statement before the Joint Economic Committee on the Economic Impacts of the 2020 Census and Business Uses of Federal Data. Retrieved from https://www.jec.senate.gov/public/_cache/files/b23fea23-8e98-4bcd-aeed-edcc061a4bc0/testimony-eberstadt-final.pdf

96. National Inventory of the Collateral Consequences of Conviction. (n.d.). *Welcome to the NICCC.* Retrieved from https://niccc.nationalreentryresourcecenter.org/

97. Lageson, S. E. (2020). *Digital punishment: Privacy, stigma, and the harms of data-driven criminal justice.* Oxford, UK: Oxford University Press.

98. Denver, M., & Ewald, A. (2018). Credentialing decisions and criminal records: A narrative approach. *Criminology, 56*(4), 715–749.

99. Pager, D. (2003). The mark of a criminal record. *American Journal of Sociology, 108*(5), 937–975.

100. Goffman, E. (1963). *Stigma: Notes on the management of a spoiled identity.* New York, NY: Touchstone.

101. Corda, A., & Lageson, S. E. (2020). Disordered punishment: Workaround technologies of criminal records disclosure and the rise of a new penal entrepreneurialism. *British Journal of Criminology, 60*(2), 245–264.

102. Uggen, C., Vuolo, M., Lageson, S., Ruhland, E, K., & Whitham, H. K. (2014). The edge of stigma: An experimental audit of the effects of low-level criminal records on employment. *Criminology, 52*(4), 627–654.

103. Leasure, P. (2019). Misdemeanor records and employment outcomes: An experimental study. *Crime & Delinquency, 65*(13), 1850–1872.

104. Denver, M., Siwach, G., & Bushway, S. D. (2017). A new look at the employment and recidivism relationship through the lens of a criminal background check. *Criminology, 55*(1), 174–204.

105. Jacobs, J. B. (2015). *The eternal criminal record.* Cambridge, MA: Harvard University Press.

106. Decker, S. H., Ortiz, N., Spohn, C., & Hedberg, E. (2015). Criminal stigma, race, and ethnicity: The consequences of imprisonment for employment. *Journal of Criminal Justice, 43*(2), 108–121.

107. Agan, A., & Starr, S. (2017). The effect of criminal records on access to employment. *American Economic Review, 107*(5), 560–564.

108. Uggen, C., Vuolo, M., Lageson, S., Ruhland, E, K., & Whitham, H. K. (2014). The edge of stigma: An experimental audit of the effects of low-level criminal records on employment. *Criminology, 52*(4), 627–654.

109. Cerda-Jara, M., Elster, A., & Hardin, D. (2020). *Criminal record stigma in the college-educated labor market and how to level the playing field.* Institute for Research on Labor and Employment. Retrieved from https://irle.berkeley.edu/files/2020/05/Criminal-Record-Stigma-in-the-College-Educated-Labor-Market-and-How-to-Level-the-Playing-Field.pdf

110. Agan, A., & Starr, S. (2017). The effect of criminal records on access to employment. *American Economic Review, 107*(5), 560–564.

111. DeWitt, S., & Denver, M. (2020). Criminal records, positive employment credentials, and race. *Journal of Research on Crime and Delinquency, 57*(3), 333–368.

112. Pager, D., Western, B., & Sugie, N. (2009). Sequencing disadvantage: Barriers to employment facing young black and white men with criminal records. *ANNALS of the American Academy of Political and Social Science, 623*(1), 195–213.

113. Herman, Z. (2020). *The national occupational licensing database.* National Conference of State Legislatures. Retrieved from https://www.ncsl.org/research/labor-and-employment/occupational-licensing-statute-database.aspx

114. Rhode, D. L. (2018). Virtue and the law: The good moral character requirement in occupational licensing, bar regulation, and immigration proceedings. *Law & Social Inquiry, 43*(3), 1027–1058.

115. Custer, B. D. (2018). Applying to university with criminal convictions: A comparative study of admissions policies in the United States and United Kingdom. *Journal of Higher Education Policy and Management, 40*(3), 239–255.

116. Stewart, R., & Uggen, C. (2020). Criminal records and college admissions: A modified experimental audit. *Criminology, 58*(1), 156–188.

117. Stewart, R., & Uggen, C. (2020). Criminal records and college admissions: A modified experimental audit. *Criminology, 58*(1), 156–188.

118. Brasil, A. (2020, August 4). *Fair housing and criminal background screening guide: Public housing and section 8 vouchers.* Fair Housing Project. Retrieved from https://www.fairhousingnc.org/2020/fair-housing-and-criminal-background-screening-guide-public-housing-and-section-8-vouchers/

119. U.S. Department of Housing and Urban Development. (2015, November 2). *Guidance for public housing agencies (PHAs) and owners of federally-assisted housing on excluding the use of arrest records in housing decisions.* Retrieved from https://www.hud.gov/sites/documents/PIH2015-19.PDF

120. Inderbitzin, M. (2019). Felony disenfranchisement. In B. Huebner (Ed.), *Oxford bibliographies – Criminology* (online). Oxford, UK: Oxford University Press.

121. American Civil Liberties Union. *Felony disenfranchisement laws* (map). Retrieved from https://www.aclu.org/issues/voting-rights/voter-restoration/felony-disenfranchisement-laws-map

122. Uggen, C., Larson, R., Shannon, S., & Pulido-Nava, A. (2020, October). *Locked out 2020: Estimates of people denied voting rights due to a felony conviction.* Sentencing Project. Retrieved from https://www.sentencingproject.org/publications/locked-out-2020-estimates-of-people-denied-voting-rights-due-to-a-felony-conviction/

123. Manza, J., & Uggen, C. (2008). *Locked out: Felon disenfranchisement and American democracy.* Oxford, UK: Oxford University Press.

124. Clegg, R., Conway III, G. T., & Lee, K. K. (2008). The case against felon voting. *University of St. Thomas Journal of Law & Public Policy, 2,* 1–19.

125. Aviram, H., Bragg, A., & Lewis, C. (2017). Felon disenfranchisement. *Annual Review of Law and Social Science, 13,* 295–311.

126. U.S. Const. amend. XIV, section II.

127. Shineman, V. (2020). Restoring voting rights: Evidence that reversing felony disenfranchisement increases political efficacy. *Policy Studies, 41*(2–3), 131–150.

128. Small, M. L., & Pager, D. (2020). Sociological perspectives on racial discrimination. *Journal of Economic Perspectives, 34*(2), 49–67.

129. Manza, J., & Uggen, C. (2008). *Locked out: Felon disenfranchisement and American democracy.* Oxford, UK: Oxford University Press.

130. Jacobs, J. B. (2015). *The eternal criminal record.* Cambridge, MA: Harvard University Press.

131. Burton, A. L., Cullen, F. T., Pickett, J. T., Burton Jr, V. S., & Thielo, A. J. (2021). Beyond the eternal criminal record: Public support for expungement. *Criminology & Public Policy, 20*(1), 123–151.

132. Lageson, S. E., Denver, M., & Pickett, J. T. (2019). Privatizing criminal stigma: Experience, intergroup contact, and public views about publicizing arrest records. *Punishment & Society, 21*(3), 315–341.

133. Adapted from Zito, R. (2020). Identifying deviant behavior. In K. Korgen & M. Atkinson (Eds.), *Sociology in action* (2nd ed.). Thousand Oaks, CA: SAGE.

134. Lageson, S. E., Denver, M., & Pickett, J. T. (2019). Privatizing criminal stigma: Experience, intergroup contact, and public views about publicizing arrest records. *Punishment & Society, 21*(3), 315–341.

135. Lageson, S. E. (2020). *Digital punishment: Privacy, stigma, and the harms of data-driven criminal justice.* New York, NY: Oxford University Press.

136. Lageson, S. E. (2020). *Digital punishment: Privacy, stigma, and the harms of data-driven criminal justice.* New York, NY: Oxford University Press.

137. Selbin, J., McCrary, J., & Epstein, J. (2018). Unmarked? Criminal record clearing and employment outcomes. *Journal of Criminal Law and Criminology, 108*(1), 1–72.

138. McCann, W., Kowalski, M. A., Hemmens, C., & Stohr, M. K. (2021). An analysis of certificates of rehabilitation in the United States. *Corrections, 6*(1), 18–44.

139. The Legal Aid Society. (n.d.). *What you need to know about certificates of relief from disabilities and certificates of good conduct.* Retrieved from https://legalaidnyc.org/get-help/employment/what-you-need-to-know-about-certificates-of-relief-and-good-conduct/

140. Leasure, P., & Andersen, T. S. (2020). Race, criminal records, and certificates of relief: An experimental pilot study. *Deviant Behavior, 41*(9), 1065–1083.

141. Leasure, P., & Andersen, T. S. (2020). Race, criminal records, and certificates of relief: An experimental pilot study. *Deviant Behavior, 41*(9), 1065–1083.

142. Raphael, S. (2021). The intended and unintended consequences of ban the box. *Annual Review of Criminology, 4,* 191–207.

143. Avery, B., & Lu, H. (2020, September 3). *Ban the box: U.S. cities, counties, and states adopt fair hiring policies.* National Employment Law Project. Retrieved from https://www.nelp.org/publication/ban-the-box-fair-chance-hiring-state-and-local-guide/

144. Raphael, S. (2021). The intended and unintended consequences of ban the box. *Annual Review of Criminology, 4,* 191–207.

145. Sugie, N. F. (2017). Criminal record questions, statistical discrimination, and equity in a ban the box era. *Criminology & Public Policy, 16,* 167–175.

146. Raphael, S. (2021). The intended and unintended consequences of ban the box. *Annual Review of Criminology, 4,* 191–207.

147. Agan, A., & Starr, S. (2018). Ban the box, criminal records, and racial discrimination: A field experiment. *Quarterly Journal of Economics, 133*(1), 191–235.

148. Rios, V. M., Prieto, G., & Ibarra, J. M. (2020). Mano suave–mano dura: Legitimacy policing and Latino stop-and-frisk. *American Sociological Review, 85*(1), 58–75.

149. Rios, V. M., Prieto, G., & Ibarra, J. M. (2020). Mano suave–mano dura: Legitimacy policing and Latino stop-and-frisk. *American Sociological Review, 85*(1), 58–75.

150. Bouffard, L., & Sherman, L. (2018). Defiance theory. In G. Bruinisma & D. Weisburd (Eds.), *Encyclopedia of criminology and criminal justice* (online). New York, NY: Springer.

151. Klein, J. L., Tolson, D., & Collins, C. (2014). Lamenting the list: A partial test of Sherman's defiance theory as applied to female sex offenders. *Contemporary Justice Review, 17*(3), 326–345.

152. Sherman, L. (1993). Defiance, deterrence, and irrelevance: A theory of the criminal sanction. *Journal of Research in Crime and Delinquency, 30,* 445–473.

153. Walters, G. D., & Bolger, P. C. (2019). Procedural justice perceptions, legitimacy beliefs, and compliance with the law: A meta-analysis. *Journal of Experimental Criminology, 15*(3), 341–372.

154. Barkworth, J. M., & Murphy, K. (2019). Procedural justice, posturing and defiant action: Exploring prisoner reactions to prison authority. *Justice Quarterly, 38*(3), 537–564.

155. Scheff, T. J. (2003). Shame in self and society. *Symbolic interaction, 26*(2), 239-262.

156. Bouffard, L., & Sherman, L. (2018). Defiance theory. In G. Bruinisma & D Weisburd (Eds.), *Encyclopedia of criminology and criminal justice* (online). New York, NY: Springer.

157. Amemiya, J., Mortenson, E., & Wang, M. T. (2020). Minor infractions are not minor: School infractions for minor misconduct may increase adolescents' defiant behavior and contribute to racial disparities in school discipline. *American Psychologist, 75*(1), 23.

158. Barkworth, J. M., & Murphy, K. (2019). Procedural justice, posturing and defiant action: Exploring prisoner reactions to prison authority. *Justice Quarterly, 38*(3), 537–564.

159. Bouffard, L., & Sherman, L. (2018). Defiance theory. In G. Bruinisma & D Weisburd (Eds.), *Encyclopedia of criminology and criminal justice* (online). New York, NY: Springer.

160. Sherman, L. W. (1993). Defiance, deterrence, and irrelevance: A theory of the criminal sanction. *Journal of Research in Crime and Delinquency, 30*(4), 445–473.

161. Kirk, D. S., & Matsuda, M. (2011). Legal cynicism, collective efficacy, and the ecology of arrest. *Criminology, 49*(2), 443–472.

162. Nagin, D. S., & Telep, C. W. (2017). Procedural justice and legal compliance. *Annual Review of Law and Social Science, 13,* 5–28.

163. Kirk, D. S., & Matsuda, M. (2011). Legal cynicism, collective efficacy, and the ecology of arrest. *Criminology, 49*(2), 443–472.

164. Sampson, R. J., & Bartusch, D. J. (1998). Legal cynicism and (subcultural?) tolerance of deviance: The neighborhood context of racial differences. *Law and Society Review, 32*(4), 777–804.

165. Gifford, F. E., & Reisig, M. D. (2019). A multidimensional model of legal cynicism. *Law and human behavior, 43*(4), 383.

166. Kaiser, K., & Reisig, M. D. (2019). Legal socialization and self-reported criminal offending: The role of procedural justice and legal orientations. *Journal of Quantitative Criminology, 35*(1), 135–154.

167. Berg, M. T., Stewart, E. A., Intravia, J., Warren, P. Y., & Simons, R. L. (2016). Cynical streets: Neighborhood social processes and perceptions of criminal injustice. *Criminology, 54*(3), 520–547.

168. Hagan, J., McCarthy, B., & Herda, D. (2020). What the study of legal cynicism and crime can tell us about reliability, validity, and versatility in law and social science research. *Annual Review of Law and Social Science, 16*, 1–20.

169. Nivette, A. E., Eisner, M., Malti, T., & Ribeaud, D. (2015). The social and developmental antecedents of legal cynicism. *Journal of Research in Crime and Delinquency, 52*(2), 270–298.

CHAPTER 12

1. Pietsch, B. (2020, December 25). Ruling on woman on death row puts her execution in doubt. *The New York Times.* Retrieved from https://www.nytimes.com/2020/12/25/us/lisa-montgomery-execution.html

2. U.S. Department of Justice. (2020, October 16). Executions scheduled for two federal inmates convicted of heinous murders. Retrieved from https://www.justice.gov/opa/pr/executions-scheduled-two-federal-inmates-convicted-heinous-murders

3. Snyder, R. L. (2020, December 18). Punch after punch, rape after rape, a murderer was made. *The New York Times.* Retrieved from https://www.nytimes.com/2020/12/18/opinion/lisa-montgomery-execution.html

4. Inter-American Commission on Human Rights. (2020, December 1). Precautionary measure no. 1048-20 – Lisa Montgomery regarding the United States of America. Retrieved from http://www.oas.org/en/iachr/decisions/pdf/2020/91-20MC1048-20-US.pdf

5. Sebba, L., & Berenblum, T. (2014). Victimology and the sociology of new disciplines: A research agenda. *International Review of Victimology, 20*(1), 7–30.

6. Smith, M., & Bouffard, L. A. (2014). Victim precipitation. In J. S. Albanese (Ed.), *The encyclopedia of criminology and criminal justice.* New York, NY: Wiley. https://ezproxy.elon.edu/login?url=https://search.credoreference.com/content/entry/wileycacj/victim_precipitation/0?institutionId=3606

7. Von Hentig, H. (1940). Remarks on the interaction of perpetrator and victim. *Journal of Criminal Law and Criminology (1931-1951), 31*(3), 303–309.

8. Hentig, H. V. (1948). *The criminal and his victim: Studies in the sociobiology of crime.* New Haven, CT: Yale University Press.

9. Mendelsohn, B. (1976). Victimology and contemporary society's trends. *Victimology, 1*(1), 8–28.

10. Wolfgang, M. (1958). *Patterns in criminal homicide.* Philadelphia: University of Pennsylvania Press.

11. Wolfgang, M. E. (1957). Victim precipitated criminal homicide. *Journal of Criminal Law, Criminology, and Police Science, 48*(1), 1–11.

12. Wolfgang, M. E. (1957). Victim precipitated criminal homicide. *Journal of Criminal Law, Criminology, and Police Science, 48*(1), 1–11.

13. Amir, M. (1967). Victim precipitated forcible rape. *Journal of Criminal Law, Criminology, and Police Science, 58*(4), 493–502.

14. Scully, D., & Marolla, J. (1984). Convicted rapists' vocabulary of motive: Excuses and justifications. *Social Problems, 31*(5), 530–544.

15. Krahé, B. (2016). Societal responses to sexual violence against women: Rape myths and the "real rape" stereotype. In H. Kury, S. Redo, & E. Shea (Eds.), *Women and children as victims and offenders: Background, prevention, reintegration* (pp. 671–700). New York, NY: Springer.

16. Hayes, R. M., Lorenz, K., & Bell, K. A. (2013). Victim blaming others: Rape myth acceptance and the just world belief. *Feminist Criminology, 8*(3), 202–220.

17. Amir, M. (1971). *Patterns in forcible rape.* Chicago, IL: University of Chicago Press.

18. Weis, K., & Borges, S. S. (1973). Victimology and rape: The case of the legitimate victim. *Issues in Criminology, 8*, 71–115.

19. Ryan, K. (2019). Rape mythology and victim blaming as a social construct. In W. O'Donohue & P. Schewe (Eds.), *Handbook of sexual assault and sexual assault prevention* (pp. 151–176). New York, NY: Springer.

20. Temkin, J., Gray, J. M., & Barrett, J. (2018). Different functions of rape myth use in court: Findings from a trial observation study. *Feminist Criminology, 13*(2), 205–226.

21. Berger, R. J., & Searles, P. (1985). Victim-offender interaction in rape: Victimological, situational, and feminist perspectives. *Women's Studies Quarterly, 13*(3/4), 9–15.

22. Dhanani, L. Y., Main, A. M., & Pueschel, A. (2020). Do you only have yourself to blame? A meta-analytic test of the victim precipitation model. *Journal of Organizational Behavior, 41*(8), 706–721.

23. Timmer, D. A., & Norman, W. H. (1984). The ideology of victim precipitation. *Criminal Justice Review, 9*(2), 63–68.

24. Felson, R. B., Messner, S. F. (1998). Disentangling the effects of gender and intimacy on victim precipitation in homicide. *Criminology, 36*, 405–423.

25. Suonpää, K., & Savolainen, J. (2019). When a woman kills her man: Gender and victim precipitation in homicide. *Journal of Interpersonal Violence, 34*(11), 2398–2413.

26. Dobash, R. P., & Dobash, R. E. (2020). *Male–male murder.* New York, NY: Routledge.

27. Lewis, J. A., Hamilton, J. C., & Elmore, J. D. (2019). Describing the ideal victim: A linguistic analysis of victim descriptions. *Current Psychology, 40*, 1–9.

28. Balfour, G., Du Mont, J., & White, D. (2018). "To this day she continues to struggle with the terror imposed upon her": Rape narratives in victim impact statements. *Women & Criminal Justice, 28*(1), 43–62.

29. Fohring, S. (2018). Revisiting the non-ideal victim. In M. Duggan (Ed.), *Revisiting the 'ideal victim': Developments in critical victimology* (pp. 195–210). Bristol, UK: Policy Press.

30. Garcia, J. (2018). Towards an inclusive victimology and a new understanding of public compassion to victims: From and beyond Christie's ideal victim. In M. Duggan (Ed.), *Revisiting the 'ideal victim': Developments in critical victimology* (pp. 297–312). Bristol, UK: Policy Press.

31. Lauritsen, J. L., & Rezey, M. L. (2018). Victimization trends and correlates: Macro-and microinfluences and new directions for research. *Annual Review of Criminology, 1*, 103–121.

32. Harrell, E. (2019, January). Victims of identity theft, 2016. *U.S. Department of Justice, Bureau of Justice Statistics.* Retrieved from https://www.bjs.gov/content/pub/pdf/vit16.pdf; Lokanan, M. E., & Liu, S. (2020). The demographic profile of victims of investment fraud: An update. *Journal of Financial Crime.*

33. Morgan, R. E., & Thompson, A. (2021, October). Criminal victimization, 2020. *National Crime Victimization Survey.* Washington, DC: U.S. Department of Justice. Retrieved from https://bjs.ojp.gov/sites/g/files/xyckuh236/files/media/document/cv20.pdf

34. Morgan, R. E., & Thompson, A. (2021, October). Criminal victimization, 2020. *National Crime Victimization Survey.* Washington, DC: U.S. Department of Justice. Retrieved from https://bjs.ojp.gov/sites/g/files/xyckuh236/files/media/document/cv20.pdf

35. Children's Bureau. (2019, June). NCANDS. *U.S. Department of Health and Human Services.* Retrieved from https://www.acf.hhs.gov/cb/research-data-technology/reporting-systems/ncands

36. United Nations. (n.d.). ICVS – International Crime Victims Survey. *United Nations Interregional Crime and Justice Research Institute.* Retrieved from http://www.unicri.it/services/library_documentation/publications/icvs/data

37. Lauritsen, J. L., & Rezey, M. L. (2018). Victimization trends and correlates: Macro-and microinfluences and new directions for research. *Annual Review of Criminology, 1*, 103–121.

38. Anderson, K. (2019). Mass-market consumer fraud in the United States: A 2017 update. *Bureau of Economics, Federal Trade Commission.* Retrieved from https://www.ftc.gov/reports/mass-market-consumer-fraud-united-states-2017-update

39. Bureau of Justice Statistics. NCVS Victimization Analysis Tool (NVAT) – Number of property victimizations, 2017 and Number of personal thefts/larcenies, 2017. *Office of Justice Programs.* Retrieved from https://www.bjs.gov/index.cfm?ty=nvat

40. Dodge, M. (2020). A black box warning: The marginalization of white-collar crime victimization. *Journal of White Collar and Corporate Crime, 1*(1), 24–33.

41. Eriksson, L., & Mazerolle, P. (2013). A general strain theory of intimate partner homicide. *Aggression and Violent Behavior, 18*, 462–470.

42. Federal Bureau of Investigation. Crime in the United States (reports for 2016–2020). *Uniform Crime Reports.*

43. Bureau of Justice Statistics. (Number of rape/sexual assaults by sex, 2016–2020). Generated using the National Crime Victimization Survey (NCVS) Dashboard (N-DASH) Tool at www.bjs.gov.

44. Fraga Dominguez, S., Storey, J. E., & Glorney, E. (2019). Help-seeking behavior in victims of elder abuse: A systematic review. *Trauma, Violence, & Abuse, 22*, 1–15.

45. Turanovic, J. J., & Pratt, T. C. (2017). Consequences of violent victimization for Native American youth in early adulthood. *Journal of Youth and Adolescence, 46*(6), 1333–1350.

46. Bureau of Justice Statistics. (Number of violent crime excluding simple assault victimizations by weapon category by race/Hispanic ethnicity, 2020). Generated using the National Crime Victimization Survey (NCVS) Dashboard (N-DASH) Tool at www.bjs.gov.

47. Wu, C. (2020). How does gun violence affect Americans' trust in each other? *Social Science Research, 91*, 102449.; Turner, H. A., Mitchell, K. J., Jones, L. M., Hamby, S., Wade Jr, R., & Beseler, C. L. (2019). Gun violence exposure and post-traumatic symptoms among children and youth. *Journal of Traumatic Stress, 32*(6), 881–889.

48. U.S. Census Bureau. (2020). Annual estimates of the resident population by sex, race, and Hispanic origin for the United States: April 1, 2010 to July 1, 2019. Retrieved from https://www.census.gov/newsroom/press-kits/2020/population-estimates-detailed.html

49. Centers for Disease Control. (2018). Table . Age-adjusted death rates for selected causes of death, by sex, race, and Hispanic origin: United States, selected years 1950–2017. Retrieved from https://www.cdc.gov/nchs/data/hus/2018/005.pdf

50. Edwards, F., Esposito, M. H., & Lee, H. (2018). Risk of police-involved death by race/ethnicity and place, United States, 2012–2018. *American Journal of Public Health, 108*(9), 1241–1248.

51. Federal Bureau of Investigation. Law enforcement officers killed and assaulted (LEOKA), 2012-2018. *Uniform Crime Reports.* Retrieved from https://ucr.fbi.gov/leoka/

52. Lauritsen, J. L., & Rezey, M. L. (2018). Victimization trends and correlates: Macro-and microinfluences and new directions for research. *Annual Review of Criminology, 1*, 103–121.

53. Nobles, M. R., Ward, J. T., & Tillyer, R. (2016). The impact of neighborhood context on spatiotemporal patterns of burglary. *Journal of Research in Crime and Delinquency, 53*(5), 711–740.

54. Gerlinger, J. (2020). Exclusionary school discipline and neighborhood crime. *Socius, 6*, 2378023120925404.

55. Anderson, E. (2019). Code of the street. In A. M. Orum (Ed.), *The Wiley Blackwell encyclopedia of urban and regional studies.* New York, NY: Wiley Blackwell.

56. Mitchell, M. M., Pyrooz, D. C., & Decker, S. H. (2020). Culture in prison, culture on the street: The convergence between the convict code and code of the street. *Journal of Crime and Justice, 44*, 1–20.

57. Peterson, R. D., & Krivo, L. J. (2010). *Divergent social worlds: Neighborhood crime and the racial-spatial divide.* New York, NY: Russell Sage Foundation.

58. Graif, C., & Matthews, S. A. (2017). The long arm of poverty: Extended and relational geographies of child victimization and neighborhood violence exposures. *Justice Quarterly, 34*(6), 1096–1125.

59. Chetty, R., & Hendren, N. (2018). The impacts of neighborhoods on intergenerational mobility I: Childhood exposure effects. *The Quarterly Journal of Economics, 133*(3), 1107–1162.

60. Annie E. Casey Foundation. (2019). Children living in high-poverty, low-opportunity areas. Retrieved from https://assets.aecf.org/m/resourcedoc/aecf-childrenlivinginhighpoverty-2019.pdf

61. Perkins, K. L., & Sampson, R. J. (2015). Compounded deprivation in the transition to adulthood: The intersection of racial and economic inequality among Chicagoans, 1995-2013. *RSF: The Russell Sage Foundation Journal of the Social Sciences, 1*(1), 35–54.

62. Renfro, P. (2020). *Stranger danger: Family values, childhood, and the American carceral state.* New York, NY: Oxford University Press.

63. McQuade, K. M. (2014). Victim-offender relationship. In J. Albanese (Ed.), *Encyclopedia of criminology and criminal justice.* New York, NY: Wiley Online.

64. Bureau of Justice Statistics. Stranger and non-stranger crime. *Office of Justice Programs.* Retrieved from https://www.bjs.gov/index.cfm?ty = tp&tid=941

65. Bureau of Justice Statistics. NCVS Victimization Analysis Tool (NVAT) – Terms and definitions. *Office of Justice Programs.* Retrieved from https://www.bjs.gov/index.cfm?ty =nvat

66. Federal Bureau of Investigation. (2019). Data declaration – Relationship of victims to offenders by offense category, 2019. *National Incident-Based Reporting Program.* Retrieved from https://ucr.fbi.gov/nibrs/2019/tables/data-tables

67. Trojan, C., & Krull, A. C. (2012). Variations in wounding by relationship intimacy in homicide cases. *Journal of Interpersonal Violence, 27*(14), 2869–2888.

68. Federal Bureau of Investigation. (2022). *Expanded homicide offense characteristics in the United States, victim's relationship to the offender, 2020. Generated using Crime Data Explorer.* Retrieved from https://crime-data-explorer.fr.cloud.gov/pages/explorer/crime/shr

69. Fairbairn, J., Jaffe, P., & Dawson, M. (2017). Challenges in defining domestic homicide: Considerations for research and practice. In M. Dawson (Ed.), *Domestic homicides and death reviews* (pp. 201–228). London: Palgrave Macmillan.

70. Wong, J. S., & Lee, C. (2018). Extra! Extra! The importance of victim–offender relationship in homicide newsworthiness. *Journal of Interpersonal Violence, 36*, 1–21.

71. Federal Bureau of Investigation. (2020). Relationship of victims to offenders by offense category, 2019. *National Incident-Based Reporting System.* Retrieved from https://ucr.fbi.gov/nibrs/2019/tables/data-tables

72. Federal Bureau of Investigation. (2020). Victims, adult and juvenile age category by offense category, 2019. *National Incident-Based Reporting System.* Retrieved from https://ucr.fbi.gov/nibrs/2019/tables/data-tables

73. Renfro, P. (2020). *Stranger danger: Family values, childhood, and the American carceral state.* New York, NY: Oxford University Press.

74. Gewirtz-Meydan, A., & Finkelhor, D. (2020). Sexual abuse and assault in a large national sample of children and adolescents. *Child Maltreatment, 25*(2), 203–214.

75. For example, https://www.kidsmartz.org/StrangerDanger

76. Azimi, A. M., Daquin, J. C., & Hoppe, S. J. (2019). Identifying poly-victimization among prisoners: An application of latent class analysis. *Journal of Interpersonal Violence, 36*, 1–25.

77. Berg, M. T., & Mulford, C. F. (2020). Reappraising and redirecting research on the victim–offender overlap. *Trauma, Violence, & Abuse, 21*(1), 16–30.

78. Berg, M. T., Stewart, E. A., Schreck, C. J., & Simons, R. L. (2012). The victim–offender overlap in context: Examining the role of neighborhood street culture. *Criminology, 50*(2), 359–390.

79. Beckley, A. L., Caspi, A., Arseneault, L., Barnes, J. C., Fisher, H. L., Harrington, H., . . . Moffitt, T. E. (2018). The developmental nature of the victim-offender overlap. *Journal of Developmental and Life-course Criminology, 4*(1), 24–49.

80. DeLong, C., & Reichert, J. (2019). *The victim-offender overlap: Examining the relationship between victimization and offending.* Chicago, IL: Illinois Criminal Justice Information Authority.

81. Muftić, L. R., & Hunt, D. E. (2013). Victim precipitation: Further understanding the linkage between victimization and offending in homicide. *Homicide Studies, 17*(3), 239–254.

82. Pizarro, J. M., Zgoba, K. M., Jennings, W. G. (2011). Assessing the interaction between offender and victim criminal lifestyles and homicide type. *Journal of Criminal Justice, 39*, 367–377.

83. Jennings, W. G., Piquero, A. R., & Reingle, J. M. (2012). On the overlap between victimization and offending: A review of the literature. *Aggression and Violent Behavior, 17*(1), 16–26.

84. Apel, R., & Burrow, J. D. (2011). Adolescent victimization and violent self-help. *Youth Violence and Juvenile Justice, 9*(2), 112–133.

85. Morselli, C., Décary-Hétu, D., Paquet-Clouston, M., & Aldridge, J. (2017). Conflict management in illicit drug cryptomarkets. *International Criminal Justice Review, 27*(4), 237–254.

86. Contreras, R. (2013). *The stickup kids: Race, drugs, violence, and the American dream.* Berkeley: University of California Press.

87. Bernasco, W., Johnson, S. D., & Ruiter, S. (2015). Learning where to offend: Effects of past on future burglary locations. *Applied Geography, 60*, 120–129.

88. Broll, R., & Huey, L. (2020). "Every time I try to get out, I get pushed back": The role of violent victimization in women's experience of multiple episodes of homelessness. *Journal of Interpersonal Violence, 35*(17–18), 3379–3404.

89. Bender, K., Brown, S. M., Thompson, S. J., Ferguson, K. M., & Langenderfer, L. (2015). Multiple victimizations before and after leaving home associated with PTSD, depression, and substance use disorder among homeless youth. *Child Maltreatment, 20*(2), 115–124.

90. Gorinas, C. (2018). A detailed analysis of childhood victimization using national registers: Forms and sequencing of violence and domestic abuse. IZA Discussion Paper No. 11398, Available at SSRN: https://ssrn.com/abstract=3153362

91. Bender, K., Brown, S. M., Thompson, S. J., Ferguson, K. M., & Langenderfer, L. (2015). Multiple victimizations before and after leaving home associated with PTSD, depression, and substance use disorder among homeless youth. *Child Maltreatment, 20*(2), 115–124.

92. Tyler, K. A., & Schmitz, R. M. (2018). Child abuse, mental health and sleeping arrangements among homeless youth: Links to physical and sexual street victimization. *Children and Youth Services Review, 95,* 327–333.

93. Tyler, K., & Wright, J. (2019). Homelessness and sexual assault. In W. O'Donohue & P. Schewe (Eds.), *Handbook of sexual assault and sexual assault prevention* (pp. 693–707). New York, NY: Springer.

94. Ellsworth, J. T. (2019). Street crime victimization among homeless adults: A review of the literature. *Victims & Offenders, 14*(1), 96–118.

95. Bureau of Justice Statistics. (2022). (Number of victimizations by crime type by medical treatment for physical injuries, 2020). Generated using the National Crime Victimization Survey (NCVS) Dashboard (N-DASH) Tool at www.bjs.gov.

96. Rui, P., & Kang, K. National Hospital Ambulatory Medical Care Survey: 2017 emergency department summary tables. *National Center for Health Statistics.* Retrieved from https://www.cdc.gov/nchs/data/nhamcs/web_tables/2017_ed_web_tables-508.pdf

97. Roberson, C., & Wallace, P. H. (2016). *Family violence: Legal, medical, and social perspectives.* New York, NY: Taylor and Francis.

98. Federal Bureau of Investigation. (2019). Crime in the United States, 2019; Table 23 – Offense analysis. *Uniform Crime Reports.* Retrieved from https://ucr.fbi.gov/crime-in-the-u.s/2019/crime-in-the-u.s.-2019/tables/table-23

99. Federal Bureau of Investigation. (2020). Crime in the United States, by volume and rate per 100,000 inhabitants, 2001-2020. Retrieved from https://crime-data-explorer.fr.cloud.gov/pages/downloads

100. Cohen, M. (2016). The costs of white-collar crime. In M. Benson & F. T. Cullen (Eds.), *The Oxford handbook of white-collar crime* (pp. 78–98). Cary, NC: Oxford University Press.

101. Association of Certified Fraud Examiners. (2020). *2020 Report to the nations on occupational fraud and abuse.* Austin, TX: ACFE.

102. Internal Revenue Service. The tax gap. Retrieved from https://www.irs.gov/newsroom/the-tax-gap

103. Anderson, K. (2019). Mass-market consumer fraud in the United States: A 2017 update. Bureau of Economics, Federal Trade Commission. Retrieved from https://www.ftc.gov/reports/mass-market-consumer-fraud-united-states-2017-update

104. Hyland, S. (2019). Justice expenditure and employment extracts, 2016 – preliminary. *Bureau of Justice Statistics.* Retrieved from https://www.bjs.gov/index.cfm?ty=pbdetail&iid=6728

105. Hochstetler, A., DeLisi, M., Jones-Johnson, G., & Johnson, W. R. (2014). The criminal victimization–depression sequela: Examining the effects of violent victimization on depression with a longitudinal propensity score design. *Crime & Delinquency, 60*(5), 785–806.

106. Rowe, A. T., Zapolski, T. C., Hensel, D. J., Fisher, S., & Barnes-Najor, J. (2019). Peer victimization, mood symptoms, and alcohol use: Examining effects among diverse high school youth. *Journal of Youth and Adolescence, 48*(5), 924–934.

107. Fissel, E. R., & Reyns, B. W. (2020). The aftermath of cyberstalking: School, work, social, and health costs of victimization. *American Journal of Criminal Justice, 45*(1), 70–87.

108. Randa, R., & Reyns, B. W. (2020). The physical and emotional toll of identity theft victimization: A situational and demographic analysis of the National Crime Victimization Survey. *Deviant Behavior, 41*(10), 1290–1304.

109. Fichera, G. P., Fattori, A., Neri, L., Musti, M., Coggiola, M., & Costa, G. (2015). Post-traumatic stress disorder among bank employee victims of robbery. *Occupational Medicine, 65*(4), 283–289.

110. Ali, P. A., & Naylor, P. B. (2013). Intimate partner violence: A narrative review of the feminist, social and ecological explanations for its causation. *Aggression and Violent Behavior, 18*(6), 611–619.

111. Maier, S. F., & Seligman, M. E. (2016). Learned helplessness at fifty: Insights from neuroscience. *Psychological Review, 123*(4), 349–367.

112. Belleville, G., Marchand, A., St-Hilaire, M. H., Martin, M., & Silva, C. (2012). PTSD and depression following armed robbery: Patterns of appearance and impact on absenteeism and use of health care services. *Journal of Traumatic Stress, 25*(4), 465–468.

113. Snipes, D. J., Calton, J. M., Green, B. A., Perrin, P. B., & Benotsch, E. G. (2017). Rape and posttraumatic stress disorder (PTSD): Examining the mediating role of explicit sex-power beliefs for men versus women. *Journal of Interpersonal Violence, 32*(16), 2453–2470.

114. Logan, T. K. (2020). Examining stalking experiences and outcomes for men and women stalked by (ex) partners and non-partners. *Journal of Family Violence, 35*(7), 729–739.

115. Brown, J., Burnette, M. L., & Cerulli, C. (2015). Correlations between sexual abuse histories, perceived danger, and PTSD among intimate partner violence victims. *Journal of Interpersonal Violence, 30*(15), 2709–2725.

116. American Psychiatric Association. (2013). Trauma and stressor related disorders. In *Diagnostic and statistical manual of mental disorders* (5th ed.). Author.

117. Chung, M. C., Stedmon, J., Hall, R., Marks, Z., Thornhill, K., & Mehrshahi, R. (2014). Posttraumatic stress reactions following burglary: The role of coping and personality. *Traumatology: An International Journal, 20*(2), 65–74.

118. Finegood, E. D., Chen, E., Kish, J., Vause, K., Leigh, A. K., Hoffer, L., & Miller, G. E. (2020). Community violence and cellular and cytokine indicators of inflammation in adolescents. *Psychoneuroendocrinology, 115,* 104; McCoy, D. C., Raver, C. C., & Sharkey, P. (2015). Children's cognitive performance

and selective attention following recent community violence. *Journal of Health and Social Behavior, 56*(1), 19–36.628.

119. McCoy, D. C., Raver, C. C., & Sharkey, P. (2015). Children's cognitive performance and selective attention following recent community violence. *Journal of Health and Social Behavior, 56*(1), 19–36.

120. Sharkey, P. (2010). The acute effect of local homicides on children's cognitive performance. *Proceedings of the National Academy of Sciences, 107*(26), 11733–11738.

121. Sharkey, P. (2018). *Uneasy peace: The great crime decline, the renewal of city life, and the next war on violence.* New York, NY: Norton.

122. Ferraro, K. F., & Grange, R. L. (1987). The measurement of fear of crime. *Sociological Inquiry, 57*(1), 70–97.

123. Collins, R. E. (2016). Addressing the inconsistencies in fear of crime research: A meta-analytic review. *Journal of Criminal Justice, 47*, 21–31.

124. Rader, N. (2017). Fear of crime. In H. Pontell (Ed.), *Research encyclopedia of criminology and criminal justice.* Cary, NC: Oxford University Press.

125. Burdick-Will, J., Stein, M. L., & Grigg, J. (2019). Danger on the way to school: Exposure to violent crime, public transportation, and absenteeism. *Sociological Science, 6*, 118–142.

126. Rader, N. E., & Haynes, S. H. (2014). Avoidance, protective, and weapons behaviors: An examination of constrained behaviors and their impact on concerns about crime. *Journal of Crime and Justice, 37*(2), 197–213.

127. Henson, B., & Reyns, B. W. (2015). The only thing we have to fear is fear itself... and crime: The current state of the fear of crime literature and where it should go next. *Sociology Compass, 9*(2), 91–103.

128. Rader, N. E., Cossman, J. S., & Porter, J. R. (2012). Fear of crime and vulnerability: Using a national sample of Americans to examine two competing paradigms. *Journal of Criminal Justice, 40*(2), 134–141.

129. Rader, N. (2017). Fear of crime. In H. Pontell (Ed.), *Research encyclopedia of criminology and criminal justice.* Cary, NC: Oxford University Press.

130. Hirtenlehner, H., & Farrall, S. (2014). Is the "shadow of sexual assault" responsible for women's higher fear of burglary? *British Journal of Criminology, 54*, 1167–1185.

131. Lane, J., Rader, N. E., Henson, B., Fisher, B. S., & May, D. C. (2014). *Fear of crime in the United States: Causes, consequences, and contradictions.* Durham, NC: Carolina Academic Press.

132. van Eijk, G. (2017). Between risk and resistance: Gender socialization, equality, and ambiguous norms in fear of crime and safekeeping. *Feminist Criminology, 12*(2), 103–124.

133. Moghe, S., & del Valle, L. (2018, January 18). Larry Nassar's abuse victims, in their own words. *CNN.* Retrieved from https://www.cnn.com/2018/01/16/us/nassar-victim-impact-statements/index.html

134. Vargas, T. (2017, November 20). Brutally killed by Charles Manson's followers, Sharon Tate became the face of victims' rights. *The Washington Post.* Retrieved from https://www.washingtonpost.com/news/retropolis/wp/2017/11/20/

brutally-killed-by-charles-mansons-followers-sharon-tate-became-the-face-of-victims-rights/

135. Booth, T. (2016). *Accommodating justice: Victim impact statements in the sentencing process.* Alexandria, NSW: Federation Press.

136. Kunst, M., de Groot, G., Meester, J., & van Doorn, J. (2020). The impact of victim impact statements on legal decisions in criminal proceedings: A systematic review of the literature across jurisdictions and decision types. *Aggression and Violent Behavior, 56*, 101512.

137. National Center for Victims of Crime. (n.d.). *Restitution.* Retrieved from https://members.victimsofcrime.org/help-for-crime-victims/get-help-bulletins-for-crime-victims/restitution

138. Sweeny, J., & Slack, J. (2017). Sexting as 'sexual behavior' under rape shield laws. *International Journal of Cyber Criminology, 11*(2), 246–260.

139. National District Attorneys Association. (2011). Rape shield statutes. *National Center for Prosecution of Child Abuse.* Retrieved from https://ndaa.org/wp-content/uploads/NCPCA-Rape-Shield-2011.pdf

140. National Crime Victim Law Institute. (2016). *Survey of select state and federal law providing victims' rights and protections that are specific to children.* Retrieved from https://law.lclark.edu/live/files/23530-survey-of-select-state-and-federal-laws-providing

141. Rentschler, C. A. (2011). *Second wounds: Victims' rights and the media in the U.S.* Durham, NC: Duke University Press.

142. Miller, E. J. (2010). The Warren Court's regulatory revolution in criminal procedure. *Connecticut Law Review, 43*(1), 1–82.

143. Ginsberg, R. (2014). Mighty crime victims: Victims' rights and neoliberalism in the American conjuncture. *Cultural Studies, 28*(5–6), 911–946.

144. Weaver, W. (1970, September 26). Agnew deplores 'permissiveness,' says his political mission is to arouse a desire for national self-discipline. *The New York Times.*

145. Patterson, M. J., Gover, A. R., & Trochmann, M. (2018). Victim rights and retribution. In O. H. Griffin & V. H. Woodward (Eds.), *Routledge handbook of corrections in the United States* (pp. 15–23). New York, NY: Routledge.

146. S.2420 - Victim and Witness Protection Act of 1982. 97th Congress (1981-1982). Retrieved from https://www.congress.gov/bill/97th-congress/senate-bill/2420

147. S.3266 - Crime Control Act of 1990. 101st Congress (1989-1990). Retrieved from https://www.congress.gov/bill/101st-congress/senate-bill/3266

148. H.R.3355 - Violent Crime Control and Law Enforcement Act of 1994. 103rd Congress (1993-1994). Retrieved from https://www.congress.gov/bill/103rd-congress/house-bill/3355/text

149. Doyle, C. (2015, December 9). Crime victims' rights act: A summary and legal analysis of 18 U.S.C. § 3771. *Congressional Research Service.* Retrieved from https://fas.org/sgp/crs/misc/RL33679.pdf

150. 18 U.S.C. § 3771. Crime victims' rights. *Office of the United States Attorneys.* Retrieved from https://www.justice.go

v/usao/resources/crime-victims-rights-ombudsman/victims-rights-act

151. Ginsberg, R. (2014). Mighty crime victims: Victims' rights and neoliberalism in the American conjuncture. *Cultural Studies, 28*(5–6), 911–946.

152. Lepore, J. (2018, May 21). The rise of the victims' rights movement. *The New Yorker Magazine*. Retrieved from https://www.newyorker.com/magazine/2018/05/21/the-rise-of-the-victims-rights-movement

153. Payne v. Tennessee, No. 90-5721, 501 US 808 (1991). https://supreme.justia.com/cases/federal/us/501/808/

154. Myers, B., Johnson, S., & Nuñez, N. (2018). Victim impact statements in capital sentencing: 25 years post-*Payne*. In M. Miller & B. Bornstein (Eds.), *Advances in psychology and law, volume 3*. New York, NY: Springer.

CHAPTER 13

1. Lussenhop, J. (2013, September 12). An oversight allowed a convicted man to walk free for thirteen years. Now the justice system wants to restart the clock. *Riverfront Times*. Retrieved from https://www.riverfronttimes.com/stlouis/an-oversight-allowed-a-convicted-man-to-walk-free-for-thirteen-years-now-the-justice-system-wants-to-restart-the-clock/Content?oid=2506702

2. Glass, Ira. (2014, February 14). 518: Except for that one thing. *This American Life*. Retrieved from https://www.thisamericanlife.org/518/except-for-that-one-thing/act-one-0

3. Glass, Ira. (2014, February 14). 518: Except for that one thing. *This American Life*. Retrieved from https://www.thisamericanlife.org/518/except-for-that-one-thing/act-one-0

4. Lussenhop, J. (2014, May 6). Cornealious Michael Anderson III, freed from prison, reunites with family. Retrieved from https://web.archive.org/web/20140508014812/http://blogs.riverfronttimes.com/dailyrft/2014/05/cornealious_michael_anderson_i.php

5. Cullen, F. T., & Jonson, C. L. (2017). *Correctional theory: Context and consequences (second edition)*. Thousand Oaks, CA: SAGE.

6. Indiana General Assembly. Retrieved from http://184.175.130.101/legislative/laws/2020/ic/titles/001

7. The Sentencing Project. Kemba Smith. Retrieved from https://www.sentencingproject.org/stories/kemba-smith/

8. Smith, K. (2011). *Poster child: The Kemba Smith story*. Sarasota, FL: First Edition Design Publishing.

9. For example, see The Last Prisoner Project. Retrieved from https://www.lastprisonerproject.org/

10. Mitchell, K. L. (2017). State sentencing guidelines: A garden full of variety. *Federal Courts Sentencing, 81*(2), 28–36.

11. Steiner, B., & Cain, C. M. (2017). Punishment within prison: An examination of the influences of prison officials' decisions to remove sentencing credits. *Law & Society Review, 51*(1), 70–98.

12. Tonry, M. (2019). Fifty years of American sentencing reform: Nine lessons. In M. Tonry (Ed.), *American sentencing: What happens and why?* Chicago, IL: University of Chicago press.

13. Luna, E. (2017). Mandatory minimums. *Reforming criminal justice: A report of the Academy for Justice on bridging the gap between scholarship and reform, 4*, 117–146.

14. United States Sentencing Commission. (2017). *An overview of mandatory minimum penalties in the federal criminal justice system*. Retrieved from https://www.ussc.gov/sites/default/files/pdf/research-and-publications/research-publications/2017/20170711_Mand-Min.pdf

15. Dujardin, P. (2021, February 22). Virginia lawmakers weigh scrapping 'mandatory minimum' sentences: Safeguard against leniency or unfair stripping of judicial discretion? *The Virginian-Pilot*. Retrieved from https://www.pilotonline.com/government/virginia/dp-nw-mandatory-minimums-20210222-tgirzpxqu5gm3jaaiy7b6cmq2u-story.html

16. Spohn, C. (2018). Reflections on the exercise of prosecutorial discretion 50 years after publication of the challenge of crime in a free society. *Criminology & Public Policy, 17*(2), 321–340.

17. Price, M. (2019). Weaponizing justice: Mandatory minimums, the trial penalty, and the purposes of punishment. *Federal Sentencing Reporter, 31*(4–5), 309–315.

18. Chalfin, A., & McCrary, J. (2017). Criminal deterrence: A review of the literature. *Journal of Economic Literature, 55*(1), 5–48.

19. *Coker v. Georgia*, 433 U.S. 584 (1977).

20. Nagin, D. S. (2013). Deterrence in the 21st century: A review of the evidence. *Crime and Justice: An Annual Review of Research, 42*, 199–263.

21. Loughran, T. A., Pogarsky, G., Piquero, A. R., & Paternoster, R. (2012). Re-examining the functional form of the certainty effect in deterrence theory. *Justice Quarterly, 29*(5), 712–741.

22. Paternoster, R. (2010). How much do we really know about criminal deterrence? *Journal of Criminal Law and Criminology, 100*(3), 765–824.

23. Braga, A. A., Weisburd, D., & Turchan, B. (2018). Focused deterrence strategies and crime control: An updated systematic review and meta-analysis of the empirical evidence. *Criminology & Public Policy, 17*(1), 205–250.

24. Barash, D. (2021, January 12). Executions don't deter murder, despite the Trump administration's push. *The Conversation*. Retrieved from https://theconversation.com/executions-dont-deter-murder-despite-the-trump-administrations-push-152207

25. Ehrlich, I. (1975). The deterrent effect of capital punishment: A question of life and death. *American Economic Review, 65*(3), 397–417.

26. *Furman v. Georgia*. 408 US 238 (1972).

27. *Gregg v. Georgia*. 428 US 153 (1976).

28. Blumstein, A., Cohen, J., & Nagin, D. (1978). *Deterrence and incapacitation: Estimating the effects of criminal sanctions on crime rates*. Washington, DC: National Academy of Sciences.

29. Nagin, D. S. (2013). Deterrence in the 21st century: A review of the evidence. *Crime and Justice: An Annual Review of Research, 42*, 199–263.

30. Death Penalty Information Center. Texas. Retrieved from https://deathpenaltyinfo.org/state-and-federal-info/state-by-state/texas

31. Baumgartner, F., Davidson, M., Johnson, K., Krishnamurthy, A., & Wilson, C. (2018). *Deadly justice: A statistical portrait of the death penalty.* New York, NY: Oxford University Press.

32. Death Penalty Information Center. (2021, July 1). Facts about the death penalty. Retrieved from https://documents.deathpenaltyinfo.org/pdf/FactSheet.pdf

33. U.S. National Weather Service. (2020, June). Number of deaths and injuries due to lightning in the U.S. from 1995 to 2019. Retrieved from https://www.statista.com/statistics/203715/injuries-and-fatalities-caused-by-lightning-in-the-us/

34. Federal Bureau of Investigation. (2021). *Expanded homicide offense counts, 2000-2020* [Expanded homicide data]. Crime Data Explorer. Retrieved from https://crime-data-explorer.app.cloud.gov/pages/explorer/crime/shr

35. Nagin, D. S., & Pepper, J. V. (2012). *Deterrence and the death penalty.* Washington, DC: National Academies Press.

36. Nagin, D. S. (2013). Deterrence in the twenty-first century. *Crime and Justice, 42*(1), 199–263.

37. Kleinstuber, R., & Coldsmith, J. (2020). Is life without parole an effective way to reduce violent crime? An empirical assessment. *Criminology & Public Policy, 19*(2), 617–651.

38. Auerhahn, K. (2017). Incapacitation. In K. Kerley (Ed.), *The encyclopedia of corrections* (online). New York, NY: Wiley.

39. Kleck, G., & Sever, B. (2017). *Punishment and crime: The limits of punitive crime control.* New York, NY: Routledge.

40. Cullen, F. T., & Jonson, C. L. (2017). *Correctional theory: Context and consequences.* Thousand Oaks, CA: SAGE.

41. Lewis, N., & Lockwood, B. (2019, December 17). The hidden cost of incarceration. *The Marshall Project.* Retrieved from https://www.themarshallproject.org/2019/12/17/the-hidden-cost-of-incarceration

42. U.S. Department of Health and Human Services. Incarceration and reentry. *Office of The Assistant Secretary for Planning and Evaluation.* Retrieved from https://aspe.hhs.gov/incarceration-reentry

43. Cullen, F. T., & Jonson, C. L. (2017). *Correctional theory: Context and consequences.* Thousand Oaks, CA: SAGE.

44. Nellis, A. (2021). No end in sight: America's enduring reliance on life imprisonment. *The Sentencing Project.* Retrieved from https://www.sentencingproject.org/publications/no-end-in-sight-americas-enduring-reliance-on-life-imprisonment/

45. Nellis, A. (2021). No end in sight: America's enduring reliance on life imprisonment. *The Sentencing Project.* Retrieved from https://www.sentencingproject.org/publications/no-end-in-sight-americas-enduring-reliance-on-life-imprisonment/

46. U.S. Department of Justice. History of risk assessment. *Public Safety Risk Assessment Clearinghouse.* Retrieved from https://bja.ojp.gov/program/psrac/basics/history-risk-assessment

47. For example, see Latessa, E., Smith, P., Lemke, R., Makarios, M., & Lowenkamp, C. (2009). *Creation and validation of the Ohio risk assessment system final report.* Retrieved from https://www.ocjs.ohio.gov/ORAS_FinalReport.pdf

48. Myhill, A., & Hohl, K. (2019). The "golden thread": Coercive control and risk assessment for domestic violence. *Journal of Interpersonal Violence, 34*(21–22), 4477–4497.

49. Desmarais, S. L., Zottola, S. A., Duhart Clarke, S. E., & Lowder, E. M. (2021). Predictive validity of pretrial risk assessments: A systematic review of the literature. *Criminal Justice and Behavior, 48*(4), 398–420.

50. Garrett, B., & Monahan, J. (2019). Assessing risk: The use of risk assessment in sentencing. *Judicature, 103*(2), 42–48.

51. Wisconsin v. Eric Loomis. 881 N.W.2d 749, 767 (Wis. 2016).

52. Jung, J., Concannon, C., Shroff, R., Goel, S., & Goldstein, D. G. (2017). Simple rules for complex decisions Available at SSRN: https://ssrn.com/abstract=2919024

53. Henry, M. (2019. December 14). Risk assessment: Explained. *The Appeal.* Retrieved from https://theappeal.org/the-lab/explainers/risk-assessment-explained/

54. Skeem, J. L., & Lowenkamp, C. T. (2016). Risk, race, and recidivism: Predictive bias and disparate impact. *Criminology, 54*(4), 680–712.

55. Angwin, J., Larson, J., Mattu, S., & Kirchner, L. (2016, May 23). Machine bias: There's software used across the country to predict future criminals. And it's biased against blacks. *ProPublica.* Retrieved from https://www.propublica.org/article/machine-bias-risk-assessments-in-criminal-sentencing

56. Skeem, J., & Lowenkamp, C. (2020). Using algorithms to address trade-offs inherent in predicting recidivism. *Behavioral Sciences & the Law, 38*(3), 259–278.

57. Yung. C. R. (2019). Civil commitment of sex offenders. In P. H. Witt & D. DeMatteo (Eds.), *Sexually violent offenders: A clinical science handbook* (pp. 21–34). New York, NY: Springer.

58. Witt, P. H., & DeMatteo, D. (2019). Sexually violent predator laws: Historical development and evolution. In P. H. Witt & D. DeMatteo (Eds.), *Sexually violent offenders: A clinical science handbook* (pp. 9–20). New York, NY: Springer.

59. Sandler, J. C., & Freeman, N. J. (2017). Evaluation of New York State's sex offender civil management assessment process recidivism outcomes. *Criminology & Public Policy, 16*(3), 913–936.

60. Tolman, A. W. (2018). Sex offender civil commitment to prison post-*Kingsley. Northwestern University Law Review, 113*(1), 155–196.

61. Steptoe, G., & Goldet, A. (2016, January 27). Why some young sex offenders are held indefinitely. *The Marshall Project.* Retrieved from https://www.themarshallproject.org/2016/01/27/why-some-young-sex-offenders-are-held-indefinitely

62. Cullen, F. T., & Jonson, C. L. (2011). *Correctional theory: Context and consequences.* Thousand Oaks, CA: SAGE.

63. Gendreau, P. (2017). Rehabilitation: What works to change offenders. In F. Cullen & C. Jonson (Eds.), *Correctional theory: Context and consequences* (pp. 171–205). Thousand Oaks, CA: SAGE.

64. Adapted from Zito, R. (2020). Identifying problems in the criminal justice system." In K. Korgen, M. Trautner, & M. Atkinson (Eds.), *Social problems in action*. Thousand Oaks, CA: SAGE.

65. Rothman, D. J. (2017). Correctional theory in crisis: America's changing context. In F. Cullen & C. Jonson (Eds.), *Correction theory: Context and consequences* (pp. 23–36). Thousand Oaks, CA: SAGE.

66. Rothman, D. J. (2017). Correctional theory in crisis: America's changing context. In F. Cullen & C. Jonson (Eds.), *Correction theory: Context and consequences* (pp. 23–36). Thousand Oaks, CA: SAGE.

67. Lemke, R. (2017). Martinson report. In C. Schreck (Ed.), *Encyclopedia of juvenile justice and delinquency* (online). New York, NY: Wiley.

68. Martinson, R. (1974) What works? Questions and answers about prison reform. *The Public Interest, 35*(Spring), 22–54.

69. Gendreau, P. (2017). Rehabilitation: What works to change offenders. In F. Cullen & C. Jonson (Eds.), Correctional theory: Context and consequences (pp. 171–205). Thousand Oaks, CA: SAGE.

70. MacKenzie, D. L., & Lattimore, P. K. (2018). To rehabilitate or not to rehabilitate: That is the question for corrections! *Criminology & Public Policy, 17*(2), 355–377.

71. Taxman, F. S. (2018). The partially clothed emperor: Evidence-based practices. *Journal of Contemporary Criminal Justice, 34*(1), 97–114.

72. MacKenzie, D. L., & Lattimore, P. K. (2018). To rehabilitate or not to rehabilitate: That is the question for corrections! *Criminology & Public Policy, 17*(2), 355–377.

73. DeMatteo, D., Heilbrun, K., Thornewill, A., & Arnold, S. (2019). *Problem-solving courts and the criminal justice system*. New York, NY: Oxford University Press.

74. Hood, B., & Ray, B. (2017). Specialty courts. In O. H. Griffin & V. H. Woodward (Eds.), *Routledge handbook of corrections in the United States* (pp. 231–242). New York, NY: Routledge.

75. DeMatteo, D., Heilbrun, K., Thornewill, A., & Arnold, S. (2019). *Problem-solving courts and the criminal justice system*. New York, NY: Oxford University Press.

76. Snedker, K. (2018). *Therapeutic justice: Crime, treatment courts, and mental illness*. Cham, Switzerland: Palgrave Macmillan.

77. Marlowe, D. B., Hardin, C. D., & Fox, C. L. (2016). Painting the current picture: A national report on drug courts and other problem-solving courts in the United States. *National Drug Court Institute*. Retrieved from https://www.ndci.org/wp-content/uploads/2016/05/Painting-the-Current-Picture-2016.pdf

78. Kaiser, K. A., & Rhodes, K. (2019). A drug court by any other name? An analysis of problem-solving court programs. *Law and Human Behavior, 43*(3), 278.

79. Wolff, N., Fabrikant, N., & Belenko, S. (2011). Mental health courts and their selection processes: Modeling variation for consistency. *Law and Human Behavior, 35*(5), 402–412.

80. Marlowe, D. B., Hardin, C. D., & Fox, C. L. (2016). Painting the current picture: A national report on drug courts and other problem-solving courts in the United States. *National Drug Court Institute*. Retrieved from https://www.ndci.org/wp-content/uploads/2016/05/Painting-the-Current-Picture-2016.pdf

81. Hood, B., & Ray, B. (2017). Specialty courts. In O. H. Griffin & V. H. Woodward (Eds.), *Routledge handbook of corrections in the United States* (pp. 231–242). New York, NY: Routledge.

82. Marlowe, D. B., Hardin, C. D., & Fox, C. L. (2016). Painting the current picture: A national report on drug courts and other problem-solving courts in the United States. *National Drug Court Institute*. Retrieved from https://www.ndci.org/wp-content/uploads/2016/05/Painting-the-Current-Picture-2016.pdf

83. Marlowe, D. B., Hardin, C. D., & Fox, C. L. (2016). Painting the current picture: A national report on drug courts and other problem-solving courts in the United States. *National Drug Court Institute*. Retrieved from https://www.ndci.org/wp-content/uploads/2016/05/Painting-the-Current-Picture-2016.pdf

84. Eley, A. (2015). Restorative justice: 'How I got an apology from my abuser.' *BBC*. Retrieved from https://www.bbc.com/news/uk-34571936

85. Wilson, D. B., Olaghere, A., & Kimbrell, C. S. (2018). Effectiveness of restorative justice principles in juvenile justice: A meta-analysis. *Inter-University Consortium for Political and Social Research*. Retrieved from https://www.ojp.gov/pdffiles1/ojjdp/grants/250872.pdf

86. Pepinsky, H. (2013). Peacemaking criminology. *Critical Criminology, 21*(3), 319–339.

87. Zehr, H. (2015). *The little book of restorative justice* (Revised & updated). New York, NY: Simon & Schuster.

88. Braithwaite, J. (2016). Reintegrative shaming. Retrieved from https://www.anu.edu.au/fellows/jbraithwaite/_documents/Articles/Reintegrative%20Shaming%20Explaining%20Criminals%20and%20Crime%20Essays%20in%20Contemporary%20Criminological%20Theory.pdf

89. Braithwate, J. (1989). *Crime, shame, and reintegration*. Cambridge, UK: Cambridge University Press.

90. Common Justice. Our work. Retrieved from https://www.commonjustice.org/our_work

91. Sered, D. (2019). *Until we reckon: Violence, mass incarceration, and a road to repair*. New York, NY: New Press.

92. Pfaff, J. (2019). Locked up. *The Baffler, 46*, 56–64.

93. Sered, D. (2017). *Accounting for violence: How to increase safety and break our failed reliance on mass incarceration*. New York, NY: Vera Institute of Justice.

94. Sered, D. (2019). *Until we reckon: Violence, mass incarceration, and a road to repair*. New York, NY: The New Press.

95. Sered, D. (2019). *Until we reckon: Violence, mass incarceration, and a road to repair*. New York, NY: New Press.

CHAPTER 14

1. Ingold, J. (2014, January 1). World's first legal recreational marijuana sales begin in Colorado. *Denver Post*. Retrieved from https://www.denverpost.com/2014/01/01/worlds-first-legal-recreational-marijuana-sales-begin-in-colorado/

2. Colorado Constitution. Article XVIII, Section16: Personal Use and Regulation of Marijuana. Retrieved from https://www.colorado.gov/pacific/sites/default/files/Section%2016%20-%20%20Retail.pdf

3. Coffman, K. (2013, December 31). World's first state-licensed marijuana retailers open doors in Colorado. *Reuters.* Retrieved from https://www.reuters.com/article/us-usa-marijuana-colorado/worlds-first-state-licensed-marijuana-retailers-open-doors-in-colorado-idUSBREA0000K20140101

4. Spalding, M. B. (2018, October 15). Colorado city 'just says no' to marijuana. Michigan cities may face the same decision. *South Bend Tribune.* Retrieved from https://www.southbendtribune.com/news/marijuana/colorado-city-just-says-no-to-marijuana-michigan-cities-may-face-the-same-decision/article_5b293e5b-5f99-59f5-afdf-f9c8a149a475.html?redir=0

5. Ferner, M. (2017, July 17). If legalizing marijuana was supposed to cause more crime, it's not doing a very good job. *Huffington Post.* Retrieved from https://www.huffpost.com/entry/marijuana-crime-denver_n_5595742

6. California Police Chiefs Association. (2009). *White paper on marijuana dispensaries.* Sacramento: California Police Chiefs Association's Task Force on Marijuana Dispensaries.

7. Bruinsma, G., & Johnson, S. (2018). Environmental criminology: Scope, history, and state of the art. In G. Bruinsma & S. Johnson (Eds.), *The Oxford handbook of environmental criminology* (pp. 1–34). Oxford: Oxford University Press.

8. Bottoms, A., & Wiles, P. (2002). Environmental criminology. In M. Maguire, R. Morgan, & R. Reiner (Eds.), *Oxford handbook of criminology* (pp. 620–656). Oxford: Oxford University Press.

9. Wilcox, P., & Cullen, F. T. (2018). Situational opportunity theories of crime. *Annual Review of Criminology, 1*, 123–148.

10. Bradley, M., & Teasdale, B. (2017). Integrating criminology and prevention research. In B. Teasdale & M. Bradley (Eds.), *Preventing crime and violence* (pp. 3–8). New York, NY: Springer.

11. Briz-Redón, Á., Martinez-Ruiz, F., & Montes, F. (2020). Reestimating a minimum acceptable geocoding hit rate for conducting a spatial analysis. *International Journal of Geographical Information Science, 34*(7), 1283–1305.

12. Andresen, M. A., & Hodgkinson, T. (2019). Place-based data, methods, and analysis: Past, present, and future. In M. Krohn, N. Hendrix, G. P. Hall, & A. Lizotte (Eds.), *Handbook on crime and deviance* (pp. 3–33). Cham, Switzerland: Springer.

13. Weisburd, D. (2015). The law of crime concentration and the criminology of place. *Criminology, 53*(2), 133–157.

14. Andresen, M. A., Curman, A. S., & Linning, S. J. (2017). The trajectories of crime at places: Understanding the patterns of disaggregated crime types. *Journal of Quantitative Criminology, 33*(3), 427–449.

15. Weisburd, D., Bushway, S., Lum, C., & Yang, S. M. (2004). Trajectories of crime at places: A longitudinal study of street segments in the city of Seattle. *Criminology, 42*(2), 283–322.

16. Braga, A. A., Papachristos, A. V., & Hureau, D. M. (2010). The concentration and stability of gun violence at micro places in Boston, 1980–2008. *Journal of Quantitative Criminology, 26*(1), 33–53.

17. Braga, A. A., Hureau, D. M., & Papachristos, A. V. (2011). The relevance of micro places to citywide robbery trends: A longitudinal analysis of robbery incidents at street corners and block faces in Boston. *Journal of Research in Crime and Delinquency, 48*(1), 7–32.

18. Gill, C., Wooditch, A., & Weisburd, D. (2017). Testing the "law of crime concentration at place" in a suburban setting: Implications for research and practice. *Journal of Quantitative Criminology, 33*(3), 519–545.

19. de Melo, S. N., Matias, L. F., & Andresen, M. A. (2015). Crime concentrations and similarities in spatial crime patterns in a Brazilian context. *Applied Geography, 62*, 314–324.

20. Andresen, M. A., Curman, A. S., & Linning, S. J. (2017). The trajectories of crime at places: Understanding the patterns of disaggregated crime types. *Journal of Quantitative Criminology, 33*(3), 427–449.

21. Levin, A., Rosenfeld, R., & Deckard, M. (2017). The law of crime concentration: An application and recommendations for future research. *Journal of Quantitative Criminology, 33*(3), 635–647.

22. Braga, A. A., Andresen, M. A., & Lawton, B. (2017). The law of crime concentration at places: Editors' introduction. *Journal of Quantitative Criminology, 33*(3), 421–426.

23. Curman, A. S., Andresen, M. A., & Brantingham, P. J. (2015). Crime and place: A longitudinal examination of street segment patterns in Vancouver, BC. *Journal of Quantitative Criminology, 31*(1), 127–147.

24. Wheeler, A. P. (2019). Quantifying the local and spatial effects of alcohol outlets on crime. *Crime & Delinquency, 65*(6), 845–871.

25. Bernasco, W., & Block, R. (2011). Robberies in Chicago: A block-level analysis of the influence of crime generators, crime attractors, and offender anchor points. *Journal of Research in Crime and Delinquency, 48*(1), 33–57.

26. Tillyer, M. S., Wilcox, P., & Walter, R. J. (2020). Crime generators in context: Examining 'place in neighborhood' propositions. *Journal of Quantitative Criminology, 37*, 1–30.

27. Bernasco, W., & Block, R. (2011). Robberies in Chicago: A block-level analysis of the influence of crime generators, crime attractors, and offender anchor points. *Journal of Research in Crime and Delinquency, 48*(1), 33–57.

28. Bernasco, W., & Block, R. (2011). Robberies in Chicago: A block-level analysis of the influence of crime generators, crime attractors, and offender anchor points. *Journal of Research in Crime and Delinquency, 48*(1), 33–57.

29. Connealy, N., Piza, E., & Hatten, D. (2020). The criminogenic effect of marijuana dispensaries in Denver, Colorado: A microsynthetic control quasi-experiment and cost-benefit analysis. *Justice Evaluation Journal, 3*(1), 69–93.

30. Connealy, N., Piza, E., & Hatten, D. (2020). The criminogenic effect of marijuana dispensaries in Denver, Colorado: A microsynthetic control quasi-experiment and cost-benefit analysis. *Justice Evaluation Journal, 3*(1), 69–93.

31. Hughes, L. A., Schaible, L. M., & Jimmerson, K. (2020). Marijuana dispensaries and neighborhood crime and

disorder in Denver, Colorado. *Justice Quarterly, 37*(3), 461–485.

32. Zakrzewski Jr, W. J., Wheeler, A. P., & Thompson, A. J. (2020). Cannabis in the capital: Exploring the spatial association between medical marijuana dispensaries and crime. *Journal of Crime and Justice, 43*(1), 1–15.

33. Wilson, J. Q., & Kelling, G. (1982). Broken windows: The police and neighborhood safety. *The Atlantic.* Retrieved from https://www.theatlantic.com/magazine/archive/1982/03/broken-windows/304465/

34. Wilson, J. Q., & Kelling, G. (1982). Broken windows: The police and neighborhood safety. *The Atlantic.* Retrieved from https://www.theatlantic.com/magazine/archive/1982/03/broken-windows/304465/

35. O'Brien, D. T., Farrell, C., & Welsh, B. C. (2019). Looking through broken windows: The impact of neighborhood disorder on aggression and fear of crime is an artifact of research design. *Annual Review of Criminology, 2,* 53–71.

36. Wilson, J. Q., & Kelling, G. (1982). Broken windows: The police and neighborhood safety. *The Atlantic.* Retrieved from https://www.theatlantic.com/magazine/archive/1982/03/broken-windows/304465/

37. Wilson, J. Q., & Kelling, G. (1982). Broken windows: The police and neighborhood safety. *The Atlantic.* Retrieved from https://www.theatlantic.com/magazine/archive/1982/03/broken-windows/304465/

38. Harcourt, B. E. (2009). *Illusion of order: The false promise of broken windows policing.* Cambridge, MA: Harvard University Press.

39. Bratton, W. (2015). Broken windows and quality of life policing in New York City. *NYPD.* Retrieved from https://www.nyc.gov/html/nypd/downloads/pdf/analysis_and_planning/qol.pdf

40. Erzen, T. (2001). Turnstile jumpers and broken windows: Policing disorder in New York City. In A. McArdle & T. Erzen (Eds.), *Zero tolerance: Quality of life and the new police brutality in New York City* (pp. 19–49). New York, NY: NYU Press.

41. Herring, C. (2019). Complaint-oriented policing: Regulating homelessness in public space. *American Sociological Review, 84*(5), 769–800.

42. Adapted from Zito, R. (2020). Identifying problems in the criminal justice system. In K. Korgen, M. Trautner, & M. Atkinson (Eds.), *Social problems in action.* Thousand Oaks, CA: SAGE.

43. Kohler-Hausmann, I. (2018). *Misdemeanorland: Criminal courts and social control in an age of broken windows policing.* Princeton, NJ; Princeton University Press.

44. Kohler-Hausmann, I. (2018). *Misdemeanorland: Criminal courts and social control in an age of broken windows policing.* Princeton, NJ; Princeton University Press.

45. Kohler-Hausmann, I. (2018). *Misdemeanorland: Criminal courts and social control in an age of broken windows policing.* Princeton, NJ; Princeton University Press.

46. Kohler-Hausmann, I. (2018). *Misdemeanorland: Criminal courts and social control in an age of broken windows policing.* Princeton, NJ; Princeton University Press.

47. Barrett, C. J. (2017). Adjudicating broken windows: A qualitative inquiry of misdemeanor case processing in the New York City's lower criminal courts. *Criminology, Criminal Justice, Law. & Society, 18,* 62–79.

48. Adapted from Zito, R. (2020). Identifying problems in the criminal justice system. In K. Korgen, M. Trautner, & M. Atkinson (Eds.), *Social problems in action.* Thousand Oaks, CA: SAGE.

49. Sampson, R. J., & Raudenbush, S. W. (2004). Seeing disorder: Neighborhood stigma and the social construction of "broken windows." *Social Psychology Quarterly, 67*(4), 319–342.

50. Skogan, W. (2015). Disorder and decline: The state of research. *Journal of Research in Crime and Delinquency, 52*(4), 464–485.

51. Brunson, R. K., & Wade, B. A. (2019). "Oh hell no, we don't talk to police" Insights on the lack of cooperation in police investigations of urban gun violence. *Criminology & Public Policy, 18*(3), 623–648.

52. Quoted in Childress, S. (2016, June 28). The problem with 'broken windows' policing. *PBS Frontline.* Retrieved from https://www.pbs.org/wgbh/frontline/article/the-problem-with-broken-windows-policing/

53. Kelling, G. (2015, August 11). Don't blame my 'broken windows' theory for poor policing. *Politico.* Retrieved from https://www.politico.com/magazine/story/2015/08/broken-windows-theory-poor-policing-ferguson-kelling-121268/

54. Thompson, K., Offler, N., Hirsch, L., Every, D., Thomas, M. J., & Dawson, D. (2012). From broken windows to a renovated research agenda: A review of the literature on vandalism and graffiti in the rail industry. *Transportation research part A: policy and practice, 46*(8), 1280–1290.

55. Shepley, M., Sachs, N., Sadatsafavi, H., Fournier, C., & Peditto, K. (2019). The impact of green space on violent crime in urban environments: An evidence synthesis. *International Journal of Environmental Research and Public Health, 16*(24), 5119.

56. Troy, A., Nunery, A., & Grove, J. M. (2016). The relationship between residential yard management and neighborhood crime: An analysis from Baltimore City and County. *Landscape and Urban Planning, 147,* 78–87.

57. Kondo, M. C., Morrison, C., Jacoby, S. F., Elliott, L., Poche, A., Theall, K. P., & Branas, C. C. (2018). Blight abatement of vacant land and crime in New Orleans. *Public Health Reports, 133*(6), 650–657.

58. Velasco, E. (2015, April 16). The battle for New Orleans: The Big Easy goes hardcore to combat blight. But can that save the lower ninth ward? *Politico.* Retrieved from https://www.politico.com/magazine/story/2015/04/new-orleans-what-works-117056/

59. City of New Orleans. Code enforcement, all violations. 2017. Retrieved from https://data.nola.gov/browse?q=Code%20Enforcement%20All%20Violations&sortBy=relevance

60. Kondo, M. C., Morrison, C., Jacoby, S. F., Elliott, L., Poche, A., Theall, K. P., & Branas, C. C. (2018). Blight abatement of vacant land and crime in New Orleans. *Public Health Reports, 133*(6), 650–657.

61. Branas, C. C., Kondo, M. C., Murphy, S. M., South, E. C., Polsky, D., & MacDonald, J. M. (2016). Urban blight remediation as a cost-beneficial solution to firearm violence. *American Journal of Public Health, 106*(12), 2158–2164.

62. Jay, J., Miratrix, L. W., Branas, C. C., Zimmerman, M. A., & Hemenway, D. (2019). Urban building demolitions, firearm violence and drug crime. *Journal of Behavioral Medicine, 42*(4), 626–634.

63. Cohen, L. E., & Felson, M. (1979). Social change and crime rate trends: A routine activity approach. *American Sociological Review, 44*, 588–608.

64. Felson, M. (2018). *Crime and everyday life* (6th ed.). Thousand Oaks, CA: SAGE Publications.

65. Wikström, P. (2018). Routine activity theories. In B. Huebner (Ed.), *Oxford bibliographies in criminology*. Cary, NC: Oxford University Press.

66. Clarke, R. V., & Felson, M. (2011). The origins of the routine activity approach and situational crime prevention. In F. Adler & C. L. Jonson (Eds.), *The origins of American criminology: Advances in criminological theory* (pp. 245–260). Piscataway, NJ: Transaction Publishers.

67. Kuhns, J., Blevins, K., & Lee, S. (2012). Understanding decisions to burglarize from the offender's perspective. *UNC-Charlotte, Alarm Industry Research and Education Foundation.*

68. Clarke, R. (2000). Hot products: A new focus for crime prevention. In S. Ballintyne, K. Pease & V. McLaren (Eds.), *Secure foundations: Key issues in crime prevention, crime reduction and community safety* (pp. 251–264). London: Institute for Public Policy Research.

69. Smith, B. T. (2018). Understanding shoplifting of fast-moving consumer goods: An application of the CRAVED model. *Security Journal, 31*(2), 428–450.

70. Miró, F. (2014). Routine activity theory. In J. M. Mitchell (Ed.), *The encyclopedia of theoretical criminology*. New York, NY: Wiley Online.

71. Bunch, J., Clay-Warner, J., & Lei, M. K. (2015). Demographic characteristics and victimization risk: Testing the mediating effects of routine activities. *Crime & Delinquency, 61*(9), 1181–1205.

72. Schnell, C., Grossman, L., & Braga, A. A. (2019). The routine activities of violent crime places: A retrospective case-control study of crime opportunities on street segments. *Journal of Criminal Justice, 60*, 140–153.

73. Ireland, L. (2020). Predicting online target hardening behaviors: An extension of routine activity theory for privacy-enhancing technologies and techniques. *Deviant Behavior, 42*, 1–17.

74. Tillyer, M. S., & Eck, J. E. (2011). Getting a handle on crime: A further extension of routine activities theory. *Security Journal, 24*(2), 179–193.

75. Eck, J. E., & Clarke, R. V. (2019). Situational crime prevention: Theory, practice and evidence. In M. Krohn, N. Hendrix, G. P. Hall, & A. Lizotte (Eds.), *Handbook on crime and deviance* (pp. 355–376). Cham, Switzerland: Springer.

76. Leukfeldt, E. R., & Yar, M. (2016). Applying routine activity theory to cybercrime: A theoretical and empirical analysis. *Deviant Behavior, 37*(3), 263–280.

77. DeLiema, M. (2018). Elder fraud and financial exploitation: Application of routine activity theory. *The Gerontologist, 58*(4), 706–718.

78. Engström, A. (2020). Conceptualizing lifestyle and routine activities in the early 21st century: A systematic review of self-report measures in studies on direct-contact offenses in young populations. *Crime & Delinquency, 67*, 1–46.

79. Pratt, T., Turanovic, J., Fox, K., & Wright, K. (2014). Self-control and victimization: A meta-analysis. *Criminology, 52*, 87–116.

80. Wilcox, P., & Cullen, F. T. (2018). Situational opportunity theories of crime. *Annual Review of Criminology, 1*, 123–148.

81. Jacobs, J. (1961). *The death and life of great American cities.* London: Jonathon Cope.

82. Newman, O. (1972). *Defensible space: People and design in the violent city.* New York, NY: Macmillan.

83. Wilcox, P., & Cullen, F. T. (2018). Situational opportunity theories of crime. *Annual Review of Criminology, 1*, 123–148.

84. Jacobs, B. A., & Cherbonneau, M. (2019). Carjacking and the management of natural surveillance. *Journal of Criminal Justice, 61*, 40–47.

85. Hollis, M. E., Felson, M., & Welsh, B. C. (2013). The capable guardian in routine activities theory: A theoretical and conceptual reappraisal. *Crime Prevention and Community Safety, 15*(1), 65–79.

86. Sohn, D. W. (2016). Residential crimes and neighbourhood built environment: Assessing the effectiveness of crime prevention through environmental design (CPTED). *Cities, 52*, 86–93.

87. Cozens, P. (2013). Crime prevention through environmental design. In R. Wortley & L. Mazerolle (Eds.), *Environmental criminology and crime analysis* (pp. 175–199). Devon, UK: Willan.

88. Jacobs, B. A., & Cherbonneau, M. (2019). Carjacking and the management of natural surveillance. *Journal of Criminal Justice, 61*, 40–47.

89. Newman, G., & Clarke, R. V. (2016). *Rational choice and situational crime prevention: Theoretical foundations.* New York, NY: Routledge.

90. Welsh, B. C., Zimmerman, G. M., & Zane, S. N. (2018). The centrality of theory in modern day crime prevention: Developments, challenges, and opportunities. *Justice Quarterly, 35*(1), 139–161.

91. Eck, J. E., & Clarke, R. V. (2019). Situational crime prevention: Theory, practice and evidence. In M. Krohn, N. Hendrix, G. P. Hall, & A. Lizotte (Eds.), *Handbook on crime and deviance* (pp. 355–376). Cham, Switzerland: Springer.

92. Eck, J. E., & Clarke, R. V. (2019). Situational crime prevention: Theory, practice and evidence. In M. Krohn, N. Hendrix, G. P. Hall, & A. Lizotte (Eds.), *Handbook on crime and deviance* (pp. 355–376). Cham, Switzerland: Springer.

93. Cornish, D. B., & Clarke, R. V. (2003). Opportunities, precipitators and criminal decisions: A reply to Wortley's critique of situational crime prevention. In M. J. Smith & D. B. Cornish (Eds.), *Theory for practice in situational crime prevention, Crime Prevention Studies* (Vol. 16, pp. 41–96). Monsey, NY: Criminal Justice Press.

94. Shariati, A., & Guertte, R. (2017). Situational crime prevention. In B. Teasdale & M. Bradley (Eds.), *Preventing crime and violence* (pp. 261–268). New York, NY: Springer.

95. Guerette, R. (2009.) The pull, push and expansion of situational crime prevention evaluation: An appraisal of thirty-seven years of research. In J. Knutsson & N. Tilley (Eds.), *Evaluating crime reduction initiatives* (pp. 28–58). Boulder, CO: Lynne Rienner Publishers.

96. Piza, E. L., Welsh, B. C., Farrington, D. P., & Thomas, A. L. (2019). CCTV surveillance for crime prevention: A 40-year systematic review with meta-analysis. *Criminology & Public Policy, 18*(1), 135–159.

97. United Nations Human Settlements Programme. (2019). United Nations system-wide guidelines on safer cities and human settlements. Kenya: UN-Habitat. Retrieved from https://unhabitat.org/sites/default/files/2020/03/un_systemwide_guidelines_on_safer_cities_and_human_settlements.pdf

98. Cozens, P., & Love, T. (2017). The dark side of crime prevention through environmental design (CPTED). In H. Pontell (Ed.), *Oxford research encyclopedia of criminology and criminal justice* (online). Oxford: Oxford University Press.

99. Cozens, P., & Love, T. (2017). The dark side of crime prevention through environmental design (CPTED). In H. Pontell (Ed.), *Oxford research encyclopedia of criminology and criminal justice* (online). Oxford: Oxford University Press.

100. Prenzler, T., & Wilson, E. (2017). The evolution of situation crime prevention. In T. Prenzler (Ed.), *Understanding crime prevention: The case study approach* (pp. 73–88). Samford Valley, Queensland: Australian Academic Press.

101. Saville, G. (2017). The missing link in CPTED theory. In B. Teasdale & M. Bradley (Eds.), *Preventing crime and violence* (pp. 297–307). New York, NY: Springer.

102. Harbour, J. L. (2019). *21st century security and CPTED: Designing for critical infrastructure protection and crime prevention.* Boca Raton, FL: CRC Press.

103. Guerette, R. T., & Bowers, K. J. (2009). Assessing the extent of crime displacement and diffusion of benefits: A review of situational crime prevention evaluations. *Criminology, 47*(4), 1331–1368.

104. Rossmo, D. K., & Summers, L. (2021). Offender decision-making and displacement. *Justice Quarterly, 38*(3), 375–405.

105. Ladegaard, I. (2019). Crime displacement in digital drug markets. *International Journal of Drug Policy, 63*, 113–121.

106. Rowe, E., Akman, T., Smith, R. G., & Tomison, A. M. (2013). Organised crime and public sector corruption: A crime scripts analysis of tactical displacement risks. *Trends and Issues in Crime and Criminal Justice, 444*, 1–7.

107. Guerette, R. T., & Bowers, K. J. (2009). Assessing the extent of crime displacement and diffusion of benefits: A review of situational crime prevention evaluations. *Criminology, 47*(4), 1331–1368.

108. Johnson, S. D., Guerette, R. T., & Bowers, K. (2014). Crime displacement: What we know, what we don't know, and what it means for crime reduction. *Journal of Experimental Criminology, 10*(4), 549–571.

INDEX